The Professional Touch

SBN No. 72340111   X

The Professional Touch

AN ENCYCLOPAEDIA OF TURF STATISTICS

Oliver Chisholm
('Traveller' of the *Sporting Chronicle*)

WOLFE PUBLISHING LTD
10 Earlham Street London WC2

Acknowledgments

The 1969 Fixture List is reproduced by courtesy of The Jockey Club

Maps reproduced by permission of the *Sporting Chronicle*

MAPS DRAWN BY REX CLIFFORD

PRINTED IN GREAT BRITAIN BY
BILLING AND SONS LIMITED, GUILDFORD AND LONDON

Contents

An Introduction

ANY AUTHOR who suggests that he might be able to provide the key to a fortune is immediately swamped with questions. Not 'How?', but 'Why?' Why should anyone spend a great deal of time and energy giving others less fortunate a leg-up on his bandwagon?

The British are generally suspicious. Many, no doubt, would not stop even for the eccentric millionaire handing out fivers in Oxford Street. But my 'generosity' is in a different form.

The only claim I make for this book is that if all the information and hints are used intelligently, readers will not only derive a great deal more pleasure out of racing but also stand a better chance of making a profit.

There is no magic formula for finding winners; whereas a large proportion of horses are successful on merit, other results are affected by luck. Luck is the chaser slipping up at the last, the sprinter facing the wrong way at the start. It sees the professional punter, prematurely grey, one day dining at the Savoy and the next in Hyde Park.

Any racing journalist worth his salt can, over a period of time, suggest ten horses that should win, with perhaps six of them living up to expectations. The reason a large number of them do not show a profit with level stakes on their selections throughout the season is that they have to tip in every race, every racing day.

I am in this position and on occasions have been forced into making a selection for a race, knowing that I am basing my assessment not on the chances of the horse winning but on it being among the least likely to finish last.

This will no doubt shock the man who relies on his favourite tipster to give him help every day with his betting—but one of the greatest assets any punter can have is Patience.

A professional, who has perhaps three or even more hefty wagers at one meeting, might then go a week without having as much as a shilling against his name in the bookmaker's ledger.

The horse, the race, the course and the conditions have to be perfect before he takes the plunge, and even the punters who bet in shillings rather than hundreds of pounds would be well advised to follow this policy.

Many newcomers to racing believe that they have only to know a few owners, trainers or jockeys to be set firmly on the road to success with information of the unbeatables, but there will never be any substitute for the form book.

From time to time I receive help from those 'in the know'. Occasionally this has proved profitable but the number of losers far outweighs the winners. If I had kept a record of these tips I am sure that it would show quite a considerable deficit.

A colleague and I once spent hours studying the 'book' for a big race and we both came up with the same horse. We were determined to have a good bet on it . . . until we were told that another horse in the same race had been scorching the gallops at home.

Needless to say we changed allegiance, fooling ourselves that a good case could be made out for the tip. But in the race he finished well behind our original choice, who scored at the rewarding odds of 10–1.

The lesson to be learned is that there is no substitute for 'form'. I know that if I had given up smoking and trained for years, Roger Bannister would still have beaten me ten times out of ten and that truism applies to horses.

The majority of winners take their prizes on merit. Sir Ivor crushed his Derby rivals not because your milkman is called Ivor but because he was better than anything else in the field . . . a fact which was pointed out in the 'book' long before the big race.

Sir Ivor had, of course, won the mile Guineas from Petingo earlier in the season and it was reckoned that, taking everything into account, including his breeding, he was likely to do just as well over the longer Derby trip.

Unfortunately not every race has such a sharply defined winner. Professional punters do almost as much research as the scientist hoping for a Nobel award. It is lucky for the bookmakers that the average race-goer casts just a casual glance in the direction of the race-card, counts his fancy's legs and then strikes a bet.

I am afraid even now that I have been making sound rather easy, for the term 'form horse' is generally a misnomer. Who can tell which it would be in a match between an animal that has been winning good handicaps and one that has run prominently in the Derby? Both horses could get votes.

Many questions have to be answered: Did horse A win his races at the expense of good rivals? Is horse B genuine and likely to reproduce his Epsom running? After these and many other investigations have been carried out, you can feel equipped to make a betting decision.

There is no better training for pin-pointing future winners than a careful study of past results. Discover why a certain horse took a certain race and you can then find the certain horse that IS to take a certain race—for racing form, like history, repeats itself over and over again.

An all-night session with the form book will certainly not bring one hundred per cent success but it will reduce the element of risk to a minimum where luck, or lack of it, refers to the horse and not to the punter.

A bad draw, slow start, poor jockeyship and, to a certain extent in National Hunt racing, sketchy jumping are all factors which cannot be foreseen when making a bet, and it is these that bring the 'shock' results.

When a long shot wins—and here I refer to horses starting at 100–8 or more— there is usually an acceptable reason. Either he was greatly underestimated or the more fancied runners had bad luck in running, with perhaps the favourite being unintentionally boxed in by other competitors.

I say 'unintentionally' with reason because, at this point, it is necessary to contradict the ideas of many losing punters, who believe that every winner they did not back was either pumped up to twice the size with a dope syringe or had been 'held' in its previous outings.

I am well aware that there are a number of shady characters in racing but they are few and far between. When they are among the ranks of trainers or jockeys it is not long before the stewards, more lively these days, root them out.

There is a world of difference between a horse being held (or stopped) and one being prepared. It is not 'legal' for the racecourse to be used as a training ground, but no steward in his senses would reprimand a jockey who, for example, does not belt the daylights out of a young horse having his first experience of racing.

It should also be remembered that no horse can maintain top form throughout the season. If a trainer announces that the intended target for one of his horses is a big race in three months' time, that animal will not necessarily win a race, no matter how small, next week. Preparation for the big day takes time.

A study of past results can give an idea of borderline trainers to watch. Another important pointer to suspicious dealings is the fluctuating bookmakers' odds. If a horse is backed in large amounts just before the start it could be inspired money or cash from the stable. If it drifts in the market, it could be a sign of connections' lack of confidence.

With continual movements in the prices, it is often possible, and sometimes even easy, to back every horse in the race and still show a profit . . . but this and, I hope, several other rewarding points will be dealt with later in the book.

I should think, however, that I am already going far too fast for the newcomers. Trusting that the more advanced 'students' will have patience, here is an explanation of the rudiments of the sport.

There are two separate groups in racing; jumping during the winter, and the flat during the summer—the two 'seasons' overlapping in both the spring and autumn.

Jumping, of course, consists of steeplechasing and hurdle events, but the best breakdown, applying to both groups, is that of handicaps and weight-for-age races.

Unlike handicaps, in which every horse is allotted a weight thought to give it an equal chance with its rivals, weight-for-age races are designed to find the best horse in the line-up. This is why all the prestige races, such as the classics, come into this category.

To a certain extent, weight for age speaks for itself in that horses of the same age carry the same weight—fillies on the flat receiving three pounds from the colts. But when horses of different ages clash, their weights are usually based on a scale devised by Admiral Rous about a century ago.

Admiral Rous spent a great deal of time following the careers of many horses and discovered that, for example, a normal two-year-old racing over six furlong in June was just over two stones inferior to the average three-year-old running over the same trip at the same time. His scale, modified only slightly, is still used by race planners and is included in this book.

While most top races follow this scale, a number of contests incorporate it with their own conditions. I quote Newbury's Peter Hastings Stakes, run in September, in which some earlier big prize winners have to carry rather more than their less successful rivals.

PETER HASTINGS STAKES, three-year-old colts and geldings 8 st 3 lb, fillies 8 st; four-year-old and up colts and geldings 8 st 10 lb, fillies 8 st 7 lb; winner of a race value £2,000 3 lb, of two races value £2,000 or one value £4,000 6 lb, of a race value £8,000 9 lb, handicaps and races won at two years old not to count for penalties.—One mile and a quarter.

Of course, weight-for-age races are not composed entirely of top-class events like the Classics, The Eclipse Stakes or jumping's Cheltenham Gold Cup. They are more often the bread-and-butter races such as maiden events and novice hurdles for horses still looking for their first win.

Obviously, it would be impossible to rate an animal before it had been seen on a racecourse. So all horses must either have won, or have run three times in, a weight-for-age race before they are eligible for handicapping, otherwise they are automatic top weight.

Entering a horse for a particular race is rather like planning the education of a child. Usually the bigger the prize the more you pay to run a horse and the earlier its name has to be put down. In the case of the three-year-olds classic races (two Guineas, Derby, Oaks and St Leger) a horse has to be entered before its two-year-old campaign but closing date for the average race is about a month before it is run.

Once the horse is entered it is given a weight, and then there are a varying number of forfeit stages—when owners pay more if they still intend to run horses—the most important stage being four days before the event, after which courses have a list of probables which are numbered with top weight as one, second highest as two, and so on.

The final stage is on the eve of the race and is called *overnight declaration*, when connections have their final chance of withdrawing their horses. This is why the numbers in your morning paper do not necessarily follow on each other.

There are, in fact, so many numbers on a race-card that, to the uninitiated, it looks rather a mathematician's nightmare. The programme itself needs explaining.

3.10 Fakenham Handicap (2 miles) for four-year-olds and upwards

Value to winner £452 2s.

```
301—0-04200 DRUMLANRIG (Lord Rotherwick) ....... W. Hern 5 8 12 ........ J. Mercer   9
303— 412140 KING OF PEACE (D) (Mr Jack Hardy) ...J. Hardy 5 8  8 ........ B. Henry    8
304— 401201 HIGH MARSHAL (C) (Mr D. Prenn).....J. Winter 5 8  7 ...... L. Piggott    2
305— 02B003 LONE WOLF (D) (Lady Brooke) ......E. Lambton 4 8  6 ..... P. Robinson   15
307—120030- CAMUS (Mr V. England) ..............P. Kearney 5 8  3 ...........D. Jelf   7
308—100-304 CORONADO (Mrs Rodney H. Edmondson)..Beeby 6 8  0 ........ D. Yates      5
309— 120320 VALERIE JOY (Mrs E. Collington) .....D. Leslie 4 8  0 ...... W. Carson  11
310—14000-0 NOTHING HIGHER (Mrs E. E. Dawnson)
                                       M. H. Easterby 4 8  0 .... L. G. Brown  14
311— 043000 C.E.D. (Mr H. L. Vickery)  ............T. Gosling 6 7 13 ....... A. Murray  13
312— 010000 BEAU LAVENDER (D2) (Mr M. R. Soames)
                                       C. J. Benstead 5 7 12 .... M. L. Thomas  12
314—2-00401 ATHLETE (C/D) (Lord Pembroke)  Boyd-Rochfort 4 7 12 ....... A. Barclay  16
316—  0-001 GALOSH (D) (Mr A. J. Massingberd-Mundy) Elsey 4 7  7 ...... E. Johnson  10
317—     00 CRESCENDO (Mrs E. M. Knox) ........D. Leslie 5 7  6 ........ C. Patton   3
318— 231300 KISS OF LIFE (Mr R. G. Angus) ..G. N. Robinson 4 7  2 ........ D. Coates   4
320—23-3400 WEALTHY SON (Mr Gerald Cooper) .J. W. Watts 4 7  0 ...... (7) J. Lowe    1
321— 000000 PETER PIPER (Mr R. E. Mason) ......R. Mason 8 7  0 .... (5) J. Higgins   6
```

All meetings operating a Totalisator Jackpot (where backers have to name all six winners) give the horse's number on the extreme left of their programme, prefixing it with a number from one to six, which refers to the race.

For example, horse 12 in the first event is 112, and horse one in the third race is 301 ... but it is still only the figure 12 or 1 that these horses carry on their saddle-cloth.

After the number of the horse are the form figures, usually six of them. They are self-explanatory with a '1' meaning it finished first, '2' second and so on to the '0' which signifies unplaced.

10

In more detailed programmes there are abbreviations of 'D' for disqualified, 'F' for fall, 'U.R.' for unseated rider, 'B' or 'B.D' for brought down or perhaps 'P' for pulled up.

The form figures are read from left to right with the extreme right referring to the horses's latest performance. In most cases where a hyphen is at either end or among the figure series there has been a break of seasons . . . thus 111-000 means that a horse won its final three outings last season but has had three attempts without success this term.

An oblique '/' instead of a hyphen indicates an absence of a season so that 111/000 means that the horse won his three races the season before last, did not race last term and has had three unrewarding ventures this campaign.

Next in the programme comes the horse's name followed sometimes by the name of the owner in brackets, though this may be left out as the trainer's name, which follows, is far more worthy of the space.

The last series of figures gives the horse's age and the weight he carries so that 4–8–7 means that the horse is four years old and carries eight-and-a-half stones. This is, of course, the weight of the jockey and, perhaps, a few pounds of lead carried in a leather holder under the saddle.

Finally, the name of the jockey. Even here there may be a figure, for apprentices are 'allowed' certain amounts of weight to put them on even terms with more experienced riders.

Boy riders are allowed 7 lb until they have ridden ten winners, 5 lb until 50 and 3 lb until 75. This appears on the programme as John Smith (7), for example, and the seven pounds has to be deducted from the listed weight of his mount.

Occasionally there are further abbreviations in the programme, usually after the horse's name. The most important of these are 'D' for a winner over the distance, 'C/D' for a course and distance winner, 'C' for a winner over the course and 'BF' meaning it started favourite last time out but let down its supporters.

The final column of figures in the programme quoted is the draw or position of the horses at the start. There is no draw in National Hunt racing and in long distances races on the flat it makes little difference, but in sprints it can have quite a considerable effect.

The horses take up their position with the lowest drawn on the left as they face the starter. If there is a left-hand bend, then low-drawn horses are favoured because they can take the shortest possible route, while those with a high number have slightly further to travel and may have to go wide round the bend. Naturally, high numbers have it when the angle is right-handed.

The effect of the draw is included with racecourse descriptions given later in the book and, perhaps, the best example of it influencing results is Chester, a tiny circuit which is turning left almost throughout. Here the winner is invariably from those drawn with a low number.

However, I am digressing. There is still one more important point to be dealt with in the programme: penalties. In most handicaps, a horse is liable to collect extra weight if, in the time between the compilation of the weights and the race itself, it wins a different event.

The amount of the penalty varies but it is usually about seven pounds. This is clearly marked in the newspaper programmes and the extra has already been added to the original weight.

There are exceptions, for if the 'interim' win was in an apprentice riders' race then the horse avoids a penalty if his target this time is a handicap in which fully fledged riders are permitted to take part.

No Grand National entry ever collects a penalty, even if it wins a dozen times between the weights being announced and the Liverpool Spring meeting. Several other handicaps have limited penalties—take the conditions for the Cambridgeshire:

CAMBRIDGESHIRE STAKES (Handicap) for three-year-olds and upwards; the lowest to be not less than 7 st, weights published August 31; winner after August 26 of a handicap value £600 to carry 4 lb, of two handicaps or of any race value £1,200 6 lb of any race value £2,000 9 lb extra but the maximum penalty for horses originally handicapped at 9 st or upwards shall be 4 lb—one mile and a furlong.

Obviously, with the risk of at least a four-pound penalty, most trainers tuning up their Cambridgeshire hopes after August 26 would have aimed them at races worth less than £600 to the winner.

The inclusion of 'conditions' with the racing programme can be a great help to winner-finding and this is one of the many points on which the specialised racing papers, such as *The Sporting Chronicle*, score over the ordinary daily newspaper, where space is short.

It often amazes me that the punter prepared to bet £1 will not spend a penny on papers, magazines and books which can tell him that there is a horse likely to beat his fancy.

There are numerous aids which should form part of a racing man's library apart from a daily racing paper.

A copy of the *Racing Calendar*—official journal of the Jockey Club and National Hunt Committee—is first with the entries and weights for future races each week, but it is expensive, and the *Handicap Book* performs almost as good a service every Friday. It gives programmes for the following week and costs just one shilling.

One of the best annuals is *Ruffs Guide*, which has many attractive features. Prominence is given to big sales of the previous year, plus breeding records. Sires are listed with winning progeny, the amount of prize money they collected and, most important, the distances of the races over which they scored.

Racehorses of 1968 is another excellent annual. Plenty of good pictures scattered throughout a massive alphabetical list of all the horses that have run in the previous year. The complete abbreviated record of each animal is given, together with a biography describing best efforts, favourite distances and going and other peculiarities.

Now, most important of all, form books. Undoubtedly the tops in this field are *Raceform* (flat) and *Chaseform* (jumping) and *Racing-Up-To-Date*. Both work out quite pricey but are worth every penny.

Raceform and *Chaseform* send out a slip, with recent results, through the post each week to be joined to the bulk. *Racing-Up-To-Date* is a complete book every Saturday.

Both have the same conformation. There is an index of horses that have run during the season, their colour, sex, breeding and reference numbers to the races in which they have taken part, brackets around the figure indicating a win.

A specimen of this index from *Racing-Up-To-Date* looks like this:

2 CHARGER b c Hard Ridden—Majestic by Buisson Ardent (Ashworth) 635, 900.
3 CHARICLES b c Bleep-Bleep—Candida by Stardust (Lambton) 675 1093², (1175), 1707, 2266, 2357⁴ (2639), 2763³, 2894.
2 CHARLATANA b or br Dumbarnie—Harvest Queen by High Profit (J. Thompson) 340, 690, 1605², 1754, 2457³, 2765, 2952².

The last set of figures in the series is the horse's latest outing and turning to that number:

2894 Ayr Gold Cup (hcap) £4,428 18s (£5,000)—6f (str)

2585*PETITE PATH (*prog to ld apprg fnl f, sn clr*) 4–7–6 (8lbx)	§⁵J. Higgins(7)1
2539 SARATOGA SKIDDY (B) (*hmpd 1½f out, fin fast*) 3–7–2	§⁵R. Still(17)2
2539 SPANIARDS INN (*effort apprg fnl f, outpcd cl home*) 5–7–11	§³R. Dicey(2)3
2885³BIRDMAN (B) (*2nd h-way, no ex fnl f*) 5–6–10	§⁷J. Lowe (4)4
2660*GREAT BEAR (*wl plcd h-way, not quicken*) 4–9–1 (4lbx)	R. Hutchinson(16)5
2402² BE FRIENDLY (fav) (*alws in tch, short-lived effort 2f out* 4–9–7	G. Lewis(12)6
2646*MATILDA III (*sn prom, no ex*) 3–7–7– (4lbx)	§⁷I. Cunningham(5)7
2763³CHARICLES (*led till 1½f out. faded*) 3–7–7	D. East(19)8
2357 ASHFORD LEA (B) (*prom till apprg fnl f, nor quicken*) 4–7–11	B. Lee(21)9
2656*KURSAAL 3–8–10 (8lbx)	P. Robinson (18)
2585 PALS PASSAGE (B) 4–8–9	J. Etherington(8)
2486 MORGAN'S PRIDE (P) 4–8–1	§³G. Sexton(9)
2328⁴HOUSE PROUD 4–8–1	B. Raymond(13)
2266 SOVEREIGN SET 5–7–10	E. Johnson(10)
2400 TINSEL (*prom h-way*) 3–7–6⁵	§⁵C. Eccleston(14)
2470 SOVEREIGN SERVICE (B) 3–7–9³	V. Faggotter(6)
2882 MILESIUS (B) 6–7–4	N.McIntosh(20)
2357 STEPHEN GEORGE (B) 5–7–0²	§⁵D. Coates(1)
2772 PERTINO 3–6–9	§⁷E. Marshall(3)
2759 ST MUNGO 5–7–0	C. Parkes(15)
2811²RED DESIRE 3–7–0	D. Noble(11)21

5/2 B Friendly (*from 7/2*), 100/8 S Skiddy (*tchd 100/6*), Charicles (*op 10's*), 100/7 PETITE PATH (*op 10's*), G. Bear, Kursaal, 100/6 A. Lea, S. Set (*tchd 18's*), 20 M. Pride, S. Inn, 25 P. Passage (*from 33's*), H. Proud, S. George, 33 Tinsel, S. Service, R Desire, 50 Matilda III, Milesius, Pertino, S. Mungo, 66 Birdman (*from 100's*). R. Mason (*Mrs R. E. Mason*), Guilsborough, Northants.
DISTANCES—2–½–2–½–½
TOTE—36/8 *Pl* 15/10, 15/2, 10/10.
TIME—1/12.83s.
Breeder—Guilsborough Stud Farm Ltd.

This form tells us a great deal. Charicles, twice a winner earlier in the season, was quite a warm fancy to land the rich £4,428 Ayr Gold Cup over six furlongs.

With a modest 7 st 3 lb in the saddle—made up in the main by David East—he started joint second favourite at 100–8 (once touching 10–1) with Saratoga Skiddy, the best backed being Be Friendly, a 5–2 chance.

13

Ayr is a very fair course (see maps and descriptions) so that his No. 19 draw in a 21-strong field meant very little. Taking advantage of his light weight the three-year-old led them all until a furlong and a half out and then faded quickly in the softish going to pass the post eighth.

The winner, Petite Path, had shot into a clear lead approaching the final furlong and still had two lengths to spare over Saratoga Skiddy at the post.

Petite Path, a 100–7 shot, had won since the weights were published, incurring a hefty eight-pound penalty, but this was partly cancelled out by the five pound claim of apprentice Higgins and she, in fact, carried 7 st 6 lb.

Under the betting we are told that she was trained by Ron Mason at Guilsborough and carried Mrs Mason's colours.

Of the others in the race: Saratoga Skiddy may have been slightly unlucky, for he was hampered when slipping into top gear a furlong and a half out, while the favourite, Be Friendly, was certainly not disgraced in carrying top weight of 9 st 7 lb into sixth position, showing up well throughout.

Finally, those figures alongside each horse. They refer to the number of the previous race in which that particular animal took part, with a star indicating that it won and the small numbers pinpointing a second, third or fourth.

14

Weights and Measures

SINCE THE HANDICAPPER spends his entire working day ensuring that the horses, although not created equal, are given an equal chance of making good, it might seem a waste of time for punters to try to pick out good bets from his assessments.

Indeed, it is an old racing belief that the only way to successful gambling comes from concentrating entirely on weight-for-age races, where the runners perform purely on their own merits.

There is undoubtedly a good deal of sense in this, but where it does misfire is in forgetting that the handicapper must treat horses as machines whereas they are, in fact, as peculiar as humans.

If two horses dead-heat one day, the assumption is that they would again share the prize if they met with the same weights a week or so later. But a change in the going, course, distance or even draw will almost certainly mean an upset in calculations.

The punter's task here is to find out which of the pair is likely to be more suited by the new conditions and, even more important, if either of the horses has improved or deteriorated since the previous clash.

In almost all other sports, handicapping means that a competitor has to run a few yards, more or less, than his rivals, but in horse racing the great leveller is weight.

The idea is that while you might be able to run quite happily for ten yards carrying a sack of coal, the next fifty would see you trailing and after a hundred you would have slowed to a walk.

* * *

After extensive experiment it has been discovered that if horse A beats horse B by a length in a flat race, they should dead-heat if horse B is set to receive THREE POUNDS from his old rival. In jumping, ONE POUND is usually enough to pull back a length.

This is obviously a fluid rule, for it might take as much as five pounds to pull back a length in a sharp sprint at Epsom, while the same amount of weight could mean ten lengths or more in the Grand National over a gruelling four and a half miles.

A simple example of handicapping is:

Past Result (one mile)
1st Sovereign 4–8–7
2nd Rome   4–8–10
3rd Bluerullah 4–9–0
Distances: neck, one length.

Taking a pound off Rome's weight would mean that he could make up the neck on Sovereign while Bluerullah should be three pounds better off with Rome to pull back the length he was beaten for runner-up spot. In theory the new handicap

        Bluerullah 4–8–10
        Rome   4–8–9
        Sovereign 4–8–7

will have a triple dead-heat!

Difficulties appear with the introduction of Follywise who, carrying 7 st 8 lb in the 'past result', finished ten lengths behind Bluerullah in sixth position.

The first thing to remember is that this ten lengths is unreal. Follywise was almost certainly not ridden out in the closing stages when it was realised that he had no chance of getting into the prize money.

Had he been pushed all the way, he would more likely have been just five lengths in arrears. Taking this line, he must now meet Bluerullah on 15 lb better terms.

It would mean 6 st 3 lb for Follywise in the new handicap but, since the minimum weight in most races is 7 st, he moves up to that mark with each of his three old rivals collecting an extra eleven pounds.

*   *   *

In examples so far I have been dealing with horses of the same age in opposition, but the process becomes rather more complicated when animals of different ages renew rivalry. Younger horses will have made more 'natural improvement' than their elders since the previous clash. The weight-for-age scale should be our guide.

March result (six furlongs)
1st So Blessed 3–7–6
2nd Willipeg   4–8–3
Winning distance: 2 lengths.

These horses are meeting again over the same six furlongs in October.

The weight-for-age scale shows that, whereas the average three-year-old is 16 lb inferior to the average four-year-old when they meet over six furlongs in March, it is only a mere five pounds in October—a difference of 11 lb.

This 11 lb natural improvement should be added to So Blessed's weight and so, too, must an extra six pounds for the two lengths he beat Willipeg on their previous meeting. So the new handicap will be:

        So Blessed 3–8–9
        Willipeg   4–8–3

*   *   *

Obviously few races are composed entirely of horses that have met before and the handicapper constantly is having to use an entirely different animal as a yardstick to the relative abilities of the two entrants.

The principle is that since horse A beat horse B by a length at level weights and horse B later beat horse C by two lengths at level weights, then horse A should give horse C nine pounds when they meet.

This form-line assessment may be none too strong, but the handicapper is even more liable to error when he has to rate a horse which, so far, has made just three appearances in weight-for-age races.

*   *   *

There are, of course, many occasions when it is quite impossible to give every would-be contender an equal chance. Some horses might be four stones inferior to the best entry, yet the complete range of most handicaps is just 2 st 7 lb (7 st to 9 st 7 lb on the flat and 10 st to 12 st 7 lb over jumps).

Faced with this quart-into-a-pint-pot situation, the handicapper will pick out his top weight and rate the other horses in relation to it until he comes to the dregs, who are all lumped on the minimum mark, even though many of them should have a good deal less.

The mighty Arkle at his peak aggravated this particular headache. He was so superior to other chasers that in putting him on the 12 st 7 lb mark, the handicapper was forced to put all but one or two of the other entries on 10 st. If the Irish chaser was later withdrawn, the title 'handicap' was a joke.

Obviously the rules had to be altered, and whenever Arkle was entered the handicapper was allowed to use an extended range of weights. If the Irish Champion was declared at the four-day forfeit stage, runners listed below 10 st were lifted to that mark, and if he was taken out, all the probables had their weights raised to fit between the limits.

This situation arose because there were so few rich weight-for-age chases and, naturally, Arkle was forced to go handicapping. Flat racing is much better balanced and handicappers are rarely put in such a tricky position.

However, there are instances of gamesmanship on the flat with a trainer entering two animals: A, a really brilliant horse, and B, extremely useful but not in the same class as his stable mate.

The pair dominate the entries. A is given top weight, a stone more than B, with the remainder cramped in the remaining stone and a half—most being on the minimum mark. A is withdrawn, leaving B to meet the majority of the opposition on far better terms than he deserves.

*   *   *

The end product of the handicapper's work across the breakfast table might seem an insoluble problem but, provided the punter is willing to spend a little time in study, he could come up with the profitable answer.

Following the principles I have described he can make up his own handicap. Comparing it with the official version he should discover a horse that, in his opinion, has been under-rated.

For confirmation or otherwise of his belief, he can then check with the horse's other engagements during the week in the *Handicap Book*, finding a race compiled by a different official handicapper—their names are listed with the programme.

There are likely to be several other runners doubly engaged, apart from the fancy, to assist with this second comparison.

*   *   *

As I mentioned earlier, the big drawback for a handicapper is that he can only rate a horse on past performances. Apart from the 'natural improvement' suggested in the weight-for-age scale, he is of course unable to foresee any unexpected progress from a particular animal.

Since the weights for most races are announced in the *Racing Calendar* about a month before the actual day of the contest, a horse has plenty of time to upset the ratings by stepping up on his earlier efforts, not necessarily by winning and thus incurring a penalty, but perhaps by finishing a creditable second.

The weights publication date is included in the conditions of all handicaps. It is always worth paying particular attention to the efforts of horses who have run since then to see if the performance is a surprise improvement—and, if so, why it came about and whether it is likely to be repeated.

Sometimes even horses who collected penalties with a recent win had so much in hand when scoring that even the extra weight is unlikely to prevent them from again going close in their follow-up bid.

*　　*　　*

One of the main reasons for 'surprise improvement' is that horses, unlike humans, share a universal birthday on January 1st, so that in theory a yearling could be 365 days old or just a few hours. There would be no doubt which would be the most able if they met as two-year-olds.

Obviously breeders try to avoid this situation and most foals are born between February and June. Calculations can go awry with the result that several horses, officially called two-year-olds are virtually little more than yearlings.

Even the four month's difference between an early and a late foal would be marked in juvenile events. It would gradually disappear as they both aged, but could sometimes account for reversed form later in their careers.

*　　*　　*

However, a more important reason for surprise improvement from a punter's point of view would be a change in distance. A horse who wins over six furlongs is not a certainty to confirm his superiority over the same opposition in a mile event.

Sensible use of the form book can provide clues. Comments against the horses names in *Racing-Up-To-Date* often say 'ran on' or 'finished strongly', suggesting that a little extra distance might be appreciated.

Then again, some tracks are a great deal easier than others—see *Description of Courses* later in the book. A mile at one meeting might be the equivalent of twelve furlongs on another.

A prime example of this is the comparison between the Epsom five furlongs and the same distance at Sandown. At Epsom runners race hell-for-leather downhill almost throughout, gathering impetus for a rising finish. A fast half-miler has his best chance here, but at Sandown the sprint track is against the collar all the way and makes demands on stamina.

Finally, breeding. It is amazing that, for example, a top-class sprinter will pass on his particular qualities to his offspring when he goes to stud, though there is occasionally the freak three-mile chaser among his progeny.

The dam, of course, also has an influence, but sires provide the best rule. I have compiled a list of the most successful with letters after their name indicating the likely best distances of their progeny.

Abernant	S	Hard Tack	S	Pinza	M
Above Suspicion	M	Henry the Seventh	S–M	Polic	S
Acropolis	M	High Hat	M	Polly's Jet	S
Aggressor	M–L	High Perch	M	Primera	M
Alcide	M–L	High Treason	S	Princely Gift	S
Arctic Storm	S–M	Hill Gail	M	Privy Councillor	S
Arctic Time	M	Honeyway	M	Psidum	M
Aureole	M–L	Hook Money	S	Quorum	S–M
Babur	S–M	Hornbeam	M	Ratification	S
Bairam II	M	Hugh Lupus	M	Red God	S
Ballymoss	M–L	Immortality	M	Relic	S–M
Blast	S	Infatuation	M	Ribot	M
Bleep-Bleep	S	Javelot	M	Right Boy	S
Cash and Courage	M	Kelly	S	Right Royal V	M
Charlottesville	M	King's Bench	S–M	Rockavon	M
Como	S	King's Troop	S	Royal Palm	S
Constable	S	Klairon	S–M	Rustam	S
Counsel	S–M	Klondyke Bill	S	Saint Crespin III	S–M
Crepello	M	Kythnos	M	St Paddy	M
Crocket	S–M	Larkspur	M	Sammy Davis	S
Darius	S–M	Le Dieu D'Or	S	Set Fair	S–M
Darling Boy	M	Le Levanstell	S–M	Shantung	M
Democratic	S	Lord of Verona	M	Sheshoon	M
Dicta Drake	M	Major Portion	S–M	Sing Sing	S
Dignitary	S	March Past	S–M	Skymaster	S
Dual	M–L	Martial	S	Sound Track	S
El Gallo	S	Matador	S	Sovereign Path	S
Ennis	S	Milesian	S–M	Star Gazer	S
Epaulette	S	Molvedo	M	Tamerlane	S–M
Eudaemon	S–M	Mossborough	M	Tiger	M
Fidalgo	M	Narrator	M	Tin Whistle	S
Firestreak	S	Never Say Die	M	Tudor Melody	S
Floribunda	S	Ossian II	M	Vienna	S–M
Fortino II	M	Our Babu	S–M	Vigo	S
French Beige	M–L	Palestine	S	Vimy	M
Galivanter	S	Pall Mall	S	Vulgan	L
Gilles de Retz	S–M	Pampered King	M	Welsh Abbot	S
Golden Cloud	S	Panaslipper	M	Whistler	S
Gratitude	S	Pandofell	M–L	Whistling Wind	S
Grey Sovereign	S	Pardal	M	Will Somers	S
Hard Ridden	M	Pardao	M	Worden II	M
Hard Sauce	S–M	Parthia	M	Zarathustra	M

I said earlier that horses have all the peculiarities of some humans, and a great many of them are just as lazy and cunning, learning that even if they do not do their best on the racecourse, they still get five-star hotel treatment back in their stables.

A set of blinkers can sometimes bring about an amazing transformation. The wearer has his attention riveted on the job in hand, which sometimes causes a surprise win. It is always worth noting an animal being fitted with blinkers for the first time.

The benefit may continue for several outings but, in many cases, the horses realise that they are being had, remembering the old saying, you can fool some of the people some of the time . . . they return to their old lack-lustre form.

*   *   *

Some horses are more at home on a right-hand-turning course than a left, some think that evening racing is an intrusion on their rest time, but they display most marked performances on the state of the going.

The flat racing season extends right through from spring until autumn, with constantly changing weather. Although form is quite reliable during the summer—a black time for the bookmakers—the coming of heavy rain washes away past results.

No other single factor has as much influence on results than the going. In studying the form book it is just as important to discover underfoot conditions when a bad performance has been turned in as when the horse gave its best display.

TRAINERS, JOCKEYS, OWNERS

The various techniques of preparing a racehorse are of little interest to the average punter. His acid test of trainers is the results they achieve with the material at their disposal.

It does not follow that the trainer collecting most prize money during a season is the best; he could be just fashionable with a host of rich owners stocking up his stable with all the top-priced buys at the previous year's sales.

A large number of these animals would win good races if their only build-up was a walk up the ramp of a horsebox. A good trainer is one who can take any horse, no matter how modest, and at a given time have it fit to run for its life, even if the target is only a selling race at Carlisle.

Noel Murless is fashionable. Any youngster in his yard that cost less than 10,000 guineas will suffer from an inferiority complex before a week is out . . . but Murless has fully earned his position at the top of the tree.

He knows he is handling valuable merchandise and behaves accordingly, showing tremendous patience with his juveniles—you rarely see one of his two-year-olds in action before Royal Ascot—and, despite a huge string, giving each of his horses individual attention.

Near neighbour Teddy Lambton pleases his patrons with quantity as much as quality, for the modest horses in his yard can build up a whole string of successes as Lambton is a master at placing his lodgers to advantage.

Harry Wragg, also based at Newmarket, can tune his horses to the second. By doing so gradually, he often fools the handicapper in big races, a commendable ability which is also possessed by Cheshire man Eric Cousins.

Dick Hern has a way with stayers, and Pat Rohan gets the ultimate out of a sprinter. George Todd can pass on the secret of eternal youth to veterans, while Tommy Robson, a veterinary surgeon as well as trainer, can work wonders with other people's cast-offs.

Every top trainer is a specialist in one particular field and a master in the others, but besides an ability to know just how much food and what exercise to give his charges, he must also be a wizard with the form book to pick out their best opportunities.

It is no good preparing a horse for the Derby and having him at his peak for Epsom when the very best that can be expected is perhaps sixth position, while if he had hung fire for a few days he would almost certainly have collected the Queen's Vase at Ascot.

Apart from reading the form book, trainers also have to be good with general bookwork, Entries close at least a month before each race, so programmes have to be planned well ahead, and one horse could be down for as many as ten races during a week.

Nearer the time, the trainer will choose his target. It is obviously worth noting a horse sent for one particular event rather than half a dozen other engagements around the same date, for this must be the race in which the horse is thought to have his best chance of success.

It follows also that if there are several entries from one stable in a race, then the final choice of representative should be given serious consideration by the punter.

In fact, common sense is the by-word. Any thinking gambler can anticipate most trainers knowing, for instance, that if an animal is sent on a 200-mile trek to one race meeting rather than fulfilling another engagement on his doorstep, there must be some reason.

Then, again, if Sam Hall has runners in all six races at Newcastle, and you spot his jovial face at Ripon, where he has just a single raider, it must be obvious which horse carries the stable's main hopes of the day.

A paddock inspection before each race should, therefore, serve a double purpose. You should see not only how your 'fancy' is looking but also who is in charge of the saddling.

*　　　*　　　*

The movements of jockeys are probably even more important than those of trainers, though to a certain extent they are dictated by the internal politics of retainers.

If a jockey accepts a retainer from a trainer at the start of the season he is paid a negotiated sum and, in return, partners all runners from that stable—weight permitting.

The *Sporting Chronicle's* 'Horses in Training', published annually, not only lists every trainer's string, but also gives the retained jockey—plus stable apprentices—and their riding weight.

Eddie Hide is retained by Sir Gordon Richards and will be aboard all horses from that stable carrying 7 st 13 lb or more—his only choice being when there are two runners from the yard in the same event or two meetings where Sir Gordon has representatives, in which cases he can decide which or where he wants to ride.

If Sir Gordon has no runners, Hide has a second retainer while some jockeys may have even a third staking claim to their services.

Freelance riding can sometimes be financially hazardous, but it does give jockeys such as Lester Piggott the freedom to pick and choose from offered mounts. They, of course, have their favourite trainers, and Lester, riding for father-in-law Sam Armstrong, or Fulke Johnson Houghton, are successful combinations.

The three major points to watch in jockeys' movements are:

1. The top-flight jockey who goes to a meeting for just one booked mount from a stable by whom he is not retained.

2. The jockey given permission to accept a mount from an outside yard when he should be partnering horses from his retaining stable.

3. The jockey who is at one of the big festivals and slips away for an afternoon to ride at a lesser meeting.

* * *

The apprentice's claim is basically meant to put him on equal terms with fully-fledged riders, but sometimes a boy is so good that his 7 lb, 5 lb or 3 lb allowance is all profit. Consequently he is in great demand.

Naturally, the trainer to whom the boy is apprenticed will charge other stables if they want to borrow him. Bearing this 'fee' in mind, it is worth noting a trainer who uses another's apprentice when he has some of his own.

* * *

Owners are delighted to win whenever and wherever they can—but pay particular attention to horses running at a meeting where their owner is a steward. There are plenty of winners amongst them.

Betting

MOST PUNTERS bet at starting price. As the name suggests, there are the odds offered about each horse by leading bookmakers on the course immediately the tapes go up or the stalls fly open.

Representatives of the *Sporting Chronicle* and *The Sporting Life*—men of the highest integrity—are on the spot to compile the lists of starting prices. Although many attempts are made to trick them, few succeed.

One S.P. man tells of the greedy bookmaker who spotted a certainty at a small jumping meeting on an Easter Monday when there were many far more important fixtures scattered throughout the country.

The horse was an obvious hot favourite yet the bookmaker—a lion among cats on that course—offered a generous 2–1 against the 'good thing'. While the animal was backed in tenners with him, he had agents backing it to win hundreds in offices up and down the land.

The S.P. man spotted the ruse and the bookmaker had an unpleasant surprise when he learned the returned price.

But this sort of thing is rare. On a normal day betting shops pass a proportion of bets via 'the blower' to the course so that the starting price really does reflect the country's opinion of a horse's chance and not just the view of a few thousand people at the meeting.

Before going into great detail about betting, I should first explain the difference between odds against and odds on:

Odds against is easy: the stake is simply multiplied by the price. Example—£2×6/4 = £3 (excluding £2 stake).

Odds on is rather more complicated. It means that the punter is acting bookmaker and buying money. 4–1 on is in fact 1–4. Example—£2×4/6 (6/4 on) = £1 6s 8d. (excluding £2 stake).

*   *   *

If there were three horses all with equal chances in a race, the obvious odds against any one of them winning must be 2–1, but the bookmaker must make his profit and by offering 7–4 against each he can collect £9 for every £109 that goes in his ledger.

In practice, however, demand for one particular horse is never constant and rarely equal to that for other animals in the race. Thus bookmakers, to ensure their necessary profit, are for ever adjusting their prices, cutting the odds of one horse and extending them on another.

The method of adjusting is to convert the odds to points and then ensure that, at any given time, the points in each contest exceed 100—but not by too much, perhaps between 110–120.

To make the conversion, work out how much money it would take at the odds to collect £100 including the stake. If the price is 3–1 then it would take £25 (25 pts) to make £100 (100 pts) with the stake included.

In many cases it is necessary to make a rough estimate in the conversion as with 2–1. An investment of £33 (33 pts) would draw £99 (99 pts), stake included, and this is close enough to make little difference in calculations.

GUIDE TO CONVERSION (points approximate)

Odds	1–4	2–7	1–3	4–11	2–5	4–9	
Points	80	77	75	73	71	69	
Odds	1–2	8–15	4–7	8–13	4–6	8–11	
Points	66	65	63	62	60	57	
Odds	4–5	10–11	Evens	11–10	5–4	11–8	
Points	55	53	50	47	44	42	
Odds	6–4	13–8	7–4	15–8	2–1	9–4	
Points	40	38	36	34	33	30	
Odds	5–2	3–1	7–2	4–1	9–2	5–1	11–2
Points	28	25	22	20	18	16	15
Odds	6–1	13–2	7–1	8–1	9–1	10–1	
Points	14	13	12	11	10	9	

Having made the conversion for each horse in the race, any number of points over the 100 is bookmaker's profit. If the total is less than 100, the book is running at a loss.

Here are simple examples of both instances. In each case there are four horses in the line-up:

The horses are on offer at 6–4, 2–1, 3–1 and 9–2. This the conversion is: 40 pts+ +33+25+18 making a total of 116, which means that the bookmaker theoretically makes £16 in every £116 that passes over his counter.

On the other hand, if the odds are 2–1, 5–2, 4–1, 6–1, the conversion will be 33 pts+28+20+14, a total of 95 pts. The punter can, therefore, back every horse in the race and show £5 profit for every £95 invested.

Unfortunately, the Chancellor of the Exchequer takes his pound of flesh in the shape of the 5 per cent betting tax, which cancels out this guaranteed £5 profit, and so the total must be below 95 pts for the punter to be on to a certainty.

The way to cash in is to back in pounds—or workable ratios of them—in place of the points. But, of course, instances of such generosity from the bookmakers are rare indeed.

Where the punter is likely to find more use for this method is if, after studying the form, he can dismiss with confidence one or two of the runners in a small field and treat the others as the only contenders.

Or it can be used in a busy market for a small field when odds are constantly fluctuating by taking advantage of generous odds about two horses, for example, and when they shorten, by backing the others as their odds are extended.

Having used common sense in picking your fancy, it would seem only natural to back intelligently. But all too many punters lose their heads and try to make a quick fortune instead of going for a slow but sure profit.

Combination bets (doubles, trebles and such) are fine provided they are not carried to excess. The William Hill client with his 175-yard betting slip had the directors' board-room shaking with laughter, not fear.

In the process of weighing up the race, it is always a good plan to compile a betting forecast with personal ideas of what prices should be offered about the chances of each horse.

If your selection goes on the bookmaker's board a great deal shorter than expected, then leave it alone. It must follow that you are not getting full value for money.

Also ignore the race if your fancy is at much longer odds than your estimate, since it is likely to be a reflection of lack of confidence by connections.

Newspapers provide a betting forecast, though how close the comparison is between this and the actual starting price varies considerably according to the astuteness of the person who compiled the list. Once again, the specialist racing papers are usually nearest the mark.

*   *   *

Ante-post odds—prices offered on race weeks or, perhaps, months before they are run—are always attractive bait but, to the unwary, they can be as deadly as an arsenic-coated carrot is to a donkey.

The odds may be tempting but a great deal can happen between the time a bet is struck and the big day. If the horse does not go to post, the money is lost.

Amazing as it might seem, however, an ante-post book rarely shows a profit for the bookmakers, and many claim they only produce the massive lists to draw new customers who will also use their ordinary day-to-day services.

The reason for this loss is that a gambler on the inside, perhaps even the owner or trainer, can place a large bet in the certain knowledge that his horse is being prepared especially for the race and is, therefore, a certain runner.

It usually pays to follow the money but there are exceptions, such as that fantastic situation a few years ago when, as a result of a well-publicised dream that El Mighty would win the Derby, the colt was backed to win millions from 200–1 to 20–1. Fools rush in . . . !

Obviously the bookmakers play by ear later on, but in the early stages, when they produce their first ante-post lists, they must back the judgment of their own private handicapper, who compares his ratings with the official weights. On occasions he has been known to slip up.

*   *   *

Another 'carrot' to treat with caution is the Tote Jackpot, which, as mentioned earlier, entails naming all six winners on the programme. Dividends are tremendously high but they are often less than the accumulated odds at starting price with a no-limit bookmaker.

Where an investment on the jackpot does prove good value is when no-one has been successful on, perhaps, the first two days of a meeting and the pool has built up for the third programme, which looks relatively simple.

* * *

Comparisons between the bookmakers and the Tote show that there is plenty to be said for both, but, in general terms, a favourite more often provides the better dividend with the book, while the tote offers more reward for picking a long-shot.

The majority of professional backers prefer the book for, after having made their selection, they know whether they are getting realistic odds. On the Tote, however, the dividend is not known until, basically, the amount staked has been added and then divided by the number of winning tickets.

I have known a few professionals who have shown a healthy profit on the Tote, mainly because of the fact that they can back their fancy for a place only and are not tied to the each-way (win and place) insistence of the bookmakers.

On the other hand, the Tote at present does not have facilities for coping with the varied small combination bets such as the Patent, Yankee, Canadian, Heinz, or Union Jack.

* * *

Patent (three horses—seven bets)
3 singles, 3 doubles, 1 treble.

Yankee (four horses—eleven bets)
6 doubles, 4 trebles, 1 accumulator.

Canadian (five horses—twenty-six bets)
10 doubles, 10 trebles, 5 four-timers, 1 accumulator.

Heinz (six horses—fifty-seven bets)
15 doubles, 20 trebles, 15 four-timers, 6 five-timers, 1 accumulator.

Union Jack (nine horses—eight bets)
8 trebles

```
1 — 2 — 3
|  \  |  /  |
4 — 5 — 6
|  /  |  \  |
7 — 8 — 9
```

Arrange the horses as above. The trebles are indicated by the lines.

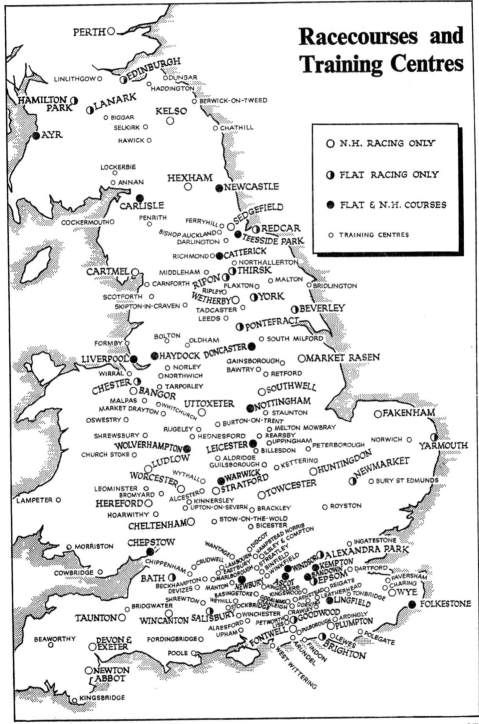

Racecourses and Training Centres

27

Where They Train

Akehurst, R. P. J.—Epsom.
Allden, P.—Newmarket.
Ancil, D.—Banbury, Oxon.
Armstrong, Fred—Newmarket.
Armytage, R. C.—East Ilsley, Newbury.
Ashworth, P. H.—Epsom.

Bacon, A. W.—Retford, Notts.
Bailey, P. G.—Wantage, Berks.
Balding, A.—Bawtry, Doncaster.
Balding, G. B.—Weyhill, Hants.
Balding, I. A.—Kingsclere, Berks.
Barclay, A. T.—Annan, Dumfriesshire.
Barclay, John.—Lockerbie, Dumfries-
 shire.
Barling, G. B.—Newmarket.
Barnes, R.—Norley, Cheshire.
Barons, D. H.—Kingsbridge, Devon.
Barratt, L. J.—Oswestry, Salop.
Bastiman, A. D.—Wetherby, Yorks.
Beadell, C. R.—Cranleigh, Surrey.
Beasley, P. T.—Malton, Yorks.
Beeby, G.—Compton, Berks.
Bell, T. C.—Biggar, Lanarkshire.
Benstead, C. J.—Epsom.
Bewicke, Maj. C.—Didcot, Berks.
Blackshaw, H. F.—Middleham, Yorks.
Blagrave, H. H. G.—Beckhampton,
 Wilts.
Blum, G.—Newmarket.
Bolton, M. J.—Ardingly, Sussex.
Boothman, C.—South Milford, Yorks.
Boyd, G. H.—Dunbar, East Lothian.
Breasley, A.—Epsom.
Brewster, A.—Doncaster.
Budgett, A. M.—Wantage, Berks.

Calvert, J. B.—Thirsk, Yorks.
Campbell, E.—Penrith, Cumberland.
Candy, D. W. J.—Wantage, Berks.
Carr, E. J.—Thirsk, Yorks.

Carr, F.—Malton, Yorks.
Carr, W.—Bolton, Lancs.
Carrod, L. N. L.—Aldridge, Staffs.
Cazalet, Maj. P. V. F.—Tonbridge,
 Kent.
Cecil, H.—Newmarket.
Champneys, Maj. E. G. S.—Lambourn.
 Berks
Charlesworth, D.—Northwich,
 Cheshire.
Chisman, P.—Alcester, Warwickshire.
Clarkson, H.—Ripley, Yorks.
Clayton, J. M.—Newmarket.
Cole, P. F. T.—Lambourn, Berks.
Collingwood, E. E.—Beverley, Yorks.
Combes, W. J.—Newmarket.
Cooper, A.—Malton, Yorks.
Corbett, T. A.—Newmarket.
Corrie, T. F.—Shrewsbury.
Cottrill, H. L.—Newmarket.
Cousins, E.—Tarporley, Cheshire.
Cousins, J. H. E.—Scotforth, Lancaster.
Craig-Brown, J. A.—Linlithgow, West
 Lothian.
Crawford, W. H.—Haddington, E.
 Lothian.
Cross, V. B.—Stockbridge, Hants.
Crossley, C. C.—Wirral, Cheshire.
Crossman, R. D.—Beaworthy, Devon.
Crump, N. F.—Middleham, Yorks.
Cundell, F. L.—Didcot, Berks.
Cundell, K. S.—Compton, Berks.

Dale, L. S.—Epsom.
Dalton, A.—Newmarket.
Davey, E.—Malton, Yorks.
Davey, P.—Newmarket.
Davies, C. H.—Chepstow.
Dawson, P. T.—Kingswood, Surrey.
Day, Reg—Newmarket.

Dennistoun, Maj. J.—Wantage, Berks,
Denson, W. R.—Cheltenham.
Dent, A.—Gainsborough, Lincs.
Dingwall, Mrs L. E.—Poole, Dorset.
Doherty, P. V.—Cheltenham.
Dowdeswell, J.—Lambourn, Berks.
Doyle, D. A.—Wetherby, Yorks.
Dunlop, J. L.—Arundel, Sussex.

East, H. J.—Northallerton, Yorks.
Easterby, M. H.—Malton, Yorks.
Easterby, M. W.—Flaxton, Yorks.
Easterby, W.—Tadcaster, Yorks.
Edmunds, J.—Wythall, Birmingham.
Elsey, W.—Malton, Yorks.
Evans, P.—Rearsby, Leics.
Evans, J. Stuart—Liss, Hants.

Fairbairn, R.—Selkirk.
Finch, T. P.—Norwich.
Fisher, W. E.—Newton Abbot, Devon.
Forster, Capt. T. A.—Wantage, Berks.
Foster, B. S.—Middleham, Yorks.
Francis, W. D.—Malpas, Cheshire.
Freeman, F. G.—Cheltenham.

Gandolfo, D. R.—Wantage, Berks.
Gates, T. I'Anson—Lewes, Sussex.
Gilman, F. H.—Uppingham, Rutland.
Gilmore, L.—Crudwell, Wilts.
Goddard, E. C.—Leatherhead, Surrey.
Goodwill, A. W.—Newmarket.
Gosling, T.—Epsom.
Goswell, M. O.—Crawley, Sussex.
Gray, W. H.—Beverley, Yorks.

Hall, A. G.—Carnforth, Lancs.
Hall, L. A.—Winchester, Hants.
Hall, N.—Burton-on-Trent, Staffs.
Hall, Miss S. E.—Middleham, Yorks.
Hall, S.—Middleham, Yorks.
Hall, W. A.—Tadcaster, Yorks.
Hanley, D. L.—Lambourn, Berks.
Hannon, H.—Marlborough, Wilts.
Hardy, J.—Staunton, Notts.
Hartigan, J. H.—Middleham, Yorks.
Harwood, G.—Pulborough, Sussex.
Hastings, D. F. G.—Lambourn, Berks.
Hern, Maj. W. R.—West Ilsley, Berks.

Hide, W. H. G.—Ludlow, Salop.
Hills, B.—Lambourn, Berks.
Hobbs, B.—Newmarket.
Hobson, R.—Doncaster.
Holden, W.—Newmarket.
Hollinshead, R.—Rugeley, Staffs.
Holt, L.—Basingstoke, Hants,
Hooton, J. K.—Polegate, Sussex.
Houghton, R. F. Johnson—Didcot,
 Berks.
Hudson, T.—Carlisle, Cumberland.
Hunter, G.—East Ilsley, Berks.

Ingham, S. W. H.—Epsom.

James, M. B. C.—Formby, Lancs.
James, S. S.—East Ilsley, Berks.
Jarvis, Sir Jack—Newmarket.
Jarvis, M. A.—Newmarket.
Jarvis, Ryan—Newmarket.
Jenkins, D. P.—Cowbridge, Glam.
Jones, Arthur—Morriston, Glam.
Jones, A. W.—Oswestry, Salop.
Jones, Earl—Hednesford, Staffs.
Jones, Herbert—Malton, Yorks.
Jones, H. Thomson—Newmarket.
Jordon, I. D.—Newcastle-on-Tyne.

Kearney, P. J.—Cheltenham.
Kennard, Mrs E.—Bridgwater,
 Somerset
Kennard, L. G.—Taunton, Somerset.
Kerr, A. M.—Dorking, Surrey.
Kilpatrick, A. S.—Marlborough, Wilts.

Lambton, E. G.—Newmarket.
Leader, H.—Newmarket.
Leader, T. E.—Newmarket.
Leslie, D. M.—Billesdon, Leics.
Lewis, I. M.—Lambourn, Berks.
Lomax, Mrs R. A.—Marlborough,
 Wilts.
Lowis, P. C.—Lambourn, Berks.

McCourt, M.—Upton-on-Severn,
 Worcs.
Magner, E.—Doncaster, Yorks.
Makin, P. J.—Wantage, Berks.
Marks, D.—Lambourn, Berks.

Marshall, B. A.—Hampstead Norris, Berks.
Marshall, W. C.—Marlborough, Wilts.
Mason, J. F.—Tarporley, Cheshire.
Mason, R. E.—Guilsborough, Northants.
Masson, T.—Lewes, Sussex.
Mather, W. D.—Chathill, Northumberland.
Maxwell, F.—Lambourn, Berks.
Meacock, J.—Alresford, Hants.
Mitchell, C. A.—Epsom.
Mitchell, V. J.—Malton, Yorks.
Molony, T.—Melton Mowbray, Leics.
Moore, P.—Newmarket.
Moore, R. A. R.—Lewes, Sussex.
Mulhall, J.—York.
Murless, Noel—Newmarket.
Murray, W.—Middleham, Yorks,

Nagle, Mrs F.—Petworth, Sussex.
Neaves, A. S.—Faversham, Kent.
Nelson, Maj. P. M.—Lambourn, Berks.
Nesbitt, S.—Oldham, Lancs.
Nesfield, C. V.—Charing, Kent.
Nicholson, D.—Stow-on-the-Wold.
Nicholson, H. C. D.—Cheltenham.
Norris, Capt. J. F.—Brackley, Northants.

O'Brien, P.—Chippenham, Wilts.
O'Donoghue, J.—Reigate, Surrey.
O'Gorman, W. G.—Newmarket.
O'Keeffe, E. D.—Leeds, Yorks.
Oliver, J. K. M.—Hawick, Roxburghshire.
Ormston, J. G.—Richmond, Yorks.
Oughton, A. D.—Findon, Sussex.
Owen, D. G.—Didcot, Berks.
Owen, G. R.—Tarporley, Cheshire.
Oxley, J. F.—Newmarket.

Parker, E. J.—Epsom.
Payne, W. J.—Eastbury, Berks.
Payne-Gallwey, Col. P.—Lambourn, Berks.
Peacock, J. H.—Ludlow, Salop.
Peacock, R. D.—Middleham, Yorks.
Pearce, J. L.—Malton, Yorks.

Pettitt, R. D.—West Wittering, Sussex.
Pitt, A. J.—Kingswood, Surrey.
Pope, Maj. M. B.—Streatley, Berks.
Poston, P. J.—Ingatestone, Essex.
Power, Jack—East Ilsley, Berks.
Price, Capt. H. Ryan—Findon, Sussex.

Ransom, P. B.—Leominster, Herefordshire.
Rayson, D.—Newmarket.
Read, R.—Lambourn, Berks.
Reavey, E. J. B.—Wantage, Berks.
Renton, R.—Ripon, Yorks.
Richards, Sir Gordon—Fordingbridge, Hants.
Richards, G. W.—Penrith, Cumberland.
Rimell, T. F.—Kinnersley, Worcs.
Roberts, J. F.—Cheltenham.
Robinson, G. N.—Berwick-on-Tweed.
Robson, R.—Newcastle-upon-Tyne.
Robson, T. W.—Penrith, Cumberland.
Roche, W.—Lambourn, Berks.
Rohan, H. P.—Malton, Yorks.

Sawyer, H.—Malton, Yorks.
Scudamore, M. J.—Hoarwithy, Hereford.
Shedden, L. H.—Wetherby, Yorks.
Shone, T. E.—Whitchurch, Salop.
Sinclair, Miss A. V.—Lewes, Sussex.
Sirett, J.—Epsom.
Smith, Denys—Bishop Auckland, Co. Durham.
Smith, Douglas—Newmarket.
Smyth, G. R.—Lewes, Sussex.
Smyth, H. E.—Epsom.
Smyth, P. V.—Epsom.
Smyth, R. V.—Epsom.
Spann, G.—Lambourn, Berks.
Speck, V. W.—Melton Mowbray, Leics.
Stamper, T. B.—Cockermouth, Cumberland.
Stephenson, W.—Royston, Herts.
Stephenson, W. A.—Bishop Auckland, Co. Durham.
Stevens, J. A. A.—Epsom.
Sturdy, R. C.—Shrewton, Wilts.
Supple, P. B.—Dartford, Kent.

Sutcliffe, J., jun.—Epsom.
Sutcliffe, J. E.—Epsom.
Swift, B. C.—Ashtead, Surrey.

Taylor, C. J.—Cheltenham.
Taylor, P. M.—Godalming, Surrey.
Thomas, A. J.—Warwick.
Thom, D. T.—Newmarket.
Thompson, J.—Wetherby, Yorks.
Todd, G. E.—Marlborough, Wilts.
Toft, G.—Beverley, Yorks.
Tree, A. J.—Marlborough, Wilts.
Turnell, A. R.—Marlborough, Wilts.

Upton, Capt. P. J.—Wantage, Berks.

Vallance, Lt.-Col. G. R. A.—Devizes, Wilts.
Van Cutsem, B. H. H.—Newmarket.
Vasey, M. A.—Middleham, Yorks.
Vergette, G. M.—Peterborough, Northants.
Vickers, J. R. P.—Darlington, Co. Durham.

Wainwright, S.—Malton, Yorks.
Walker, I. S.—Newmarket.
Wallace, G.—Kettering, Northants.
Wallington, H. G.—Epsom.
Walsh, J.—Winkfield, Berks.
Walwyn, Fulke—Lambourn, Berks.
Walwyn, P. T.—Lambourn, Berks.
Watson, Alfred—Skipton-in-Craven, Yorks.

Watts, J. F.—Newmarket.
Watts, J. W.—Newmarket.
Watts, W. C.—Bridlington, Yorks.
Waugh, Jack A. J.—Newmarket.
Waugh, John A.—Newmarket.
Waugh, T. A.—Newmarket.
Weeden, D. E.—Bury St Edmunds, Suffolk.
Weymes, E.—Middleham, Yorks.
Wharton, H.—Gainsborough, Lincs.
Wharton, W.—Richmond, Yorks.
Whelan, D.—Epsom.
Whiston, W. R.—Market Drayton, Salop.
Wightman, W. G. R.—Upham, Hants.
Wilkinson, B.—Middleham, Yorks.
Williams, D. H.—Ferryhill, Co. Durham.
Williams, N. B.—Churchstoke, Montgomery.
Wilmot, Miss Norah—Binfield, Berks.
Wilson, R.—Lambourn, Berks.
Wilton-Clark, J. W.—Lampeter, Cardiganshire.
Winter, F. T.—Lambourn, Berks.
Winter, J. R.—Newmarket.
Wragg, H.—Newmarket.
Wright, J. S.—Bromyard, Herefordshire.

Yeoman, D.—Catterick, Yorks.

How Far Is It ?

THIS LIST of racecourses (Flat) gives the approximate distances in miles from (*L*) London, (*M*) Manchester, (*B*) Birmingham and (*N*) Newcastle; the counties in which they are situated and the nearest principal towns.

Meeting	(L)	(M)	(B)	(N)	County	Principal Nearest Town
Alexandra Park .	5	190	112	274	Middlesex	London
Ascot	29	212	125	285	Berkshire	Windsor
Ayr	405	214	303	150	Ayrshire	Ayr
Bath	105	180	97	295	Somerset	Bath
Beverley	205	98	129	114	Yorkshire	Hull
Brighton	50	234	155	315	Sussex	Brighton
Carlisle	299	121	188	60	Cumberland	Carlisle
Catterick Bridge .	243	116	168	40	Yorkshire	Stockton
Chepstow	141	160	88	330	Monmouthshire	Newport
Chester	179	40	75	170	Cheshire	Chester
Doncaster.......	156	52	92	112	Yorkshire	Doncaster
Edinburgh	393	224	288	124	Midlothian	Edinburgh
Epsom	16	195	127	280	Surrey	Epsom
Folkestone	70	253	185	330	Kent	Folkestone
Goodwood	70	258	160	310	Sussex	Chichester
Hamilton Park .	391	235	288	170	Lanarkshire	Glasgow
Haydock Park ..	210	21	91	160	Lancashire	{ Manchester & Liverpool
Kempton	18	198	112	280	Middlesex	London
Lanark	337	255	288	160	Lanarkshire	Glasgow
Leicester	99	90	40	188	Leicestershire	Leicester
Lingfield	26	209	127	290	Surrey	Epsom
Liverpool	193	36	90	160	Lancashire	Liverpool
Newbury	53	230	93	281	Berkshire	Reading
Newcastle	268	143	204	—	Northumberland	Newcastle
Newmarket	70	171	115	236	Cambs.	Newmarket
Nottingham	126	78	51	167	Notts.	Nottingham
Pontefract	183	57	112	102	Yorkshire	Leeds
Redcar	246	118	180	55	Yorkshire	Redcar
Ripon	214	73	143	67	Yorkshire	Ripon
Salisbury	83	217	134	343	Wiltshire	Salisbury
Sandown	14	198	112	280	Surrey	London
Teesside Park (Stockton) ...	243	112	168	40	Yorkshire	Stockton
Thirsk	210	90	143	58	Yorkshire	Thirsk

Warwick	89	...108	... 21	...220	...Warwickshire	.....Warwick
Windsor	21	...200	...125	...284	...Berkshire	........Windsor
Wolverhampton	125	... 71	... 12	...199	...Staffordshire	......Wolverhampton
Yarmouth	121	...225	...166	...296	...Norfolk	..........Yarmouth
York	188	... 68	...124	... 80	...Yorkshire	........York

Racecourses

Maps, descriptions and statistics of all the flat racecourses, plus a few of the important National Hunt circuits.

There are two figures after the names of the courses, separated by a stroke. The first is a mark for the standard of racing and the second for the course's treatment of the public—amenities, lay-out, etc. Both marks are out of five.

ALEXANDRA PARK (1/1)

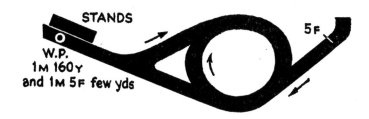

For obvious reasons, Alexandra Park is known as the 'frying pan' with its small circuit attached to the sprint course. This loop is so cramped that runners for both 1-mile-160-yards and 1-mile-5 furlongs events start in front of the stands and then race on the turn almost throughout. A horse needs to be pretty handy to win here while the climbing finish calls for stamina as well. The sprint course has a marked right-hand bend at half way. This means high numbers in the draw have quite an advantage.

Trainers to Note: F. Armstrong, Sir G. Richards, S. Ingham, T. Corbett, J. Sirett.
Best Race for Favourites—SECOND; **for Second Favourites**—THIRD
Worst Race for Favourites—FIRST; **for Second Favourites**—SIXTH.

ASCOT (5/4)

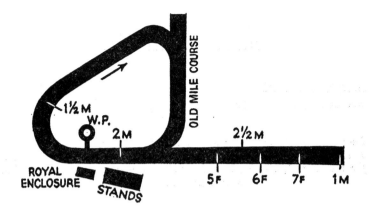

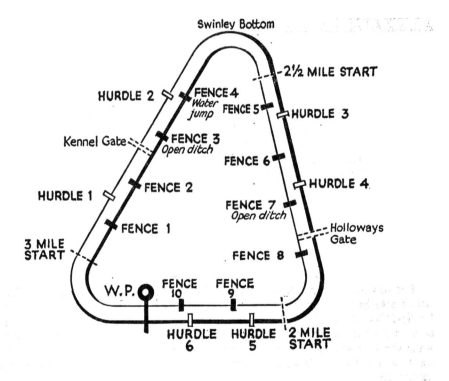

Ascot is an attractive course from the racegoer's point of view, with first-class facilities. Horses probably have a different opinion, for the track itself is one of the most testing. The bends on the fourteen-furlong circuit are easy, with nothing to upset the rhythm of a strong galloper, but while the first half of the 'triangle' is mainly downhill, the last seven furlongs or so to the post is an uphill slog which proves gruelling, especially in long-distance races when the going is soft. The straight mile is no place for the chicken-hearted either and from the point it is joined by the circuit—three furlongs from home—there is a stiff climb. The draw seems to give no advantage.

> **Trainers to Note:** In Ireland, N. Murless, W. Hern, J. Jarvis, H. Wragg I. Balding.
> **Best Race for Favourites—FOURTH; for Second Favourites—THIRD.**
> **Worst Race for Favourites—THIRD; for Second Favourites—FIFTH.**

NATIONAL HUNT

> **Trainers to Note:** P. Cazalet, H. Price, F. Cundell, K. Cundell.
> **Best Race for Favourites—FIFTH; for Second Favourites—THIRD.**
> **Worst Race for Favourites—FIRST; for Second Favourites—FIFTH.**

AYR (3/3+)

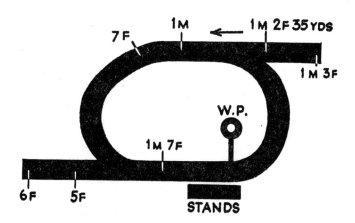

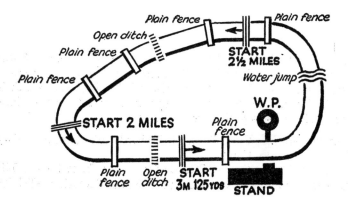

There can be few excuses for Ayr failures: it is one of the fairest courses in the country with an excellent surface and well-graded bends. The straight six furlongs is roomy and the draw bestows no favours. However in races of seven furlongs or more, which start on the circuit and join the 'straight' about four furlongs from home, horses drawn with low numbers have a better chance.

Trainers to Note: S. Hall, G. Boyd, R. Barnes, E. Lambton.
Best Race for Favourites—THIRD; **for Second Favourites**—FIRST.
Worst Race for Favourites—FIFTH; **for Second Favourites**—SIXTH.

NATIONAL HUNT

Trainers to Note: R. Fairbairn, W. A. Stephenson, J. Oliver, John Barclay, R. Hall.
Best Race for Favourites—THIRD; **for Second Favourites**—SECOND.
Worst Race for Favourites—FIRST; **for Second Favourites**—FOURTH.

BATH (1/1)

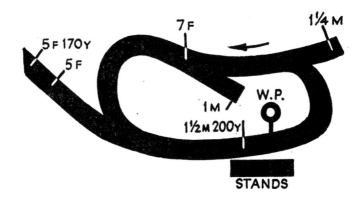

Bath caters mainly for second-raters but, despite an absence of stars, sport is usually competitive. The mile-and-a-half-circuit is galloping rather than sharp and the interesting feature here is the steadily rising half-mile run-in which has a slight bend to the left. This angle can be quite important in sprints, as the winners seem to come rather more from a low position in the draw.

Trainers to Note: K. Cundell, Sir G. Richards, W. Hern, P. Walwyn, D. Candy.
Best Race for Favourites—SECOND; **for Second Favourites**—FOURTH.
Worst Race for Favourites—FIRST; **for Second Favourites**—THIRD.

BEVERLEY (2/3)

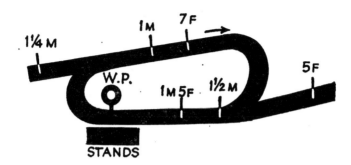

Early season two-year-old form is often turned upside down at Beverley. The five-furlong straight is against the collar throughout and takes some getting, particularly when there is mud about. A fractional right bend gives high-drawn horses a slight advantage. The oval circuit is galloping in nature but there is a downhill turn into the straight and the run-in is short.

Trainers to Note: S. Hall, M. H. Easterby, E. Lambton, H. Rohan, W. Elsey.
Best Race for Favourites—SECOND; for Second Favourites—FIRST.
Worst Race for Favourites—SIXTH; for Second Favourites—FOURTH.

BRIGHTON (2/2)

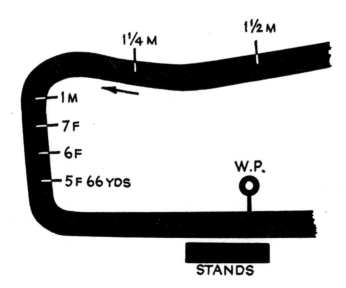

The turns at Brighton are easier than they might seem from the map, but even so can be quite a handicap to the big, long-striding galloper. A medium-sized fluent mover is far more at home. The straight run-in is about three and a half furlongs and has a slight rise a quarter of a mile out until levelling again a hundred yards from the post. Although a low number in the draw is favoured it is perhaps even more important for the sprinters to be fast away.

Trainers to Note: P. Nelson, N. Murless, C. J. Benstead, Sir G. Richards, J. Dunlop.
Best Race for Favourites—FOURTH; for Second Favourites—SECOND.
Worst Race for Favourites—SECOND; for Second Favourites—FIRST.

CARLISLE (1/1)

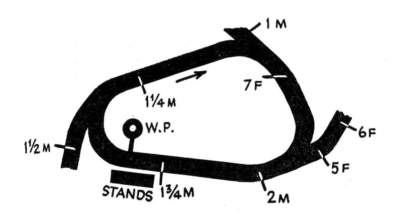

The course at Carlisle is about twelve furlongs in circumference—undulating throughout—with three separate off-shoots; one for the five- and six-furlong starts, another for the mile and the third for the mile and a half. The six-furlong track is quite a severe test, especially for two-year-olds, since it is a steady climb throughout, bending to the right until half way to give high-drawn horses an advantage. In longer races the draw is not so important.

Trainers to Note: S. Hall, M. H. Easterby, W. Elsey, G. Boyd, E. G. Lambton.
Best Race for Favourites—THIRD; for Second Favourites—SECOND.
Worst Race for Favourites—FIFTH; for Second Favourites—FIFTH.

CATTERICK (1/2+)

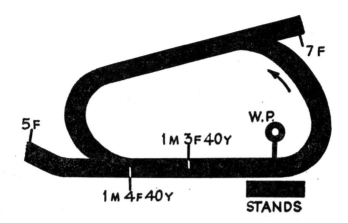

Catterick is just the place for course specialists. It is exceptionally tricky and good jockeyship is essential. Five-furlong sprints are downhill all the way. There is a slight left-hand bend at the junction with the round course, giving low numbers in the draw a slight advantage—though it is even more important to get a quick break. In seven-furlong races a low draw is also favoured. The whole course is sharp and totally unsuited to a big, long-striding horse.

Trainers to Note: W. Elsey, S. Hall, Denys Smith, J. Calvert, W. Gray.
Best Race for Favourites—SIXTH; for Second Favourites—THIRD.
Worst Race for Favourites—FIRST; for Second Favourites—FOURTH.

CHELTENHAM

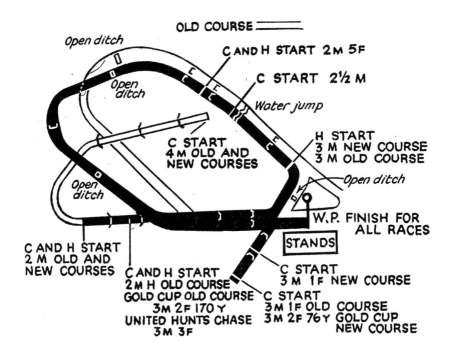

Trainers to Note: R. Turnell, F. Walwyn, In Ireland, T. F. Rimell.
Best Race for Favourites—SEVENTH/SIXTH; for Second Favourites—SIXTH
Worst Race for Favourites—FIRST; for Second Favourites—FOURTH

CHEPSTOW (2+/3+)

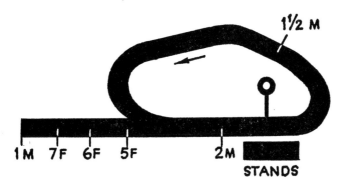

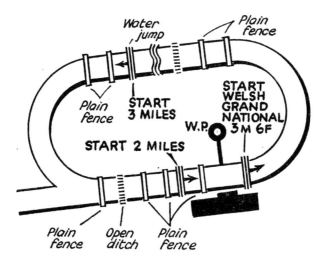

There is plenty of room at Chepstow, but it is certainly not an ideal galloping course because of pronounced changing gradients. On the straight mile, runners go downhill until about half way and then there is a sharp climb for two furlongs followed by a fairly level run to the post. High numbers are slightly favoured in the draw on the straight course. The opening of the Severn Bridge has meant that Chepstow is drawing bigger attendances and the standard of racing is rising accordingly.

Trainers to Note: P. Nelson, P. Walwyn, D. Candy, C. Davies, W. Hern.
Best Race for Favourites—FOURTH; **for Second Favourites**—FIFTH.
Worst Race for Favourites—THIRD; **for Second Favourites**—FOURTH

NATIONAL HUNT

Trainers to Note: C. H. Davies, R. Turnell, F. Walwyn, T. F. Rimell.
Best Race for Favourites—EIGHTH/FIFTH; **for Second Favourites**—FIRST.
Worst Race for Favourites—FOURTH; **for Second Favourites**—SECOND.

CHESTER (2+/2)

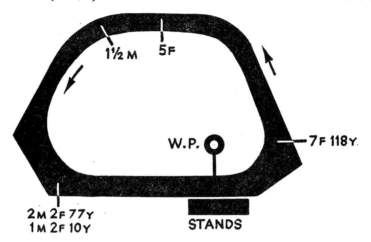

Chester has the smallest circuit in Great Britain and small, or rather medium-sized horses do best here. It does take a tough, resolute stayer to land the long-distance Chester Cup, but in other races a handy, sharp-actioned horse is far more at home. The course is about a mile round and on the turn almost throughout, except for an almost straight two-furlong run-in. A low draw is essential in all races up to seven and a half furlongs and a fast get-away is also important.

> **Trainers to Note:** N. Murless, H. Rohan, E. Cousins, B. van Cutsem, R. J. Houghton.
> **Best Race for Favourites**—THIRD; **for Second Favourites**—SECOND.
> **Worst Race for Favourites**—SIXTH; **for Second Favourites**—SIXTH.

CURRAGH

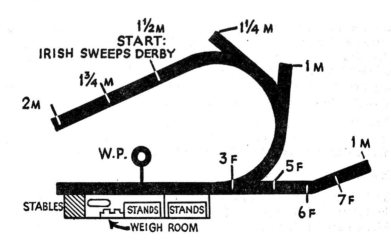

DONCASTER (3+/1*)

(*Likely to be 5 when rebuilding completed in Autumn 1969.)

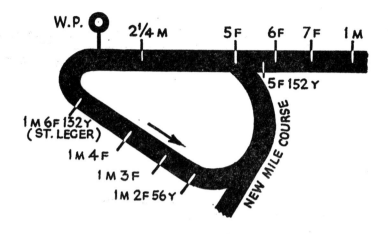

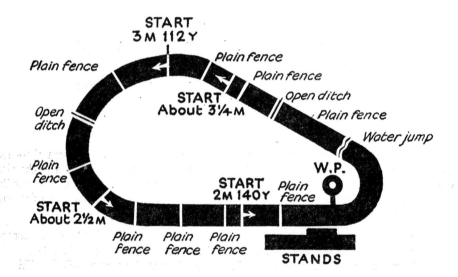

Doncaster is a very fair course and a worthy home for the St Leger. The Classic and other distance races usually go to a big long-striding stayer, for the course is completely flat and there is a sweeping bend into a long run-in with nothing to interrupt the rhythm. The straight mile is extremely wide—it needs to be to accommodate Lincoln Handicap fields. Sprints are run on this course and a high number in the draw can be a great advantage, particularly when the going is soft.

Trainers to Note: F. Armstrong, In Ireland, W. O'Gorman, H. Rohan, B. van Cutsem, J. F. Watts.
Best Race for Favourites—FIRST; **for Second Favourites**—SEVENTH/FIRST.
Worst Race for Favourites—SIXTH; **for Second Favourites**—SECOND.

NATIONAL HUNT

Trainers to Note: W. A. Stephenson, T. F. Rimell, N. Crump, Denys Smith.
Best Race for Favourites—FIRST; **for Second Favourites**—FIFTH.
Worst Race for Favourites—SECOND, **for Second Favourites**—FIRST.

EDINBURGH (1/1)

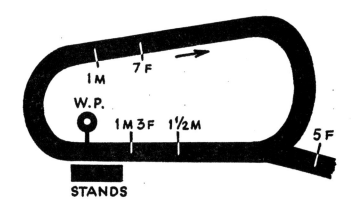

Edinburgh is flat, but sharp bends—particularly the one into the straight—are against the big horses and favour the handy, adaptable types. There is a slight rise over the last few yards to the post, but sprinters over the straight five furlongs hardly notice this. With a quick break they can notch up fast times here. In seven-furlong and mile events the draw favours high numbers.

Trainers to Note: J. Jarvis, H. Rohan, A. Barclay, G. Boyd, M. W. Easterby.
Best Race for Favourites—FOURTH; **for Second Favourites**—SECOND.
Worst Race for Favourites—SECOND; **for Second Favourites**—FOURTH.

EPSOM (4/2)

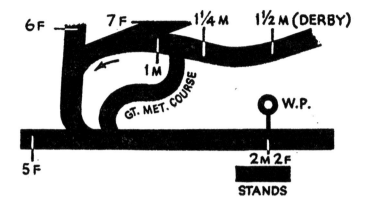

There is no course in the country more suitable for our premier Classic than Epsom. Sweeping bends and downhill gradients offer the supreme test. Derby fields run uphill for the first half mile, fairly level for a couple of furlongs and then swing sharply downhill to join the straight sprinting track. The half-mile run-in ends with a climb over the last 300 yards. Sprints over five furlongs are run at a tremendous pace as there is a downhill start which gives impetus for the rising finish. Speed from the gate is also important in six- and seven-furlong events so this is no place for the inexperienced youngster. A low number in the draw can be an advantage in mile and ten-furlong races.

Trainers to Note: S. Ingham, J. Jarvis, N. Murless, F. Armstrong, R. Smyth.
Best Race for Favourites—FOURTH; Second Favourites—SIXTH.
Worst Race for Favourites—FIRST; for Second Favourites—SECOND.

FOLKESTONE (1/2)

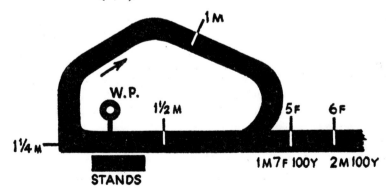

Folkestone is a slightly undulating course, wide and with easy turns . . . even so it certainly cannot be classed as a galloping track. There is a gentle rise over the final furlong and on the straight course, with the five- and six-furlong starts, the winners seem to come rather more often from those drawn with low numbers.

> **Trainers to Note:** R. Smyth, Ryan Jarvis, P. Ashworth, J. Dunlop, R. J. Houghton.
> **Best Race for Favourites**—FOURTH; **for Second Favourites**—THIRD.
> **Worst Race for Favourites**—FIRST; **for Second Favourites**—SECOND.

GOODWOOD (4/2+)

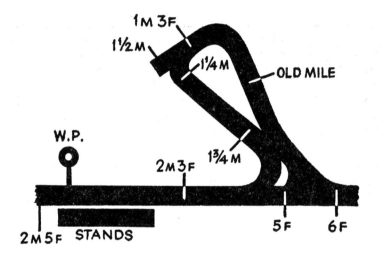

Until 1965, Goodwood's programme was just one Festival meeting each year. Much more use is being made of the course nowadays and sponsors have stepped in to boost the new fixtures. But while the general standard is quite high, fields are usually on the small side. It is an unusual-shaped course with a long run-in but a sharp loop joined on the far end with some steep downhill gradients put the long-striding horse at a disadvantage in races up to a mile and a half. Longer events provide a really tough test. The five furlongs is very fast and speed from the gate is more important than a high number in the draw.

> **Trainers to Note:** G. Richards, G. Todd, Ireland, N. Murless, J. Dunlop.
> **Best Race for Favourites**—FIRST; **for Second Favourites**—SECOND.
> **Worst Race for Favourites**—THIRD; **for Second Favourites**—SIXTH.

HAMILTON PARK (1/2)

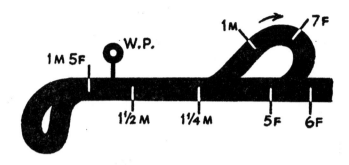

About three and a half furlongs from the Hamilton Park winning post, the runners drop into a hollow. This has been the 'grave' of many a hot fancy, for the rest of the race is a sharp climb. The shape of the course is a straight six furlongs with a pear-shaped loop attached. Turns are easy and, apart from the hollow, the surface is only gently undulating. Past sprinting results show that low-drawn horses are at a disadvantage.

Trainers to Note: G. Boyd, A. Balding, R. Peacock, H. Rohan, M. H. Easterby, J. Ormston.
Best Race for Favourites—SECOND; **for Second Favourites**—FIRST.
Worst Race for Favourites—THIRD; **for Second Favourites**—SECOND.

HAYDOCK (2+/3)

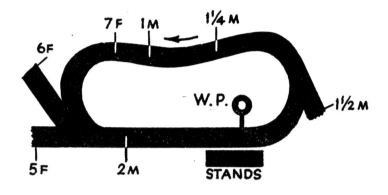

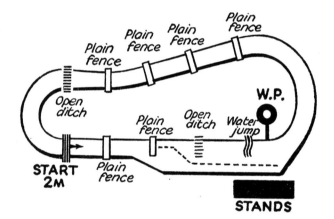

Haydock is a very fair course but if it does bestow favours then the big, long-striding gallopers receive the benefit. It provides a fair test of stamina with a slightly rising four-furlong run-in helping to see to this. With the exception of five-furlong events, races of up to a mile seem to go more to the low-drawn horses. Over the minimum trip the high numbers have an edge, particularly when there is mud about.

Trainers to Note: M. H. Easterby, E. Cousins, W. Elsey, H. Rohan, J. F. Watts.
Best Race for Favourites—SEVENTH, n.b. SECOND; for Second Favourites—
FIFTH.
Worst Race for Favourites—THIRD; for Second Favourites—SIXTH.

NATIONAL HUNT

Trainers to Note: G. Owen, N. Crump, W. A. Stephenson, T. F. Rimell.
Best Race for Favourites—SECOND; for Second Favourites—SECOND.
Worst Race for Favourites—FIFTH; for Second Favourites—FIFTH.

KEMPTON PARK (3/3)

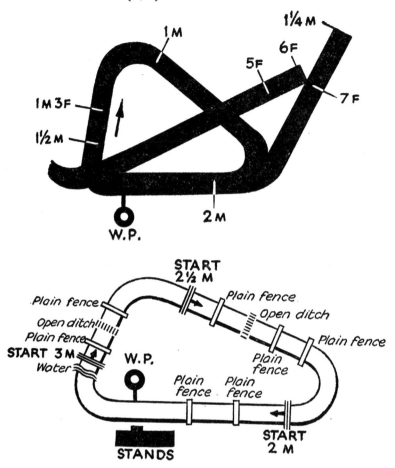

Kempton is one of the best courses in the London area, both for amentities and the standard of racing. Since it is perfectly flat, spectators have a clear view of proceedings throughout. The course is basically triangular with an extension for the mile-and-a-quarter Jubilee start which includes the seven-furlong gate. There is a separate sprint course with the finishing line at rather a deceptive angle from the stands. The draw seems to have little bearing on results in any races.

Trainers to Note: G. Smyth, P. Nelson, S. Ingham, T. Corbett, J. Jarvis.
Best Race for Favourites—THIRD; for Second Favourites—FOURTH.
Worst Race for Favourites—FOURTH; for Second Favourites—THIRD.

NATIONAL HUNT

Trainers to Note: P. Cazalet, F. Cundell, F. Walwyn, R. Turnell, H. Price.
Best Race for Favourites—SECOND; for Second Favourites—FIFTH.
Worst Race for Favourites—FIRST; for Second Favourites—SECOND.

LANARK (1/2)

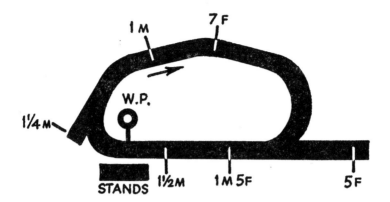

Lanark provides only second-class sport but, if you do not mind the absence of stars, the meetings here are usually a good day out. The course is perfectly flat throughout with the ten-furlong round circuit joining the straight five furlongs about half a mile from the finish. The bends are easy enough, but a big powerful galloper may not find them to his liking. On the round course, high numbers are worth watching, but the opposite side has preference in sprints on the straight course.

Trainers to Note: J. Ormston, E. Davey, S. Hall, I. Walker, M. H. Easterby.
Best Race for Favourites—FIRST; for Second Favourites—THIRD.
Worst Race for Favourites—SECOND; for Second Favourites—FOURTH.

LEICESTER (1/1)

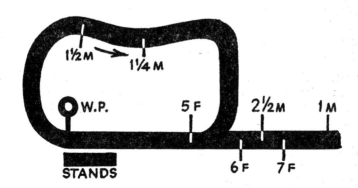

All races of a mile or less at Leicester are run on the straight course. The first half of this is downhill, then comes a steady rise for two furlongs with a level stretch to the post. Of course in five-furlong dashes the climb comes shortly after the start, so this can prove quite a test for two-year-olds early on in the season. High numbers in the draw are believed to have a slight advantage. The circuit is a good size and a strong galloper is at home.

Trainers to Note: F. Armstrong, J. A. J. Waugh, R. Hollinshead, W. Stephenson, B. Hobbs.

Best Race for Favourites—THIRD; **for Second Favourites**—FIFTH.
Worst Race for Favourites—FOURTH; **for Second Favourites**—SIXTH.

LINGFIELD (2/3)

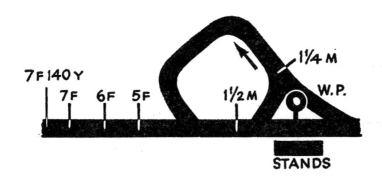

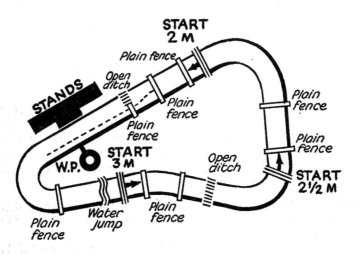

53

The Lingfield Derby Trial often has a bearing on the Classic result, for the mile-and-a-half course here bears a close resemblance to Epsom with a climb and later a downhill turn into the straight, calling for plenty of speed and adaptability. The course as a whole is easy and, apart from two-mile races, stamina is of only secondary importance. The straight 7-furlong-140-yard course is downhill almost throughout and a quick break is important, though the draw does play some part in results, high numbers usually having an advantage. Low numbers come into their own when the going is on the soft side.

> **Trainers to Note:** G. Todd, J. Jarvis, A. Budgett, C. Benstead, R. Smyth.
> **Best Race for Favourites—FIFTH; for Second Favourites—FOURTH.**
> **Worst Race for Favourites—FOURTH; for Second Favourites—FIRST.**

NATIONAL HUNT

> **Trainers to Note:** P. Cazalet, R. Turnell, H. Price, F. Cundell.
> **Best Race for Favourites—THIRD; for Second Favourites—FIFTH.**
> **Worst Race for Favourites—FIFTH; for Second Favourites—SIXTH.**

LIVERPOOL (1*/1)
(*Without the Grand National.)

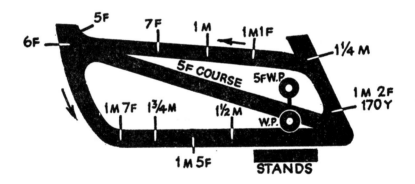

At present Liverpool has just one meeting a year with the Grand National as its centre-piece. The flat racing is rather poorly supported but there are plans to make more use of the course: this would mean not only improved racing but also better amenities for the public. The circuit is perfectly flat with a half-mile run-in, low numbers having an advantage in six-furlong and one-mile races. But on the separate five-furlong course, high-drawn horses are worth watching.

> **Trainers to Note:** H. Rohan, B. van Cutsem, W. Elsey, F. Armstrong, In Ireland.
> **Best Race for Favourites—FOURTH; for Second Favourites—SEVENTH/**
> FOURTH.
> **Worst Race for Favourites—FIFTH; for Second Favourites—SIXTH.**

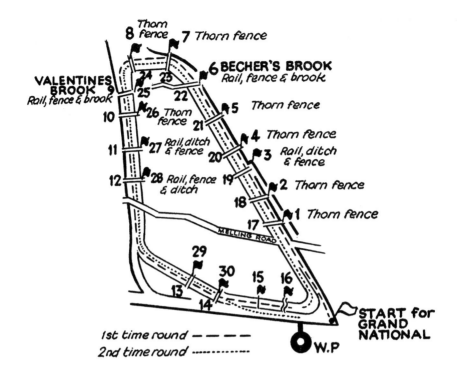

1st time round — — — —
2nd time round ··············

NATIONAL HUNT

Trainers to Note: T. F. Rimell, W. A. Stephenson, In Ireland.
Best Race for Favourites—THIRD; **for Second Favourites**—FIRST.
Worst Race for Favourites—FIRST; **for Second Favourites**—THIRD.

NEWBURY (4/4+)

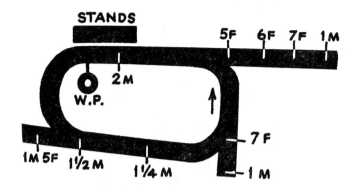

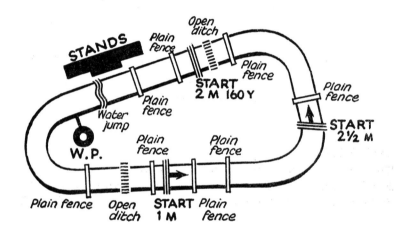

Newbury sets a high standard in racing, but an even greater one in its consideration of the public with everything (stands, parade ring, bars and tote) in easy reach—the only drawback being a poor car park. The circuit is about fifteen furlongs, joining the slightly undulating straight mile just over half a mile from the post. It is a fair, galloping course. On the straight mile it is ability that counts with the draw offering no favours.

> **Trainers to Note:** N. Murless, A. J. Tree, W. Hern, G. Richards, I. Balding, P. Nelson.
> **Best Race for Favourites—FIRST; for Second Favourites—THIRD.**
> **Worst Race for Favourites—THIRD; for Second Favourites—FIFTH.**

NATIONAL HUNT

> **Trainers to Note:** P. Cazalet, F. Walwyn, H. Price, R. Turnell.
> **Best Race for Favourites—FOURTH; for Second Favourites—FIRST.**
> **Worst Race for Favourites—FIRST; for Second Favourites—FOURTH.**

NEWCASTLE (3/4)

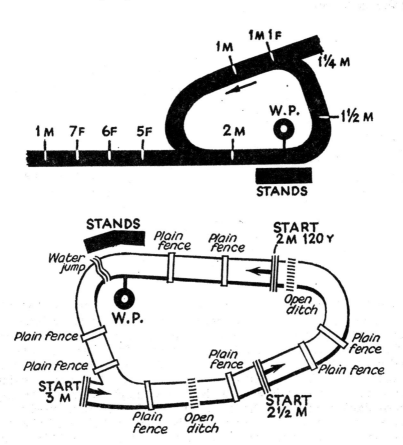

Newcastle is a really tough course with the last half mile of every race being uphill to the post. Events like the gruelling two-mile Northumberland Plate always go to a really stout resolute galloper with plenty of stamina. Ability to see the journey out is essential in all events. Sprinters have the climbing finish and two-year-olds can find this a particularly severe test. This course has more than its fair share of sponsors and the standard of racing is quite high.

Trainers to Note: W. Elsey, J. Calvert, R. Peacock, H. Rohan, H. Blackshaw.
Best Race for Favourites—SEVENTH/SIXTH; for Second Favourites—FIFTH.
Worst Race for Favourites—THIRD; for Second Favourites—FIRST.

NATIONAL HUNT

Trainers to Note: J. Oliver, N. Crump, W. A. Stephenson, R. Fairbairn.
Best Race for Favourites—FIFTH; for Second Favourites—SIXTH.
Worst Race for Favourites—FIRST; for Second Favourites—THIRD.

NEWMARKET (4+/4+*)

(*3 for Summer Course)

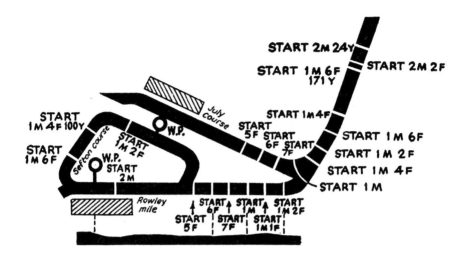

Newmarket, the headquarters of racing, has two courses; the Rowley Mile and Summer. They are best dealt with separately although, in some long-distance races, runners cover 'common ground' and they have similar characteristics in that both make the big long-striding horse at home and offer no favours from the draw.

Rowley Mile. The eighteen-furlong Cesarewitch course runs downhill for almost a mile and then there is a sharp rise into the right-hand bend taking runners into the mile-and-a-quarter straight. There is a plan of the straight just below the map and this shows clearly the famous 'Dip' about a furlong from home followed by a steep rise to the post, ensuring Guineas winners really do get a mile. The right-hand Sefton course—two miles in extent—circles round to join the Rowley Mile about four furlongs from home.

Summer Course. Long-distance horses use part of the Cesarewitch course, but bear off right into their own straight Bunbury Mile shortly before the Rowley Mile turn. The Bunbury Mile has slight undulations for about four furlongs, then a downhill stretch until the runners start to climb again a furlong out.

> **Trainers to Note:** J. Jarvis, H. Leader, N. Murless, F. Armstrong, G. Barling, J. F. Watts.
> **Best Race for Favourites**—SEVENTH/SIXTH; **for Second Favourites**—FIRST.
> **Worst Race for Favourites**—FIRST; **for Second Favourites**—SIXTH.

NOTTINGHAM (1+/1+)

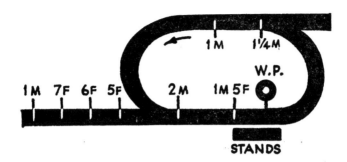

The standard of racing at Nottingham is on the upgrade, which is fitting for this is quite an interesting course. The mile-and-a-half circuit is flat, with easy turns and generally on the sharp side, but just over a quarter of a mile from home there is a hump which gives the long-striding galloper a few difficult moments. This hump also affects runners on the straight mile. The draw makes little difference on the round course, but on the straight mile low numbers do have a slight advantage.

Trainers to Note: F. Armstrong, J. Jarvis, Ryan Jarvis, J. A. J. Waugh, J. Clayton.
Best Race for Favourites—FIFTH; **for Second Favourites**—FOURTH.
Worst Race for Favourites—THIRD; **for Second Favourites**—SIXTH.

PONTEFRACT (1/1)

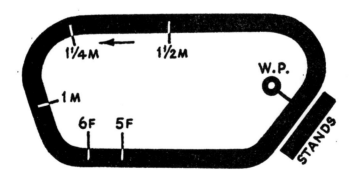

Pontefract is quite a testing course: there are marked gradients throughout and the last three furlongs is all hard, uphill slog which calls for plenty of stamina. There is no straight course and the run-in for all races—sprints included—is a mere two furlongs. The bend in the sprint track gives low numbers in the draw an advantage, but any horse getting a fast break takes a great deal of catching.

> **Trainers to Note:** F. Armstrong, E. Lambton, Ryan Jarvis, S. Hall, E. Weymes.
> **Best Race for Favourites**—FIRST; **for Second Favourites**—SECOND.
> **Worst Race for Favourites**—SECOND; **for Second Favourites**—THIRD.

REDCAR (3/4)

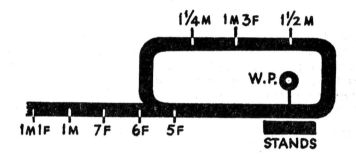

Redcar is a really well-equipped seaside course and an obvious home for sponsors with its Hill Gold Cup, Vaux Gold Tankard and Andy Capp Handicap. The two-mile circuit—joining the straight about five furlongs from home—is perfectly flat and is a good gallop throughout, while the straight nine furlong is very fair, giving only a slight advantage to low-drawn horses.

> **Trainers to Note:** S. Hall, W. Elsey, L. Sheddon, M. H. Easterby, W. A. Stephenson.
> **Best Race for Favourites**—FIRST; **for Second Favourites**—FIFTH.
> **Worst Race for Favourites**—SECOND; **for Second Favourites**—SIXTH.

RIPON (2+/3+)

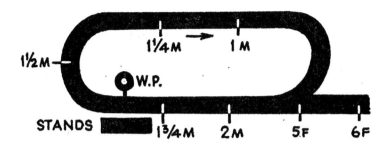

Bends on the Ripon circuit are cramped and make this a rather sharp course, while on the straight five-furlong run-in there are surface undulations with a marked dip approaching the final furlong. On the whole, therefore, the strapping, resolute gallopers are at a disadvantage. The effect of the draw is debatable but it is generally believed that low numbers are slightly favoured on the straight course, while high numbers have it on the round.

> **Trainers to Note:** S. Hall, M. H. Easterby, W. A. Stephenson, E. Weymes, W. Hern.
> **Best Race for Favourites**—SECOND; **for Second Favourites**—FIFTH.
> **Worst Race for Favourites**—SIXTH; **for Second Favourites**—SECOND.

SALISBURY (1+/2)

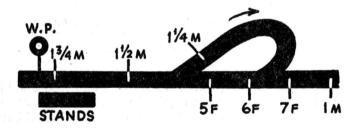

The standard of racing at Salisbury is low—but keep an eye on the two-year-old races: many local trainers, including Sir Gordon Richards, like to give their youngsters a first airing here and these include many would-be stars. The course is a straight mile with loop attached, galloping in nature. An uphill climb for the last half mile can provide quite a test of stamina. High numbers in the draw should be watched on the straight course.

> **Trainers to Note:** Sir G. Richards, A. J. Tree, W. Hern, P. Nelson, P. Walwyn.
> **Best Race for Favourites**—SECOND; **for Second Favourites**—FIFTH.
> **Worst Race for Favourites**—THIRD; **for Second Favourites**—FIRST.

61

SANDOWN (4+/3+)

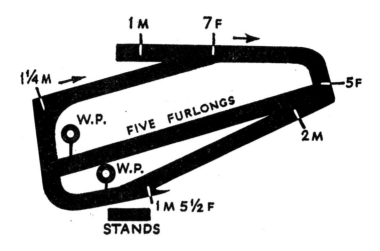

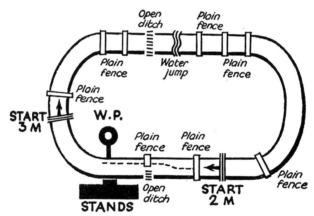

Sandown Park provides a combination of fine racing with good amenities. It also makes sure that its prizes are worthily won, for the oval galloping course provides a severe test and the rising four furlongs to the post is quick death to all but the stout-hearted. On the round course, high numbers in the draw seem to come off best. But on the separate five-furlong course, which is on the rise throughout, low numbers are slightly favoured.

Trainers to Note: N. Murless, S. Ingham, J. F. Watts, C. J. Benstead, J. Jarvis.
Best Race for Favourites—FIRST; for Second Favourites—EIGHT/SECOND.
Worst Race for Favourites—THIRD; for Second Favourites—FIFTH.

NATIONAL HUNT

Trainers to Note: P. Cazalet, R. Turnell, H. Price, F. Walwyn, F. Cundell.
Best Race for Favourites—SECOND; for Second Favourites—THIRD.
Worst Race for Favourites—FIFTH; for Second Favourites—SECOND.

STRATFORD-UPON-AVON

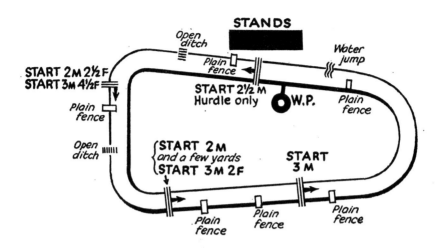

Trainers to Note: T. F. Rimell, F. Walwyn, D. Ancil, T. Forster, H. Price.
Best Race for Favourites—SECOND; for Second Favourites—FIFTH.
Worst Race for Favourites—FIRST; for Second Favourites—SECOND.

TEESSIDE PARK (STOCKTON) (1/1+)

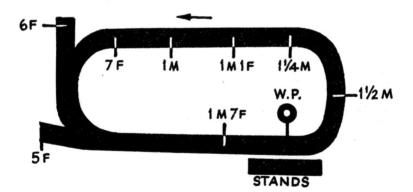

Teesside Park is perfectly flat with easy bends. So it is a very sharp course and races are usually run at a cracking pace, particularly when the going is on the firm side. The five-furlong offshoot start joins the run-in on a leftish incline about a half mile out, while in six-furlong races there is a two-furlong run before the bend. In these sprints, speed from the gate is important but a low draw is worth noting. This is not so much marked in longer events.

Trainers to Note: M. W. Easterby, L. Sheddon, W. Elsey, S. Hall.
Best Race for Favourites—FIRST; **for Second Favourites**—SIXTH.
Worst Race for Favourites—SIXTH; **for Second Favourites**—FIFTH.

THIRSK (2/2)

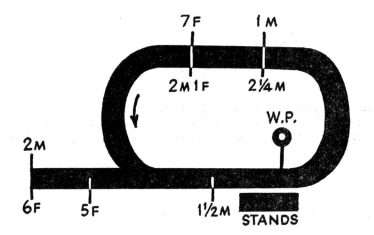

The circuit at Thirsk is quite small, measuring a mere ten furlongs in circumference, but even so the bends are quite easy. In the main it is perfectly flat, but the half-mile run-in—like the whole of the straight six-furlong—is gently undulating. The course as a whole is on the sharp side and in all but long-distance races, horses must be quickly into their stride. This is of great importance in sprints and a smart break plus a high number in the draw on the straight course is usually the winning formula.

Trainers to Note: W. Elsey, H. P. Rohan, S. Hall, J. Calvert, W. Gray.
Best Race for Favourites—THIRD; **for Second Favourites**—FIFTH.
Worst Race for Favourites—FOURTH; **for Second Favourites**—SIXTH.

WARWICK (1/1)

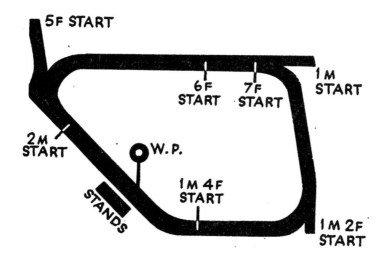

There is no straight course at Warwick and in sprints over the minimum trip—started on an extension from the circuit—runners cover a quarter of a mile and then take a left turn into the three-furlong run-in. This angle gives low numbers in the draw quite an edge, which also applies in longer events. The accent is on speed here and this is no place for the horse who takes time to settle down.

Trainers to Note: H. Leader, V. Cross, E. Reavey, F. Armstrong, Ryan Jarvis.
Best Race for Favourites—FIRST; **for Second Favourites**—SECOND.
Worst Race for Favourites—FOURTH; **for Second Favourites**—SIXTH.

C

WINDSOR (1/2)

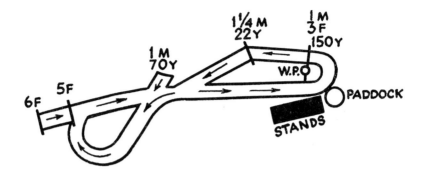

Improvements were made to the course at Windsor last year (1968), easing the bottom loop of this figure of eight. It is still on the sharp side but, with an almost straight five-furlong run-in, the longer races call for plenty of stamina. Big horses, usually at home on a galloping track, take their fair share of prizes here. In sprints, high numbers are favoured in the draw but they must be smartly away to avoid bunching at the slight right-hand elbow.

Trainers to Note: G. Smyth, I. Balding, K. Cundell, G. Richards, F. Armstrong.
Best Race for Favourites—FIRST; **for Second Favourites**—FOURTH.
Worst Race for Favourites—SIXTH; **for Second Favourites**—SECOND.

WOLVERHAMPTON (1/1)

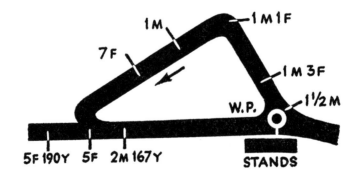

Racing at Wolverhampton is rather poor, but it is quite a good course. The circuit is about a mile and a half round with a five-furlong run-in. Sprints on the straight course are fair, giving no favour in the draw, but in seven-furlong and mile races there is a left-hand bend which gives low numbers a slight advantage.

> **Trainers to Note:** W. Hern, F. Armstrong, P. Walwyn, A. Budgett, A. Goodwill.
> **Best Race for Favourites**—FOURTH; **for Second Favourites**—FIRST.
> **Worst Race for Favourites**—THIRD; **for Second Favourites**—SECOND.

YARMOUTH (2/2)

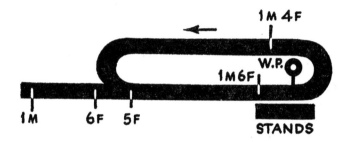

Yarmouth is quite close to Newmarket and, not surprisingly, a great number of the runners on this course come from headquarters. In spite of this, however, the standard of racing is rather low, mainly due to a lack of attractive prizes. The course is a narrow oval with a slight fall before the perfectly flat five-furlong run-in. The straight mile is quite fast and it is questioned whether high-drawn horses have any advantage.

> **Trainers to Note:** H. Leader, J. Jarvis, J. A. J. Waugh, F. Armstrong, J. Oxley.
> **Best Race for Favourites**—FIRST; **for Second Favourites**—SIXTH.
> **Worst Race for Favourites**—THIRD; **for Second Favourites**—THIRD.

YORK (4/5)

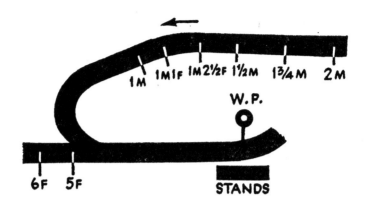

York is the Ascot of the north. Although a few other courses have a slightly higher standard of racing, nowhere offers the public a better deal. The two-mile 'U'-shaped course is wide and perfectly flat. The sweeping bend into the five-furlong run-in makes it ideal for the long-striding powerful gallopers. If a horse is good enough, it will win here for the course is very fair and the draw has no effect on results.

Trainers to Note: S. Hall, J. Oxley, In Ireland, W. Elsey, F. Armstrong, N. Murless.

Best Race for Favourites—SECOND; **for Second Favourites**—FIRST.

Worst Race for Favourites—FIRST; **for Second Favourites**—SIXTH.

Expensive Yearlings of 1968

(Sales; G=Goff's September Yearlings Sales, N.O.=Newmarket October Sales, N.H.=Newmarket Houghton Sales   N.A.=Newmarket Autumn Sales)

Yearling	Vendor	Sales and Date	Buyer	Price (Gns)
B c by Ribot—Montea	Anne, Duchess of Westminster	N.H. (Oct 17)	Anglo Irish Agency	37,000
Ch c by Mourne—Tinta	Airlie and Snailwell Stud Co.	N.O. (Oct 4)	Capt M Lemos	25,000
B c by Charlottesville—Romp Home	William Hill Studs	N.H. (Oct 17)	Lady Beaverbrook	24,000
Ch f by Never Say Die—Miss Doree	Woodpark Ltd.	N.O. (Oct 4)	Anglo Irish Agency	22,000
Ch c by Exbury—Reel In	Mr J R S Coggan	N.O. (Oct 3)	Mr F Armstrong	21,000
B c by Ragusa—Samaria	Mrs A Levins Moore	N.H. (Oct 18)	Lord Harrington	20,000
Gr c by Grey Sovereign—Nona	Mr W F Davidson	N.H. (Oct 19)	Lady Beaverbrook	19,500
Gleam of Gold Ch f by Roan Rocket—Winter Gleam	Ballymorris Studs	N.O. (Oct 4)	Mr W Lyde	18,500
Ch c by Princely Gift—Mor'a Bai	Fort Union Stud	N.H. (Oct 17)	Mr D McCall	18,500
Ch f by Relko—Alice Delysia	Brook Stud Company	N.O. (Oct 3)	Mr G S. Forbes	17,500
Ch c by Crepello—Honeymoon House	Mr E Cooper Bland	N.H. (Oct 17)	Mr B Swift	17,000
Gr f by Sovereign Path—Flattering	Mr F F Tuthill	N.H. (Oct 17)	British Bloodstock Agency	17,000
B c by Princely Gift—Mwanza	Ribblesdale Stud	N.H. (Oct 16)	Mr B Swift	16,500
Gr c by Sovereign Path—Wedding Cake	Middleton Park Stud	N.H. (Oct 18)	Lady Beaverbrook	16,500
B or Gr c by Firestreak—Welsh Mistress	Brook Stud Company	N.O. (Oct 3)	Lady Beaverbrook	16,000
B f by Larkspur—Lumina	Mr A R Tarry	N.O. (Oct 2)	Mr William Hill	15,500
B c by Crepello—Trip to the Moon	Mr E Nicholas Hall	N.H. (Oct 17)	Mr J P Bartholomew	15,500
Ch c by St Paddy—Lucky Stream	Ribblesdale Stud	N.H. (Oct 16)	Lord Harrington	15,000
B c by Tudor Melody—Alphabet	Woodcote Stud	N.O. (Oct 1)	Lord Harrington	14,500
Ch c by Henry the Seventh—Loidien	Burton Agnes Stud	N.H. (Oct 18)	Mr D McCall	14,000
B c by Crepello—No Saint	Cleaboy Stud	N.H. (Oct 19)	Mr M V O'Brien	14,000
B f by Narrator—High Powered	Cleaboy Stud	N.H. (Oct 19)	Capt G T Booth Jones	14,000
B or Br c by Relko—Skylarking	Philip A Love	G. (Sep 17)	Mr G Harwood	13,000

Pedigree	Vendor	Sale	Buyer	Price
B f by Mourne—Fair Bid	Mr A Percy Harris	N.H. (Oct 18)	Lord Harrington	13,000
B f by Tudor Melody—Crepina	Sassoon Studs	N.A. (Nov. 8)	Mr. P. Burrell	13,000
B c by Tudor Melody—Bridge of Stars	Stackallan	G. (Sep 17)	Lord Harrington	12,500
B f by Charlottesville—Coriander	Burton Agnes Stud	N.H. (Oct 18)	Mr J Lambton	12,500
B c by Star Gazer—Solarist	Riversdale Stud	G. (Sep 17)	Cragwood Estates	12,000
B c by Princely Gift—Wildsteps	Riversdale Stud	G. (Sep 17)	Mrs A M Ford	12,000
B c by Santa Claus—Armeria	Stackallan	G. (Sep 17)	Lord Harrington	12,000
Gr c by Grey Sovereign—Polly Gilles	Thoroughbred Breeding Ltd	N.O. (Oct 4)	Mr A J Scratchley	12,000
Dandy Lion Ch c by Relko—Nun Neater	Mr E Coupey	N.O. (Oct 5)	Curragh Bloodstock Agency	12,000
B c by Ragusa—Esquire Girl	Burton Agnes Stud	N.H. (Oct 18)	Mr M Cosgrove	12,000
Gr c by Ballymoss—My Poppet	Banstead Manor Stud	N.H. (Oct 19)	Lord Harrington	12,000
Ch c by Mossborough—Bernice	Mr W J McEnery	N.H. (Oct 19)	Mr B van Cutsem	12,000
B f by Tudor Melody—Jeanne d'Arc	Major J H de Burgh	N.H. (Oct 16)	Major P Nelson	11,500
Ch c by Ballymoss—Asmara	William Hill Studs	N.H. (Oct 17)	Mrs S Jacobson	11,500
B c by Tamerlane—Donna Lollo	Southdown Stud Company	N.H. (Oct 17)	Mr J Tree	11,500
Br c by Relko—My Mother	Mr A Percy Harris	N.O. (Oct 2)	Mr C A Rogers	11,000
B c by Crepello—My Game	Eyrefield Stud Co Ltd	N.H. (Oct 16)	Mr G Forbes	11,000
B f by Pall Mall—Northern Beauty	Middleton Park Stud	N.H. (Oct 18)	Mr B Hobbs	11,000
Ch f by Crepello—Quail	Mr R More O'Ferrall and Farmleigh Estates Company	N.H. (Oct 19)	Mr C F N Murless	11,000
Ch c by Charlottesville—Meadow Pipit	Mr Philip A Love	G. (Sep 17)	Lord Harrington	10,500
Ch f by Whistling Wind—Ballymiss	Mr P Burns	N.O. (Oct 1)	Capt M Lemos	10,500
B c by Sing Sing—Miss McTaffy	Overbury Stud	N.H. (Oct 16)	Anglo Irish Agency	10,500
B f by Santa Claus—Lania	Burton Agnes Stud	N.H. (Oct 18)	Mr W Hern	10,500
B c by Sing Sing—Queen of Peru	West Grinstead Stud Ltd	N.O. (Oct 3)	Mr W Burmann	10,000
Br c by Molvedo—Mistress Grace	Mr E Nicholas Hall	N.H. (Oct 17)	Anglo Irish Agency	10,000
Ch c by Princely Gift—Riches	William Hill Studs	N.H. (Oct 17)	Lady Beaverbrook	10,000
B c by Alcide—Be Careful	William Hill Studs	N.H. (Oct 17)	Mr F Armstrong	10,000
Ch f by Pall Mall—Floral Park	Knockaney Stud	N.H. (Oct 19)	British Bloodstock Agency	10,000
B c by Shantung—Near the Line	Banstead Manor Stud	N.H. (Oct 19)	M E Pollet	10,000
B c by Hethersett—Who Can Tell	Cleaboy Stud	N.H. (Oct 19)	Anglo Irish Agency	10,000

Full Free Handicap Weights
Since 1957

Horses in capital letters were subsequently placed in a Classic.
2G—2,000 Guineas; 1G—1,000 Guineas; O—Oaks; D—Derby;
L—St Leger.

1957

Name	st.	lb.	Name	st.	lb.	Name	st.	lb.
MAJOR PORTION (2nd, 2G)	9	7	Medina	8	6	Glendawn	7	13
Neptune II	9	6	Light Catch	8	5	Capponcina	7	13
Rich and Rare	9	4	Lavandier	8	5	Masquerade	7	13
Coup de Vent	9	2	Cool Debate	8	5	Kandy-Sugar	7	13
Kelly	9	1	Vestal King	8	5	Selindra	7	13
Pheidippides	9	1	Welsh Abbot	8	5	Lightning Flash	7	13
Pinched	9	1	Wonder Belle	8	5	Logarithm	7	13
PALL MALL (First, 2G)	9	0	Chandelier	8	5	Cameo	7	12
Aggressor	9	0	Meissa	8	4	Abbey Oaks	7	12
Abelia	8	13	Miniature	8	4	Holiday Time	7	12
Promulgation	8	12	ALCIDE (First, L)	8	4	Pleiades	7	12
Idler	8	12	Zanzibar	8	4	Elisha	7	12
ALPINE BLOOM (3rd, 1G)	8	12	Barleycroft	8	4	Welsh Rake	7	11
Liberal Lady	8	11	Angelo	8	4	Long John Silver	7	11
Munch	8	10	MOTHER GOOSE (2nd, O)	8	3	Pebble Ridge	7	11
Torbella III	8	10	Davenport	8	3	Casse Noisette	7	11
Vegeo	8	9	Galley Hill	8	3	Arcure	7	11
Boccaccio	8	9	Ruthin	8	3	Rock Event	7	11
Trimmer	8	9	Mr Snake	8	3	General Pil	7	11
Cornplaster	8	9	Kinglike	8	3	Silver Mistress	7	11
Prime Boy	8	9	Okaye	8	3	Astrol	7	10
Patroness	8	8	Supreme Joy	8	2	Linger Not	7	10
Poplin	8	8	Inkerman	8	2	Starboard	7	10
Butterfly Net	8	7	Satan's Slide	8	2	Sufi	7	10
NAGAMI (3rd, 2G; 3rd, D; 3rd, L)	8	7	Lacydon	8	2	Bromelia	7	10
Troubadour	8	7	Hope Arose	8	2	Forensic	7	10
NONE NICER (2nd, L)	8	7	Guersillus	8	2	Rhythmic	7	9
High Camber	8	7	Kingroy	8	1	Faultless Speech	7	9
Jack & Jill	8	7	Rolled Gold	8	1	Orarca	7	9
Darlene	8	6	Open View	8	1	Rosebag	7	9
			Pacifico	8	0	Snapdragon	7	9
			Ben Arthur	7	13	Mistra	7	9
			Gay Song	7	13	Proud Galleon	7	8
			Cocked Hat	7	13	Hot Money	7	8
						Trial Note	7	8
						Welsh Vote	7	6

1958

	st.	lb.		st.	lb.		st.	lb.
Tudor Melody	9	7	Phantom Star	8	7	Oserian	8	0
MASHAM	9	5	Sue	8	7	Pale Sapphire	8	0
(2nd, 2G)			Archbishop	8	6	Stratus	8	0
CARNOUSTIE	9	3	Grey Marsh	8	6	Decor	8	0
(3rd, 2G)			Thyra Lee	8	6	Solo Singer	8	0
Captain Kidd	9	3	Scarlet Plume	8	6	Capuchon	8	0
Dan Cupid	9	3	PETITE ETOILE	8	6	Court Imperial	8	0
Lindsay	9	2	(First, 1G; First, O)			Yucatan	8	0
ROSALBA	9	2	Donjon	8	6	Street Song	7	13
(2nd, 1G)			Major General	8	5	Lindrick	7	13
Be Careful	9	1	Donna	8	5	Dear Gazelle	7	13
Bill of Rights	9	1	Solvilio	8	4	Cashel	7	13
Billum	9	1	Spice	8	4	Dunoon Star	7	13
Hieroglyph	9	0	Ricky Joe	8	3	Obscurity	7	13
Firestreak	9	0	High Perch	8	3	Chris	7	13
Greek Sovereign	8	12	Chanter	8	3	Kesteven	7	13
Fan Light	8	12	Traviata	8	2	Falling in Love	7	12
PARAGUANA	8	11	Sutton Harbour	8	2	Euphorbia	7	12
(3rd, 1G)			A.20	8	2	Danube	7	12
Krakenwake	8	11	Kindling Chips	8	2	Number One	7	12
Bleep-Bleep	8	10	Brixham	8	2	Reprimand	7	12
Compere	8	10	Connaissance	8	2	Double Flight	7	12
Sovereign Path	8	10	PINDARI	8	2	Piranha	7	12
Seascape	8	10	(3rd, L)			Starlet	7	11
CANTELO	8	9	Cortachy	8	2	Mayflower	7	11
(2nd, O; First, L)			Gol Brig	8	2	Confidential	7	10
Ink Spot	8	9	Parrotia	8	2	Benchers	7	10
Tesso	8	9	Arragon	8	2	Decoy	7	10
Anthelion	8	8	King's Mark	8	2	Saturnetta	7	10
Crystal Palace	8	8	Whistle Stop	8	2	Bellisle	7	10
Dominate	8	8	Persian Beauty	8	1	Court Caprice	7	10
Fortune's Darling	8	8	Short Sentence	8	1	Tritonia	7	9
Marsh Meadow	8	8	Dame Melba	8	1	Catalpa	7	9
Imagine	8	7	Signal Boy	8	1	Royal Clyde	7	9
ROSE OF MEDINA	8	7	Helen Rosa	8	1	Chappaqua	7	7
(3rd, O)			Charmed Life	8	0	Tribune	7	7

1959

	st.	lb.		st.	lb.		st.	lb.
Sing Sing	9	7	Goose Creek	8	3	Shy Girl	7	11
VENTURE VII	9	4	Jet Stream	8	3	Not Guilty	7	11
(2nd, 2G)			Midsummer Night II	8	3	Pretty Cage	7	11
Paddy's Sister	9	1	Dollar Piece	8	2	Chinky Bu	7	11
Newbus	9	0	St Mark	8	2	Keryl	7	10
ST PADDY	8	13	Memorable	8	2	Inga	7	10
(First, D; First, L)			Beau Ideal	8	1	No Saint	7	10
Queensberry	8	12	Fascinator	8	1	Morgat	7	10
Oak Ridge	8	12	Spaniards Close	8	1	Star Minstrel	7	10
MARTIAL	8	11	Mozart	8	0	Calypso	7	9
(First, 2G)			Braga	8	0	Jeanne Michelle	7	9
Intervener	8	11	Western Sky	8	0	San Siro	7	9
Panga	8	11	Sonomag	8	0	Comobeau	7	9
Sound Track	8	10	Whinchat	7	13	Gideon	7	9
Red Gauntlet	8	10	Enticement	7	13	Pardoner	7	9
Fair Reward	8	10	Purim	7	13	Mr Higgins	7	9
Optimist	8	9	Gentiana	7	13	LADY IN		
Blast	8	9	Palmural	7	13	TROUBLE	7	8
Be Cautious	8	8	Red Sugar	7	13	(2nd, 1G)		
Arctic Hope	8	8	Pugnacious	7	13	Gallows Gal	7	8
Ironic	8	7	Whistlers Daughter	7	13	Higher Level	7	8
Tywydd Teg	8	7	High Pitch	7	12	Demoiselle	7	8
Carnival Dancer	8	7	Laminate	7	12	Scala	7	8
Monet	8	7	Balsarroch Boy	7	12	Lentolia	7	8
Arion	8	7	Carpaccio	7	12	Royal Glen	7	8
Tulyartos	8	7	Pampered	7	12	Pink Paraffin	7	7
King of the Clyde	8	6	Monamolin	7	12	Heat Haze	7	7
Diffidence	8	5	Maritime	7	12	Gay Natasha	7	7
St Anne	8	5	Mickey Finn	7	12	Arbell	7	7
Lombard	8	4	Queen of the Roses	7	12	Eternal Goddess	7	7
Astrador	8	4	Romper Lad	7	12	Daily Sketch	7	6
Tudor Court	8	4	Chota Hazri	7	12	Dance Time	7	6
Grasp	8	4	Petticoat Law	7	12	Syndale Valley	7	6
RUNNING BLUE	8	4	Chiara	7	11	Comat	7	6
(3rd, 1G)			Honeymug	7	11	Denial	7	6
						Sind	7	6

1960

	st.	lb.		st.	lb.		st.	lb.
Opaline II	9	7	Italian Riviera	8	6	Grisetta	7	13
Typhoon	9	6	Crowded Room	8	6	Fantastic Command	7	13
Floribunda	9	5	Royal Salic	8	5	Aqua Regia	7	13
Kathy Too	9	4	Ribelle	8	5	Alanix	7	13
SWEET SOLERA	9	2	The Axe	8	4	New Blood	7	13
(First, 1G; First, O)			PSIDIUM	8	4	Prized	7	13
Cynara	9	2	(First, D)			Prince Orsini	7	12
AMBERGRIS	9	2	Prosecutor	8	4	Royal Stretch	7	12
(2nd, 1G; 2nd, O)			Tender Word	8	4	Klondyke Bill	7	12
Favorita	9	1	Blue Sash	8	4	Blue Palm	7	12
Test Case	9	1	PARDAO	8	4	State Offence	7	12
Skymaster	8	12	(3rd, D)			Rain Coat	7	12
Kerrabee	8	12	Who's Caprice	8	4	Wild Night	7	12
TIME GREINE	8	12	Neroncy	8	3	Marche d'Or	7	12
(3rd, 2G)			Miss Biffin	8	3	Ayrshire Bard	7	12
Primus	8	10	BOUNTEOUS	8	2	Munificent	7	11
King's Son	8	9	(2nd, L)			Piero	7	11
PRINCE TUDOR	8	9	Lawful	8	2	Treasure Island	7	11
(2nd, 2G)			Andromache	8	2	Tudor Warning	7	11
Prince Midge	8	9	Diophantes	8	2	Sybil's Comb	7	11
King Frank			Recitatif	8	2	Go Man Go	7	11
(late Praise)	8	8	Laughing Cheese	8	2	Deetease	7	11
Gallant Knight	8	8	No Fiddling	8	2	Who Can Tell	7	10
Beta	8	8	Non Proven	8	2	Vinnie	7	10
Blue Sails	8	8	Royal Pennant	8	2	Blue Wand	7	10
Scandale	8	8	Bordone	8	1	Divine Comedy	7	9
Palatina	8	8	Smuggler's Joy	8	1	Covert Side	7	9
Colour Blind	8	8	Rins of Clyde	8	1	Gittern	7	9
Mythical Return	8	7	Oakville	8	1	Watersmeet	7	9
New Move	8	7	Elegant Stephen	8	1	Violetta III	7	8
Dual	8	7	Sunspeck	8	0	Bury Hill	7	8
Eagle	8	7	Barbizon	8	0	Flower Drum	7	8
Sticky Case	8	6	Swingtime	8	0	Limitless	7	8
Abanilla	8	6	Checkendon	8	0	Storymount	7	8
Crisper	8	6	Morning Star	8	0	Admonish	7	8
Erudite	8	6	Fury Royal	8	0	Weather Way	7	8

77

1961

	st.	lb.		st.	lb.		st.	lb.
La Tendresse	9	7	Victorina	8	4	Set Going	7	11
DISPLAY	9	3	Writ of Error	8	4	Peacock Throne	7	11
(2nd, 1G)			Vendeuse	8	3	Light on his Feet	7	11
MIRALGO	9	1	Windmill	8	3	Maeandon	7	11
(3rd, L)			Brother	8	3	Young Lochinvar	7	11
Escort	9	0	Gustave Dore	8	3	Overdue	7	10
Gay Mairi	9	0	Songedor	8	3	PRIVY COUNCILLOR		
Caerphilly	9	0	Olympius	8	3	(First, 2G)	7	10
Gustav	8	12	Conspirator	8	2	Fiacre	7	10
Sovereign Lord	8	11	Nerissa	8	2	Laggan	7	10
Compensation	8	10	Hidden Meaning	8	2	Quince	7	10
PRINCE POPPA	8	10	Couloir	8	2	Fortunella	7	10
(3rd, 2G)			Persian Wonder	8	2	Exhibitor	7	10
Blaze of Glory II	8	9	Catchpole	8	1	Soueida	7	10
Valentine	8	9	Principal	8	1	Tamerlo	7	9
Clear Sound	8	9	Windbag	8	1	Pegs Fancy	7	9
ROMULUS	8	9	Bonny Creeper	8	0	Scribbler	7	9
(2nd, 2G)			High Noon	8	0	Champ	7	9
River Chanter	8	9	Our Guile	8	0	Pervinca	7	9
Xerxes	8	9	Oliver Hardy	8	0	Crepello's Daughter	7	8
HETHERSETT	8	8	Tacitus	8	0	Tart	7	8
(First, L)			Oroondates	8	0	Coogee	7	8
Bow Tie	8	8	Secret Step	7	13	Marchendeer	7	8
Heron	8	8	Naturalist	7	13	Black Nanny	7	8
All-a-Gogg	8	8	Chalkey	7	12	Tournella	7	8
Prince Tor	8	8	Will Reward	7	12	Light Case	7	8
French Plea	8	7	Kingbenitch	7	12	Exhibition	7	8
Burning Thoughts	8	7	Polly's Beau	7	12	Palanna	7	8
Aznip	8	7	Fast Beat	7	12	Remainder	7	7
Cyrus	8	7	Liege Lord	7	12	Miss Klaire II	7	7
ABERMAID	8	6	Windfields	7	12	Nereus	7	7
(First, 1G)			Tipstaff	7	12	Rustana	7	7
Kathyanga	8	4	Nortia	7	12	Scots Fusilier	7	7
Miletus	8	4	Next to Nothing	7	12	Star Prize	7	7
Alpine Scent	8	4	Jibuti	7	12	Fircone	7	7
Polly Toogood	8	4				Themides	7	7

1962

	st.	lb.		st.	lb.		st.	lb.
Crocket	9	7	In the Gloaming	8	7	Gallop On	8	0
NOBLESSE	9	4	The Bo'sun	8	7	Honey Portion	8	0
(First, O)			Fast Company	8	7	Abaddon	8	0
Happy Omen	9	2	Executor	8	7	Chartered		
IONIAN	8	13	Polybius	8	7	Accountant	8	0
(2nd, 2G)			Tarara	8	7	Oh! Do	7	13
Daybreak	8	13	King's Case	8	6	Marzipan	7	13
Fair Astronomer	8	13	Portofino	8	6	Majority	7	13
Magic Carpet	8	13	Hejaz	8	6	Santa Maria	7	13
Queen's Hussar	8	13	Guinea Sparrow	8	6	Proclamation	7	13
Romantic	8	12	Didon	8	6	Prince's Error	7	13
Partholon	8	12	Golden Plume	8	5	Marcher	7	13
Summer Day	8	11	Narrow Escape	8	5	Sultana's Pet	7	12
STAR MOSS	8	11	Tzigane	8	5	Flashing Light	7	12
(2nd, L)			FIGHTING SHIP	8	5	Plymouth Sound	7	12
Molino	8	11	(3rd, L)			True North	7	12
Dunce Cap	8	10	Dilly Boy	8	4	Tandlebury	7	12
Royal Indiscretion	8	10	Sammy Davis	8	4	Marazion	7	12
My Goodness Me	8	9	Idomeneo	8	4	High Flown	7	12
Matatina	8	9	Tierra del Fuego	8	4	Seymour	7	11
King's Favourite	8	9	Snark	8	3	Born Free	7	11
King of Babylon	8	9	Lunatic	8	3	Ampney Princess	7	11
Trafalgar	8	9	Palm Springs	8	3	Nautch Dance	7	11
Tudor Grey	8	9	Aubusson	8	3	Fiji	7	11
Fidelio	8	9	High Flying	8	3	Barleycroft Bay	7	11
Follow Suit	8	8	Confidence	8	3	Saltarello	7	10
Hera	8	8	All of a Kind	8	2	Ernie	7	10
Scholar Gypsy	8	8	Visualise	8	2	Pornic	7	10
Top of the Milk	8	8	Lucky Gwen	8	2	Ruffino	7	10
Young David	8	8	Tumbrel	8	2	Ros Rock	7	9
Zaleucus	8	8	Bourguignon	8	2	Mrs Gail	7	9
My Myosotis	8	8	Lady Astronaut	8	1	Zucchini	7	9
Harbinger	8	8	Clinkers	8	1	Orleans	7	9
Bandarilla	8	7	Vijay	8	1	Mandamus	7	9
Forearmed	8	7	Fear Not	8	1	Empetrum	7	8

1963

	st.	lb.		st.	lb.		st.	lb.
Talahasse	9	7	Flattering	8	7	London Melody	8	1
Showdown	9	6	Penny Stall	8	7	French Vintage	8	1
Derring-Do	9	4	Causerie	8	6	Cumshaw	8	1
Althrey Don	9	2	Peter le Grand	8	6	Aristo	8	1
Pushful	9	2	King's Lane	8	6	Alborada	8	1
Mesopotamia	9	2	Silver Churn	8	6	Chopine	8	1
Goldhill	9	1	SODERINI	8	6	Spring Fever	8	1
Dondeen	9	1	(3rd, L)			George's Gem	8	1
Gentle Art	9	0	Bivouac	8	5	Honey Wax	8	0
Crimea II	9	0	Water Eaton	8	5	Paddy Paws	8	0
Smooth Jet	8	13	Sweet Moss	8	5	Gipsy Kelly	8	0
POURPARLER	8	13	Cursorial	8	5	Willow Red	8	0
(First, 1G)			Corinth	8	5	Avektos	8	0
FABERGE II	8	12	Fideve	8	4	Young Turnabout	7	13
(2nd, 2G)			GWEN	8	4	Boys Delighta	7	13
Roan Rocket	8	12	(2nd, 1G)			Conchita	7	13
Runnymede	8	12	Mara River	8	4	No Danger	7	13
Casabianca	8	12	Touchbutton	8	4	Words and Music	7	13
Takawalk II	8	11	Monkey Palm	8	4	Free Style	7	13
Casserola	8	11	Mark Hopkins	8	4	Gallegos	7	13
Golden Apollo	8	10	Round Trip	8	4	Fair Valley	7	13
Lerida	8	10	Royal Justice	8	4	Ballymacad	7	13
Young Christopher	8	10	High Powered	8	3	Matterhorn	7	13
Endless Honey	8	10	Golden Ruffle	8	3	Quo Banco	7	12
Palm	8	9	Make Haste	8	3	Foxford Boy	7	12
Port Merion	8	9	Prince of Orange	8	3	Umgeni Poort	7	12
Quentin	8	9	Pilgrims Journey	8	3	Tamerslip	7	12
Dumpy	8	9	Sterner Stuff	8	2	Viceroy	7	12
Con Brio	8	9	Daylight Robbery	8	2	Wisley	7	12
Atbara	8	8	Julieta	8	2	Fair Bonza	7	11
Impact	8	8	Whistling Fool	8	2	Stone the Crows	7	11
Piccadilly	8	8	Solennis	8	2	Irish Rhythm	7	11
News Item	8	8	Zingaline	8	1	Somerville	7	11
Palinda	8	8	Shoulder Strap	8	1	Scottish Society	7	10
Travel Man	8	7				Mahbub Aly	7	10

1964

	st.	lb.		st.	lb.		st.	lb.
Double Jump	10	0	Abscond	8	11	Nearside	8	6
Hardicanute	9	12	Siliconn	8	11	Milesius	8	6
Spanish Express	9	12	Convamore	8	10	Pally	8	6
Prominer	9	9	Zaloba	8	10	Silent Trust	8	6
Ragtime	9	8	Street Fighter	8	10	Pamade	8	6
Leonardo	9	8	Alan Adare	8	10	Quissett	8	5
Holborn	9	7	Dunlin	8	10	Forlorn River	8	5
SILLY SEASON	9	5	Valoroso	8	10	Flare	8	5
(2nd, 2G)			Sunacelli	8	10	Off the Hook	8	5
Rehearsed	9	5	Old Bailey	8	9	Sweet Sovereign	8	5
Polyfoto	9	5	Barnie's Image	8	9	Pamir	8	5
NIGHT OFF	9	5	London Way	8	9	Sky Cracker	8	5
(First, 1G)			Greybeard	8	9	Ballycotton	8	5
Brave Knight	9	3	Caruso	8	9	Take a Chance	8	5
Gulf Pearl	9	3	Welsh Mistress	8	9	Alcalde	8	5
Never a Fear	9	3	Dashing	8	9	Short Commons	8	4
Foothill	9	3	Veroussa	8	8	Unity	8	4
Spaniards Mount	9	2	Hell's Delight	8	8	Langley Park	8	3
Crispian	9	2	Vivat Rex	8	8	Defender	8	3
King Log	9	1	Enrico	8	8	Seeded	8	3
Tamino	9	1	Isola d'Asti	8	8	Atonement	8	3
Attitude	9	1	Young Nelson	8	8	Spanish Moon	8	3
Royalgo	9	0	Selina	8	7	Prince of Paris	8	2
Audience	9	0	Wind Song	8	7	River Rhine	8	2
Pugnacity	9	0	Palm Way	8	7	Goupi	8	2
Greengage	8	13	Sandro	8	7	Vitruvius	8	2
Potier	8	13	Hornblower	8	7	The Sheriff	8	2
Nentego	8	13	The Beatle	8	7	Valdesta	8	2
Air Patrol	8	13	Royal Rubicon	8	7	Blind Eye	8	1
Merry Madcap	8	12	Astrellita	8	7	Duke Street	8	1
Manolete	8	12	Grey Silk	8	7	MABEL	8	1
Runnello	8	12	Hasty Cast	8	6	(3rd, 1G; 2nd, O)		
RUBY'S PRINCESS	8	11	Boulderwood	8	6	Dynamic	8	1
(2nd, O)			Pinsun	8	6	Unpredictable	8	1
High Proof	8	11				Bognor Camp	8	0

1965

Name	st.	lb.	Name	st.	lb.	Name	st.	lb.
Young Emperor	10	0	Gay Palm	8	9	Galvanic	8	5
PRETENDRE	9	10	Comonisi	8	9	Allenheads	8	5
(2nd, D)			Persian Empire	8	9	Kew	8	5
CHARLOTTOWN	9	9	Caterina	8	9	At-a-Venture	8	5
(First, D; 2nd, L)			Regal Light	8	9	Coventry Blue	8	5
Soft Angels	9	7	Audrey Joan	8	9	Welsh Harvest	8	5
Le Cordonnier	9	7	Auskerry	8	9	Every Blessing	8	5
Tin King	9	6	Harolds Cross	8	9	Corinto	8	5
Track Spare	9	5	Master of Belcombe	8	8	Marcus Brutus	8	5
Troopfire	9	4	Downing Street	8	8	Bouchard	8	5
Khalekan	9	4	My Swanee	8	8	Bolting	8	4
CELTIC SONG	9	3	Military	8	8	Truvox	8	4
(3rd, 2G)			Pick Me Up	8	8	Ship Yard	8	4
The Ritz	9	3	Out of Orbit	8	8	Bugle Boy	8	4
SODIUM	9	3	Giuro	8	8	Lunar Princess	8	4
(First, L)			Marandis	8	8	Nancy	8	4
Double-U-Jay	9	2	Just Lucky II	8	8	French Parade	8	4
Lanark	9	2	Vibrant	8	8	Kibenka	8	4
Visp	9	1	Lincoln	8	7	Irish Minstrel	8	3
BERKELEY			Fleece	8	7	Saints and Sinners	8	3
SPRINGS	9	0	Irish Guard	8	7	Corbalton	8	3
(2nd, 1G; 2nd, O)			Royal Request	8	7	Castlenik	8	3
Sky Gipsy	9	0	Miss Togs	8	7	Snow Dale	8	3
Jet Aura	9	0	Selvedge	8	7	Chantmarle	8	3
Golden Summer	9	0	Queen of the Troops	8	7	DAVID JACK	8	3
Regular Guy	8	13	From Russia with			(3rd, L)		
Right of the Line	8	12	Love	8	7	St Puckle	8	3
Lucky Coin	8	12	Full Toss	8	7	Tape Recorder	8	3
GLAD RAGS	8	12	Eze	8	7	Southern Belle	8	2
(First, 1G)			New Conqueror	8	6	High Table	8	2
BLACK PRINCE II	8	12	Rennet	8	6	Lad's Love	8	2
(3rd, D)			Swiftest	8	6	Rosambre	8	2
Conjuror	8	11	GREAT NEPHEW	8	6	Gallic	8	2
Reet Lass	8	11	(2nd, 2G)			Regal Bell		
Procession	8	11	Garter Lady	8	6	Secret Affair	8	2
Zahedan	8	11	Gyropolis	8	6	Timarum	8	2
Whispering II	8	10	Saulisa	8	5	Fontex	8	2
Lumley Road	8	10						

1966

	st.	lb.		st.	lb.		st.	lb.
Bold Lad	9	7	PIA	8	4	View Mistress	7	13
ROYAL PALACE	9	4	(First, O)			Hidden Key	7	13
(First, 2G; First, D)			Hully Gully	8	4	First Date	7	13
RIBOCCO	9	3	Rose of Tralee	8	4	Rougeway	7	13
(2nd, D; First, L)			Galipar	8	3	Brent	7	13
Falcon	9	1	DART BOARD	8	3	Helluvafella	7	13
Reform	9	0	(3rd, D)			Majetta	7	13
Hambleden	8	13	Bunratty Castle	8	3	LUDHAM	7	13
Speed of Sound	8	13	Nantagos	8	3	(3rd, O)		
Florescence	8	13	Sir Herbert	8	3	Abbeyfield	7	13
On Your Mark	8	13	St Chad	8	3	London Boy	7	13
Be Friendly	8	11	Privy Seal	8	2	March of Time	7	12
Golden Horus	8	11	El Mighty	8	2	Poupette	7	12
Starry Halo	8	10	Maeander	8	2	Supreme Sovereign	7	12
FLEET	8	10	Solar Call	8	2	Cantadora	7	12
(First, 1G)			French Vine	8	2	Negotiator	7	12
Golden Dipper	8	9	Marble Court	8	1	Grey Venture	7	12
Heath Rose	8	9	Agile	8	1	Gay Glory	7	12
Kedge	8	9	LACQUER	8	1	Karpathos	7	12
Alamo City	8	9	(3rd, 1G)			Flower Patch	7	12
Manacle	8	9	Heavenly Sound	8	1	Wolver Hollow	7	12
Royal Saint	8	8	Countermarch	8	1	Nip Away	7	12
Tordo	8	8	Aiguillette	8	1	Massasoit	7	12
Quy	8	8	Que Guapo	8	1	Mountain Ash	7	12
Aglojo	8	8	Paddykin	8	0	Blanquette	7	11
Starboard Watch	8	7	Pennant	8	0	Field Mouse	7	11
Slip Stitch	8	7	Floosie	8	0	Greek Skittle	7	11
Horned Moon	8	6	Smooth	8	0	My Enigma	7	11
Green Park	8	6	Sharp Work	8	0	Bayarin	7	11
Ulpion	8	6	Boot Camp	8	0	Attacker	7	11
Apex II	8	6	In Command	8	0	St Cuthbert	7	11
Broadway Melody	8	6	The Ambion	8	0	Common Sergeant	7	11
Plotina	8	6	Good Match	8	0	St Padarn	7	11
Alcan	8	5	Winkie	7	13	Mary Tudor	7	11
Fab	8	5	Night Patrol	7	13	Fancy Smith	7	11
Above Water	8	4				Full Stretch	7	11

1967

	st.	lb.		st.	lb.		st.	lb.
PETINGO	9	7	Storm Bird	8	3	Exchange	7	11
(2nd, 2G)			Cease Fire	8	3	Belgrave Square	7	11
Vaguely Noble	9	6	Czar Alexander	8	3	How Far	7	11
Remand	9	5	PHOTO FLASH	8	2	Saufina	7	11
So Blessed	9	4	(2nd, 1G)			Red Sunset III	7	11
SOVEREIGN	9	1	Dahban	8	2	Sing Again	7	10
(3rd, 1G)			Right-Winger	8	2	Ilkley Moor	7	10
Lalibela	8	13	Wing-Commander II	8	2	Sovereign Service	7	10
Berber	8	12	Pseudonym	8	2	Sapper	7	10
Dalry	8	11	Last Shoe	8	2	Arctic Jelly	7	10
Hametus	8	10	Montana Girl	8	2	Saratoga Skiddy	7	10
Chebs Lad	8	9	Aunt Audrey	8	1	Daniel	7	10
D'Urberville	8	9	Miss Tarara	8	1	Profile	7	10
Doon	8	8	Scottish Dignity	8	1	Our Ruby	7	10
Mountain Call	8	8	Don Florestan	8	0	Matilda III	7	10
Mark Royal	8	7	Raffingora	8	0	Patriotic Alibi	7	10
The Viscount	8	7	Hardiesse	8	0	Panpiper	7	10
Lorenzaccio	8	7	Epe-Dor	8	0	Pertino	7	9
Front Row	8	7	Vitalgo	8	0	Arrival	7	9
Riboccare	8	7	Milltown	7	13	Homespun	7	9
Star and Garter	8	6	Abbie West	7	13	Whiz	7	9
Attalus	8	6	Virginia Gentleman	7	13	Covey	7	9
Lucky Finish	8	5	Relentless	7	13	Fly Past	7	9
Fairy Path	8	5	Canteen	7	13	Oraculus	7	9
Heathen	8	5	Sky Rocket	7	13	Ilium	7	8
Constans	8	4	Battle Flame	7	13	Heathtolt	7	8
Porto Bello	8	4	Maria Helena	7	12	Whiffle	7	8
Saraceno	8	4	Sovereign Ruler	7	12	Foggy Bell	7	8
Lowna	8	4	Loveridge	7	12	Calendula	7	7
Stansfield	8	4	CAERGWRLE	7	12	Lucky Toss	7	7
Hurry Hurry	8	4	(First, 1G)			Atopolis	7	6
Honey Bear	8	4	The Rift	7	12	Volunteer	7	6
Kursaal	8	4	Chico	7	12	Raffaello	7	6
La Mome	8	4	Stop Thief	7	12	Winter's Quota	7	6
Alaska Way	8	3	Freda Rose	7	11			

1968

	st.	lb.		st.	lb.		st.	lb.
Ribofilio	9	7	Mount Melody	8	4	Frontier Goddess	7	13
Right Tack	9	5	Timon	8	4	Smeralda	7	13
Tower Walk	9	3	Flying Legs	8	4	Blakeney	7	13
Folle Rousse	9	3	Adropejo	8	4	Vital Match	7	13
Tudor Music	9	2	Symona	8	4	Harbour Flower	7	13
Burglar	9	0	Laxmi	8	4	The Square	7	13
The Elk	9	0	Mitsouko	8	3	Tantivy	7	12
Hopiana	8	13	Quen Tanner	8	3	Shoemaker	7	12
Mige	8	13	Silverware	8	3	Grey Portal	7	12
The Erne	8	12	Lady's View	8	3	Concord Hymn	7	12
Deep Run	8	11	Caliban	8	3	Knotty Pine	7	11
Welsh Pageant	8	10	Perfect Friday	8	2	Sleeping Partner	7	11
Intermezzo	8	10	Whistling Top	8	2	Bogesund	7	11
Lucyrowe	8	10	Royal Captive	8	2	Silver Spray	7	11
Stung	8	9	Red Rose Prince	8	2	Miss Dollyrocker	7	11
Blue Yonder	8	8	Royal Smoke	8	2	Nedda	7	11
Hill Run	8	8	Sea Lavender	8	2	Polsky	7	11
Song	8	8	Harmony Hall	8	1	Anzio Jo	7	10
Hotfoot	8	8	Meldrum	8	1	Aggravate	7	10
Lord John	8	7	Nevetta	8	1	Jukebox	7	10
Star Story	8	7	Carsina	8	1	Beauty	7	10
Zarco	8	7	Margera	8	1	Dover Castle	7	10
Murrayfield	8	7	River Peace	8	0	New Chapter	7	10
Crooner	8	7	Fascination	8	0	Lovely Clare	7	10
Grey Goose	8	7	Brother Scot	8	0	Paul Mary	7	10
Mistral	8	7	Eldo	8	0	Golden Orange	7	10
Keep Going	8	6	Balidar	8	0	Gambola	7	10
Above and Beyond	8	6	Virginia Boy	8	0	Madlin	7	10
Dutch Bells	8	5	Ready Wit	7	13	Affric	7	10
Stoned	8	5	Ribomar	7	13	Grasper	7	10
Laser Light	8	5	Pindarique	7	13	Polly Peck	7	10
French Tutor	8	5	Buckler	7	13	Acquit	7	9
Sica Dan	8	5	Full Dress II	7	13	Nell Gwyn	7	9
White Fang	8	5						

Scale of Weight for Age

FLAT

The Scale of Weight for Age is published under the sanction of the Stewards of the Jockey Club as a guide to Managers of Race Meetings, but is not intended to be imperative, especially as regards the weights of two- and three-year-olds relatively to the older horses in selling races early in the year. It is founded on the scale published by Admiral Rous, and revised by him in 1873, but has been modified in accordance with suggestions from the principal trainers and practical authorities, and has been further revised since.

Note. The alteration of Rule 116, which came into force on March 1, 1931, requires the minimum weight in all races to be 6st 7lb (except in races confined to apprentices).

FIVE FURLONGS

AGE	MAR. & APR. st. lb.	MAY st. lb.	JUNE st. lb.	JULY st. lb.	AUG. st. lb.	SEPT. st. lb.	OCT. st. lb.	NOV. st. lb.
Two	6 0	6 2	6 7	6 10	7 2	7 7	7 9	7 12
Three	8 4	8 3	8 5	8 7	8 9	8 12	8 12	8 13
Four	9 4	9 0	9 0	9 0	9 0	9 0	9 0	9 0
Five, six & aged	9 5	9 0	9 0	9 0	9 0	9 0	9 0	9 0

SIX FURLONGS

AGE	MAR. & APR. st. lb.	MAY st. lb.	JUNE st. lb.	JULY st. lb.	AUG. st. lb.	SEPT. st. lb.	OCT. st. lb.	NOV. st. lb.
Two	—	6 4	6 7	6 11	7 0	7 6	7 9	7 13
Three	8 5	8 6	8 8	8 10	8 12	9 0	9 2	9 3
Four	9 7	9 7	9 7	9 7	9 7	9 7	9 7	9 7
Five, six & aged	9 9	9 8	9 7	9 7	9 7	9 7	9 7	9 7

ONE MILE

AGE	MAR. & APR. st. lb.	MAY st. lb.	JUNE st. lb.	JULY st. lb.	AUG. st. lb.	SEPT. st. lb.	OCT. st. lb.	NOV. st. lb.
Two.............	—	7 11	7 13	—	—	6 7	6 9	6 12
Three	7 8	9 0	9 0	8 2	8 4	8 6	8 7	8 8
Four	9 0	9 0	9 0	9 0	9 0	9 0	9 0	9 0
Five, six & aged	9 4	9 3	9 2	9 0	9 0	9 0	9 0	9 0

ONE MILE AND A HALF

AGE	MAR. & APR. st. lb.	MAY st. lb.	JUNE st. lb.	JULY st. lb.	AUG. st. lb.	SEPT. st. lb.	OCT. st. lb.	NOV. st. lb.
Two.............	—	7 9	7 11	7 13	8 1	6 0	6 4	6 7
Three	7 7	9 0	9 0	9 0	9 0	8 3	8 5	8 7
Four	9 0	9 0	9 0	9 0	9 0	9 0	9 0	9 0
Five, six & aged	9 5	9 4	9 3	9 2	9 1	9 0	9 0	9 0

TWO MILES

AGE	MAR. & APR. st. lb.	MAY st. lb.	JUNE st. lb.	JULY st. lb.	AUG. st. lb.	SEPT. st. lb.	OCT. st. lb.	NOV. st. lb.
Two.............	—	7 11	7 12	8 0	8 3	6 0	6 2	6 2
Three	7 8	9 4	9 4	9 4	9 4	8 4	8 5	8 5
Four	9 4	9 4	9 4	9 4	9 4	9 4	9 4	9 4
Five, six, & aged	9 10	9 9	9 8	9 7	9 6	9 5	9 4	9 4

THREE MILES

AGE	MAR. & APR. st. lb.	MAY st. lb.	JUNE st. lb.	JULY st. lb.	AUG. st. lb.	SEPT. st. lb.	OCT. st. lb.	NOV. st. lb.
Three	7 1	7 4	7 5	7 7	7 9	7 11	7 13	7 13
Four	9 0	9 0	9 0	9 0	9 0	9 0	9 0	9 0
Five	9 8	9 7	9 6	9 5	9 5	9 4	9 3	9 3
Six & aged	9 10	9 8	9 7	9 6	9 5	9 4	9 3	9 3

Scale of Weight for Age

NATIONAL HUNT

The National Hunt Committee recommend the following Scale of Weight-for-Age:

STEEPLECHASE TWO MILES

AGE	JAN.	FEB.	MAR.	APR.	MAY.	JUNE	AUG.	SEPT.	OCT.	NOV.	DEC.
	st. lb.	st. lb.	st. lb.	st. lb.	st. lb.	st. lb.	st. lb.	st. lb.	st. lb.	st. lb.	st. lb.
Four	10 9	10 10	10 11	10 12	10 13	11 0	11 2	11 3	11 4	11 5	11 6
Five	11 8	11 9	11 9	11 10	11 10	11 10	11 11	11 12	11 13	12 0	12 1
Six and aged	12 3	12 3	12 3	12 3	12 3	12 3	12 3	12 3	12 3	12 3	12 3

STEEPLECHASE TWO MILES AND A HALF

AGE	JAN.	FEB.	MAR.	APR.	MAY	JUNE	AUG.	SEPT.	OCT.	NOV.	DEC.
	st. lb.	st. lb.	st. lb.	st. lb.	st. lb.	st. lb.	st. lb.	st. lb.	st. lb.	st. lb.	st. lb.
Four	10 7	10 8	10 9	10 11	10 12	10 13	11 2	11 3	11 4	11 5	11 6
Five	11 8	11 8	11 9	11 10	11 10	11 10	11 11	11 12	11 13	12 0	12 1
Six and aged	12 3	12 3	12 3	12 3	12 3	12 3	12 3	12 3	12 3	12 3	12 3

STEEPLECHASE   THREE MILES

AGE	JAN.		FEB.		MAR.		APR.		MAY		JUNE		AUG.		SEPT.		OCT.		NOV.		DEC.	
	st.	lb.	st.	lb.	st.	lb.	st.	lb.	st.	lb.	st.	lb.	st.	lb.	st.	lb.	st.	lb.	st.	lb.	st.	lb.
Four	10	3	10	5	10	7	10	9	10	10	10	11	11	0	11	1	11	2	11	4	11	6
Five	11	8	11	8	11	9	11	10	11	10	11	10	11	10	11	11	11	12	11	13	12	1
Six and aged	12	3	12	3	12	3	12	3	12	3	12	3	12	3	12	3	12	3	12	3	12	3

HURDLE RACES   TWO MILES

AGE	JAN.		FEB.		MAR.		APR.		MAY		JUNE		AUG.		SEPT.		OCT.		NOV.		DEC.	
	st.	lb.	st.	lb.	st.	lb.	st.	lb.	st.	lb.	st.	lb.	st.	lb.	st.	lb.	st.	lb.	st.	lb.	st.	lb.
Three	—		—		—		—		—		11	9	10	7	10	7	10	9	10	11	11	0
Four	11	3	11	5	11	7	11	9	11	9	11	9	11	12	11	12	11	12	11	12	11	12
Five	11	13	12	0	12	1	12	2	12	2	12	2	12	3	12	3	12	3	12	3	12	3
Six and aged	12	3	12	3	12	3	12	3	12	3	12	3	12	3	12	3	12	3	12	3	12	3

Index of Races

The races in each section are in approximate chronological order

Section One: CLASSICS

Section Two: TWO-YEAR-OLD EVENTS

Race	32.	Champagne Stakes (7f)	Doncaster
Race	33.	Norfolk Stakes (5f)	Doncaster
Race	34.	Crookham Stakes (7f 60y)	Newbury
Race	35.	Champion Two-Year-Old Trophy (6f)	Ripon
Race	36.	National Stakes (7f)	Curragh
Race	37.	Imperial Stakes (6f)	Kempton
Race	38.	Larkspur Stakes (7f)	Leopardstown
Race	39.	Royal Lodge Stakes (1m)	Ascot
Race	40.	Blue Seal Stakes (6f)	Ascot
Race	41.	Beresford Stakes (1m)	Curragh
Race	42.	Middle Park Stakes (6f)	Newmarket
Race	43.	Cheveley Park Stakes (6f)	Newmarket
Race	44.	Cornwallis Stakes (5f)	Ascot
Race	45.	Duke of Edinburgh Stakes (6f)	Ascot
Race	46.	Dewhurst Stakes (7f)	Newmarket
Race	47.	Houghton Stakes (7f)	Newmarket
Race	48.	Horris Hill Stakes (7f 60y)	Newbury
Race	49.	Observer Gold Cup (1m)	Doncaster

Section Three: WEIGHT-FOR-AGE-EVENTS

Race	59.	2,000 Guineas Trial Stakes (7f)	Kempton
Race	60.	Coventry Stakes (1m)	Kempton
Race	61.	1,000 Guineas Trial Stakes (7f)	Kempton
Race	62.	Gladness Stakes (1m)	Curragh
Race	63.	Players' Navy Cut Trial Stakes (1m)	Phoenix Park
Race	64.	Ballymoss Stakes (1m 2f)	Curragh
Race	65.	Tetrarch Stakes (7f)	Curragh
Race	66.	Athasi Stakes (7f)	Curragh
Race	67.	Craven Stakes (1m)	Newmarket
Race	68.	Wood Ditton Stakes (1m)	Newmarket
Race	69.	Nell Gwyn Stakes (7f)	Newmarket
Race	70.	Greenham Stakes (7f)	Newbury
Race	71.	Fred Darling Stakes (7f 60y)	Newbury
Race	72.	John Porter Stakes (1m 4f)	Newbury
Race	73.	Thirsk Classic Trial Stakes (1m)	Thirsk
Race	74.	Blue Riband Trial Stakes (1m 110y)	Epsom
Race	75.	Princess Elizabeth Stakes (1m 110y)	Epsom
Race	76.	Royal Stakes (1m 2f)	Sandown
Race	77.	Coronation Stakes (1m 2f)	Sandown
Race	78.	Jockey Club Stakes (1m 4f)	Newmarket
Race	79.	Palace House Stakes (5f)	Newmarket
Race	80.	White Rose Maiden Stakes (1m 2f)	Ascot
Race	81.	Paradise Stakes (2m)	Ascot
Race	82.	Chester Vase (1m 4f 53y)	Chester
Race	83.	Cheshire Oaks (1m 4f 53y)	Chester
Race	84.	Ormonde Stakes (1m 5f 75y)	Chester

Race	85.	Dee Stakes (1m 2f 10y)	Chester
Race	86.	Irish 1,000 Guineas (1m)	Curragh
Race	87.	Irish 2,000 Guineas (1m)	Curragh
Race	88.	Brighton Derby Trial (1m 4f)	Brighton
Race	89.	Dante Stakes (1m 2½f)	York
Race	90.	Musidora Stakes (1m 2½f)	York
Race	91.	Yorkshire Cup (1m 6f)	York
Race	92.	Lingfield Derby Trial (1m 4f)	Lingfield
Race	93.	Lingfield Oaks Trial (1m 4f)	Lingfield
Race	94.	Pretty Polly Stakes (1m 2f)	Newmarket
Race	95.	Henry II Stakes (2m)	Sandown
Race	96.	Westbury Stakes (1m 2f)	Sandown
Race	97.	Sandleford Priory Stakes (1m 2f)	Newbury
Race	98.	Lockinge Stakes (1m)	Newbury
Race	99.	St James Stakes (1m 110y)	Epsom
Race	100.	Coronation Cup (1m 4f)	Epsom
Race	101.	Ebbisham Stakes (1m 110y)	Epsom
Race	102.	Gallinule Stakes (1m 2f)	Curragh
Race	103.	Queen Anne Stakes (1m)	Royal Ascot
Race	104.	Queen's Vase (2m)	Royal Ascot
Race	105.	St James's Palace Stakes (1m)	Royal Ascot
Race	106.	Jersey Stakes (7f)	Royal Ascot
Race	107.	Coronation Stakes (1m)	Royal Ascot
Race	108.	Ribblesdale Stakes (1m 4f)	Royal Ascot
Race	109.	Cork and Orrery Stakes (6f)	Royal Ascot
Race	110.	Ascot Gold Cup (2m 4f)	Royal Ascot
Race	111.	King Edward VII Stakes (1m 4f)	Royal Ascot
Race	112.	Prince of Wales Stakes (1m 2f)	Royal Ascot
Race	113.	Hardwicke Stakes (1m 4f)	Royal Ascot
Race	114.	Queen Alexandra Stakes (2m 6f 34y)	Royal Ascot
Race	115.	King's Stand Stakes (5f)	Royal Ascot
Race	116.	Churchill Stakes (1m 4f)	Ascot
Race	117.	Irish Sweeps Derby (1m 4f)	Curragh
Race	118.	Pretty Polly Stakes (1m 2f)	Curragh
Race	119.	Eclipse Stakes (1m 2f)	Sandown
Race	120.	Princess of Wales's Stakes (1m 4f)	Newmarket
Race	121.	Falmouth Stakes (1m)	Newmarket
Race	122.	July Cup (6f)	Newmarket
Race	123.	Rous Memorial Stakes (1m 2f)	Ascot
Race	124.	King George VI & Queen Elizabeth Stakes (1m 4f)	Ascot
Race	125.	Sussex Stakes (1m)	Goodwood
Race	126.	King George Stakes (5f)	Goodwood
Race	127.	Goodwood Cup (2m 5f)	Goodwood
Race	128.	Gordon Stakes (1m 3f 200y)	Goodwood
Race	129.	Nassau Stakes (1m 2f)	Goodwood
Race	130.	Warren Stakes (1m 3f 200y)	Goodwood
Race	131.	Irish Guinness Oaks (1m 4f)	Curragh
Race	132.	Hungerford Stakes (7f 60y)	Newbury

Race 133.	Oxfordshire Stakes (1m 5f 60y)	Newbury
Race 134.	Yorkshire Oaks (1m 4f)	York
Race 135.	Great Voltigeur Stakes (1m 4f)	York
Race 136.	Nunthorpe Stakes (5f)	York
Race 137.	Wills Mile (1m)	Goodwood
Race 138.	Fifinella Fillies Stakes (1m 2f)	Epsom
Race 139.	Park Hill Stakes (1m 6f 132y)	Doncaster
Race 140.	Doncaster Cup (2m 2f)	Doncaster
Race 141.	Peter Hastings Stakes (1m 2f)	Newbury
Race 142.	Irish St Leger (1m 6f)	Curragh
Race 143.	Doonside Cup (1m 3f)	Ayr
Race 144.	Queen Elizabeth II Stakes (1m)	Ascot
Race 145.	Princess Royal Stakes (1m 4f)	Ascot
Race 146.	Diadem Stakes (6f)	Ascot
Race 147.	Sun Chariot Stakes (1m 2f)	Newmarket
Race 148.	Jockey Club Cup (2m)	Newmarket
Race 149.	Champion Stakes (1m 2f)	Newmarket
Race 150.	Challenge Stakes (6f)	Newmarket
Race 151.	Vernons November Sprint Cup (6f)	Haydock

Section Four: HANDICAP EVENTS

Race 161.	Doncaster Spring Handicap (1m 6f 132y)	Doncaster
Race 162.	Lincoln Handicap (1m)	Doncaster
Race 163.	Irish Lincoln (1m)	Curragh
Race 164.	Rosebery Stakes (1m 2f)	Kempton
Race 165.	Queen's Prize (2m)	Kempton
Race 166.	Northern Free Handicap (7f)	Newcastle
Race 167.	Free Handicap (7f)	Newmarket
Race 168.	Newbury Spring Cup (1m)	Newbury
Race 169.	Great Metropolitan Handicap (2m 2f)	Epsom
Race 170.	City and Suburban Handicap (1m 2f)	Epsom
Race 171.	Totalisator Spring Handicap (1m)	Newmarket
Race 172.	March Handicap (2m)	Newmarket
Race 173.	Crocker Bulteel Stakes (7f)	Ascot
Race 174.	Victoria Cup (7f)	Ascot
Race 175.	Chester Cup (2m 2f 77y)	Chester
Race 176.	Scottish and Newcastle Breweries Handicap (1m 2f 30y)	Newcastle
Race 177.	Usher-Vaux Brewery Gold Tankard (1m 7f)	Ayr
Race 178.	Great Jubilee Handicap (1m 2f)	Kempton
Race 179.	Airey of Leeds Spring Cup (7f) (formerly 6f Spring H'cap)	York
Race 180.	John Davies Handicap (1m 4f)	Haydock
Race 181.	Cecil Frail Handicap (1m)	Haydock
Race 182.	Thirsk Hunt Cup (1m)	Thirsk
Race 183.	Harewood Handicap (1m 4f)	Doncaster
Race 184.	Zetland Handicap (1m)	Doncaster
Race 185.	Zetland Gold Cup (1m 2f)	Redcar

Race 186.	Sandown Park Whitsun Cup (1m)	Sandown
Race 187.	Pavilion Handicap (1m 2f)	Brighton
Race 188.	Brighthelmstone Handicap (7f)	Brighton
Race 189.	Rosebery Memorial Handicap (2m 2f)	Epsom
Race 190.	Newbury Summer Cup (1m 4f)	Newbury
Race 191.	Ascot Stakes (2m 4f)	Royal Ascot
Race 192.	Britannia Stakes (1m)	Royal Ascot
Race 193.	Royal Hunt Cup (1m)	Royal Ascot
Race 194.	Bessborough Stakes (1m 4f)	Royal Ascot
Race 195.	King George V Stakes (1m 4f)	Royal Ascot
Race 196.	Wokingham Stakes (6f)	Royal Ascot
Race 197.	Fern Hill Handicap (1m)	Ascot
Race 198.	Andy Capp Handicap (1m 2f)	Redcar
Race 199.	Northumberland Plate (2m)	Newcastle
Race 200.	Brighton Mile (1m)	Brighton
Race 201.	Greenall Whitley Gold Challenge Trophy (2m 2f 77y)	Chester
Race 202.	Old Chester Handicap (1m 2f 10y)	Chester
Race 203.	Sandown Anniversary Handicap (1m)	Sandown
Race 204.	Bunbury Cup (7f)	Newmarket
Race 205.	Seaview Handicap (1m)	Brighton
Race 206.	Southern Handicap (1m 2f)	Brighton
Race 207.	Old Newton Cup (1m 4f)	Haydock
Race 208.	Magnet Cup (1m 2½f)	York
Race 209.	Tennent Trophy (1m 7f)	Ayr
Race 210.	Chesterfield Cup (1m 2f)	Goodwood
Race 211.	Stewards' Cup (6f)	Goodwood
Race 212.	Goodwood Stakes (2m 3f)	Goodwood
Race 213.	News of the World Stakes (1m 2f)	Goodwood
Race 214.	Vaux Gold Tankard (1m 6f 132y)	Redcar
Race 215.	William Hill Gold Cup (1m)	Redcar
Race 216.	Nottingham Stewards' Handicap (6f)	Nottingham
Race 217.	Great St Wilfred Handicap (6f)	Ripon
Race 218.	Rose of York Handicap (1m)	York
Race 219.	Harewood Handicap (5f)	York
Race 220.	Ebor Handicap (1m 6f)	York
Race 221.	Melrose Handicap (1m 6f)	York
Race 222.	Northern Goldsmiths' Handicap (1m)	Newcastle
Race 223.	Steve Donoghue Apprentice Handicap (1m 4f)	Epsom
Race 224.	Ripon Rowels Handicap (1m)	Ripon
Race 225.	Lanark Silver Bell (1m 4f)	Lanark
Race 226.	Great Yorkshire Handicap (1m 6f 132y)	Doncaster
Race 227.	Doncaster Handicap (1m)	Doncaster
Race 228.	Portland Handicap (5f 152y)	Doncaster
Race 229.	Newbury Autumn Cup (2m)	Newbury
Race 230.	Ayr Gold Cup (6f)	Ayr
Race 231.	Irish Cambridgeshire (1m)	Curragh
Race 232.	Cesarewitch Stakes (2m 2f)	Newmarket
Race 233.	Cambridgeshire Stakes (1m 1f)	Newmarket

Race 234. Irish Cesarewitch (2m)   Curragh
Race 235. Manchester Handicap (1m 4f)   Doncaster

Section Five: NATIONAL HUNT EVENTS

Race 245. Grand National (4m 856y)   Liverpool
Race 246. Mackeson Gold Cup (2m 4f)   Cheltenham
Race 247. Mackeson Handicap Hurdle (2m 200y)   Cheltenham
Race 248. Kirk and Kirk Handicap Chase (3m)   Ascot
Race 249. Black and White Gold Cup (2m)   Ascot
Race 250. Hennessy Gold Cup (3m 2f 82y)   Newbury
Race 251. Rhymney Breweries Handicap Chase (3m)   Chepstow
Race 252. Massey-Ferguson Gold Cup (2m 4f)   Cheltenham
Race 253. Henry VIII Chase (2m 18y)   Sandown
Race 254. King George VI Chase (3m)   Kempton
Race 255. Fred Withington Handicap Chase (4m)   Cheltenham
Race 256. Mildmay Memorial Handicap Chase (3m 5f)   Sandown
Race 257. Mandarin Handicap Chase (3m 2f 82y)   Newbury
Race 258. Thyestes Handicap Chase (3m 170y)   Gowran Park
Race 259. Great Yorkshire Handicap Chase (3m 2f)   Doncaster
Race 260. Haydock Park National Trial (3m 4f)   Haydock
Race 261. Eider Handicap Chase (4m 350y)   Newcastle
Race 262. Stone's Ginger Wine Handicap Chase (2m 4f 68y)   Sandown
Race 263. Schweppes Gold Trophy (2m)   Newbury
Race 264. Manifesto Handicap Chase (3m)   Lingfield
Race 265. Leopardstown Chase (3m)   Leopardstown
Race 266. Victor Ludorum Hurdle (2m)   Haydock
Race 267. Tom Coulthwaite Handicap Chase (3m)   Haydock
Race 268. Princess Royal Handicap Hurdle (2m 140y)   Doncaster
Race 269. K.P. Hurdle (2m)   Kempton
Race 270. Gloucestershire Hurdle (2m 200y)   Cheltenham
Race 271. Totalisator Champion Novices' Chase (3m 2f 170y)   Cheltenham
Race 272. National Hunt Handicap Chase (3m 1f)   Cheltenham
Race 273. National Hunt Two Mile Champion Chase (2m)   Cheltenham
Race 274. National Hunt Chase (4m)   Cheltenham
Race 275. Cotswold Chase (2m)   Cheltenham
Race 276. Grand Annual Chase (2m)   Cheltenham
Race 277. Champion Hurdle (2m 200y)   Cheltenham
Race 278. United Hunts Challenge Cup (3m 2f 170y)   Cheltenham
Race 279. George Duller Handicap Hurdle (3m)   Cheltenham
Race 280. Kim Muir Memorial Challenge Cup (3m 1f)   Cheltenham
Race 281. Mildmay of Flete Challenge Cup (2m 4f)   Cheltenham
Race 282. Foxhunters Challenge Cup (4m)   Cheltenham
Race 283. Daily Express Triumph Hurdle (2m 200y)   Cheltenham
Race 284. Cheltenham Gold Cup (3m 2f 76y)   Cheltenham
Race 285. County Handicap Hurdle (2m 200y)   Cheltenham
Race 286. Cathcart Challenge Cup (2m)   Cheltenham

Race 287. Imperial Cup (2m)   Sandown
Race 288. Topham Trophy Handicap Chase (2m 6f)   Liverpool
Race 289. Spa Hurdle (3m)   Cheltenham
Race 290. Irish Grand National (3m 2f)   Fairyhouse
Race 291. Scottish Grand National (4m 120y)   Ayr
Race 292. Whitbread Gold Cup (3m 5f 18y)   Sandown
Race 293. Final Champion Hunters' Chase (3m 2f)   Stratford

Section One: Classics

Race 1: 2,000 GUINEAS
1 mile. Newmarket. Three-year-olds.

1809 Wizard	(8)	**1840** Crucifix	(6)
1810 Hephestion	(9)	**1841** Ralph	(8)
1811 Trophonius	(11)	**1842** Meteor	(8)
1812 Cwrw	(7)	**1843** Cotherstone	(3)
1813 Smolensko	(12)	**1844** The Ugly Buck	(7)
1814 Olive	(14)	**1845** Idas	(5)
1815 Tigris	(10)	**1846** Sir Tatton Sykes	(6)
1816 Nectar	(12)	**1847** Conyngham	(10)
1817 Manfred	(8)	**1848** Flatcatcher	(5)
1818 Interpreter	(9)	**1849** Nunnykirk	(8)
1819 Antar	(6)	**1850** Pitsford	(5)
1820 Pindarrie	(5)	**1851** Hernandez	(10)
1821 Reginald	(4)	**1852** Stockwell	(9)
1822 Pastille	(3)	**1853** West Australian	(7)
1823 Nicolo	(7)	**1854** The Hermit	(9)
1824 Schahriar	(7)	**1855** Lord of the Isles	(9)
1825 Enamel	(6)	**1856** Fazzoletto	(10)
1826 Dervise	(7)	**1857** Vedette	(21)
1827 Turcoman	(5)	**1858** Fitz-Roland	(14)
1828 Cadland	(5)	**1859** The Promised	
1829 Patron	(2)	Land	(9)
1830 Augustus	(2)	**1860** The Wizard	(15)
1831 Riddlesworth	(6)	**1861** Diophantus	(16)
1832 Archibald	(7)	**1862** The Marquis	(17)
1833 Clearwell	(6)	**1863** Macaroni	(9)
1834 Glencoe	(7)	**1864** General Peel	(13)
1835 Ibrahim	(4)	**1865** Gladiateur	(18)
1836 Bay Middleton	(6)	**1866** Lord Lyon	(15)
1837 Achmet	(8)	**1867** Vauban	(18)
1838 Grey Momus	(6)	**1868** Moslem and	
1839 The Corsair	(3)	Formosa	(14)

1869 Pretender	(19)
1870 Macgregor	(10)
1871 Bothwell	(13)
1872 Prince Charlie	(14)
1873 Gang Forward	(10)
1874 Atlantic	(12)
1875 Camballo	(13)
1876 Petrarch	(14)
1877 Chamant	(11)
1878 Pilgrimage	(10)
1879 Charibert	(15)
1880 Petronel	(17)
1881 Peregrine	(14)
1882 Shotover	(18)
1883 Galliard	(14)
1884 Scot Free	(10)
1885 Paradox	(7)
1886 Ormonde	(6)
1887 Enterprise	(8)
1888 Ayrshire	(6)
1889 Enthusiast	(9)
1890 Surefoot	(9)
1891 Common	(9)
1892 Bonavista	(14)
1893 Isinglass	(10)
1894 Ladas	(8)
1895 Kirkconnel	(8)
1896 St. Frusquin	(7)
1897 Galtee More	(8)
1898 Disraeli	(14)
1899 Flying Fox	(8)

1900 Diamond Jubilee (11–4) H. Jones (H.R.H. The Prince of Wales) R. Marsh
     2. Bonarosa,   3. Sidus.   4, ¾.   10 ran
1901 Handicapper (33–1) Halsey (Sir E. Cassel) F. W. Day
     2. Doricles,   3. Osboch.   2, Nk.   17 ran

1902 Sceptre (4–1) Randall (Mr R. S. Sievier) R. S. Sievier
  2. Pistol,   **3.** Ard Patrick. 2, 3.   14 ran
1903 Rock Sand (6–4) J. H. Martin (Sir J. Miller) G. Blackwell
  2. Flotsam,   **3.** Rabelais. 1½, 2.   11 ran
1904 St Amant (11–4) K. Cannon (Mr Leopold de Rothschild) A. Hayhoe
  2. John o'Gaunt,   **3.** Henry the First. 4, 2.   14 ran
1905 Vedas (11–2) H. Jones (Mr W. F. de Wend-Fenton) W. Robinson
  2. Signorino,   **3.** Llangibby. 2, Hd.   13 ran
1906 Gorgos (20–1) H. Jones (Mr Arthur James) R. Marsh
  2. Sancy,   **3.** Ramrod. Hd, Nk.   12 ran
1907 Slieve Gallion (4–11) W. Higgs (Capt. Greer) S. Darling
  2. Bezonian,   **3.** Linacre. 3, ¾.   10 ran
1908 Norman III (25–1) O. Madden (Mr August Belmont) J. Watson
  2. Sir Archibald,   **3.** White Eagle. 3, ¾.   17 ran
1909 Minoru (4–1) H. Jones (His Majesty) R. Marsh
  2. Phaleron,   **3.** Louviers. 2, 1½.   11 ran
1910 Neil Gow (2–1) D. Maher (Lord Rosebery) P. Peck
  2. Lemberg,   **3.** Whisk Broom. Sht Hd, 2. 13 ran
1911 Sunstar (5–1) G. Stern (Mr J. B. Joel) C. Morton
  2. Stedfast,   **3.** Lycaon. 2, ½.   14 ran
1912 Sweeper II (6–1) D. Maher (Mr H. B. Duryea) H. S. Persse
  2. Jaeger,   **3.** Hall Cross. 1, ½.   14 ran
1913 Louvois (25–1) J. Reiff (Mr W. Raphael) D. Waugh
  2. Craganour,   **3.** Meeting House. Hd, 2.   15 ran
1914 Kennymore (2–1) G. Stern (Sir J. Thursby) Alec Taylor
  2. Corcyra,   **3.** Black Jester. Sht Hd, 2. 18 ran
1915 Pommern (2–1) S. Donoghue (Mr Sol Joel) C. Peck
  2. Tournament,   **3.** The Vizier. 3, Hd.   16 ran
1916 Clarissimus (100–7) J. Clark (Lord Falmouth) W. Waugh
  2. Kwang-Su,   **3.** Nassovian. ¾, ½.   17 ran
1917 Gay Crusader (9–4) S. Donoghue (Mr Fairie) Alec Taylor
  2. Magpie,   **3.** Athdara. Hd, 3.   14 ran
1918 Gainsborough (4–1) J. Childs (Lady James Douglas) Alec Taylor
  2. Somme Kiss,   **3.** Blink. 1½, 6.   13 ran
1919 The Panther (10–1) R. Cooper (Sir A. Black) G. Manser
  2. Buchan,   **3.** Dominion. Nk, ¾.   12 ran
1920 Tetratema (2–1) B. Carslake (Maj. D. McCalmont) H. S. Persse
  2. Allenby,   **3.** Paragon. ½, 3.   17 ran
1921 Craig an Eran (100–6) J. Brennan (Lord Astor) Alec Taylor
  2. Lemonora,   **3.** Humorist. ¾, ¾.   26 ran
1922 St Louis (6–1) G. Archibald (Lord Queensborough) P. P. Gilpin
  2. Pondoland,   **3.** Captain Cuttle. 3, 4.   22 ran
1923 Ellangowan (7–1) C. Elliott (Lord Rosebery) J. L. Jarvis
  2. Knockando,   **3.** D'Orsay. Hd, ½.   18 ran
1924 Diophon (11–2) G. Hulme (H. H. Aga Khan) R. Dawson
  2. Bright Knight,   **3.** Green Fire. Hd, Nk.   20 ran
1925 Manna (100–8) S. Donoghue (Mr H. E. Morriss) F. Darling
  2. St Becan,   **3.** Oojah. 2, 4.   13 ran

1926 Colorado (100–8) T. Weston (Lord Derby) Hon. G. Lambton
    2. Coronach,   3. Apple Sammy.   5, 3.   **19 ran**

1927 Adam's Apple (20–1) J. Leach (Mr C. W. Whitburn) H. L. Cottrill
    2. Call Boy,   3. Sickle.   Sht Hd, ¼.   **23 ran**

1928 Flamingo (5–1) C. Elliott (Sir L. Philipp) J. L. Jarvis
    2. Royal Minstrel,   3. O'Curry.   Hd, 1½.   **17 ran**

1929 Mr Jinks (5–2) H. Beasley (Maj. D. McCalmont) H. S. Persse
    2. Cragadour,   3. Gay Day.   Hd, 1½.   **22 ran**

1930 Diolite (10–1) F. Fox (Sir H. Hirst) F. Templeman
    2. Paradine,   3. Silver Flare.   2, 1.   **28 ran**

1931 Cameronian (100–8) J. Childs (Mr J. A. Dewar) F. Darling
    2. Goyescas,   3. Orpen.   2, 3.   **24 ran**

1932 Orwell (Evens) R. A. Jones (Mr W. M. G. Singer) J. Lawson
    2. Dastur,   3. Hesperus.   2, 1½.   **11 ran**

1933 Rodosto (9–1) R. Brethes (Princesse de Faucigny-Lucinge) H. Count (France)
    2. King Salmon,   3. Gino.   1, ¾.   **27 ran**

1934 Colombo (2–7) W. Johnstone (Lord Glanely) T. Hogg
    2. Easton,   3. Badruddin.   1, 1½.   **12 ran**

1935 Bahram (7–2) F. Fox (H. H. Aga Khan) Frank Butters
    2. Theft,   3. Sea Bequest,   1½, 2.   **16 ran**

1936 Pay Up (11–2) R. Dick (Lord Astor) J. Lawson
    2. Mahmoud,   3. Thankerton.   Sht Hd, 3.   **19 ran**

1937 Le Ksar (20–1) C. Semblat (M. E. de St Alary) F. Carter (France)
    2. Goya II,   3. Mid-day Sun.   4, ½.   **18 ran**

1938 Pasch (5–2) G. Richards (Mr H. E. Morriss) F. Darling
    2. Scottish Union,   3. Mirza II.   2, 1½.   **18 ran**

1939 Blue Peter (5–1) E. Smith (Lord Rosebery) J. L. Jarvis
    2. Admiral's Walk,   3. Fairstone.   ½, ¾.   **25 ran**

1940 Djebel (9–4) C. Elliott (M. M. Boussac) A. Swann (France)
    2. Stardust,   3. Tant Mieux.   2, Hd.   **21 ran**

1941 Lambert Simnel (10–1) C. Elliott (Duke of Westminster) F. Templeman
    2. Morogoro,   3. Sun Castle.   2, 1½.   **19 ran**

1942 Big Game (8–11) G. Richards (His Majesty) F. Darling
    2. Watling Street,   3. Gold Nib.   4, 2.   **14 ran**

1943 Kingsway (18–1) S. Wragg (Mr A. E. Saunders) J. Lawson
    2. Pink Flower,   3. Way In.   Sht Hd, Hd.   **19 ran**

1944 Garden Path (5–1) H. Wragg (Lord Derby) W. Earl
    2. Growing Confidence,   3. Tehran.   Hd, 1½.   **26 ran**

1945 Court Martial (13–2) C. Richards (Lord Astor) J. Lawson
    2. Dante,   3. Royal Charger.   Nk, 2.   **20 ran**

1946 Happy Knight (28–1) T. Weston (Sir W. Cooke) H. Jelliss
    2. Khaled,   3. Radiotherapy.   4, Hd.   **13 ran**

1947 Tudor Minstrel (11–8) G. Richards (Mr J. A. Dewar) F. Darling
    2. Saravan,   3. Sayajirao.   8, Sht Hd.   **15 ran**

1948 My Babu (2–1) C. Smirke (H. H. Maharaja of Baroda) F. Armstrong
    2. The Cobbler,   3. Pride of India,   Hd, 4.   **18 ran**

1949 Nimbus (10–1) E. C. Elliott (Mrs M. Glenister) G. S. Colling
    2. Abernant,   3. Barnes Park.   Sht Hd, 4.   **13 ran**

1950 Palestine (4–1) C. Smirke (H. H. Aga Khan) M. Marsh
    2. Prince Simon,   **3.** Masked Light.   Sht Hd, 5.   19 ran

1951 Ki Ming (100–8) A. Breasley (Mr Ley On) M. Beary
    2. Stokes,   **3.** Malka's Boy.   1½, Sht Hd.   27 ran

1952 Thunderhead II (100–7) R. Poincelet (M. E. Constant) E. Pollet (France)
    2. King's Bench,   **3.** Argur.   5, ½.   26 ran

1953 Nearula (2–1) E. Britt (Mr W. Humble) C. F. Elsey
    2. Bebe Grande,   **3.** Oleandrin.   4, 3.   16 ran

1954 Darius (8–1) E. Mercer (Sir Percy Loraine) H. Wragg
    2. Ferriol,   **3.** Poona.   1, 5.   19 ran

1955 Our Babu (13–2) D. Smith (Mr D. Robinson) G. Brooke
    2. Tamerlane,   **3.** Klairon.   Nk, Sht Hd.   23 ran

1956 Gilles de Retz (50–1) F. Barlow (Mr A. G. Samuel) C. Jerdein
    2. Chantelsey,   **3.** Buisson Ardent.   1, 1½.   19 ran

1957 CREPELLO (7–2) L. Piggott (£13,598) (Sir Victor Sassoon) N. Murless
    2. Quorum (A. Russell),   **3.** Pipe of Peace (A. Breasley) (100–30f),
    4. Tyrone,   **5.** Wayne II,
    6. Bellborough.   Extended distances, ½, Hd, 6, 1½, 2.   15 ran

1958 PALL MALL (20–1) D. Smith (£13,917) (The Queen) C. Boyd-Rochfort
    2. Major Portion (E. Smith),   **3.** Nagami (J. Mercer),
    4. Val d'Oisans,   **5.** Paresa,
    6. Kingroy.
        (Bald Eagle 7–4f–7th.) Extended distances, ½, 3, Nk, 4, Nk.   14 ran

1959 TABOUN (5–2f) G. Moore (£15,341) (Prince Aly Khan) A. Head (France)
    2. Masham (D. Smith),   **3.** Carnoustie (L. Piggott),
    4. Lindrick,   **5.** My Aladdin,
    6. Dan Cupid.   Extended distances, 3, Nk, 1, Hd, Nk.   13 ran

1960 MARTIAL (18–1) R. Hutchinson (£16,854) (R. N. Webster) P. J. Prendergast
    2. Venture VII   **3.** Auroy (T. Gosling),
        (G. Moore) (6–4f),
    4. Tulyartos,   **5.** High Hat,
    6. St Paddy.   Extended distances, Hd, 4, ½, ½, ¾.   17 ran

1961 ROCKAVON (66–1) N. Stirk (£22,801) (T. C. Yuill) G. Boyd
    2. Prince Tudor   **3.** Time Greine (W. Williamson),
        (W. Rickaby)
    4. Pinturischio (7–4f),   **5.** Bally Vimy,
    6. L'Epinay.   Extended distances, 2, Sht Hd, Hd, Sht Hd, Hd.   22 ran

1962 PRIVY COUNCILLOR (100–6) W. Rickaby (£32,839) (Maj. G. Glover)
    T. Waugh
    2. Romulus (W. Swinburn),   **3.** Prince Poppa (W. Carr),
    4. Clear Sound,   **5.** High Noon,
    6. Catchpole.
        (Escort 11–2f–8th.) Extended distances, 3, 2, ½, Hd, 1½.   19 ran

1963 ONLY FOR LIFE (33–1) J. Lindley (£31,369) (Miss M. Sheriffe) J. Tree
    2. Ionian (L. Ward),   **3.** Corpora (A. Mulley),
    4. Fidelio,   **5.** King of Babylon,
    6. Aigle Gris.
        (Crocket 5–2f–last.) Extended distances, Sht Hd, 3, 1½, 1½, Nk.   21 ran

1964 BALDRIC II (20–1) W. Pyers (£40,302) (Mrs H. E. Jackson) E. Fellows (France)

    2. Faberge II (J. Mercer),   **3.** Balustrade (W. Williamson),
    4. Showdown (5–1f),   **5.** Minor Portion,
    6. Acer.   Extended distances, 2, 1, Sht Hd, 1, Nk.   27 ran

1965 NIKSAR (100–8) D. Keith (£30,230) (W. Harvey) W. Nightingall

    2. Silly Season   **3.** Present II (M. Depalmas),
      (G. Lewis) (13–2f),
    4. Coronado,   **5.** Abscond,
    6. Enrico.   Extended distances, 1, 1, Nk, 4, 3.   22 ran

1966 KASHMIR II (7–1) J. Lindley (£30,595) (P. Butler) C. Bartholomew (France)

    2. Great Nephew   **3.** Celtic Song (D. Lake),
      (W. Rickaby),
    4. Young Emperor,   **5.** Ambericos,
    6. Village Square.

    (Pretendre 9–4f–8th.) Extended distances, Sht Hd, 2½, Sht Hd, Nk, 1¼.   25 ran

1967 ROYAL PALACE (100–30jf) G. Moore (£31,080) (H. J. Joel) N. Murless

    2. Taj Dewan (F. Head),   **3.** Missile (L. Ward),
    4. Golden Horus,   **5.** Bold Lad (100–30jf),
    6. Above Water.   Extended distances, Sht Hd, 1½, 4, Nk, 2.   18 ran

1968 SIR IVOR (11–8f) L. Piggott (£22,587) (Raymond R. Guest) M. V. O'Brien

    2. Petingo (J. Mercer),   **3.** Jimmy Reppin (G. Lewis),
    4. So Blessed,   **5.** Chebs Lad,
    6. Dalry.   Extended distances, 1½, 2½, Nk, 1, ½.   10 ran

Race 2: 1,000 GUINEAS

1 mile. Newmarket. Three-year-old fillies

Year	Horse	Pos	Year	Horse	Pos	Year	Horse	Pos
1814	Charlotte	(5)	1831	Galantine	(8)	1847	Clementina	(5)
1815	br f. by Selim	(4)	1832	Galata	(4)	1848	Canezou	(9)
1816	Rhoda	(6)	1833	Tarantella	(10)	1849	Flea	(10)
1817	Neva	(10)	1834	May Day	(7)	1850	f by Slane	(5)
1818	Corinne	(8)	1835	Preserve	(3)	1851	Aphrodite	(6)
1819	Catgut	(7)	1836	Destiny	(7)	1852	Kate	(6)
1820	Rowena	(6)	1837	Chapeau		1853	Mentmore Lass	(11)
1821	Zeal	(6)		d'Espagne	(5)	1854	Virago	(3)
1822	Whizgig	(4)	1838	Barcarolle	(6)	1855	Habena	(11)
1823	Zinc	(5)	1839	Cara	(5)	1856	Manganese	(5)
1824	Cobweb	(4)	1840	Crucifix	(4)	1857	Imperieuse	(8)
1825	Tontine	(w. o.)	1841	Potentia	(5)	1858	Governess	(9)
1826	Problem	(5)	1842	Firebrand	(6)	1859	Mayonaise	(4)
1827	Arab	(7)	1843	Extempore	(9)	1860	Sagitta	(13)
1828	Zoe	(7)	1844	Sorella	(9)	1861	Nemesis	(9)
1829	Godolphin	(4)	1845	Picnic	(8)	1862	Hurricane	(11)
1830	Charlotte West	(7)	1846	Mendicant	(7)	1863	Lady Augusta	(10)

1864	Tomato	(15)	1876	Camelia	(13)	1888	Briar Root	(14)
1865	Siberia	(11)	1877	Belphoebe	(19)	1889	Minthe	(14)
1866	Repulse	(9)	1878	Pilgrimage	(9)	1890	Semolina	(10)
1867	Achievement	(7)	1879	Wheel of		1891	Mimi	(12)
1868	Formosa	(8)		Fortune	(8)	1892	La Fleche	(7)
1869	Scottish Queen	(9)	1880	Elizabeth	(10)	1893	Siffleuse	(11)
1870	Hester	(10)	1881	Thebais	(13)	1894	Amiable	(13)
1871	Hannah	(7)	1882	St Marguerite	(6)	1895	Galeottia	(15)
1872	Reine	(11)	1883	Hauteur	(9)	1896	Thais	(19)
1873	Cecilia	(14)	1884	Busybody	(6)	1897	Chelandry	(9)
1874	Apology	(9)	1885	Farewell	(16)	1898	Nun Nicer	(15)
1875	Spinaway	(6)	1886	Miss Jummy	(10)	1899	Sibola	(14)
			1887	Reve d'Or	(12)			

1900 Winifreda (11–2) S. Loates (Mr L. Brassey) T. Jennings jun.
  2. Inquisitive, **3.** Vain Duchess. $\frac{3}{4}$, 2. 10 ran
1901 Aida (13–8) Maher (Sir J. Miller) G. Blackwell
  2. Fleur d'Ete, **3.** Santa Brigida. Nk, 2. 15 ran
1902 Sceptre (1–2) Randall (R. S. Sievier) R. S. Sievier
  2. St Windeline, **3.** Black Fancy. $1\frac{1}{2}$, 4. 15 ran
1903 Quintessence (4–1) Randall (Lord Falmouth) J. Chandler
  2. Sun-Rose, **3.** Skyscraper. $1\frac{1}{2}$, 2. 12 ran
1904 Pretty Polly (1–4) W. Lane (Maj. E. Loder) P. P. Gilpin
  2. Leucadia, **3.** Flamma. 3, 4. 7 ran
1905 Cherry Lass (5–4) G. McCall (Mr W. Hall Walker) W. Robinson
  2. Koorhaan, **3.** Jongleuse. 1, 3. 19 ran
1906 Flair (10–11) B. Dillon (Sir Daniel Cooper) P. P. Gilpin
  2. Lischana, **3.** Paid Up. 3, $\frac{3}{4}$. 12 ran
1907 Witch Elm (4–1) B. Lynham (Mr W. Hall Walker) W. Robinson
  2. Frugality, **3.** Sixty. 3, $1\frac{1}{2}$. 17 ran
1908 Rhodora (100–8) L. Lyne (Mr R. Crocker) G. Allen
  2. Bracelet, **3.** Ardentrive. 2, Nk. 19 ran
1909 Electra (9–1) B. Dillon (Mr L. Neumann) P. P. Gilpin
  2. Princesse de Galles, **3.** Perola. 1, 4. 10 ran
1910 Winkipop (5–2) B. Lynham (Mr W. Astor) W. Waugh
  2. Maid of Corinth, **3.** Rosedrop. $1\frac{1}{2}$, Hd. 13 ran
1911 Atmah (7–1) F. Fox (Mr J. A. de Rothschild) F. Pratt
  2. Radiancy, **3.** Knockfeerna. Sht Hd, 2. 16 ran
1912 Tagalie (20–1) L. Hewitt (Mr W. Raphael) D. Waugh
  2. Alope, **3.** Belleisle. $1\frac{1}{2}$, $\frac{3}{4}$. 13 ran
1913 Jest (9–1) F. Rickaby (Mr J. B. Joel) C. Morton
  2. Taslett, **3.** Prue. Hd, $\frac{1}{2}$. 22 ran
1914 Princess Dorrie (100–9) W. Huxley (Mr J. B. Joel) C. Morton
  2. Glorvina, **3.** Torchlight. $\frac{3}{4}$, Nk. 13 ran
1915 Vaucluse (5–2) F. Rickaby (Lord Rosebery) F. Hartigan
  2. Silver Tag, **3.** Bright. $\frac{3}{4}$, $1\frac{1}{2}$. 15 ran
1916 Canyon (9–4) F. Rickaby (Lord Derby) Hon. G. Lambton
  2. Fifinella, **3.** Salamandra. $\frac{3}{4}$, 3. 10 ran

1917 Diadem (6–4) F. Rickaby (Lord d'Abernon) Hon. G. Lambton
    2. Sunny Jane,   **3.** Nonpariel. $\frac{1}{2}$, 4.   14 ran
1918 Ferry (50–1) B. Carslake (Lord Derby) Hon. G. Lambton
    2. My Dear,   **3.** Herself.   2, 3.   8 ran
1919 Roseway (2–1) A. Whalley (Sir E. Hulton) F. Hartigan
    2. Britannia,   **3.** Glaciale.   6, $1\frac{1}{2}$.   15 ran
1920 Cinna (4–1) Wm. Griggs (Sir R. W. B. Jardine) T. Waugh
    2. Cicerole,   **3.** Valescure.   3, 1.   21 ran
1921 Bettina (33–1) G. Bellhouse (Mr W. Raphael) P. Linton
    2. Petrea,   **3.** Pompadour. $1\frac{1}{2}$, $\frac{3}{4}$.   24 ran
1922 Silver Urn (10–1) B. Carslake (Mr B. W. Parr) H. S. Persse
    2. Soubriquet,   **3.** Golden Corn.   2, $\frac{3}{4}$.   20 ran
1923 Tranquil (5–2) E. Gardner (Lord Derby) Hon. G. Lambton
    2. Cos,   **3.** Shrove. $1\frac{1}{2}$, 1.   16 ran
1924 Plack (8–1) C. Elliott (Lord Rosebery) J. L. Jarvis
    2. Mumtaz Mahal,   **3.** Straitlace. $\frac{1}{2}$, $\frac{1}{2}$.   16 ran
1925 Saucy Sue (1–4) F. Bullock (Lord Astor) Alec Taylor
    2. Miss Gadabout,   **3.** Firouze Mahal.   6, 2.   11 ran
1926 Pillion (25–1) R. Perryman (Mr A. de Rothschild) J. Watson
    2. Trilogy,   **3.** Short Story.   1, $\frac{1}{2}$.   29 ran
1927 Cresta Run (10–1) A. Balding (Lt.-Col. G. Loder) P. P. Gilpin
    2. Book Law and   **2.** Endowment.   2, Dd Ht.   28 ran
1928 Scuttle (15–8) J. Childs (His Majesty) W. Jarvis
    2. Jurisdiction,   **3.** Toboggan.   1, 6.   14 ran
1929 Taj Mah (33–1) W. Sibbritt (M. Simon Guthmann) J. Torterolo (France)
    2. Sister Anne,   **3.** Ellanvale. $\frac{3}{4}$, Sht Hd.   19 ran
1930 Fair Isle (7–4) T. Weston (Lord Derby) Frank Butters
    2. Torchere,   **3.** Sister Clover.   Sht Hd, Nk.   19 ran
1931 Four Course (100–9) C. Elliott (Lord Ellesmere) Fred Darling
    2. Lady Marjorie,   **3.** Lindos Ojos.   Hd, 1.   20 ran
1932 Kandy (33–1) C. Elliott (M. E. de St Alary) F. Carter (France)
    2. Thorndean,   **3.** Safe Return.   1, 1.   19 ran
1933 Brown Betty (8–1) J. Childs (Mr Wm. Woodward) C. Boyd-Rochfort
    2. Fur Tor,   **3.** Myrobella. $\frac{1}{2}$, $\frac{3}{4}$.   22 ran
1934 Campanula (2–5) H. Wragg (Sir G. Bullough) J. L. Jarvis
    2. Light Brocade,   **3.** Spend a Penny.   1, 6.   10 ran
1935 Mesa (8–1) W. Johnstone (M. Pierre Wertheimer) M. P. Corbiere (France)
    2. Hyndford Bridge,   **3.** Caretta.   3, $1\frac{1}{2}$.   22 ran
1936 Tide-way (100–30) R. Perryman (Lord Derby) C. Leader
    2. Feola,   **3.** Ferrybridge. $1\frac{1}{2}$, Nk.   22 ran
1937 Exhibitionist (10–1) S. Donoghue (Sir V. Sassoon) J. Lawson
    2. Spray,   **3.** Gainsborough $\frac{1}{2}$, Hd.   20 ran
                                      Lass.
1938 Rockfel (8–1) S. Wragg (Sir H. Cunliffe-Owen) O. Bell
    2. Laughing Water,   **3.** Solar Flower. $1\frac{1}{2}$, 3.   20 ran
1939 Galatea II (6–1) R. A. Jones (Mr R. S. Clark) J. Lawson
    2. Aurora,   **3.** Olein,   3, $\frac{1}{2}$.   18 ran

1940 Godiva (10–1) D. Marks (Lord Rothermere) W. Jarvis
    2. Golden Penny,   **3.** Allure.   5, 4.   11 ran
1941 Dancing Time (100–8) R. Perryman (Lord Glanely) J. Lawson
    2. Beausite,   **3.** Keystone.   1, 2.   13 ran
1942 Sun Chariot (Evens) G. Richards (His Majesty) Fred Darling
    2. Perfect Peace,   **3.** Light of Day.   4, 2.   18 ran
1943 Herringbone (15–2) H. Wragg (Lord Derby) W. Earl
    2. Ribbon,   **3.** Cincture.   Nk, 1½.   12 ran
1944 Picture Play (15–2) C. Elliott (Mr H. J. Joel) J. Watts
    2. Grande Corniche,   **3.** Superior.   4, 2.   11 ran
1945 Sun Stream (5–2) H. Wragg (Lord Derby) W. Earl
    2. Blue Smoke,   **3.** Mrs Feather.   3, 2.   14 ran
1946 Hypericum (100–6) D. Smith (His Majesty) C. Boyd-Rochfort
    2. Neolight,   **3.** Iona.   1½, ¾.   13 ran
1947 Imprudence (4–1) W. Johnstone (Mme P. Corbiere) J. Lieux (France)
    2. Rose O'Lynn,   **3.** Wild Child.   Nk, Hd.   20 ran
1948 Queenpot (6–1) G. Richards (Sir P. Loraine) N. Murless
    2. Ariostar,   **3.** Duplicity.   Hd, 1½.   22 ran
1949 Musidora (100–8) E. Britt (Mr N. P. Donaldson) C. F. Elsey
    2. Unknown Quantity,   **3.** Solar Myth.   1½, 2.   18 ran
1950 Camaree (10–1) W. Johnstone (M. J. Ternynck) A. Lieux (France)
    2. Catchit and   **2.** Tambara.   3, Dd Ht.   17 ran
1951 Belle of All (4–1) G. Richards (Mr H. S. Tufton) N. Bertie
    2. Subtle Difference,   **3.** Bob Run.   Nk, 2.   18 ran
1952 Zabara (7–1) K. Gethin (Sir M. McAlpine) V. Smyth
    2. La Mirambule,   **3.** Refreshed.   ½, 5.   20 ran
1953 Happy Laughter (10–1) E. Mercer (Mr H. D. H. Wills) J. L. Jarvis
    2. Tessa Gillian,   **3.** Bebe Grande.   2, 5.   14 ran
1954 Festoon (9–2) A. Breasley (Mr J. A. Dewar) N. Cannon
    2. Big Berry,   **3.** Welsh Fairy.   2, 1.   12 ran
1955 Meld (11–4) W. Carr (Lady Zia Wernher) C. Boyd-Rochfort
    2. Aberlady,   **3.** Feria.   2, 1½.   12 ran
1956 Honeylight (100–6) E. Britt (Sir Victor Sassoon) C. F. Elsey
    2. Midget II,   **3.** Arietta.   2, 3.   19 ran
1957 ROSE ROYALE II (6–1) C. Smirke (£13,602) (H. H. Aga Khan) A. Head
    (France)
    2. Sensualita (J. Massard),   **3.** Angelet (E. Hide) (4–1f),
    4. Carrozza,   **5.** Silken Glider,
    6. Nagaika.   Extended distances, 1, 2, 1½, Nk, ½.   20 ran
1958 BELLA PAOLA (8–11f) S. Boullenger (£12,773) (F. Dupre) F. Mathet
    (France)
    2. Amante (J. Massard),   **3.** Alpine Bloom (E. Mercer),
    4. Persian Wheel,   **5.** Darlene,
    6. Mother Goose.   Extended distances, 1½, 5, 3, Nk, 1½.   11 ran
1959 PETITE ETOILE (8–1) D. Smith (£13,254) (Prince Aly Khan) N. Murless
    2. Rosalba (J. Mercer) (9–4f), **3.** Paraguana (G. Moore),
    4. Rose of Medina,   **5.** Lindsay,
    6. Mirnaya.   Extended distances, 1, 4, ½, ½, Sht Hd.   14 ran

1960 NEVER TOO LATE II (8–11f) R. Poincelet (£14,023) (Mrs H. E. Jackson)
E. Pollet (France)

    2. Lady in Trouble   **3.** Running Blue (E. Larkin),
       (A. Breasley),
    4. Queensberry,   **5.** Panga,
    6. Release.   Extended distances, 2, $\frac{1}{2}$, 4, 2, Nk.   14 ran

1961 SWEET SOLERA (4–1jf) W. Rickaby (£16,234) (Mrs S. M. Castello)
Reg Day

    2. Ambergris (J. Lindley),   **3.** Indian Melody (A. Breasley),
    4. Verbena,   **5.** Mystify (4–1jf),
    6. Covert Side.   Extended distances, $1\frac{1}{2}$, 6, $\frac{1}{2}$, 1, Nk.   14 ran

1962 ABERMAID (100–6) W. Williamson (£21,597) (R. More O'Ferrall)
H. Wragg

    2. Display (G. Bougoure)   **3.** West Side Story (E. Smith),
       (5–2f),
    4. Pervinca,   **5.** Anassa,
    6. Fool's Gold.   Extended distances, $\frac{1}{2}$, $\frac{3}{4}$, 3, 4, Nk.   14 ran

1963 HULA DANCER (1–2f) R. Poincelet (£22,830) (Mrs P. A. B. Widener)
E. Pollet (France)

    2. Spree (J. Lindley),   **3.** Royal Cypher (A. Breasley),
    4. Dunce Cap,   **5.** Hera,
    6. Top of the Milk.   Extended distances, 1, 1, Hd, 4, Nk.   12 ran

1964 POURPARLER (11–2) G. Bougoure (£29,103) (Beatrice Lady Granard)
P. J. Prendergast

    2. Gwen (P. Robinson),   **3.** Royal Danseuse (J. Roe) and
                    3. Petite Gina (R. P. Elliott),
   5. Crimea II,   **6.** King's Mistress.
     (Texanita 100–30f) Extended distances, 1, $1\frac{1}{2}$, Dd Ht, $1\frac{1}{2}$, $\frac{1}{2}$. 18 ran

1965 NIGHT OFF (9–2f) W. Williamson (£22,570) (Major L. B. Holliday)
W. Wharton

    2. Yami (J. Desaint),   **3.** Mabel (R. Hutchinson),
    4. Long Look,   **5.** Rose of Mooncoin,
    6. Miba.   Extended distances, Nk, 3, $1\frac{1}{2}$, $1\frac{1}{2}$, 2.   16 ran

1966 GLAD RAGS (100–6) P. Cook (£25,214) (Mrs J. P. Mills) M. V. O'Brien

    2. Berkeley Springs   **3.** Miliza II (Y. Saint-Martin) (10–11f),
       (G. Lewis),
    4. Sea Lichen,   **5.** Soft Angels,
    6. Hiding Place.   Extended distances, Nk, 2, 2, $\frac{3}{4}$, Hd.   21 ran

1967 FLEET (11–2) G. Moore (£24,848) (R. C. Boucher) N. Murless

    2. St Pauli Girl   **3.** Lacquer (R. Hutchinson),
       (B. Raymond),
    4. Pia,   **5.** Jadeite,
    6. Palatch.
     (Fix the Date 11–10f–8th.) Extended distances, $\frac{1}{2}$, Hd, Hd, 2, $\frac{3}{4}$. 16 ran

1968 CAERGWRLE (4–1f) A. Barclay (£19,682) (Mrs N. Murless) N. Murless

    2. Photo Flash (J. Lindley),   **3.** Sovereign (R. Hutchinson),
    4. Ileana,   **5.** Hill Shade,
    6. Travelling Fair.   Extended distances, 1, Sht Hd, 8, Hd, Nk. 14 ran

Race 3: THE DERBY
1 mile 4 furlongs. Epsom. Three-year-olds

1780 Diomed	(9)	1822 Moses	(12)	1861 Kettledrum	(18)
1781 Young Eclipse	(15)	1823 Emilius	(11)	1862 Caractacus	(34)
1782 Assassin	(13)	1824 Cedric	(17)	1863 Macaroni	(31)
1783 Saltram	(6)	1825 Middleton	(18)	1864 Blair Athol	(30)
1784 Sergeant	(11)	1826 Lap-dog	(19)	1865 Gladiateur	(30)
1785 Aimwell	(10)	1827 Mameluke	(23)	1866 Lord Lyon	(26)
1786 Noble	(15)	1828 Cadland	(15)	1867 Hermit	(30)
1787 Sir Peter Teazle	(7)	1829 Frederick	(17)	1868 Blue Gown	(18)
1788 Sir Thomas	(11)	1830 Priam	(23)	1869 Pretender	(22)
1789 Skyscraper	(11)	1831 Spaniel	(23)	1870 Kingcraft	(15)
1790 Rhadamanthus	(10)	1832 St Giles	(22)	1871 Favonius	(17)
1791 Eager	(9)	1833 Dangerous	(25)	1872 Cremorne	(23)
1792 John Bull	(7)	1834 Plenipotentiary	(22)	1873 Doncaster	(12)
1793 Waxy	(13)	1835 Mundig	(14)	1874 George	
1794 Dadalus	(4)	1836 Bay Middleton	(21)	Frederick	(20)
1795 Spread Eagle	(11)	1837 Phosphorus	(17)	1875 Galopin	(18)
1796 Didelot	(11)	1838 Amato	(23)	1876 Kisber	(15)
1797 c by Fidget	(7)	1839 Bloomsbury	(21)	1877 Silvio	(17)
1798 Sir Harry	(10)	1840 Little Wonder	(17)	1878 Sefton	(22)
1799 Archduke	(11)	1841 Coronation	(29)	1879 Sir Bevys	(23)
1800 Champion	(13)	1842 Attila	(24)	1880 Bend Or	(19)
1801 Eleanor	(11)	1843 Cotherstone	(23)	1881 Iroquois	(15)
1802 Tyrant	(9)	1844 Orlando	(29)	1882 Shotover	(14)
1803 Ditto	(6)	1845 The Merry		1883 St Blaise	(11)
1804 Hannibal	(8)	Monarch	(31)	1884 St Gatien and	
1805 Cardinal		1846 Pyrrhus the		Harvester	(15)
Beaufort	(15)	First	(27)	1885 Melton	(12)
1806 Paris	(12)	1847 Cossack	(32)	1886 Ormonde	(9)
1807 Election	(13)	1848 Surplice	(17)	1887 Merry Hampton	(11)
1808 Pan	(10)	1849 The Flying		1888 Ayrshire	(9)
1809 Pope	(10)	Dutchman	(26)	1889 Donovan	(13)
1810 Whalebone	(11)	1850 Voltigeur	(24)	1890 Sainfoin	(8)
1811 Phantom	(16)	1851 Teddington	(33)	1891 Common	(11)
1812 Octavius	(14)	1852 Daniel		1892 Sir Hugo	(13)
1813 Smolensko	(12)	O'Rourke	(27)	1893 Isinglass	(11)
1814 Blucher	(14)	1853 West Australian	(28)	1894 Ladas	(7)
1815 Whisker	(13)	1854 Andover	(27)	1895 Sir Visto	(15)
1816 Prince Leopold	(11)	1855 Wild Dayrell	(12)	1896 Persimmon	(11)
1817 Azor	(13)	1856 Ellington	(24)	1897 Galtee More	(11)
1818 Sam	(16)	1857 Blink Bonny	(30)	1898 Jeddah	(18)
1819 Tiresias	(16)	1858 Beadsman	(23)	1899 Flying Fox	(12)
1820 Sailor	(15)	1859 Musjid	(30)		
1821 Gustavus	(13)	1860 Thormanby	(30)		

1900 Diamond Jubilee (6–4) H. Jones (H. R. H. the Prince of Wales) R. Marsh
    2. Simon Dale,   **3.** Disguise II. $\frac{1}{2}$, 1.   14 ran
1901 Volodyovski (5–2) L. Reiff (Mr Whitney) J. Huggins
    2. William the Third,   **3.** Veronese. $1\frac{3}{4}$, 4.   25 ran
1902 Ard Patrick (100–14) J. H. Martin (Mr J. Gubbins) S. Darling
    2. Rising Glass,   **3.** Friar Tuck.   3, 3.   18 ran
1903 Rock Sand (4–6) Maher (Sir J. Miller) G. Blackwell
    2. Vinicius,   **3.** Flotsam.   2, 2.   7 ran
1904 St Amant (5–1) K. Cannon (Mr L de Rothschild) A. Hayhoe
    2. John o'Gaunt,   **3.** St Denis.   3, 6.   8 ran
1905 Cicero (4–11) Maher (Lord Rosebery) P. P. Peck
    2. Jardy,   **3.** Signorino. $\frac{3}{4}$, Hd.   9 ran
1906 Spearmint (6–1) D. Maher (Maj. E. Loder) P. Gilpin
    2. Picton,   **3.** Troutbeck. $1\frac{1}{2}$, 2.   22 ran
1907 Orby (100–9) J. Reiff (Mr R. Croker) J. Allen
    2. Wool Winder,   **3.** Slieve Gallion.   2, $\frac{1}{2}$.   9 ran
1908 Signorinetta (100–1) W. Bullock (Chev E. Ginistrelli) Chev Ginistrelli
    2. Primer,   **3.** Llangwm.   2, Nk.   18 ran
1909 Minoru (7–2) H. Jones (His Majesty) R. Marsh
    2. Louviers,   **3.** William the
         Fourth   Sht Hd, $\frac{1}{2}$.   15 ran
1910 Lemberg (7–4) B. Dillon (Mr Fairie) Alec Taylor
    2. Greenback,   **3.** Charles O'Malley. Nk, 2.   15 ran
1911 Sunstar (13–8) G. Stern (Mr J. B. Joel) C. Morton
    2. Stedfast,   **3.** Royal Tender.   2, 4.   26 ran
1912 Tagalie (100–8) J. Reiff (Mr Raphael) D. Waugh
    2. Jaeger,   **3.** Tracery.   4, 2.   20 ran
1913 Aboyeur (100–1) E. Piper (Mr A. B. Cunliffe) T. Lewis
    2. Louvois,   **3.** Great Sport.
         (Craganour first, disqualified.) Original distances, Hd, Nk.   15 ran
1914 Durbar II (20–1) M. MacGee (Mr H. Duryea) T. Murphy
    2. Hapsburg,   **3.** Peter the Hermit. 3, $1\frac{1}{2}$.   30 ran

AT NEWMARKET

1915 Pommern (11–10) S. Donoghue (Mr S. Joel) C. Peck
    2. Let Fly,   **3.** Rossendale.   2, 3.   17 ran
1916 Fifinella (11–2) J. Childs (Mr E. Hulton) R. Dawson
    2. Kwang-Su,   **3.** Nassovian.   Nk, Hd.   10 ran
1917 Gay Crusader (7–4) S. Donoghue (Mr A. W. Cox) Alec Taylor
    2. Dansellon,   **3.** Dark Legend.   4, Hd.   12 ran
1918 Gainsborough (8–13) J. Childs (Lady J. Douglas) Alec Taylor
    2. Blink,   **3.** Treclare. $1\frac{1}{2}$, 2.   13 ran

AT EPSOM

1919 Grand Parade (33–1) F. Templeman (Lord Glanely) F. Barling
    2. Buchan,   **3.** Paper Money. $\frac{1}{2}$, 2.   13 ran
1920 Spion Kop (100–6) F. O'Neill (Maj. G. Loder) P. P. Gilpin
    2. Archaic,   **3.** Orpheus.   2, $1\frac{1}{2}$.   19 ran

1921 Humorist (6–1) S. Donoghue (Mr J. B. Joel) C. Morton
    2. Craig an Eran,   **3.** Lemonora.   Nk, 3.   23 ran
1922 Captain Cuttle (10–1) S. Donoghue (Lord Woolavington) F. Darling
    2. Tamar,   **3.** Craigangower.   4, 3.   30 ran
1923 Papyrus (100–15) S. Donoghue (Mr B. Irish) B. Jarvis
    2. Pharos,   **3.** Parth.   1, 1½.   19 ran
1924 Sansovino (9–2) T. Weston (Lord Derby) Hon. G. Lambton
    2. St Germans,   **3.** Hurstwood.   6, Nk.   27 ran
1925 Manna (9–1) S. Donoghue (Mr H. E. Morriss) F. Darling
    2. Zionist,   **3.** The Sirdar.   8, 2.   27 ran
1926 Coronach (11–2) J. Childs (Lord Woolavington) F. Darling
    2. Lancegaye,   **3.** Colorado.   5, Sht Hd.   19 ran
1927 Call Boy (4–1) C. Elliott (Mr F. Curzon) J. Watts
    2. Hot Night,   **3.** Shian Mor.   2, 8.   23 ran
1928 Felstead (33–1) H. Wragg (Sir H. Cunliffe-Owen) O. Bell
    2. Flamingo,   **3.** Black Watch.   1½, 6.   19 ran
1929 Trigo (33–1) J. Marshall (Mr W. Barnett) R. Dawson
    2. Walter Gay,   **3.** Brienz.   1½, 2.   26 ran
1930 Blenheim (18–1) H. Wragg (H. H. Aga Khan) R. Dawson
    2. Iliad,   **3.** Diolite.   1, 2.   17 ran
1931 Cameronian (7–2) F. Fox (Mr J. A. Dewar) F. Darling
    2. Orpen,   **3.** Sandwich.   ¾, ¾.   25 ran
1932 April the Fifth (100–6) F. Lane (Mr T. Walls) T. Walls
    2. Dastur,   **3.** Miracle.   ¾, Sht Hd.   21 ran
1933 Hyperion (6–1) T. Weston (Lord Derby) Hon. G. Lambton
    2. King Salmon,   **3.** Statesman.   4, 1.   24 ran
1934 Windsor Lad (15–2) C. Smirke (H. H. Maharaja of Rajpipla) M. Marsh
    2. Easton,   **3.** Colombo.   1, Nk.   19 ran
1935 Bahram (5–4) F. Fox (H. H. Aga Khan) Frank Butters
    2. Robin Goodfellow,   **3.** Field Trial.   2, ½.   16 ran
1936 Mahmoud (100–8) C. Smirke (H. H. Aga Khan) Frank Butters
    2. Taj Akbar,   **3.** Thankerton.   3, ¾.   22 ran
1937 Mid-day Sun (100–7) M. Beary (Mrs G. B. Miller) F. S. Butters
    2. Sandsprite,   **3.** Le Grand Duc.   1½, 1½.   21 ran
1938 Bois Roussel (20–1) C. Elliott (Mr P. Beatty) F. Darling
    2. Scottish Union,   **3.** Pasch.   4, 2.   22 ran
1939 Blue Peter (7–2) E. Smith (Lord Rosebery) J. L. Jarvis
    2. Fox Cub,   **3.** Heliopolis.   4, 3.   27 ran

AT NEWMARKET

1940 Pont l'Eveque (10–1) S. Wragg (Mr F. Darling) F. Darling
    2. Turkhan,   **3.** Lighthouse II.   3, Sht Hd.   16 ran
1941 Owen Tudor (25–1) W. Nevett (Mrs Macdonald Buchanan) F. Darling
    2. Morogoro,   **3.** Firoze Din.   1½, 2.   20 ran
1942 Watling Street (8–1) H. Wragg (Lord Derby) W. Earl
    2. Hyperides,   **3.** Ujiji.   Nk, 2.   13 ran
1943 Straight Deal (100–6) T. Carey (Miss D. Paget) W. Nightingall
    2. Umiddad,   **3.** Nasrullah.   Hd, ½.   23 ran

1944 Ocean Swell (28–1) W. Nevett (Lord Rosebery) J. L. Jarvis
    2. Tehran,   **3.** Happy Landing.   Nk, Sht Hd.   20 ran
1945 Dante (100–30) W. Nevett (Sir E. Ohlson) M. Peacock
    2. Midas,   **3.** Court Martial.   2, Hd.   27 ran

AT EPSOM

1946 Airborne (50–1) T. Lowrey (Mr J. E. Ferguson) R. Perryman
    2. Gulf Stream,   **3.** Radiotherapy.   1, 2.   17 ran
1947 Pearl Diver (40–1) G. Bridgland (Baron G. de Waldner) W. Halsey
    2. Migoli,   **3.** Sayajirao.   4, ¾.   15 ran
1948 My Love (100–9) W. Johnstone (H. H. Aga Khan) R. Carver (France)
    2. Royal Drake,   **3.** Noor.   1½, 4.   32 ran
1949 Nimbus (7–1) E. C. Elliott (Mrs M. Glenister) G. S. Colling
    2. Amour Drake,   **3.** Swallow Tail.   Hd, Hd.   32 ran
1950 Galcador (100–9) W. Johnstone (M. M. Boussac) C. H. Semblat (France)
    2. Prince Simon,   **3.** Double Eclipse.   Hd, 4.   25 ran
1951 Arctic Prince (28–1) C. Spares (Mr J. McGrath) W. Stephenson
    2. Sybil's Nephew,   **3.** Signal Box.   6, Hd.   33 ran
1952 Tulyar (11–2) C. Smirke (H. H. Aga Khan) M. Marsh
    2. Gay Time,   **3.** Faubourg II.   ¾, 1.   33 ran
1953 Pinza (5–1) G. Richards (Sir Victor Sassoon) N. Bertie
    2. Aureole,   **3.** Pink Horse,   4, 1½.   27 ran
1954 Never Say Die (33–1) L. Piggott (Mr R. S. Clark) J. Lawson
    2. Arabian Night,   **3.** Darius.   2, Nk.   22 ran
1955 Phil Drake (100–8) F. Palmer (Mme Leon Volterra) F. Mathet (France)
    2. Panaslipper,   **3.** Acropolis.   1½, 3.   23 ran
1956 Lavandin (7–1) W. Johnstone (M Pierre Wertheimer) A. Head (France)
    2. Montaval,   **3.** Roistar.   Nk, 2.   27 ran
1957 CREPELLO (6–4f) L. Piggott (£18,659) (Sir Victor Sassoon) N. Murless
    2. Ballymoss (T. P. Burns),   **3.** Pipe of Peace (A. Breasley),
    4. Tempest,   **5.** Royaumont,
    6. Messmate.   Extended distances, 1½, 1, ¾, Nk, 6.   22 ran
1958 HARD RIDDEN (18–1) C. Smirke (£20,036) (Sir Victor Sassoon) J. Rogers
    2. Paddy's Point   **3.** Nagami (J. Mercer),
    (G. W. Robinson),
    4. Baroco II,   **5.** Guersillus,
    6. Miner's Lamp and   **6.** Alberta Blue.
    (Wallaby II 4–1f.) Extended distances, 5, 1½, Sht Hd, Hd, Nk.   20 ran
1959 PARTHIA (10–1) W. Carr (£36,078) (Sir H. de Trafford) C. Boyd-Rochfort
    2. Fidalgo (J. Mercer),   **3.** Shantung (F. Palmer) (11–2f),
    4. Saint Crespin III,   **5.** Above Suspicion.
    6. Carnoustie.   Extended distances, 1½, 1½, Hd, 1½, 2.   20 ran
1960 ST PADDY (7–1) L. Piggott (£33,052) (Sir Victor Sassoon) N. Murless
    2. Alcaeus (A. Breasley),   **3.** Kythnos (R. Hutchinson),
    4. Auroy,   **5.** Proud Chieftain,
    6. Die Hard.
    (Angers 2–1f.) Extended distances, 3, ½, 2, Hd, 1½.   17 ran

1961 PSIDIUM (66–1) R. Poincelet (£34,548) (Mrs Arpad Plesch) H. Wragg
    2. Dicta Drake (M. Garcia),   **3.** Pardao (W. Carr),
    4. Sovrango,   **5.** Cipriani,
    6. Latin Lover.
          (Moutiers 5–1f.)   Extended distances, 2, Nk, 2, Hd, $1\frac{1}{2}$.   28 ran

1962 LARKSPUR (22–1) N. Sellwood (£34,786) (R. R. Guest) M. V. O'Brien
    2. Arcor (R. Poincelet),   **3.** Le Cantilien (Y. Saint-Martin),
    4. Escort,   **5.** Sebring,
    6. Prince d'Amour.
          (Hethersett 9–2f–fell.)   Extended distances, 2, $\frac{1}{2}$, $\frac{3}{4}$, Nk, $\frac{3}{4}$.   26 ran

1963 RELKO (5–1f) Y. Saint-Martin (£35,338) (F. Dupre) F. Mathet (France)
    2. Merchant Venturer   **3.** Ragusa (G. Bougoure),
    (G. Starkey),
    4. Tarqogan,   **5.** Corpora,
    6. Portofino.   Extended distances, 6, 3, Nk, $\frac{3}{4}$, 8.   26 ran

1964 SANTA CLAUS (15–8f) A. Breasley (£72,067) (J. Ismay) J. Rogers
    2. Indiana (J. Lindley),   **3.** Dilettante II (P. Matthews),
    4. Anselmo,   **5.** Baldric II,
    6. Crete.   Extended distances, 1, 2, Nk, 3, Sht Hd.   17 ran

1965 SEA BIRD II (7–4f) T. P. Glennon (£65,301) (M. J. Ternynck) E. Pollet
(France)
    2. Meadow Court   **3.** I Say (R. Poincelet),
    (L. Piggott)
    4. Niksar,   **5.** Convamore,
    6. Cambridge.   Extended distances, 2, $1\frac{1}{2}$, 4, Nk, 1.   22 ran

1966 CHARLOTTOWN (5–1) A. Breasley (£74,489) (Lady Zia Wernher) G. Smyth
    2. Pretendre (P. Cook)   **3.** Black Prince II (J. Lindley),
    (9–2jf),
    4. Sodium,   **5.** Crisp and Even,
    6. Ambericos.
    (Right Noble 9–2jf—9th.)   Extended distances, Nk, 5, $1\frac{1}{2}$, 5, $1\frac{1}{2}$,   25 ran

1967 ROYAL PALACE (7–4f) G. Moore (£61,918) (Mr H. J. Joel) N. Murless
    2. Ribocco (L. Piggott),   **3.** Dart Board (A. Breasley),
    4. Royal Sword,   **5.** Helluvafella,
    6. Landigou.   Extended distances, $2\frac{1}{2}$, 2, $1\frac{1}{2}$, $\frac{1}{2}$, Nk.   22 ran

1968 SIR IVOR (4–5f) L. Piggott (£58,525) (Raymond R. Guest) M. V. O'Brien
    2. Connaught (A. Barclay),   **3.** Mount Athos (R. Hutchinson),
    4. Remand,   **5.** Society,
    6. Torpid.   Extended distances, $1\frac{1}{2}$, $2\frac{1}{2}$, 1, $1\frac{1}{2}$, 8.   13 ran

Race 4: THE OAKS

1 mile 4 furlongs. Epsom. Three-year-old fillies

1779 Bridget	(12)	**1820** Caroline	(13)	**1861** Brown Duchess	(17)
1780 Teetotum	(11)	**1821** Augusta	(7)	**1862** Feu de Joie	(19)
1781 Faith	(6)	**1822** Pastille	(10)	**1863** Queen Bertha	(20)
1782 Ceres	(12)	**1823** Zinc	(10)	**1864** Fille de l'Air	(19)
1783 Maid of the		**1824** Cobweb	(13)	**1865** Regalia	(18)
Oakes	(10)	**1825** Wings	(10)	**1866** Tormentor	(17)
1784 Stella	(10)	**1826** Lilias	(15)	**1867** Hippla	(8)
1785 Trifle	(8)	**1827** Gulnare	(19)	**1868** Formosa	(9)
1786 Perdita filly	(13)	**1828** Turquoise	(14)	**1869** Brigantine	(15)
1787 Annette	(8)	**1829** Green Mantle	(14)	**1870** Gamos	(7)
1788 Nightshade	(7)	**1830** Variation	(18)	**1871** Hannah	(9)
1789 Tag	(7)	**1831** Oxygen	(21)	**1872** Reine	(17)
1790 Hippolyta	(12)	**1832** Galata	(19)	**1873** Marie Stuart	(18)
1791 Portia	(9)	**1833** Vespa	(19)	**1874** Apology	(11)
1792 Volante	(11)	**1834** Pussy	(15)	**1875** Spinaway	(7)
1793 Caelia	(10)	**1835** Queen of		**1876** Enguerrande and	
1794 Hermione	(8)	Trumps	(10)	Camelia	(14)
1795 Platina	(11)	**1836** Cyprian	(12)	**1877** Placida	(9)
1796 Parissot	(13)	**1837** Miss Letty	(13)	**1878** Jannette	(8)
1797 Nike	(5)	**1838** Industry	(16)	**1879** Wheel of	
1798 Bellissima	(7)	**1839** Deception	(13)	Fortune	(8)
1799 Bellina	(4)	**1840** Crucifix	(15)	**1880** Jenny Howlet	(13)
1800 Ephemera	(8)	**1841** Ghuznee	(22)	**1881** Thebats	(12)
1801 Eleanor	(6)	**1842** Our Nell	(16)	**1882** Geheimniss	(5)
1802 Scotia	(6)	**1843** Poison	(23)	**1883** Bonny Jean	(14)
1803 Theophania	(7)	**1844** The Princess	(25)	**1884** Busybody	(9)
1804 Pelisse	(8)	**1845** Refraction	(21)	**1885** Lonely	(10)
1805 Meteora	(8)	**1846** Mendicant	(24)	**1886** Miss Jummy	(12)
1806 Bronze	(12)	**1847** Miami	(23)	**1887** Reve d'Or	(9)
1807 Briseis	(13)	**1848** Cymba	(26)	**1888** Seabreeze	(6)
1808 Morel	(10)	**1849** Lady Evelyn	(15)	**1889** L'Abbesse	(12)
1809 Maid of		**1850** Rhedycina	(15)	**1890** Memoir	(7)
Orleans	(11)	**1851** Iris	(15)	**1891** Mimi	(6)
1810 Oriana	(11)	**1852** Songstress	(14)	**1892** La Fleche	(7)
1811 Sorcery	(12)	**1853** Catherine		**1893** Mrs Butterwick	(17)
1812 Manuella	(12)	Hayes	(17)	**1894** Amiable	(11)
1813 Music	(9)	**1854** Mincemeat	(15)	**1895** La Sagesse	(15)
1814 Medora	(9)	**1855** Marchioness	(11)	**1896** Canterbury	
1815 Minuet	(11)	**1856** Mincepie	(10)	Pilgrim	(11)
1816 Landscape	(11)	**1857** Blink Bonny	(13)	**1897** Limasol	(8)
1817 Neva	(11)	**1858** Governess	(13)	**1898** Airs and Graces	(13)
1818 Corinne	(10)	**1859** Summerside	(15)	**1899** Musa	(12)
1819 Shoveler	(10)	**1860** Butterfly	(13)		

1900 La Roche (5–1) M. Cannon (Duke of Portland) J. Porter
  2. Merry Gal,   3. Lady Schomberg. 3, Bad.   14 ran
1901 Cap and Bells II (9–4) Henry (Mr Foxhall Keene) S. Darling
  2. Sabrinetta,   3. Minnie Dee.   6, 2.   21 ran
1902 Sceptre (5–2) Randall (Mr R. S. Sievier) R. S. Sievier
  2. Glass Jug,   3. Elba.   3, 1½.   14 ran
1903 Our Lassie (6–1) M. Cannon (Mr J. B. Joel) C. Morton
  2. Hammerkop,   3. Skyscraper.   3, Hd.   14 ran
1904 Pretty Polly (8–100) W. Lane (Maj. E. Loder) P. P. Gilpin
  2. Bitters,   3. Fiancee.   3, Bad.   4 ran
1905 Cherry Lass (4–5) H. Jones (Mr W. Hall Walker) W. T. Robinson
  2. Queen of the Earth,   3. Amitie.   3, 6.   12 ran
1906 Keystone II (5–2) D. Maher (Lord Derby) G. Lambton
  2. Gold Riach,   3. Snow-Glory.   3, 1½.   12 ran
1907 Glass Doll (25–1) H. Randall (Mr J. B. Joel) C. Morton
  2. Laomedia,   3. Lady Hasty.   ½, ¾.   14 ran
1908 Signorinetta (3–1) W. Bullock (Chev E. Ginistrelli) Chev E. Ginistrelli
  2. Courtesy,   3. Santeve.   ¾, 2.   13 ran
1909 Perola (5–1) F. Wotton (Mr W. C. Cooper) G. Davies
  2. Princesse de Galles,   3. Verne.   2, 2.   14 ran
1910 Rosedrop (7–1) C. Trigg (Sir W. Bass) Alec Taylor
  2. Evolution,   3. Pernelle.   4, Nk.   11 ran
1911 Cherimoya (25–1) F. Winter (Mr W. Brodrick Cloetes) C. Marsh
  2. Tootles,   3. Hair Trigger II.   3, 5.   21 ran
1912 Mirska (33–1) J. Childs (M. J. Prat) T. Jennings
  2. Equitable,   3. Bill and Coo.   3, ¾.   14 ran
1913 Jest (8–1) F. Rickaby (Mr J. B. Joel) C. Morton
  2. Depeche,   3. Arda.   2, ½.   12 ran
1914 Princess Dorrie (11–4) W. Huxley (Mr J. B. Joel) C. Morton
  2. Wassilissa,   3. Torchlight.   2, 4.   21 ran

AT NEWMARKET

1915 Snow Marten (20–1) Walter Griggs (Mr L. Neumann) P. P. Gilpin
  2. Bright,   3. Silver Tag.   4, Hd.   11 ran
1916 Fifinella (8–13) J. Childs (Mr E. Hulton) R. Dawson
  2. Salamandra,   3. Market Girl.   5, ½.   7 ran
1917 Sunny Jane (4–1) O. Madden (Maj. W. Astor) Alec Taylor
  2. Diadem,   3. Moravia.   ½, 4.   11 ran
1918 My Dear (3–1) S. Donoghue (Mr A. W. Cox) Alec Taylor
  2. Ferry and 2 Silver Bullet.
    (Stony Ford first, disqualified.)   Original distances, 1, 4.   15 ran

AT EPSOM

1919 Bayuda (100–7) J. Childs (Lady James Douglas) Alec Taylor
  2. Roseway,   3. Mapledurham.   1½, 1½.   10 ran
1920 Charlebelle (7–2) A. Whalley (Mr A. P. Cunliffe) H. Braime
  2. Cinna,   3. Roselet.   Nk, 4.   17 ran

114

1921 Love in Idleness (5–1) J. Childs (Mr Jos Watson) Alec Taylor
    2. Lady Sleipner,   **3.** Long Suit.   3, Nk.   22 ran
1922 Pogrom (5–4) E. Gardner (Lord Astor) Alec Taylor
    2. Soubriquet,   **3.** Mysia. $\frac{3}{4}$, 3.   11 ran
1923 Brownhylda (10–1) V. Smyth (Vicomte de Fontarce) R. Dawson
    2. Shrove,   **3.** Teresina.   Nk, Hd.   12 ran
1924 Straitlace (100–30) F. O'Neill (Sir E. Hulton) D. Waugh
    2. Plack,   **3.** Mink. $1\frac{1}{2}$, Hd.   12 ran
1925 Saucy Sue (30–100) F. Bullock (Lord Astor) Alec Taylor
    2. Miss Gadabout,   **3.** Riding Light.   8, 8.   12 ran
1926 Short Story (5–1) R. A. Jones (Lord Astor) Alec Taylor
    2. Resplendent,   **3.** Gay Bird.   4, 2.   16 ran
1927 Beam (4–1) T. Weston (Lord Durham) Frank Butters
    2. Book Law,   **3.** Grande Vitesse.   Hd, 6.   16 ran
1928 Toboggan (100–15) T. Weston (Lord Derby) Frank Butters
    2. Scuttle,   **3.** Flegere.   4, 6.   13 ran
1929 Pennycomequick (11–10) H. Jelliss (Lord Astor) J. Lawson
    2. Golden Silence,   **3.** Sister Anne.   5, 2.   13 ran
1930 Rose of England (7–1) G. Richards (Lord Glanely) T. Hogg
    2. Wedding Favour,   **3.** Micmac.   3, 2.   15 ran
1931 Brulette (7–2) C. Elliott (Lt.-Col. C. Birkin) F. Carter (France)
    2. Four Course,   **3.** Links Tor.   1, $\frac{3}{4}$.   15 ran
1932 Udaipur (10–1) M. Beary (H. H. Aga Khan) Frank Butters
    2. Will o' the Wisp,   **3.** Giudecca.   2, 2.   12 ran
1933 Chatelaine (25–1) S. Wragg (Mr E. Thornton-Smith) F. Templeman
    2. Solfatara,   **3.** Fur Tor. $1\frac{1}{2}$, 2.   14 ran
1934 Light Brocade (7–4) B. Carslake (Lord Durham) Frank Butters
    2. Zelina,   **3.** Instantaneous. $1\frac{1}{2}$, $\frac{1}{2}$.   8 ran
1935 Quashed (33–1) H. Jellis (Lord Stanley) C. Leader
    2. Ankaret,   **3.** Mesa.   Sht Hd, 1.   17 ran
1936 Lovely Rosa (33–1) T. Weston (Sir Abe Bailey) H. L. Cottrill
    2. Barrowby Gem,   **3.** Feola. $\frac{3}{4}$, 2.   17 ran
1937 Exhibitionist (3–1) S. Donoghue (Sir V. Sassoon) J. Lawson
    2. Sweet Content,   **3.** Sculpture.   3, Hd.   13 ran
1938 Rockfel (3–1) H. Wragg (Sir H. Cunliffe-Owen) O. Bell
    2. Radiant,   **3.** Solar Flower.   4, $1\frac{1}{2}$.   14 ran
1939 Galatea II (10–11) R. A. Jones (Mr R. S. Clark) J. Lawson
    2. White Fox,   **3.** Superbe.   Hd, 3.   21 ran

AT NEWMARKET

1940 Godiva (7–4) D. Marks (Lord Rothermere) W. Jarvis
    2. Silverlace II,   **3.** Valeraine.   3, 4.   14 ran
1941 Commotion (8–1) H. Wragg (Mr J. A. Dewar) Fred Darling
    2. Turkana,   **3.** Dancing Time.   2, $\frac{3}{4}$.   12 ran
1942 Sun Chariot (1–4) G. Richards (His Majesty) Fred Darling
    2. Afterthought,   **3.** Feberion.   1, $1\frac{1}{2}$.   12 ran
1943 Why Hurry (7–1) C. Elliott (Mr J. V. Rank) N. Cannon
    2. Ribbon,   **3.** Tropical Sun.   Nk, 1.   13 ran

1944 Hycilla (8–1) G. Bridgland (Mr W. Woodward) C. Boyd-Rochfort
    2. Monsoon,   **3.** Kannabis. $1\frac{1}{2}$, $1\frac{1}{2}$.   16 ran
1945 Sun Stream (6–4) H. Wragg (Lord Derby) W. Earl
    2. Naishapur,   **3.** Solar Princess.   Sht Hd, 3.   16 ran

AT EPSOM

1946 Steady Aim (7–1) H. Wragg (Sir A. Butt) Frank Butters
    2. Iona,   **3.** Nelia.   3, 3.   10 ran
1947 Imprudence (7–4) W. Johnstone (Mme P. Corbiere) L. Lieux (France)
    2. Netherton Maid,   **3.** Mermaid.   5, 2.   11 ran
1948 Masaka (7–1) W. Nevett (H. H. Aga Khan) Frank Butters
    2. Angelola,   **3.** Folie II.   6, 3.   25 ran
1949 Musidora (4–1) E. Britt (Mr N. P. Donaldson) C. F. Elsey
    2. Coronation V,   **3.** Vice Versa II.   Nk, 2.   17 ran
1950 Asmena (5–1) W. Johnstone (M. M. Boussac) C. H. Semblat (France)
    2. Plume II,   **3.** Stella Polaris.   1, $1\frac{1}{2}$.   19 ran
1951 Neasham Belle (33–1) S. Clayton (Maj. L. B. Holliday) G. T. Brooke
    2. Chinese Cracker,   **3.** Belle of All.   4, 2.   16 ran
1952 Frieze (100–7) E. Britt (Capt. A. M. Keith) C. F. Elsey
    2. Zabara,   **3.** Moon Star.   3, $1\frac{1}{2}$.   19 ran
1953 Ambiguity (18–1) J. Mercer (Lord Astor) R. J. Colling
    2. Kerkeb,   **3.** Noemi.   1, 1.   21 ran
1954 Sun Cap (100–8) W. Johnstone (Mme R. Forget) R. Carver (France)
    2. Altana,   **3.** Philante.   6, 1.   21 ran
1955 Meld (7–4) W. Carr (Lady Zia Wernher) C. Boyd-Rochfort
    2. Ark Royal,   **3.** Reel In.   6, 3.   13 ran
1956 Sicarelle (3–1) F. Palmer (Mme Leon Volterra) F. Mathet (France)
    2. Janiari,   **3.** Yasmin.   3, 6.   14 ran
1957 CARROZZA (100–8) L. Piggott (£16,101) (The Queen) N. Murless
    2. Silken Glider (J. Eddery),   **3,** Rose Royale II (J. Massard) (11–10f)
    4. Taittinger,   **5.** Crotchet,
    6. Lady Salisbury.   Extended distances, Sht Hd, 3, 5, 3, $1\frac{1}{2}$.   11 ran
1958 BELLA PAOLA (6–4f) M. Garcia (£15,557) (F. Dupre) F. Mathet (France)
    2. Mother Goose (W. Carr),   **3.** Cutter (E. Mercer),
    4. None Nicer,   **5.** Torbella III,
    6. Princess Lora.   Extended distances, 3, 3, Nk, $\frac{3}{4}$, 1.   17 ran
1959 PETITE ETOILE (11–2) L. Piggott (£21,155) (Prince Aly Khan) N. Murless
    2. Cantelo (E. Hide) (7–4f),   **3.** Rose of Medina (E. Smith),
    4. Collyria,   **5.** Calceolaria,
    6. Mirnaya.   Extended distances, 3, 5, 2, Sht Hd, 8.   11 ran
1960 NEVER TOO LATE II (6–5f) R. Poincelet (£17,836) (Mrs H. E. Jackson)
    E. Pollet (France)
    2. Paimpont (G. Thiboeuf),   **3.** Imberline (J. Boullenger),
    4. Io,   **5.** No Saint,
    6. Saint Anne.   Extended distances, Hd, 2, Hd, $\frac{3}{4}$, $1\frac{1}{2}$.   10 ran
1961 SWEET SOLERA (11–4f) W. Rickaby (£18,104) (Mrs S. M. Castello) R. Day
    2. Ambergris (J. Lindley),   **3.** Anne la Douce (G. Thiboeuf),

    4. Tuna Gail,   **5.** La Bergerette,
    6. Indian Melody.   Extended distances, 1½, Nk, Nk, 2, 4.   12 ran

1962 MONADE (7–1) Y. St Martin (£18,435) (G. P. Goulandris) J. Lieux (France)
    2. West Side Story   **3.** Tender Annie (G. Bougoure),
       (E. Smith) (3–1f),
    4. Moira II,   **5.** Romantica,
    6. Nortia.   Extended distances, Sht Hd, 1½, 1½, 2, ¾. 18 ran

1963 NOBLESSE (4–11f) G. Bougoure (£18,129) (Mrs J. M. Olin) P. J. Prendergast
    2. Spree (J. Lindley),   **3.** Pouponne (A. Breasley),
    4. Sunsuit,   **5.** Amicable,
    6. Elite Royale.   Extended distances, 10, Nk, 1, 2, 6. 9 ran

1964 HOMEWARD BOUND (100–7) G. Starkey (£32,311) (Sir Foster Robinson) J. Oxley
    2. Windmill Girl   **3.** La Bamba (J. Deforge),
       (J. Mercer),
    4. Patti (3–1f),   **5.** All Saved,
    6. Beaufront.   Extended distances, 2, 1, ¾, 2, ¾. 18 ran

1965 LONG LOOK (100–7) J. Purtell (£30,747) (J. Cox Brady) M. V. O'Brien
    2. Mabel (J. Lindley),   **3.** Ruby's Princess (K. Temple-Nidd),
    4. Queen Anne's Lace,   **5.** Hilary Term,
    6. Miba.
    (Never a Fear 85–40f—10th.) Extended distances, 1½, ¾, 6, Hd, 3. 18 ran

1966 VALORIS (11–10f) L. Piggott (£35,711) (Charles Clore) M. V. O'Brien
    2. Berkeley Springs   **3.** Varinia (S. Clayton),
       (G. Lewis),
    4. Bombazine,   **5.** Black Gold,
    6. Hiding Place.   Extended distances, 2½, 3, 4, 1½, 5. 13 ran

1967 PIA (100–7) E. Hide (£28,137) (Countess Margit Batthyany) W. Elsey
    2. St Pauli Girl   **3.** Ludham (A. Breasley),
       (B. Raymond),
    4. Fleet (3–1f),   **5.** Hannah Darling,
    6. Palatch.   Extended distances, ¾, 2, 1, 1, ¾.   12 ran

1968 LA LAGUNE (11–8f) G. Thiboeuf (£28,774) (M. H. Berlin) F. Boutin (France)
    2. Glad One   **3.** Pandora Bay (M. Thomas),
       (W. Williamson),
    4. Hardiesse,   **5.** Kylin,
    6. Hill Shade.   Extended distances, 5, Sht Hd, 3, Hd, Hd. 14 ran

Race 5: ST. LEGER
1 mile 6 furlongs 132 yards. Doncaster. Three-year-olds

Year	Horse	(No.)	Year	Horse	(No.)	Year	Horse	(No.)
1776	Allabaculia	(5)	1820	St. Patrick	(27)	1858	Sunbeam	(18)
1777	Bourbon	(10)	1821	Jack Spiggot	(13)	1859	Gamester	(11)
1778	Hollandaise	(8)	1822	Theodore	(23)	1860	St Albans	(15)
1779	Tommy	(10)	1823	Barefoot	(12)	1861	Caller Ou	(18)
1780	Ruler	(7)	1824	Jerry	(23)	1862	The Marquis	(15)
1781	Serina	(9)	1825	Memnon	(30)	1863	Lord Clifden	(19)
1782	Imperatrix	(5)	1826	Tarrare	(27)	1864	Blair Athol	(10)
1783	Phoenomenon	(4)	1827	Matilda	(2)	1865	Gladiateur	(14)
1784	Omphale	(7)	1828	The Colonel	(19)	1866	Lord Lyon	(11)
1785	Cowslip	(4)	1829	Rowton	(19)	1867	Achievement	(12)
1786	Paragon	(8)	1830	Birmingham	(28)	1868	Formosa	(12)
1787	Spadille	(6)	1831	Chorister	(24)	1869	Pero Gomez	(11)
1788	Young Flora	(5)	1832	Margrave	(17)	1870	Hawthornden	(19)
1789	Pewett	(6)	1833	Rockingham	(20)	1871	Hannah	(10)
1790	Ambidexter	(8)	1834	Touchstone	(11)	1872	Wenlock	(17)
1791	Y. Traveller	(8)	1835	Queen of		1873	Marie Stuart	(8)
1792	Tartar	(11)		Trumps	(11)	1874	Apology	(13)
1793	Ninety-three	(8)	1836	Elis	(14)	1875	Craig Millar	(13)
1794	Beningbrough	(8)	1837	Mango	(13)	1876	Pertarch	(9)
1795	Hambletonian	(5)	1838	Don John	(7)	1877	Silvio	(14)
1796	Ambrosio	(7)	1839	Charles the		1878	Jannette	(14)
1797	Lounger	(8)		Twelfth	(14)	1879	Rayon d'Or	(17)
1798	Symmetry	(10)	1840	Launcelot	(11)	1880	Robert the	
1799	Cockfighter	(7)	1841	Satirist	(11)		Devil	(12)
1800	Champion	(10)	1842	Blue Bonnet	(17)	1881	Iroquois	(15)
1801	Quiz	(8)	1843	Nutwith	(9)	1882	Dutch Oven	(14)
1802	Orville	(7)	1844	Foig a Ballagh	(9)	1883	Ossian	(9)
1803	Remembrancer	(8)	1845	The Baron	(15)	1884	The Lambkin	(13)
1804	Sancho	(11)	1846	Sir Tatton		1885	Melton	(10)
1805	Staveley	(10)		Sykes	(12)	1886	Ormonde	(7)
1806	Fyldener	(15)	1847	Van Tromp	(8)	1887	Kilwarlin	(9)
1807	Paulina	(16)	1848	Surplice	(9)	1888	Seabreeze	(16)
1808	Petronius	(12)	1849	The Flying		1889	Donovan	(12)
1809	Ashton	(14)		Dutchman	(10)	1890	Memoir	(15)
1810	Octavian	(8)	1850	Voltigeur	(8)	1891	Common	(9)
1811	Soothsayer	(24)	1851	Newminster	(18)	1892	La Fleche	(11)
1812	Ottrington	(24)	1852	Stockwell	(6)	1893	Isinglass	(7)
1813	Altisidora	(17)	1853	West		1894	Throstle	(8)
1814	William	(12)		Australian	(10)	1895	Sir Visto	(11)
1815	Filho da Puta	(15)	1854	Knight of St.		1896	Persimmon	(7)
1816	The Duchess	(13)		George	(18)	1897	Galtee More	(5)
1817	Ebor	(18)	1855	Saucebox	(12)	1898	Wildfowler	(12)
1818	Reveller	(21)	1856	Warlock	(9)	1899	Flying Fox	(6)
1819	Antonio	(14)	1857	Imperieuse	(11)			

1900 Diamond Jubilee (2–7) H. Jones (Prince of Wales) R. Marsh
    2. Elopement,   **3.** Courlan.   1, 2.   11 ran
1901 Doricles (40–1) K. Cannon (Mr L. de Rothschild) A. Hayhoe
    2. Volodyovski,   **3.** Revenue.   Nk, 3.   13 ran
1902 Sceptre (100–30) Hardy (Mr R. Sievier) R. S. Sievier
    2. Rising Glass,   **3.** Friar Tuck.   3, 2.   12 ran
1903 Rock Sand (2–5) D. Maher (Sir J. Miller) G. Blackwell
    2. William Rufus,   **3.** Mead.   4, $\frac{1}{2}$.   5 ran
1904 Pretty Polly (2–5) W. Lane (Maj. E. Loder) P. P. Gilpin
    2. Henry the First,   **3.** Almscliff.   3, 6.   6 ran
1905 Challacombe (100–7) O. Madden (Mr W. Singer) Alec Taylor
    2. Polymelus,   **3.** Cherry Lass.   3, 3.   8 ran
1906 Troutbeck (5–1) G. Stern (Duke of Westminster) W. Waugh
    2. Prince William,   **3.** Beppo.   Hd, Hd.   12 ran
1907 Wool Winder (11–10) W. Halsey (Col. E. W. Baird) H. Enoch
    2. Baltinglass,   **3.** Acclaim.   6, $\frac{1}{2}$.   12 ran
1908 Your Majesty (11–8) Wal Griggs (Mr J. B. Joel) C. Morton
    2. White Eagle,   **3.** Santo Strato. $\frac{1}{2}$, 4.   10 ran
1909 Bayardo (10–11) D. Maher (Mr Fairie) Alec Taylor
    2. Valens,   **3.** Mirador. $1\frac{1}{2}$, $\frac{1}{2}$.   7 ran
1910 Swynford (9–2) F. Wootton (Lord Derby) Hon. G. Lambton
    2. Bronzino,   **3.** Lemberg.   Hd, $1\frac{1}{2}$.   11 ran
1911 Prince Palatine (100–30) F. O'Neill (Mr T. Pilkington) H. Beardsley
    2. Lycaon,   **3.** King William.   6, 3.   8 ran
1912 Tracery (8–1) G. Bellhouse (Mr A. Belmont) J. Watson
    2. Maiden Erlegh,   **3.** Hector.   5, $\frac{3}{4}$.   14 ran
1913 Night Hawk (50–1) E. Wheatley (Col. Hall-Walker) W. Robinson
    2. White Magic,   **3.** Seremond.   2, 3.   12 ran
1914 Black Jester (10–1) Wal Griggs (Mr J. Joel) C. Morton
    2. Kennymore,   **3.** Cressingham.   5, 3.   18 ran

AT NEWMARKET

1915 Pommern (1–3) S. Donoghue (Mr S. Joel) C. Peck
    2. Snow Marten,   **3.** Achtoi.   2, 6.   7 ran
1916 Hurry On (11–10) C. Childs (Mr J. Buchanan) F. Darling
    2. Clarissimus,   **3.** Atheling.   3, 5.   5 ran
1917 Gay Crusader (2–11) S. Donoghue (Mr Fairie) Alec Taylor
    2. Kingston Black,   **3.** Dansellon.   6, Bad.   3 ran
1918 Gainsborough (4–11) J. Childs (Lady Jas Douglas) Alec Taylor
    2. My Dear,   **3.** Prince Chimay.   3, 4.   5 ran

AT DONCASTER

1919 Keysoe (100–8) B. Carslake (Lord Derby) Hon. G. Lambton
    2. Dominion,   **3.** Buchan.   6 2.   10 ran
1920 Caligula (100–6) A. Smith (Mr M. Goculdas) H. Leader
    2. Silvern,   **3.** Manton. $\frac{1}{2}$, 3.   14 ran
1921 Polemarch (50–1) J. Childs (Lord Londonderry) T. Green
    2. Franklin,   **3.** Westward Ho. $1\frac{1}{2}$, 3.   9 ran

1922 Royal Lancer (33–1) R. Jones (Lord Lonsdale) A. D. Sadler jun.
    2. Silurian,   **3.** Ceylonese.   2, 2.   24 ran

1923 Tranquil (100–9) T. Weston (Lord Derby) C. Morton
    2. Papyrus,   **3.** Teresina.   2, 1½.   13 ran

1924 Salmon-Trout (6–1) B. Carslake (H. H. Aga Khan) R. C. Dawson
    2. Santorb,   **3.** Polyphontes.   2, ½.   17 ran

1925 Solario (7–2) J. Childs (Sir J. Rutherford) R. Day
    2. Zambo,   **3.** Warden of the   3, 3.   15 ran
                                  Marches.

1926 Coronach (8–15) J. Childs (Lord Woolavington) F. Darling
    2. Caissot,   **3.** Foliation.   2, 6.   12 ran

1927 Book Law (7–4) H. Jelliss (Lord Astor) Alec Taylor
    2. Hot Night,   **3.** Son and Heir.   3, 5.   16 ran

1928 Fairway (7–4) T. Weston (Lord Derby) Frank Butters
    2. Palais Royal II,   **3.** Cyclonic.   1½, 1.   13 ran

1929 Trigo (5–1) M. Beary (Mr W. Barnett) R. C. Dawson
    2. Bosworth,   **3.** Horus.   Sht Hd, ¾.   14 ran

1930 Singapore (4–1) G. Richards (Lord Glanely) T. Hogg
    2. Parenthesis,   **3.** Rustom Pasha.   1½, ¾.   13 ran

1931 Sandwich (9–1) H. Wragg (Lord Rosebery) J. L. Jarvis
    2. Orpen,   **3.** Sir Andrew.   4, 1.   10 ran

1932 Firdaussi (20–1) F. Fox (H. H. Aga Khan) Frank Butters
    2. Dastur,   **3.** Silvermere.   Nk, 4.   19 ran

1933 Hyperion (6–4) T. Weston (Lord Derby) Hon. G. Lambton
    2. Felicitation,   **3.** Scarlet Tiger.   3, Nk.   14 ran

1934 Windsor Lad (4–9) C. Smirke (Mr M. H. Benson) M. Marsh
    2. Tiberius,   **3.** Lo Zingaro.   2, 2.   10 ran

1935 Bahram (4–11) C. Smirke (H. H. Aga Khan) Frank Butters
    2. Solar Ray,   **3.** Buckleigh.   5, 3.   8 ran

1936 Boswell (20–1) P. Beasley (Mr W. Woodward) C. Boyd-Rochfort
    2. Fearless Fox,   **3.** Mahmoud.   ¾, 3.   13 ran

1937 Chulmleigh (18–1) G. Richards (Lord Glanely) T. Hogg
    2. Fair Copy,   **3.** Mid-day Sun.   ½, ¾.   15 ran

1938 Scottish Union (7–1) B. Carslake (Mr J. V. Rank) N. Cannon
    2. Challenge,   **3.** Pasch.   Nk, 4.   9 ran

1939 Abandoned owing to outbreak of war.

AT THIRSK

1940 Turkhan (4–1) G. Richards (H. H. Aga Khan) Frank Butters
    2. Stardust,   **3.** Hippius.   ¾, ¾.   6 ran

AT MANCHESTER

1941 Sun Castle (10–1) G. Bridgland (Lord Portal) C. Boyd-Rochfort
    2. Chateau Larose,   **3.** Dancing Time.   Hd, 1.   16 ran

AT DONCASTER

1942 Sun Chariot (9–4) G. Richards (His Majesty) F. Darling
    2. Watling Street,   **3.** Hyperides.   3, 5.   8 ran

1943 Herringbone (100–6) H. Wragg (Lord Derby) W. Earl
    2. Ribbon,   **3.** Straight Deal.   Sht Hd, $\frac{3}{4}$.   12 ran
1944 Tehran (9–2) G. Richards (H. H. Aga Khan) Frank Butters
    2. Borealis,   **3.** Ocean Swell. $1\frac{1}{2}$, 1.   17 ran

AT YORK

1945 Chamossaire (11–2) T. Lowrey (Sq.-Ldr. S. Joel) R. Perryman
    2. Rising Light,   **3.** Stirling Castle.   2, $\frac{3}{4}$.   10 ran

AT DONCASTER

1946 Airborne (3–1) T. Lowrey (Mr J. E. Ferguson) R. Perryman
    2. Murren,   **3.** Fast and Fair. $1\frac{1}{2}$, 3.   11 ran
1947 Sayajirao (9–2) E. Britt (H. H. Maharaja of Baroda) F. Armstrong
    2. Arbar,   **3.** Migoli.   Hd, 3.   11 ran
1948 Black Tarquin (15–2) E. Britt (Mr W. Woodward) C. Boyd-Rochfort
    2. Alycidon,   **3.** Solar Slipper. $1\frac{1}{2}$, 5.   14 ran
1949 Ridge Wood (100–7) M. Beary (Mr G. R. H. Smith) N. Murless
    2. Dust Devil,   **3.** Lone Eagle.   2, $\frac{3}{4}$.   16 ran
1950 Scratch II (9–2) W. Johnstone (M. M. Boussac) C. H. Semblat (France)
    2. Vieux Manoir,   **3.** Sanlinea.   1, 5.   15 ran
1951 Talma II (7–1) W. Johnstone (M. M. Boussac) C. H. Semblat (France)
    2. Fraise du Bois II,   **3.** Medway.   10, 4.   18 ran
1952 Tulyar (10–11) C. Smirke (H. H. Aga Khan) M. Marsh
    2. Kingsfold,   **3.** Alcinus.   3, 4.   12 ran
1953 Premonition (10–1) E. Smith (Brig. W. P. Wyatt) C. Boyd-Rochfort
    2. Northern Light,   **3.** Aureole.   3, 3.   11 ran
1954 Never Say Die (100–30) C. Smirke (Mr R. S. Clark) J. Lawson
    2. Elopement,   **3.** Estremadur.   12, 4.   16 ran
1955 Meld (10–11) W. Carr (Lady Zia Wernher) C. Boyd-Rochfort
    2. Nucleus,   **3.** Beau Prince. $\frac{3}{4}$, 3.   8 ran
1956 Cambremer (8–1) F. Palmer (Mr R. B. Strassburger) G. Bridgland (France)
    2. Hornbeam,   **3.** French Beige. $\frac{3}{4}$, $1\frac{1}{2}$.   13 ran
1957 BALLYMOSS (8–1) T. P. Burns (£14,575) (J. McShain) M. V. O'Brien
    2. Court Harwell   **3.** Brioche (E. Hide)
        (A. Breasley),   (6–1f),
    4. Tempest,   **5.** Supreme Courage,
    6. Brave Buck.   Extended distances, 1, $\frac{3}{4}$, $1\frac{1}{2}$, 2, Nk.   16 ran
1958 ALCIDE (4–9f) W. Carr (£15,196) (Sir H. de Trafford) C. Boyd-Rochfort
    2. None Nicer (S. Clayton),   **3.** Nagami (J. Mercer),
    4. Restoration,   **5.** Trimmer,
    6. Illinois.   Extended distances, 8, $\frac{3}{4}$, 4, 5, 2.   8 ran
1959 CANTELO (100–7) E. Hide (£28,636) (Wm. Hill) C. Elsey
    2. Fidalgo (J. Mercer),   **3.** Pindari (L. Piggott),
    4. Parthia (8–13f),   **5.** Agricola,
    6. Sheshoon.   Extended distances, $1\frac{1}{2}$, 3, $\frac{3}{4}$, 1, Hd.   11 ran

1960 ST PADDY (4–6f) L. Piggott (£30,379) (Sir Victor Sassoon) N. Murless
   2. Die Hard (G. Bougoure),   **3.** Vienna (T. Gosling),
   4. Oak Ridge,   **5.** Off Key,
   6. Chrysler III.   Extended distances, 3, 1½, Nk, 2, Nk.   9 ran

1961 AURELIUS (9–2) L. Piggott (£29,818) (Mrs V. Lilley) N. Murless
   2. Bounteous (J. Sime),   **3.** Dicta Drake (M. Garcia) (6–4f),
   4. Pardao,   **5.** Sempervivum,
   6. Sovrango.   Extended distances, ¾, ¾, 2, 4, 3.   13 ran

1962 HETHERSETT (100–8) W. Carr (£31,407) (Maj. L. B. Holliday) W. Hern
   2. Monterrico (A. Breasley),   **3.** Miralgo (W. Williamson),
   4. March Wind,   **5.** Sebring,
   6. Larkspur.
       (Antelami 7–2f—11th.) Extended distances, 4, 1, 1½, Nk, ½.   15 ran

1963 RAGUSA (2–5f) G. Bougoure (£32,338) (J. R. Mullion) P. J. Prendergast
   2. Star Moss (E. Smith),   **3.** Fighting Ship (S. Smith),
   4. Merchant Venturer,   **5.** Blueroy,
   6. Moriarty.   Extended distances, 6, Sht Hd, Sht Hd, 3, 2.   7 ran

1964 INDIANA (100–7) J. Lindley (£43,558) (C. W. Engelhard) J. F. Watts
   2. Patti (W. Williamson),   **3.** Soderini (G. Lewis),
   4. I Titan (5–1jf),   **5.** Oncidium,
   6. White Label II (5–1jf).   Extended distances, Hd, 4, Nk, 8, 4.   15 ran

1965 PROVOKE (28–1) J. Mercer (£42,432) (J. J. Astor) W. Hern
   2. Meadow Court   **3.** Solstice (E. Eldin),
      (L. Piggott) (4–11f),
   4. Ballymarais,   **5.** As Before,
   6. Donato.   Extended distances, 10, 5, 6, 2, 15.   11 ran

1966 SODIUM (7–1) F. Durr (£41,178) (R. J. Sigtia) G. Todd
   2. Charlottown   **3.** David Jack (L. Piggott),
      (J. Lindley) (11–10f),
   4. Crisp and Even,   **5.** Hermes,
   6. Pretendre.   Extended distances, Hd, 1½, 2, 4, 2.   9 ran

1967 RIBOCCO (7–2jf) L. Piggott (£42,696) (C. W. Engelhard) R. Houghton
   2. Hopeful Venture   **3.** Ruysdael II (C. Ferrari),
      (G. Moore) (7–2jf),
   4. Dart Board,   **5.** Great Host,
   6. Dominion Day.   Extended distances, 1½, ½, 1½, 10, 4.   9 ran

1968 RIBERO (100–30) L. Piggott (£33,437) (C. W. Engelhard) R. Houghton
   2. Canterbury   **3.** Cold Storage (R. Greenaway),
      (W. Williamson),
   4. Alignment,   **5.** Connaught (10–11f),
   6. Riboccare.   Extended distances, Sht Hd, 6, 2, 8, 2.   8 ran

Section Two: Two-Year-Old Events

Race 6: BROCKLESBY PLATE

5 furlongs. Doncaster. Two-year-olds. Run at Lincoln until 1965.

1957 Offspring (5–1) W. Snaith (£446) H. Cottrill
    2. Baiser,   **3.** Argosy Royal.   ¾, 2.   15 ran
1958 Plaudit (13–8f) S. Clayton (£429) W. Hern
    2. Grey Marsh,   **3.** Chantha.   3, 3.   12 ran
1959 Near Naples (100–6) E. Britt (£703) C. Elsey
    2. Amstel,   **3.** Chatellerault.   2, Hd.   10 ran
1960 Indian Lad (7–4f) E. Smith (£747) T. Leader
    2. Rover,   **3.** Coralinda.   ¾, 6.   15 ran
1961 Dipper (11–8f) E. Larkin (£724) J. Jarvis
    2. Quince,   **3.** Millibar.   6, ½.   14 ran
1962 Siren (7–2jf) D. Smith (£642) G. Brooke
    2. Matatina,   **3.** Star Whistler.   Hd, 3.   16 ran
1963 Colony (4–1) D. Ryan (£642) W. Stephenson
    2. Brooky,   **3.** Hazy.   1½, Nk.   17 ran
1964 Grey Wave (20–1) B. Taylor (£841) H. Leader
    2. Pugnacity,   **3.** Rothesay.   1½, 3.   23 ran
1965 America (100–7) E. Hide (£690) W. Elsey
    2. Madras,   **3.** Shylock.   3, 4.   19 ran
1966 Palasrullah (7–4f) B. Raymond (£690) H. Cottrill
    2. Royalty Cash,   **3.** Metropolita.   3, 1½.   16 ran
1967 Chebs Lad (5–1) B. Connorton (£690) W. Gray
    2. Ormolu II,   **3.** Heathtolt.   4, 3.   9 ran
1968 Merry Hell (11–8f) J. Wilson (£690) B. Swift
    2. Port Soderick,   **3.** Maystreak.   6, 3.   12 ran

Race 7: WOODCOTE STAKES

6 furlongs. Epsom. Two-year-olds. First run 1807

1900 Toddington	(6)	**1905** Serenata	(7)	**1910** Seaforth	(13)
1901 Sceptre	(11)	**1906** Traquair	(10)	**1911** White Star	(8)
1902 Rock Sand	(11)	**1907** White Eagle	(11)	**1912** Shogun	(8)
1903 Merryman	(5)	**1908** Perola	(12)	**1913** The Tetrarch	(11)
1904 Cicero	(13)	**1909** Varco	(8)	**1914** Cattistock	(8)

1915–18 No race		1932 Montrose	(11)	[AT EPSOM]	
1919 Poltava	(4)	1933 The Old		1946 Bhishma	(6)
1920 Humorist	(11)	Pretender	(6)	1947 Lerins (renamed	
1921 Reecho	(8)	1934 Bagman	(7)	My Babu)	(6)
1922 Duncan Gray	(9)	1935 Lady Abbess f.	(7)	1948 River Tay	(9)
1923 Tippler	(11)	1936 Hartington	(7)	1949 Full Dress	(8)
1924 Iron Mask	(11)	1937 Caerloptic	(12)	1950 Crocodile	(8)
1925 Jessel	(7)	1938 Quarteroon	(10)	1951 Fairforall	(9)
1926 Birthright	(13)	1939 Tant Mieux	(8)	1952 Candaules	(8)
1927 Rose Willow c.	(7)	1940 No race		1953 Blue Prince II	(11)
1928 Osiris	(8)			1954 Royal Palm	(12)
1929 Lady Abbess	(8)	[AT NEWBURY]		1955 Idle Rocks	(9)
1930 Arthos	(11)	1941 Ujiji	(14)	1956 Mansbridge	(7)
1931 Dastur	(9)	1942–45 No race			

1957 Mr Snake (11–10f) W. Carr (£2,053) C. Boyd-Rochfort
    2. After Twelve,   3. Welsh Rake. $\frac{1}{2}$, 5.   3 ran

1958 Loyal Lady (7–4) J. Longden (£2,002) T. H. Carey
    2. Tylers Hill,   3. Caliph.   2, 3.   5 ran

1959 Tulyartos (5–2f) J. Eddery (£2,278) S. McGrath
    2. Primary,   3. Koppernik.   5, 5.   11 ran

1960 Morning Star (100–8) D. Smith (£2,172) G. Brooke
    2. New Blood,   3. First Sea Lord.   Nk, 2.   8 ran

1961 Xerxes (13–2) D. Smith (£2,635) G. Brooke
    2. River Chanter,   3. Zurina.   5, 4.   9 ran

1962 Tierra del Fuego (10–1) W. Carr (£2,690) H. L. Cottrill
    2. Zaleucus,   3. Campaign.   Hd, $\frac{3}{4}$.   9 ran

1963 Gentle Art (1–7f) R. Hutchinson (£2,630) J. Jarvis
    2. Kings Petition,   3. Prince Pan.   3, $1\frac{1}{2}$.   4 ran

1964 Presto (100–8) J. Mercer (£2,828) P. Ashworth
    2. Call of the Wild,   3. Warrior Prince.   3, $1\frac{1}{2}$.   8 ran

1965 Visp (11–8f) J. Lindley (£1,479) J. F. Watts
    2. Running Words,   3. Warsite.   3, 1.   6 ran

1966 Bunratty Castle (5–4f) R. Hutchinson (£1,180) J. Dunlop
    2. Hand in Hand,   3. Paddy Boy. $\frac{1}{2}$, $\frac{3}{4}$.   5 ran

1967 Last Shoe (7–2) J. Wilson (£1,559) B. Swift
    2. Arctic Jelly,   3. My Horace .   Nk, 3.   10 ran

1968 Silverware (4–7f) L. Piggott (£1,663) R. Houghton
    2. Dutch Bells,   3. Knotty Pine.   Hd, 2.   6 ran

Race 8: LONSDALE STAKES

5 furlongs. Epsom. Two-year-olds. Run over 6 furlongs until 1960

1957 MAJOR PORTION (7–2) E. Smith (£4,149) T. Leader
    2. Paresa,   3. Kinglike.   2, 2.   6 ran

1958 Dominate (7–2) D. Smith (£4,060) J. F. Watts
    2. Ink Spot,   **3.** Never Say No.   Nk, 1½.   14 ran
1959 Mozart (15–2) E. Hide (£4,721) C. Elsey
    2. Avon's Pride,   **3.** Royal Heiress.   Nk, 5.   7 ran
1960 Flyover (4–7f) A. Breasley (£2,019) W. Smyth
    2. Who's Caprice,   **3.** Vanita.   Hd, 4.   6 ran
1961 Nerissa (4–6f) D. Smith (£1,836) G. Brooke
    2. Coogee,   **3.** Island Lore.   4, 1½.   5 ran
1962 Golden Plume (8–13f) A. Breasley (£1,644) G. Smyth
    2. Double Handful,   **3.** White Rajah.   Nk, 4.   5 ran
1963 Welford Lad (33–1) F. Durr (£1,695) R. Mason
    2. Persian Lamb,   **3.** Golden Hind.   Hd, Sht Hd.   6 ran
1964 Sweet Sovereign (5–2jf) R. Hutchinson (£1,810) J. Jarvis
    2. Night Signal,   **3.** Caruso.   2, 3.   5 ran
1965 Kibenka (100–9) R. P. Elliott (£814) T. Corbett
    2. Sky Gipsy,   **3.** Timarum.   Hd, 4.   9 ran
1966 Flying By (2–1) R. Hutchinson (£844) G. Smyth
    2. Alamo City,   **3.** Nikimas.   6, 2.   10 ran
1967 Porto Bello (1–2f) G. Lewis (£817) S. Ingham
    2. Rift,   **3.** Spin Out.   Nk, 8.   7 ran
1968 Lady's View (5–6f) D. Keith (£1,586) P. Ashworth
    2. Art Nouveau,   **3.** David's Boy.   4, Sht Hd.   4 ran

Race 9: ACORN STAKES

5 furlongs. Epsom. Two-year-old fillies

1957 Ruthin (7–2) J. Egan (£2,176) J. Jarvis
    2. Light Fantastic,   **3.** Cloth of Gold.   4, ¾.   5 ran
1958 Sans Souci (6–1) E. Mercer (£2,465) D. Whelan
    2. Morin,   **3.** Catherine.   1, 5.   5 ran
1959 Morgat (2–1f) E. Mercer (£2,410) J. Jarvis
    2. Princess Nuri,   **3.** Nova Gail.   2, 2.   7 ran
1960 Kerrabee (11–2) A. Breasley (£2,665) S. Ingham
    2. Close Up,   **3.** Sunspeck.   3, 1.   5 ran
1961 Rosaura (100–8) A. Breasley (£2,333) N. Bertie
    2. Pillar of Fire,   **3.** Get There.   1, Sht Hd.   7 ran
1962 Gallop On (6–4f) J. Mercer (£1,666) W. Hern
    2. Faerie Ring,   **3.** Veejlee.   2, 1.   6 ran
1963 Flattering (5–6f) A. Breasley (£1,694) S. Ingham
    2. Gaska,   **3.** Clean Verdict.   3, 5.   8 ran
1964 Welsh Mistress (11–2) A. Breasley (£1,703) S. Ingham
    2. Hasty Cast,   **3.** Toffee Nose and
                            3. Welsh Reine.   2, Nk.   8 ran
1965 Kew (100–30f) L. Piggott (£880) F. Armstrong
    2. Impeached,   **3.** America.   3, Nk.   11 ran

1966 Cantadora (15–2) R. Maddock (£865) D. Thom
    2. Scottish Mary,   **3.** First Date.   1, Sht Hd.   9 ran
1967 Canteen (4–5f) M. Thomas (£1,614) G. Barling
    2. Idle Dreams,   **3.** Silvia.   Sht Hd, 2½.   7 ran
1968 Folle Rousse (evens jf) R. Hutchinson (£1,586) J. Winter
    2. Mistress Sophie,   **3.** Margera.   1½, 15.   3 ran

Race 10: COVENTRY STAKES

6 furlongs. Royal Ascot. Two-year-olds. First run 1890

[5 FURLONGS]		1923	Knight of the		[AT NEWMARKET]	
1900	Good Morning (11)		Garter	(10)	1941 Big Game	(5)
1901	Sterling Balm (14)	1924	Iceberg	(9)	1942 Nasrullah	(7)
1902	Rock Sand (13)	1925	Colorada	(11)	1943 Orestes	(11)
1903	St Amant (13)	1926	Knight of the		1944 Dante	(6)
1904	Cicero (7)		Grail	(9)		
1905	Black Arrow (9)	1927	Fairway	(20)	[AT ROYAL ASCOT]	
1906	Traquair (7)	1928	Reflector	(14)	1945 Khaled	(8)
1907	Prospector (11)	1929	Diolite	(12)	1946 Tudor Minstrel	(6)
1908	Louviers (11)	1930	Lemnarchus	(12)	1947 The Cobbler	(12)
1909	Admiral Hawke (18)	1931	Cockpen	(8)	1948 Royal Forest	(14)
1910	Radiancy (18)	1932	Manitoba	(12)	1949 Palestine	(12)
1911	Lady Americus (10)	1933	Medieval Knight (9)		1950 Big Dipper	(11)
1912	Shogun (10)	1934	Mairan	(9)	1951 King's Bench	(11)
1913	The Tetrarch (8)	1935	Black Speck	(11)	1952 Whistler	(7)
1914	Lady Josephine (7)	1936	Early School	(18)	1953 The Pie King	(12)
1915–18	No race	1937	Mirza II	(11)	1954 Noble Chieftain	(8)
1919	Sarchedon (8)	1938	Panorama	(12)	[6 FURLONGS]	
1920	Milesius (13)	1939	Turkhan	(16)	1955 Ratification	(7)
1921	Pondoland (15)	1940	No race		1956 Messmate	(17)
1922	Drake (16)					

1957 Amerigo (7–4f) E. Smith (£2,436) J. A. Waugh
    2. Trimmer,   **3.** Ballyrullah.   8, 5.   10 ran
1958 Hieroglyph (10–1) W. Carr (£2,674) C. Boyd-Rochfort
    2. TABOUN,   **3.** New Warrior.   1, 2.   14 ran
1959 MARTIAL (11–10f) W. Swinburn (£2,382) P. J. Prendergast
    2. Blast,   **3.** RUNNING BLUE. Sht Hd, 4.   13 ran
1960 Typhoon (evens f) R. Hutchinson (£2,484) P. J. Prendergast
    2. Blue Sails,   **3.** Bold Lover.   1, 5.   9 ran
1961 Xerxes (9–2) D. Smith (£2,556) G. Brooke
    2. Torero,   **3.** Court Sentence.   1½, 3.   17 ran
1962 Crocket (9–4f) D. Smith (£2,480) G. Brooke
    2. Happy Omen,   **3.** King's Case.   5, 4.   14 ran
1963 Showdown (6–1) D. Smith (£4,060) F. Winter
    2. Travel Man,   **3.** Piccadilly.   3, 1.   12 ran

1964 SILLY SEASON (13–2) G. Lewis (£3,388) I. Balding
    2. Barrymore,   **3.** Sandro.   Hd, 3.   19 ran
1965 Young Emperor (9–4f) L. Piggott (£5,969) P. J. Prendergast
    2. At-A-Venture,   **3.** Bull Dancer.   6, 1½.   13 ran
1966 Bold Lad (4–6f) D. Lake (£6,020) P. J. Prendergast
    2. Donated,   **3.** Bosworth Field.   4, ½.   16 ran
1967 Mark Royal (13–2) A. Breasley (£4,596) P. Norris
    2. Star and Garter,   **3.** Storm Bird.   Nk, 1½.   16 ran
1968 Murrayfield (15–2) G. Lewis (£4,757) I. Balding
    2. Royal Smoke,   **3.** Whistling Top.   1½, ¾.   16 ran

Race 11: QUEEN MARY STAKES
5 furlongs. Royal Ascot. Two-year-old fillies

1935 Fair Ranee	(20)	**1945** Rivaz	(5)	**1951** Primavera	(20)
1936 Night Song	(35)	**1946** Apparition	(14)	**1952** Devon Vintage	(23)
1937 Queen of Simla	(31)	**1947** Masaka	(18)	**1953** Sybil's Niece	(24)
1938 Belle Travers	(29)	**1948** Coronation V	(28)	**1954** Bride Elect	(16)
1939 Snowberry	(28)	**1949** Diableretta	(18)	**1955** Weeber	(16)
1940–44 No race		**1950** Rose Linnet	(16)	**1956** Pharsalia	(19)

1957 Abelia (11–2) L. Piggott (£3,558) N. Murless
    2. Patroness,   **3.** Liberal Lady.   2, 2.   14 ran
1958 A.20 (5–1f) W. Rickaby (£3,618) F. Sutherland
    2. ROSE OF MEDINA,   **3.** Pale Sapphire.   Hd, ½.   23 ran
1959 Paddy's Sister (15–8f) G. Moore (£2,875) P. J. Prendergast
    2. Queensberry,   **3.** Queen of the   2, 5.   21 ran
                                      Roses.
1960 Cynara (evens f) W. Carr (£3,058) H. Wragg
    2. Crisper,   **3.** SWEET   5, 1.   17 ran
                                        SOLERA.
1961 My Dream (2–1) D. Smith (£2,922) G. Brooke
    2. Gay Mairi,   **3.** Silken Glade.   3, 4.   11 ran
1962 Shot Silk (100–8) D. Smith (£2,820) G. Brooke
    2. Hera,   **3.** Guinea Sparrow.   3, 2.   14 ran
1963 Lerida (9–2) J. Lindley (£4,617) J. A. Waugh
    2. High Powered,   **3.** St Cecilia.   2, 6.   15 ran
1964 Brassia (7–2) J. Purtell (£3,571) M. V. O'Brien
    2. Wind Song,   **3.** Toffee Nose.   3, 1½.   17 ran
1965 Visp (6–4f) J. Lindley (£5,927) J. F. Watts
    2. Procession,   **3.** Loyalty.   ½, 2.   10 ran
1966 Petite Path (33–1) J. Lindley (£5,740) R. Mason
    2. Broadway Melody,   **3.** Floosie.   Sht Hd, 2½.   13 ran
1967 SOVEREIGN (10–11f) R. Hutchinson (£4,442) H. Wragg
    2. Cease Fire,   **3.** Sing Again.   5, 1.   12 ran
1968 Grizel (5–2f) W. Williamson (£4,616) P. J. Prendergast
    2. Stung,   **3.** Carsina.   Hd, 4.   13 ran

Race 12: NEW STAKES

5 furlongs. Royal Ascot. Two-year-olds. First run 1843

1900 Bay Melton (11)	**1920** Alan Breck (16)	**1938** Meadow (22)
1901 Duke of	**1921** Scamp (11)	**1939** Tant Mieux (13)
Westminster (10)	**1922** Town Guard (11)	**1940–45** No race
1902 Sermon (13)	**1923** Druids Orb (14)	**1946** Petition (10)
1903 Montem (14)	**1924** Black Friar (15)	**1947** Lerins (renamed
1904 Llangibby (9)	**1925** Buckler (12)	My Babu)
1905 Colonia (7)	**1926** Damon (19)	and Delirium (12)
1906 Slieve Gallion (9)	**1927** Hakim (16)	**1948** Makarpura (22)
1907 Sir Archibald (16)	**1928** Mr Jinks (18)	**1949** Master Gunner (12)
1908 Bayardo (13)	**1929** Blenheim (17)	**1950** Bay Meadows (10)
1909 Lemberg (12)	**1930** Lightning Star (19)	**1951** Bob Major (10)
1910 Seaforth (16)	**1931** Spenser (17)	**1952** Blue Lamp (14)
1911 Lomond (12)	**1932** Hyperion (22)	**1953** Hydrologist (14)
1912 Craganour (15)	**1933** Colombo (17)	**1954** Tamerlane (9)
1913 Hapsburg (17)	**1934** Eppie Adair c. (21)	**1955** Gratitude (7)
1914 Let Fly (15)	**1935** Bossover c. (18)	**1956** Skindles Hotel (15)
1915–18 No race	**1936** Le Grand Duc (19)	
1919 Orpheus (7)	**1937** Ramtapa (18)	

1957 PALL MALL (6–1) W. Carr (£2,589) C. Boyd-Rochfort
    2. Troubadour,   **3.** Will Somers.   1, 2.   8 ran

1958 MASHAM (8–1) D. Smith (£2,547) G. Brooke
    2. Galivanter,   **3.** Spithead.   1½, Hd.   8 ran

1959 Sound Track (1–5f) G. Lewis (£2,361) W. Smyth
    2. Godiva's Pink Flower,   **3.** Golden Merle.   1½, 3.   5 ran

1960 Floribunda (2–7f) R. Hutchinson (£2,403) P. J. Prendergast
    2. Praise,   **3.** Foxstar.   8, Hd.   7 ran

1961 ABERMAID (3–1jf) L. Piggott (£2,420) H. Wragg
    2. Princely Strath,   **3.** Golden   Hd, 3.   13 ran
                             Sovereign.

1962 Daybreak (13–8f) R. Hutchinson (£2,280) J. Jarvis
    2. Romantic,   **3.** Tierra del Fuego.   Sht Hd, 5.   10 ran

1963 Ballymacad (9–4) R. Hutchinson (£3,499) G. Smyth
    2. Dark Sovereign,   **3.** Blue Marine.   1, 2.   8 ran

1964 Abandoned

1965 Tin King (4–7f) L. Piggott (£5,400) R. Houghton
    2. Track Spare,   **3.** Village Cross.   ½, 6.   8 ran

1966 Falcon (11–8f) L. Piggott (£5,204) R. Houghton
    2. Wolver Hollow,   **3.** Above Water.   4, Hd.   8 ran

1967 Porto Bello (7–4) G. Lewis (£4,054) S. Ingham
    2. Sovereign Service,   **3.** Whiz.   2½, 1.   4 ran

1968 Song (8–1) J. Mercer (£4,335) D. Candy
    2. Lord John,   **3.** Silverware.   Sht Hd, 2½.   12 ran

Race 13: CHESHAM STAKES

6 furlongs. Royal Ascot. Two-year-olds. Run over 5 furlongs until 1963

1957 MAJOR PORTION (11–10f) E. Smith (£3, 486) T. Leader
    2. Procedure,   **3.** Lynch Law.   Hd. 5.   10 ran
1958 Tudor Melody (4–5f) E. Hide (£3,805) R. Peacock
    2. Gail Prince,   **3.** Connaissance.   5, 1½.   11 ran
1959 Newbus (5–1) E. Britt (£1,630) C. Elsey
    2. Beau Court,   **3.** No Saint.   ½, 1½.   6 ran
1960 New Move (4–6f) L. Piggott (£1,698) P. Walwyn
    2. Marche d'Or,   **3.** Rain Coat.   3, ¾.   9 ran
1961 Kathyanga (13–8f) R. Hutchinson (£1,651) P. J. Prendergast
    2. Tacitus,   **3.** Sudden Thought.   1, 5.   7 ran
1962 Narrow Escape (9–4f) J. Mercer (£1,625) W. Hern
    2. Visualise,   **3.** Ampney Princess.   3, 3.   9 ran
1963 Mesopotamia (6–4f) P. Boothman (£2,245) R. Fetherstonhaugh
    2. Zodiac,   **3.** Frigolet.   10, ¾.   12 ran
1964 Abandoned
1965 Swift Harmony (6–1) L. Piggott (£2,200) E. Reavey
    2. Guano,   **3.** Maldavan.   Hd, ¾.   19 ran
1966 Hambleden (10–11f) A. Breasley (£2,139) T. Corbett
    2. Catterline,   **3.** Hand in Hand.   Nk, Hd.   11 ran
1967 Riboccare (7–1) J. Lindley (£1,836) J. Tree
    2. Czar Alexander,   **3.** Laudamus.   Nk, 2½.   8 ran
1968 Ribofilio (7–2) L. Piggott (£2,020) R. Houghton
    2. Timon,   **3.** Pindarique.   1, 2½.   11 ran

Race 14: WINDSOR CASTLE STAKES

5 furlongs. Royal Ascot. Two-year-olds

1957 Rich and Rare (11–10f) E. Mercer (£1,850) J. Jarvis
    2. Tom Pom,   **3.** Budge Blue.   3, 2.   6 ran
1958 CARNOUSTIE (25–1) L. Piggott (£2,071) N. Murless
    2. Greek Sovereign,   **3.** Edwalton Boy.   ½, 8.   15 ran
1959 Monamolin (6–1) E. Cracknell (£1,961) F. Walwyn
    2. Tywydd Teg,   **3.** Nice Guy.   ½, 2.   8 ran
1960 Skymaster (100–8) A. Breasley (£1,940) W. Smyth
    2. Coney Island,   **3.** Palatina.   Nk, Nk,   15 ran
1961 Prince Tor (13–8f) G. Lewis (£1,919) R. N. Fetherstonhaugh
    2. Polly Toogood,   **3.** Bow Tie.   2, ½.   14 ran
1962 Summer Day (1–2f) E. Smith (£1,885) J. A. Waugh
    2. Queen's Hussar,   **3.** Vijay.   2, ½.   5 ran
1963 Goldhill (6–4f) J. Etherington (£1,944) M. H. Easterby
    2. Quentin,   **3.** Gainstrive.   2, 3.   6 ran

1964 Abandoned
1965 Sky Gipsy (8–1) R. Hutchinson (£1,915) G. Smyth
      2. Impeached,   **3.** Blue Streak.   3, Hd.   17 ran
1966 On Your Mark (9–4f) L. Piggott (£1,862) F. Armstrong
      2. Night Patrol,   **3.** My Enigma.   6, ¾.   10 ran
1967 D'Urberville (100–9) J. Lindley (£1,665) J. Tree
      2. Stop Thief,   **3.** Canteen.   2½, Sht Hd.   12 ran
1968 Hopiana (5–1) A. Barclay (£1,728) A. Budgett
      2. Burglar,   **3.** Mistral.   1, 5.   9 ran

Race 15: CURRAGH STAKES

5 furlongs. Curragh. Two-year-olds. Called Curragh Foal Stakes until 1959

1957 Golden Game (1–3f) T. M. Burns (£1,256) P. J. Prendergast
      2. Lady Arctic,   **3.** Rusheen.   6, 2.   5 ran
1958 His Legend (5–2f) D. Page (£1,134) S. H. Nugent
      2. Andromeda Nebula,   **3.** Lawrence.   3, Nk.   13 ran
1959 Hobson (6–1) N. Brennan (£1,115) H. V. S. Murless
      2. Diamonds Galore,   **3.** Foreign Account. 1½, 3.   9 ran
1960 Dorney Common (6–1) P. Powell jn. (£1,238) T. D. Ainsworth
      2. Loquacious,   **3.** Tuna Gail.   Hd, Nk.   10 ran
1961 Golden Sovereign (8–11f) G. Bougoure (£1,260) A. S. O'Brien
      2. Warwick,   **3.** Hardy Annual.   Nk, 1½.   7 ran
1962 Majority Rule (4–6f) T. P. Glennon (£1,469) M. Connolly
      2. Tarqogan,   **3.** Migologan.   2, 1½.   5 ran
1963 Blue Marine (6–4f) G. Bougoure (£1,535) P. J. Prendergast
      2. Sayitagain,   **3.** Jet Age.   Nk, 2.   9 ran
1964 Adriatic Star (100–7) J. Roe (£1,633) S. McGrath
      2. Twelve Oaks,   **3.** Royal Garden.   Nk, Nk.   8 ran
1965 Lady Matador (100–6) T. Murphy (£839) C. Magnier
      2. Red Spice,   **3.** Irish Guard.   Nk, 3.   9 ran
1966 Jadeite (4–6f) M. Kennedy (£1,563) J. M. Rogers
      2. Royal Scot,   **3.** Ranunculus.   8, 2.   7 ran
1967 Sorrentina (9–2) P. Powell jun. (£1,531) M. Hurley
      2. Polar Gold,   **3.** Bonda.   2, 1½.   8 ran
1968 Soho Lad (3–1jf) W. Williamson (£1,489) M. Connolly
      2. Marcia Royal,   **3.** Shortcastle.   Hd, Nk.   7 ran

Race 16: JULY STAKES

6 furlongs. Newmarket. Two-year-olds. Run over 5 furlongs until 1961. First run 1786

1900	Doricles and		**1918**	Buchan	(3)	**1938**	Prometheus	(4)
	Veles	(7)	**1919**	Sarchedon	(4)	**1939**	Rose of	
1901	Sceptre	(7)	**1920**	Monarch	(6)		England c.	(5)
1902	Hammerkop	(9)	**1921**	Lembach	(5)	**1940**	No race	
1903	Montem	(8)	**1922**	Legality	(7)	**1941**	Ujiji	(5)
1904	Cicero	(5)	**1923**	Diophon	(12)	**1942–44**	No race	
1905	Gorgos	(7)	**1924**	Runnymede	(11)	**1945**	Rivaz	(3)
1906	Traquair	(3)	**1925**	Apple Sammy	(6)	**1946**	Miss Stripes	(7)
1907	Pearl of the		**1926**	The Satrap	(7)	**1947**	Masaka	(9)
	Loch	(13)	**1927**	Fairway	(9)	**1948**	Nimbus	(7)
1908	Battleaxe	(5)	**1928**	Mr Jinks	(5)	**1949**	Diableretta	(2)
1909	Prince Rupert	(12)	**1929**	Teacup	(4)	**1950**	Big Dipper	(4)
1910	St Anton	(7)	**1930**	Four Course	(6)	**1951**	Bob Major	(6)
1911	White Star	(11)	**1931**	Riot	(6)	**1952**	Empire Honey	(5)
1912	Rock Flint	(10)	**1932**	Colorow	(6)	**1953**	Darius	(3)
1913	Ambassador	(11)	**1933**	Alishah	(3)	**1954**	Tamerlane	(9)
1914	Rose Land	(4)	**1934**	Hilla	(2)	**1955**	Edmundo	(8)
1915	Figaro	(12)	**1935**	Daytona	(6)	**1956**	Earl Marshal	(5)
1916	Grand Fleet	(6)	**1936**	Foray	(7)			
1917	Abandoned		**1937**	Mirza II	(4)			

1957 Abelia (1–2f) L. Piggott (£2,086) N. Murless
    2. PALL MALL,   3. Lavandier.   ¾, 3.   4 ran
1958 Greek Sovereign (11–4) A. Breasley (£1,413) R. Read
    2. Captain Kidd,   3. Galivanter.   1, ¾.   4 ran
1959 Sound Track (2–5f) W. Rickaby (£1,501) W. Smyth
    2. Monet.   ¾.   2 ran
1960 Favorita (100–30) L. Piggott (£1,549) N. Murless
    2. Praise,   3. Kathy Too.   1½, 3.   6 ran
1961 Burning Thoughts (3–1) W. Carr (£2,704) W. Hern
    2. Cyrus,   3. Torero.   Hd, 4.   6 ran
1962 Romantic (4–11f) A. Breasley (£2,526) N. Murless
    2. Tudor Grey,   3. Golden Inca.   3, Hd.   5 ran
1963 Endless Honey (100–8) R. Hutchinson (£2,657) J. Jarvis
    2. Bivouac,   3. London Melody.   1, Hd.   5 ran
1964 Ragtime (7–2) R. Hutchinson (£2,027) G. Smyth
    2. Palm Way,   3. Dunlin.   ¾, Sht Hd.   10 ran
1965 Sky Gipsy (11–8f) R. Hutchinson (£1,487) G. Smyth
    2. Tin King,   3. Kibenka.   Nk, 3.   5 ran
1966 Golden Horus (2–1) L. Piggott (£1,472) W. O'Gorman
    2. Manacle,   3. Gay Glory.   Hd, 4.   3 ran
1967 Lorenzaccio (5–1) G. Moore (£1,201) N. Murless
    2. Last Shoe,   3. Whiz.   2, 3.   5 ran

1968 Burglar (4–7f) R. Hutchinson (£1,222) J. Dunlop
    2. Welsh Pageant,   **3.** Grey Portal.   2, 5.   6 ran

Race 17: CHERRY HINTON STAKES

6 furlongs. Newmarket. Two-year-old fillies

1957 Munch (8–13f) D. Smith (£1,512) R. Jarvis
    2. Bromelia,   **3.** ALPINE   6, Nk.   8 ran
                                     BLOOM.
1958 Fan Light (2–5f) E. Mercer (£1,594) G. Colling
    2. Grecian Urn II,   **3.** Margaret Ann.   2, 6.   4 ran
1959 Panga (4–7f) E. Smith (£1,590) B. van Cutsem
    2. Rave,   **3.** Galloping Shoe.   6, 1½.   8 ran
1960 SWEET SOLERA (4–5f) W. Rickaby (£1,788) R. Day
    2. Palatina,   **3.** Secret Session.   5, 1½.   10 ran
1961 Crepello's Daughter (3–1) E. Larkin (£1,494) J. Jarvis
    2. Joyful Scene,   **3.** Rustana.   ½, 2.   5 ran
1962 Tzigane (13–8f) A. Breasley (£2,551) Sir G. Richards
    2. Guinea Sparrow,   **3.** Gallop On.   1, 6.   7 ran
1963 Round Trip (5–1) W. Williamson (£2,747) H. Wragg
    2. Royal Justice,   **3.** Fine Feathers.   5, 2.   8 ran
1964 Greengage (9–2) A Breasley (£1,519) Sir G. Richards
    2. RUBY'S PRINCESS,   **3.** Valdesta.   2, Hd.   10 ran
1965 Chrona (7–1) A. Breasley (£861) R. Houghton
    2. Impeached,   **3.** Lunar Princess.   Hd, Sht Hd.   10 ran
1966 PIA (8–1) E. Hide (£1,495) W. Elsey
    2. ST PAULI GIRL,   **3.** Aiguillette.   ½, 2.   9 ran
1967 Cease Fire (4–7f) B. Taylor (£1,161) H. Leader
    2. Ash Lawn,   **3.** Quinita.   5, ½.   4 ran
1968 Symona (2–1f) G. Starkey (£1,266) H. Leader
    2. Lovely Light,   **3.** Hot Penny.   1, Nk.   6 ran

Race 18: NATIONAL STAKES

5 furlongs. Sandown. Two-year-olds. First run 1889.
Called the National Breeders' Produce Stakes until 1960

1900 Star Shoot and		**1906** Traquair	(13)	**1913** The Tetrarch	(9)
Ian	(15)	**1907** White Eagle	(9)	**1914** Redfern	(15)
1901 Game Chick	(13)	**1908** Bayardo	(14)	**1915–18** No race	
1902 Rabelais	(9)	**1909** Neil Gow	(17)	**1919** Tetratema	(13)
1903 Pretty Polly	(11)	**1910** Cellini ·	(18)	**1920** Polly Flinders	(4)
1904 Cicero	(8)	**1911** Mountain Mint	(19)	**1921** Polyhistor	(10)
1905 Sarcelle	(8)	**1912** Prue	(13)	**1922** Town Guard	(7)

1923 Mumtaz Mahal (6)	1934 Bahram (10)	[AT SANDOWN]			
1924 Garden of Allah (12)	1935 Wyndham (13)	1947 The Cobbler	(5)		
1925 Kate Coventry (12)	1936 Full Sail (17)	1948 Abernant	(5)		
1926 Priscilla (13)	1937 Portmarnock (12)	1949 Palestine	(3)		
1927 Flamingo (21)	1938 Rogerstone	1950 Belle of All	(9)		
1928 Tiffin (13)	Castle (14)	1951 Constantia	(11)		
1929 Queen of the	1939 Stardust (8)	1952 Bebe Grande	(5)		
Nore (8)	1940–45 No race	1953 Tudor Honey	(6)		
1930 Thyestes (15)		1954 Courageous	(12)		
1931 Orwell (12)	[AT ASCOT]	1955 Rustam	(11)		
1932 Myrobella (13)	1946 Tudor Minstrel (7)	1956 Military Law	(11)		
1933 Colombo (10)					

1957 Promulgation (8–1) E. Smith (£6,540) T. Leader
    2. Trimmer,   3. Amerigo.   Sht Hd, 3   7 ran
1958 Captain Kidd (7–1) E. Mercer (£6,623) J. Jarvis
    2. Ink Spot,   3. British Empire.   2, 1.   14 ran
1959 Sing Sing (11–4f) D. Smith (£7,259) J. F. Watts
    2. Red Gauntlet,   3. Lombard. $1\frac{1}{2}$, 3.   9 ran
1960 Kerrabee (6–1) A. Breasley (£5,407) S. Ingham
    2. Crisper,   3. Panastar. $\frac{3}{4}$, 2.   10 ran
1961 DISPLAY (6–5f) R. Hutchinson (£4,788) P. J. Prendergast
    2. Lima,   3. My Dream.   6, 2.   7 ran
1962 Whistling Wind (8–13f) G. Bougoure (£5,961) P. J. Prendergast
    2. Dunce Cap,   3. Nun Neater.   4, $\frac{3}{4}$.   5 ran
1963 POURPARLER (3–1f) G. Bougoure (£5,748) P. J. Prendergast
    2. Derring-Do,   3. Gentle Art.   Nk, 3.   10 ran
1964 Double Jump (evens f) J. Lindley (£6,121) J. Tree
    2. Caruso,   3. Milesius.   3, $1\frac{1}{2}$.   4 ran
1965 Zahedan (11–8f) L. Piggott (£8,057) N. Murless
    2. Lad's Love,   3. Miss Togs.   4, $1\frac{1}{2}$.   11 ran
1966 Falcon (8–13f) L. Piggott (£6,951) R. Houghton
    2. Majetta,   3. Floosie.   5, $\frac{3}{4}$.   6 ran
1967 SOVEREIGN (8–11f) R. Hutchinson (£6,097) H. Wragg
    2. Porto Bello,   3. How Far.   5, 3.   4 ran
1968 Tower Walk (7–4) M. Thomas (£6,680) G. Barling
    2. Red Rose Prince and   2. Silverware. $2\frac{1}{2}$, Dd Ht.   8 ran

Race 19: HYPERION STAKES

6 furlongs. Ascot. Two-year-olds

1961 Blaze of Glory II (9–1) R. Poincelet (£1,794) E. Pollet (France) and
    Alpine Scent (7–2) E. Larkin (£1,794) J. Jarvis
    3. Poet and Peasant.   Dd Ht, 3.   8 ran
1962 Top of the Milk (9–1) D. Smith (£3,285) G. Brooke
    2. King's Favourite,   3. Vertigo.   6, $\frac{3}{4}$.   7 ran

1963 Talahasse (2–1) A. Breasley (£2,941) T. Corbett
    2. Mesopotamia,   **3.** Ombrello. $1\frac{1}{2}$, 15.   4 ran
1964 Pugnacity (7–1) J. Mercer (£3,106) W. Wharton
    2. Potier,   **3.** RUBY'S   1, 2.   5 ran
                            PRINCESS.
1965 Auskerry (2–1) R. Hutchinson (£3,040) J. Jarvis
    2. Kibenka ,   **3.** Water Diviner. $2\frac{1}{2}$, 2.   6 ran
1966 Tordo (8–13f) L. Piggott (£2,897) M. V. O'Brien
    2. Bunratty Castle,   **3.** Bosworth Field. $1\frac{1}{2}$, 6.   5 ran
1967 Chebs Lad (1–2f) B. Connorton (£2,460) W. Gray
    2. Pari-Passu,   **3.** Scipio. $1\frac{1}{2}$, $\frac{1}{2}$.   4 ran
1968 Hill Run (11–2) A. Barclay (£2,562) N. Murless
    2. French Tutor,   **3.** Carsina.   1, Sht Hd.   5 ran

Race 20: PRINCESS MARGARET STAKES

6 furlongs. Ascot. Two-year-olds. Run over 5 furlongs until 1962

1957 Medina (6–5f) A. Breasley (£895) S. Ingham
    2. Quaver,   **3.** Pebble Ridge.   Sht Hd, Hd.   7 ran
1958 Parrotia (8–15f) L. Piggott (£993) N. Murless
    2. Tana Dante,   **3.** Golden Rain.   3, 6.   4 ran
1959 Lady Advocate (7–2) G. Lewis (£1,469) W. Nightingall
    2. Extra Time,   **3.** Miss Pixie. $\frac{3}{4}$, 2.   10 ran
1960 Abanilla (9–4) J. Mercer (£1,466) H. Wragg
    2. Mythical Return,   **3.** Miss Wong.   5, 2.   5 ran
1961 Parquetta (100–30) L. Piggott (£1,496) H. Wragg
    2. Pretty Swift,   **3.** Pronunciation.   1, 2.   8 ran
1962 Palm Springs (4–1) A. Breasley (£2,458) Sir G. Richards
    2. Twosome,   **3.** Vi.   1, Hd.   11 ran
1963 High Powered (6–4f) S. Clayton (£2,220) S. James
    2. Golden Harmony,   **3.** Snow White.   1, 2.   6 ran
1964 Attitude (3–1f) J. Mercer (£2,313) W. Hern
    2. Unity,   **3.** Flare.   2, 4.   10 ran
1965 Soft Angels (100–30) L. Piggott (£2,231) N. Murless
    2. Moon Dancer,   **3.** Aerial Lady. $1\frac{1}{2}$, $\frac{1}{2}$.   11 ran
1966 FLEET (4–6f) L. Piggott (£1,996) N. Murless
    2. Gift Token,   **3.** Negotiator. $2\frac{1}{2}$, 1.   6 ran
1967 PHOTO FLASH (7–2) J. Lindley (£1,716) T. Leader
    2. Exchange,   **3.** Celina. $\frac{3}{4}$, Hd.   6 ran
1968 Star Story (4–1) L. Piggott (£1,920) R. Houghton
    2. Hot Penny,   **3.** Natterer. $\frac{3}{4}$, Hd.   8 ran

Race 21: HORN BLOWER STAKES

5 furlongs. Ripon. Two-year-olds. Called Horn Blower Plate until 1964

1958 Anne of Hollins (13–8) E. Hide (£1,185) C. F. Elsey
    2. Whistle Stop,   **3.** Mentone.   2, 1½.   6 ran
1959 Shy Girl (25–1) S. Clayton (£1,185) W. Hern
    2. Tin Whistle,   **3.** Nimgem.   4, 2.   4 ran
1960 Irma La Douce (20–1) E. Hide (£685) C. Elsey and Europa (33–1) F. Durr (£685) L. Sheddon
    3. E.B.S.   Dd Ht, Hd.   9 ran
1961 Gay Mairi (5–1) F. Durr (£1,580) G. Laurence
    2. Brother,   **3.** Superstition.   ½, 6.   9 ran
1962 Hera (evens f) W. Williamson (£1,580) H. Wragg
    2. West Shaw,   **3.** Gyroscope.   3, Sht Hd.   11 ran
1963 Pushful (5–4f) R. Maddock (£1,580) S. Meaney
    2. Birdbrook,   **3.** Acer.   Hd, 2.   11 ran
1964 Seacroft (4–6f) B. Henry (£1,578) A. Vasey
    2. Racing Demon,   **3.** Nimble Runner.   4, 5.   8 ran
1965 Sea Lichen (8–13f) F. Durr (£1,242) H. Wragg
    2. Gaynora,   **3.** Grey Streak.   3, 5.   7 ran
1966 Midsummer Dream (5–2f) Donald Morris (£1,221) J. Thompson
    2. Welsh Warrior,   **3.** King Aziru.   1, 1.   11 ran
1967 Dan Somers (100–9) C. Williams (£1,105) W. O'Gorman
    2. Rift,   **3.** Privy Vale.   Sht Hd, ½.   10 ran
1968 My Sett (11–2) A. Russell (£948) D. Doyle
    2. Heavenly Boss,   **3.** Sica Dan.   2, 2.   9 ran

Race 22: RICHMOND STAKES

6 furlongs. Goodwood. Two-year-olds. First run 1877

1900 Handicapper	(5)	**1913** Black Jester	(7)	**1929** Challenger	(9)
1901 Duke of		**1914** Pommern	(10)	**1930** Four Course	(11)
Westminster	(6)	**1915–18** No race		**1931** Spenser	(7)
1902 Mead	(7)	**1919** Golden Guinea	(4)	**1932** Solar Boy	(7)
1903 Queen's Holiday	(6)	**1920** Sunblaze	(4)	**1933** Colombo	(8)
1904 Polymelus	(7)	**1921** Fodder	(5)	**1934** Bobsleigh	(11)
1905 Lally	(4)	**1922** Bombay Duck	(2)	**1935** Mahmoud	(11)
1906 Weathercock	(8)	**1923** Halcyon	(5)	**1936** Perifox	(12)
1907 Bolted	(9)	**1924** Manna	(9)	**1937** Unbreakable	(8)
1908 Bayardo	(4)	**1925** Pantera	(6)	**1938** Chancery	(13)
1909 Charles O'Malley	(5)	**1926** The Satrap	(4)	**1939** Moradabad	(8)
1910 Pietri	(9)	**1927** Gang Warily	(13)	**1940–45** No race	
1911 Sweeper II	(6)	**1928** Rattlin the		**1946** Petition	(4)
1912 Seremond	(9)	Reefer	(7)		

1947	Birthday		1950	Grey Sovereign	(7)	1954	Eubulides	(7)
	Greetings	(10)	1951	Gay Time	(4)	1955	Ratification	(4)
1948	Star King	(10)	1952	Artane	(5)	1956	Red God	(5)
1949	Palestine	(3)	1953	The Pie King	(6)			

1957 Promulgation (11–8f) E. Smith (£3,004) T. Leader
    2. Pinched,   **3.** Kelly.   2, 3.   7 ran
1958 Hieroglyph (9–4) W. Carr (£2,986) C. Boyd-Rochfort
    2. Bleep-Bleep,   **3.** British Empire.   ½, 3.   7 ran
1959 Dollar Piece (100–6) J. Mercer (£2,852) H. Cottrill
    2. Newbus,   **3.** Colour Plate.   ½, 5.   4 ran
1960 Typhoon (4–11f) R. Hutchinson (£3,081) P. J. Prendergast
    2. PARDAO,   **3.** Tudor Tale.   1½, 3.   5 ran
1961 Sovereign Lord (8–1) G. Lewis (£3,037) G. Smyth
    2. Honey Line,   **3.** Kathyanga.   Hd, 3.   7 ran
1962 Romantic (8–11f) L. Piggott (£3,215) N. Murless
    2. Daybreak,   **3.** Snark.   1, ¾.   5 ran
1963 Gentle Art (8–11f) R. Hutchinson (£3,301) J. Jarvis
    2. Quentin,   **3.** Travel Man.   ½, 3.   5 ran
1964 Ragtime (13–8) R. Hutchinson (£2,631) G. Smyth
    2. Sovereign Crest,   **3.** Dunlin.   ½, 4.   3 ran
1965 Sky Gipsy (3–1) R. Hutchinson (£1,843) G. Smyth
    2. Marandis,   **3.** Young Emperor.   Sht Hd, Bad.   3 ran
1966 Hambleden (2–1f) A. Breasley (£1,904) T. Corbett
    2. Golden Horus,   **3.** Massasoit.   2½, 5.   7 ran
1967 Berber (8–11f) A. Breasley (£6,225) Sir G. Richards
    2. Mark Royal,   **3.** Honey Bear.   1½, 8.   3 ran
1968 Tudor Music (5–1) F. Durr (£6,421) M. Jarvis
    2. Burglar,   **3.** Alceste.   2½, 6.   3 ran

Race 23: MOLECOMB STAKES
5 furlongs. Goodwood. Two-year-old fillies

1957 Abelia (1–5f) L. Piggott (£2,975) N. Murless
    2. Ruthin,   **3.** Frederique II.   3, 2.   4 ran
1958 Krakenwake (11–4) A. Breasley (£2,940) N. Bertie
    2. PETITE ETOILE,   **3.** Anthelion.   2, 4.   8 ran
1959 Queensberry (5–4jf) E. Smith (£2,839) J. A. Waugh
    2. Lady Advocate,   **3.** Grey Fashion.   6, 3.   5 ran
1960 Cynara (2–9f) J. Mercer (£2,876) H. Wragg
    2. Kerrabee,   **3.** Sybil's Comb.   3, 1½.   4 ran
1961 La Tendresse (evens f) R. Hutchinson (£3,460) P. J. Prendergast
    2. Alpine Scent,   **3.** Nerissa.   6, 2.   7 ran
1962 Royal Indiscretion (11–8f) G. Bougoure (£3,497) P. J. Prendergast
    2. Matatina,   **3.** Lucky Gwen.   Hd, 3.   7 ran
1963 Crimea II (11–2) W. Carr (£3,484) C. Boyd-Rochfort
    2. Lerida,   **3.** Flattering.   ½, 3.   8 ran

1964 Regal Pink (5–2f) G. Bougoure (£2,646) P. J. Prendergast
    2. Welsh Mistress,   **3.** Wind Song.   3, 2.   7 ran
1965 Reet Lass (100–9) B. Connorton (£1,921) W. Gray
    2. Saulisa,   **3.** Procession. $1\frac{1}{2}$, Sht Hd.   6 ran
1966 Smooth (9–2) L. Piggott (£1,847) R. Houghton
    2. My Enigma,   **3.** Luciennes. $1\frac{1}{2}$, $1\frac{1}{2}$.   5 ran
1967 Lowna (7–4f) G. Moore (£1,628) N. Murless
    2. Sing Again,   **3.** Canteen.   4, $\frac{3}{4}$.   7 ran
1968 Flying Legs (4–1) L. Piggott (£1,700) M. Jarvis
    2. Grizel,   **3.** Hazy Sky. $\frac{1}{2}$, 6.   5 ran

Race 24: SEATON DELAVAL STAKES

5 furlongs. Newcastle. Two-year-olds

1935 Sister Anne c	(6)	**1947** Gold Mist	(5)	**1952** Good Brandy	(7)
1936 Royal Romance	(9)	**1948** Ballisland	(7)	**1953** Tiger Kloof	(7)
1937 Tete a Tete f	(10)	**1949** Peter Anthony	(6)	**1954** North Cone	(8)
1938 Buoyant	(7)	**1950** Judith Paris	(8)	**1955** Vigo	(7)
1939 Tullyford	(10)	**1951** Dornoch	(5)	**1956** Lunar Way	(8)

1940–46 No race

1957 Pinched (10–11f) L. Piggott (£2,360) N. Murless
    2. Poplin,   **3.** Kandy-Sugar.   2, 3.   6 ran
1958 Lindsay (100–8) E. Larkin (£2,297) R. Peacock
    2. Gol Brig,   **3.** Macmartin.   3, 3.   7 ran
1959 Tin Whistle (4–9f) L. Piggott (£1,805) H. Rohan
    2. Starry Rock,   **3.** Hopsack.   4, $\frac{1}{2}$.   6 ran
1960 China Clipper (1–4f) L. Ward (£2,731) T. Shaw
    2. Derry,   **3.** Alba Rock. $1\frac{1}{2}$, 6.   6 ran
1961 La Tendresse (6–1) R. Hutchinson (£2,734) P. J. Prendergast
    2. Gay Mairi,   **3.** Catchpenny.   4, Nk.   10 ran
1962 Dunce Cap (3–1 jf) D. W. Morris (£4,038) C. Boyd-Rochfort
    2. Tudor Grey,   **3.** Vi. $1\frac{1}{2}$, 3.   8 ran
1963 Abandoned
1964 Unity (7–2) M. Thomas (£4,422) G. Barling
    2. Seacroft,   **3.** Kimono.   4, 2.   5 ran
1965 Gay Palm (100–8) J. Seagrave (£5,809) H. Rohan
    2. Queen of Helena,   **3.** Sea Lichen. $\frac{1}{2}$, $1\frac{1}{2}$.   6 ran
1966 Galipar (5–1) M. Thomas (£1,957) G. Barling
    2. Melodic Air,   **3.** Welsh Warrior.   4, 2.   11 ran
1967 Sky Rocket (5–1) L. Piggott (£1,617) F. Armstrong
    2. Pertino,   **3.** Heathen.   1, 1.   9 ran
1968 Lady's View (100–8) D. Keith (£1,704) P. Ashworth
    2. Sica Dan,   **3.** Zarco.   Hd, 3.   7 ran

Race 25: PHOENIX STAKES

5 furlongs. Phoenix Park. Two-year-olds

1957 Vestogan (20–1) J. Wright (£1,939) S. McGrath
    2. Denim,   **3.** Precious Hoard.   4, $\frac{3}{4}$.   11 ran
1958 Getaway (6–1) L. Piggott (£1,972) E. M. Quirke
    2. Sovereign Path,   **3.** Lillet.   4, $\frac{1}{2}$.   11 ran
1959 Gigi (5–2) T. P. Burns (£2,107) R. J. McCormick
    2. Nice Guy,   **3.** Arodstown Boy. $1\frac{1}{4}$, Sht Hd.   8 ran
1960 Kathy Too (6–4f) R. Hutchinson (£2,129) P. J. Prendergast
    2. Silken Yogan,   **3.** Ritudyr. $1\frac{1}{2}$, 2.   10 ran
1961 PRINCE POPPA (20–1) W. Burke (£2,119) J. M. Rogers
    2. Arctic Storm and   **2.** Shandon Belle.   Sht Hd, Dd Ht. 12 ran
1962 Irish Chorus (evens f) G. McGrath (£2,477) K. Kerr
    2. Majority Rule,   **3.** Marshal Grey. $1\frac{1}{2}$, $1\frac{1}{2}$.   9 ran
1963 Right Strath (100–7) D. Page (£2,302) C. Weld
    2. Victoria Quay,   **3.** Quisling. $\frac{3}{4}$, 3.   11 ran
1964 Adriatic Star (100–9) J. Roe (£3,725) S. McGrath
    2. Ernest Henry,   **3.** Royal Garden.   Sht Hd, Nk.   7 ran
1965 Current Coin (9–2) W. Williamson (£4,226) J. Oxx
    2. Red Taffy (first, disq.)   **3.** Irish Guard.
                        Original distances Nk, $1\frac{1}{2}$.   7 ran
1966 Jadeite (4–9f) M. Kennedy (£4,384) J. M. Rogers
    2. Graunuaile,   **3.** Storm Inn. $\frac{3}{4}$, 5.   7 ran
1967 Fatima's Gift (15–2) R. F. Parnell (£3,860) S. Quirke
    2. Polar Gold,   **3.** Viscount. $2\frac{1}{2}$, Sht Hd.   11 ran
1968 Lord John (6–4f) A. C. McGarrity (£3,800) P. J. Prendergast
    2. Centra,   **3.** Marcia Royal.   2, Sht Hd.   8 ran

Race 26: ACOMB STAKES

6 furlongs. York. Two-year-olds

1957 Cool Debate (5–1) D. Ryan (£1,595) W. Stephenson
    2. Brilliant Stone,   **3.** Tantalizer.   3, $\frac{1}{2}$.   16 ran
1958 Anthelion (100–30) E. Mercer (£1,690) J. Jarvis
    2. Maratea,   **3.** Reactor.   1, 3.   23 ran
1959 Beau Ideal (100–6) D. Keith (£1,388) D. Gunn
    2. King's Decision,   **3.** Eratosthenes.   Sht Hd, $1\frac{1}{2}$.   18 ran
1960 Tender Word (100–8) J. Mercer (£1,484) R. J. Colling
    2. Viburnum,   **3.** Prevale.   2, Nk.   24 ran
1961 Cyrus (6–4f) D. Smith (£1,504) G. Brooke
    2. Sherry Netherland,   **3.** Chevalier.   Hd, 3.   25 ran
1962 Confidence (3–1) G. Bougoure (£1,418) P. J. Prendergast
    2. Campaign,   **3.** Plymouth Sound. $\frac{1}{2}$, 1.   21 ran

1963 Causerie (11–2) G. Starkey (£1,464) J. Oxley
    2. Feliptica,   **3.** Ominous.   5, 2.   18 ran
1964 Royalgo (15–2) W. Williamson (£1,588) H. Wragg
    2. Foothill,   **3.** Super Gay.   3, Nk.   23 ran
1965 Le Cordonnier (7–2) G. Lewis (£1,330) S. Ingham
    2. Marcus Brutus,   **3.** Southern Belle.   2½, 3.   9 ran
1966 ROYAL PALACE (7–2) L. Piggott (£1,408) N. Murless
    2. Imagination,   **3.** Countermarch.   2, ½.   13 ran
1967 Alaska Way (7–1) B. Raymond (£1,043) H. Cottrill
    2. Honey Bear,   **3.** Heathen.   Hd, ¾.   10 ran
1968 Dieudonne (3–1f) L. Piggott (£1,158) R. Houghton
    2. Rebel Prince,   **3.** Anguilla.   Sht Hd, 1½.   15 ran

Race 27: CONVIVIAL MAIDEN STAKES

6 furlongs. York. Two-year-olds. Run over 5 furlongs until 1962

1957 NONE NICER (10–11f) W. Snaith (£1,560) H. L. Cottrill
    2. Persuasive,   **3.** Will Somers.   ½, ½.   12 ran
1958 ROSALBA (100–6) W. Carr (£1,510) R. J. Colling
    2. Compere,   **3.** Tana Dante.   1, 3.   12 ran
1959 Monet (5–6f) J. Lindley (£1,285) J. Tree
    2. Fusion,   **3.** Clever Dick.   2, 3.   13 ran
1960 Daisy Belle (10–1) D. Page (£1,476) C. Magnier
    2. Royal Whistler,   **3.** Fair Future.   Nk, Sht Hd.   21 ran
1961 True Course (10–1) W. Williamson (£1,440) S. McGrath
    2. Miss Butterfly,   **3.** Oliver Hardy.   4, 2.   22 ran
1962 Molino (7–1) G. Bougoure (£1,678) P. J. Prendergast
    2. Sammy Davis,   **3.** Loyal Monarch.   2, Nk.   31 ran
1963 Daylight Robbery (100–8) J. Lindley (£1,604) A. Budgett
    2. Desaix,   **3.** Tuba.   5, 3.   20 ran
1964 Audience (6–1) D. Smith (£1,734) G. Brooke
    2. Ark,   **3.** Appoline.   3, Nk.   20 ran
1965 Lucky Coin (7–1) J. Mercer (£1,646) R. Houghton
    2. Crazy Paving,   **3.** Brief Chorus.   4, 1½.   28 ran
1966 Prince Piper (5–1) D. Lake (£1,616) P. J. Prendergast
    2. Montesano,   **3.** Bosworth Field.   Hd, 1¼.   28 ran
1967 Miss Tarara (100–8) L. Piggott (£1,359) R. Houghton
    2. Royal Chant,   **3.** Snake Charmer.   3, Nk.   20 ran
    (Connaught 5–2f withdrawn, bookmakers deduct 6s. in £)
1968 Explode (13–8f) R. Hutchinson (£1,512) H. Wragg
    2. Brand New,   **3.** Solar Beam.   ¾, 1½.   17 ran

Race 28: GIMCRACK STAKES

6 furlongs. York. Two-year-olds. First run 1846

1900	Garb Or	(13)	1921 Scamp	(12)	1937	Golden Sovereign	(6)
1901	Sterling Balm	(12)	1922 Town Guard	(8)	1938	Cockpit	(11)
1902	Chaucer	(10)	1923 Sansovino	(7)	1939	Tant Mieux	(14)
1903	Barbette	(12)	1924 Game Shot	(7)	1940–44	No race	
1904	Desiree	(14)	1925 Lex	(7)	1945	Gulf Stream	(4)
1905	Colonia	(10)	1926 Bold Archer	(14)	1946	Petition	(5)
1906	Polar Star	(11)	1927 Black Watch	(14)	1947	Black Tarquin	(7)
1907	Royal Realm	(11)	1928 The Black		1948	Star King	(12)
1908	Blankney II	(13)	Abbot	(10)	1949	Palestine	(2)
1909	Lily Rose	(10)	1929 Roral	(7)	1950	Cortil	(10)
1910	Pietri	(9)	1930 Four Course	(13)	1951	Windy City	(10)
1911	Lomond	(6)	1931 Miracle	(7)	1952	Bebe Grande	(10)
1912	Flippant	(8)	1932 Young Lover	(7)	1953	The Pie King	(9)
1913	Stornoway	(11)	1933 Mrs Rustom	(10)	1954	Precast	(11)
1914–18	No race		1934 Bahram	(5)	1955	Idle Rocks	(5)
1919	Southern	(7)	1935 Paul Beg	(8)	1956	Eudaemon	(7)
1920	Polemarch	(9)	1936 Goya II	(15)			

1957 Pheidippides (100–8) D. Smith (£5,577) C. F. Elsey
      2. Pinched,   3. PALL MALL.   1, ½.   9 ran
1958 Be Careful (10–1) E. Hide (£5,526) C. F. Elsey
      2. Captain Kidd,   3. Ink Spot.   3, 2.   12 ran
1959 Paddy's Sister (4–11f) G. Moore (£5,883) P. J. Prendergast
      2. Newbus,   3. Oak Ridge.   3, 2.   10 ran
1960 Test Case (100–7) E. Larkin (£5,449) J. Jarvis
      2. PRINCE TUDOR,   3. Floribunda.   2, 2.   7 ran
1961 Sovereign Lord (10–1) A. Breasley (£5,917) G. Smyth
      2. PRINCE POPPA,   3. MIRALGO.   Nk, Sht Hd.   11 ran
1962 Crocket (2–5f) D. Smith (£5,798) G. Brooke
      2. Young David,   3. King of Babylon. 2, 2.   5 ran
1963 Talahasse (11–8f) L. Piggott (£7,260) T. Corbett
      2. Gentle Art,   3. Metellus.   2, 4.   7 ran
1964 Double Jump (evens f) J. Lindley (£6,988) J. Tree
      2. Ragtime,   3. Strand Station.   1½, 3.   7 ran
1965 Young Emperor (5–6f) L. Piggott (£6,809) P. J. Prendergast
      2. Lanark,   3. Mr Dolittle.   6, 4.   8 ran
1966 Golden Horus (7–1) J. Mercer (£6,546) W. O'Gorman
      2. Falcon,   3. Pennant.   2, 1½.   9 ran
1967 PETINGO (7–4f) L. Piggott (£5,079) F. Armstrong
      2. Chebs Lad,   3. Scipio.   6, ½.   9 ran
1968 Tudor Music (10–11f) F. Durr (£5,149) M. Jarvis
      2. Song,   3. Zarco.   4, 1.   7 ran

Race 29: LOWTHER STAKES
5 furlongs. York. Two-year-old fillies

1957 Liberal Lady (100–8) K. Gethin (£2,360) P. Thrale			
2. Abelia,	**3.** High Camber.	2, 1½.	3 ran
1958 Fortune's Darling (20–1) S. Clayton (£2,660) W. Hern			
2. Fan Light,	**3.** Marsh Meadow.	½, 5.	8 ran
1959 Queensberry (10–11f) E. Smith (£2,361) J. A. Waugh			
2. Palmural,	**3.** Pretty Cage.	4, 1.	10 ran
1960 Kathy Too (9–2) R. Hutchinson (£2,300) P. J. Prendergast			
2. Cynara,	**3.** Favorita.	1½, Hd.	4 ran
1961 La Tendresse (2–7f) R. Hutchinson (£2,275) P. J. Prendergast			
2. Alpine Scent,	**3.** Pervinca.	12, 3.	5 ran
1962 Dunce Cap (6–1) W. Carr (£2,360) C. Boyd-Rochfort			
2. Guinea Sparrow,	**3.** Top of the Milk.	Nk, 2.	7 ran
1963 POURPARLER (7–2) G. Bougoure (£2,495) P. J. Prendergast			
2. Flattering,	**3.** GWEN.	Nk, 1.	13 ran
1964 Pugnacity (4–6f) J. Mercer (£2,295) W. Wharton			
2. Sweet Sovereign,	**3.** Atonement.	1½, ½.	6 ran
1965 Reet Lass (3–1) B. Connorton (£2,336) W. Gray			
2. Harolds Cross,	**3.** Barlow Fold.	½, 4.	9 ran
1966 PIA (100–9) E. Hide (£2,292) W. Elsey			
2. Maeander,	**3.** Winkie.	Hd, ¾.	10 ran
1967 SOVEREIGN (1–9f) R. Hutchinson (£2,163) H. Wragg			
2. Abbie West.		1.	2 ran
1968 Flying Legs (9–4) F. Durr (£2,030) M. Jarvis			
2. Sea Lavender,	**3.** Grizel.	½, 4.	3 ran

Race 30: ANGLESEY STAKES
6 furlongs 63 yards. Curragh. Two-year-olds

1957 Daffodil (3–1) L. Ward (£907) J. M. Rogers			
2. Precious Hoard,	**3.** Ballyrullah.	2, 4.	7 ran
1958 Sauchrie (11–2) John Power (£1,413) J. Oxx			
2. His Legend,	**3.** Bois Belleau.	1½, ½.	13 ran
1959 Arctic Sea (7–2) G. Bougoure (£1,335) M. V. O'Brien			
2. Jamipego,	**3.** Sabot d'Or.	Hd, 4.	6 ran
1960 Indian Conquest (5–1) L. Ward (£1,412) J. M. Rogers			
2. Georges,	**3.** Fight On.	¾, 1½.	11 ran
1961 Richmond (20–1) P. Hughes (£1,531) R. Fetherstonhaugh			
2. Arctic Storm,	**3.** Olympius.	Hd, 2.	16 ran
1962 Philemon (8–11f) T. P. Glennon (£1,669) M. V. O'Brien			
2. Partholon,	**3.** Vertigo.	8, Nk.	16 ran
1963 Dromoland (10–1) P. Boothman (£1,756) R. Fetherstonhaugh			
2. Smooth Jet,	**3.** Chamarre.	2, 6.	16 ran

1964 Green Banner (9–2) G. McGrath (£2,045) K. Kerr
    2. Rose d'Or,   3. Messene.   5, Nk.   9 ran
1965 Bravery (2–1f) J. Purtell (£1,990) M. V. O'Brien
    2. Martian Lady,   3. Farandole.   4, 2.   11 ran
1966 Archangel Gabriel (9–4) D. Lake (£2,377) P. J. Prendergast
    2. Michaelis,   3. Lama.   5, 1.   10 ran
1967 Society (5–1) W. Williamson (£2,432) P. J. Prendergast
    2. Polar Gold,   3. Bianconi Lady.   2½, ¾.   10 ran
1968 Marcia Royal (9–4) M. Kennedy (£2,177) P. Norris
    2. Tirconail,   3. Blue Wolf.   Nk, ¾.   5 ran

Race 31: SOLARIO STAKES

7 furlongs. Sandown. Two-year-olds

1957 Aggressor (7–1) J. Lindley (£1,885) J. Gosden
    2. Pandour,   3. Munch.   2, ¾.   12 ran
1958 PINDARI (20–1) L. Piggott (£1,953) N. Murless
    2. Romsey,   3. Piona.   1, ½.   15 ran
1959 Intervener (4–1) W. Snaith (£3,228) H. Cottrill
    2. No Saint,   3. Goose Creek.   ½, 2.   13 ran
1960 Dual (7–1) J. Lindley (£1,897) J. Gosden
    2. Crowded Room,   3. PARDAO.   3, 1½.   17 ran
1961 Hidden Meaning (2–1f) E. Smith (£1,948) H. Leader
    2. Oroondates,   3. Deauville Dandy. 2, 1½.   9 ran
1962 Happy Omen (5–2) W. Carr (£1,893) W. Hern
    2. Idomeneo,   3. STAR MOSS.   Hd, 3.   9 ran
1963 Penny Stall (33–1) D. Keith (£2,016) W. Nightingall
    2. Tamerslip,   3. Somerville.   2, Nk.   11 ran
1964 Rehearsed (5–2) J. Lindley (£2,640) J. Gosden
    2. Potier,   3. Brave Knight.   3, 2.   9 ran
1965 CHARLOTTOWN (3–1jf) J. Lindley (£1,947) J. Gosden
    2. Bugle Boy,   3. Zimbie.   8, 3.   9 ran
1966 Speed of Sound (4–7f) L. Piggott (£1,802) N. Murless
    2. Ulpion,   3. Princes Street. 1½, 6.   9 ran
1967 Remand (8–15f) L. Piggott (£1,710) W. Hern
    2. Milltown,   3. First Pick.   ¾, 4.   5 ran
1968 Murrayfield (8–13f) G. Lewis (£1,812) I. Balding
    2. Adropejo,   3. Mitsouko.   Sht Hd, 1.   7 ran

HORSES IN CAPITAL LETTERS
WERE TO BE, OR HAD BEEN,
PLACED IN THE CLASSICS

Race 32: CHAMPAGNE STAKES

7 furlongs. Doncaster. Two-year-olds. Run over 6 furlongs until 1962. First run 1823

1900 Orchid	(6)	**1921** Golden Corn	(7)		**[AT NEWBURY]**	
1901 Game Chick	(7)	**1922** Drake	(10)	**1941** Big Game		(6)
1902 Rock Sand	(4)	**1923** Mumtaz Mahal	(5)	**1942–45** No race		
1903 Pretty Polly	(5)	**1924** Bucellas	(6)			
1904 Galangal and		**1925** Coronach	(12)		**[AT DONCASTER]**	
Vedriana	(10)	**1926** Damon	(8)	**1946** Petition		(3)
1905 Achilles	(8)	**1927** Fairway	(9)	**1947** Lerins (renamed		
1906 Slieve Gallion	(7)	**1928** Arabella	(10)		My Babu)	(4)
1907 Lesbia	(5)	**1929** Fair Diana	(6)	**1948** Abernant		(3)
1908 Duke Michael	(6)	**1930** Portlaw	(8)	**1949** Palestine		(3)
1909 Neil Gow	(4)	**1931** Orwell	(5)	**1950** Big Dipper		(7)
1910 Pietri	(4)	**1932** Myrobella	(8)	**1951** Orgoglio		(7)
1911 White Star	(7)	**1933** Blazonry	(8)	**1952** Bebe Grande		(5)
1912 Craganour	(4)	**1934** Kingsem	(7)	**1953** Darius		(6)
1913 The Tetrarch	(3)	**1935** Mahmoud	(11)	**1954** Our Babu		(9)
1914 Redfern	(6)	**1936** Foray	(10)	**1955** Rustam		(3)
1915–18 No race		**1937** Portmarnock	(8)	**1956** Eudaemon		(4)
1919 Tetratema	(5)	**1938** Panorama	(7)			
1920 Lemonora	(5)	**1939–40** No race				

1957 Kelly (10–1) J. Purtell (£4,830) N. Cannon
    2. PALL MALL,   3. Promulgation.   Sht Hd, 4.   5 ran

1958 Be Careful (4–7f) E. Hide (£4,907) C. F. Elsey
    2. CARNOUSTIE,   3. Dominate.   Nk, 12.   5 ran

1959 Paddy's Sister (8–15f) G. Moore (£4,660) P. J. Prendergast
    2. Newbus,   3. Tudor Court.   ¾, 6.   6 ran

1960 AMBERGRIS (7–2) J. Lindley (£5,102) H. Wragg
    2. Henry the Seventh,   3. War Dancer.   2, 1½.   9 ran

1961 Clear Sound (3–1) R. Hutchinson (£5,850) P. J. Prendergast
    2. ROMULUS,   3. Brother.   Nk, 3.   8 ran

1962 King of Babylon (100–7) E. Hide (£5,612) W. Elsey
    2. Romantic,   3. Young David.   2, ½.   10 ran

1963 Talahasse (4–7f) A. Breasley (£5,935) T. Corbett
    2. News Item,   3. FABERGE II.   Nk, ¾.   7 ran

1964 Hardicanute (7–1) G. Bougoure (£5,014) P. J. Prendergast
    2. Crispian,   3. Air Patrol.   Sht Hd, 2.   11 ran

1965 CELTIC SONG (2–1) L. Piggott (£5,168) P. J. Prendergast
    2. Lucky Coin,   3. Conjuror.   1, 1½.   8 ran

1966 Bold Lad (8–11f) D. Lake (£5,336) P. J. Prendergast
    2. RIBOCCO,   3. Hambleden.   ¾, 1½.   5 ran

1967 Chebs Lad (7–1) B. Connorton (£5,152) W. Gray
    2. Lorenzaccio,   3. Fairullah.   1, 3.   6 ran

1968 Ribofilio (7–2) L. Piggott (£5,273) R. Houghton
    2. Tudor Music,   3. Hotfoot.   2, 2.   7 ran

Race 33: NORFOLK STAKES
5 furlongs. Doncaster. Two-year-olds

1967 D'Urberville (4–5f) J. Lindley (£2,316) J. Tree
    2. Mountain Call,   **3.** PHOTO FLASH. 1½, Hd.   5 ran
1968 Tower Walk (6–4 jf) M. Thomas (£2,320) G. Barling
    2. French Tutor   **3.** Sica Dan   5, Hd.   6 ran

Race 34: CROOKHAM STAKES
7 furlongs 60 yards. Newbury. Two-year-olds

1958 Seascape (7–2) E. Smith (£1,485) T. Leader
    2. Anthelion,   **3.** Ricky Joe.   8, 4.   14 ran
1959 No Saint (2–1jf) S. Clayton (£1,349) W. Hern
    2. Optimist,   **3.** Scala.   Hd, 3.   11 ran
1960 Colour Blind (13–8f) G. Lewis (£1,328) T. Corbett
    2. Lucem,   **3.** Xan.   ½, 5.   6 ran
1961 All-a-Gogg (9–4jf) D. Smith (£1,383) G. Brooke
    2. Gustav,   **3,** Set Going.   1½, 3.   9 ran
1962 My Myosotis (11–8f) B. Taylor (£1,290) H. Leader
    2. Arise,   **3.** Regiment.   2, 3.   9 ran
1963 SODERINI (25–1) J. Wilson (£2,441) S. Ingham
    2. Young Christopher,   **3.** Smooth Jet.   ½, 2.   20 ran
1964 Audience (2–1f) J. Lindley (£2,195) G. Brooke
    2. Look Sharp,   **3.** NIKSAR.   ½, Nk.   14 ran
1965 Fontex (9–2jf) B. Taylor (£2,024) H. Leader
    2. Royal Flirt,   **3.** Golden Bolt.   ½, 2½.   11 ran
1966 Karpathos (15–2) R. Hutchinson (£970) J. Dunlop
    2. Aldium,   **3,** St Padarn.   ¾, ½.   17 ran
1967 Hurry Hurry (evens f) G. Moore (£1,698) N. Murless
    2. Exchange,   **3.** Trumpet Major. 1½, 5.   10 ran
1968 Full Dress II (9–2) R. Hutchinson (£1,757) H. Wragg
    2. Aggravate,   **3.** Shoemaker.   4, Nk.   11 ran

Race 35: CHAMPION TWO-YEAR-OLD TROPHY
6 furlongs. Ripon. Two-year-olds. Run over 1 mile until 1965

1960 Vinnie (7–1) N. McIntosh (£1,757) S. Hall
    2. Smuggler's Joy,   **3.** Salmon King.   3, 8.   13 ran
1961 Lucky Brief (100–8) B. Connorton (£2,014) W. Gray
    2. Oroondates,   **3.** Musical Hall.   Sht Hd, 1½.   8 ran
1962 Zaleucus (11–2) D. Smith (£2,014) G. Brooke
    2. Young David,   **3.** Narrow Escape.   1½, 1½.   7 ran

1963 Con Brio (8–11f) M. Hayes (£1,862) F. Armstrong
    2. Siesta Time,   **3.** Shotley Mill.   ½, 3.   10 ran
1964 Never a Fear (11–10jf) A. Robson (£1,523) W. Wharton
    2. Isola d'Asti,   **3.** Centaurus.   2, 1½.   3 ran
1965 Audrey Joan (100–9) G. Cadwaladr (£1,537) E. Cousins
    2. Fleece,   **3.** Queen of Helena. 3, Nk.   8 ran
1966 Horned Moon (9–4jf) J. Sime (£1,560) R. Day
    2. Brent,   **3.** Persister.   Hd, 4.   7 ran
1967 Chebs Lad (2–5f) B. Connorton (£1,323) W. Gray
    2. Sky Rocket,   **3.** Proud Stone.   4, 2.   3 ran
1968 Meldrum (7–2) P. Hetherington (£1,386) E. Weymes
    2. Rebel Prince,   **3.** Marton Lady.   1½, Nk.   7 ran

Race 36: NATIONAL STAKES

7 furlongs. Curragh. Two-year-olds.
Called National Produce Stakes, run over 6 furlongs 63 yards until 1960

1957 Talmud (2–5f) T. M. Burns (£1,630) P. J. Prendergast
    2. Sous Etoile,   **3.** Fair Journey.   2, 1.   8 ran
1958 Babu (6–4f) G. Cooney (£1,600) D. Rogers
    2. Goody Two Shoes,   **3.** Bois Belleau.   6, 1.   12 ran
1959 His Story (100–8) P. Powell jn. (£1,619) Sir Hugh Nugent
    2. Le Levanstell,   **3.** Say No More.   1½, 1¼.   10 ran
1960 Paris Princess (20–1) F. Langan (£2,392) S. McGrath
    2. Gailowind,   **3.** Light Year,   1, 2.   15 ran
1961 Mystery (4–1) L. Ward (£2,531) T. Shaw
    2. Richmond,   **3.** LARKSPUR.   Sht Hd, ¾.   17 ran
1962 Partholon (10–1) L. Ward (£2,914) T. Shaw.
    2. Molino,   **3.** Turbo Jet.   Nk, ½.   11 ran
1963 SANTA CLAUS (4–1) W. Burke (£2,584) J. M. Rogers
    2. Mesopotamia,   **3.** Chamarre.   8, 1.   12 ran
1964 Prominer (25–1) T. P. Burns (£3,027) P. J. Prendergast
    2. Rose d'Or,   **3.** Wedding Present. 3, ¾.   16 ran
1965 Reubens (100–7) P. Sullivan (£3,775) H. V. S. Murless
    2. Radbrook,   **3.** Democrat.   1, 1¼.   13 ran
1966 House Proud (17–2) P. Boothman (£4,427) R. Fetherstonhaugh
    2. Dominion Day,   **3.** Rhinelander.   2, ¾.   15 ran
1967 SIR IVOR (5–2) L. Ward (£4,460) M. V. O'Brien
    2. Candy Cane,   **3.** Society.   3, 4.   9 ran
1968 Thataboy (5–1) W. Williamson (£4,235) P. J. Prendergast
    2. Sahib,   **3.** Winden.   Hd, 6.   10 ran

Race 37: IMPERIAL STAKES

6 furlongs. Kempton. Two-year-olds. First run 1889

1900 Aida	(9)	**1919** Tetratema	(3)	**1936** Lover's Path	(11)
1901 Ard Patrick	(8)	**1920** Pompadour	(4)	**1937** Glen Loan	(16)
1902 Flotsam	(8)	**1921** Lord of Burghley	(4)	**1938** Heliopolis	(19)
1903 Lancashire	(7)	**1922** Cos	(6)	**1939–46** No race	
1904 Khammurabi	(14)	**1923** Arcade	(8)	**1947** Henley-in-Arden	
1905 Flair	(11)	**1924** Picaroon	(5)	and Ottoman	(6)
1906 Galvani	(8)	**1925** Tolgus	(9)	**1948** Gigantic	(6)
1907 Vamose and		**1926** Cresta Run	(12)	**1949** Kisaki	(8)
Lesbia	(6)	**1927** Buland	(11)	**1950** Clutha	(8)
1908 Vivid	(12)	**1928** Arabella	(11)	**1951** Zabara	(15)
1909 Neil Gow	(3)	**1929** Roral	(7)	**1952** Bluefin	(10)
1910 Prince Palatine	(10)	**1930** Doctor Dolittle	(11)	**1953** Fluorescent	(11)
1911 Fruition	(10)	**1931** Orwell	(5)	**1954** Grass Court	(20)
1912 Radiant	(7)	**1932** Gino	(14)	**1955** Milesian	(6)
1913 By George	(9)	**1933** Colombo	(11)	**1956** Sarcelle	(13)
1914 Pommern	(4)	**1934** Shahali	(15)		
1915–18 No race		**1935** Harina	(17)		

1957 Pin Wheel (6–1) L. Piggott (£6,931) N. Murless
    2. Trimmer,   3. Asiago.   5, ½.   7 ran

1958 Saint Crespin III (5–1f) M. Garcia (£7,945) A. Head (France)
    2. Collyria,   3. Chanter.   ¾, 4.   16 ran

1959 VENTURE VII (7–4f) G. Moore (£7,730) A. Head (France)
    2. Extra Time,   3. Palmural.   1½, 3.   8 ran

1960 Axe (20–1) S. Clayton (£1,903) C. Boyd-Rochfort
    2. PRINCE TUDOR and   2. Mystify.   2, Dd Ht.   8 ran

1961 Compensation (11–2) S. Smith (£3,117) E. Lambton
    2. Pipaway,   3. Chevalier.   5, 5.   7 ran

1962 Saucepan (100–8) G. Starkey (£3,073) H. Thomson Jones
    2. Hera,   3. Candid Picture.   ½, 1.   8 ran

1963 Derring-Do (2–1f) L. Piggott (£6,702) A. Budgett
    2. Whistling Buoy,   3. Camisado.   4, ½.   18 ran

1964 Gulf Pearl (50–1) J. Lindley (£6,149) J. Tree
    2. Weaver Bird,   3. Spanish Express.   Sht Hd, ½.   10 ran

1965 Conjuror (2–1f) R. Hutchinson (£9,417) W. Wharton
    2. Military,   3. Water Diviner.   1½, ½.   11 ran

1966 Heath Rose (20–1) W. Williamson (£9,200) W. Wharton
    2. Ulpion,   3. Fab.   3, ½.   13 ran

1967 Hametus (20–1) R. Hutchinson (£1,281) W. Nightingall
    2. Fairy Path,   3. Big Deal.   Nk, 1½.   8 ran

1968 Right Tack (3–1jf) G. Lewis (£8,707) J. Sutcliffe jun.
    2. Perfect Friday,   3. Mount Melody.   2, 4.   8 ran

Race 38: LARKSPUR STAKES

7 furlongs. Leopardstown. Two-year-old colts and geldings

1965 Current Coin (100–30) W. Williamson (£2,507) J. Oxx
    2. Grey Moss,   **3.** Floral Mile.   1¾, 3.   12 ran
1966 Hespero (11–10f) L. Ward (£2,740) M. V. O'Brien
    2. Skamander,   **3.** Saint   Sht Hd, 3.   7 ran
                              Christopher.
1967 Ballygoran (11–2) L. Ward (£2,897) M. V. O'Brien
    2. Mistigo,   **3.** Laurence O.   4, ¾.   10 ran
1968 Star Marine (evens f) W. Williamson (£2,057) P. J. Prendergast
    2. Glad Hand,   **3.** Enchanter.   ¾, ¾,   7 ran

Race 39: ROYAL LODGE STAKES

1 mile. Ascot. Two-year-olds. *Run at Newbury

1946 Royal Barge	(4)	1950 Fraise du Bois II	(5)	1954 Solarium	(12)
1947 Black Tarquin	(5)	1951 Khor-Mousa	(5)	1955 Royal Splendour	(4)
1948 Swallow Tail	(8)	1952 Neemah	(4)	1956 Noble Venture	(10)
1949 Tabriz	(5)	1953 Infatuation	(9)		

1957 Pinched (evens f) L. Piggott (£3,840) N. Murless
    2. Miner's Lamp,   **3.** Lacydon.   3, ¾.   6 ran
1958 CANTELO (5–4f) E. Hide (£3,419) C. F. Elsey
    2. Last Line,   **3.** PINDARI.   2, Nk.   7 ran
1959 ST PADDY (11–4jf) L. Piggott (£3,082) N. Murless
    2. Goose Creek,   **3.** Jet Stream.   5, Hd.   5 ran
*1960 Beta (9–4) E. Larkin (£3,218) J. Jarvis
    2. Dual,   **3.** Orbit.   1, 3.   10 ran
1961 Escort (9–2) J. Mercer (£3,520) R. J. Colling
    2. Heron,   **3.** Aznip.   1, Hd.   12 ran
1962 STAR MOSS (5–1) E. Smith (£3,635) J. A. Waugh
    2. Coliseum,   **3.** MERCHANT   3, ¾.   9 ran
                           VENTURER.
*1963 Casabianca (4–1) L. Piggott (£3,852) N. Murless
    2. Desaix,   **3.** Oncidium.   Nk, 5.   12 ran
1964 Prominer (3–1) G. Bougoure (£9,793) P. J. Prendergast
    2. Never a Fear,   **3.** Rehearsed.   Sht Hd, 2.   13 ran
1965 Soft Angels (5–2f) L. Piggott (£5,687) N. Murless
    2. SODIUM,   **3.** GLAD RAGS.   3, 4.   11 ran
1966 ROYAL PALACE (6–4f) L. Piggott (£5,500) N. Murless
    2. Slip Stitch,   **3.** Starry Halo.   1½, 4.   5 ran
1967 Remand (13–8f) L. Piggott (£4,526) W. Hern
    2. Riboccare,   **3.** Attalus.   4, ½.   7 ran
1968 Dutch Bells (100–7) A. Murray (£4,325) H. Price
    2. Adropejo,   **3.** Murrayfield.   ¾, 2.   4 ran

Race 40: BLUE SEAL STAKES

6 furlongs. Ascot. Two-year-old fillies. *Run at Newbury

1957 Brilliant Stone (7–4f) L. Piggott (£1,565) N. Murless		
2. Petronella,	3. St Lucia.	$1\frac{1}{2}$, $1\frac{1}{2}$. 13 ran
1958 Number One (100–6) J. Lindley (£1,595) W. Hern		
2. Dame Melba,	3. Wanjohe.	$\frac{3}{4}$, 5. 13 ran
1959 High Pitch (9–1) L. Piggott (£2, 356) N. Murless		
2. Extra Time,	3. Ergina.	3, 2. 10 ran
***1960** Stype (8–1) W. Carr (£2,517) P. Nelson		
2. Keld,	3. Adowa,	Hd, $\frac{3}{4}$. 8 ran
1961 Barnegat (20–1) D. Smith (£2,640) G. Brooke		
2. Secret Step,	3. Gail Royal.	4, 3. 20 ran
1962 NOBLESSE (11–8f) G. Bougoure (£2,462) P. J. Prendergast		
2. Dinant,	3. There She Goes.	5, 2. 21 ran
***1963** King's Mistress (10–1) A. Breasley (£2,152) A. Budgett		
2. Alzara,	3. Lupina.	Hd, $1\frac{1}{2}$. 14 ran
1964 Hell's Angels (11–10f) R. Hutchinson (£2,164) C. Magnier		
2. Grecian Bridge,	3. Crisp Piece.	3, Hd. 9 ran
1965 Ballette (100–8) J. Mercer (£2,153) W. Wharton		
2. VALORIS,	3. Ysolda.	$1\frac{1}{2}$, $\frac{3}{4}$. 18 ran
1966 Fab (4–11f) L. Piggott (£1,996) N. Murless		
2. Death Duties,	3. All Hail.	6, $\frac{3}{4}$. 7 ran
1967 Denosa (15–8f) L. Piggott (£1,920) M. V. O'Brien		
2. Mary Mine,	3. Hill Shade.	$1\frac{1}{2}$, Sht Hd. 12 ran
1968 Peace (9–2) L. Piggott (£1,844) J. Tree		
2. Mayhaw,	3. Lullaby.	4, $1\frac{1}{2}$. 11 ran

Race 41: BERESFORD STAKES

1 mile. Curragh. Two-year-olds

1957 Arcticeelagh (5–1) J. Wright (£941) S. McGrath		
2. PADDY'S POINT,	3. Precious Hoard.	4, Sht Hd. 9 ran
1958 Sunny Court (6–1) W. Burke (£920) J. M. Rogers		
2. Sinna,	3. Dusky Boy.	2, Sht Hd. 6 ran
1959 Lynchris (100–8) P. Sullivan (£1,037) J. Oxx		
2. Tulyartos,	3. Hans Andersen.	$\frac{1}{2}$, $2\frac{1}{2}$. 10 ran
1960 Paris Princess (8–11f) G. Bougoure (£1,004) S. McGrath		
2. Wild Fast,	3. Prescience.	1, 4. 5 ran
1961 Richmond (5–1) D. Page (£1,217) R. Fetherstonhaugh		
2. Feevagh Hill,	3. Islam.	Hd, Sht Hd. 10 ran
1962 Pontifex (6–4f) T. P. Glennon (£1,550) M. V. O'Brien		
2. Profit Refused,	3. Gladys.	$1\frac{1}{2}$, $\frac{3}{4}$. 16 ran
1963 Scissors (10–1) L. Ward (£1,648) T. Shaw		
2. All Saved,	3. Cuaran Riona.	$1\frac{1}{2}$, $1\frac{1}{2}$. 10 ran

1964 Jealous (8–1) P. Sullivan (£2,031) J. Oxx
    2. Ragazzo,   **3.** Soldier.   2½, Sht Hd.   19 ran
1965 Boleslas (10–1) J. Lindley (£2,799) P. J. Prendergast
    2. Right Noble,   **3.** Paveh.   Nk, Sht Hd.   14 ran
1966 Sovereign Slipper (10–1) T. P. Burns (£4,016) P. Murphy
    2. House Proud,   **3.** Zaracarn.   2, ½.   14 ran
1967 Hibernian (9–4f) L. Ward (£4,962) M. V. O'Brien
    2. Kylin,   **3.** Grey Hawk.   2, Nk.   10 ran
1968 Deep Run (100–8) C. Williams (£4,520) H. V. S. Murless
    2. Mongolia II,   **3.** Arctic Lace.   5, Nk.   9 ran

Race 42: MIDDLE PARK STAKES
6 furlongs. Newmarket. Two-year-olds. First run 1866

1900 Floriform	(10)	**1921** Golden Corn	(5)	**[AT NOTTINGHAM]**	
1901 Minstead	(9)	**1922** Drake	(7)	**1940** Hyacinthus	(7)
1902 Flotsam	(8)	**1923** Diophon	(11)		
1903 Pretty Polly	(7)	**1924** Picaroon	(8)	**[AT NEWMARKET]**	
1904 Jardy	(9)	**1925** Lex	(3)	**1941** Sun Chariot	(4)
1905 Flair	(7)	**1926** Call Boy	(12)	**1942** Ribbon	(8)
1906 Galvani	(5)	**1927** Pharamond	(8)	**1943** Orestes	(9)
1907 Lesbia	(7)	**1928** Costaki Pasha	(13)	**1944** Dante	(4)
1908 Bayardo	(4)	**1929** Press Gang	(4)	**1945** Khaled	(6)
1909 Lemberg	(8)	**1930** Portlaw	(8)	**1946** Saravan	(8)
1910 Borrow	(5)	**1931** Orwell	(5)	**1947** The Cobbler	(4)
1911 Absurd	(10)	**1932** Felicitation		**1948** Abernant	(3)
1912 Craganour	(7)	(Manitoba disq.)	(6)	**1949** Masked Light	(5)
1913 Corcyra	(7)	**1933** Medieval Knight	(11)	**1950** Big Dipper	(5)
1914 Friar Marcus	(7)	**1934** Bahram	(6)	**1951** King's Bench	(8)
1915 Argos	(10)	**1935** Abjer	(13)	**1952** Nearula	(9)
1916 North Star	(7)	**1936** Fair Copy	(7)	**1953** Royal	
1917 Benevente	(6)	**1937** Scottish Union	(5)	Challenger	(5)
1918 Stefan the Great	(9)	**1938** Foxbrough II	(10)	**1954** Our Babu	(10)
1919 Tetratema	(5)	**1939** Djebel	(20)	**1955** Buisson Ardent	(6)
1920 Monarch	(8)			**1956** Pipe of Peace	(8)

1957 MAJOR PORTION (11–2) E. Smith (£3,361) T. Leader
    2. Neptune II,   **3.** Kelly.   ½, 2.   7 ran
1958 MASHAM (2–1f) D. Smith (£3,468) G. Brooke
    2. Dan Cupid,   **3.** Hieroglyph.   1, ¾.   5 ran
1959 VENTURE VII (1–4f) G. Moore (£3,472) A. Head (France)
    2. Blast,   **3.** Arctic Hope.   2, Hd.   5 ran
1960 Skymaster (100–30) A. Breasley (£3,816) W. Smyth
    2. Uncle Percy,   **3.** China Clipper. ½, 2.   4 ran
1961 Gustav (100–6) J. Lindley (£5,672) J. Tree
    2. Sovereign Lord, **3.** Sturdy Man.   ½, 4.   7 ran

1962 Crocket (5–4f) E. Smith (£5,383) G. Brooke
    2. Happy Omen,   **3.** Romantic. $1\frac{1}{2}$, 2.   4 ran
1963 Showdown (100–30) D. Smith (£14,941) F. Winter
    2. Smooth Jet,   **3.** FABERGE II.   3, $\frac{1}{2}$.   11 ran
1964 Spanish Express (9–1) J. Mercer (£18,184) L. Hall
    2. Ragtime,   **3.** Sovereign Edition.   4, 2.   4 ran
1965 Track Spare (10–1) J. Lindley (£17,704) R. Mason
    2. Ritz,   **3.** Legal Measure. $\frac{1}{2}$, $2\frac{1}{2}$.   9 ran
1966 Bold Lad (2–7f) D. Lake (£9,284) P. J. Prendergast
    2. Golden Horus,   **3.** Golden Dipper. $2\frac{1}{2}$, Nk.   5 ran
1967 PETINGO (1–4f) L. Piggott (£7,908) F. Armstrong
    2. Berber,   **3.** Lucky Finish. $1\frac{1}{2}$, Hd.   3 ran
1968 Right Tack (11–2) G. Lewis (£7,910) J. Sutcliffe jun.
    2. Tower Walk,   **3.** Burglar. $\frac{1}{2}$, $\frac{3}{4}$.   7 ran

Race 43: CHEVELEY PARK STAKES
6 furlongs. Newmarket. Two-year-old fillies. First run in 1870

1900 Alruna	(6)	1918 Bayuda	(10)	1937 Stafaralla	(9)
1901 Punctilio	(14)	1919 Bright Folly	(9)	1938 Seaway	(13)
1902 Skyscraper	(7)	1920 Romana	(11)	1939–41 No race	
1903 Pretty Polly	(7)	1921 Selene	(7)	1942 Lady Sybil	(11)
1904 Galantine	(5)	1922 Paola	(12)	1943 Fair Fame	(9)
1905 Colonia	(4)	1923 Chronometer	(16)	1944 Sweet Cygnet	(8)
1906 Witch Elm	(6)	1924 Miss Gadabout	(10)	1945 Neolight	(3)
1907 Bracelet	(5)	1925 Karra	(14)	1946 Djerba	(6)
1908 Sceptre f by		1926 Nipisiquit	(22)	1947 Ash Blonde	(7)
Cyllene	(5)	1927 Scuttle	(8)	1948 Pambidian	(7)
1909 Maid of Corinth	(11)	1928 Tiffin	(8)	1949 Corejada	(3)
1910 Knockfeerna	(5)	1929 Merry Wife	(12)	1950 Belle of All	(8)
1911 Belleisle	(5)	1930 The Leopard	(16)	1951 Zabara	(8)
1912 Merula	(17)	1931 Concordia	(10)	1952 Bebe Grande	(6)
1913 Shake Down	(15)	1932 Brown Betty	(10)	1953 Sixpence	(6)
1914 Lady of Asia	(9)	1933 Light Brocade	(8)	1954 Gloria Nicky	(10)
1915 Fifinella	(4)	1934 Lady Gabriel	(12)	1955 Midget II	(8)
1916 Molly Desmond	(8)	1935 Ferrybridge	(17)	1956 Sarcella	(7)
1917 Freesia	(5)	1936 Celestial Way	(12)		

1957 Rich and Rare (5–1) E. Mercer (£3,604) J. Jarvis
    2. Abelia,   **3.** NONE NICER.   3, 2.   8 ran
1958 Lindsay (100–8) E. Mercer (£3,888) R. Peacock
    2. ROSALBA,   **3.** PARAGUANA.   Nk, 3.   15 ran
1959 Queensberry (2–5f) E. Smith (£3,638) J. A. Waugh
    2. Release,   **3.** Whistler's   5, 3.   6 ran
                               Daughter.
1960 Opaline II (11–10f) G. Moore (£3,935) A. Head (France)
    2. Kerrabee,   **3.** Abanilla.   3, 3.   6 ran

1961 DISPLAY (8–11f) R. Hutchinson (£5,507) P. J. Prendergast
    2. WEST SIDE STORY,   **3.** Couloir.   2, 5.   10 ran
1962 My Goodness Me (100–8) E. Smith (£5,341) G. Brooke
    2. Dunce Cap,   **3.** Didon. $\frac{3}{4}$, $1\frac{1}{2}$.   10 ran
1963 Crimea II (9–1) W. Carr (£5,664) C. Boyd-Rochfort
    2. Palinda,   **3.** Flattering.   3, Sht Hd.   12 ran
1964 NIGHT OFF (20–1) J. Mercer (£4,330) W. Wharton
    2. Fall in Love II,   **3.** Greengage.   1, $1\frac{1}{2}$.   6 ran
1965 BERKELEY SPRINGS (100–8) G. Lewis (£7,198) I. Balding
    2. Right of the Line,   **3.** Bravery. $\frac{1}{2}$, 2.   11 ran
1966 FLEET (5–2jf) L. Piggott (£9,467) N. Murless
    2. PIA,   **3.** Maeander. $1\frac{1}{2}$, $\frac{3}{4}$.   8 ran
1967 Lalibela (5–1) L. Piggott (£7,742) M. V. O'Brien
    2. Fairy Path,   **3.** Alaska Way.   4, $\frac{3}{4}$.   5 ran
1968 Mige (5–2) J. Taillard (£8,412) A. Head (France)
    2. Lucyrowe,   **3.** Grey Goose. $\frac{1}{2}$, 2.   18 ran

Race 44: CORNWALLIS STAKES

5 furlongs. Ascot. Two-year-olds. *Run at Kempton

1957 Abelia (5–4f) L. Piggott (£1, 578) N. Murless
    2. Promulgation,   **3.** Prime Boy.   3, $\frac{3}{4}$.   6 ran
1958 ROSALBA (11–4) J. Mercer (£1,595) R. J. Colling
    2. Greek Sovereign,   **3.** Sundown.   4, Sht Hd.   7 ran
1959 Sing Sing (4–6f) D. Smith (£1,973) J. F. Watts
    2. Queensberry,   **3.** Sound Track. $1\frac{1}{2}$, 3.   4 ran
*1960 Favorita (11–10f) L. Piggott (£2,181) N. Murless
    2. Silver Tor,   **3.** Mythical Return.   Hd, 6.   9 ran
1961 Prince Tor (11–8) W. Rickaby (£2,203) R. N. Fetherstonhaugh
    2. French Plea.   Hd.   2 ran
1962 Fair Astronomer (7–2) G. Bougoure (£2,232) J. Lenehan
    2. Matatina,   **3.** Hera.   2, Nk.   11 ran
*1963 Derring-Do (8–13f) A. Breasley (£2,088) A. Budgett
    2. Golden Apollo,   **3.** Trident Jet.   Sht Hd, 2.   4 ran
1964 Spaniards Mount (9–4f) A. Breasley (£2,156) F. Winter
    2. Tamino,   **3.** Audience.   Sht Hd, 4.   5 ran
1965 Tin King (8–11f) L. Piggott (£1,884) R. Houghton
    2. Comonisi,   **3.** Saulisa.   3, 3.   4 ran
1966 Green Park (5–1) J. Lindley (£7,580) J. Tree
    2. St Chad,   **3.** Turn Coat. $1\frac{1}{2}$, $2\frac{1}{2}$.   8 ran
1967 So Blessed (4–5f) F. Durr (£5,431) P. Davey
    2. Constans,   **3.** Tudor Black.   4, 4.   7 ran
1968 Abandoned

Race 45: DUKE OF EDINBURGH STAKES

6 furlongs. Ascot. Two-year-olds. *Run at Kempton

1957 Bald Eagle (6–5f) W. Carr (£1,688) C. Boyd-Rochfort
    2. Barleycroft,   **3.** Teynham.   1, ½.   8 ran
1958 Cortachy (2–1f) E. Mercer (£1,620) J. Jarvis
    2. Aura,   **3.** Frangipan.   Hd, 6.   8 ran
1959 Arion (15–8jf) J. Mercer (£2,402) H. Wragg
    2. Ergina,   **3.** Raccolto,   5, 3.   9 ran
*1960 PSIDIUM (9–4) L. Piggott (£2,500) H. Wragg
    2. Path of Glory,   **3.** Meridian.   2, 1.   4 ran
1961 HETHERSETT (100–6) W. Carr (£2,929) W. Hern
    2. Palmistry,   **3.** Nardus.   5, ¾.   13 ran
1962 IONIAN (2–1f) L. Ward (£2,347) T. Shaw
    2. Nadir Shah,   **3.** Parthenia.   4, Nk.   7 ran
*1963 Marco Polo (9–4f) L. Ward (£2,207) T. Shaw
    2. Tamerella,   **3.** Bush Fire.   ¾, Sht Hd.   9 ran
1964 Carlemont (2–5f) R. Hutchinson (£2,555) P. J. Prendergast
    2. Coronado,   **3.** Aurianda.   3, 3.   8 ran
1965 Persian Empire (33–1) E. Smith (£2,231) T. Leader
    2. Double-U-Jay,   **3.** Tok.   1½, 4.   14 ran
1966 Apex II (4–1) J. Mercer (£2,102) P. Walwyn
    2. High Order,   **3.** Zimone Boy.   2, 4.   11 ran
1967 Dalry (5–2) W. Williamson (£1,796) P. J. Prendergast
    2. Hill Shade,   **3.** Path.   ¾, 6.   9 ran
1968 Stoned (7–4f) D. Keith (£2,008) P. Walwyn
    2. Straight Arrow,   **3.** Lutine.   2, 12.   6 ran

Race 46: DEWHURST STAKES

7 furlongs. Newmarket. Two-year-olds. First run 1875. Until 1921 known as Dewhurst Plate

1900 Lord Bobs	(10)	1912 Louvois	(8)	1925 Review Order	(6)
1901 Game Chick	(10)	1913 Kennymore	(7)	1926 Money Maker	(6)
1902 Rock Sand	(8)	1914 Let Fly	(7)	1927 Toboggan	(7)
1903 Henry the First	(9)	1915 Atheling	(10)	1928 Brienz	(10)
1904 Rouge Croix	(9)	1916 Telephus	(6)	1929 Grace Dalrymple	(7)
1905 Picton	(7)	1917 My Dear	(6)	1930 Sangre	(8)
1906 My Pet II	(5)	1918 Knight of Blyth	(6)	1931 Firdaussi	(6)
1907 Rhodora	(9)	1919 Prince Galahad	(7)	1932 Hyperion	(6)
1908 Bayardo	(6)	1920 No race		1933 Mrs Rustom	(9)
1909 Lemberg	(2)	1921 Lembach	(4)	1934 Hairan	(5)
1910 King William		1922 Hurry Off	(9)	1935 Bala Hissar	(12)
and Phryxus	(7)	1923 Salmon-Trout	(6)	1936 Sultan Mohamed	(6)
1911 White Star	(6)	1924 Zionist	(6)	1937 Manorite	(7)

1938	Casanova	(4)	1944	Paper Weight	(5)	1950	Turco II	(6)
1939	No race		1945	Hypericum	(10)	1951	Marsyad	(11)
1940	Fettes	(9)	1946	Migoli	(8)	1952	Pinza	(9)
1941	Canyonero	(5)	1947	Pride of India	(11)	1953	Infatuation	(5)
1942	Umidadd	(8)	1948	Royal Forest	(11)	1954	My Smokey	(9)
1943	Effervescence	(10)	1949	Emperor II	(7)	1955	Dacian	(10)
						1956	Crepello	(4)

1957 Torbella III (9–4) A. Breasley (£1,977) W. Clout (France)
    2. NAGAMI,   **3.** Long John Silver. 1, 4.   7 ran
1958 Billum (6–1) E. Hide (£2,288) C. F. Elsey
    2. Traviata,   **3.** PARTHIA.   2, $\frac{3}{4}$.   8 ran
1959 Ancient Lights (100–7) E. Smith (£2,228) T. Leader
    2. Intervener,   **3.** Midsummer $1\frac{1}{2}$, 3.   12 ran
            Night II.
1960 BOUNTEOUS (2–1f) J. Sime (£2,407) P. Beasley
    2. PSIDIUM,   **3.** Flambeau. $\frac{3}{4}$, $1\frac{1}{2}$.   7 ran
1961 River Chanter (100–30) J. Mercer (£4,309) G. Todd
    2. Aznip,   **3.** Catchpole.   1, $\frac{3}{4}$.   8 ran
1962 Follow Suit (10–1) L. Piggott (£4,500) N. Murless
    2. Forearmed,   **3.** King's Favourite. Nk, 2.   10 ran
1963 King's Lane (10–1) J. Sime (£4,352) S. Hall
    2. SODERINI,   **3.** London Melody. $1\frac{1}{2}$, Hd.   9 ran
1964 SILLY SEASON (13–2) G. Lewis (£3,291) I. Balding
    2. King Log,   **3.** Nentego.   Sht Hd, 1.   11 ran
1965 PRETENDRE (11–2) R. Hutchinson (£2,217) J. Jarvis
    2. Khalekan,   **3.** Le Cordonnier. $\frac{1}{2}$, 4.   11 ran
1966 DART BOARD (10–1) D. Smith (£9,867) Sir G. Richards
    2. French Vine,   **3.** Countermarch. Hd, Nk.   13 ran
1967 Hametus (100–9) F. Durr (£8,151) W. Nightingall
    2. D'Urberville,   **3.** Heathen.   Hd, $1\frac{1}{2}$.   7 ran
1968 Ribofilio (8–11f) L. Piggott (£8,580) R. Houghton
    2. Deep Run,   **3.** Murrayfield.   3, $2\frac{1}{2}$.   11 ran

Race 47: HOUGHTON STAKES

7 furlongs. Newmarket. Two-year-olds. Race run over 1 mile in '57, '58; 6 furlongs in '59, '60, '61

1957 Rich and Rare (5–6f) E. Mercer (£937) J. Jarvis
    2. Aggressor,   **3.** Glendawn. $1\frac{1}{2}$, 8.   3 ran
1958 Anthelion (5–4f) E. Mercer (£954) J. Jarvis
    2. FIDALGO,   **3.** Decree.   1, 5.   6 ran
1959 Demagog (5–2) A. Breasley (£424) S. Ingham
    2. Christmas Night,   **3.** Miss Caroline.   1, Hd.   19 ran
1960 Jebanette (7–2f) B. Swift (£499) T. H. Carey
    2. Golden Sands,   **3.** Performance. $1\frac{1}{2}$, 4.   27 ran

1961 Kings Regulations (8–1) E. Smith (£584) T. Leader

    2. Windscale,   **3.** Allurement.   2, 6.   23 ran

1962 There She Goes (5–2f) F. Durr (£561) W. Hern

    2. Dumelle,   **3.** Greek Honey.   1, 3.   12 ran

1963 Royal Desire (11–10f) L. Piggott (£1,787) N. Murless

    2. Paddy's Song,   **3.** Hotroy.   ¾, 3.   5 ran

1964 Alan Adare (11–8f) L. Piggott (£1,939) N. Murless

    2. Go Shell,   **3.** Inquisitor.   Hd, 2.   29 ran

1965 Hermes (10–1) G. Starkey (£1,826) J. Oxley

    2. Salvo,   **3.** VARINIA.   Hd, 5.   24 ran

1966 Love for Sale (11–4) L. Piggott (£1,693) N. Murless

    2. Chapmans Peak,   **3.** Meyerling.   Sht Hd, 2½.   17 ran

1967 Ilium (5–1) D. Smith (£1,474) G. Brooke

    2. Torpid,   **3.** Pardon.   4, 2.   16 ran

1968 Blakeney (7–1) E. Johnson (£1,573) A. Budgett

    2. Prince de Galles,   **3.** Favour.   ½, 1.   27 ran

Race 48: HORRIS HILL STAKES

7 furlongs 60 yards. Newbury. Two-year-olds

1957 ALCIDE (5–1) W. Carr (£1,424) C. Boyd-Rochfort

    2. Bengal Lancer,   **3.** Rapin.   1½, 2.   10 ran

1958 Seascape (1–7f) E. Smith (£1,388) T. Leader

    2. Open Sky,   **3.** Harley Street.   6, 8.   4 ran

1959 Ironic (100–8) W. Carr (£1,522) D. Candy

    2. Arctic Sea,   **3.** Astrador.   Nk, 1½.   11 ran

1960 Gallant Knight (4–5f) E. Smith (£1,586) T. Leader

    2. PSIDIUM,   **3.** Apache.   1½, 10.   5 ran

1961 Valentine (9–4) D. Smith (£2,339) G. Brooke

    2. Heron,   **3.** Palmistry.   3, Nk.   11 ran

1962 Scholar Gypsy (10–1) R. Hutchinson (£2,318) R. Jarvis

    2. Forearmed,   **3.** Hill Town.   Hd, 1½.   13 ran

1963 Atbara (15–8f) A. Breasley (£3,918) Sir G. Richards

    2. London Melody,   **3.** Woolhampton.

    (Penny Stall second, disqualified.) Original distances, Sht Hd, 4, Hd.   6 ran

1964 Foothill (7–1) J. Mercer (£4,226) W. Hern

    2. Kirsch Flambee,   **3.** Shai.   ½, ¾.   17 ran

1965 CHARLOTTOWN (11–10f) J. Lindley (£5,508) J. Gosden

    2. Red Rumour,   **3.** Bright Will.   2½, Sht Hd.   13 ran

1966 Alcan (13–2) B. Raymond (£6,395) H. Cottrill

    2. Good Match,   **3.** Attacker.   Nk, Sht Hd.   12 ran

1967 Dalry (11–8f) R. Poincelet (£5,178) P. J. Prendergast

    2. Country Path,   **3.** Swallow Tail II.   1½, 12.   10 ran

1968 Sentier (11–2) A. Breasley (£5,352) K. Cundell

    2. Stoned,   **3.** Polar Venture.   ½, 5.   7 ran

154

Race 49: OBSERVER GOLD CUP

1 mile. Doncaster. Two-year-olds. Run as Timeform Gold Cup until 1965

1961 MIRALGO (10–1) W. Williamson (£21,894) H. Wragg
      2. Escort,   **3.** PRINCE POPPA. Nk, 2.   13 ran
1962 NOBLESSE (11–10f) G. Bougoure (£23,339) P. J. Prendergast
      2. Partholon,   **3.** STAR MOSS.   3, ¾.   12 ran
1963 Pushful (100–6) W. Carr (£23,377) S. Meaney
      2. Scissors (first, disq.)   **3.** All Saved.
                             Original distances, Nk, 1½.   10 ran
1964 Hardicanute (13–8f) W. Williamson (£24,830) P. J. Prendergast
      2. Leonardo,   **3.** Brave Knight.   Nk, 2.   11 ran
1965 PRETENDRE (6–1) R. Hutchinson (£21,719) J. Jarvis
      2. Le Cordonnier,   **3.** Khalekan.   1, 2.   13 ran
1966 RIBOCCO (4–9f) L. Piggott (£20,155) R. Houghton
      2. Starry Halo,   **3.** El Mighty.   ¾, 4.   11 ran
1967 Vaguely Noble (8–1) W. Williamson (£16,945) W. Wharton
      2. Doon,   **3.** Riboccare.   7, Hd.   8 ran
1968 Elk (10–1) W. Pyers (£19,430) J. Tree
      2. Intermezzo,   **3.** Blue Yonder.   1½, ¾.   11 ran

---

*HORSES IN CAPITAL LETTERS
WERE TO BE, OR HAD BEEN,
PLACED IN THE CLASSICS*

155

HORSES IN CAPITAL LETTERS
WERE TO BE, OR HAD BEEN,
PLACED IN THE CLASSICS

Section Three:
Weight for Age Events

Race 59: 2,000 GUINEAS TRIAL STAKES

7 furlongs. Kempton. Three-year-olds

1957 Doutelle (2–1f) W. Carr (£1,238) C. Boyd-Rochfort
    2. Super Snipe,   **3.** Copenhagen.   1½, 4.   7 ran
1958 Aggressor (100–30) J. Lindley (£1,170) J. Gosden
    2. Welsh Abbot,   **3.** Mr Snake.   4, 3.   8 ran
1959 Connaissance (7–1) W. Rickaby (£1,161) R. Day
    2. Sovereign Path,   **3.** Franciscan.   ½, 5.   8 ran
1960 Nice Guy (100–8) T. Gosling (£1,227) P. J. Prendergast
    2. AUROY,   **3.** Le Levanstell.   ½, ½.   9 ran
1961 Dual (9–4) J. Lindley (£1,228) J. Gosden
    2. Good Old Days,   **3.** PSIDIUM.   Nk, 1½.   9 ran
1962 Miletus (3–1f) W. Rickaby (£1,259) F. Winter
    2. French Plea,   **3.** Writ of Error.   1, 5.   8 ran
1963 Turbo Jet (7–4f) L. Piggott (£2,067) M. V. O'Brien
    2. Zaleucus,   **3.** Gyroscope.   1, 1.   8 ran
1964 Penny Stall (20–1) D. Keith (£2,092) W. Nightingall
    2. Make Haste,   **3.** Showdown.   Hd, 1½.   11 ran
1965 NIKSAR (100–6) D. Keith (£1,418) W. Nightingall
    2. Streetfighter,   **3.** Holborn.   6, 3.   6 ran
1966 Lucky Biscuit (10–1) B. Taylor (£1,438) H. Leader
    2. At-A-Venture,   **3.** Young Emperor.   1½, Hd.   9 ran
1967 Be Friendly (7–2jf) A. Breasley (£1,184) C. Mitchell
    2. Quy,   **3.** Above Water.   Sht Hd, 2½.   10 ran
1968 Constans (5–2) J. Lindley (£1,167) J. Tree
    2. Viscount,   **3.** Hametus.   Nk, 2½.   3 ran

Race 60: COVENTRY STAKES

1 mile. Kempton. Three-year-olds

1957 Agreement (8–1) W. Carr (£1,026) C. Boyd-Rochfort
    2. Mossarco,   **3.** Sovereign Flame.   1½, 4.   9 ran

1958 Blackness (10–11f) E. Mercer (£899) J. Jarvis
    2. Davy Crockett,   **3.** Long John $\frac{3}{4}$, 2.   4 ran
        Silver.
1959 Dickens (15–2) W. Carr (£1,026) C. Boyd-Rochfort
    2. My Aladdin,   **3.** Arctic Run. $\frac{1}{2}$, 5.   13 ran
1960 Bookmarker (9–2) J. Lindley (£908) J. Gosden
    2. Tudor Period,   **3.** Blast. $\frac{1}{2}$, 2.   13 ran
1961 Morgan (100–7) E. Smith (£884) J. F. Watts
    2. Penhill,   **3.** Phoenix Star. $\frac{1}{2}$, Sht Hd.   15 ran
1962 Pablo (20–1) D. Smith (£1,357) G. Brooke
    2. Albatros,   **3.** Superstition.   Hd, 4.   10 ran
1963 Campaign (10–1) S. Smith (£2,245) J. Jarvis
    2. Dumelle,   **3.** Fine Bid. $1\frac{1}{2}$, 4.   11 ran
1964 Frigolet (100–7) R. Hutchinson (£2,319) J. Jarvis
    2. Pretentious,   **3.** Oncidium.   3, 2.   15 ran
1965 Bastion (7–1) J. Mercer (£1,527) W. Hern
    2. Yankee Clipper,   **3.** Quick Thought. $1\frac{1}{2}$, 8.   9 ran
1966 Lay About (20–1) J. Lindley (£1,618) J. Tree
    2. Italiano,   **3.** Maldavan.   4, $\frac{3}{4}$.   17 ran
1967 Starry Halo (8–13f) L. Piggott (£1,222) J. Thompson
    2. Straight Master,   **3.** Hipster. $\frac{1}{2}$, 3.   10 ran
1968 Moorings (100–30f) A. Barclay (£1,237) N, Murless
    2. Cheval,   **3.** Principal Boy.   3, 2.   11 ran

Race 61: 1,000 GUINEAS TRIAL STAKES

7 furlongs. Kempton. Three-year-old fillies

1957 Even Star (100–6) F. Durr (£1,518) R. Day
    2. Refined,   **3.** Picture Light.   6, 1.   14 ran
1958 MOTHER GOOSE (4–7f) L. Piggott (£1,294) W. Nightingall
    2. Tropical Breeze.   6.   2 ran
1959 Spice (11–2) G. Lewis (£1,378) M. Feakes
    2. Donna,   **3.** Be Careful.   Sht Hd, 6.   12 ran
1960 Queensberry (7–2) E. Smith (£1,384) J. A. Waugh
    2. Diffidence,   **3.** Shy Girl.   Hd, Hd.   15 ran
1961 SWEET SOLERA (4–7f) W. Rickaby (£1,204) Reg Day
    2. Who Can Tell,   **3.** Tender Word. $\frac{1}{2}$, 3.   7 ran
1962 Hidden Meaning (11–2) E. Smith (£1,374) H. Leader
    2. Victorina,   **3.** Bryonia. $\frac{1}{2}$, 8.   10 ran
1963 Hera (7–2) W. Carr (£2,075) H. Wragg
    2. Fair Astronomer,   **3.** My Goodness Me. $1\frac{1}{2}$, Sht Hd.   7 ran
1964 GWEN (11–4) S. Smith (£2,088) J. Jarvis
    2. POURPARLER,   **3.** Siesta Time. $\frac{3}{4}$, 3.   11 ran
1965 Valdesta (13–8) D. Smith (£1,443) G. Brooke
    2. Coup,   **3.** La Gamberge.   Hd, 2.   5 ran

1966 Orabella II (8–1) B. Taylor (£1,599) H. Leader
    2. Sea Lichen,   **3.** America.   1, 3.   20 ran
1967 Broadway Melody (9–4f) G. Lewis (£1,197) S. Ingham
    2. My Enigma,   **3.** Jabula.   Sht Hd, 5.   12 ran
1968 CAERGWRLE (2–1f) A. Barclay (£1,237) N. Murless
    2. Grandpa's Legacy,   **3.** Milistrina.   4, ¾.   10 ran

Race 62: GLADNESS STAKES

1 mile. Curragh

1963 Christmas Island (100–30) G. Bougoure (£1,624) P. J. Prendergast, 3 yrs
    2. Tristram,   **3.** Cagliari.   1½, 2.   9 ran
1964 Khalkis (7–4f) G. Bougoure (£1,534) P. J. Prendergast, 4 yrs
    2. Ashavan,   **3.** Master Buck.   2, Nk.   14 ran
1965 Western Wind (100–6) L. Ward (£2,227) M. Dawson, 3 yrs
    2. MEADOW COURT,   **3.** Flaming Red.   2, 1¼.   15 ran
1966 Not So Cold (100–8) P. Powell jun. (£2,355) M. Hurley, 3 yrs
    2. Ambericos,   **3.** Reubens.   3, 2½.   15 ran
1967 Sparrow Hawk (11–2) M. Kennedy (£2,152) J. M. Rogers, 5 yrs
    2. Crepe Clover,   **3.** Sofico.   1½, 1½.   8 ran
1968 Signa Infesta (9–2) G. McGrath (£2,192) S. McGrath, 4 yrs
    2. Hibernian,   **3.** World Cup.   1, 2.   12 ran

Race 63: PLAYERS' NAVY CUT TRIAL STAKES

1 mile. Phoenix Park. Three-year-olds. Run over 1 mile 1 furlong in 1960

1960 DIE HARD (1–2f) G. Bougoure (£1,196) M. V. O'Brien, 3 yrs
    2. His Story,   **3.** Sunny Court.   Nk, 4.   15 ran
1961 Bally Vimy (100–8) N. Brennan (£942) C. Collins, 3 yrs, and
    Dorney Common (100–6) P. Powell jun. (£942) T. D. Ainsworth, 3 yrs
        3. Dusky Boy.   Dd. Ht, 2.   23 ran
1962 Sebring (8–13f) T. P. Glennon (£1,811) M. V. O'Brien, 3 yrs
    2. Richmond,   **3.** Mystery.   Nk, Sht Hd.   12 ran
1963 Lock Hard (33–1) P. Boothman (£2,287) M. Hurley
    2. Final Move,   **3.** Deep Gulf.   3. 3.   14 ran
1964 Marco Polo (100–6) L. Ward (£2,550) T. Shaw
    2. Persian Spark,   **3.** Glenrowan.   Nk, 1¼.   17 ran
1965 Prominer (8–15f) T. P. Burns (£2,461) P. J. Prendergast
    2. Sandiment,   **3.** Dante's Hill.   Nk, 5.   7 ran
1966 Paveh (5–1) P. Powell jun. (£2,597) T. D. Ainsworth
    2. Golden Scene,   **3.** Acrania.   3, 2½.   10 ran
1967 Signa Infesta (9–1) G. McGrath (£2,524) S. McGrath
    2. Rome,   **3.** Gay Henry.   2, 1.   13 ran

1968 Giolla Mear (10–1) P. Powell jun. (£2,403) M. Hurley
    2. Meadsville,   **3.** Mistigo.   5, 3.   11 ran

Race 64: BALLYMOSS STAKES
1 mile 2 furlongs. Curragh

1964 Glenrowan (5–1jf) G. McGrath (£1,612) P. Norris, 3 yrs
    2. Cassim,   **3.** AURELIUS.   2¼, Nk.   12 ran
1965 Hardicanute (4–11f) G. Bougoure (£2,092) P. J. Prendergast, 3 yrs
    2. Cassim,   **3.** Test Ban.   Nk, 2½.   5 ran
1966 Radbrook (2–1f) M. Kennedy (£2,205) J. M. Rogers, 3 yrs
    2. Pieces of Eight,   **3.** Al-'Alawi.   6, 4.   8 ran
1967 White Gloves (10–1) L. Ward (£2,145) M. V. O'Brien, 4 yrs
    2. My Kuda,   **3.** Royal Sword.   2½, Hd.   9 ran
1968 Candy Cane (evens f) M. Kennedy (£2,043) J. M. Rogers, 3 yrs
    2. Signa Infesta,   **3.** World Cup.   5, 6.   8 ran

Race 65: TETRARCH STAKES
7 furlongs. Curragh. Three-year-old colts

1957 Jack Ketch (5–4f) N. Brennan (£718) E. M. Quirke
    2. English Slipper,   **3.** Ballyprecious.   3, 1½.   10 ran
1958 Tharp (5–1) L. Browne (£751) C. Brabazon
    2. HARD RIDDEN,   **3.** Mesembryanthe- Sht Hd, 1¾.   10 ran
                                       mum.
1959 Sovereign Path (3–1f) C. Smirke (£790) C. Brabazon
    2. Ross Sea,   **3.** Larkspur Bloom. ¾, 8.   15 ran
1960 KYTHNOS (5–2) R. Hutchinson (£805) P. J. Prendergast
    2. Our Charger,   **3.** Ti Amo.   ½, ¾.   14 ran
1961 TIME GREINE (100–7) W. Willamson (£1,029) S. McGrath
    2. Light Year,   **3.** Bun Penny.   Nk, Sht Hd.   15 ran
1962 Assurance (100–8) P. Powell jun. (£984) T. D. Ainsworth
    2. Prince Tor,   **3.** Ahascragh.   1, 3.   9 ran
1963 Vertigo (8–1) T. Gosling (£1,191) J. M. Rogers
    2. Profit Refused,   **3.** Vic Mo Chroi (first, disq.)
                        Original distances, Hd, Sht Hd.   11 ran
1964 Majority Blue (4–1) W. Wiliamson (£1,272) J. Oxx
    2. Ordonez,   **3.** Cold Slipper. 3, Sht Hd.   7 ran
1965 Quintillian (9–2) L. Piggott (£1,427) P. J. Prendergast
    2. Green Banner,   **3.** Tomahawk IV. 3, Nk.   5 ran
1966 Ultimate II (8–1) P. Sullivan (£2,042) H. V. S. Murless
    2. Golden Scene,   **3.** Indian Scene. 1½, 8.   11 ran

1967 Bold Lad (1–3f) D. Lake (£1,945) P. J. Prendergast
    2. Mark Scott,   **3.** Sovereign Slipper. Nk, 2.   9 ran
1968 Harry (4–1jf) L. Ward (£1,967) M. V. O'Brien
    2. Noblesse Oblige,   **3.** Polar Gold.   ½, Hd.   9 ran

Race 66: ATHASI STAKES

7 furlongs. Curragh. Three-year-old fillies

1957 After the Show (7–1) P. Matthews (£736) M. Hurley
    2. Gorm Abu,   **3.** Refined.   4, 2½.   14 ran
1958 Minou (7–1) T. P. Burns (£742) D. Rogers
    2. Rising Wings,   **3.** Daffodil.   2½, ½.   11 ran
1959 Pastime Penny (100–8) N. Brennan (£787) D. St. John Gough
    2. Truly,   **3.** Princess Marie.   2, ½.   12 ran
1960 Gilboa (100–7) P. Sullivan (£760) J. Oxx
    2. Zenobia,   **3.** Davedasee   1¼, 2.   13 ran
1961 Tuna Gail (evens f) W. Williamson (£939) S. McGrath
    2. Peeress,   **3.** Eglee.   Sht Hd, 2½.   10 ran
1962 Lovely Gale (2–1f) T. P. Glennon (£995) M. V. O'Brien
    2. Top Song,   **3.** George's Girl.   Sht Hd, 2.   17 ran
1963 Evening Shoe (100–8) P. Sullivan (£1,236) J. Oxx
    2. Hibernia III,   **3.** Confidence.   3, 1.   15 ran
1964 ROYAL DANSEUSE, (7–2f) J. Roe (£1,218) S. McGrath
    2. Shoubad,   **3.** Courtwell.   1, 8.   10 ran
1965 Arctic Melody (100–30) G. Bougoure (£1,467) Patrick Prendergast jun.
    2. Brassia,   **3.** Ashling.   5, 4.   8 ran
1966 Loyalty (2–1) J. Roe (£1,915) J. Oxx
    2. Honey Lake,   **3.** Black Gold.   ¾, Nk.   6 ran
1967 Jadeite (7–2) M. Kennedy (£2,035) J. M. Rogers
    2. Regality,   **3.** Princess Ribot.
    (Regal Cloud third, disqualified.) Original distances, ¾, Sht Hd, 1½.   12 ran
1968 Rimark (3–1f) L. Ward (£2,065) M. V. O'Brien
    2. Windy Gay,   **3.** Sorrentina.   ½, 5.   11 ran

Race 67: CRAVEN STAKES

1 mile. Newmarket. Three-year-olds. First run 1878

1900	Headpiece	(7)	1907	Slieve Gallion	(12)	1913	Sanquhar	(9)
1901	Rigo	(12)	1908	No race		1914	Kenny More	(8)
1902	Port Blair	(12)	1909	Howick	(9)	1915	Rossendale	(7)
1903	Countermark	(9)	1910	Neil Gow	(6)	1916	Sir Dighton and	
1904	Airlie	(10)	1911	Irish King	(5)		Roi d'Ecosse	(6)
1905	St Oswald	(10)	1912	Jingling		1917	Dansellon	(9)
1906	His Eminence	(5)		Geordie	(12)	1918	Benevente	(8)

1919	Buchan (8)	1931	Philae (12)	1946	Gulf Stream (8)
1920	Daylight Patrol (11)	1932	Loaningdale (7)	1947	Migoli (6)
1921	Not run	1933	Lochiel (8)	1948	My Babu (9)
1922	Collaborator (19)	1934	Colombo (7)	1949	Moondust (8)
1923	Light Hand (11)	1935	Buckleigh (16)	1950	Rising Flame (6)
1924	St Germans (12)	1936	Monument (13)	1951	Claudius (13)
1925	Picaroon (6)	1937	Snowfall (14)	1952	Kara Tepe (11)
1926	Harpagon (11)	1938	Challenge (6)	1953	Oleandrin (7)
1927	Tattoo (15)	1939	Signal Light (13)	1954	Ambler II (8)
1928	Royal Minstrel (10)	1940	Prince Tetra (14)	1955	True Cavalier (9)
1929	Cragadour (13)	1941	Morogoro (16)	1956	Pirate King (15)
1930	Writ (13)	1942–45	No race		

1957 Shearwater (10–1) L. Piggott (£735) N. Murless
    2. Alan A'Dale,   **3.** Just Verdict.   Nk, 2.   7 ran

1958 Bald Eagle (7–2) W. Carr (£716) C. Boyd-Rochfort
    2. NAGAMI,   **3.** Pinched.   1, 3.   6 ran

1959 PINDARI (6–1) L. Piggott (£758) N. Murless
    2. Winning Move,   **3.** British Empire.   4, 4.   7 ran

1960 Tudorich (11–4jf) A. Breasley (£796) Sir G. Richards
    2. Armour Star,   **3.** Palisander.   1½, Hd.   13 ran

1961 AURELIUS (8–1) L. Piggott (£724) N. Murless
    2. Eagle,   **3.** Pinzon,   2, 1.   6 ran

1962 High Noon (5–2) E. Hide (£1,239) W. Elsey
    2. Writ of Error,   **3.** Valentine.   ½, 4.   7 ran

1963 Crocket (4–11f) D. Smith (£1,196) G. Brooke
    2. Victory Way,   **3.** MERCHANT   Hd, 3.   5 ran
                                     VENTURER.

1964 Young Christopher (100–7) R. Sheather (£1,154) F. Maxwell
    2. BALUSTRADE,   **3.** Lionhearted.   1½, 2.   12 ran

1965 Corifi (20–1) G. Lewis (£829) S. Ingham
    2. Potier,   **3.** Pepperpot.   ¾, 3.   7 ran

1966 Salvo (3–1f) F. Durr (£831) H. Wragg
    2. Out of Orbit,   **3.** Parbury.   ½, Hd.   11 ran

1967 Sloop (7–1) G. Starkey (£1,234) J. Oxley
    2. Palatch,   **3.** Persister.   1½, 1½.   11 ran

1968 PETINGO (2–5f) J. Mercer (£1,159) F. Armstrong
    2. Milltown,   **3.** Relentless.   4, ½.   4 ran

Race 68: WOOD DITTON STAKES

1 mile. Newmarket. Three-year-olds

1957 London Cry (6–4f) A. Breasley (£569) N. Bertie
    2. Our Girl,   **3.** Stoneborer.   4, 1.   11 ran

1958 Presentiment (9–4jf) W. Rickaby (£543) M. Marsh
    2. Bella Voce,   **3.** Nicky's Double.   6, ¾.   9 ran

1959 Everanick (5–1) W. Rickaby (£568) M. Marsh
    2. Yola,   **3.** Love and   3, ¾.   9 ran
                                   Marriage.
1960 Net (100–30) J. Lindley (£662) H. Leader
    2. Welsh Border,   **3.** Wraith.   2, 3.   15 ran
1961 Pinturischio (2–5f) L. Piggott (£559) N. Murless
    2. Nicomedus,   **3.** Sagacity.   1, 5.   7 ran
1962 Anaphora (20–1) J. Mercer (£467) C. Boyd-Rochfort
    2. Canarina,   **3.** Harvest Gold.   3, 1½.   7 ran
1963 Olgiata (5–2f) G. Starkey (£516) J. Oxley
    2. Whiskey a Go Go,   **3.** Acros.   4, 3.   12 ran
1964 Canisbay (7–1) W. Carr (£909) C. Boyd-Rochfort
    2. Finish Fast,   **3.** St Antonius.   ¾, 1½.   15 ran
1965 Craighouse (85–40) J. Mercer (£826) W. Hern
    2. Hadji Mourad,   **3.** Fort Knox II.   5, 4.   6 ran
1966 Tesco Boy (11–4f) G. Lewis (£861) S. Ingham
    2. Rock Tan,   **3.** General Gordon. 1½, Sht Hd.   16 ran
1967 HOPEFUL VENTURE (4–1) G. Moore (£795) N. Murless
    2. Epidauros,   **3.** Town Life.   1½, ½.   8 ran
1968 Sugar Apple (3–1f) A. Barclay (£851) N. Murless
    2. Driven,   **3.** Great Occasion. ½, ¾.   15 ran

Race 69: NELL GWYN STAKES

7 furlongs. Newmarket. Three-year-old fillies. *Called Spring Fillies Stakes

*1961 Verbena (6–1) D. Smith (£1,332) G. Brooke
    2. Lady Senator,   **3.** Tudor Top.   Hd, 1.   10 ran
1962 WEST SIDE STORY (5–4f) E. Smith (£1,273) T. Leader
    2. Fool's Gold,   **3.** Widden.   2, 4.   6 ran
1963 Amicable (100–7) W. Carr (£1,341) C. Boyd-Rochfort
    2. Dinant,   **3.** Honeysuckle. Sht Hd, 1½.   12 ran
1964 Alborada (9–4) G. Starkey (£1,058) J. Oxley
    2. Triona,   **3.** Zingaline.   1, 1½.   6 ran
1965 Gently (7–4f) A. Breasley (£805) Sir G. Richards
    2. Mirella,   **3.** Crisp Piece.   Hd, 1.   4 ran
1966 Hiding Place (4–1f) A. Breasley (£857) J. Clayton
    2. Padante,   **3.** Pen-Emma   1½, Hd.   11 ran
1967 Cranberry Sauce (7–4f) G. Moore (£1,205) N. Murless
    2. Vital Error,   **3.** Wide Awake.   3, 4.   9 ran
1968 Abbie West (10–11f) A. Barclay (£1,182) N. Murless
    2. She Wolf,   **3.** Sing Again.   1, 5.   4 ran

Race 70: GREENHAM STAKES

7 furlongs. Newbury. Three-year-olds. Prior to 1949 the race was run over 1 mile

1935 Theft	(10)	**1940** Tant Mieux	(16)	**1952** Serpenyoe	(10)
1936 Noble King	(20)	**1941–48** No race		**1953** March Past	(14)
1937 Fairford	(18)	**1949** Star King	(10)	**1954** Infatuation	(13)
1938 Mirza II	(7)	**1950** Port o'Light	(12)	**1955** Counsel	(11)
1939 Fairstone	(22)	**1951** No race		**1956** Ratification	(10)

1957 PIPE OF PEACE (evens f) A. Breasley (£1,523) Sir G. Richards
    2. Crampon,   **3.** Queen's Tankard. Sht Hd, 4.   10 ran
1958 Paresa (15–2) W. Rickaby (£1,463) R. Day
    2. Parma,   **3.** Talisman. $1\frac{1}{2}$, 2.   12 ran
1959 MASHAM (11–10f) D. Smith (£2,112) G. Brooke
    2. Franciscan,   **3.** Rio Santo.   2, 2.   8 ran
1960 Filipepi (100–8) G. Lewis (£2,125) R. Smyth
    2. Taurus,   **3.** Red Gauntlet.   6, Sht Hd.   10 ran
1961 Primus (7–4f) D. Smith (£2,074) Sir G. Richards
    2. Tudor Treasure,   **3.** Golden Voice.   Sht Hd, 3.   8 ran
1962 ROMULUS (9–4f) W. Swinburn (£2,661) R. Houghton
    2. Tacitus,   **3.** Rescind,   3, 5.   12 ran
1963 FIGHTING SHIP (15–2) S. Smith (£2,590) J. Jarvis
    2. Willies,   **3.** ONLY FOR   Hd, 4.   9 ran
    LIFE.
1964 Excel (8–1) F. Durr (£4,691) T. Gosling
    2. Frigolet,   **3.** Pan's Surprise.   Hd, 3.   10 ran
1965 SILLY SEASON (100–30f) G. Lewis (£4,769) I. Balding
    2. Spanish Express,   **3.** Golden Sicamore. $\frac{3}{4}$, 3.   11 ran
1966 Abandoned
1967 Play High (100–8) D. Keith (£3,320) W. Nightingall
    2. Reform,   **3.** Wolver Hollow.   Nk, Hd.   8 ran
1968 Heathen (10–1) J. Mercer (£3,380) W. Hern
    2. Jacobus,   **3.** So Blessed. $\frac{1}{2}$, 2.   8 ran
(CONNAUGHT withdrawn. 2s. in £ deducted from winnings.)

Race 71: FRED DARLING STAKES

7 furlongs 60 yards. Newbury. Three-year-old fillies. *Race run over 7 furlongs only

1957 Sijui (20–1) L. Piggott (£1,207) N. Murless
    2. Even Star,   **3.** Resurge. $1\frac{1}{2}$, Sht Hd.   20 ran
1958 Nicaria (25–1) J. Mercer (£1,141) R. J. Colling
    2. ALPINE BLOOM,   **3.** Bacchanalia. $\frac{1}{2}$, 3.   11 ran
1959 ROSALBA (6–4f) J. Mercer (£1,285) R. J. Colling
    2. Alice Delysia,   **3.** Donna.   3, 5.   8 ran

1960 Soldier's Song (100–6) J. Lindley (£1,307) J. Tree
    2. LADY IN TROUBLE,   **3.** Desert Beauty.   Hd, 5.   23 ran
1961 Who Can Tell (5–1) R. P. Elliott (£1,791) W. Hern
    2. Tenacity,   **3.** Princess Ray.   Nk, 3.   11 ran
*1962 Anassa (11–2) J. Lindley (£1,859) J. Gosden
    2. Mona Louise,   **3.** Jibuti.   ½, 3.   14 ran
*1963 Gazpacho (7–1) G. Bougoure (£3,206) P. J. Prendergast
    2. SPREE,   **3.** Guinea Sparrow.   ½, 3.   13 ran
*1964 Ela Marita (5–4f) G. Bougoure (£3,177) P. J. Prendergast
    2. Analupus,   **3.** Tamerella.   3, ½.   16 ran
1965 Night Appeal (100–7) J. Lindley (£2,326) A. Budgett
    2. Attitude,   **3.** Ashling.   Sht Hd, ½.   7 ran
1966 Abandoned
1967 Royal Saint (8–11f) L. Piggott (£2,316) N. Murless
    2. Whirled,   **3.** Secret Ray.   Nk, Nk.   11 ran
1968 Raymonda (100–6) G. Starkey (£2,226) J. Oxley
    2. Celina,   **3.** Aunt Audrey.   Nk, 3.   5 ran

Race 72: JOHN PORTER STAKES
1 mile 4 furlongs. Newbury

1957 China Rock (100–6) F. Durr (£553) H. G. Blagrave, 4 yrs
    2. Shikar II,   **3.** Court Command. 1, 1½.   10 ran
1958 Doutelle (5–6f) W. Carr (£784) C. Boyd-Rochfort, 4 yrs
    2. COURT HARWELL,   **3.** China Rock.   3, Sht Hd.   4 ran
1959 CUTTER (11–8) J. Lindley (£968) J. Oxley, 4 yrs
    2. Induna,   **3.** Jalan-Besar.   5, Bad.   3 ran
1960 Aggressor (11–8f) J. Lindley (£1,297) J. Gosden, 5 yrs
    2. Agricola,   **3.** Light Horseman.   8, 1½.   12 ran
1961 High Perch (6–4f) J. Lindley (£1,297) J. Gosden, 5 yrs
    2. Pandofell,   **3.** His Story.   1½, 4.   8 ran
1962 Hot Brandy (4–1) D. Keith (£1,241) W. Nightingall, 4 yrs
    2. Sovrango,   **3.** Dual.   ½, ¾.   9 ran
1963 Peter Jones (4–1) E. Smith (£1,927) A. M. Budgett, 4 yrs
    2. Hot Brandy,   **3.** Young Lochinvar. 2, ¾.   11 ran
1964 Royal Avenue (100–8) L. Piggott (£1,966) N. Murless, 6 yrs
    2. ONLY FOR LIFE,   **3.** Stavros II.   Nk, 4.   12 ran
1965 SODERINI (4–1) G. Lewis (£1,913) S. Ingham, 4 yrs
    2. Cassim,   **3.** Earldom.   ¾, ½.   7 ran
1966 Abandoned
1967 CHARLOTTOWN (4–6f) J. Lindley (£2,238) G. Smyth, 4 yrs
    2. Salvo,   **3.** Hermes.   Hd, 5.   8 ran
1968 Fortissimo (3–1) G. Lewis (£2,245) R. N. Fetherstonhaugh, 4 yrs
    2. Hermes,   **3.** Gay Garland.   Sht Hd, 6.   9 ran

Race 73: THIRSK CLASSIC TRIAL STAKES
1 mile. Thirsk. Three-year-olds

1957 Orycida (11–2) E. Hide (£1,378) C. F. Elsey
    2. Earl Marshal,   **3.** BRIOCHE.   ¾, Hd.   6 ran
1958 PALL MALL (100–30) W. Rickaby (£1,155) C. Boyd-Rochfort
    2. Pleiades,   **3.** Pheidippides.   1, 3.   5 ran
1959 CARNOUSTIE (7–4f) L. Piggott (£1,164) N. Murless
    2. Agricola,   **3.** Billum.   1½, 2.   7 ran
1960 Newbus (9–4f) E. Hide (£1,549) C. F. Elsey
    2. MARTIAL,   **3.** Great Faith.   3, 5.   10 ran
1961 SWEET SOLERA (7–4jf) W. Rickaby (£1,447) R. Day
    2. Henry the Seventh,   **3.** Oakville.   ¾, Nk.   6 ran
1962 Windscale (4–1) J. Sime (£2,054) S. Hall
    2. Escort,   **3.** Aznip.   ¾, 2.   6 ran
1963 King of Babylon (7–4) E. Hide (£1,973) W. Elsey
    2. Wiljotur,   **3.** Zaleucus.   4, ¾.   5 ran
1964 Signal Rocket (8–1) E. Hide (£1,579) W. Elsey
    2. SWEET MOSS,   **3.** Pretentious.   ¾, Hd.   10 ran
1965 Hornblower (3–1) E. Hide (£1,449) W. Elsey
    2. Fair Saying,   **3.** Royalgo.   2, 2½.   6 ran
1966 Hermes (7–4f) G. Starkey (£1,436) J. Oxley
    2. North Copse,   **3.** Marcus Brutus.   1½, 3.   6 ran
1967 Pennant (7–1) E. Larkin (£2,046) S. Hall
    2. Melodic Air,   **3.** Pals Passage.   2, 1.   9 ran
1968 Chebs Lad (evens jf) B. Connorton (£1,901) W. Gray
    2. Strathallander,   **3.** Laureate.   5, 1½.   5 ran

Race 74: BLUE RIBAND TRIAL STAKES
1 mile 110 yards. Epsom. Three-year-olds

1937 Printer	(8)	1948 King's Counsel	(11)	1953 Premonition	(8)
1938 Chatsworth	(5)	1949 Grani	(7)	1954 Ambler II	(6)
1939 Blue Peter	(9)	1950 Port o'Light	(10)	1955 Sierra Nevada	(9)
1940–46 No race		1951 Zucchero	(11)	1956 Monterey	(11)
1947 Combat	(4)	1952 Castleton	(9)		

1957 Tempest (6–4f) W. Carr (£4,829) C. Boyd-Rochfort
    2. Supreme Courage,   **3.** Guarani.   Nk, 1½.   7 ran
1958 Miner's Lamp (4–5f) W. Carr (£4,735) C. Boyd-Rochfort
    2. Kingroy,   **3.** Barleycroft.   4, 1.   7 ran
1959 My Aladdin (10–1) S. Clayton (£5,330) W. Nightingall
    2. Arvak,   **3.** Vallauris.   1½, 6.   10 ran
1960 VIENNA (7–4f) G. Lewis (£6,087) W. Nightingall
    2. Torullo,   **3.** Woodforest.   2, ¾.   12 ran

1961 No Fiddling (10–1) J. Lindley (£5,995) R. Greenhill
    2. Marsolve,   **3.** So Cozy. $\frac{1}{2}$, 5.   11 ran
1962 Cyrus (100–7) W. Rickaby (£5,619) G. Brooke
    2. Silver Cloud,   **3.** Marsh King.   4, Nk.   12 ran
1963 Bo'sun (5–1) S. Smith (£3,692) J. Jarvis
    2. Whiskey A Go Go,   **3.** Iron Peg.   Nk, Hd.   6 ran
1964 Minor Portion (8–1) J. Lindley (£4,434) J. Tree
    2. El Giza,   **3.** Turn Right.   4, Nk.   14 ran
1965 Cambridge (100–9) W. Snaith (£4,551) B. Hobbs
    2. Brave Knight,   **3.** Abscond. $1\frac{1}{2}$, 1.   8 ran
1966 PRETENDRE (7–4f) P. Cook (£3,365) J. Jarvis
    2. Le Cordonnier,   **3.** Right Honour-
                able Gentleman.   6, Hd.   10 ran
1967 Starry Halo (8–13f) L. Piggott (£3,223) J. Thompson
    2. Great Pleasure,   **3.** Privy Seal.   3, 1.   10 ran
1968 Society (2–1) W. Williamson (£3,364) P. J. Prendergast
    2. Attalus,   **3.** Sovereign Ruler.   Hd, 5.   5 ran

Race 75: PRINCESS ELIZABETH STAKES

1 mile 110 yards. Epsom. Three-year-old fillies

1947 Netherton Maid	(6)	**1950** One for the		**1953** Noemi	(16)
1948 La Chipotte	(11)	Road	(12)	**1954** Bara Bibi	(5)
1949 Jet Plane	(10)	**1951** Staffa	(8)	**1955** Pappagena	(12)
		1952 Brighton Belle	(14)	**1956** Victoria Cross	(10)

1957 CARROZZA (10–1) L. Piggott (£6,461) N. Murless
    2. ROSE ROYALE II,   **3.** Street Singer. $\frac{1}{2}$, 2.   18 ran
1958 Princess Lora (9–4f) J. Massard (£5,883) A. Head (France)
    2. Persian Wheel,   **3.** Mistress Gwynne. Nk, 3.   16 ran
1959 ROSE OF MEDINA (5–2) L. Piggott (£5,806) N. Murless
    2. Fiorentina,   **3.** Minnie.   Hd, 4.   6 ran
1960 Plump (6–4f) L. Piggott (£6,410) N. Murless
    2. Owlet,   **3.** Release.   3, Nk.   11 ran
1961 Mystify (4–1) D. Smith (£6,639) G. Brooke
    2. Atrevida,   **3.** Lady Pilot.   2, 3.   14 ran
1962 Almiranta (10–1) J. Sime (£6,202) J. A. Waugh
    2. Tahiri,   **3.** Grischuna. $\frac{3}{4}$, 1.   10 ran
1963 Amorella (11–2) L. Piggott (£4,436) N. Murless
    2. Honey Portion,   **3.** Mythic.   Hd, 5.   9 ran
1964 HOMEWARD BOUND (10–1) G. Starkey (£4,414) J. Oxley
    2. Feather Bed,   **3.** Rose Rock.   3, 3.   11 ran
1965 Miba (11–4) L. Piggott (£4,005) H. Cottrill
    2. Wimpole Street,   **3.** Appoline. $2\frac{1}{2}$, Sht Hd.   7 ran
1966 Every Blessing (5–1) L. Piggott (£2,724) N. Murless
    2. Aerial Lady,   **3.** Pure Folly.   3, $\frac{1}{2}$.   8 ran

1967 Pytchley Princess (20–1) R. Maddock (£2,325) R. Day
    2. Golden Reward,   **3.** Pertinacity.   Sht Hd, 2¼.   9 ran
1968 La Mome (6–1) J. Mercer (£3,471) W. Hern
    2. Hill Shade,   **3.** Denosa.   Nk, 2.   8 ran

Race 76: ROYAL STAKES

1 mile 2 furlongs. Sandown. Three-year-olds

1957 Sun Charger (7–1) L. Piggott (£1,727) N. Murless
    2. Brave Buck,   **3.** Rose Argent.   4, 1.   9 ran
1958 Snow Cat (11–2) L. Piggott (£1,744) N. Murless
    2. ALCIDE,   **3.** Veneer.   Sht Hd, 3.   7 ran
1959 Casque (20–1) A. Breasley (£1,715) H. Blagrave
    2. Above Suspicion,   **3.** Arctic Run.   3, Sht Hd.   7 ran
1960 Marengo (6–1) R. Fawdon (£1,838) M. Marsh
    2. Radiation,   **3.** Marshall Hall.   4, 3.   13 ran
1961 Just Great (7–2f) G. Lewis (£1,804) S. Ingham
    2. Magnificat,   **3.** Flambeau.   1½, Hd.   11 ran
1962 Ferneley (4–1) L. Piggott (£1,825) N. Murless
    2. Heron,   **3.** Triborough.   2, 1½.   8 ran
1963 Raise You Ten (100–8) W. Carr (£1,795) C. Boyd-Rochfort
    2. In The Gloaming,   **3.** Never Beat.   Sht Hd, Sht Hd. 7 ran
1964 Oncidium (7–2) E. Smith (£1,970) J. A. Waugh
    2. INDIANA,   **3.** Pushful.   6, ¾.   14 ran
1965 Nearside (11–8f) J. Mercer (£1,332) W. Hern
    2. Beneficiary,   **3.** Wiskhert.   2, 3.   7 ran
1966 Mehari (10–1) D. Smith (£1,384) J. Winter
    2. Gaulois,   **3.** Twister.   6, 1½.   13 ran
1967 Sun Rock (9–4f) L. Piggott (£1,264) N. Murless
    2. Good Match,   **3.** Mariner.   ½, 2½.   7 ran
1968 Safety Match (100–8) G. Starkey (£1,220) J. Oxley
    2. Scipio,   **3.** Heron's Plume.   1½, 1.   9 ran

Race 77: CORONATION STAKES

1 mile 2 furlongs. Sandown

1957 GILLES DE RETZ (100–6) F. Barlow (£967) P. Walwyn, 4 yrs
    2. Talgo,   **3.** Le Pretendant.   3, 3.   5 ran
1958 Arctic Explorer (11–4) L. Piggott (£984) N. Murless, 4 yrs
    2. Rabbi,   **3.** Induna.   Sht Hd, Hd.   5 ran
1959 Aggressor (7–2) J. Lindley (£980) J. Gosden, 4 yrs
    2. Glyndebourne,   **3.** London Cry.   2, 6.   7 ran
1960 Lucky Guy (8–1) W. Williamson (£1,035) S. McGrath, 4. yrs
    2. Barclay,   **3.** Aggressor.   ½, 1.   4 ran

1961 PETITE ETOILE (4–9f) L. Piggott (£986) N. Murless, 5 yrs
    2. Wordpam,   **3.** Stupor Mundi.   Nk, 10.   4 ran
1962 Cipriani (9–2) G. Bougoure (£1,112) P. J. Prendergast, 4 yrs
    2. VIENNA,   **3.** Dual. $\frac{1}{2}$, 2.   8 ran
1963 Tacitus (15–2) G. Lewis (£1,061) W. Nightingall, 4 yrs
    2. Royal Avenue,   **3.** Propriano.   1, 4.   7 ran
1964 Tacitus (13–2) D. Keith (£1,143) W. Nightingall, 5 yrs
    2. Best Song,   **3.** Khalkis.   1, 4.   8 ran
1965 Philanderer (4–9f) J. Mercer (£781) W. Wharton, 4 yrs
    2. Man the Rail,   **3.** Bargello.   6, $\frac{3}{4}$.   3 ran
1966 Super Sam (6–1) J. Lindley (£1,484) J. F. Watts, 4 yrs
    2. Pugnacity,   **3.** Ballymarais.   3, 3.   6 ran
1967 Busted (3–1) G. Moore (£2,276) N. Murless, 4 yrs
    2. Haymaking,   **3.** Bluerullah.   3, Sht Hd.   7 ran
1968 ROYAL PALACE (8–15f) A. Barclay (£2,220) N. Murless, 4 yrs
    2. Sidon,   **3.** Royal Falcon.   1, 6.   5 ran

Race 78: JOCKEY CLUB STAKES

1 mile 4 furlongs. Newmarket. First run 1894. Run over 1 mile 6 furlongs until 1963

1900 Disguise II, 3	(8)	**1917** Race abandoned		**1935** Plassy, 3	(7)
1901 Pietermaritz-		**1918** Prince Chimay, 3	(7)	**1936** Precipitation, 3	(7)
burg, 3	(8)	**1919** Race abandoned		**1937** Solfo, 3	(6)
1902 Rising Glass, 3	(11)	**1920** Torelore, 3	(6)	**1938** Challenge, 3	(8)
1903 Sceptre, 4	(5)	**1921** Milenko, 3	(8)	**1939–44** No race	
1904 Rock Sand, 4	(10)	**1922** Lady Juror, 3	(8)	**1945** Black Peter, 3	(4)
1905 St Amant, 4	(6)	**1923** Inkerman, 3	(6)	**1946** Rising Light, 4	(7)
1906 Beppo, 3	(5)	**1924** Teresina, 4	(11)	**1947** Esprit de	
1907 Sancy, 4	(6)	**1925** Tatra, 3	(4)	France, 3	(5)
1908 Siberia, 3	(10)	**1926** Foxlaw, 4	(5)	**1948** Alycidon, 3	(5)
1909 Phaleron, 3	(10)	**1927** Book Law, 3	(8)	**1949** Dust Devil, 3	(4)
1910 Lemberg, 3	(9)	**1928** Toboggan, 3	(9)	**1950** Holmbush, 3	(6)
1911 Stedfast, 3	(5)	**1929** Cyclonic, 4	(8)	**1951** Pardal, 4	(4)
1912 Prince		**1930** Pyramid, 3	(7)	**1952** Mister Cube, 3	(5)
Palatine, 4	(9)	**1931** Shell		**1953** Buckhound, 4	(7)
1913 Cantilever, 3	(7)	Transport, 3	(11)	**1954** Brilliant Green, 3	(5)
1914 Trois Temps, 3	(11)	**1932** Firdaussi, 3	(7)	**1955** Nucleus, 3	(5)
1915 Lanius, 4	(11)	**1933** Tai-Yang, 3	(7)	**1956** Kurun, 4	(7)
1916 Cannobie, 3	(12)	**1934** Umidwar, 3	(11)		

1957 COURT HARWELL (8–11f) A. Breasley (£3,987) Sir G. Richards, 3. yrs
    2. Alexis,   **3.** Ommeyad. $\frac{1}{2}$, $\frac{3}{4}$.   6 ran
1958 All Serene (10–1) D. Smith (£4,975) N. Bertie, 3 yrs
    2. COURT HARWELL,   **3.** Ommeyad.   4, Nk.   5 ran

F*

1959 Court Prince (100–30) L. Piggott (£4,431) N. Murless, 3 yrs
    2. Restoration,   **3.** Duplex.   2, Sht Hd.   5 ran
1960 Prolific (10–11f) D. Keith (£2,184) W. Nightingall, 3 yrs
    2. Exar.   5.   2 ran
1961 ST PADDY (4–6f) L. Piggott (£2,282) N. Murless, 4 yrs
    2. High Hat,   **3.** Pinzon.   1, 2.   5 ran
1962 Gaul (100–8) G. Lewis (£2,214) P. Hastings-Bass, 3 yrs
    2. Pindaric,   **3.** Oakville.   Hd, 3.   11 ran
1963 Darling Boy (11–2) J. Mercer (£1,600) W. Hern, 5 yrs
    2. HETHERSETT,   **3.** Hot Brandy.   1, 3.   7 ran
1964 FIGHTING SHIP (5–1) P. Robinson (£1,483) J. Jarvis, 4 yrs
    2. Crepone,   **3.** Young Lochinvar. 4, 5.   6 ran
1965 Bal Masque (5–1) W. Pyers (£1,357) E. Fellows (France), 5 yrs
    2. Le Pirate,   **3.** Autre Prince.   1½, 5.   3 ran
1966 Alcalde (7–2) D. Smith (£1,546) B. van Cutsem, 4 yrs
    2. Donato,   **3.** St Puckle.   ¾, 1.   13 ran
1967 Acrania (100–8) J. Lindley (£2,196) G. Harwood, 4 yrs
    2. Hermes,   **3.** DAVID JACK.   4, Hd.   3 ran
1968 Crozier (7–1) D. Keith (£2,309) P. Walwyn, 5 yrs
    2. Palatch,   **3.** Sun Rock.   1, 1½.   7 ran

Race 79: PALACE HOUSE STAKES

5 furlongs. Newmarket

1961 Galivanter (15–8) R. P. Elliott (£1,460) W. Hern, 5 yrs
    2. Whistling Willie,   **3.** Tudor Warning. 1, Sht Hd.   11 ran
1962 Crisper (4–1f) W. Carr (£1,281) W. Hern, 4 yrs
    2. Derry,   **3.** Bonny Creeper.   ½, 1.   13 ran
1963 Sammy Davis (9–4f) D. Smith (£1,141) G. Brooke, 3 yrs
    2. Polybius,   **3.** Queen's Hussar. 4, 2.   14 ran
1964 Ruby Laser (5–2) R. Hutchinson (£973) G. Smyth, 3 yrs
    2. Matatina,   **3.** Pilgrims Journey. 3, 1½.   9 ran
1965 Runnymede (7–2jf) D. Keith (£824) W. Wightman, 4 yrs
    2. Holborn,   **3.** Polyfoto.   2, 3.   10 ran
1966 Tamino (10–1) R. Hutchinson (£875) J. Dunlop, 4 yrs
    2. Eze,   **3.** Fauvallon.   Nk, 2.   19 ran
1967 Heavenly Sound (10–1) A. Barclay (£2,393) T. Waugh, 3 yrs
    2. Quy,   **3.** Vital Error.   Nk, 2.   8 ran
1968 Mountain Call (5–2f) R. Maddock (£2,372) B. van Cutsem, 3 yrs
    2. Golden Pal,   **3.** Constans.   2, Hd.   9 ran
    (Dahban withdrawn, 4s. in £ deducted from winnings.)

Race 80: WHITE ROSE MAIDEN STAKES

1 mile 2 furlongs. Ascot. Three-year-olds. Up to and including '62 run at Hurst Park. *Run over 1 mile 4 furlongs. †Run at Newbury

1957 Heswall Honey (5–1) B. Swift (£765) R. A. Thrale				
2. Sway,	**3.** COURT HARWELL.	Sht Hd, 1½.	10 ran
1958 Crystal Bay (8–1) W. Carr (£1,409) D. Candy				
2. Tantalizer,	**3.** Kulak.	1, ½.	8 ran
1959 PARTHIA (3–1f) W. Carr (£1,498) C. Boyd-Rochfort				
2. Gerome,	**3.** My Aladdin.	3, Hd.	16 ran
1960 Tudor Period (11–10f) W. Rickaby (£1,604) W. Smyth				
2. Tobago,	**3.** Pannier.	½, 6.	8 ran
1961 Scatter (100–8) J. Mercer (£1,331) R. J. Colling				
2. Sure Shot,	**3.** So Cozy.	5, 1.	13 ran
1962 Samothraki (9–4f) L. Piggott (£1,336) F. Maxwell				
2. Pindaric,	**3.** Anaphora.	½, 5.	16 ran
*1963 Fern (100–7) W. Carr (£2,394) J. Rogers				
2. Prado,	**3.** Hullabaloo.	3, 6.	19 ran
*†1964 Beaufront (10–1) D. Smith (£2,407) J. F. Watts				
2. Ravel,	**3.** Crest of the Wave.	½, 4.	11 ran
*1965 I SAY (1–2f) D. Keith (£2,170) W. Nightingall				
2. Sweet Story,	**3.** Parthian Shot.	5, ¾.	8 ran
*1966 Right Noble (11–4) L. Piggott (£2,370) M. V. O'Brien				
2. Castle Yard,	**3.** SODIUM.	6, ¾.	19 ran
1967 Great Society (100–8) G. Moore (£2,016) C. Boyd-Rochfort				
2. Persian Genius,	**3.** Covent Garden.	Sht Hd, ¾.	13 ran
1968 Torpid (5–2f) G. Starkey (£2,096) J. Oxley				
2. Harry Lauder,	**3.** Zorba II.	1½, ¾.	15 ran

Race 81: PARADISE STAKES

2 miles. Ascot. Up to and including '62 run over 1 mile 6 furlongs 66 yards Hurst Park. †Run at Newbury

1957 China Rock (9–4f) F. Durr (£546) H. G. Blagrave, 4 yrs				
2. Prince Barle,	**3.** Double Red.	Nk, 3.	9 ran
1958 Sway (4–1) A. Breasley (£615) S. Ingham, 4 yrs				
2. Compromise,	**3.** Alizio.	½, 5.	5 ran
1959 Vacarme (13–2) A. Breasley (£636) N. Bertie, 5 yrs				
2. Papy,	**3.** Ticklish.	3, Hd.	8 ran
1960 PARTHIA (1–10f) W. Carr (£964) C. Boyd-Rochfort, 4 yrs				
2. Roman Empire,	**3.** Genius.	4, 5.	5 ran
1961 High Hat (10–1) D. Keith (£987) W. Nightingall, 4 yrs				
2. Pandofell,	**3.** Jet Stream.	2, 4.	6 ran

1962 Pinzon (9–4f) R. Hutchinson (£1,038) J. Jarvis, 4 yrs
    2. Oakville,   **3.** Sagacity.   2, 1½.   10 ran
1963 Orchardist (4–1) A. Breasley (£1,956) C. J. Benstead, 4 yrs
    2. MONTERRICO,   **3.** Young Lochinvar. 3, 3.   8 ran
†1964 Oakville (3–1) W. Carr (£1,935) W. Elsey, 6 yrs
    2. ONLY FOR LIFE,   **3.** Stavros II.   Hd, 4.   7 ran
1965 Anselmo (10–11f)L. Piggott (£1,833) K. Piggott, 4 yrs
    2. Bargello,   **3.** Stavros II.   2½, 1½.   4 ran
1966 Vivat Rex (100–8) W. Williamson (£1,908) W. Wharton, 4 yrs
    2. Chandulal,   **3.** Fighting Charlie. Hd, 8.   8 ran
1967 Mehari (11–4f) D. Smith (£1,696) J. Winter, 4 yrs
    2. Acrania,   **3.** Parbury.   5, 4.   8 ran
1968 Parbury (9–1) J. Mercer (£1,644) D. Candy, 5 yrs
    2. Sweet Story,   **3.** Dan Kano.   1½, Hd.   8 ran

Race 82: CHESTER VASE

1 mile 4 furlongs 53 yards. Chester. Until 1959 for three and four-year-olds over 1 mile 5 furlongs 75 yards

1935 Valerius, 4	(6)	**1946** Sky High, 3	(5)	**1952** Summer Rain, 3	(5)
1936 Taj Akbar, 3	(11)	**1947** Edward Tudor, 4	(3)	**1953** Empire Honey, 3	(4)
1937 Merry		**1948** Valognes, 3	(8)	**1954** Blue Rod, 3	(7)
Mathew, 3	(15)	**1949** Swallow Tail, 3	(4)	**1955** Daemon, 3	(5)
1938 Cave Man, 3	(12)	**1950** Castle Rock, 3	(6)	**1956** Articulate, 3	(7)
1939 Heliopolis, 3	(10)	**1951** Supreme			
1940–45 No race		Court, 3	(8)		

1957 King Babar (9–2) P. Robinson (£1,523) P. J. Prendergast
    2. Donald,   **3.** Papayer.   Sht Hd, 4.   5 ran
1958 ALCIDE (15–8f) W. Snaith (£1,660) C. Boyd-Rochfort, 3 yrs
    2. Veronese,   **3.** Hero's Mead.   ¾, 2.   7 ran
1959 FIDALGO (10–1) S. Clayton (£1,603) H. Wragg
    2. Reactor,   **3.** Dominate.   6, 5.   9 ran
1960 Mr Higgins (10–1) W. Carr (£1,650) H. Cottrill
    2. Proud Chieftain,   **3.** Pinerolo.   3, 2.   6 ran
1961 Sovrango (7–1) J. Mercer (£1,633) H. Wragg
    2. Cracksman,   **3.** BOUNTEOUS. 5, ¾.   10 ran
1962 Silver Cloud (5–1) R. Hutchinson (£1,472) J. Jarvis
    2. Young Lochinvar,   **3.** MIRALGO.   ½, 1.   6 ran
1963 Christmas Island (100–8) L. Piggott (£2,253) P. J. Prendergast
    2. FIGHTING SHIP,   **3.** Coliseum.   3, Sht Hd.   7 ran
1964 INDIANA (11–4f) J. Mercer (£2,788) J. F. Watts
    2. Con Brio,   **3.** El Giza.   2, 3.   8 ran
1965 Gulf Pearl (7–1) J. Lindley (£4,284) J. Tree
    2. Foothill,   **3.** Quintillian.   1½, ½.   6 ran

1966 General Gordon (6–1) P. Cook (£4,305) J. Jarvis
    2. Allenheads,   **3.** BLACK   3, 3.   9 ran
                                            PRINCE II.
1967 Great Host (2–1) D. Lake (£3,300) P. J. Prendergast
    2. Sun Rock,   **3.** Tapis Rose.   2½, 1.   7 ran
1968 Remand (4–11f) J. Mercer (£3,337) W. Hern
    2. CONNAUGHT,   **3.** Middleham Matt. ½, 15.   4 ran

Race 83: CHESHIRE OAKS

1 mile 4 furlongs 53 yards. Chester. Three-year-old fillies

1957 Mulberry Harbour (11–8f) W. Carr (£1,341) C. Boyd-Rochfort
    2. Crotchet,   **3.** Midnight Press.   Nk, 3.   7 ran
1958 Scryer (8–1) G. Littlewood (£1,630) G. Barling
    2. St Lucia,   **3.** Pleasure Cruise.   Nk, 5.   10 ran
1959 CANTELO (2–1jf) E. Hide (£1,638) C. Elsey
    2. Anthelion,   **3.** Seascape.   6, Bad.   7 ran
1960 Courtesan (7–1) A. Rawlinson (£1,587) J. Fawcus
    2. Shahlala,   **3.** Chota Hazri.   4, Sht Hd.   9 ran
1961 Bernie (50–1) W. Carr (£1,549) R. Ward
    2. Aphrodita,   **3.** Peeress.   1, Nk.   7 ran
1962 Tropic Star (11–2) E. Smith (£1,647) D. Whelan
    2. Crystal Clear,   **3.** Windbag.   2, 1.   13 ran
1963 Elite Royale (10–1) G. Lewis (£1,562) D. Whelan
    2. Born Free,   **3.** Crepe de Chine.   3, 3.   9 ran
1964 Paddy's Song (9–2) J. Sime (£1,613) S. Hall
    2. Montella,   **3.** Triona.   ½, 2.   12 ran
1965 Bell Top (4–11f) J. Mercer (£1,510) W. Hern
    2. Shamrock Cross.   12.   2 ran
1966 Lucaya (13–1) E. Hide (£1,523) W. Elsey
    2. VARINIA,   **3.** Daphne.   1½, 2.   9 ran
1967 Pink Gem (6–4f) G. Moore (£1,192) N. Murless
    2. LUDHAM,   **3.** Resilience II.   Hd, 4.   6 ran
1968 Hardiesse (7–4) A. Barclay (£1,178) N. Murless
    2. COLD STORAGE,   **3.** PANDORA   ¾, 2½.   3 ran
                                            BAY.

HORSES IN CAPITAL LETTERS
WERE TO BE, OR HAD BEEN,
PLACED IN THE CLASSICS

Race 84: ORMONDE STAKES

1 mile 5 furlongs 75 yards. Chester. Prior to 1936 the race was for two-year-olds over 5 furlongs

1936 Quashed, 4	(9)	**1946** High Stakes, 4	(4)	**1952** Tulyar, 3	(4)
1937 Young		**1947** Turkish Tune, 4	(4)	**1953** Wyandank, 4	(5)
England, 4	(11)	**1948** Goyama, 5	(5)	**1954** Stem King, 4	(5)
1938 Senor, 4	(5)	**1949** Alycidon, 4	(4)	**1955** North Cone, 3	(9)
1939 Tricameron, 3	(6)	**1950** Oleins Grace, 4	(6)	**1956** Stephanotis, 3	(8)
1940–45 No race		**1951** Cagire II, 4	(7)		

1957 Hindu Festival (3–1) T. Gosling (£1,459) P. J. Prendergast, 3 yrs
    2. Arctic Flower,   3. Baron's Folly. $\frac{3}{4}$, 3.   5 ran

1958 Doutelle (11–8f) W. Carr (£2,419) C. Boyd-Rochfort, 4 yrs
    2. BALLYMOSS,   3. BRIOCHE.   1$\frac{1}{2}$, 3.   6 ran

1959 Primera (11–8f) L. Piggott (£2,346) N. Murless, 5 yrs
    2. Supreme Courage,   3. NAGAMI.   Nk, 3.   6 ran

1960 Light Horseman (4–1) R. Hutchinson (£2,443) P. J. Prendergast, 4 yrs
    2. Primera,   3. Must Fly.   1, 5.   4 ran

1961 ALCAEUS (4–11f) A. Breasley (£1,976) P. J. Prendergast, 4 yrs
    2. Azurine,   3. Honest Boy.   Nk, Bad.   4 ran

1962 Sovrango (11–10f) W. Williamson (£2,001) H. Wragg, 4 yrs
    2. PARDAO,   3. Magga Dan.   12, 5.   6 ran

1963 Sovrango (11–4f) W. Williamson (£2,044) H. Wragg, 5 yrs
    2. Gaul,   3. Espresso. $\frac{1}{2}$, 2.   7 ran

1964 Arctic Vale (6–5f) L. Piggott (£1,976) P. J. Prendergast, 5 yrs
    2. Sovrango,   3. Wily Trout.   3, 3.   3 ran

1965 INDIANA (4–11f) J. Lindley (£1,354) J. F. Watts, 4 yrs
    2. Autre Prince,   3. Philanderer. $\frac{3}{4}$, 12.   4 ran

1966 Biomydrin (11–2) L. Piggott (£1,426) N. Murless, 4 yrs
    2. Prominer,   3. SOLSTICE.   3, 8.   8 ran

1967 DAVID JACK (8–13f) L. Piggott (£1,156) E. Lambton, 4 yrs
    2. Suvretta,   3. St Puckle.   3, 3.   4 ran

1968 HOPEFUL VENTURE (evens f) A. Barclay (£1,108) N. Murless, 4 yrs
    2. Park Top,   3. Starry Halo.   5, 10.   3 ran

Race 85: DEE STAKES

1 mile 2 furlongs 10 yards. Chester. Three-year-olds

1957 Palor (9–2) E. Smith (£1,501) R. Day
    2. Messmate,   3. Albergo.   Nk, 2.   6 ran

1958 Pandour (9–4jf) S. Clayton (£1,549) W. Hern
    2. Mr Snake,   3. Blackness.   Nk, 4.   6 ran

1959 PARTHIA (4–5f) W. Carr (£1,613) C. Boyd-Rochfort
    2. Shining Orb,   3. Gerome.   Nk, 1$\frac{1}{2}$.   5 ran

1960 ALCAEUS (5–4f) R. Hutchinson (£1,710) P. J. Prendergast
    2. Jet Stream,   **3.** Iron Blue.   4, 2.   8 ran
1961 Oakville (5–1) E. Hide (£1,587) W. Elsey
    2. Cipriani,   **3.** Lawful.
        (Deton first, disq.)   Original distances, $\frac{3}{4}$, $\frac{1}{2}$, 6.   7 ran
1962 Persian Wonder (3–1jf) J. Mercer (£1,502) R. J. Colling
    2. Xerxes,   **3.** Will Reward. $\frac{1}{2}$, 5.   6 ran
1963 My Myosotis (9–4) B. Taylor (£2,335) H. Leader
    2. RAGUSA,   **3.** Early to Rise. $\frac{3}{4}$, 5.   4 ran
1964 Sweet Moss (5–4f) L. Piggott (£2,420) N. Murless
    2. Make Haste,   **3.** Devastation.   Hd, 5.   7 ran
1965 Look Sharp (7–4f) D. Smith (£2,367) B. van Cutsem
    2. Abscond,   **3.** Beatle.   5, 2.   5 ran
1966 Grey Moss (9–4jf) P. Cook (£2,555) M. V. O'Brien
    2. Sejamus,   **3.** Hedge Rose.   20, 3.   7 ran
1967 French Vine (20–1) E. Hide (£1,924) W. Elsey
    2. RIBOCCO,   **3.** El Mighty.   2, 6.   4 ran
1968 Laureate (7–1) W. Carson (£1,938) B. van Cutsem
    2. Attalus,   **3.** Honey Bear. $\frac{1}{2}$, 4.   4 ran

Race 86: IRISH 1,000 GUINEAS

1 mile. Curragh. Three-year-old fillies

1922 Lady Violette	(11)	**1934** Kyloe	(6)	**1946** Ella Retford	(13)
1923 Glenshesk	(6)	**1935** Smokeless	(9)	**1947** Sea Symphony	(20)
1924 Volto	(6)	**1936** Harvest Star	(6)	**1948** Morning Wings	(16)
1925 Flying Dinah	(11)	**1937** Sol Speranga	(7)	**1949** Sunlit Ride	(18)
1926 Resplendent	(12)	**1938** Lapel	(12)	**1950** Princess Trudy	(18)
1927 West Indies	(9)	**1939** Serpent Star	(7)	**1951** Queen of Sheba	(16)
1928 Moucheron	(13)	**1940** Gainsworth	(12)	**1952** Nashua	(14)
1929 Soloptic	(9)	**1941** Milady Rose	(9)	**1953** Northern Gleam	(15)
1930 Star of Egypt	(9)	**1942** Majideh	(13)	**1954** Pantomime	
1931 Spiral	(7)	**1943** Suntop	(11)	Queen	(16)
1932 Petoni	(12)	**1944** Annetta	(10)	**1955** Dark Issue	(17)
1933 Spy-Ann	(17)	**1945** Panastrid	(16)	**1956** Pederoba	(16)

1957 Even Star (6–1) F. Durr (£2,527) R. Day
    2. After the Show,   **3.** ANGELET.   1, $2\frac{1}{4}$.   15 ran
1958 Butiaba (2–1f) J. Massard (£2,395) A. Head (France)
    2. Owenello,   **3.** Bedecked. $\frac{1}{2}$, $\frac{3}{4}$.   15 ran
1959 Fiorentina (evens f) G. Moore (£2,319) A. Head (France)
    2. Lillet,   **3.** Clara Bow.   Nk, Sht Hd.   19 ran
1960 Zenobia (100–8) L. Ward (£2,436) T. Shaw
    2. Young Empress,   **3.** Azurine.   Sht Hd, $\frac{1}{2}$.   15 ran
1961 Lady Senator (6–4f) T. Gosling (£2,503) P. Ashworth
    2. Tuna Gail,   **3.** Atrevida. $\frac{1}{2}$, Hd,   12 ran

1962 Shandon Belle (20–1) T. P. Burns (£3,356) R. Fetherstonhaugh
    2. Lovely Gale,   **3.** ABERMAID.   1, Nk.   16 ran
1963 Gazpacho (9–1) F. Palmer (£3,475) P. J. Prendergast
    2. Hibernia III,   **3.** Evening Shoe.   2½, 1.   18 ran
1964 ROYAL DANSEUSE (7–4f) J. Roe (£4,247) S. McGrath
    2. Feather Bed,   **3.** Mesopotamia.   4, 2.   13 ran
1965 Ardent Dancer (5–1) W. Rickaby (£5,394) T. Gosling
    2. Aurabella,   **3.** Brassia.   ½, Hd.   13 ran
1966 VALORIS (9–1) John Power (£6,020) M. V. O'Brien
    2. Loyalty,   **3.** Lady Clodagh.   3, Nk.   15 ran
1967 LACQUER (4–1) R. Hutchinson (£6,164) H. Wragg
    2. Hannah Darling,   **3.** Lauravella.   4, Sht Hd.   15 ran
1968 Front Row (7–1) E. Eldin (£7,512) R. Jarvis
    2. GLAD ONE,   **3.** Kylin.   ½, 4.   13 ran

Race 87: IRISH 2,000 GUINEAS

1 mile. Curragh. Three-year-olds

1921 Soldennis	(10)	**1934** Cariff	(10)	**1945** Stalino	(20)
1922 Spike Island	(11)	**1935** Museum	(11)	**1946** Claro	(14)
1923 Soldumeno	(9)	**1936** Hocus Pocus	(9)	**1947** Grand Weather	(8)
1924 Grand Joy	(8)	**1937** Phideas	(9)	**1948** Beau-Sabreur	(12)
1925 St Donagh	(8)	**1938** Nearchus	(12)	**1949** Solonaway	(12)
1926 Embargo	(10)	**1939** Cornfield	(16)	**1950** Mighty Atom	(10)
1927 Fourth Hand	(9)	**1940** Teasel	(6)	**1951** Signal Box	(16)
1928 Baytown	(8)	**1941** Khosro	(14)	**1952** D.C.M.	(11)
1929 Salisbury	(7)	**1942** Windsor Slipper	(12)	**1953** Sea Charger	(13)
1930 Glannarg	(10)	**1943** The Phoenix	(12)	**1954** Arctic Wind	(14)
1931 Double Arch	(10)	**1944** Slide on and		**1955** Hugh Lupus	(20)
1932 Lindley	(12)	Good Morn-		**1956** Lucero	(13)
1933 Canteener	(12)	ing	(14)		

1957 Jack Ketch (7–4f) C. Smirke (£3,710) E. M. Quirke
    2. Ballyprecious,   **3.** Hindu Festival.   1, ½.   13 ran
1958 HARD RIDDEN (9–2f) C. Smirke (£3,574) J. M. Rogers
    2. Sindon,   **3.** PADDY'S   4, 3.   13 ran
                          POINT.
1959 El Toro (100–9) T. P. Burns (£3,716) M. V. O'Brien
    2. Red Ross,   **3.** Vallauris.   2½, ½.   15 ran
1960 KYTHNOS (5–4f) R. Hutchinson (£4,121) P. J. Prendergast
    2. Exchange Student,   **3.** Arctic Sea.   3, 3.   14 ran
1961 Light Year (6–1) G. Bougoure (£4,121) A. S. O'Brien
    2. Royal Avenue,   **3.** Ritudyr and   2½, 2.   21 ran
                        3. Travel Light.
1962 Arctic Storm (20–1) W. Williamson (£5,585) J. Oxx
    2. Saint Denys,   **3.** Catchpole.   1¼, ¾.   17 ran

1963 Linacre (40–1) P. Matthews (£5,289) P. J. Prendergast
    2. Turbo Jet,   **3.** L'Homme Arme. 1½, 1.   14 ran
1964 SANTA CLAUS (evens f) W. Burke (£6.311) J. M. Rogers
    2. Young Christopher,   **3.** Crete.   3, ½.   16 ran
1965 Green Banner (100–7) N. Brennan (£7,706) K. R. Kerr
    2. Dandini,   **3.** Sovereign   2½, 2.   21 ran
                         Edition.
1966 Paveh (9–1) T. P. Burns (£8,356) T. D. Ainsworth
    2. Ultimate II,   **3.** Not so Cold.   ¾, 8.   15 ran
1967 Atherstone Wood (100–7) R. F. Parnell (£8,576) S. Quirke
    2. Kingfisher   **3.** Rare Jewel.
    (first, disqualified),   Original distances, 1½, 1. 19 ran
1968 Mistigo (10–1) R. F. Parnell (£10,196) S. Quirke
    2. Dalry,   **3.** Panpiper.   Hd, Sht Hd.   15 ran

Race 88: BRIGHTON DERBY TRIAL

1 mile 4 furlongs. Brighton. Three-year-olds

1961 Just Great (6–4f) A. Breasley (£3,124) S. Ingham
    2. Dual,   **3.** Polyktor.   Hd, 6.   10 ran
1962 HETHERSETT (9–4) W. Carr (£2,890) W. Hern
    2. River Chanter,   **3.** Heron.   5, 6.   3 ran
1963 Portofino (11–4) W. Rickaby (£3,665) H. Cottrill
    2. Happy Omen,   **3.** Whiskey A   2, 1½.   6 ran
                          Go Go.
1964 Con Brio (9–2) A. Breasley (£3,079) F. Armstrong
    2. Canisbay,   **3.** Beige Lee.   4, Sht Hd.   10 ran
1965 No race
1966 SODIUM (2–5f) F. Durr (£2,747) G. Todd
    2. Crisp and Even,   **3.** Mont Blanc II. ¾, ¾.   4 ran
1967 DART BOARD (5–1) D. Smith (£2,385) Sir G. Richards
    2. Landigou,   **3.** Hambleden. 2½, 2.   8 ran
1968 No race

Race 89: DANTE STAKES

1 mile 2½ furlongs. York. Three-year-olds

1958 Bald Eagle (11–10f) W. Carr (£3,190) C. Boyd-Rochfort
    2. Carbon Copy,   **3.** Mongoose.   1½, 2.   7 ran
1959 Dickens (100–8) W. Carr (£1,895) C. Boyd-Rochfort
    2. Piping Rock,   **3.** Firecracker. 1½, 1.   9 ran
1960 ST PADDY (8–11f) L. Piggott (£1,875) N. Murless
    2. Ancient Lights,   **3.** Balaji.   3, 2.   10 ran

1961 Gallant Knight (3–1) E. Smith (£1,820) T. Leader
    2. Soslaio,   **3.** Fury Royal.   2, 1½.   5 ran
1962 Lucky Brief (9–2) B. Connorton (£1,775) W. Gray
    2. Ferneley,   **3.** Kings   8, Hd.   5 ran
                       Regulations.
1963 MERCHANT VENTURER (9–2) G. Starkey (£2,625) J. Oxley
    2. Raise You Ten,   **3.** Moon Shot.   2, 2.   6 ran
1964 Sweet Moss (3–1jf) L. Piggott (£2,790) N. Murless
    2. New South Wales,   **3.** Pan's Surprise.   3, 3.   9 ran
1965 Ballymarais (10–1) W. Pyers (£2,648) W. Gray
    2. MEADOW COURT,   **3.** Fort Knox II.   ½, 1½.   11 ran
1966 Hermes (3–1jf) G. Starkey (£2,630) J. Oxley
    2. Mehari,   **3.** Salvo.   2, 4.   9 ran
1967 Gay Garland (100–7) R. Hutchinson (£1,951) H. Wragg
    2. Sloop,   **3.** Kiss of Life.   5, ¾.   5 ran
1968 Lucky Finish (10–1) B. Taylor (£2,119) H. Leader
    2. Rangong,   **3.** RIBERO.   Hd, Sht Hd.   10 ran

Race 90: MUSIDORA STAKES

1 mile 2½ furlongs. York. Three-year-old fillies

1961 AMBERGRIS (4–9f) L. Piggott (£1,186) H. Wragg
    2. Tender Word,   **3.** Verbena.   3, 3.   8 ran
1962 Fool's Gold (8–11f) W. Carr (£1,670) C. Boyd-Rochfort
    2. Illuminous,   **3.** Bleu Azur.   1, Nk.   6 ran
1963 NOBLESSE (evens f) G. Bougoure (£2,514) P. J. Prendergast
    2. Olgiata,   **3.** Crenelle.   6, 1½.   8 ran
1964 Ela Marita (20–21f) G. Bougoure (£2,518) P. J. Prendergast
    2. Alborada,   **3.** Gloomy Portal.   1½, Nk.   9 ran
1965 Arctic Melody (5–4) G. Bougoure (£2,454) P. J. Prendergast Jnr.
    2. Aunt Edith,   **3.** Wimpole Street.   Hd, 5.   5 ran
1966 Orabella II (8–1) B. Taylor (£2,498) H. Leader
    2. Lucaya,   **3.** Soft Angels.   2½, 2½.   9 ran
1967 Palatch (9–1) B. Taylor (£1,526) H. Leader
    2. Pink Gem,   **3.** PIA.   Hd, 5.   7 ran
1968 Exchange (11–4jf) B. Taylor (£1,604) H. Leader
    2. Border Bounty,   **3.** Country Path.   4, 2½.   7 ran

Race 91: YORKSHIRE CUP

1 mile 6 furlongs. York. Up to and including '65 run over 2 miles

1957 Souverlone (50–1) J. Sime (£1,815) H. Peacock, 4 yrs
    2. HORNBEAM,   **3.** Maelsheachlainn.
    (FRENCH BEIGE third, disqualified.) Original distances, Hd, 2, Nk.   11 ran

1958 BRIOCHE (5–6f) E. Britt (£1,705) C. F. Elsey, 4 yrs
    2. HORNBEAM,   **3.** Devon Brew.   Sht Hd, Bad   4 ran
1959 CUTTER (5–2) E. Mercer (£1,650) J. Oxley, 4 yrs
    2. Agreement,   **3.** Miss McTaffy.   3, 1½.   5 ran
1960 Dickens (11–2) W. Carr (£1,765) C. Boyd-Rochfort, 4 yrs
    2. Exar,   **3.** Beau Normand.   ½, 3.   9 ran
1961 Pandofell (11–4f) L. Piggott (£1,760) F. Maxwell, 4 yrs
    2. Poetic Licence,   **3.** New Brig.   1½, Nk.   6 ran
1962 Sagacity (15–2) W. Carr (£2,235) C. Boyd-Rochfort, 4 yrs
    2. Pinzon,   **3.** Minute Gun.   5, 5.   7 ran
1963 Honour Bound (9–2) D. Smith (£3,080) T. F. Rimell, 5 yrs
    2. Orchardist,   **3.** Escort.   3, ¾.   7 ran
1964 Raise You Ten (5–1) W. Carr (£3,115) C. Boyd-Rochfort, 4 yrs
    2. Arctic Vale,   **3.** Grey of Falloden.   ½, 3.   8 ran
1965 Apprentice (33–1) S. Clayton (£2,932) C. Boyd-Rochfort, 5 yrs
    2. INDIANA,   **3.** Philemon.   ¾, 3.   5 ran
1966 Aunt Edith (4–5f) L. Piggott (£3,043) N. Murless, 4 yrs
    2. Fighting Charlie,   **3.** Mintmaster.   4, 1½.   6 ran
1967 Salvo (8–11f) R. Hutchinson (£2,236) H. Wragg, 4 yrs
    2. Mintmaster,   **3.** Mossy Bank.   5, ¾.   5 ran
1968 Sweet Story (3–1) J. Etherington (£2,364) R. Peacock, 6 yrs
    2. Palatch,   **3.** Fortissimo.   3, 2.   9 ran

Race 92: DERBY TRIAL STAKES

1 mile 4 furlongs. Lingfield. Three-year-olds

1932 April the Fifth (13)	**1939** Hypnotist (12)	**1951** North Carolina (8)
1933 Myosotis (13)	**1940–45** No race	**1952** Tulyar (12)
1934 Medieval Knight (5)	**1946** Fast and Fair (9)	**1953** Aureole (6)
1935 Field Trial (7)	**1947** Sayajirao (9)	**1954** Rowston Manor (6)
1936 Barrystar (8)	**1948** Black Tarquin (4)	**1955** True Cavalier (8)
1937 Midday Sun (7)	**1949** Brown Rover (5)	**1956** Induna (8)
1938 Blandstar (13)	**1950** Tramper (10)	

1957 Doutelle (11–4f) W. Carr (£2,742) C. Boyd-Rochfort
    2. Alcastus,   **3.** Sun Charger.   Nk, 1.   10 ran
1958 ALCIDE (2–1f) W. Carr (£2,776) C. Boyd-Rochfort
    2. Paresa,   **3.** Casey.   12, 1½.   9 ran
1959 PARTHIA (4–11f) W. Carr (£2,674) C. Boyd-Rochfort
    2. Casque,   **3.** Beau Tudor.   ¾, 8.   5 ran
1960 Jet Stream (100–8) D. Smith (£2,878) C. Boyd-Rochfort
    2. Iron Blue,   **3.** AUROY.   3, 1½.   10 ran
1961 PARDAO (4–1) W. Carr (£2,691) C. Boyd-Rochfort
    2. Nicomedus,   **3.** Scatter.   2, Sht Hd.   7 ran
1962 Pindaric (100–9) R. P. Elliott (£2,521) T. Masson
    2. MIRALGO,   **3.** London Gazette.   Nk, 1½.   10 ran

1963 Duplation (100–7) J. Lindley (£3,461) J. Gosden
    2. My Myosotis,   **3.** In the Gloaming. 3, 3.   11 ran
1964 Oncidium (11–2) E. Smith (£6,349) J. A. Waugh
    2. Pushful,   **3.** Lionhearted.   5, Hd.   16 ran
1965 SOLSTICE (20–1) J. Lindley (£7,931) J. F. Watts
    2. Alcalde,   **3.** Foothill.   Sht Hd, Hd.   15 ran
1966 BLACK PRINCE II (20–1) B. Taylor (£6,614) J. F. Watts
    2. CHARLOTTOWN,   **2.** St Puckle.   3, 2.   12 ran
1967 Heave Ho (100–6) W. Williamson (£2,530) S. McGrath
    2. Great Pleasure,   **3.** Attacker.   Hd, $\frac{3}{4}$.   10 ran
1968 Laureate (5–1) W. Carson (£2,404) B. van Cutsem
    2. Torpid,   **3.** Hurry Hurry.   1, 6.   9 ran

Race 93: OAKS TRIAL STAKES
1 mile 4 furlongs. Lingfield. Three-year-old fillies

1933 Look Alive	(7)	**1940–45** No race		**1952** Zabara	(7)
1934 Shining Cloud	(3)	**1946** Iona	(8)	**1953** Nectarine	(11)
1935 Milldoria	(7)	**1947** Solpax	(8)	**1954** Angel Bright	(7)
1936 Miss Windsor	(8)	**1948** Angelola	(6)	**1955** Ark Royal	(7)
1937 Ruby Red	(8)	**1949** Squall	(10)	**1956** No Pretender	(4)
1938 Night Bird	(11)	**1950** Stella Polaris	(4)		
1939 Foxcraft	(13)	**1951** Chinese Cracker	(10)		

1957 Crotchet (8–11f) W. Snaith (£1,816) H. Cottrill
    2. Lobelia,   **3.** Almeria, $1\frac{1}{2}$, Hd.   6 ran
1958 NONE NICER (5–2) S. Clayton (£1,782) W. Hern
    2. MOTHER GOOSE,   **3.** Persian Wheel.   Nk, 2.   8 ran
1959 Mirnaya (4–6f) W. Carr (£1,892) C. Boyd-Rochfort
    2. Discorea,   **3.** Number One.   5, Sht Hd.   3 ran
1960 RUNNING BLUE (2–1) E. Larkin (£1,977) J. Jarvis
    2. Saint Anne,   **3.** Green Opal. $\frac{1}{2}$, 5.   14 ran
1961 Impudent (7–1) W. Carr (£1,761) C. Boyd-Rochfort
    2. Sure Shot,   **3.** Comma.   Hd, $1\frac{1}{2}$.   7 ran
1962 Nortia (10–1) J. Mercer (£1,877) W. Hern
    2. Arbitrate,   **3.** Little Miss $\frac{1}{2}$, Nk.   13 ran
                                           Muffett.
1963 Amicable (2–1f) W. Carr (£2,706) C. Boyd-Rochfort
    2. Top of the Milk,   **3.** Shadow.   5, 4.   7 ran
1964 Beaufront (9–2) D. Smith (£3,911) J. F. Watts
    2. Cursorial,   **3.** Alzara.   5, $1\frac{1}{2}$.   10 ran
1965 Quita II (100–8) D. Keith (£3,053) W. Nightingall
    2. Never a Fear,   **3.** Eucumbene.   2, Sht Hd.   6 ran
1966 VARINIA (evens f) S. Clayton (£2,644) N. Murless
    2. Parthian Glance,   **3.** Aerial Lady.   1, 6.   5 ran

1967 Javata (10–1) D. Keith (£1,182) W. Wightman
    2. My Mary,   **3.** Royal Saint.   2, 1.   6 ran
1968 Our Ruby (3–1) J. Lindley (£1,334) J. W. Watts
    2. Lady Kyth,   **3.** Fair Patricia.   6, 6.   5 ran

Race 94: PRETTY POLLY STAKES
1 mile 2 furlongs. Newmarket. Three-year-old fillies

1962 Military Pickle (15–2) W. Rickaby (£862) R. Day
    2. Eutrippa,   **3.** Tuesday Eve. $\frac{3}{4}$, $1\frac{1}{2}$.   9 ran
1963 Fair Astronomer (evens f) B. Taylor (£1,012) H. Leader
    2. Zamarra,   **3.** Amorella.   1, Sht Hd.   9 ran
1964 Young Man's Fancy (9–1) D. Smith (£917) G. Brooke
    2. Nanette,   **3.** Cracker.   1, 2.   7 ran
1965 Miba (5–1) E. Smith (£851) H. Cottrill
    2. Aurianda,   **3.** Machella. $\frac{3}{4}$, $\frac{3}{4}$.   10 ran
1966 Orabella II (4–11f) B. Taylor (£831) H. Leader
    2. Ice Ballet,   **3.** Sicilia.   2, $1\frac{1}{2}$.   7 ran
1967 Cranberry Sauce (8–15f) G. Moore (£1,192) N. Murless
    2. Resilience II,   **3.** Caramel.   Nk, 4.   4 ran
1968 Celina (8–13f) A. Barclay (£1,312) N. Murless
    2. Vivara,   **3.** Flying Fur.   6, $\frac{1}{2}$.   5 ran

Race 95: HENRY II STAKES
2 miles. Sandown

1963 Gaul (6–1) G. Lewis (£1,569) P. Hastings-Bass, 4 yrs
    2. Twilight Alley,   **3.** Escort. $1\frac{1}{2}$, 3.   6 ran
1964 FIGHTING SHIP (5–2f) P. Robinson (£2,143) J. Jarvis, 4 yrs
    2. Gaul,   **3.** Grey of Falloden. $1\frac{1}{2}$, 2.   7 ran
1965 Grey of Falloden (10–11f) J. Mercer (£1,648) W. Hern, 6 yrs
    2. Fighting Charlie,   **3.** Ulster Prince. $1\frac{1}{2}$, 1.   4 ran
1966 Fighting Charlie (9–4f) G. Starkey (£1,672) F. Maxwell, 5 yrs
    2. AURELIUS,   **3.** Goupi. $\frac{1}{2}$, Sht Hd.   6 ran
1967 Parbury (7–1) R. Hutchinson (£1,582) D. Candy, 4 yrs
    2. Piaco,   **3.** Mehari.   3, 4.   10 ran
1968 Chicago (7–2) A. Barclay (£1,554) H. Wragg 4 yrs
    2. Tubalcain,   **3.** Parbury. $1\frac{1}{2}$, 6.   7 ran

Race 96: WESTBURY STAKES

1 mile 2 furlongs. Sandown

1963 MIRALGO (7–2) W. Williamson (£1,290) H. Wragg, 4 yrs
    2. Amber Light,   3. Propriano.   3, 4.   6 ran
1964 Tacitus (11–8jf) D. Keith (£1,791) W. Nightingall, 5 yrs
    2. Silver Cloud,   3. FABERGE II.   2, 8.   4 ran
1965 Goupi (2–1) G. Lewis (£1,666) S. Ingham, 3 yrs
    2. Tarqogan,   3. Beneficiary.   ¾, 2.   3 ran
1966 Super Sam (8–13f) B. Taylor (£1,654) J. F. Watts, 4 yrs
    2. Tesco Boy,   3. Gulf Pearl.   1, 10.   3 ran
1967 Chinwag (5–2) A. Barclay (£1,495) A. Budgett, 3 yrs
    2. Italiano,   3. Haymaking.   3, 2.   4 ran
1968 Sidon (4–6f) L. Piggott (£1,654) Sir G. Richards, 4 yrs
    2. Fair Winter,   3. My Swanee.   2½, 1.   8 ran

Race 97: SANDLEFORD PRIORY STAKES

1 mile 2 furlongs. Newbury. Three-year-old fillies. Called National Playing Fields Stakes in 1961

1959 Dame Melba (2–1f) L. Piggott (£1,133) N. Murless
    2. Blue Riband,   3. Priddy Fair.   ½, Nk.   9 ran
1960 Green Opal (9–4) E. Smith (£1,311) N. Murless
    2. French Fern,   3. Sunny Cove.   1½, 2.   9 ran
1961 Tender Word (5–2) J. Mercer (£1,066) R. J. Colling
    2. Sweet Lola,   3. Futurama.   Sht Hd, 1.   7 ran
1962 Illuminous (9–4jf) E. Smith (£1,385) T. Leader
    2. Tropic Star,   3. Miss   ½, 1.   11 ran
                               Worthington.
1963 Tanned (3–1f) J. Mercer (£2,095) W. Hern
    2. Born Free,   3. Orleans.   1½, 1½.   11 ran
1964 Words and Music (17–2) R. Hutchinson (£2,064) H. Blagrave
    2. Slag,   3. Bewilder.   2, 4.   10 ran
1965 Cloudy Symbol (100–6) T. Carter (£2,035) I. Balding
    2. Pretty Wit,   3. Royalties.   2, Hd.   15 ran
1966 Royal Flirt (33–1) R. Hutchinson (£2,048) G. Brooke
    2. Anippe,   3. Gyropolis.   2, 1½.   11 ran
1967 Resilience II (9–2) B. Taylor (£1,629) H. Leader
    2. Plotina,   3. Tamasha.   ¾, 1½.   11 ran
1968 Tudor Gal (20–1) G. Lewis (£1,618) I. Balding
    2. Bringley,   3. Grandpa's   1½, 10.   6 ran
                               Legacy.

Race 98: LOCKINGE STAKES

1 mile. Newbury

1958 PALL MALL (4–6f) W. Carr (£1,039) C. Boyd-Rochfort, 3 yrs
    2. PIPE OF PEACE,   **3.** Angel Baby,   5, 5.   **4 ran**
1959 PALL MALL (1–2f) W. Carr (£1,024) C. Boyd-Rochfort, 4 yrs
    2. Rexequus,   **3.** Rhythmic Light.   2, 5.   **5 ran**
1960 Sovereign Path (7–4f) L. Piggott (£1,203) R. Mason, 4 yrs
    2. Connaissance,   **3.** Babu.   Sht Hd, 6.   **5 ran**
1961 Prince Midge (11–2) D. Keith (£1,231) R. J. Colling, 3 yrs
    2. Connaissance,   **3.** Scotch   4, 2.   **8 ran**
                                          Woodcock.
1962 Superstition (100–30f) D. W. Morris (£1,259) C. Boyd-Rochfort, 3 yrs
    2. Eagle,   **3.** Persian Wonder.   Nk, 1.   **10 ran**
1963 Queen's Hussar (9–2) A. Breasley (£2,379) T. Corbett, 3 yrs
    2. Cyrus,   **3.** ROMULUS.   Sht Hd, ¾.   **10 ran**
1964 Creditor (10–11f) L. Piggott (£2,316) N. Murless, 4 yrs
    2. Young Christopher,   **3.** Passenger.   3, 1½.   **6 ran**
1965 Young Christopher (6–1) W. Williamson (£3,421) F. Maxwell, 4 yrs
    2. Showdown,   **3.** Roan Rocket.   ½, Sht Hd.   **10 ran**
1966 SILLY SEASON (7–1) G. Lewis (£4,072) I. Balding, 4 yrs
    2. GREAT NEPHEW,   **3.** Pally.   Hd, Hd.   **13 ran**
1967 Bluerullah (4–1) W. Williamson (£3,903) S. McGrath, 4 yrs
    2. Bold Lad,   **3.** Kibenka.   ¾, Nk.   **5 ran**
1968 Supreme Sovereign (5–6f) R. Hutchinson (£3,836) H. Wragg, 4 yrs
    2. Rome,   **3.** Morris Dancer.   3, 2.   **5 ran**

Race 99: ST. JAMES STAKES

1 mile 110 yards. Epsom. Three-year-old colts

1957 Monsieur Roc (10–11f) A. Breasley (£2,351) N. Bertie
    2. Copenhagen,   **3.** Papayer.   1½, 4.   **4 ran**
1958 Pinched (4–6f) L. Piggott (£2,431) N. Murless
    2. Pheidippides,   **3.** Game Ball.   4, 1½.   **5 ran**
1959 Ongar (4–5f) G. Moore (£2,533) A. Head (France)
    2. Pal Fast,   **3.** Ram Lamb.   ½, 6.   **4 ran**
1960 Polo (100–8) D. Smith (£2,733) C. Boyd-Rochfort
    2. Mozart,   **3.** Astrador.   ¾, 4.   **6 ran**
1961 Dalesa (100–30) W. Rickaby (£2,820) R. Day
    2. Good Old Days,   **3.** New Blood.   ½, 2.   **5 ran**
1962 Principal (4–1) E. Hide (£2,521) F. Armstrong
    2. Catchpole,   **3.** Via Tenerana.   1½, Hd.   **7 ran**
1963 Aubusson (9–1) W. Carr (£3,001) C. Boyd-Rochfort
    2. Whisky A Go Go,   **3.** No Argument.   Sht Hd, Nk.   **10 ran**

1964 Gentle Art (15–8f) R. Hutchinson (£2,240) J. Jarvis
    2. Turn Right,   **3.** Polar Legend and ¾, 5.   7 ran
                            3. Burning Torch.
1965 Enrico (11–2) J. Lindley (£2,177) B. Hobbs
    2. Alan Adare,   **3.** Siliconn.   ½, Hd.   6 ran
1966 Kibenka (9–1) A. Breasley (£2,372) T. Corbett
    2. Double-u-Jay,   **3.** GREAT   2½, 1½.   7 ran
                            NEPHEW.
1967 Reform (11–8f) A. Breasley (£2,356) Sir G. Richards
    2. Golden Horus,   **3.** Kedge.   1, 1.   8 ran
1968 Berber (6–1) L. Piggott (£3,273) Sir G. Richards
    2. Chebs Lad and   **2.** JIMMY REPPIN. 4, Dd Ht.   4 ran

Race 100: CORONATION CUP

1 mile 4 furlongs. Epsom

1902 Osboch, 4	(6)	**1920** Manilardo, 4	(8)	**[AT NEWBURY]**		
1903 Valenza, 5	(6)	**1921** Silvern, 4	(6)	**1941** Winterhalter, 4	(17)
1904 Zinfandel, 4	(4)	**1922** Franklin, 4	(7)	**1942** No race	
1905 Pretty Polly, 4	(3)	**1923** Condover, 4	(8)		
1906 Pretty Polly, 5	(3)	**1924** Verdict, 4	(7)	**[AT NEWMARKET]**	
1907 The White		**1925** St Germans, 4	(7)	**1943** Hyperides, 4	(7)
Knight, 4	(4)	**1926** Solario, 4	(5)	**1944** Persian Gulf, 4	(6)
1908 The White		**1927** Coronach, 4	(3)	**1945** Borealis, 4	(4)
Knight, 5	(5)	**1928** Apelle, 5	(4)	**[AT EPSOM]**	
1909 Dean Swift, a	(6)	**1929** Reigh Count, 4	(9)	**1946** Ardan, 5	(3)
1910 Sir Martin, 4	(9)	**1930** Plantago, 5	(6)	**1947** Chanteur II, 5	(5)
1911 Lemberg, 4	(8)	**1931** Parenthesis, 4	(11)	**1948** Goyama, 5	(5)
1912 Stedfast, 4	(5)	**1932** Salmon Leap, 5	(8)	**1949** Beau Sabreur, 4	(3)
1913 Prince Palatine, 5	(4)	**1933** Dastur, 4	(4)	**1950** Amour Drake, 4	(6)
1914 Blue Stone, 4	(7)	**1934** King Salmon, 4	(3)	**1951** Tantieme, 4	(5)
		1935 Windsor Lad, 4	(4)	**1952** Nuccio, 4	(5)
[AT NEWMARKET]		**1936** Plassy, 4	(8)	**1953** Zucchero, 5	(10)
1915 Black Jester, 4	(16)	**1937** Cecil, 6 and		**1954** Aureole, 4	(8)
1916 Pommern, 4	(6)	His Grace, 4	(8)	**1955** Narrator, 4	(12)
1917–18 No Race		**1938** Monument, 5	(7)	**1956** Tropique, 4	(6)
		1939 Scottish Union, 4	(6)		
[AT EPSOM]		**1940** No race			
1919 He, 4	(3)				

1957 Fric (7–2jf) J. Deforge (£2,542) P. Lallie (France), 5 yrs
    2. Donald,   **3.** High Veldt.   1½, 2.   8 ran
1958 BALLYMOSS (evens f) A. Breasley (£3,371) M. V. O'Brien, 4 yrs
    2. Fric,   **3.** Ommeyad.   2, Hd.   5 ran
1959 NAGAMI (5–4f) L. Piggott (£3,265) H. Wragg, 4 yrs
    2. Al Mabsoot,   **3.** London Cry.   3, 2.   3 ran

1960 PETITE ETOILE (1–3f) L. Piggott (£2,966) N. Murless, 4 yrs
    2. PARTHIA,   **3.** Above Suspicion. 1½, 1½.   3 ran
1961 PETITE ETOILE (2–5f) L. Piggott (£3,894) N. Murless, 5 yrs
    2. VIENNA,   **3.** Proud Chieftain. Nk, 1.   5 ran
1962 DICTA DRAKE (2–1f) Y. Saint-Martin (£3,970) F. Mathet (France), 4 yrs
    2. Your Highness,   **3.** Proud Chieftain. Nk, 3.   7 ran
1963 Exbury (11–8f) J. Deforge (£13,456) G. Watson (France), 4 yrs
    2. HETHERSETT,   **3.** Picfort.   6, Hd.   9 ran
1964 RELKO (4–6f) Y. Saint-Martin (£14,221) F. Mathet (France), 4 yrs
    2. Khalkis,   **3.** Royal Avenue. Nk, 4.   7 ran
1965 Oncidium (11–2) A. Breasley (£14,483) G. Todd, 4 yrs
    2. SODERINI,   **3.** HOMEWARD   1½, 5.   10 ran
                                                BOUND.
1966 I SAY (10–1) D. Keith (£14,415) W. Nightingall, 4 yrs
    2. Prominer,   **3.** Atilla.   2, 3.   7 ran
1967 CHARLOTTOWN (11–8f) J. Lindley (£11,363) G. Smyth, 4 yrs
    2. Nelcius,   **3.** White Gloves.   2, Hd.   7 ran
1968 ROYAL PALACE (4–9f) A. Barclay (£11,095) N. Murless, 4 yrs
    2. Bamboozle,   **3.** Dan Kano.   2, Nk.   4 ran

Race 101: EBBISHAM STAKES

1 mile 110 yards. Epsom. Three-year-old fillies

1957 Caperer (4–1) E. Hide (£2,967) C. Boyd-Rochfort
    2. Picture Light,   **3.** Sunburnt   Nk, 3.   9 ran
                                                Country.
1958 Night Court (4–1) E. Britt (£3,099) C. F. Elsey
    2. Trial Note,   **3.** Nougat.   3, ½.   6 ran
1959 Whipsnade (4–1) D. Smith (£3,443) N. Murless
    2. Princess Yasmin,   **3.** Minnie.   1½, 2.   7 ran
1960 Release (2–1) G. Lewis (£3,553) W. Nightingall
    2. LADY IN TROUBLE,   **3.** Reckless.   ¾, 2.   5 ran
1961 Sunspeck (5–1) W. Carr (£3,549) C. Boyd-Rochfort
    2. Irristable,   **3.** Secret Session.   2, 2.   9 ran
1962 Jibuti (8–1) D. Smith (£3,468) G. Brooke
    2. Ribes,   **3.** Tahiri.   3, ½.   7 ran
1963 Lachine (7–2) A. Breasley (£2,564) Sir G. Richards
    2. Plymouth Sound,   **3.** Sun Rose.   ½, 4.   7 ran
1964 High Powered (7–2) D. Smith (£2,459) W. Wharton
    2. Causerie,   **3.** PETITE GINA. 4, 4.   5 ran
1965 Greengage (11–8f) A. Breasley (£2,352) Sir G. Richards
    2. Aurianda,   **3.** Red Quill,   Nk, 1.   8 ran
1966 Daisy Chain (100–7) G. Starkey (£2,465) J. Oxley
    2. Every Blessing,   **3.** Pretty Asset. 3, 3.   7 ran
1967 Wide Awake (2–1f) A. Breasley (£2,402) J. Clayton
    2. Maeander,   **3.** Broken Doll.   ¾, 1½.   7 ran

1968 Ileana (7–2) R. Hutchinson (£3,260) H. Wragg
    2. CAERGWRLE,   **3.** Travelling Fair.   1, 4.   4 ran

Race 102: GALLINULE STAKES
1 mile 2 furlongs. Curragh. Three-year-olds

1957 After the Show (5–4f) P. Matthews (£781) M. Hurley
    2. Star Prince,   **3.** Valentine   2, 4.   6 ran
                                        Slipper.
1958 Tharp (7–4f) L. Browne (£793) C. Brabazon
    2. Arcticeelagh,   **3.** Sindon.   Nk, 1.   8 ran
1959 Anthony (18–1) J. Mullane (£817) J. M. Rogers
    2. Sinna,   **3.** Sunny Court.   1, $\frac{3}{4}$.   15 ran
1960 Chamour (evens f) G. Bougoure (£811) A. S. O'Brien
    2. His Story,   **3.** Djebe Boy.   3, $\frac{1}{2}$.   9 ran
1961 Royal Avenue (7–4f) L. Ward (£1,055) K. Kerr
    2. Anner Banks,   **3.** Soysambu. $\frac{3}{4}$, Nk.   13 ran
1962 Saint Denys (8–1) P. Canty (£939) M. Hurley
    2. Le Pirate,   **3.** Gay Challenger.   4, 1.   12 ran
1963 Vic Mo Chroi (100–9) P. Boothman (£1,485) M. Hurley
    2. Little Sandy,   **3.** Gladys. $\frac{1}{2}$, 5.   8 ran
1964 Master Buck (8–1) R. F. Parnell (£1,560) M. Hurley
    2. Fray Bentos,   **3.** Hovercraft. $2\frac{1}{4}$, 3.   13 ran
1965 Baljour (5–1) J. Purtell (£1,617) M. V. O'Brien
    2. Khalife,   **3.** Kilcoran.   2, 4.   14 ran
1966 Busted (8–1) P. Boothman (£2,005) R. N. Fetherstonhaugh
    2. Pieces of Eight,   **3.** Not So Cold.   Hd, 10.   11 ran
1967 Atherstone Wood (8–1) R. F. Parnell (£2,020) S. Quirke
    2. Crepe Clover,   **3.** House Proud.   Sht Hd, $1\frac{1}{2}$.   10 ran
1968 Giolla Mear (4–1) P. Powell jun. (£1,945) M. Hurley
    2. Ballygoran,   **3.** Laudamus. $\frac{3}{4}$, 3.   7 ran

Race 103: QUEEN ANNE STAKES
1 mile. Royal Ascot

1957 Baron's Folly (100–7) E. Britt (£1,548) P. Beasley, 3 yrs
    2. Fairy Stone,   **3.** Westmarsh. $\frac{1}{2}$, 2.   10 ran
1958 Teynham (15–2) D. W. Morris (£1,769) G. Colling, 3 yrs
    2. Tharp,   **3.** QUORUM. $\frac{1}{2}$, 5.   8 ran
1959 Lucky Guy (100–8) J. Sime (£1,702) S. McGrath, 3 yrs
    2. Rexequus,   **3.** Glyndebourne.   Nk, 2.   9 ran
1960 Blast (100–7) W. Snaith (£1,791) A. Budgett, 3 yrs
    2. Givenaway,   **3.** Fagus.   1, $\frac{3}{4}$.   12 ran

1961 Amber Light (9–1) D. Smith (£1,821) F. Winter, 3 yrs
    2. Lucky Guy,   **3.** Abat Jour.   3, 4.   10 ran
1962 Nereus (8–1) P. Robinson (£1,727) K. Cundell, 3 yrs
    2. Le Prince,   **3.** Persian Wonder. 3, 1½.   11 ran
1963 Welsh Rake (8–1) R. Hutchinson (£1,727) J. Jarvis, 8 yrs
    2. Royal Agreement,   **3.** My Myosotis.   3, 4.   12 ran
1964 Princelone (100–8) R. Maddock (£1,757) W. Nightingall, 3 yrs
    2. Piccadilly,   **3.** Crepone.   Hd, Hd.   8 ran
1965 Showdown (5–4f) D. Smith (£1,594) F. N. Winter, 4 yrs
    2. Pally,   **3.** Noble Record.   ¾, 12.   9 ran
1966 Tesco Boy (8–1) R. Hutchinson (£1,548) S. Ingham, 3 yrs
    2. Orabella II,   **3.** GREAT
                                  NEPHEW.
    (Ballyciptic first disqualified.) Original distances, Hd, 4, 2.   10 ran
1967 Good Match (6–1jf) D. East (£1,341) J. Tree, 3 yrs
    2. Arenaria,   **3.** Town Life.   Nk, 2.   13 ran
1968 Virginia Gentleman (9–2) A. Barclay (£1,428) Doug Smith, 3 yrs
    2. Frankincense,   **3.** Starry Halo.   1½, 3.   10 ran

Race 104: QUEEN'S VASE

2 miles. Royal Ascot. Run as Gold Vase until 1960. First run 1838

1900	Solitaire, 4	(5)	**1914**	Glorvina, 3	(11)	**1935**	Flash Bye, 3	(19)
1901	Mackintosh, 3	(4)	**1915–18**	No race		**1936**	Rondo, 3	(17)
1902	Ice Maiden, 3	(9)	**1919**	Silonyx, 3	(8)	**1937**	Fearless Fox, 4	(13)
1903	Zinfandel, 3	(4)	**1920**	Kentish Cob, 4	(8)	**1938**	Foxglove II, 3	(21)
1904	Bachelor's		**1921**	Copyright, 3	(6)	**1939**	Atout Maitre, 3	(17)
	Button, 5	(5)	**1922**	Golden Myth, 4	(9)	**1940–45**	No race	
1905	Bachelor's		**1923**	Puttendem, 4	(5)	**1946**	Look Ahead, 3	(10)
	Button, 6	(10)	**1924**	Audlem, 3	(11)	**1947**	Auralia, 4	(20)
1906	The White		**1925**	Kentish		**1948**	Estoc, 3	(20)
	Knight, 3	(4)		Knock, 3	(12)	**1949**	Lone Eagle, 3	(15)
1907	Golden		**1926**	High Art, 3	(14)	**1950**	Fastlad, 4	(19)
	Measure, 5	(12)	**1927**	Adieu, 3	(10)	**1951**	Faux Pas, 3	(15)
1908	Pillo, 3	(4)	**1928**	Maid of Perth, 4	(12)	**1952**	Souepi, 4	(21)
1909	Amadis, 3	(8)	**1929**	Covenden, 4	(20)	**1953**	Absolve, 5	(21)
1910	Charles		**1930**	Trimdon, 4	(10)	**1954**	Prescription, 3	(14)
	O'Malley, 3	(10)	**1931**	Pomme d'Api, 3	(11)	**1955**	Prince Barle, 3	(11)
1911	Martingale II, 3	(4)	**1932**	Silvermere, 3	(11)	**1956**	French Beige, 3	(22)
1912	Tidal Wave, 3	(11)	**1933**	Gainslaw, 4	(14)			
1913	Shogun, 3	(3)	**1934**	Duplicate, 3	(13)			

1957 Tenterhooks (6–1) E. Britt (£1,952) C. F. Elsey, 3 yrs
    2. Palor,   **3.** Compromise.   1½, ¾.   13 ran
1958 Even Money (9–4f) A. Breasley (£2,198) M. V. O'Brien, 3 yrs
    2. Owen Glendower,   **3.** Red Dragon.   5, 1½.   18 ran

1959 Vivi Tarquin (100–8) D. Greening (£2,581) S. McGrath, 3 yrs
    2. Lemnos,   **3.** Supreme Courage. Nk, 3.   12 ran
1960 Prolific (5–2f) D. Keith (£2,632) W. Nightingall, 3 yrs
    2. Farrney Fox,   **3.** Poetic Licence.   5, 2.   18 ran
1961 Black King (100–8) E. Hide (£2,560) W. Elsey, 3 yrs
    2. Polyktor,   **3.** Sagacity.   4, 1½.   10 ran
1962 Pavot (10–1) J. Sime (£2,547) P. J. Prendergast, 3 yrs
    2. Parthaon,   **3.** Tamper.   2, 1.   14 ran
1963 Hereford (20–1) James Hunter (£3,752) H. V. S. Murless, 3 yrs
    2. Credo,   **3.** Apprentice,   12, Sht Hd.   25 ran
1964 I Titan (10–1) M. Giovannelli (£3,752) N. Murless, 3 yrs
    2. Mahbub Aly,   **3.** Minotaur.   1½, 4.   22 ran
1965 Beddard (9–1) J. Sime (£3,666) H. V. S. Murless, 3 yrs
    2. Hillgrove,   **3.** Zulu.   4, 1.   24 ran
1966 Bally Russe (5–1f) A. Breasley (£3,416) N. Murless, 4 yrs
    2. Vrai,   **3.** Gaulois.   5, 2½.   16 ran
1967 Accuser (15–2) F. Durr (£3,145) W. Hern, 3 yrs
    2. Lead the Way,   **3.** Burn the Candle. 4, 1.   14 ran
1968 Zorba II (10–1) R. Hutchinson (£3,091) P. J. Prendergast, 3 yrs
    2. Hurry Hurry,   **3.** Ophite.   1, Hd.   14 ran

Race 105: ST. JAMES'S PALACE STAKES

1 mile. Royal Ascot. Three-year-olds

1925 Zambo	(9)	**1936** Rhodes Scholar	(5)	**1947** Tudor Minstrel	(3)
1926 Coronach	(3)	**1937** Goya II	(6)	**1948** Black Tarquin	(5)
1927 Kincardine	(10)	**1938** Scottish Union	(8)	**1949** Faux Tirage	(8)
1928 Royal Minstrel	(8)	**1939** Admiral's Walk	(6)	**1950** Palestine	(4)
1929 Mr Jinks	(8)	**1940** No race		**1951** Turco II	(10)
1930 Christopher				**1952** King's Bench	(7)
Robin	(6)	**[AT NEWMARKET]**		**1953** Nearula	(6)
1931 Cameronian	(6)	**1941** Orthodox	(7)	**1954** Darius	(7)
1932 Andrea	(10)	**1942–45** No race		**1955** Tamerlane	(5)
1933 Canon Law	(9)			**1956** Pirate King	(6)
1934 Flamenco	(4)	**[AT ASCOT]**			
1935 Bahram	(5)	**1946** Khaled (5)			

1957 Chevastrid (8–1) J. Eddery (£4,949) S. McGrath
    2. Tempest,   **3.** PIPE OF   Hd, 1.   5 ran
                            PEACE.
1958 MAJOR PORTION (evens f) E. Smith (£4,864) T. Leader
    2. Guersillus,   **3.** Bald Eagle.   2, 1.   5 ran
1959 Above Suspicion (9–4) W. Carr (£3,919) C. Boyd-Rochfort
    2. CARNOUSTIE,   **3.** Piping Rock.   2, 1½.   5 ran
1960 VENTURE VII (1–33f) G. Moore (£3,206) A. Head (France)
    2. Riverdare.   6.   2 ran

1961 Tudor Treasure (11–4f) D. Smith (£3,265) J. F. Watts
    2. Eagle,   **3.** Test Case.   4, 1½.   9 ran
1962 Court Sentence (100–8) E. Smith (£3,427) T. Leader
    2. Sovereign Lord,   **3.** Cyrus.   ½, ¾.   8 ran
1963 Crocket (9–2) D. Smith (£3,257) G. Brooke
    2. Follow Suit,   **3.** IONIAN.   6, 1½.   10 ran
1964 Roan Rocket (5–4f) L. Piggott (£9,049) G. Todd
    2. Acer,   **3.** New South   1½, 1½.   8 ran
                        Wales.
1965 SILLY SEASON (5–1f) G. Lewis (£8,934) I. Balding
    2. Kirsch Flambee,   **3.** Sovereign   Hd, 10.   12 ran
                        Edition.
1966 Track Spare (100–9) J. Lindley (£5,254) R. Mason
    2. Watergate,   **3.** Double-U-Jay.   ¾, 3.   7 ran
1967 Reform (4–6f) A. Breasley (£4,265) Sir G. Richards
    2. Chinwag,   **3.** Bold Lad.   Hd, ¾.   5 ran
1968 PETINGO (10–11f) L. Piggott (£4,311) F. Armstrong
    2. Atopolis,   **3.** Berber.   1½, 1½.   3 ran

Race 106: JERSEY STAKES

7 furlongs. Royal Ascot. Three-year-olds

1957 QUORUM (4–6f) A. Russell (£1,715) W. Hyde
    2. Kings Barn,   **3.** Fuel.   4, ½.   7 ran
1958 Faith Healer (11–2) J. Sime (£2,033) P. Beasley
    2. Two Francs,   **3.** Game Ball.   Nk, ½.   13 ran
1959 Welsh Guard (4–1) W. Carr (£2,021) C. Boyd-Rochfort
    2. Sallymount,   **3.** Gang Warily.   2, 3.   10 ran
1960 Red Gauntlet (100–8) E. Smith (£2,012) T. Leader
    2. Le Levanstell,   **3.** Gilboa.   1½, 1.   13 ran
1961 Favorita (5–4f) L. Piggott (£1,910) N. Murless
    2. Indian Conquest,   **3.** Erudite.   Sht Hd, 8.   9 ran
1962 Catchpole (13–2) D. Smith (£1,812) G. Brooke
    2. ABERMAID,   **3.** Featheredge.   ½, ¾.   10 ran
1963 Creditor (11–2jf) L. Piggott (£1,817) N. Murless
    2. Brief Flight,   **3.** Queen's Hussar.   3, 4.   17 ran
1964 Young Christopher (5–4f) L. Piggott (£1,829) F. Maxwell
    2. Prince Hansel,   **3.** Whistling Buoy.   Hd, 1.   16 ran
1965 Fortezza (100–6) F. Durr (£1,852) H. Wragg
    2. Go Shell,   **3.** Hassan.   ¾, 1½.   26 ran
1966 Vibrant (4–1) P. Robinson (£1,699) E. Lambton
    2. All A'Light,   **3.** Kibenka.   2, 1.   14 ran
1967 St Chad (11–2) G. Moore (£1,437) N. Murless
    2. Broadway Melody,   **3.** Mark Scott.   ½, 2.   11 ran
1968 World Cup (15–8f) W. Williamson (£1,380) P. J. Prendergast
    2. Town Crier,   **3.** Paddy Me.   1½, 1.   10 ran

Race 107: CORONATION STAKES

1 mile. Royal Ascot. Three-year-old fillies. First run 1870

1900	Winifreda and Sainte Nitouche	(9)	**1919**	Flying Spear	(11)	
1901	Bella Gallina	(13)	**1920**	Cinna	(12)	
1902	Doctrine	(13)	**1921**	Donna Branca	(9)	
1903	Oriole	(10)	**1922**	Pogrom	(10)	
1904	Pretty Polly	(8)	**1923**	Paola	(7)	
1905	Commune	(12)	**1924**	Straitlace	(7)	
1906	Keystone II	(5)	**1925**	Saucy Sue	(4)	
1907	Frugality	(11)	**1926**	Moti Mahal	(9)	
1908	Lesbia	(8)	**1927**	Book Law	(7)	
1909	Princesse de Galles	(7)	**1928**	Toboggan	(10)	
1910	Winkipop	(10)	**1929**	Daumont	(8)	
1911	Knockfeerna	(7)	**1930**	Qurrat-al-Ain	(14)	
1912	Polkerris	(11)	**1931**	Sunny Devon	(9)	
1913	Prue	(13)	**1932**	Udaipur	(10)	
1914	Wassilissa	(16)	**1933**	Betty	(11)	
1915–18	No race		**1934**	Foxcroft	(11)	
			1935	Ankaret	(13)	
			1936	Traffic Light	(18)	

1937	Gainsborough Lass	(17)
1938	Solar Flower	(15)
1939	Olein	(11)
1940–45	No race	
1946	Neolight	(7)
1947	Saucy Sal	(9)
1948	Fortuity	(8)
1949	Avila	(15)
1950	Tambara	(7)
1951	Belle of All	(11)
1952	Zabara	(7)
1953	Happy Laughter	(7)
1954	Festoon	(6)
1955	Meld	(5)
1956	Midget II	(7)

1957 Toro (3–1f) J. Massard (£4,914) A. Head (France)
    2. ANGELET,   3. Sarcelle.   4, 4.   11 ran

1958 St Lucia (100–8) G. Lewis (£4,582) P. Hastings-Bass
    2. Yla,   3. Persian Wheel.   Sht Hd, Hd.   8 ran

1959 ROSALBA (11–8f) J. Mercer (£4,540) R. J. Colling
    2. Ginetta,   3. Mirnaya.   1, Hd.   8 ran

1960 Barbaresque (9–2) G. Moore (£3,554) W. Clout (France)
    2. RUNNING BLUE,   3. LADY IN TROUBLE.   6, ½.   6 ran

1961 Aiming High (100–8) L. Piggott (£3,563) N. Murless
    2. Opaline II,   3. AMBERGRIS.   ½, 3.   6 ran

1962 DISPLAY (3–1) G. Bougoure (£3,886) P. J. Prendergast
    2. Mona Louise,   3. Lovely Gale.   ½, 3.   8 ran

1963 Fiji (7–2) G. Starkey (£3,529) J. Oxley
    2. Crevette,   3. Honey Portion.   2, 4.   7 ran

1964 Ocean (7–1) G. Starkey (£9,784) J. Oxley
    2. Words and Music,   3. POURPARLER.   Nk, 3.   6 ran

1965 Greengage (5–4f) A. Breasley (£9,325) Sir G. Richards
    2. NIGHT OFF,   3. Quita II.   Sht Hd, ½.   8 ran

1966 Haymaking (100–7) J. Mercer (£5,560) R. Houghton
    2. Bravery,   3. GLAD RAGS.   3, Hd.   8 ran

1967 FLEET (15–8) G. Moore (£4,285) N. Murless
    2. Royal Saint,   3. Whirled.   ¾, 1.   8 ran

1968 SOVEREIGN (3–1) R. Hutchinson (£4,271) H. Wragg
    2. Front Row,   3. Pseudonym.   6, 2½.   6 ran

Race 108: RIBBLESDALE STAKES

1 mile 4 furlongs. Royal Ascot. Three-year-old fillies. Prior to 1948 race was for three- and four-year-olds over 1 mile

1935 Easton, 4	(6)	**1940–47** No race			**1953** Skye	(12)	
1936 Can-Can, 3	(11)	**1948** Sandastre	(8)		**1954** Sweet One	(8)	
1937 Rhodes		**1949** Colonist II	(8)		**1955** Ark Royal	(11)	
Scholar, 4	(11)	**1950** La Baille	(9)		**1956** Milady	(13)	
1938 River Prince, 3	(10)	**1951** Chinese Cracker	(9)				
1939 Ombro, 3	(11)	**1952** Esquilla	(13)				

1957 Almeria (13–8f) W. Carr (£4,225) C. Boyd-Rochfort
　　　　2. Blue Galleon, 　　　　3. Donna Lydia. 　5, 3. 　　　9 ran
1958 NONE NICER (11–2) S. Clayton (£4,370) W. Hern
　　　　2. Tantalizer, 　　　　3. AMANTE. 　1½, Nk. 　12 ran
1959 CANTELO (5–4f) E. Hide (£4,174) C. Elsey
　　　　2. La Coquenne, 　　　　3. Dame Melba. 　1½, Nk. 　8 ran
1960 French Fern (8–1) G. Lewis (£3,444) J. A. Waugh
　　　　2. No Saint, 　　　　3. Green Opal. 　3, 1. 　　8 ran
1961 Futurama (9–2) A. Breasley (£3,405) H. Wragg
　　　　2. Verbena, 　　　　3. Paris Princess. 　½, 3. 　12 ran
1962 TENDER ANNIE (5–4f) G. Bougoure (£3,737) P. J. Prendergast
　　　　2. Desert Moss, 　　　　3. Tendentious. 　1, Nk. 　15 ran
1963 Ostrya (100–9) J. Lindley (£3,584) J. A. Waugh
　　　　2. Shadow, 　　　　3. Cretencia. 　3, 2. 　　8 ran
1964 WINDMILL GIRL (9–4f) A. Breasley (£9,338) A. Budgett
　　　　2. Fusil, 　　　　3. Lochailort. 　1½, ½. 　15 ran
1965 Bracey Bridge (5–1) L. Piggott (£9,147) N. Murless
　　　　2. Miba, 　　　　3. Wimpole Street, 　3, Hd. 　9 ran
1966 Parthian Glance (11–2) R. Hutchinson (£5,968) G. Todd
　　　　2. VARINIA, 　　　　3. Gyropolis. 　3, 5. 　13 ran
1967 Park Top (9–2) R. Maddock (£4,606) B. van Cutsem
　　　　2. ST PAULI GIRL, 　　　　3. Plotina. 　½, 2. 　12 ran
1968 PANDORA BAY (11–4jf) M. Thomas (£4,479) G. Barling
　　　　2. Exchange, 　　　　3. Celina. 　1, Hd. 　9 ran

Race 109: CORK AND ORRERY STAKES

6 furlongs. Royal Ascot

1957 Matador (13–8f) E. Smith (£1,477) J. A. Waugh, 4 yrs
　　　　2. Wasps Fifteen, 　　　　3. Tudor Grand. 　4, 3. 　6 ran
1958 Right Boy (5–6f) L. Piggott (£1,668) W. Dutton, 4 yrs
　　　　2. Alastair, 　　　　3. Rampant. 　1½, 15. 　5 ran
1959 Right Boy (11–4) L. Piggott (£1,740) H. Rohan, 5 yrs
　　　　2. Red Sovereign, 　　　　3. Capuchon. 　¾, Nk, 　9 ran

1960 Tin Whistle (8–13f) L. Piggott (£1,630) H. Rohan, 3 yrs
    2. Sovereign Path,   **3.** Title Deed.   4, 1.   7 ran
1961 Bun Penny (2–1) D. Smith (£1,604) R. Fetherstonhaugh, 3 yrs
    2. Irish Gambol,   **3.** Loquacious.   3, 3.   8 ran
1962 Compensation (4–1) J. Lindley (£1,659) E. Lambton, 3 yrs
    2. Top Song,   **3.** Prince Tor.   5, 5.   9 ran
1963 El Gallo (20–1) L. Piggott (£1,642) N. Murless, 4 yrs
    2. Turbo Jet,   **3.** Scabbard. $\frac{3}{4}$, Sht Hd.   7 ran
1964 Abandoned
1965 Majority Blue (100–8) W. Williamson (£1,640) J. Oxx, 4 yrs
    2. Prince of Orange,   **3.** Port Merion. $1\frac{1}{2}$, $\frac{3}{4}$.   13 ran
1966 Current Coin (100–8) J. Roe (£1,500) J. Oxx, 3 yrs
    2. Quisling,   **3.** Prince of Orange. $2\frac{1}{2}$, Sht Hd.   10 ran
1967 Siliconn (5–2f) G. Moore (£1,299) T. Corbett, 5 yrs
    2. Empress Sissi,   **3.** Holborn.   4, 5.   8 ran
1968 Mountain Call (8–15f) L. Piggott (£1,299) B. van Cutsem, 3 yrs
    2. Abbie West,   **3.** Welshman. $1\frac{1}{2}$, Sht Hd.   7 ran

Race 110: ASCOT GOLD CUP

2 miles 4 furlongs. Royal Ascot. First run 1807

1900	Merman, a	(6)	1918	Gainsborough, 3	(3)	1939	Flyon, 4	(9)
1901	Santoi, 4	(6)				1940	No race	
1902	William the			**[AT ASCOT]**				
	Third, 4	(11)	1919	By Jingo, 5	(4)		**[AT NEWMARKET]**	
1903	Maximum II, 4	(4)	1920	Tangiers, 4	(6)	1941	Finis, 6	(7)
1904	Throwaway, 5	(4)	1921	Periosteum, 4	(7)	1942	Owen Tudor, 4	(9)
1905	Zinfandel, 5	(5)	1922	Golden Myth, 4	(10)	1943	Ujiji, 4	(8)
1906	Bachelor's		1923	Happy Man, 7	(8)	1944	Umiddad, 4	(5)
	Button, a	(5)	1924	Massine, 4	(11)			
1907	The White		1925	Santorb, 4	(6)		**[AT ASCOT]**	
	Knight, 4	(8)	1926	Solario, 4	(6)	1945	Ocean Swell, 4	(10)
1908	The White		1927	Foxlaw, 5	(8)	1946	Caracalla II, 4	(7)
	Knight, 5	(6)	1928	Invershin, 6	(10)	1947	Souverain, 4	(6)
1909	Bomba, 3	(6)	1929	Invershin, 7	(13)	1948	Arbar, 4	(8)
1910	Bayardo, 4	(13)	1930	Bosworth, 4	(7)	1949	Alycidon, 4	(7)
1911	Willonyx, 4	(6)	1931	Trimdon, 5	(10)	1950	Supertello, 4	(13)
1912	Prince Palatine, 4	(7)	1932	Trimdon, 6	(9)	1951	Pan II, 4	(11)
1913	Prince Palatine, 5	(8)	1933	Foxhunter, 4	(10)	1952	Aquino II, 4	(6)
1914	Aleppo, 5	(10)	1934	Felicitation, 4	(10)	1953	Souepi, 5	(10)
1915–16	abandoned		1935	Tiberius, 4	(6)	1954	Elpenor, 4	(11)
			1936	Quashed, 4	(9)	1955	Botticelli, 4	(6)
	[AT NEWMARKET]		1937	Precipitation, 4	(12)	1956	Macip, 4	(10)
1917	Gay Crusader, 3	(3)	1938	Flares, 5	(10)			

1957 Zarathustra (6–1) L. Piggott (£11,587) C. Boyd-Rochfort
    2. CAMBREMER,   **3.** Tissot.   1½, ½.   9 ran
1958 Gladness (3–1jf) L. Piggott (£10,950) M. V. O'Brien, 5 yrs
    2. HORNBEAM,   **3.** Doutelle.   1, 5.   8 ran
1959 Wallaby II (9–4) F. Palmer (£10,950) P. Carter (France), 4 yrs
    2. ALCIDE,   **3.** FRENCH   Sht Hd, ¾.   6 ran
                             BEIGE.
1960 Sheshoon (7–4f) G. Moore (£10,929) A. Head (France), 4 yrs
    2. Exar,   **3.** Le Loup Garou.   1½, Hd.   6 ran
1961 Pandofell (100–8) L. Piggott (£11,205) F. Maxwell, 4 yrs
    2. Jet Stream,   **3.** Prolific.   5, Nk.   10 ran
1962 Balto (7–4f) F. Palmer (£11,205) M. Bonaventure (France), 4 yrs
    2. Sagacity,   **3.** Prolific.   ¾, ½.   7 ran
1963 Twilight Alley (100–30) L. Piggott (£10,397) N. Murless, 4 yrs
    2. Misti IV,   **3.** Taine.   1, 3.   7 ran
1964 Abandoned
1965 Fighting Charlie (6–1) L. Piggott (£10,801) F. Maxwell, 4 yrs
    2. Waldmeister,   **3.** Autre Prince.   2½, 8.   7 ran
1966 Fighting Charlie (15–8f) G. Starkey (£10,355) F. Maxwell, 5 yrs
    2. Biomydrin,   **3.** Mintmaster.   8, Hd.   7 ran
1967 Parbury (7–1) J. Mercer (£8,409) D. Candy, 4 yrs
    2. Mehari,   **3.** Danseur.   Sht Hd, 4.   7 ran
1968 Pardallo II (13–2) W. Pyers (£8,459) C. Bartholomew (France), 5 yrs
    2. Samos,   **3.** Petrone.   1, 2½.   9 ran

Race 111: KING EDWARD VII STAKES

1 mile 4 furlongs. Royal Ascot. Three-year-olds

1926 Finglas	(6)	1935 Field Trial	(7)	1949 Swallow Tail	(7)
1927 Buckfast	(10)	1936 Precipitation	(10)	1950 Babu's Pet	(4)
1928 Cyclonic	(10)	1937 Solfo	(7)	1951 Supreme Court	(9)
1929 Horus	(7)	1938 Foroughi	(11)	1952 Castleton	(10)
1930 Pinxit	(8)	1939 Hypnotist	(10)	1953 Skyraider	(9)
1931 Sandwich	(3)	1940–45 No race		1954 Rashleigh	(8)
1932 Dastur	(6)	1946 Field Day	(8)	1955 Nucleus	(10)
1933 Sans Peine	(7)	1947 Migoli	(5)	1956 Court	
1934 Berestoi	(8)	1948 Vic Day	(14)	Command	(12)

1957 Arctic Explorer (6–1) L. Piggott (£5,101) N. Murless
    2. BRIOCHE,   **3.** Messmate.   3, ¾.   8 ran
1958 Restoration (6–1) W. Carr (£5,177) C. Boyd-Rochfort
    2. Capitaine Corcoran,   **3.** All Serene.   2, 3.   10 ran
1959 PINDARI (13–8f) L. Piggott (£5,237) N. Murless
    2. Hieroglyph,   **3.** Peterman.   ¾, ½.   12 ran
1960 Atrax (4–1) R. Poincelet (£3,350) H. Nicholas (France)
    2. Faust,   **3.** Jet Stream.   1½, 5.   12 ran

1961 AURELIUS (11–4) L. Piggott (£3,499) N. Murless
    2. Pinzon,   **3.** Gailowind.   2, 3.   10 ran
1962 Gaul (20–1) G. Lewis (£3,546) P. Hastings-Bass
    2. Escort,   **3.** Silver Cloud. $\frac{3}{4}$, 3.   9 ran
1963 ONLY FOR LIFE (3–1f) J. Lindley (£3,329) J. Tree
    2. Nadir Shah,   **3.** FIGHTING   2, 1$\frac{1}{2}$.   7 ran
                                        SHIP.
1964 Abandoned
1965 Convamore (13–2) J. Mercer (£9,648) R. Smyth
    2. Bally Russe,   **3.** Alcalde.   Nk, 1$\frac{1}{2}$.   12 ran
1966 PRETENDRE (1–2f) P. Cook (£5,957) J. Jarvis
    2. Crozier,   **3.** Crisp and Even.   2$\frac{1}{2}$, 2.   8 ran
1967 Mariner (8–1) G. Starkey (£4,573) J. Oxley
    2. HOPEFUL VENTURE,   **3.** Dancing Moss.   Sht Hd, Sht Hd. 10 ran
1968 CONNAUGHT (1–2f) A. Barclay (£4,452) N. Murless
    2. RIBERO,   **3.** Karabas.   12, 4.   5 ran

Race 112: PRINCE OF WALES STAKES
1 mile 2 furlongs. Royal Ascot

1968 ROYAL PALACE (1–4f) A. Barclay (£4,630) N. Murless, 4 yrs
    2. Djehad.   2.   2 ran

Race 113: HARDWICKE STAKES
1 mile 4 furlongs. Royal Ascot. First run 1879

1900	Boniface, 4	(7)	1919	Sir Douglas, 3	(2)	1935 J. R. Smith, 3 (9)
1901	Merry Gal, 4	(5)	1920	Black		1936 Corrida, 4 (11)
1902	Joshua, 3	(11)		Gauntlet, 3	(10)	1937 Mid-day Sun, 3 (5)
1903	Sceptre, 4	(7)	1921	Franklin, 3	(12)	1938 Maranta, 4 (7)
1904	Rock Sand, 4	(4)	1922	Welsh Spear, 3	(7)	1939 Pointis, 3 (11)
1905	Bachelor's		1923	Chosroes, 3	(6)	1940–45 No race
	Button, 6	(5)	1924	Chosroes, 4	(13)	1946 Priam II, 5 (4)
1906	Wombwell, 3	(3)	1925	Hurstwood, 4	(7)	1947 Nirgal, 4 (5)
1907	Beppo, 4	(8)	1926	Lancegaye, 3	(3)	1948 Sayajirao, 4 (3)
1908	Bembo, 3	(5)	1927	Coronach, 4	(4)	1949 Helioscope, 3 (8)
1909	Primer, 4	(10)	1928	Foliation, 5	(9)	1950 Peter Flower, 4 (4)
1910	Swynford, 3	(7)	1929	Posterity, 3	(8)	1951 Saturn, 4 (5)
1911	Swynford, 4	(5)	1930	Alcester, 4	(9)	1952 Dynamiter, 4 (4)
1912	Stedfast, 4	(8)	1931	Orpen, 3	(11)	1953 Guersant, 4 (4)
1913	Lancaster, 4	(4)	1932	Goyescas, 4	(12)	1954 Aureole, 4 (4)
1914	Peter the		1933	Limelight, 4	(8)	1955 Elopement, 4 (2)
	Hermit, 3	(10)	1934	Cotoneaster, 4	(9)	1956 Hugh Lupus, 4 (6)
1915–18	No race					

1957 Fric (11–10f) J. Deforge (£4,269) J. Lawson, 5 yrs
    2. Pirate King,   **3.** High Veldt.   1½, 4.   6 ran
1958 BRIOCHE (7–2) E. Britt (£3,636) C. F. Elsey, 4 yrs
    2. China Rock,   **3.** True Code.   2, 6.   5 ran
1959 Impatient (10–1) J. Lindley (£3,477) J. Gosden, 4 yrs
    2. Restoration,   **3.** Guersillus.   4, 4.   5 ran
1960 Aggressor (7–2) J. Lindley (£2,398) J. Gosden, 5 yrs
    2. PARTHIA,   **3.** Barclay.   1½, 3.   5 ran
1961 ST PADDY (4–9f) L. Piggott (£2,504) N. Murless, 4 yrs
    2. VIENNA,   **3.** DIE HARD.   1, 1½.   4 ran
1962 AURELIUS (8–13f) A. Breasley (£3,761) N. Murless, 4 yrs
    2. Hot Brandy,   **3.** Dahabeah.   ¾, 8.   4 ran
1963 MIRALGO (100–30) W. Williamson (£3,701) H. Wragg, 4 yrs
    2. Best Song,   **3.** TENDER   4, 1½.   8 ran
                                ANNIE.
1964 Abandoned
1965 SODERINI (3–1) G. Lewis (£11,936) S. Ingham, 4 yrs
    2. Earldom,   **3.** Bally Joy.   Nk, 5.   9 ran
1966 Prominer (4–1) D. Lake (£10,015) P. J. Prendergast, 4 yrs
    2. Rehearsed,   **3.** I SAY.   6, 2½.   6 ran
1967 Salvo (7–4jf) R. Hutchinson (£7,923) H. Wragg, 4 yrs
    2. SODIUM,   **3.** My Kuda.   ½, 7.   8 ran
1968 HOPEFUL VENTURE (4–6f) A. Barclay (£8,007) N. Murless, 4 yrs
    2. Tapis Rose,   **3.** Fortissimo.   2, 1½.   6 ran

Race 114: QUEEN ALEXANDRA STAKES

2 miles 6 furlongs 34 yards. Royal Ascot. First run 1865

2M 6F 75Y					
1900 Gadfly, 4	(4)	**1919** St Eloi, a	(3)	**1937** Valerian, 4	(6)
1901 Kilmarnock		**1920** Haki, a	(5)	**1938** Epigram, 5	(6)
II, 4	(10)	**1921** Spearwort, 4	(6)	**1939** Pretender II, 5	(5)
1902 William the		**1922** Air Balloon, 5	(7)	**1940–45** No race	
Third, 4	(6)	**1923** Bucks Hussar, 4	(7)	**1946** Marsyas II, 6	(5)
1903 Arizona, 4	(6)	**1924** Rose Prince, 5	(9)	**1947** Monsieur	
1904 Zinfandel, 4	(6)	**1925** Seclin, 4	(7)	l'Amiral, 6	(6)
1905 Hammerkop, 5	(5)	**1926** Vermilion		**1948** Vulgan, 5	(7)
1906 Hammerkop, 6	(4)	Pencil, 4	(5)	**1949** Alindrake, 4	(9)
1907 Torpoint, a	(5)	**1927** Finglas, 4	(7)	**1950** Aldborough, 5	(7)
1908 Torpoint, a	(4)	**1928** Finglas, 5	(5)	**1951** Strathspey, 6	(5)
1909 Pure Gem, 5	(8)	**1929** Brown Jack, 5	(9)	**1952** Medway, 4	(3)
1910 Lagos, 5	(6)	**1930** Brown Jack, 6	(6)	**1953** Lord Fox, 4	(9)
1911 Royal Realm, 6	(3)	**1931** Brown Jack, 7	(7)	**1954** Bitter Sweet, 5	(9)
1912 Jackdaw, 4	(7)	**1932** Brown Jack, 8	(7)		
1913 Rivoli, 4	(7)	**1933** Brown Jack, 9	(4)	2M 6F 34Y	
1914 Fiz Yama, 5	(10)	**1934** Brown Jack, 10	(9)	**1955** Bitter Sweet, 6	(5)
1915–18 No race		**1935** Enfield, 4	(6)	**1956** Borghetto, 5	(5)
		1936 Cecil, 5	(9)		

1957 Flying Flag II (evens f) L. Flavien (£1,518) J. Laumain (France), 4 yrs
    2. Strait-jacket,   **3.** Borghetto.   Nk, 2.   5 ran
1958 Rally (6–5f) J. Mercer (£1,679) R. J. Colling, 6 yrs
    2. Induna,   **3.** Magic North.   1½, 2.   4 ran
1959 Bali Ha'i III (15–8f) W. Carr (£2,173) C. Boyd-Rochfort, 6 yrs
    2. Smiley,   **3.** Havasnack.   ½, 6.   4 ran
1960 Predominate (8–15f) E. Smith (£2,096) T. Leader, 8 yrs
    2. Fabius,   **3.** Colchicum.   6, ½.   4 ran
1961 Moss Bank (9–4jf) W. Williamson (£2,088) T. O'Brien, 5 yrs
    2. Agreement,   **3.** Farrney Fox.   8, Sht Hd.   7 ran
1962 Trelawny (6–5f) A. Breasley (£1,926) G. Todd, 6 yrs
    2. Agreement,   **3.** Moss Bank.   1½, 2.   6 ran
1963 Trelawny (11–8f) A. Breasley (£1,994) G. Todd, 7 yrs
    2. Grey of Falloden,   **3.** Sannazaro.   3, 20.   8 ran
1964 Abandoned
1965 Grey of Falloden (4–5f) J. Mercer (£1,809) W. Hern, 6 yrs
    2. Cold Slipper,   **3.** Liberty Truck.   12, 1½.   6 ran
1966 Panic (5–1) J. Roe (£1,911) J. Oxx, 5 yrs
    2. Apprentice,   **3.** Valentine's Day.   5, ½.   9 ran
1967 Alciglide (6–1) W. Williamson (£1,760) S. McGrath, 4 yrs
    2. Apprentice,   **3.** Grey of Falloden.   8, 5.   10 ran
1968 Tubalcain (9–4f) G. Lewis (£1,644) E. Goddard, 7 yrs
    2. Valoroso,   **3.** Landigou.   3, 2½.   7 ran

Race 115: KING'S STAND STAKES

5 furlongs. Royal Ascot

1957 Right Boy (4–1) L. Piggott (£1,484) W. Dutton, 3 yrs
    2. Edmundo,   **3.** Nanavati.   1, 3.   8 ran
1958 Drum Beat (2–1jf) A. Breasley (£2,066) W. O'Gorman, 5 yrs
    2. Texana,   **3.** Abelia.   6, Sht Hd.   5 ran
1959 Chris (9–4jf) J. Sime (£2,198) W. Nevett, 3 yrs
    2. Welsh Abbot,   **3.** Krakenwake.   Hd, 6.   8 ran
1960 Sound Track (8–1) A. Breasley (£2,084) A. S. O'Brien, 3 yrs
    2. Sing Sing,   **3.** Monet.   Nk, 4.   8 ran
1961 Silver Tor (7–4f) G. Lewis (£2,139) R. Fetherstonhaugh, 3 yrs
    2. Floribunda,   **3.** Tin Whistle.   4, 4.   8 ran
1962 Cassarate (5–1) N. Sellwood (£2,105) M. V. O'Brien, 3 yrs
    2. La Tendresse,   **3.** Silver Tor.   2, 1½.   7 ran
1963 Majority Rule (100–8) L. Piggott (£2,084) W. O'Gorman, 3 yrs
    2. Matatina,   **3.** My Goodness Me.   Nk, Hd.   9 ran
1964 Abandoned
1965 Goldhill (10–1) J. Etherington (£2,051) M. H. Easterby, 4 yrs
    2. Spaniards Mount,   **3.** Golden Apollo.   4, 1½.   11 ran
1966 Roughlyn (20–1) G. Cadwaladr (£1,989) W. D. Francis, 5 yrs
    2. Zahedan,   **3.** Washington.   1½, 2.   10 ran

1967 Be Friendly (3–1) A. Breasley (£2,622) C. Mitchell, 3 yrs
    2. Yours,   **3.** Heavenly Sound. $\frac{1}{2}$, $1\frac{1}{2}$.   **10 ran**
1968 D'Urberville (4–1) J. Mercer (£2,622) J. Tree, 3 yrs
    2. So Blessed,   **3.** Porto Bello.   2, 3.   **12 ran**

Race 116: CHURCHILL STAKES

1 mile 4 furlongs. Ascot

1957 Sway (5–4f) A. Breasley (£1,229) S. Ingham, 3 yrs
    2. Ahmose,   **3.** Le Pretendant.   1, 4.   **4 ran**
1958 Primera (10–11f) L. Piggott (£1,370) N. Murless, 4 yrs
    2. Double Red,   **3.** Arcticeelagh.   4, 1.   **4 ran**
1959 Amourrou (9–4) P. Robinson (£1,549) J. Gosden, 3 yrs
    2. Primera,   **3.** Blue Net II.   Hd, 5.   **4 ran**
1960 Sunny Court (3–1) W. Carr (£1,553) J. Rogers, 4 yrs
    2. Apostle,   **3.** Paul Jones. $\frac{1}{2}$, 3.   **10 ran**
1961 Brocade Slipper (10–1) J. Mercer (£1,630) R. J. Colling, 4 yrs
    2. His Story,   **3.** Arctic Sea.   1, 2.   **8 ran**
1962 Darling Boy (100–8) J. Mercer (£1,566) R. J. Colling, 4 yrs
    2. Gay Challenger,   **3.** Snow Court. $\frac{1}{2}$, 3.   **9 ran**
1963 London Gazette (11–2) G. Starkey (£1,621) H. Thomson-Jones, 4 yrs
    2. Young Lochinvar,   **3.** Hot Brandy and $\frac{1}{2}$, Nk.   **10 ran**
                                3. Redoubt.
1964 Abandoned
1965 Goupi (4–1) G. Lewis (£1,492) S. Ingham, 3 yrs
    2. Mahbub Aly,   **3.** Canisbay. $\frac{3}{4}$, 4.   **7 ran**
1966 Lomond (6–1) L. Piggott (£1,507) R. Jarvis, 6 yrs
    2. Royal Rubicon,   **3.** Bowzen. $2\frac{1}{2}$, 2.   **9 ran**
1967 Wage War (9–2) G. Moore (£1,263) T. Leader, 4 yrs
    2. Wrekin Rambler,   **3.** St Puckle.   2, $1\frac{1}{2}$.   **3 ran**
1968 Richmond Fair (100–8) B. Taylor (£1,251) Sir J. Jarvis, 4 yrs
    2. Wage War,   **3.** Lucky Match.   2, $2\frac{1}{2}$.   **6 ran**

Race 117: IRISH SWEEPS DERBY

1 mile 4 furlongs. Curragh. Three-year-olds. First run 1866: until 1962 called Irish Derby

1900 Gallinaria	(12)	**1906** Killeagh	(9)	**1911** Shanballymore	(10)
1901 Carrigavalla	(9)	**1907** Orby	(7)	**1912** Civility	(5)
1902 St Brendan	(11)	**1908** Wild Bouquet	(8)	**1913** Bachelor's	
1903 Lord Rossmore	(8)	**1909** Bachelor's		Wedding	(8)
1904 Royal Arch	(8)	Double	(7)	**1914** Land of Song	(6)
1905 Flax Park	(11)	**1910** Aviator	(9)	**1915** Ballaghtobin	(12)

1916 Furore	(10)	**1929** Kopi	(9)	**1943** The Phoenix	(9)
1917 First Flier	(10)	**1930** Rock Star	(12)	**1944** Slide On	(7)
1918 King John	(7)	**1931** Sea Serpent	(6)	**1945** Piccadilly	(8)
1919 Loch Lomond	(8)	**1932** Dastur	(10)	**1946** Bright News	(14)
1920 He Goes	(8)	**1933** Harinero	(8)	**1947** Sayajirao	(11)
1921 Ballyheron	(10)	**1934** Primero and		**1948** Nathoo	(12)
1922 Spike Island	(12)	Patriot King	(6)	**1949** Hindostan	(12)
1923 Waygood	(15)	**1935** Museum	(8)	**1950** Dark Warrior	(8)
1924 Zodiac and		**1936** Raeburn	(9)	**1951** Fraise du Bois II	(16)
Haine	(7)	**1937** Phideas	(6)	**1952** Thirteen of	
1925 Zionist	(8)	**1938** Rosewell	(9)	Diamonds	(10)
1926 Embargo	(10)	**1939** Mondragon	(9)	**1953** Chamier	(13)
1927 Knight of the		**1940** Turkhan	(7)	**1954** Zarathustra	(11)
Grail	(6)	**1941** Sol Oriens	(10)	**1955** Panaslipper	(13)
1928 Baytown	(10)	**1942** Windsor Slipper	(13)	**1956** Talgo	(10)

1957 BALLYMOSS (4–9f) T. P. Burns (£6,790) M. V. O'Brien
      2. Hindu Festival,   **3.** Valentine Slipper. 4, 1.   8 ran
1958 Sindon (100–8) L. Ward (£7,345) M. Dawson
      2. PADDY'S POINT,   **3.** Royal Highway. Sht Hd, 4.   12 ran
1959 FIDALGO (1–2f) J. Mercer (£7,212) H. Wragg
      2. Bois Belleau,   **3.** Anthony. 4, ½.   11 ran
1960 Chamour (3–1) G. Bougoure (£7,442) A. S. O'Brien
      2. ALCAEUS,   **3.** Prince Chamier. 1, 5.   7 ran
1961 Your Highness (33–1) Herbert Holmes (£7,921) H. Cottrill
      2. Soysambu,   **3.** Haven. ½, 2¼.   18 ran
1962 Tambourine II (15–2) R. Poincelet (£50, 027) E. Pollet (France)
      2. Arctic Storm,   **3.** Sebring. Sht Hd, 5.   24 ran
1963 RAGUSA (100–7) G. Bougoure (£48,732) P. J. Prendergast
      2. Vic Mo Chroi,   **3.** Tiger. 2½, 2.   16 ran
(RELKO (8–11) withdrawn and bookmakers deducted 10s. in £1 from winnings.)
1964 SANTA CLAUS (4–7f) W. Burke (£53,725) J. Rogers
      2. Lionhearted,   **3.** Sunseeker. 4, Sht Hd.   19 ran
1965 MEADOW COURT (11–10f) L. Piggott (£55,950) P. J. Prendergast
      2. Convamore,   **3.** Wedding Present. 2, ¾.   21 ran
1966 SODIUM (13–2) F. Durr (£52,307) G. Todd
      2. CHARLOTTOWN,   **3.** Paveh. 1, 2½.   23 ran
1967 RIBOCCO (5–2f) L. Piggott (£57,590) R. Houghton
      2. Sucaryl,   **3.** DART BOARD. ¾, 3.   23 ran
1968 RIBERO (100–6) L. Piggott (£55,340) R. Houghton
      2. SIR IVOR,   **3.** Val d'Aoste. 2, 2.   14 ran

HORSES IN CAPITAL LETTERS
WERE TO BE, OR HAD BEEN,
PLACED IN THE CLASSICS

Race 118: PRETTY POLLY STAKES

1 mile 2 furlongs. Curragh. Three-year-old fillies

1957 After the Show (2–7f) P. Matthews (£709) M. Hurley
    2. Sail Aniar,   3. Meriana.   Nk, 3.   5 ran
1958 Owenello (7–4f) L. Browne (£736) J. M. Rogers
    2. Ticklish,   3. Padus.   4, 2½.   8 ran
1959 Little Mo (9–2) G. Bougoure (£769) M. V. O'Brien
    2. Sinna,   3. Fleur de Lys.   1¼, 4.   13 ran
1960 Young Empress (8–11f) R. Hutchinson (£736) P. J. Prendergast
    2. Azurine,   3. Willowtale.   1, 4.   8 ran
1961 Icy Look (1–2f) W. Williamson (£882) S. McGrath
    2. Eglee,   3. Orofino.   Sht Hd, 2¼.   4 ran
1962 Tropic Star (6–4f) E. Smith (£911) D. Whelan
    2. George's Girl,   3. Sally Stream.   ½, ¾.   11 ran
1963 Hibernia III (evens f) W. Williamson (£1,455) J. Oxx
    2. Ashavan,   3. Southern Cross.   2, 2.   11 ran
1964 Ancasta (11–10f) J. Purtell (£1,395) M. V. O'Brien
    2. Miss Success,   3. ROYAL DANSEUSE.   2½, ½.   8 ran
1965 Messene (7–2) G. McGrath (£1,453) S. McGrath
    2. Livia,   3. Lucky Pigeon.   1½, 1¼.   13 ran
1966 Black Gold (13–8f) A. Breasley (£1,967) M. Hurley
    2. Royal Display,   3. Marians.   Nk, 6.   11 ran
1967 Iskereen (9–4) L. Ward (£1,885) M. V. O'Brien
    2. Pampalina,   3. Marie's Daughter.   ½, 4.   11 ran
1968 Rimark (3–1) L. Ward (£2,117) M. V. O'Brien
    2. Never Red,   3. Kylin.   Nk, Nk.   16 ran

Race 119: ECLIPSE STAKES

1 mile 2 furlongs. Sandown. First run 1886

1900 Diamond Jubilee, 3 (9)	**1911** Swynford, 4 (7)	**1927** Colorado, 4 (3)
1901 Epsom Lad, 4 (13)	**1912** Prince Palatine, 4 (8)	**1928** Fairway, 3 (12)
1902 Cheers, 3 (12)	**1913** Tracery, 4 (7)	**1929** Royal Minstrel, 4 (8)
1903 Ard Patrick, 4 (5)	**1914** Hapsburg, 3 (13)	**1930** Rustom Pasha, 3 (11)
1904 Darley Dale, 3 (7)	**1915–18** No race	**1931** Caerleon, 4 (11)
1905 Val d'Or, 3 (6)	**1919** Buchan, 3 (7)	**1932** Miracle, 3 (13)
1906 Llangibby, 4 (9)	**1920** Buchan, 4 (7)	**1933** Loaningdale, 4 (10)
1907 Lally, 4 (7)	**1921** Craig an Eran, 3 (5)	**1934** King Salmon, 4 (10)
1908 Your Majesty, 3 (10)	**1922** Golden Myth, 4 (12)	**1935** Windsor Lad, 4 (5)
1909 Bayardo, 3 (4)	**1923** Saltash, 3 (9)	**1936** Rhodes Scholar, 3 (9)
1910 Lemberg, 3 and Neil Gow, 3 (6)	**1924** Polyphontes, 3 (8)	**1937** Boswell, 4 (6)
	1925 Polyphontes, 4 (13)	**1938** Pasch, 3 (6)
	1926 Coronach, 3 (8)	

1939 Blue Peter, 3	(8)	[AT SANDOWN]		1952 Tulyar, 3	(7)
1940–45 No race		1947 Migoli, 3	(5)	1953 Argur, 4	(7)
		1948 Petition, 4	(8)	1954 King of the	
[AT ASCOT]		1949 Djeddah, 4	(7)	Tudors, 4	(6)
1946 Gulf Stream, 3	(5)	1950 Flocon, 4	(6)	1955 Darius, 4	(7)
		1951 Mystery IX, 3	(8)	1956 Tropique, 4	(8)

1957 Arctic Explorer (100–30) L. Piggott (£7,673) N. Murless, 3 yrs
    2. Pirate King,   **3.** MONTAVAL.   1, 4.   5 ran

1958 BALLYMOSS (8–11f) A. Breasley (£11,672) M. V. O'Brien, 4 yrs
    2. Restoration,   **3.** Arctic Explorer.   6, Sht Hd.   7 ran

1959 Saint Crespin III (5–2) G. Moore (£11,681) A. Head (France), 3 yrs
    2. Javelot,   **3.** Vif Argent.   Nk, ½.   9 ran

1960 Javelot (4–1) F. Palmer (£16,185) P. Carter (France), 4 yrs
    2. Tulyartos,   **3.** Blast.   ½, 4.   9 ran

1961 ST PADDY (2–13f) L. Piggott (£17,056) N. Murless, 4 yrs
    2. Proud Chieftain,   **3.** Blast.   1½, 6.   7 ran

1962 Henry the Seventh (8–11f) E. Hide (£15,045) W. Elsey, 4 yrs
    2. Valentine,   **3.** Ferneley.   3, 1.   7 ran

1963 Khalkis (7–4f) G. Bougoure (£15,247) P. J. Prendergast, 3 yrs
    2. MIRALGO,   **3.** Tang.   Hd, 2.   9 ran

1964 RAGUSA (4–6f) G. Bougoure (£29,996) P. J. Prendergast, 4 yrs
    2. BALDRIC II,   **3.** Tarqogan.   1½, 6.   11 ran

1965 Canisbay (20–1) S. Clayton (£29,451) C. Boyd-Rochfort, 4 yrs
    2. Roan Rocket,   **3.** Red Vagabonde.   Sht Hd, 2.   8 ran

1966 Pieces of Eight (15–2) L. Piggott (£27,326) M. V. O'Brien, 3 yrs
    2. Ballyciptic,   **3.** PRETENDRE.   2, ½.   10 ran

1967 Busted (8–1) W. Rickaby (£22,697) N. Murless, 4 yrs
    2. GREAT NEPHEW,   **3.** Appiani II.   2½, 1½.   9 ran

1968 ROYAL PALACE (9–4) A. Barclay (£22,077) N. Murless, 4 yrs
    2. TAJ DEWAN,   **3.** SIR IVOR.   Sht Hd, ¾.   5 ran

Race 120: PRINCESS OF WALES'S STAKES
1 mile 4 furlongs. Newmarket. First run 1894

1900 Merry Gal, 3	(8)	1911 Swynford, 4	(5)	1923 Triumph, 4	(7)
1901 Epsom Lad, 4	(12)	1912 Lance Chest, 3	(10)	1924 Salmon Trout, 3	(8)
1902 Veles, 4	(6)	1913 Lance Chest, 4	(11)	1925 Solario, 3	(7)
1903 Ard Patrick, 4	(9)	1914 The Curragh, 4	(6)	1926 Tournesol, 4	(7)
1904 Rock Sand, 4	(5)	1915 Rosendale, 3	(6)	1927 Colorado, 4	(5)
1905 St Denis, 4	(9)	1916 Nassovian, 3	(6)	1928 Tourist, 3	(11)
1906 Dinneford, 4	(6)	1917 Abandoned		1929 Fairway, 4	(4)
1907 Polymelus, 5	(9)	1918 Blink, 3	(3)	1930 Press Gang, 3	(4)
1908 Queen's		1919 Buchan, 3	(4)	1931 The Recorder, 4	
Advocate, 4	(9)	1920 Attilius, 3	(11)	and Shell	
1909 Dark Ronald, 4	(10)	1921 Orpheus, 4	(7)	Transport, 3	(7)
1910 Ulster King, 3	(9)	1922 Blandford, 3	(9)	1932 Jacopo, 4	(8)

1933 Raymond, 3	(11)	**1940–44** No race		**1951** Pardal, 4	(5)
1934 Bright Bird, 3	(7)	**1945** Stirling Castle, 3	(7)	**1952** Zucchero, 4	(7)
1935 Fairbairn, 3	(9)	**1946** Airborne, 3	(4)	**1953** Rawson, 4	(4)
1936 Taj Akbar, 3	(6)	**1947** Nirgal, 4	(9)	**1954** Woodcut, 3	(5)
1937 Flares, 4	(6)	**1948** Alycidon, 3	(5)	**1955** Cobetto, 3	(8)
1938 Pound Foolish, 3	(9)	**1949** Dogger Bank, 3	(6)	**1956** Cash and	
1939 Heliopolis, 3	(8)	**1950** Double Eclipse, 3	(6)	Courage, 3	(8)

1957 Wake Up! (9–4f) D. Smith (£2,817) J. F. Watts, 3 yrs
    2. Messmate,   3. Sun Charger.   Sht Hd, 1.   7 ran
1958 Miner's Lamp (3–1jf) W. Carr (£2,732) C. Boyd-Rochfort, 3 yrs
    2. Primera,   3. Hyphen.   Nk, 4.   7 ran
1959 Primera (4–5f) L. Piggott (£2,588) N. Murless, 5 yrs
    2. Duplex,   3. Belafonte. $\frac{1}{2}$, $1\frac{1}{2}$.   4 ran
1960 Primera (9–4f) L. Piggott (£2,775) N. Murless, 6 yrs
    2. Balaji,   3. Iron Blue. $1\frac{1}{2}$, $\frac{1}{2}$.   6 ran
1961 Apostle (4–6f) L. Piggott (£2,520) S. Ingham, 4 yrs
    2. Pinzon,   3. Sagacity.   Hd, $1\frac{1}{2}$.   6 ran
1962 Silver Cloud (5–1) E. Smith (£2,163) J. Jarvis, 3 yrs
    2. Royal Avenue,   3. Your Highness. $\frac{1}{2}$, $\frac{3}{4}$.   4 ran
1963 Trafalgar (15–2) A. Breasley (£2,129) Sir G. Richards, 3 yrs
    2. London Gazette,   3. Follow Suit.   Hd, $\frac{1}{2}$.   6 ran
1964 Carrack (5–1jf) D. Cullen (£1,676) J. Oxley, 3 yrs
    2. King Chesnut,   3. Silver Cloud.   4, Nk.   8 ran
1965 Lomond (10–1) E. Eldin (£1,492) R. Jarvis, 5 yrs
    2. Goupi,   3. Sandro. $1\frac{1}{2}$, 2.   7 ran
1966 Lomond (3–1) E. Eldin (£1,418) R. Jarvis, 6 yrs
    2. Royal Rubicon,   3. Suvretta.   2, Hd.   5 ran
1967 HOPEFUL VENTURE (13–8f) G. Moore (£2,452) N. Murless, 3 yrs
    2. Sloop,   3. Tumbled. $\frac{3}{4}$, $\frac{3}{4}$.   7 ran
1968 MOUNT ATHOS (3–1) R. Hutchinson (£2,469) J. Dunlop, 3 yrs
    2. Attalus,   3. Principal Boy.   2, 3.   10 ran

Race 121: FALMOUTH STAKES
1 mile. Newmarket. Three-year-old fillies

1957 Sylphide (11–2) L. Piggott (£1,358) N. Murless
    2. Instow,   3. Martial Air. $1\frac{1}{2}$, 3.   13 ran
1958 Court One (6–1) D. Smith (£1,309) N. Murless
    2. ALPINE BLOOM,   3. Blizzard.   4, Hd.   8 ran
1959 Crystal Palace (15–8) E. Smith (£1,343) T. Leader
    2. Anthelion,   3. Yola.   4, $\frac{3}{4}$.   6 ran
1960 Green Opal (9–4) L. Piggott (£1,354) N. Murless
    2. LADY IN TROUBLE,   3. Extra Time.   Hd, 3.   3 ran
1961 Aphrodita (4–6f) J. Mercer (£1,433) H. Wragg
    2. Sticky Case,   3. Brittle II.   Hd, 8.   3 ran

1962 Tournella (11–4) W. Rickaby (£1,413) F. Sutherland
    2. Pellegrino,   **3.** ABERMAID.   Hd, 1½.   6 ran
1963 Crevette (6–1) D. Smith (£1,455) G. Brooke
    2. Fair Astronomer,   **3.** Donatellina II.   2, 6.   8 ran
1964 Alborada (8–11f) G. Starkey (£1,098) J. Oxley
    2. Mara River,   **3.** Honeysucker.   ½, 2.   7 ran
1965 Pugnacity (4–5f) J. Mercer (£816) W. Wharton
    2. Short Commons,   **3.** Lindosa.   1, 2½.   8 ran
1966 Chrona (9–1) L. Piggott (£781) R. Houghton
    2. Orabella II,   **3.** Gem of Gems.   1½, 4.   6 ran
1967 Resilience II (10–1) B. Taylor (£1,161) H. Leader
    2. Whirled,   **3.** Fab.   Nk, 3.   6 ran
1968 Ileana (7–4) R. Hutchinson (£1,167) H. Wragg
    2. Magic Thrust,   **3.** Montana Girl.   1, ¾.   4 ran

Race 122: JULY CUP
6 furlongs. Newmarket. First run 1876

1900 Running Stream, 2 (5)	**1920** Diadem, 6 (w.o.)	**1939** Porto Bello, 3 (10)
1901 Lord Bobs, 3 (5)	**1921** Tetratema, 4 (3)	**1940** No race
1902 Sundridge, 4 (6)	**1922** Pharmacie, 4 (4)	**1941** Comatas, 4 (8)
1903 Sundridge, 5 (2)	**1923** Golden Corn, 4 (2)	**1942–44** No race
1904 Sundridge, 6 (3)	**1924** Drake, 4 (5)	**1945** Honeyway, 4 (4)
1905 Delaunay, 4 (2)	**1925** Diomedes, 3 (w.o.)	**1946** The Bug, 3 (3)
1906 Thrush, 4 (2)	**1926** Diomedes, 4 and	**1947** Falls of Clyde, 3 (5)
1907 Dinneford, 5 (5)	Phalaros, 4 (3)	**1948** Palm Vista, 3 (9)
1908 Lesbia, 3 (6)	**1927** Highborn II, 4 (4)	**1949** Abernant, 3 (3)
1909 Jack Snipe, 4 (8)	**1928** Golden Oracle, 3 (4)	**1950** Abernant, 4 (6)
1910 Amore, 3 (3)	**1929** Tiffin, 3 (3)	**1951** Hard Sauce, 3 (6)
1911 Sunder, 4 (3)	**1930** Sir Cosmo, 4 (10)	**1952** Set Fair, 3 (4)
1912 Spanish Prince, 5 (4)	**1931** Xandover, 4 (4)	**1953** Devon Vintage, 3 (5)
1913 Spanish Prince, 6 (3)	**1932** Concerto, 4 (6)	**1954** Vilmoray, 4 (4)
1914 Golden Sun, 4 (5)	**1933** Myrobella, 3 (4)	**1955** Pappa
1915 Volta, 3 (4)	**1934** Coroado, 4 (7)	Fourway, 3 (3)
1916 Torloisk, 4 (4)	**1935** Bellacose, 3 (11)	**1956** Matador, 3 (5)
1917 No race	**1936** Bellacose, 4 (6)	
1918 Irish Elegance, 3 (7)	**1937** Mickey the	
1919 Diadem, 5 (2)	Greek, 3 (6)	
	1938 Shalfleet, 7 (5)	

1957 Vigo (7–2) L. Piggott (£1,195) W. Dutton, 4 yrs
    2. Drum Beat,   **3.** Dentivate.   3, 15.   4 ran
1958 Right Boy (4–5f) L. Piggott (£1,178) W. Dutton, 4 yrs
    2. Pendlehill,   **3.** Rampant.   2, 6.   4 ran
1959 Right Boy (11–10f) L. Piggott (£1,930) H. Rohan, 5 yrs
    2. Welsh Abbot,   **3.** ROSALBA.   2, 3.   6 ran

1960	Tin Whistle L. Piggott (£2,130) H. Rohan, 3 yrs			walked over
1961	Galivanter (9–2) W. Carr (£1,879) W. Hern, 5 yrs			
	2. Tin Whistle,	3. Favorita.	3, Nk.	3 ran
1962	Marsolve (5–1) W. Rickaby (£1,943) Reg Day, 4 yrs			
	2. Klondyke Bill,	3. Victorina.	Hd, 1½.	4 ran
1963	Secret Step (2–1f) G. Lewis (£2,814) P. Hastings-Bass, 4 yrs			
	2. Matatina,	3. Brother.	¾, 1½.	8 ran
1964	Daylight Robbery (100–9) A. Breasley (£2,839) A. Budgett, 3 yrs			
	2. Matatina,	3. Marcher.	Hd, 3.	7 ran
1965	Merry Madcap (100–8) R. Hutchinson (£3,035) F. Maxwell, 3 yrs			
	2. Port Merion,	3. Goldhill.	Nk, Hd.	14 ran
1966	Lucasland (100–6) E. Eldin (£3,091) J. A. Waugh, 4 yrs			
	2. Dondeen,	3. Spark.	½, 2½.	18 ran
1967	Forlorn River (8–1) B. Raymond (£2,410) W. A. Stephenson, 5 yrs			
	2. Lunar Princess,	3. Hard Water.	¾, 1½.	9 ran
1968	So Blessed (7–2) F. Durr (£2,288) M. Jarvis, 3 yrs			
	2. Mountain Call,	3. Majetta.	4, 1.	7 ran

Race 123: ROUS MEMORIAL STAKES

1 mile 2 furlongs. Ascot. First run 1878

7F 166Y

1900	Champ de Mars, 5	(8)
1901	Sonatura, 4 and Lord Bobs, 3	(6)
1902	Royal Lancer, 3	(7)
1903	Duke of Westminster, 4	(3)
1904	Wild Oats, 4	(5)
1905	Hackler's Pride, 5	(2)
1906	Andover, 5	(6)
1907	Sancy, 4	(3)
1908	Polar Star, 4	(2)
1909	Sir Archibald, 4	(4)
1910	Greenback, 3	(w. o.)
1911	The Story, 5	(2)
1912	Spanish Prince, 5	(2)
1913	Spanish Prince, 6	(2)
1914	Maiden Erlegh, 5	(5)

1915–18	No race	
1919	Diadem, 5	(3)
1920	Diadem, 6	(w. o.)
1921	Monarch, 3	(3)
1922	Sicyon, 3	(6)
1923	My Lord, 3	(5)
1924	Twelve Pointer, 4	(5)
1925	Caravel, 4	(4)
1926	Warden of the Marches, 4	(4)
1927	Colorado, 4	(5)
1928	Delius, 5	(6)
1929	Fairway, 4	(4)
1930	Lansdowne, 3	(6)
1931	The Recorder, 4	(2)
1932	Heronslea, 5	(5)
1933	Loaningdale, 4 and Mannamead, 4	(7)
1934	Alishah, 3	(5)

1935	Windsor Lad, 4	(3)
1936	Fair Trial, 4	(4)
1937	Dan Bulger, 4	(6)
1938	Khan Bahadur, 3	(5)
1939	Glen Loan, 4	(7)
1940–45	No race	
1946	Hobo, 4	(4)
1947	Combat, 3	(4)
1948	Oros, 4	(2)
	1 MILE	
1949	Silver Gate, 4	(8)
1950	Krakatao, 4	(6)
1951	Red Tabs, 3	(6)
1952	Wilwyn, 4	(7)
1953	Chavey Down, 4	(7)
1954	Landau, 3	(8)
1955	Whiranek, 3	· (5)
1956	Chantelsey, 3	(8)

1957	Meldon (2–1) E. Hide (£1,221) P. Beasley, 3 yrs			
	2. SENSUALITA,	3. Traitress.	5, 1½.	4 ran
1958	Snow Cat (100–8) E. Smith (£1,561) N. Murless, 3 yrs			
	2. QUORUM,	3. Shut Up II.	1½, ½.	8 ran

1959 Pinicola (7–2) E. Smith (£1,515) N. Murless, 3 yrs
    2. Eyrefield,   **3.** Cortachy. $1\frac{1}{2}$, 4.   4 ran
1960 Firestreak (8–11f) L. Piggott (£1,553) P. Nelson, 4 yrs
    2. His Story,   **3.** Midsummer   1, $1\frac{1}{2}$.   6 ran
                                Night II.
1961 PETITE ETOILE (2–15f) L. Piggott (£1,528) N. Murless, 5 yrs
    2. Right of Way,   **3.** Don't Look.   1, 6.   5 ran
1962 Henry the Seventh (5–4f) E. Hide (£1,540) W. Elsey, 4 yrs
    2. Royal Avenue,   **3.** Eagle. $1\frac{1}{2}$, Nk.   8 ran
1963 Fair Astronomer (6–4f) E. Smith (£1,553) H. Leader, 3 yrs
    2. High Flown,   **3.** Miletus.   3, $1\frac{1}{2}$.   6 ran
1964 Abandoned
1965 Sweet Moss (4–1) L. Piggott (£1,375) N. Murless, 4 yrs
    2. BALUSTRADE,   **3.** Tarqogan. $1\frac{1}{2}$, $1\frac{1}{2}$.   6 ran
1966 Hill Rise (20–1) W. Rickaby (£1,426) N. Murless, 5 yrs
    2. SILLY SEASON,   **3.** Sweet Moss.   Hd, Hd.   7 ran
1967 Morris Dancer (8–1) G. Lewis (£1,215) I. Balding, 6 yrs
    2. Haymaking,   **3.** Golden Horus.   1, $\frac{1}{2}$.   7 ran

1 MILE 2 FURLONGS

1968 Birdbrook (7–2) R. Hutchinson (£826) M. Pope, 7 yrs
    2. Midnight Marauder,   **3.** Game All. $\frac{3}{4}$, 2.   4 ran

Race 124: KING GEORGE VI AND
QUEEN ELIZABETH STAKES

1 mile 4 furlongs. Ascot Heath

1951 Supreme Court, 3 (19)	**1953** Pinza, 3	(13)	**1955** Vimy, 3	(10)
1952 Tulyar, 3 (15)	**1954** Aureole, 4	(17)	**1956** Ribot, 4	(9)

1957 MONTAVAL (20–1) F. Palmer (£23,090) G. Bridgland (France), 4 yrs
    2. Al Mabsoot,   **3.** Tribord.   Sht Hd, 2.   12 ran
1958 BALLYMOSS (7–4f) A. Breasley (£23,642) M. V. O'Brien, 4 yrs
    2. Almeria,   **3.** Doutelle.   3, $\frac{3}{4}$.   8 ran
1959 ALCIDE (2–1f) W. Carr (£23,642) C. Boyd-Rochfort, 4 yrs
    2. Gladness,   **3.** Balbo.   2, $\frac{3}{4}$.   11 ran
1960 Aggressor (100–8) J. Lindley (£23,345) J. Gosden, 5 yrs
    2. PETITE ETOILE,   **3.** KYTHNOS. $\frac{1}{2}$, 4.   8 ran
1961 Right Royal V (6–4) R. Poincelet (£23,090) E. Pollet (France), 3 yrs
    2. ST PADDY,   **3.** ROCKAVON.   3, 4.   4 ran
1962 Match III (9–2jf) Y. Saint-Martin (£23,515) F. Mathet (France), 4 yrs
    2. AURELIUS,   **3.** Arctic Storm. $\frac{3}{4}$, Nk.   11 ran
1963 RAGUSA (4–1) G. Bougoure (£28, 742) P. J. Prendergast, 3 yrs
    2. MIRALGO,   **3.** Tarqogan.   4, 5.   10 ran
1964 Nasram II (100–7) W. Pyers (£30,740) E. Fellows (France), 4 yrs
    2. SANTA CLAUS,   **3.** Royal Avenue.   2, 4.   4 ran

1965 MEADOW COURT (6–5f) L. Piggott (£31,207) P. J. Prendergast, 3 yrs
    2. SODERINI,   3. Oncidium.   2, 3.   12 ran
1966 Aunt Edith (7–2) L. Piggott (£29,167) N. Murless, 4 yrs
    2. SODIUM,   3. Prominer.   ½, 2.   5 ran
1967 Busted (4–1) G. Moore (£24,389) N. Murless, 4 yrs
    2. Salvo,   3. RIBOCCO.   3, Nk.   9 ran
1968 ROYAL PALACE (4–7f) A. Barclay (£24,020) N. Murless, 4 yrs
    2. Felicio II,   3. Topyo.   ½, Sht Hd.   7 ran

Race 125: SUSSEX STAKES

1 mile. Goodwood. First run 1841. Three-year-olds only until 1960, then three- and four-year-olds

1900	The Raft	(5)	1920	Braishfield	(6)	1937 Pascal	(6)
1901	Energetic	(9)	1921	Sunblaze	(5)	1938 Faroe	(6)
1902	Royal Lancer	(5)	1922	Diligence	(3)	1939 Olein	(7)
1903	Stephanas	(5)	1923	Hurry Off	(4)	1940–45 No race	
1904	Mousqueton	(5)	1924	Burslem	(4)	1946 Radiotherapy	(6)
1905	Thrush	(2)	1925	The Monk	(8)	1947 Combat	(2)
1906	Troutbeck	(3)	1926	Plimsol	(6)	1948 My Babu	(2)
1907	Wool Winder	(6)	1927	Rosalia	(7)	1949 Krakatao	(2)
1908	White Eagle	(5)	1928	Marconigram	(6)	1950 Palestine	(4)
1909	Minoru	(3)	1929	Le Phare	(6)	1951 Le Sage	(7)
1910	Winkipop	(5)	1930	Paradine	(7)	1952 Agitator	(5)
1911	Stedfast	(3)	1931	Inglesant	(6)	1953 King of the	
1912	Tracery	(5)	1932	Dastur	(2)	Tudors	(4)
1913	Sun Yat	(5)	1933	The Abbot	(7)	1954 Landau	(4)
1914	Black Jester	(5)	1934	Badruddin	(3)	1955 My Kingdom	(5)
1915–18	No race		1935	Hairan	(7)	1956 Lucero	(6)
1919	Glanmerin	(4)	1936	Corpach	(5)		

1957 QUORUM (10–11f) A. Russell (£2,760) W. Lyde
    2. Sylphide,   3. Tempest.   ¾, 4.   4 ran
1958 MAJOR PORTION (8–11f) E. Smith (£2,658) T. Leader
    2. PALL MALL,   3. Two Francs.   1, 2.   5 ran
1959 PETITE ETOILE (1–10f) L. Piggott (£2,730) N. Murless
    2. Piping Rock,   3. Welsh Guard.   ¾, Sht Hd.   6 ran
1960 VENTURE VII (13–8f) G. Moore (£2,790) A. Head (France), 3 yrs
    2. MARTIAL,   3. Sovereign Path.   ½, ½.   6 ran
1961 Le Levanstell (100–7) W. Williamson (£2,820) S. McGrath, 4 yrs
    2. Eagle,   3. Lady Senator.   Nk, Sht Hd.   11 ran
1962 ROMULUS (9–1) W. Swinburn (£2,803) R. Houghton, 3 yrs
    2. Cipriani,   3. Songedor.   4, ¾.   8 ran
1963 Queen's Hussar (25–1) R. Hutchinson (£14,766) T. Corbett, 3 yrs
    2. Linacre,   3. Nereus.   Hd, 3.   10 ran

1964 Roan Rocket (4–6f) L. Piggott (£15,011) G. Todd, 3 yrs
    2. Derring-Do,   **3.** BALUSTRADE. $\frac{1}{2}$, $\frac{3}{4}$.   8 ran
1965 Carlemont (7–2) R. Hutchinson (£15,635) P. J. Prendergast, 3 yrs
    2. Roan Rocket,   **3.** Showdown.   3, $\frac{3}{4}$.   11 ran
1966 Paveh (5–1) R. Hutchinson (£15,351) T. Ainsworth, 3 yrs
    2. SILLY SEASON,   **3.** Tesco Boy.   Sht Hd, $2\frac{1}{2}$.   7 ran
1967 Reform (evens f) A. Breasley (£12,841) Sir G. Richards, 3 yrs
    2. Supreme Sovereign,   **3.** Bluerullah. $1\frac{1}{2}$, 2.   10 ran
1968 PETINGO (6–4f) L. Piggott (£12,114) F. Armstrong, 3 yrs
    2. World Cup,   **3.** Frankincense.   4, $1\frac{1}{2}$.   6 ran

Race 126: KING GEORGE STAKES

5 furlongs. Goodwood

1957 Refined (5–2) D. Smith (£1,055) P. J. Prendergast, 3 yrs
    2. Gratitude,   **3.** Ennis. $\frac{1}{2}$, 4.   4 ran
1958 Right Boy (8–13f) L. Piggott (£1,038) W. Dutton, 4 yrs
    2. Hard Tack,   **3.** Ennis. $1\frac{1}{2}$, 3.   5 ran
1959 Right Boy (8–13f) L. Piggott (£1,119) H. Rohan, 5 yrs
    2. Welsh Abbot,   **3.** Compere.   2, Hd.   5 ran
1960 Bleep-Bleep (100–8) W. Carr (£1,408) H. Cottrill, 4 yrs
    2. Sing Sing,   **3.** Tin Whistle.   Hd, 3.   3 ran
1961 Floribunda (4–6f) R. Hutchinson (£1,446) P. J. Prendergast, 3 yrs
    2. Cynara,   **2.** Bleep-Bleep.   3, 2.   4 ran
1962 La Tendresse (11–10) G. Bougoure (£1,455) P. J. Prendergast, 3 yrs
    2. Nerium,   **3.** Caerphilly. $\frac{1}{2}$, 6.   3 ran
1963 Secret Step (11–10f) A. Breasley (£1,510) P. Hastings-Bass, 4 yrs
    2. Tudor Grey,   **3.** Vent Neurf.   1, 4.   5 ran
1964 Matatina (evens f) L. Piggott (£1,421) F. Armstrong, 4 yrs
    2. Crimea II,   **3.** Willie's Kuda.   Hd, 5.   5 ran
1965 Pugnacity (9–4) L. Piggott (£1,431) W. Wharton, 3 yrs
    2. Spaniards Mount,   **3.** Golden Apollo.   1, 2.   4 ran
1966 Polyfoto (8–1) B. Taylor (£1,428) E. Reavey, 4 yrs
    2. Caterina,   **3.** Zahedan.   1, 3.   9 ran
1967 Right Strath (100–6) J. Mercer (£1,203) W. Nightingall, 6 yrs
    2. Florescence,   **3.** Flying By. $\frac{3}{4}$, 2.   5 ran
1968 So Blessed (4–5f) F. Durr (£1,197) M. Jarvis, 3 yrs
    2. St Alphage,   **3.** Willipeg.   1, Nk.   5 ran

Race 127: GOODWOOD CUP
2 miles 5 furlongs. First run 1812

1900 Mazagan, 4	(8)	**1919** Queens Square, 4	(5)	**1936** Cecil, 5	(9)
1901 Fortunatus, 3	(5)	**1920** Mount Royal, 3	(4)	**1937** Fearless Fox, 4	(6)
1902 Perseus, 3	(6)	**1921** Bucks, 3	(5)	**1938** Epigram, 5	(11)
1903 Rabelais, 3	(8)	**1922** Flamboyant, 4	(5)	**1939** Dubonnet, 4	(5)
1904 Saltpetre, 4	(5)	**1923** Triumph, 4	(3)	**1940–45** No race	
1905 Red Robe, 4	(5)	**1924** Teresina, 4	(6)	**1946** Marsyas II, 6	(4)
1906 Plum Tree, 3	(8)	**1925** Cloudbank, 4	(6)	**1947** Monsieur	
1907 The White		**1926** Glommen, 4	(9)	l'Amiral, 6	(4)
Knight, 4	(6)	**1927** Dark Japan, 4	(3)	**1948** Tenerani, 4	(4)
1908 Radium, 5	(6)	**1928** Kinchinjunga, 4	(7)	**1949** Alycidon, 4	(5)
1909 Carrousel, 3	(5)	**1929** Old Orkney, 5	(6)	**1950** Val Drake, 4	(4)
1910 Magic, 3	(3)	**1930** Brown Jack, 6	(5)	**1951** Pan II, 4	(4)
1911 Kilbroney, 4	(5)	**1931** Salmon Leap, 4	(6)	**1952** Medway, 4	(4)
1912 Tullibardine, 4	(3)	**1932** Brulette, 4	(5)	**1953** Souepi, 5	(8)
1913 Catmint, 4	(6)	**1933** Sans Peine, 3	(5)	**1954** Blarney Stone, 5	(5)
1914 Son-in-Law, 3	(5)	**1934** Loosestrife, 5	(4)	**1955** Double Bore, 4	(8)
1915–18 No race		**1935** Tiberius, 4	(3)	**1956** Zarathustra, 5	(4)

1957 Tenterhooks (2–1f) E. Britt (£3,371) C. Elsey, 3 yrs
    2. Macip,   **3.** Donald. $\frac{1}{2}$, 5.   7 ran

1958 Gladness (1–2f) L. Piggott (£3,414) M. V. O'Brien, 5 yrs
    2. Ranchiquito,   **3.** Clichy. $1\frac{1}{2}$, 8.   4 ran

1959 Dickens (9–4) D. Smith (£3,265) C. Boyd-Rochfort, 3 yrs
    2. FRENCH BEIGE,   **3.** Sandiacre. $\frac{3}{4}$, 8.   4 ran

1960 Exar (4–9f) L. Piggott (£3,137) N. Murless, 4 yrs
    2. Predominate,   **3.** Bel Baraka.   2, Nk.   4 ran

1961 Predominate (11–4) E. Smith (£3,222) T. Leader, 9 yrs
    2. Shatter,   **3.** Agreement.   Sht Hd, 3.   4 ran

1962 Sagacity (5–1) W. Carr (£3,265) C. Boyd-Rochfort, 4 yrs
    2. Trelawny,   **3.** Balto.   2, 4.   4 ran

1963 Trelawny (8–13f) A. Breasley (£3,278) G. Todd, 7 yrs
    2. Raise You Ten,   **3.** Sannazaro.   6, 3.   4 ran

1964 Raise You Ten (evens f) S. Clayton (£3,275) C. Boyd-Rochfort, 4 yrs
    2. Credo,   **3.** Timber King. $\frac{3}{4}$, 5.   5 ran

1965 Apprentice (8–1) S. Clayton (£3,194) C. Boyd-Rochfort, 5 yrs
    2. SODERINI,   **3.** Philemon. $2\frac{1}{2}$, $\frac{3}{4}$.   5 ran

1966 Gaulois (15–2) R. Hutchinson (£3,233) C. Boyd-Rochfort, 3 yrs
    2. Vivat Rex,   **3.** Bally Russe.   3, 4.   7 ran

1967 Wrekin Rambler (2–1f) A. Breasley (£3,149) Sir G. Richards, 4 yrs
    2. Piaco,   **3.** Parbury. $1\frac{1}{2}$, 5.   5 ran

1968 Ovaltine (5–2jf) B. Taylor (£3,260) J. F. Watts, 4 yrs
    2. Parbury,   **3.** My Kuda. $2\frac{1}{2}$, $\frac{1}{2}$.   7 ran

Race 128: GORDON STAKES

1 mile 3 furlongs 200 yards. Goodwood. Three-year-olds

1 MILE		**1920** The Alder	(2)	**1936** Magnet	(9)
1902 Osbech a	(3)	**1921** Stanislaus	(4)	**1937** Perifox	(5)
1903 Zindafel	(3)	**1922** Tamar	(3)	**1938** Valedictory	(7)
1904 Delaunay	(3)	**1923** Bold and Bad	(3)	**1939** Wheatland	(4)
1905 Dinneford	(6)	**1924** Black Sheep	(3)	**1940–45** No race	
1906 Victorious	(3)	**1925** Kentish Knock	(4)		
1907 Galvani	(7)	**1926** Thistledown		**1M 3F 200Y**	
1908 Putchamin	(7)	(after dd ht		**1946** Fast and Fair	(5)
		with Pantera)	(4)	**1947** Merry Quip	(4)
1M 4F		**1927** Tiger Hill	(6)	**1948** Nathoo	(6)
1909 Moscato	(5)	**1928** Cyclonic	(10)	**1949** Royal Forest	(3)
1910 Cardinal		**1929** Defoe	(7)	**1950** Foxboro	(8)
Beaufort	(5)	**1930** Press Gang and		**1951** Prince d'Ouilly	(3)
1911 Prince Palatine	(4)	Ut Majeur	(4)	**1952** Gay Time	(3)
1912 Fantasio	(4)	**1931** Rose en Soleil	(6)	**1953** Prince Canarina	(4)
1913 Augur	(8)	**1932** Firdaussi	(5)	**1954** Brilliant Green	(9)
1914 My Prince	(6)	**1933** Tavern	(4)	**1955** Manati	(7)
1915–18 No race		**1934** Bright Bird	(4)	**1956** Dacian	(6)
1919 Sir Douglas	(2)	**1935** Bideford Bay	(5)		

1957 PIPE OF PEACE (4–6f) A. Breasley (£1,744) Sir G. Richards
    2. Sun Charger,   **3.** Albergo.   ½, 1½.   6 ran
1958 Guersillus (13–8) E. Hide (£5,254) C. Elsey
    2. NONE NICER,   **3.** Chinese Sun.   5, 10.   5 ran
1959 Above Suspicion (evens f) D. Smith (£5,306) C. Boyd-Rochfort
    2. CARNOUSTIE,   **3.** Fatralo.   Nk, 8.   4 ran
1960 Kipling (6–1) G. Lewis (£5,619) P. Hastings-Bass
    2. ST PADDY,   **3.** Balaji.   ½, 5.   8 ran
1961 PARDAO (10–11f) W. Carr (£5,451) C. Boyd-Rochfort
    2. Gailowind,   **3.** Tudor Tale.   1½, 1½.   5 ran
1962 Gay Challenger (5–1) R. Hutchinson (£5,355) J. Oxx
    2. Atlantis,   **3.** MIRALGO.   2, 2.   9 ran
1963 Tiger (100–30) A. Breasley (£5,361) Sir G. Richards
    2. MERCHANT   **3.** Follow Suit.   2, ½.   9 ran
    VENTURER,
1964 Sweet Moss (11–2) L. Piggott (£4,963) N. Murless
    2. Crete,   **3.** Lionhearted.   1½, 3.   7 ran
1965 King Log (4–1) R. Hutchinson (£6,121) G. Todd
    2. Ballymarais,   **3.** As Before.   3, Hd.   6 ran
1966 Khalekan (2–1f) D. Lake (£6,219) P. J. Prendergast
    2. Crozier,   **3.** Castle Yard.   2½, 1½.   6 ran
1967 Sun Rock (11–4jf) G. Moore (£4,704) N. Murless
    2. Gay Garland,   **3.** French Vine.   Hd, 4.   7 ran
1968 MOUNT ATHOS (4–7f) R. Hutchinson (£4,279) J. Dunlop
    2. Royal Rocket,   **3.** Torpid.   1, 2.   3 ran

Race 129: NASSAU STAKES
1 mile 2 furlongs. Goodwood. Three-year-old fillies

1957 Swallow Swift (100–9) E. Mercer (£2,190) G. Colling
        2. Blue-Galleon,   3. Cadenza.   1, Nk.   8 ran
1958 Darlene (100–30) A. Breasley (£2,298) Sir G. Richards
        2. MOTHER GOOSE,   3. Persian Wheel.   3, 3.   6 ran
1959 Crystal Palace (3–1) E. Smith (£2,233) T. Leader
        2. ROSE OF MEDINA,   3. Mistlethrush.   Hd, 5.   6 ran
1960 Desert Beauty (2–1) A. Breasley (£2,322) Sir G. Richards
        2. Green Opal,   3. Bebop. $\frac{1}{2}$, 3.   5 ran
1961 Rachel (7–2) J. Lindley (£2,285) J. Gosden
        2. Secret Session,   3. Vitality Plus. $1\frac{1}{2}$, Sht Hd.   6 ran
1962 Nortia (100–30jf) J. Mercer (£2,396) W. Hern
        2. Romantica,   3. Pellegrino. $\frac{1}{2}$, 3.   7 ran
1963 SPREE (15–8f) J. Lindley (£2,350) J. Tree
        2. Wishful Thinking,   3. POUPONNE.   Hd, 5.   4 ran
1964 Cracker (10–1) J. Mercer (£2,456) W. Wharton
        2. Sound of Music,   3. Lochailort. $1\frac{1}{2}$, 2.   6 ran
1965 Aunt Edith (7–4f) L. Piggott (£2,948) N. Murless
        2. Eucumbene,   3. Toffee Nose.   4, 10.   6 ran
1966 Haymaking (13–2) L. Piggott (£2,006) R. Houghton
        2. Corbalton,   3. Last Case.   3, $2\frac{1}{2}$.   9 ran
1967 Fair Winter (7–2) J. Mercer (£1,660) D. Candy
        2. Autumn Melody,   3. Geraldine Too.   6, $1\frac{1}{2}$.   5 ran
1968 Hill Shade (5–6f) A. Barclay (£1,656) N. Murless
        2. Pseudonym,   3. Grandpa's   3, 4.   7 ran
                                            Legacy.

Race 130: WARREN STAKES
1 mile 3 furlongs 200 yards. Goodwood

1957 COURT HARWELL (6–4f) A. Breasley (£597) Sir G. Richards, 3 yrs
        2. Super Snipe,   3. Praetorian. $\frac{1}{2}$, $1\frac{1}{2}$.   6 ran
1958 Castro (5–1) W. Carr (£567) C. Boyd-Rochfort, 3 yrs
        2. Hyphen,   3. Attractor. $1\frac{1}{2}$, 4.   8 ran
1959 Admiral's Lark (5–1) E. Mercer (£565) D. Whelan, 3 yrs
        2. Light Horseman,   3. Lemnos.   Sht Hd, $\frac{1}{2}$.   5 ran
1960 Menelek (5–1) D. Smith (£817) G. Brooke, 3 yrs
        2. Lysander,   3. Iron Blue. $\frac{3}{4}$, 2.   5 ran
1961 Hot Brandy (5–1) D. Keith (£595) W. Nightingall, 3 yrs
        2. Perfect Knight,   3. Night Porter.   Nk, $1\frac{1}{2}$.   9 ran
1962 Idle Hour (7–4f) D. Smith (£975) J. F. Watts, 3 yrs
        2. Neanderthal,   3. Blackwood.   Nk, $\frac{3}{4}$.   7 ran

1963 In the Gloaming (7–4f) A. Breasley (£1,005) Sir G. Richards, 3 yrs
    2. Rebirth,   **3.** Hanassi.   1½, 2.   7 ran
1964 DILETTANTE II (4–6f) G. Bougoure (£1,218) P. J. Prendergast, 3 yrs
    2. Cursorial,   **3.** Ruantallan.   2, ½.   10 ran
1965 Suvretta (5–2f) J. Mercer (£1,156) B. Hobbs, 3 yrs
    2. High Proof,   **3.** Gondolier.   ½, 6.   7 ran
1966 Crisp and Even (5–4f) G. Bougoure (£1,146). A. Budgett, 3 yrs
    2. Saints and Sinners,   **3.** Tatarin   3, ¾.   3 ran
1967 In Command (5–2f) B. Taylor (£1,212) H. Leader, 3 yrs
    2. Proconsul,   **3.** Promethean.   Sht Hd, Hd.   8 ran
1968 Karabas (5–1) W. Williamson (£1,184) P. J. Prendergast, 3 yrs
    2. Scipio,   **3.** Heron's Plume.   2½, Sht Hd.   7 ran

Race 131: IRISH GUINNESS OAKS

1 mile 4 furlongs. Curragh. Three-year-old fillies. First run 1895. Sponsored by Guinness since 1964

1 MILE		**1918** Judea	(4)	**1938** Conversation	
1900 May Race	(6)	**1919** Snow Maiden	(6)	Piece	(8)
1901 Royal Mantle	(5)	**1920** Place Royale	(6)	**1939** Superb	(8)
1902 Marievale	(5)	**1921** The Kiwi	(7)	**1940** Queen of Shiray	(11)
1903 Mary Lester	(5)	**1922** Miss Hazelwood	(10)	**1941** Uvira	(5)
1904 f–Copestone	(5)	**1923** Becka	(10)	**1942** Majideh	(8)
1905 Blakestown	(3)	**1924** Amethystine	(8)	**1943** Suntop	(12)
1906 Juliet II	(6)	**1925** Ixia	(6)	**1944** Avoca	(9)
1907 Reina	(2)	**1926** Resplendent	(7)	**1945** Admirable	(14)
1908 Queen of Peace	(5)	**1927** Cinq a Sept	(7)	**1946** Linaria	(10)
1909 Fredith	(7)	**1928** Haintonette	(7)	**1947** Desert Drive	(14)
1910 Blair Royal	(5)	**1929** Soliptic	(4)	**1948** Masaka	(10)
1911 Tullynacree	(6)	**1930** Therisina	(8)	**1949** Circus Lady	(12)
1912 Shining Way	(6)	**1931** Nitsichin	(9)	**1950** Corejada	(16)
1913 Athgreany	(7)	**1932** Santaria	(9)	**1951** Djebellica	(13)
1914 May Edgar	(6)	**1933** Salar	(14)	**1952** Five Spots	(13)
		1934 Foxcroft	(5)	**1953** Noory	(11)
		1935 Smokeless	(8)	**1954** Pantomime	
1M 4F		**1936** Silversol	(6)	Queen	(15)
1915 Latharna	(9)	**1937** Sol Speranza	(7)	**1955** Agar's Plough	(12)
1916 Captive Princess	(6)			**1956** Garden State	(8)
1917 Golden Maid	(8)				

1957 SILKEN GLIDER (11–4) J. Eddery (£4,021) S. McGrath
    2. Chatting,   **3.** Sail Aniar.   4, Sht Hd.   15 ran
1958 AMANTE (11–4) L. Ward (£3,969) A. Head (France)
    2. Torbella III,   **3.** Tantalizer.   5, 1.   11 ran
1959 Discorea (100–7) E. Mercer (£3,852) H. Wragg
    2. La Coquenne,   **3.** Minnehaha.   ¾, 1¼.   9 ran
1960 Lynchris (11–4f) W. Williamson (£3,781) J. Oxx
    2. Sunny Cove,   **3.** Nubena.   6, 2¼,   17 ran

1961 AMBERGRIS (6–4f) J. Lindley (£3,867) H. Wragg
    2. INDIAN MELODY,   3. Choir Practice.   2½, 2.   10 ran
1962 French Cream (100–9) W. Rickaby (£5,030) G. Brooke
    2. Cherry,   3. Anitra.   2, 2.   12 ran
1963 Hibernia III (6–4f) W. Williamson (£5,674) J. Oxx
    2. Kazanlik,   3. Ashavan.   1½, 2¼.   15 ran
1964 Ancasta (3–1) J. Purtell (£11,461) M. V. O'Brien
    2. PATTI,   3. WINDMILL   Nk, 2.   9 ran
                         GIRL.
1965 Aurabella (22–1) L. Ward (£19,846) M. V. O'Brien
    2. LONG LOOK,   3. Bracey Bridge.   ¾, ½.   10 ran
1966 Merry Mate (100–9) W. Williamson (£18,599) J. Oxx
    2. Black Gold,   3. Loyalty.   Nk, 6.   10 ran
1967 Pampalina (100–8) J. Roe (£20,571) J. Oxx
    2. Iskereen,   3. Arawak.   2½, ¾.   14 ran
1968 Celina (4–1) A. Barclay (£20,371) N. Murless
    2. Kylin,   3. GLAD ONE.   5, 1.   12 ran

Race 132: HUNGERFORD STAKES
7 furlongs 60 yards. Newbury

1957 Picture Light (100–30) E. Smith (£550) T. Leader, 3 yrs
    2. Primera,   3. Kings Barn.   2, 2.   4 ran
1958 Lovestone (2–1) D. Smith (£514) H. Murless, 3 yrs
    2. Troubadour,   3. Snow Cat.   1½, 1½.   4 ran
1959 Agile (5–2) G. Bougoure (£571) M. V. O'Brien, 3 yrs
    2. Gang Warily,   3. Kindling Chips.   2, 3.   8 ran
1960 Fagus (10–11f) A. Breasley (£529) Sir G. Richards, 3 yrs
    2. Gilboa,   3. Optimist.   1½, Nk.   6 ran
1961 Eagle (4–7f) G. Starkey (£536) J. Oxley, 3 yrs
    2. Restaurant,   3. Ruffian. 1½, 4.   6 ran
1962 ROMULUS (4–6f) W. Swinburn (£522) R. Houghton, 3 yrs
    2. Torero,   3. Panthera.   Sht Hd, 8.   5 ran
1963 Dunce Cap (9–4f) D. Smith (£1,413) C. Boyd-Rochfort, 3 yrs
    2. Queen's Hussar,   3. Nereus.   Nk, 3.   8 ran
1964 Derring-Do (2–1f) A. Breasley (£1,432) A. Budgett, 3 yrs
    2. Feather Bed,   3. Piccadilly.   1, 3.   7 ran
1965 Roan Rocket (1–2f) L. Piggott (£1,884) G. Todd, 4 yrs
    2. Siliconn,   3. Ragtime.   ¾, 1.   8 ran
1966 SILLY SEASON (10–11f) G. Lewis (£1,899) I. Balding, 4 yrs
    2. Enrico,   3. Red Slipper.   ¾, 2.   7 ran
1967 St Chad (4–5f) G. Moore (£1,524) N. Murless, 3 yrs
    2. Quisling,   3. Kibenka.   2½, Sht Hd.   4 ran
1968 JIMMY REPPIN (10–11f) G. Lewis (£1,542) J. Sutcliffe jun., 3 yrs
    2. Sidon,   3. Town Crier.   5, 2½.   6 ran

Race 133: OXFORDSHIRE STAKES

1 mile 5 furlongs 60 yards. Newbury. For three-year-olds only until 1961

1957 COURT HARWELL (5–2) A. Breasley (£1,081) Sir G. Richards
    2. Superfluous,   **3.** Heswall Honey.   1½, Nk.   6 ran
1958 Owen Glendower (13–8f) G. Lewis (£1,069) P. Hastings-Bass
    2. Royal Highway,   **3.** All Serene.   1½, 5.   4 ran
1959 Kalydon (evens f) E. Smith (£961) B. van Cutsem
    2. Pinicola,   **3.** Honest Boy.   6, 8.   4 ran
1960 High Hat (7–1) W. Carr (£1,094) W. Nightingall
    2. Tobago,   **3.** Dusky Prince.   5, ½.   6 ran
1961 Sagacity (5–1) E. Smith (£2,698) C. Boyd-Rochfort, 3 yrs
    2. High Perch,   **3.** High Hat (second, disq.)
            Original distances, ¾, 3.   4 ran
1962 Sovrango (15–8) W. Williamson (£2,613) H. Wragg, 4 yrs
    2. Icarus,   **3.** Gaul.   Nk, 4.   6 ran
1963 Sovrango (5–2jf) W. Williamson (£4,101) H. Wragg, 5 yrs
    2. Christmas Island,   **3.** Crepes d'Enfer.   5. 2.   5 ran
1964 Sunseeker (6–1) J. Purtell (£3,004) M. V. O'Brien, 3 yrs
    2. Gaul,   **3.** Credo.   Hd, 5.   8 ran
1965 Court Gift (4–1) S. Clayton (£3,557) B. Hobbs, 3 yrs
    2. Oncidium,   **3.** Bally Russe.   1½, 6.   5 ran
1966 CHARLOTTOWN (11–8) J. Lindley (£3,585) G. Smyth, 3 yrs
    2. Desert Call II,   **3.** SODIUM.   5, 8.   4 ran
1967 HOPEFUL VENTURE (4–7f) G. Moore (£3,347) N. Murless, 3 yrs
    2. Nip Away,   **3.** Matchim.   5, 2½.   6 ran
1968 Levmoss (100–6) B. Taylor (£3,548) S. McGrath, 3 yrs
    2. CANTERBURY,   **3.** Park Top.   Nk, Hd.   10 ran

Race 134: YORKSHIRE OAKS

1 mile 4 furlongs. York. Three-year-old fillies

1957 Almeria (11–10f) W. Carr (£6,938) C. Boyd-Rochfort
    2. Blue Galleon,   **3.** Crotchet.   6, 6.   7 ran
1958 NONE NICER (4–1) S. Clayton (£6,802) W. Hern
    2. Darlene,   **3.** Chambord.   2, 1.   8 ran
1959 PETITE ETOILE (2–15f) L. Piggott (£7,048) N. Murless
    2. Mirnaya,   **3.** Phantom Star.   ¾, 5.   3 ran
1960 Lynchris (5–4f) W. Williamson (£3,744) J. Oxx
    2. No Saint,   **3.** Green Opal.   ½, Hd.   7 ran
1961 Tenacity (7–1) A. Breasley (£3,574) Sir G. Richards
    2. Irristable,   **3.** Wistful.   2, 2.   7 ran

1962 WEST SIDE STORY (2–1f) E. Smith (£3,650) T. Leader
    2. Almiranta,   **3.** Nortia.   Hd, 2.   5 ran
1963 Outcrop (9–1) E. Smith (£4,866) G. Barling
    2. Amicable,   **3.** Kazanlik.   1, ½.   11 ran
1964 HOMEWARD BOUND (2–1) G. Starkey (£4,418) J. Oxley
    2. Beaufront,   **3.** Ancasta.   3, 2.   7 ran
1965 MABEL (7–4f) J. Mercer (£4,465) P. Walwyn
    2. Eucumbene,   **3.** Bracey Bridge.   1½, 1½.   5 ran
1966 Parthian Glance (3–1) L. Piggott (£4,490) G. Todd
    2. Predicament,   **3.** Brief Chorus.   1, Nk.   8 ran
1967 Palatch (7–1) B. Taylor (£3,364) H. Leader
    2. Cranberry Sauce,   **3.** Arawak.   Nk, 2½.   6 ran
1968 Exchange (7–2) B. Taylor (£3,457) H. Leader
    2. Border Bounty,   **3.** Hardiesse.   ¾, 1½.   8 ran

Race 135: GREAT VOLTIGEUR STAKES

1 mile 4 furlongs. York. Three-year-olds. Until 1957 run as Voltigeur Sweepstakes for three-year-old colts

1950 Castle Rock   (5)   **1953** Premonition   (6)   **1955** Acropolis   (5)
1951 Border Legend   (13)   **1954** Blue Sail   (9)   **1956** Hornbeam   (4)
1952 Childe Harold   (7)

1957 BRIOCHE (100–6) E. Britt (£8,264) C. F. Elsey
    2. BALLYMOSS,   **3.** Tempest.   4, ½.   7 ran
1958 ALCIDE (3–1) W. Carr (£8,374) C. Boyd-Rochfort
    2. Arcticeelagh,   **3.** Guersillus.   12, 3.   5 ran
1959 PINDARI (11–10f) L. Piggott (£10,508) N. Murless
    2. Sheshoon,   **3.** Agricola.   1½, 3.   4 ran
1960 ST PADDY (4–11f) L. Piggott (£5,951) N. Murless
    2. Apostle,   **3.** Oak Ridge.   ¾, 8.   4 ran
1961 Just Great (3–1jf) A. Breasley (£4,217) S. Ingham
    2. AURELIUS,   **3.** PARDAO.   ¾, 4.   8 ran
1962 HETHERSETT (15–2) F. Durr (£4,200) W. Hern
    2. MIRALGO,   **3.** MONTERRICO. Sht Hd, 3.   11 ran
1963 RAGUSA (2–5f) G. Bougoure (£4,931) P. J. Prendergast
    2. ONLY FOR LIFE,   **3.** MERCHANT Hd. 6.   5 ran
                                    VENTURER.
1964 INDIANA (4–7f) J. Lindley (£4,473) J. F. Watts
    2. Fighting Charlie,   **3.** DILETTANTE II.
                                      Hd, 5.   6 ran
1965 Ragazzo (13–8f) L. Piggott (£4,524) P. J. Prendergast
    2. Ballymarais,   **3.** Craighouse.   2, Hd.   6 ran
1966 Hermes (15–2) G. Starkey (£4,558) J. Oxley
    2. BLACK PRINCE II,   **3.** Agogo.   Sht Hd, 1.   8 ran

1967 Great Host (3–1) W. Williamson (£3,323) P. J. Prendergast
    2. Accuser,   **3.** Mariner.   5, 2½.   6 ran
1968 CONNAUGHT (1–3f) A. Barclay (£3,263) N. Murless
    2. Riboccare (first, disq.)   **3.** Laurence. O.
                      Original distances, Nk, 4.   4 ran

Race 136: NUNTHORPE STAKES
5 furlongs. York

1957 Gratitude (7–2) W. Snaith (£1,740) H. L. Cottrill, 4 yrs
    2. Right Boy,   **3.** Vigo.   ¾, 2.   5 ran
1958 Right Boy (8–100f) L. Piggott (£1,600) W. Dutton, 4 yrs
    2. Abadesa,   **3.** High Finance.   ½, Bad.   3 ran
1959 Right Boy (4–9f) L. Piggott (£2,207) H. Rohan, 5 yrs
    2. Galivanter,   **3.** Welsh Abbot.   ½, ½.   6 ran
1960 Bleep-Bleep (9–2) W. Carr (£2,300) H. Cottrill, 4 yrs
    2. Kerrabee,   **3.** Tin Whistle.   Nk, 2.   7 ran
1961 Floribunda (4–1) R. Hutchinson (£2,235) P. J. Prendergast, 3 yrs
    2. Cynara,   **3.** Silver Tor.   4, 1.   6 ran
1962 Gay Mairi (100–8) A. Breasley (£2,235) H. Whiteman, 3 yrs
    2. French Plea,   **3.** Cassarate.   ¾, 1.   9 ran
1963 Matatina (7–2) L. Piggott (£3,945) F. Armstrong, 3.
    2. Secret Step,   **3.** Runnymede.   1, ½.   6 ran
1964 Althrey Don (3–1) R. Maddock (£3,673) H. Rohan, 3 yrs
    2. Matatina,   **3.** Siliconn.   2, Hd.   10 ran
1965 Polyfoto (20–1) J. Wilson (£3,741) E. Reavey, 3 yrs
    2. Caterina,   **3.** Granville Greta.   ½, 1.   8 ran
1966 Caterina (13–2) L. Piggott (£3,754) F. Armstrong, 3 yrs
    2. Lucasland,   **3.** Alamo City.   1, 3.   11 ran
1967 Forlorn River (6–1) B. Raymond (£2,921) W. A. Stephenson, 5 yrs
    2. Empress Sissi,   **3.** Flying By.   Sht Hd, ¾.   12 ran
1968 So Blessed (4–6f) F. Durr (£2,814) M. Jarvis, 3 yrs
    2. Be Friendly,   **3.** Manacle.   ½, 2½.   5 ran

Race 137: WILLS MILE
1 mile. Goodwood

1967 St Chad (9–4) G. Moore (£6,893) N. Murless, 3 yrs
    2. Reform,   **3.** Atherstone Wood. 1, 1.   7 ran
1968 JIMMY REPPIN (5–1) G. Lewis (£9,806) J. Sutcliffe jun., 3 yrs
    2. PETINGO,   **3.** Majetta.   2, 8.   6 ran

Race 138: FIFINELLA FILLIES STAKES

1 mile 2 furlongs. Epsom. Three-year-olds. For maidens at closing until 1961

1960 Reckless (13–2) E. Smith (£1,817) R. J. Colling
    2. Tudor Love,   3. Alcoa.   Sht Hd, 1.   7 ran
1961 Miss Biffin (5–2) G. Lewis (£1,383) P. Hastings-Bass
    2. Bluecourt,   3. Piero.   Hd, 2.   5 ran
1962 George's Girl (100–30) W. Williamson (£1,395) M. Connolly
    2. Bleu Azur,   3. Tropic Star.   6, Sht Hd.   5 ran
1963 Lachine (5–4f) A. Breasley (£1,401) Sir G. Richards
    2. Crenelle,   3. Born Free.   1½, nk.   6 ran
1964 Young Man's Fancy (7–2) D. Smith (£1,396) G. Brooke
    2. Causerie,   3. Sound of Music. Nk, 3.   6 ran
1965 Mlle Barker (7–1) J. Purtell (£1,421) M. V. O'Brien
    2. Lindosa,   3. Kitimat.   Nk, Sht Hd.   7 ran
1966 Green Halo (1–3f) L. Piggott (£1,421) N. Murless
    2. Hedge Rose.   4.   2 ran
1967 ST PAULI GIRL (4–11f) L. Piggott (£1,163) H. Cottrill
    2. Chasmarella,   3. Aura.   1½, 12.   3 ran
1968 Mahal (11–2) L. Piggott (£1,116) P. Walwyn
    2. Ash Lawn,   3. Fair Patricia,   4, ½.   5 ran

Race 139: PARK HILL STAKES

1 mile 6 furlongs 132 yards. Doncaster. Three-year-old fillies. First run 1839

1900 Goosander	(8)	1919 Flying Spear	(5)	1935 Fox Lair	(6)
1901 St Aldegonde	(9)	1920 Redhead	(5)	1936 Traffic Light	(5)
1902 Elba	(4)	1921 Love in Idleness	(5)	1937 Nadushka	(11)
1903 Quintessence	(6)	1922 Selene	(2)	1938 Gainly	(10)
1904 Pretty Polly	(5)	1923 Brownhylda	(4)	1939–45 No race	
1905 Adula	(6)	1924 Charley's Mount	(7)	1946 Procne	(4)
1906 Demure	(4)	1925 Juldi	(4)	1947 Mitrailleuse	(8)
1907 Jubilee	(8)	1926 Glasheen	(7)	1948 Vertencia	(9)
1908 Siberia	(4)	1927 Cinq a Sept	(7)	1949 Sea Idol	(12)
1909 Electra	(4)	1928 Girandola	(8)	1950 La Baille	(14)
1910 Yellow Slave	(4)	1929 Nuwara Eliya	(3)	1951 Verse	(5)
1911 Hair Trigger II	(3)	1930 Glorious Devon	(10)	1952 Moon Star	(14)
1912 Eufrosina	(5)	1931 Volume	(8)	1953 Kerkeb	(9)
1913 Arda	(7)	1932 Fury	(5)	1954 Bara Bibi	(14)
1914 First Spear	(6)	1933 Typhonic	(7)	1955 Ark Royal	(5)
1915–18 No race		1934 Poker	(3)	1956 Kyak	(10)

1957 Almeria (2–7f) W. Carr (£5,475) C. Boyd-Rochfort
    2. Crotchet,   **3.** SILKEN   2, 8.   5 ran
                            GLIDER.
1958 CUTTER (100–8) E. Mercer (£5,186) G. Colling
    2. Chambord,   **3.** MOTHER   5, 1½.   8 ran
                            GOOSE.
1959 Collyria (33–1) E. Smith (£5,203) N. Murless
    2. CANTELO,   **3.** Discorea.   1½, 3.   7 ran
1960 Sunny Cove (5–1) A. Breasley (£4,159) Sir G. Richards
    2. French Fern,   **3.** Annotation.   Nk, 5.   6 ran
1961 Never Say (7–2) J. Mercer (£4,235) R. J. Colling
    2. Irristable,   **3.** Icy Look.   3, Nk.   8 ran
1962 Almiranta (7–2) W. Carr (£4,405) J. A. Waugh
    2. WEST SIDE STORY,   **3.** Romantica.   1, 6.   9 ran
1963 Outcrop (4–1) E. Smith (£4,626) G. Barling
    2. Ostrya,   **3.** Olgiata.   1½, ½.   9 ran
1964 Cursorial (100–6) J. Mercer (£3,796) W. Wharton
    2. Ancasta,   **3.** Alzara.   ¾, 5.   5 ran
1965 Bracey Bridge (7–2) L. Piggott (£3,929) N. Murless
    2. MABEL,   **3.** Miba.   2, 1½.   5 ran
1966 Parthian Glance (4–5f) L. Piggott (£3,901) G. Todd
    2. Predicament,   **3.** VARINIA.   2½, 3.   7 ran
1967 PIA (7–2) E. Hide (£2,383) W. Elsey and
    Pink Gem (2–1f) G. Moore (£2,383) N. Murless
    3. ST PAULI GIRL.   Dd Ht, 2.   7 ran
1968 Bringley (3–1) B. Taylor (£3,571) H. Leader
    2. Border Bounty,   **3.** Sunland.   2, 3.   8 ran

Race 140: DONCASTER CUP
2 miles 2 furlongs. Doncaster. First run 1801

1900 King's		**1909** Amadis, 3	(6)	**1927** Bythorne, 3	(4)
Courier, 3	(5)	**1910** Bronzino, 3	(5)	**1928** Pons	
1901 Merry Gal, 4 and		**1911** Lemberg, 4	(6)	Asinorum, 6	(3)
Sidus, 4	(4)	**1912** Prince Palatine, 4	(2)	**1929** Athford, 4	(4)
1902 William the		**1913** Long Set, 6	(2)	**1930** Brown Jack, 6	(5)
Third, 4	(3)	**1914** Willbrook, 3	(9)	**1931** Singapore, 4	(6)
1903 Wavelet's		**1915–18** No race		**1932** Foxhunter, 3	(6)
Pride, 6	(8)	**1919** Haki, a	(3)	**1933** Colorado Kid, 4	(2)
1904 Robert le		**1920** Buchan, 4	(7)	**1934** Alcazar, 3	(3)
Diable, 5	(3)	**1921** Flamboyant, 3	(6)	**1935** Black Devil, 4	(5)
1905 Bachelor's		**1922** Devizes, 5	(4)	**1936** Buckleigh, 4	(6)
Button, 6	(5)	**1923** Silurian, 4	(5)	**1937** Haulfryn, 4	(6)
1906 Velocity, 4	(5)	**1924** Santorb, 3	(6)	**1938** Epigram, 5	(5)
1907 Velocity, 5	(6)	**1925** St Germans, 4	(9)	**1939–45** No race	
1908 Radium, 5	(7)	**1926** Bongrace, 3	(7)	**1946** Marsyas II, 6	(4)

1947 Trimbush, 7	(7)	1951 Fast Fox, 4	(7)	1954 Osborne, 7	(9)
1948 Auralia, 5	(9)	1952 Aquino II, 4	(7)	1955 Entente	
1949 Alycidon, 4	(4)	1953 Souepi, 5 and		Cordiale, 4	(4)
1950 Aldborough, 5	(8)	Nick La		1956 Atlas, 3	(8)
		Rocca, 4	(7)		

1957 FRENCH BEIGE (5–1) G. Littlewood (£3,540) H. Peacock, 4 yrs
    2. HORNBEAM,   **3.** Court Command. Sht Hd, 15.   4 ran

1958 Agreement (25–1) D. Smith (£3,400) C. Boyd-Rochfort, 4 yrs
    2. Almeria,   **3.** BRIOCHE.   Nk, 2.   7 ran

1959 Agreement (11–4) W. Carr (£3,438) C. Boyd-Rochfort, 5 yrs
    2. FRENCH BEIGE and   **2.** Alexis.   1, Dd Ht.   4 ran

1960 Exar (6–100f) L. Piggott (£3,390) N. Murless, 4 yrs
    2. Jongleur.   1½.   2 ran

1961 Pandofell (9–4jf) L. Piggott (£3,174) F. Maxwell, 4 yrs
    2. Sagacity,   **3.** Negresco II.   3, 4.   5 ran

1962 Bonnard (6–1) R. Hutchinson (£3,115) J. Clayton, 4 yrs
    2. Oakville,   **3.** Sagacity.   2, 4.   6 ran

1963 Raise You Ten (5–1) D. Smith (£3,166) C. Boyd-Rochfort, 3 yrs
    2. Arctic Vale,   **3.** Oakville.   3, 1.   4 ran

1964 Grey of Falloden (8–1) J. Mercer (£2,783) W. Hern, 5 yrs
    2. Raise You Ten,   **3.** Oakville.   ¾, ½.   6 ran

1965 Prince Hansel (2–1f) D. Yates (£2,759) D. Thom, 4 yrs
    2. HOMEWARD BOUND,   **3.** Grey of Falloden. 6, 4.   6 ran

1966 Piaco (11–8f) M. Thomas (£2,780) G. Barling, 3 yrs
    2. Suvretta,   **3.** Desert Call II.   3, 1.   6 ran

1967 Crozier (20–1) F. Durr (£2,292) P. Walwyn, 4 yrs
    2. Hermes,   **3.** Wrekin Rambler. ½, 4.   6 ran

1968 Accuser (2–1) J. Mercer (£2,306) W. Hern, 4 yrs
    2. Fortissimo,   **3.** Ovaltine.   3, 1½.   4 ran

Race 141: PETER HASTINGS STAKES

1 mile 2 furlongs. Newbury

1966 Double-U-Jay (11–4) D. Smith (£3,498) J. Winter, 3 yrs
    2. Ballyciptic,   **3.** Pieces of Eight.   Sht Hd, ½.   4 ran

1967 Sun Rock (15–8f) G. Moore (£3,387) N. Murless, 3 yrs
    2. Good Match,   **3.** Lucky Biscuit.   ¾, Nk.   6 ran

1968 Abandoned

> *HORSES IN CAPITAL LETTERS*
> *WERE TO BE, OR HAD BEEN,*
> *PLACED IN THE CLASSICS*

Race 142: IRISH ST. LEGER
1 mile 6 furlongs. Curragh. Three-year-olds

1915 La Poloma	(6)	**1930** Sol de Terre	(4)	**1945** Spam	(9)
1916 Captive Princess	(8)	**1931** Beaudelaire	(2)	**1946** Cassock	(9)
1917 Double Scotch	(5)	**1932** Hill Song	(4)	**1947** Esprit de France	(5)
1918 Dionysos	(7)	**1933** Harinero	(6)	**1948** Beau Sabreur	(8)
1919 Cheap Popularity	(5)	**1934** Primero	(8)	**1949** Brown Rover	(13)
1920 Kirk Alloway	(3)	**1935** Museum	(5)	**1950** Morning	
1921 Kircubbin	(5)	**1936** Battle Song	(4)	Madam	(12)
1922 Royal Lancer	(8)	**1937** Owenstown	(5)	**1951** Do Well	(10)
1923 O'Dempsey	(5)	**1938** Ochiltree	(7)	**1952** Judicate	(7)
1924 Zodiac	(8)	**1939** Skoiter	(6)	**1953** Sea Charger	(10)
1925 Spelthorne	(6)	**1940** Harvest Feast	(5)	**1954** Zarathustra	(5)
1926 Sunny View	(2)	**1941** Etoile de Lyons	(6)	**1955** Diamond Slipper	(9)
1927 Ballyvoy	(4)	**1942** Windsor Slipper	(8)	**1956** Magnetic North	(8)
1928 Law Suit	(4)	**1943** Solferino	(4)		
1929 Trigo	(5)	**1944** Water Street	(7)		

1957 Ommeyad (5–4f) J. Massard (£3,665) A. Head (France)
    2. Primera,   3. Solartickle.   1, Sht Hd.   11 ran
1958 Royal Highway (7–4jf) N. Brennan (£3,742) H. V. S. Murless
    2. Sindon,   3. Irish Penny.   2, 10.   6 ran
1959 Barclay (1–2f) G. Bougoure (£3,859) M. V. O'Brien
    2. Light Horseman,   3. Capitaine.   Sht Hd, Nk.   7 ran
1960 Lynchris (4–6f) W. Williamson (£4,149) J. Oxx
    2. Our Charger,   3. Avril Sprite.   6, 3.   8 ran
1961 Vimadee (100–9) T. P. Burns (£3,950) T. Burns
    2. Your Highness,   3. Silver Moon.   1½, 2.   10 ran
1962 Arctic Vale (40–1) P. Matthews (£5,094) P. J. Prendergast
    2. Nos Royalistes,   3. Torano.   ¾, 1½.   9 ran
1963 Christmas Island (6–1) G. Bougoure (£5,405) P. J. Prendergast
    2. Ashavan,   3. Philemon.   1½, 2½.   10 ran
1964 Biscayne (4–1) W. Williamson (£6,414) J. Oxx
    2. Sunseeker,   3. Tired Monarch.   10, 3.   8 ran
1965 Craighouse (6–1) J. Mercer (£8,585) W. Hern
    2. Alcalde,   3. Khalife.   2, 5.   14 ran
1966 White Gloves (4–1) L. Ward (£8,240) M. V. O'Brien
    2. Khalekan,   3. Wrekin Rambler.   1, Nk.   14 ran
1967 Dan Kano (evens f) L. Piggott (£8,471) J. Lenehan
    2. Dancing Moss,   3. Zaracarn.   6, 8.   8 ran
1968 Giolla Mear (8–1) F. Berry (£11,045) M. Hurley
    2. Saragan,   3. Laurence O.   5, 3.   10 ran

Race 143: DOONSIDE CUP

1 mile 3 furlongs. Ayr. Three-year-olds only until 1967. Called Doonside Stakes until 1961

1957 Taittinger (4–6f) E. Britt (£1,273) C. F. Elsey
    2. Northmayne,   **3.** Regal Rock.   8, 2.   5 ran
1958 Aggressor (7–4) J. Lindley (£1,358) J. Gosden
    2. Legal Tie,   **3.** Paridel.   10, 1.   5 ran
1959 Connaissance (7–2) W. Rickaby (£1,286) R. Day
    2. High Perch,   **3.** Solo Singer.   ½, 8.   4 ran
1960 Caistor Top (2–7f) J. Sime (£1,443) S. Hall
    2. Star Combine,   **3.** Scottish Court.   4, 10.   3 ran
1961 Dual (2–1) E. Hide (£1,052) J. Gosden
    2. Flower Drum,   **3.** Garland Knight.   5, Nk.   9 ran
1962 River Whistle (7–1) J. Lindley (£583) H. Murless and
    Trade Wind (100–7) E. Hide (£583) W. Elsey
                                    3. No Bidders.   Dd Ht, 6.   6 ran
1963 Thik Hai (20–1) B. Connorton (£2,123) W. Gray
    2. Fidelio,   **3.** Follow Suit.   5, 4.   8 ran
1964 Devastation (7–1) J. Sime (£1,911) S. Hall
    2. Mowden Magic,   **3.** Gloomy Portal.   15, 2.   9 ran
1965 Rehearsed (4–9f) R. P. Elliott (£1,955) J. Gosden
    2. Indian Order,   **3.** Epaulard.   6, Nk.   4 ran
1966 Reubens (5–1) J. Sime (£1,952) H. Murless
    2. St Puckle,   **3.** High Table.   ½, 2½.   6 ran
1967 LUDHAM (7–1) D. Letherby (£1,783) E. Cousins, 3 yrs
    2. Marcus Brutus,   **3.** Showman's Fair.   10, 2½.   13 ran
1968 Attalus (9–4) A. Barclay (£1,612) N. Murless, 3 yrs
    2. Deep Sapphire,   **3.** GLAD ONE.   1, ½.   7 ran

Race 144: QUEEN ELIZABETH II STAKES

1 mile. Ascot. *Run at Newbury

              1955 Hafiz II 3   (8)   **1956** Cigalon 3   (11)
1957 MIDGET II (5–6f) A. Breasley (£6,230) A. Head (France), 4 yrs
    2. Bellborough,   **3.** El Relicario.   ½, 1.   7 ran
1958 MAJOR PORTION (1–3f) E. Smith (£5,839) T. Leader, 3 yrs
    2. Babur,   **3.** Blockhaus.   Hd, ½.   4 ran
1959 ROSALBA (5–2) J. Mercer (£5,356) R. J. Colling, 3 yrs
    2. Sallymount,   **3.** Crystal Palace.   Hd, 4.   6 ran
*1960 Sovereign Path (13–8) W. Carr (£5,245) R. Mason, 4 yrs
    2. Release,   **3.** Djebel Traffic.   ¾, 6.   4 ran
1961 Le Levanstell (20–1) W. Williamson (£5,747) S. McGrath, 4 yrs
    2. PETITE ETOILE,   **3.** Eagle.   ½, Sht Hd.   6 ran

1962 ROMULUS (7–4f) W. Swinburn (£5,432) R. Houghton, 3 yrs
    2. Cyrus,   **3.** Eagle.   1, 2.   7 ran
*1963 Creditor (5–4f) L. Piggott (£5,186) N, Murless, 3 yrs
    2. SPREE,   **3.** Lock Hard.   5, Nk.   9 ran
1964 Linacre (11–10f) L. Piggott (£5,449) P. J. Prendergast, 4 yrs
    2. Derring-Do,   **3.** Feather Bed.   1, 1.   5 ran
1965 Derring-Do (9–4f) A. Breasley (£5,781) A. Budgett, 4 yrs
    2. Ballyciptic,   **3.** Minor Portion.   2, ¾.   6 ran
1966 Hill Rise (7–2) L. Piggott (£5,203) N. Murless, 5 yrs
    2. SILLY SEASON,   **3.** Tesco Boy.   Nk, 2½.   6 ran
1967 Reform (6–5f) A. Breasley (£3,742) Sir G. Richards, 3 yrs
    2. Track Spare,   **3.** St Chad.   10, 5.   4 ran
1968 World Cup (7–2) W. Williamson (£3,769) P. J. Prendergast, 3 yrs
    2. Wolver Hollow,   **3.** Lorenzaccio.   4, 3.   5 ran

Race 145: PRINCESS ROYAL STAKES

1 mile 4 furlongs. Ascot. Three-year-old fillies. *Run at Newbury

1957 Nagaika (5–1) W. Carr (£1,574) W. Smyth
    2. Crotchet,   **3.** Heritiere.   ½, 2.   7 ran
1958 MOTHER GOOSE (3–1f) W. Carr (£1,956) W. Nightingall
    2. St Lucia,   **3.** Miss McTaffy.   4, 3.   9 ran
1959 ROSE OF MEDINA (8–13f) L. Piggott (£2,398) N. Murless
    2. Dame Melba,   **3.** Mirnaya.   3, ½.   3 ran
*1960 Green Opal (3–1) L. Piggott (£2,368) N. Murless
    2. Desert Beauty,   **3.** No Saint.   ½, 1.   3 ran
1961 Tenacity (6–4f) A. Breasley (£2,241) Sir G. Richards
    2. Tender Word,   **3.** Paris Princess. Nk, 4.   7 ran
1962 Romantica (5–2f) W. Williamson (£2,058) H. Wragg
    2. Crystal Clear,   **3.** Black Nanny. 1½, 8.   9 ran
*1963 Vhairi (11–4f) L. Piggott (1,994) P. Beasley
    2. Olgiata,   **3.** Elite Royale. Nk, 3.   11 ran
1964 French Possession (15–8f) D. Smith (£1,982) G. Brooke
    2. Lochailort,   **3.** Sound of Music. 2, Nk.   8 ran
1965 Bracey Bridge (6–4f) L. Piggott (£1,949) N. Murless
    2. Miba,   **3.** Livia.   Nk, 4.   7 ran
1966 Predicament (1–6f) R. Hutchinson (£1,894) J. Dunlop
    2. Frozen Blonde,   **3.** Shamrock Queen. 10, 2½.   3 ran
1967 Bamboozle (7–2f) L. Piggott (£1,724) F. Armstrong
    2. Pertinacity,   **3.** Quarterings, ½, 6.   10 ran
1968 Abandoned

Race 146: DIADEM STAKES

6 furlongs. Ascot. *Run at Kempton

1957 Arcandy (7–4f) T. Gosling (£1,219) G. Beeby, 4 yrs
    2. Game Hide,   **3.** Drum Beat.   1, Nk.   4 ran
1958 Jack & Jill (20–1) S. Clayton (£1,916) W. Nightingall 3 yrs
    2. Welsh Abbot,   **3.** Stanmar.   1, Nk.   5 ran
1959 Jack & Jill (6–1) W. Carr (£2,907) W. Nightingall, 4 yrs
    2. Anxious Lady,   **3.** Galivanter.   Nk, 2.   7 ran
***1960** Zanzibar (15–8) W. Rickaby (£2,762) J. Oxley, 5 yrs
    2. Shamrock Star,   **3.** Deer Leap. $\frac{3}{4}$, 5.   3 ran
1961 Satan (100–8) J. Mercer (£2,898) T. Shaw, 3 yrs
    2. Ritudyr,   **3.** Skymaster.   Hd, 6.   5 ran
1962 La Belle (10–1) W. Williamson (£3,166) H. Wragg, 3 yrs
    2. Featheredge,   **3.** Daisy Belle.   Nk, 2.   13 ran
***1963** Sammy Davis (4–1) D. Smith (£2,830) G. Brooke, 3 yrs
    2. Secret Step,   **3.** Windscale. $1\frac{1}{2}$, 3.   6 ran
1964 Ampney Princess (25–1) F. Durr (£2,996) H. Hannon, 4 yrs
    2. Weeper's Boy,   **3.** Dondeen.   3, 5.   13 ran
1965 Majority Blue (3–1f) W. Williamson (£2,953) J. Oxx, 4 yrs
    2. Merry Madcap,   **3.** Compensation.   Nk, 2.   12 ran
1966 Lucasland (7–2f) E. Eldin (£3,071) J. A. Waugh, 4 yrs
    2. Dondeen,   **3.** Current Coin. $\frac{3}{4}$, 4.   13 ran
1967 Great Bear (11–2) R. Hutchinson (£2,538) J. Dunlop, 3 yrs
    2. Desert Call,   **3.** Quy.   Hd, $2\frac{1}{2}$.   8 ran
1968 Secret Ray (11–2) A. Barclay (£2,924) Doug Smith, 4 yrs
    2. Great Bear,   **3.** Mountain Call. $1\frac{1}{2}$, 5.   4 ran

Race 147: SUN CHARIOT STAKES

1 mile 2 furlongs. Newmarket. Three-year-old fillies

1966 Lucaya (100–8) J. Lindley (£2,872) W. Elsey
    2. Predicament,   **3.** Petite Marmite.   1, Sht Hd.   11 ran
1967 Cranberry Sauce (7–2) G. Moore (£2,284) N. Murless
    2. ST PAULI GIRL,   **3.** Iskereen.   1, $\frac{3}{4}$.   6 ran
1968 Hill Shade (4–5f) A. Barclay (£2,330) N. Murless
    2. Wenona,   **3.** Parthica and
                    3. Mahal.   5, $\frac{1}{2}$.   6 ran

HORSES IN CAPITAL LETTERS
WERE TO BE, OR HAD BEEN,
PLACED IN THE CLASSICS

Race 148: JOCKEY CLUB CUP

2 miles. Newmarket. First run 1873

	2M 2F			1919	Gay Lord, 3	(2)
1900	Osbech, 5	(5)		1920	No race	
1901	King's Courier, 4	(4)		1921	Nippon, 3	(3)
1902	Black Sand, 5	(3)		1922	Bucks Hussar, 3	(5)
1903	Mead, 3	(3)		1923	Tranquil, 3	(2)
1904	Zinfandel, 4	(5)		1924	Plack, 3	(3)
1905	Pretty Polly, 4	(4)		1925	Bucellas, 3	(5)
1906	Bachelor's			1926	Bongrace, 3	(5)
	Button, a	(2)		1927	Mont Bernina, 4	(6)
1907	Radium, 4	(3)		1928	Invershin, 6	(2)
1908	Radium, 5	(2)		1929	Fairway, 4	(3)
1909	Amadis, 3	(2)		1930	Brumeux, 5	(3)
1910	Lagos, 5	(5)		1931	Noble Star, 4	(3)
1911	Willonyx, 4	(2)		1932	Brulette, 4	(w. o.)
1912	Aleppo, 3	(2)		1933	Nitsichin, 5	(3)
1913	Aleppo, 4	(3)		1934	Felicitation, 4	(3)
1914	Son-in-Law, 3	(2)		1935	Quashed, 3	(3)
1915	Son-in-Law, 4	(5)		1936	Quashed, 4	(2)
1916	Hurry On, 3	(3)		1937	Buckleigh, 5	(4)
1917	Brown's Prince, 3	(5)		1938	Foxglove II, 3	(5)
1918	Queen's Square, 3	(3)		1939	No race	

	[AT NOTTINGHAM]	
1940	Atout Maitre, 4	(7)
1941	No race	
	[AT NEWMARKET]	
1942	Afterthought, 3	(12)
1943	Shahpoor, 4	(6)
1944	Ocean Swell, 3	(7)
1945	Amber Flash, 3	(4)
1946	Felix II, 3	(4)
1947	Laurentis, 4	(5)
1948	Vic Day, 3	(w. o.)
1949	Vic Day, 4	(4)
1950	Colonist II, 4	(3)
1951	Eastern	
	Emperor, 3	(4)
1952	Blarney Stone, 3	(4)
1953	Ambiguity, 3	(4)
1954	Yorick II, 3	(8)
1955	Romany Air, 4	(5)
1956	Donald, 3	(5)

1957 Flying Flag II (11–4) F. Palmer (£2,054) J. Laumain (France), 4 yrs
    2. FRENCH BEIGE,   **3.** China Rock.   Nk, 5.   3 ran
1958 FRENCH BEIGE (3–1) G. Littlewood (£1,943) H. Peacock, 5 yrs
    2. BRIOCHE,   **3.** Jongleur. $\frac{3}{4}$, Bad.   5 ran

1 MILE 4 FURLONGS

1959 Vacarme (7–2) A. Breasley (£997) N. Bertie, 5 yrs
    2. ALCIDE,   **3.** Royal Highway.   Sht Hd, 8.   6 ran
1960 PARTHIA (10–11f) W Carr (£960) C. Boyd-Rochfort, 4 yrs
    2. Court Prince,   **3.** Arcticeelagh.   4, 15.   4 ran
1961 Apostle (13–2) E. Hide (£1,562) S. Ingham, 4 yrs
    2. Proud Chieftain,   **3.** Illinois. $\frac{3}{4}$, Nk.   8 ran
1962 PARDAO (2–1f) W. Carr (£1,545) C. Boyd-Rochfort, 4 yrs
    2. Hot Brandy,   **3.** Entanglement.   Hd, Nk.   7 ran

2 MILES

1963 Gaul (2–1) G. Lewis (£2,180) P. Hastings-Bass, 4 yrs
    2. Grey of Falloden,   **3.** MONTERRICO. 3, Bad.   3 ran
1964 Oncidium (7–2) A. Breasley (£1,888) G. Todd, 3 yrs
    2. Ruantallan,   **3.** Oakville.   3, 1½.   7 ran
1965 Goupi (10–11f) G. Lewis (£1,840) S. Ingham, 3 yrs
    2. Prince Hansel,   **3.** Lomond.   2, 4.   4 ran

1966 Hermes (7–1) G. Starkey (£2,897) J. Oxley, 3 yrs
    2. Parbury,   **3.** BLACK   ½, Sht Hd.   10 ran
                                      PRINCE II.
1967 Dancing Moss (6–1) G. Lewis (£2,389) R. Fetherstonhaugh, 3 yrs
    2. Mariner,   **3.** Accuser.   Nk, 2½.   11 ran
1968 Riboccare (6–1) L. Piggott (£2,330) J. Tree, 3 yrs
    2. Fortissimo,   **3.** Double Quick.   ½, 1.   8 ran

Race 149: CHAMPION STAKES
1 mile 2 furlongs. Newmarket. First run 1877

1900 Solitaire, 4	(4)	**1920** Orpheus, 3	(6)	**1937** Flares, 4	(4)
1901 Osbech, 3	(3)	**1921** Orpheus, 4	(4)	**1938** Rockfel, 3	(5)
1902 Veles, 4	(4)	**1922** Franklin, 4	(5)	**1939** No race	
1903 Sceptre, 4	(3)	**1923** Ellangowan, 3	(4)	**1940** Hippius, 3	(8)
1904 Bachelor's		**1924** Pharos, 4	(5)	**1941** Hippius, 4	(5)
Button, 5	(4)	**1925** Picaroon, 3	(2)	**1942** Big Game, 3	(5)
1905 Pretty Polly, 4	(2)	**1926** Warden of the		**1943** Nasrullah, 3	(6)
1906 Polymelus, 4	(2)	Marches, 4	(4)	**1944** Hycilla, 3	(17)
1907 Galvani, 3	(6)	**1927** Asterus, 4	(3)	**1945** Court Martial, 3	(4)
1908 Llangwm, 3	(2)	**1928** Fairway, 3	(4)	**1946** Honeyway, 5	(8)
1909 Bayardo, 3	(3)	**1929** Fairway, 4	(2)	**1947** Migoli, 3	(4)
1910 Lemberg, 3	(2)	**1930** Rustom Pasha, 3	(9)	**1948** Solar Slipper, 3	(7)
1911 Lemberg, 4	(w. o.)	**1931** Goyescas, 3	(5)	**1949** Djeddah, 4	(5)
1912 Stedfast, 4	(3)	**1932** Cameronian, 4	(6)	**1950** Peter Flower, 4	(7)
1913 Tracery, 4	(2)	**1933** Dastur, 4 and		**1951** Dynamiter, 3	(19)
1914 Hapsburg, 3	(2)	Chatelaine, 3	(3)	**1952** Dynamiter, 4	(5)
1915 Let Fly, 3	(5)	**1934** Umidwar, 3	(9)	**1953** Nearula, 3	(7)
1916 Clarissimus, 3	(3)	**1935** Wychwood		**1954** Narrator, 3	(6)
1917 Gay Crusader, 3	(4)	Abbot, 4	(7)	**1955** Hafiiz II, 3	(5)
1918 My Dear, 3	(4)	**1936** Wychwood		**1956** Hugh Lupus, 4	(11)
1919 Buchan, 3	(5)	Abbot, 5	(4)		

1957 ROSE ROYALE II (5–2) J. Massard (£4,965) A. Head (France), 3 yrs
    2. No Complaint,   **3.** Fric.   6, ½.   7 ran
1958 BELLA PAOLA (4–1) G. Lequeux (£6,673) F. Mathet (France), 3 yrs
    2. Sindon,   **3.** MAJOR   1½, 2.   7 ran
                                      PORTION.
1959 PETITE ETOILE (2–11f) L. Piggott (£10,406) N. Murless, 3 yrs
    2. Barclay,   **3.** Javelot.   ½, Nk.   3 ran
1960 Marguerite Vernaut (9–4) E. Camici (£10,223) U. Penco (Italy), 3 yrs
    2. NEVER TOO LATE II,   **3.** Apostle.   ½, 6.   4 ran
1961 Bobar II (100–8) M. Garcia (£10,512) R. Corme (France), 3 yrs
    2. ST PADDY,   **3.** Proud Chieftain. ¾, 1.   8 ran
1962 Arctic Storm (6–1) W. Williamson (£10,083) J. Oxx, 3 yrs
    2. HETHERSETT,   **3.** Lebon M. L. and 3, Nk.   7 ran
                              3. VIENNA.

1963 HULA DANCER (9–2) J. Deforge (£28,018) E. Pollet (France), 3 yrs
    2. Linacre,   **3.** Creditor.   1, 2.   11 ran
1964 BALDRIC II (7–2) W. Pyers (£27,227) E. Fellows (France), 3 yrs
    2. Linacre,   **3.** Papaya II.   1, 1.   9 ran
1965 SILLY SEASON (100–8) G. Lewis (£28,315) I. Balding, 3 yrs
    2. Tadolina,   **3.** NIKSAR.   1, ½.   13 ran
1966 Pieces of Eight (5–4f) L. Piggott (£26,972) M. V. O'Brien, 3 yrs
    2. Ballyciptic,   **3.** Tesco Boy.   Sht Hd, ½.   8 ran
1967 Reform (100–30) A. Breasley (£14,720) Sir G. Richards, 3 yrs
    2. TAJ DEWAN,   **3.** ROYAL   2, 1½.   7 ran
                               PALACE.
1968 SIR IVOR (8–11f) L. Piggott (£14,673) M. V. O'Brien, 3 yrs
    2. Locris,   **3.** Candy Cane.   2½, 2.   6 ran

Race 150: CHALLENGE STAKES

6 furlongs. Newmarket

1967 Forlorn River (6–4f) L. Piggott (£2,326) W. A. Stephenson, 5 yrs
    2. Great Bear,   **3.** Florescence.   2½, 1½.   6 ran
1968 Mountain Call (2–1f) L. Piggott (£2,372) B. van Cutsem, 3 yrs
    2. Desert Call,   **3.** Great Bear.   Nk, Hd.   8 ran

Race 151: VERNONS NOVEMBER SPRINT CUP

6 furlongs. Haydock

1966 Be Friendly (15–2) C. Williams (£5,337) C. Mitchell, 2 yrs
    2. Green Park,   **3.** Dondeen.   2, 2.   15 ran
1967 Be Friendly (2–1f) A. Breasley (£4,282) C. Mitchell, 3 yrs
    2. Mountain Call,   **3.** Forlorn River.   Nk, 5.   9 ran
1968 Abandoned

Section Four: Handicap Events

Race 161: DONCASTER SPRING HANDICAP
1 mile 6 furlongs 132 yards. Doncaster. Run over 2 miles at Lincoln as Spring Handicap until 1965

1957 Bonhomie (100–8) P. Tulk (£276) E. Cousins, 8–7–5
    2. Lord Provost,   **3.** Hammal II.   Sht Hd, ¾.   13 ran
1958 Straight Lad (3–1f) E. Mercer (£345) H. Nicholson, 8–9–1
    2. Souvrillus,   **3.** Magnifitant.   2, 1.   9 ran
1959 Bothered (11–2) E. Smith (£207) F. Cundell, 5–8–3
    2. Laird o'Montrose,   **3.** Paysan.   3, Nk.   14 ran
1960 Royal Cavalier (8–1) G. Littlewood (£132) H. Peacock, 4–7–12 and
Ferncliffe (100–9) C. Parkes (£132) J. Calvert, 5–7–0
    3. Ceremony.   Dd Ht, ¾.   16 ran
1961 Hard Master (100–8) N. McIntosh (£207) W. A. Stephenson, 4–7–6
    2. Usurper,   **3.** Hurada.   Sht Hd, 4.   6 ran
1962 Eiger (100–8) D. Ryan (£132) P. Moore, 8–9–3 and
Starliner (7–2f) G. Starkey (£132) M. Pope, 6–8–8
    3. Curry's Kin.   Dd Ht, 2.   14 ran
1963 Byng (8–1) D. Cullen (£403) D. Griffiths, 6–8–1
    2. Vital Link,   **3.** Exhorbitant.   2, Nk.   12 ran
1964 Magic Court (2–1f) L. G. Brown (£1,691) T. Robson, 6–9–4
    2. Kanthral,   **3.** Delmere.   4, ½.   13 ran
1965 Fez (11–2) G. Lewis (£1,566) S. Ingham, 4–7–11
    2. Le Pirate,   **3.** Cagirama.   8, 4.   13 ran
1966 Valoroso (7–1) G. Lewis (£1,676) S. Ingham, 4–8–11
    2. French Patrol,   **3.** Compton Martin. 1½, ½.   18 ran
1967 Sandro (9–2) B. Taylor (£1,297) T. E. Leader, 5–9–2
    2. Allenheads,   **3.** Royal Ridge.   2, ¾.   11 ran
1968 King of Peace (100–8) E. Johnson (£1,304) J. Hardy, 5–7–3
    2. Inyanga,   **3.** Jacthelot.   ½, 1½.   15 ran

---

*HORSES IN CAPITAL LETTERS
WERE TO BE, OR HAD BEEN,
PLACED IN THE CLASSICS*

H

Race 162: LINCOLN HANDICAP
1 mile. Doncaster. Run at Lincoln until 1965. First run 1853

1900 Sir Geoffrey, 5–8–6	(25)	1931 Knight Error, 5–7–7	(35)
1901 Little Eva, 6–7–5	(28)	1932 Jerome Fandor, 4–6–13	(36)
1902 St Maclou, 4–7–12	(23)	1933 Dorigen, 4–9–1	(28)
1903 Over Norton, 6–7–6	(20)	1934 Play On, 4–7–8	(26)
1904 Uninsured, 4–7–10	(23)	1935 Flamenco, 4–9–0	(34)
1905 Sansovino, 4–7–6	(18)	1936 Over Coat, 5–7–12	(34)
1906 Ob, 5–8–0	(24)	1937 Marmaduke Jinks, 5–8–0	(32)
1907 Ob, 6–8–10	(24)	1938 Phakos, 4–8–3	(27)
1908 Kaffir Chief, 6–7–11	(20)	1939 Squadron Castle, 6–7–7	(38)
1909 Duke of Sparta, 5–6–11	(23)	1940 Quartier-Maitre, 5–8–1	(21)
1910 Cinderello, 5–7–2	(27)	1941 Gloaming, 4–7–4	(19)
1911 Mercutio, 6–8–4	(32)		

[AT PONTEFRACT]

1912 Long Set, 5–8–2	(17)	1942 Cuerdley, 4–9–4	(12)
1913 Berrilldon, 4–7–4	(22)	1943 Lady Electra, 4–8–10	(17)
1914 Outram, 5–7–1	(22)	1944 Backbite, 5–7–8	(24)
1915 View Law, 4–6–1	(23)	1945 Double Harness, 4–6–10	(25)

1916–18 No race

[AT LINCOLN]

1919 Royal Bucks, 6–7–5	(15)	1946 Langton Abbot, 4–8–2	(37)
1920 Furious, 4–7–4	(29)	1947 Jockey Treble, 5–6–0	(46)
1921 Soranus, 4–8–4	(30)	1948 Commissar, 8–8–9	(58)
1922 Granely, 4–7–9	(32)	1949 Fair Judgement, 4–7–10	(43)
1923 White Bud, 6–6–5	(30)	1950 Dramatic, 5–8–13	(40)
1924 Sir Gallahad III, 4–8–5	(27)	1951 Barnes Park, 5–8–0	(35)
1925 Tapin, 4–8–7	(26)	1952 Phariza, 5–6–12	(40)
1926 King of Clubs, 6–6–2	(26)	1953 Sailing Light, 4–7–11	(41)
1927 Priory Park, 5–7–7	(30)	1954 Nahar, 7–8–0	(32)
1928 Dark Warrior, 4–8–2	(26)	1955 Military Court, 5–8–2	(29)
1929 Elton, 4–7–2	(35)	1956 Three Star II, 8–6–13	(41)
1930 Leonidas II, 5–8–0	(31)		

1957 Babur (25–1) E. Hide (£2,816) C. F. Elsey, 4–7–13
    2. Setting Star,   3. Nicholas   1, Hd.   32 ran
    Nickleby.

1958 Babur (25–1) E. Britt (£2,460) C. F. Elsey, 5–9–0
    2. Who You,   3. Statfold.   1½, 3.   37 ran

1959 Marshal Pil (15–2f) P. Robinson (£3,299) S. Hall, 5–7–13
    2. Chalk Stream and
    2. Precious Heather.   ¾, Dd Ht.   32 ran

1960 Mustavon (8–1) N. McIntosh (£3,545) S. Hall, 5–6–13
    2. Major General,   3. Lavandier.   ¾, Sht Hd.   31 ran

1961 Johns Court (25–1) B. Lee (£3,724) E. Cousins, 6–7–7
    2. Honeycomb Rock,   3. Honeymoor.   3, ¾.   37 ran

1962 Hill Royal (50–1) J. Sime (£4,009) E. Cousins, 4–7–9
    2. Robson's Choice,   3. Honeymoor.   Nk, 2.   40 ran

1963 Monawin (25–1) J. Sime (£4,089) R. Mason, 8–7–9
    2. Kalimnos,   **3.** Becket.   2, 1½.   40 ran
1964 Mighty Gurkha (33–1) P. Robinson (£4,550) E. Lambton, 5–7–8
    2. Fair Astronomer,   **3.** Vijay.   Nk, 2.   45 ran
1965 Old Tom (22–1) A. Breasley (£8,398) M. H. Easterby, 6–8–7
    2. Tarqogan,   **3.** Printer.   ½, Hd.   38 ran
1966 Riot Act (8–1f) A. Breasley (£9,190) F. Armstrong, 4–8–3
    2. Le Garcon,   **3.** Christmas Review.
         ½, 1½.   49 ran
1967 Ben Novus (22–1) P. Robinson (£6,583) W. Hide, 5–7–10
    2. Aberdeen,   **3.** Danella.   ½, 4.   24 ran
1968 Frankincense (100–8) G. Starkey (£6,616) J. Oxley, 4–9–5
    2. Waterloo Place,   **3.** Norton Priory.   ½, 2.   31 ran

Race 163: IRISH LINCOLN
1 mile handicap. Curragh

1957 End Money (100–7) J. Gifford (£1,000) J. M. Rogers, 4–8–4
    2. Gladness,   **3.** But Why.   2½, Sht Hd.   20 ran
1958 Clear Round (100–6) J. Mullane (£1,015) J. Oxx, 4–7–13
    2. Courts Appeal,   **3.** Luran.   Sht Hd, 1.   21 ran
1959 Bright Talk (2–1f) L. Browne (£1,001) T. J. Taaffe, 6–8–9
    2. Clear Round,   **3.** Gleniry.   5, Nk.   20 ran
1960 Farrney Fox (6–1) W. Berg (£1,014) C. Weld, 5–8–9
    2. Lavella,   **3.** Sunny Court.   ½, 2½.   25 ran
1961 Brunton (33–1) T. Enright (£989) C. Collins, 8–6–7
    2. Arctic Sea,   **3.** Farrney Fox.   Nk, 2½.   19 ran
1962 K.O. (100–7) P. Roche (£1,039) C. McCartan jun., 5–7–4
    2. Starlight Flight,   **3.** Brackley.   4, 1½.   29 ran
1963 Barney Fagan (50–1) T. Roche (£1,059) C. McCartan jun., 6–6–7
    2. Cassim,   **3.** Gilroy.   1, 2.   28 ran
1964 Cassim (9–2jf) W. Williamson (£994) J. Oxx, 5–8–9
    2. K.O.,   **3.** Wily Trout.   Nk, Sht Hd.   19 ran
1965 Red Slipper (9–2f) M. Kennedy (£1,030) Sir Hugh Nugent, 5–10–0
    2. Joker,   **3.** Lully Boy.   2½, 1½.   22 ran
1966 Night Star (7–1) A. Barclay (£989) A. D. Turner, 5–7–3
    2. Bagoas,   **3.** K.O.   8, ¾.   20 ran
1967 Al-'Alawi (100–9) W. Williamson (£2,087) M. Connelly, 4–8–5
    2. Intrepid,   **3.** Marble Step (second, disqualified).
         Original distances, 3, 2½.   25 ran
1968 Little Hawk (100–7) C. Williams (£1,900) H. V. S. Murless, 4–8–4
    2. Marcia's Mark,   **3.** Gail Time.   1, 1.   23 ran

Race 164: ROSEBERY STAKES

1 mile 2 furlongs handicap. Kempton

1957 Royal Chief (20–1) R. Reader (£1,685) H. G. Blagrave, 4–7–0
    2. Orinthia,   **3.** Barton Street.   Nk, 1.   15 ran
1958 Abandoned because of snow
1959 Red Letter (100–8) A. Breasley (£1,596) W. Smyth, 5–8–5
    2. Pardonez-Moi,   **3.** Empire Way.   Nk, 1.   13 ran
1960 Falls of Shin (10–1) L. Piggott (£1,693) E. Parker, 7–8–9
    2. Marshal Pil,   **3.** Red Letter.   Sht Hd, Hd.   13 ran
1961 Proud Chieftain (100–7) T. Gosling (£1,886) W. Hern, 4–9–3
    2. Nerograph,   **3.** Powder Rock.   1, 1½.   20 ran
1962 Damredub (7–1) D. W. Morris (£1,781) J. Gosden, 5–7–9
    2. Rockamour,   **3.** Bob Barker.   1½, 3.   13 ran
1963 Wilhelmina Henrietta (100–8) D. Greening (£2,895) M. Bolton, 4–7–9
    2. Redoubt,   **3.** London Gazette.   3, 1.   23 ran
1964 Red Tears (15–2) J. Mercer (£2,354) W. Hern, 4–8–4
    2. Crepone,   **3.** Tacitus.   Sht Hd, 4.   17 ran
1965 Noorose (10–1) R. Reader (£1,942) E. Parker, 4–7–7
    2. Antiquarian,   **3.** Yellow Sovereign. Sht Hd, 2.   7 ran
1966 Rehearsed (100–30) R. Hutchinson (£2,079) G. Smyth, 4–9–1
    2. Beatle,   **3.** Hotroy.   2, 1½.   18 ran
1967 Hotroy (7–1) D. Keith (£1,680) W. Nightingall, 6–9–2
    2. St Puckle,   **3.** Le Cordonnier.   1, 2½.   14 ran
1968 Midnight Marauder (100–7) J. Lindley (£1,710) J. Tree, 6–8–9
    2. Lexicon,   **3.** Shady Knight.   Nk, ½.   13 ran

Race 165: QUEEN'S PRIZE

2 miles handicap. Kempton. First run 1891

1M 6F			
1900 Chevening, 3–6–9	(12)	**1911** Origo, 5–6–11	(12)
1M 2F		**1912** Duke of Sparta II, 5–6–6	(13)
1901 Hulcot, 4–7–2	(12)	**1913** Rivoli, 4–7–2	(12)
1902 Wabun, 4–6–7	(10)	**1914** China Cock, 4–8–0	(21)
1903 Fighting Furley, 6–7–9	(12)	**1915** Frustration, 4–6–6	(16)
1904 Ypsilanti, 6–9–0	(11)	**1916–18** No race	
1M		**1M 5F**	
1905 Glenamoy, 4–7–10	(12)	**1919** Race Rock, a–7–9	(6)
1M 4F		**1M 2F**	
1906 Burgundy, 5–7–7	(13)	**1920** Bridgewater, 4–7–2	(15)
1907 Bridge of Canny, 4–9–0	(8)	**1M 4F**	
1908 Glacis, 4–6–0	(12)	**1921** Trespasser, 5–8–4	(18)
1909 Wuffy, 6–8–4	(10)	**1922** Golden Myth, 4–7–6	(14)
1910 Old China, 6–8–2	(14)	**1923** Bhuidhaonach, 4–7–12	(15)

1924	Evander, 6–8–2 and		
	Scapino, 4–6–13	(10)	
1925	Cloudbank, 4–7–13	(12)	

2M

1926	Confirmation, 6–8–4	(12)
1927	Tournesol, 5–9–3	(11)
1928	Zeno, 5–8–13	(14)
1929	Glenhazel, 4–8–11	(16)
1930	Cacao, 5–8–12	(21)
1931	Trimdon, 5–8–13	(16)
1932	Scardroy, 5–7–9	(17)
1933	Foxhunter, 4–9–2	(13)
1934	Negro, 5–7–12	(24)
1935	Apple Peel, 5–7–9	(13)
1936	Guiscard, 8–7–8	(16)
1937	Solar Bear, 5–8–2	(17)
1938	Senor, 4–8–5 and	
	Bendex, 6–8–3	(12)

1939	Vergilius, 5–7–10	(9)
1940–45	No race	

[AT HURST PARK]

1946	Triumvir, 6–8–13	(12)

[AT KEMPTON]

1947	Gremlin, 6–7–10	(12)
1948	Kolper, 5–8–6	(8)
1949	White Heather, 5–7–8	(12)
1950	Sports Master, 5–8–1	(12)
1951	Father Thames, 5–8–12	(16)
1952	Sports Master, 7–8–5	(15)
1953	Milcote Manor, 4–8–2	(22)
1954	Romney Legend, 5–6–10	(12)
1955	Running Water, 6–9–2	(10)
1956	Purple Sand, 4–7–12	(13)

1957 Persian Flag (10–1) W. Carr (£1,685) W. Nightingall, 4–8–3
    2. Icarian,   **3.** Partner.   ¾, 4.   12 ran

1958 Hollyhock (100–8) S. Millbanks (£1,600) A. M. Budgett, 6–7–3
    2. Master of Arts,   **3.** Gudmenarmist.   8, ¾.   15 ran

1959 Sacarole (9–2f) D. W. Morris (£1,659) D. Hastings, 5–7–9
    2. Amazons Choice,   **3.** Prefairy.   Sht Hd, Nk.   17 ran

1960 Eborneezer (8–1) A. Breasley (£1,719) H. Price, 5–8–0
    2. Printemps,   **3.** Elf-Arrow.   5, 3.   18 ran

1961 Pandofell (100–8) J. Lindley (£1,826) F. Maxwell, 4–8–8
    2. Lucky White Heather,   **3.** Fourth of June.   4, 1.   19 ran

1962 Minute Gun (8–1) E. Smith (£1,818) W. Hern, 5–8–10
    2. Iron Blue,   **3.** Agreement.   1½, 1.   13 ran

1963 Grey of Falloden (100–8) J. Mercer (£2,734) W. Hern 4–9–7
    2. Spartan General,   **3.** Ulster Ranger.   2, Sht Hd.   18 ran

1964 Orchardist (11–2) A. Breasley (£2,259) C. Benstead, 5–9–3
    2. Proper Pride,   **3.** Grey of Falloden. Hd, 1.   14 ran

1965 Ulster Prince (4–1) J. Lindley (£1,962) C. Mitchell, 7–8–12
    2. Fez,   **3.** Grey of Falloden. Hd, 1½.   6 ran

1966 Aegean Blue (5–1) A. Breasley (£2,155) R. Houghton, 4–8–4
    2. Zaloba,   **3.** Sans Pareil.   Sht Hd, 5.   21 ran

1967 Royal Ridge (10–1) A. Barclay (£1,747) M. Pope, 5–7–7
    2. Belmura,   **3.** Colonel Imp.   3, 3.   20 ran

1968 Que Guapo (10–1) G. Lewis (£1,761) S. Ingham, 4–8–0
    2. Colonel Imp,   **3.** Hipster.   4, 2.   14 ran

Race 166: NORTHERN FREE HANDICAP

7 furlongs. Newcastle. Three-year-olds

1961 Pouncer (7–1) R. Maddock (£1,014) J. Clark, 7–9			
2. Kamasu,	3. Foxstar.	4, Hd.	21 ran
1962 Pervinca (9–2f) E. Hide (£931) W. Elsey, 8–13			
2. Luminous Sun,	3. Old Tom.	$\frac{3}{4}$, $\frac{1}{2}$.	22 ran
1963 Brief Flight (15–2) V. Faggotter (£933) W. Lyde, 8–5			
2. Aberflight,	3. Marieson.	3, 5.	15 ran
1964 Shotley Mill (33–1) B. Henry (£951) A. Vasey, 9–5			
2. Lanarkshire,	3. Sutherland.	$\frac{1}{2}$, 2.	16 ran
1965 Bluest (7–2) J. Sime (£839) S. Hall, 8–6			
2. Pamaloo,	3. Sing High.	Nk, 4.	7 ran
1966 Norton Priory (33–1) W. Bentley (£1,505) A. Vasey, 7–6			
2. Tracker,	3. Johns Key.	1, 2.	18 ran
1967 Minho (11–2) J. Seagrave (£1,314) H. Rohan, 8–5			
2. Pals Passage,	3. Swinging Bird.	2, 4.	22 ran
1968 Alloway Lad (9–2jf) J. Sime (£1,341) H. Whiteman, 8–6			
2. Wild Root,	3. Alignment.	Sht Hd, 7.	18 ran

Race 167: FREE HANDICAP

7 furlongs. Newmarket. Three-year-olds

1957 QUORUM (15–2) A. Russell (£935) W. Lyde, 8–7			
2. Petersfield,	3. Camille.	3, $1\frac{1}{2}$.	13 ran
1958 Faultless Speech (10–1) E. Smith (£914) H. Wallington, 8–4			
2. Masquerade,	3. Okaye.	Nk, 1.	14 ran
1959 PETITE ETOILE (9–1) G. Moore (£893) N. Murless, 9–0			
2. Chappaqua,	3. Charmed Life.	3, $\frac{1}{2}$.	10 ran
1960 RUNNING BLUE (100–7) J. Limb (£1,008) J. Jarvis, 8–4			
2. Optimist,	3. Morgat.	$\frac{3}{4}$, $\frac{3}{4}$.	20 ran
1961 Erudite (100–6) J. Etherington (£1,390) R. Peacock, 8–6			
2. Smuggler's Joy,	3. Rins of Clyde.	$1\frac{1}{2}$, 2.	19 ran
1962 PRIVY COUNCILLOR (100–7) J. Sime (£1,284) T. Waugh, 8–4			
2. Miletus,	3. Tournella.	1, 4.	18 ran
1963 Ros Rock (25–1) P. Tulk (£3,001) J. Tree, 8–1			
2. Prince's Error,	3. Honey Portion.	1, 2.	16 ran
1964 Port Merion (100–8) A. Breasley (£3,099) Sir G. Richards, 8–9			
2. Whistling Fool,	3. Piccadilly.	2, $\frac{1}{2}$.	23 ran
1965 Short Commons (100–8) R. Maddock (£1,999) H. Rohan, 8–4			
2. Unity,	3. Spaniards Mount. 4, Sht Hd.		11 ran
1966 Kibenka (10–1) R. Hutchinson (£2,051) T. Corbett, 8–4			
2. Persian Empire,	3. Lincoln.	Nk, 5.	16 ran
1967 Supreme Sovereign (7–1) P. Robinson (£1,666) A. Vasey, 8–1			
2. Golden Horus,	3. St Chad.	2, $\frac{3}{4}$.	15 ran

1968 Panpiper (100–7) E. Johnson (£1,682) R. Smyth, 7–13
    2. Lorenzaccio,   **3.** PHOTO FLASH. Nk, 1½.   13 ran

Race 168: NEWBURY SPRING CUP
1 mile handicap. Newbury

1957 Orthopaedic (8–1) J. Mercer (£1,344) J. Gosden, 6–8–5
    2. Aberdovey,   **3.** Nicholas
                                  Nickleby.   ¾, ¾.   19 ran
1958 Nicholas Nickleby (7–1) J. Mercer (£1,327) W. O'Gorman, 7–8–2
    2. Rose Argent,   **3.** Rose Knight.   ½, ¾.   17 ran
1959 Precious Heather (3–1jf) J. Limb (£1,297) J. Gosden, 7–7–7
    2. Doctor Tadgh,   **3.** Chinese Sun.   ½, ½.   9 ran
1960 Line Shooter (100–7) D. Greening (£1,438) B. van Cutsem, 6–7–1
    2. Orthology,   **3.** Major General.   3, 1½.   21 ran
1961 Zanzibar (8–1) E. Smith (£1,477) J. Oxley, 6–9–4
    2. Chino,   **3.** Fuel.   3, ¾.   19 ran
1962 Pardoner (100–9) W. Rickaby (£1,443) John Waugh, 5–8–8
    2. Dats One,   **3.** Tenet.   1½, ½.   22 ran
1963 Owl (10–1) G. Lewis (£1,553) P. Hastings-Bass, 4–8–3
    2. Mona Louise,   **3.** Guard of Honour.
                                        1½, Sht Hd.   15 ran
1964 March Wonder (100–6) S. Millbanks (£1,417) V. Cross, 4–7–11
    2. Dunme,   **3.** Smuggler's Joy.   2, Nk.   15 ran
1965 Scots Fusilier (20–1) J. Wilson (£1,599) T. Corbett, 6–7–10
    2. Prince of Orange,   **3.** Aberdeen.   Nk, 3.   16 ran
1966 Abandoned
1967 Last Case (100–7) A. Breasley (£1,375) P. Nelson, 4–9–5
    2. Shady Knight (first, disq.) **3.** Morris Dancer.
                            Original distances, Hd, 3.   20 ran
1968 Owen Anthony (10–1) A. Barclay (£1,396) D. Smith, 4–7–13
    2. Cumshaw,   **3.** Danella.   1½, Sht Hd.   23 ran

Race 169: GREAT METROPOLITAN HANDICAP
2 miles 2 furlongs. Epsom. First run 1846

1900 King's Messenger, 5–8–8   (15)   **1907** Father Blind, 4–6–2   (14)
1901 Evasit, 4–7–7   (17)   **1908** Father Blind, 5–7–11   (15)
1902 Congratulation, 4–6–13   (15)   **1909** Laughing Mirror, 4–6–0 (17)
1903 Wavelet's Pride, 6–7–3   (9)   **1910** Lagos, 4–9–0   (21)
1904 Elba, 5–8–7   (13)   **1911** Kilbroney, 4–7–1   (16)
1905 Long Tom, 6–7–5   (12)   **1912** Accurate, 6–7–10   (15)
1906 Whinbloom, 5–6–12   (9)   **1913** Annecy, 4–6–5   (19)

1914	Annecy, 5–7–13	(19)	1935	Crawley Wood, 5–8–0	(21)
1915	Fiz Yama, 6–8–11	(20)	1936	Quashed, 4–9–4 and	
1916–18	No race			Jack Tar, 6–7–6	(19)
1919	Langdon Hills, 4–6–8	(12)	1937	Corofin, 5–6–11	(15)
1920	Viaduct, 4–6–0	(15)	1938	Irish Stew, 6–7–13	(13)
1921	Not run		1939	Lillibullero, 4–6–12	(13)
1922	Sangrail, 4–6–13	(16)	1940–45	No race	
1923	Glass Idol, 5–6–7	(18)	1946	Golden Horus, 4–8–11	(4)
1924	Kwannon, 4–6–8	(13)	1947	Star Song, 7–7–9	(19)
1925	Brisl, 5–8–9	(16)	1948	Now or Never, 4–9–0	(15)
1926	Kyra, 5–7–10	(15)	1949	Yoyo, 5–7–12	(12)
1927	Kinnaird, 7–8–8	(22)	1950	Blue Fox II, 4–7–8	(13)
1928	Alacrity, 5–8–3	(20)	1951	Barnacle, 5–7–10	(17)
1929	Jugo, 5–9–0	(13)	1952	French Squadron, 6–8–11	(14)
1930	Servus, 7–7–10	(17)	1953	Father Thames, 7–8–9	(12)
1931	Summer Princess, 5–7–6	(16)	1954	Luxury Hotel, 4–8–4	(11)
1932	Roi de Paris, 4–6–8	(18)	1955	Babylonian, 5–8–6	(14)
1933	Joyous Greeting, 9–7–12	(12)	1956	Curry, 5–8–3	(11)
1934	Annihilation, 4–8–3	(20)			

1957 Gay Ballad (100–8) J. Lynch (£1,111) G. Brooke, 4–6–8
    2. Curry,   **3.** Clear Night.   5, 20.   11 ran

1958 Hollyhock (9–1) S. Millbanks (£1,596) A. M. Budgett, 6–8–4
    2. Sacarole,   **3.** Beyond the Moss. 2, ½.   16 ran

1959 Miss McTaffy (10–1) L. Piggott (£1,515) P. Walwyn, 4–9–2
    2. Prefairy,   **3.** Kadir Cup.   ½, 1½.   12 ran

1960 Kaffirboom (5–1) W. Snaith (£1,586) F. Armstrong, 4–8–0
    2. Domesday,   **3.** Alcastus.   Nk, 2.   13 ran

1961 Little Buskins (20–1) W. Snaith (£2,194) C. Boyd-Rochfort, 4–7–11
    2. Poetic Licence,   **3.** Avon's Pride.   2, 2.   19 ran

1962 Narratus (100–7) E. Smith (£2,024) D. Thom, 4–8–1
    2. Avon's Pride,   **3.** Parnear.   1½, 2.   12 ran

1963 Byng (100–7) D. Cullen (£2,254) D. Griffiths, 6–7–8
    2. Narratus,   **3.** Ulster Ranger (second, disqualified).
    Original distances, 2, 1.   20 ran

1964 Gold Aura (11–2) J. Sime (£2,594) C. Boyd-Rochfort, 4–7–9
    2. Orchardist,   **3.** Minehead Camp. 1½, 6.   17 ran

1965 Romp Home (15–8f) Donald Morris (£1,962) W. Elsey, 4–8–3
    2. Sonnet II,   **3.** Exhorbitant.
    (Aureate third, disqualified.) Original distances, 2, 4, Hd.   8 ran

1966 Cullen (100–6) F. Messer (£1,839) M. Tate, 5–6–12
    2. Gypsy Refrain,   **3.** Colonel Imp.   2, 2½.   18 ran

1967 Moon Storm (33–1) A. Murray (£1,357) K. Cundell, 4–7–2
    2. Colonel Imp,   **3.** Sandro.   Hd, 1½.   23 ran

1968 Pick Me Up (6–1jf) L. Piggott (£1,730) T. F. Rimell, 5–9–4
    2. Ginger Boy,   **3.** Colonel Imp.   ¾, 2½.   14 ran

Race 170: CITY AND SUBURBAN HANDICAP
1 mile 2 furlongs. Epsom. First run 1851

Year	Horse		Year	Horse	
1900	The Grafter, a–8–10	(19)	1927	Embargo, 4–8–11	(22)
1901	Australian Star, 5–7–10	(15)	1928	Priory Park, 6–8–12	(18)
1902	First Principal, 5–7–6	(20)	1929	Parwiz, 4–8–1	(21)
1903	Brambilla, 3–7–1	(15)	1930	Lucky Tor, 5–7–6	(16)
1904	Robert le Diable, 5–8–2	(21)	1931	Anthurium, 4–7–1	(17)
1905	Pharisee, 6–8–5	(19)	1932	Clogheen, 4–7–4	(16)
1906	Dean Swift, 5–7–11	(18)	1933	Great Scot, 7–8–4	(13)
1907	Velocity, 5–9–2	(13)	1934	Light Sussex, 4–8–6	(14)
1908	Dean Swift, 7–8–12	(16)	1935	Montrose, 5–8–13	(15)
1909	White Eagle, 4–8–7	(18)	1936	His Reverence, 5–8–12	(18)
1910	Bachelor's Double, 4–8–0	(14)	1937	William of Valence, 5–9–6	(15)
1911	Mushroom, 3–7–0	(15)	1938	Pigskin, 6–7–5	(18)
1912	Chili II, 4–6–13	(14)	1939	Bistolfi, 4–8–10	(14)
1913	Drinmore, 5–7–3	(18)	1940–45	No race	
1914	Maiden Erlegh, 5–8–9	(20)	1946	Hobo, 4–9–0	(8)
1915	Black Jester, 4–9–0	(14)	1947	Banco, 4–7–13	(12)
1916–18	No race		1948	Fast Soap, 5–9–0	(16)
1919	Royal Bucks, 6–7–9	(13)	1949	Impeccable, 5–9–0	(10)
1920	Corn Sack, 4–7–5	(16)	1950	Iron Duke, 4–8–7	(12)
1921	No race		1951	Burnt Brown, 5–9–3	(17)
1922	Paragon, 5–9–0	(10)	1952	Sunny Brae, 4–8–4	(14)
1923	Dry Toast, 4–7–12	(13)	1953	Damremont, 6–8–11	(12)
1924	Ulula, a–6–5	(10)	1954	Sunny Brae, 6–9–3	(10)
1925	Greek Bachelor, 5–6–10	(18)	1955	Coronation Year, 4–7–13	(14)
1926	Warden of the		1956	Great Pacha, 6–8–1	(12)
	Marches, 4–9–0	(12)			

1957 Coronation Year (5–1) D. Smith (£1,637) A. J. Thomas, 6–8–11
    2. Andros,   3. Prince Moon.   ¾. Nk.   11 ran
1958 Setting Star (100–9) S. Clayton (£2,521) W. Hern, 6–8–9
    2. Prince Moon,   3. Wheatley.   Sht Hd, 1½.   12 ran
1959 Guersillus (9–4f) E. Hide (£2,580) C. Elsey, 4–9–3
    2. Pardonez-Moi,   3. Hard as Nails.   Nk, 2.   15 ran
1960 Firestreak (11–4f) L. Piggott (£2,627) P. Nelson, 4–9–5
    2. Rocky Royale,   3. Lavandier.   Sht Hd, Nk.   15 ran
1961 Nerograph (8–1) T. Carter (£2,550) G. Todd, 5–7–3
    2. VIENNA,   3. Golden Vision.   2, 2.   15 ran
1962 Eastern Nip (5–1) B. Raymond (£2,504) W. Stephenson, 4–7–0
    2. Darling Boy,   3. Rigvada.   ¾, ¾.   12 ran
1963 Tahiri (10–1) S. Clayton (£2,631) J. Gosden, 4–8–4
    2. Kalimnos,   3. Touroy.   Nk, 3.   17 ran
1964 Bo'sun (4–1f) S. Smith (£3,031) J. Jarvis, 4–9–0
    2. Paramour,   3. Nahum.   Nk, 3.   15 ran
1965 Minor Portion (2–1f) J. Lindley (£4,431) J. Tree, 4–8–6
    2. Noorose,   3. Picture Palace.   4, Sht Hd.   8 ran

1966 Abandoned
1967 Hotroy (100–7) D. Keith (£2,055) W. Nightingall, 6–9–11
    2. Swift Harmony,   **3.** St Puckle.   3, Hd.   16 ran
1968 My Swanee (11–2) L. Piggott (£2,059) W. Marshall, 5–9–6
    2. Le Garcon,   **3.** Hully Gully.   ½, ½.   11 ran

Race 171: TOTALISATOR SPRING HANDICAP

1 mile. Newmarket

1964 Smartie (100–6) J. Wilson (£6,356) R. Mason, 6–7–7
    2. Nahum,   **3.** Connamara Kid.   ¾, 2.   19 ran
1965 Barwin (9–1) D. Letherby (£6,402) W. Stephenson 6–7–1
    2. Happy Omen,   **3.** Ocean Diamond.   3, ¾.   12 ran
1966 Christmas Review (9–1) C. Williams (£6,893) H. Leader, 5–7–9
    2. Pally,   **3.** Le Garcon.   Sht Hd, 1½.   32 ran
1967 Kibenka (8–1) A. Breasley (£5,779) T. Corbett, 4–9–0
    2. Danella,   **3.** Aberdeen.   3, 4.   18 ran
1968 Golden Mean (20–1) F. Durr (£5,956) C. Crossley, 5–8–2
    2. Waterloo Place,   **3.** Owen Anthony.   4, 1½.   21 ran

Race 172: MARCH HANDICAP

2 miles. Newmarket. *Run over 1 mile 6 furlongs

1958 Gads Hill (5–1jf) D. Smith (£948) F. Winter, 7–9–2
    2. Garibaldi,   **3.** Raggoty Ann.   ¾, Nk.   12 ran
1959 Paridel (9–1) E. Hide (£987) C. Elsey, 4–7–13
    2. Agreement,   **3.** Ocho Rios.   ½, 1.   13 ran
1960 Sultry Day (3–1) S. Clayton (£961) J. Fawcus, 5–8–5
    2. Site Plan,   **3.** Induna.   3, 1½.   3 ran
*1961 Bravi (100–8) R. P. Elliott (£1,182) K. Cundell, 6–7–12
    2. Lysander,   **3.** Off Key.   5, ½.   8 ran
1962 Domesday (7–1) S. Smith (£1,124) J. Jarvis, 6–8–2
    2. Golden Fire,   **3.** Carrigeen Duff.   1, 12.   12 ran
1963 Ultima (8–1) F. Durr (£1,192) S. James, 4–8–6
    2. Koolabah,   **3.** Black King.   1½, 3.   13 ran
1964 Le Pirate (100–8) W. Williamson (£1,075) H. Thomson Jones, 5–9–3
    2. Delmere,   **3.** Aureate.   ½, 1½.   16 ran
1965 New Liskeard (100–8) G. Cadwaladr (£771) E. Cousins, 4–7–11
    2. Spare Filly,   **3.** Cagirama.   1½, 3.   5 ran
1966 Sandro (15–2) R. Maddock (£1,658) T. Leader, 4–8–7
    2. Armagnac Monarch,   **3.** Zugela.   2½, ¾.   20 ran
1967 Cagirama (5–1) F. Durr (£814) G. Boyd, 8–8–11 and
    Beau Lavender (5–1) A. Breasley (£814) C. Benstead, 4–8–2
                3. Montecello.   Dd Ht, 6.   11 ran

1968 Quartette (9–1) A. Murray (£1,327) T. Gosling, 4–7–12
   2. Fuchsia Cottage,   3. Que Guapo.   ½, 2.   14 ran

Race 173: CROCKER BULTEEL STAKES

7 furlongs handicap. Ascot. Three-year-olds. Run at Hurst Park until 1963. *Run at Newbury

1957 Red Letter (100–8) G. Lewis (£2,254) W. Smyth, 8–2
   2. Martial Air,   3. Flash Past.   ½, ½.   16 ran
1958 Kingroy (5–1) W. Carr (£2,177) W. Nightingall, 8–9
   2. Faultless Speech,   3. Masquerade.   1, 5.   12 ran
1959 Starlet (4–1f) P. Boothman (£2,275) H. Wragg, 8–5
   2. Sanctum,   3. Short Sentence.   ¾, ½.   15 ran
1960 Fulshaw Cross (5–2f) A. Breasley (£2,237) H. Wallington, 8–0
   2. Midsummer Night II,   3. Young Love.   Nk, Sht Hd.   12 ran
1961 King of Saba (100–9) Donald Morris (£2,360) W. Elsey, 8–0
   2. Lastime,   2. Indian Conquest.   1, 1½.   19 ran
1962 Remainder (6–1) R. P. Elliott (£1,964) J. A. Waugh, 8–5
   2. Golden Gloves,   3. Catchpenny.   Nk, 1½.   15 ran
1963 Hard Match (100–7) E. Davies (£2,317) C. Mitchell, 7–9
   2. Loyal Monarch,   3. Prince's Error.   1½, 3.   17 ran
*1964 Filey Camp (20–1) E. Davies (£2,279) R. Smyth, 7–5
   2. Prince of Orange,   3. Whistling Fool.   1½, ½.   9 ran
1965 Turret (100–7) G. Lewis (£2,289) G. Smyth, 8–0
   2. Gratin,   3. Roaming Star.   ½, Nk.   19 ran
1966 Hadrian (8–1) D. Keith (£2,244) W. Nightingall, 8–9
   2. Grey Imp,   3. Welsh Violet.   2½, 6.   14 ran
1967 Come April (13–2) G. Lewis (£1,944) S. Ingham, 8–8
   2. Polistina,   3. Colonel in Chief.   ¾, 2½.   12 ran
1968 Marmaduke (11–2) L. Piggott (£2,012) K. Cundell, 8–5
   2. Town Crier,   3. Delayed Tip.   2½, 4.   14 ran

Race 174: VICTORIA CUP

7 furlongs handicap. Ascot. Run at Hurst Park until 1963. *Run at Newbury. First run 1904

1M 2F		7F	
1904 Cottager, 6–7–13	(16)	1908 Llangwm, 3–7–2	(18)
1905 Antonio, 4–8–6	(9)	1909 Sir Archibald, 4–8–6	(14)
6F		1910 Senseless, 5–7–4	(18)
1906 Catapult, 3–7–11	(10)	1911 Spanish Prince, 4–8–0	(9)
1907 No race		1912 Whisk Broom, 5–9–2	(14)

1913 Aldegond, 3–7–10	(14)	**1934** Alluvial, 6–8–8	(18)
1914 Jameson, 4–7–4	(19)	**1935** Precious Pearl, 4–7–5	(19)
1915 Volta, 3–7–9	(16)	**1936** Hairan, 4–8–12	(18)
1916–18 No race		**1937** Fairplay, 4–7–8	(18)
1919 Carados, 4–7–11	(9)	**1938** Phakos, 4–8–8	(18)
1920 Paragua, 4–7–9	(17)	**1939** Unbreakable, 4–9–2	(19)
1921 Polydipsia, 4–7–6	(16)	**1940** Time Step, 4–8–4	(21)
1922 The Yellow Dwarf, 4–7–10	(18)	**1941–45** No race	
1923 Top Gallant, 3–7–13	(24)	**1946** Honeyway, 5–9–7	(17)
1924 Jarvie, 4–7–9	(11)	**1947** Fairey Fulmar, 4–8–7	(16)
1925 Creolian, 4–6–9	(13)	**1948** Petition, 4–9–3	(19)
1926 Phalaros, 4–8–3	(17)	**1949** My Babu, 4–9–7	(14)
1927 Herbalist, 4–7–3	(16)	**1950** Star Signal, 5–8–0	(14)
1928 Fohanaun, 5–8–10	(23)	**1951** Fastnet Rock, 4–8–2	(21)
1929 Royal Minstrel, 4–8–8	(16)	**1952** Star Signal, 7–7–9	(15)
1930 Ecilath, 4–7–4	(21)	**1953** Orgoglio, 4–8–7	(15)
1931 Fleeting Memory, 6–8–7	(18)	**1954** Chivalry, 5–7–9	(15)
1932 Knight Error, 6–7–11	(17)	**1955** Alf's Caprice, 4–7–9	(19)
1933 Fonab, 4–8–1	(23)	**1956** Coronation Year, 5–8–9	(25)

1957 Dionisio (7–1) E. Hide (£2,469) C. F. Elsey, 4–8–3
    2. Nonchalance,   3. Aberdovey.   Nk, Sht Hd.   14 ran

1958 Red Letter (10–1) G. Lewis (£2,392) W. Smyth, 4–8–5
    2. Alf's Caprice,   3. Nicholas   ¾, 1.   17 ran
                             Nickleby.

1959 Alf's Caprice (20–1) E. Cracknell (£1,471) H. Wallington, 8–7–13 and
D.T.J. (20–1) W. Snaith (£1,471) W. Lyde, 5–7–9
                       3. Magic Moment.   Dd Ht, Sht Hd 20 ran

1960 Sanctum (9–1) A. Breasley (£3,374) A. Smyth, 4–8–4
    2. Sovereign Path,   3. Welsh Rake.   1, Hd.   20 ran

1961 Bass Rock (7–1) P. Robinson (£3,370) J. Jarvis, 4–7–12
    2. Fulshaw Cross,   3. Welsh Rake.   1½, Nk.   21 ran

1962 Spaniards Close (20–1) D. Smith (£2,554) F. Winter, 5–9–3
    2. Robson's Choice,   3. King of Saba.   Sht Hd, Nk.   21 ran

1963 Tudor Treasure (100–7) D. Leah (£3,735) E. Cousins, 5–9–0
    2. Miletus,   3. Welsh Rake.   1½, 1.   35 ran

*1964 Blazing Scent (25–1) R. Hutchinson (£3,327) G. Todd, 5–7–11
    2. Campaign,   3. No Fiddling and Nk, Sht Hd.   19 ran
                       3. Old Tom.

1965 Princelone (10–1) D. Keith (£3,055) W. Nightingall, 4–9–7
    2. Young Christopher,   3. King's Leap.   3, ½.   9 ran

1966 Enrico (11–2) L. Piggott (£3,275) J. Thompson, 4–9–10
    2. Petty Cash,   3. Creole.   ¾, 2½.   14 ran

1967 Hadrian (9–1) A. Murray (£2,934) W. Nightingall, 4–7–11
    2. Prince of Orange,   3. Minera.   5, 1½.   17 ran

1968 Rome (20–1) B. Taylor (£2,868) K. Cundell, 4–8–6
    2. Quy,   3. Supreme   ¾, Hd.   15 ran
                     Sovereign.

Race 175: CHESTER CUP
2 miles 2 furlongs 77 yards handicap. Chester. First run 1824

1900	Roughside, a–7–5	(14)	**1927**	Dark Japan, 4–8–11	(16)
1901	David Garrick, 4–8–10	(16)	**1928**	St Mary's Kirk, 5–7–0	(17)
1902	Carabine, 4–7–5	(16)	**1929**	First Flight, 4–7–7	(22)
1903	Vendale, 4–6–6	(15)	**1930**	Mountain Lad, 5–7–11	(18)
1904	Sandboy, 4–6–2	(12)	**1931**	Brown Jack, 7–9–6	(19)
1905	Imari, 4–7–4	(10)	**1932**	Bonny Brighteyes, 4–7–3	(17)
1906	Feather Bed, 4–6–9	(15)	**1933**	Dick Turpin, 4–7–10	(14)
1907	Querido, 4–8–0	(12)	**1934**	Blue Vision, 7–7–11	(20)
1908	Glacis, 4–7–8	(13)	**1935**	Damascus, 4–7–1	(17)
1909	Santo Strato, 4–9–0	(10)	**1936**	Cho-Sen, 4–7–2	(13)
1910	Elizabetta, 4–6–11	(21)	**1937**	Faites vos Jeux, 6–7–4	(17)
1911	Willonyx, 4–8–2	(14)	**1938**	Mr Grundy, 4–7–5	(17)
1912	Rathlea, a–7–5	(12)	**1939**	Winnebar, 5–7–12	(18)
1913	The Guller, 4–6–6	(19)	**1940–45**	No race	
1914	Aleppo, 5–8–4	(17)	**1946**	Retsel, 4–7–9	(8)
1915	Hare Hill, 5–7–10	(10)	**1947**	Asmodee II, 4–9–1	(14)
1916–18	No race		**1948**	Billet, 4–8–3	(12)
1919	Tom Pepper, 4–7–4	(11)	**1949**	John Moore, 5–6–10	(16)
1920	Our Stephen, 4–7–1	(15)	**1950**	Heron Bridge, 6–9–7	(15)
1921	No race		**1951**	Wood Leopard, 4–7–5	(19)
1922	Chivalrous, 4–7–5	(22)	**1952**	Le Tellier, 7–8–11	(14)
1923	Chivalrous, 5–8–11	(17)	**1953**	Eastern Emperor, 5–9–2	(13)
1924	Rugeley, 4–6–4	(13)	**1954**	Peperium, 4–8–6	(16)
1925	Spithead, 6–8–7	(20)	**1955**	Prescription, 4–8–9	(23)
1926	Hidennis, 5–7–0	(10)	**1956**	Golovine, 6–8–2	(18)

1957 Curry (11–4) J. Gifford (£2,093) F. Armstrong, 6–8–0
　　　　2. Atlas, 　　　　　　　**3.** Combatant. 　　6, 2. 　　　　11 ran
1958 Sandiacre (15–2) L. Piggott (£2,556) W. Dutton, 6–8–5
　　　　2. Induna, 　　　　　　　**3.** Compromise. 　Nk, 2. 　　　15 ran
1959 Agreement (3–1f) W. Carr (£2,524) C. Boyd-Rochfort, 5–9–4
　　　　2. Papy, 　　　　　　　　**3.** Sandiacre. 　Nk, 1½. 　　　14 ran
1960 Trelawny (100–6) F. Durr (£2,659) S. Mercer, 4–7–11
　　　　2. Doctor F., 　　　　　　**3.** Mistlethrush. 　½, 3. 　　　16 ran
1961 Hoy (15–2) G. Lewis (£2,729) L. Dale, 5–8–0
　　　　2. Trelawny, 　　　　　　**3.** Aristarchus. 　Sht Hd, 2. 　16 ran
1962 Golden Fire (7–1) D. Yates (£2,954) D. Marks, 4–7–9
　　　　2. El Surpriso, 　　　　　**3.** Trelawny. 　½, 10. 　　　19 ran
1963 Narratus (8–1) D. Yates (£4,948) D. Thom, 5–7–5
　　　　2. Arctic Vale, 　　　　　**3.** Grey of Falloden. ¾, ½. 　21 ran
1964 Credo (4–1f) P. Cook (£4,654) P. J. Prendergast, 4–8–3
　　　　2. Utrillo, 　　　　　　　**3.** Proper Pride and 　Nk, 4. 　13 ran
　　　　　　　　　　　　　　　　3. Gypsy Refrain.
1965 Harvest Gold (11–2) F. Durr (£6,590) T. Robson, 6–7–11
　　　　2. Aureate, 　　　　　　　**3.** Peter Piper. 　1½, 3. 　　10 ran

1966 Aegean Blue (22–1) L. Piggott (£5,349) R. Houghton, 4–8–7
    2. Alcalde,   **3.** Zaloba.   5, 5.   22 ran
1967 Mahbub Aly (7–1) P. Cook (£4,750) W. Hern, 6–8–1
    2. Belmura,   **3.** Allenheads.   6, 2½.   14 ran
1968 Major Rose (11–4f) L. Piggott (£4,896) H. Price, 6–8–7
    2. Frog,   **3.** Shira.   ½, 6.   15 ran

Race 176: SCOTTISH AND NEWCASTLE BREWERIES HANDICAP

1 mile 2 furlongs 30 yards. Newcastle. Three-year-olds

1965 Ballymarais (evens f) C. Parkes (£4,932) W. Gray, 7–4
    2. Goupi,   **3.** Latour.   6, 3.   10 ran
1966 DAVID JACK (5–1) P. Robinson (£5,578) E. Lambton, 8–6
    2. Sereno,   **3.** Flip-A-Disc.   4, 1½.   17 ran
1967 Tiber (20–1) P. Tulk (£4,864) J. Tree, 7–13
    2. Hang On,   **3.** Thoralgo.   Sht Hd, 3.   23 ran
1968 MOUNT ATHOS (100–9) R. Hutchinson (£4,670) J. Dunlop, 8–5
    2. Big Hat,   **3.** Alignment.   1, 7.   23 ran

Race 177: USHER-VAUX BREWERY GOLD TANKARD

1 mile 7 furlongs handicap. Ayr

1962 Rosie Wings (10–1) Donald Morris (£4,884) H. Whiteman, 5–8–7
    2. Bordone,   **3.** Hard Master.   5, ¾.   15 ran
1963 By Jupiter! (9–1) B. Lee (£5,086) Sir G. Richards, 4–7–5
    2. Magic Court,   **3.** Champ.   1½, 2.   20 ran
1964 Pluit (100–6) Brian Lee (£5,115) G. N. Robinson, 7–7–12
    2. Chinese Lacquer,   **3.** Cagirama.   Sht Hd, ¾.   13 ran
1965 Marsh King (6–1jf) C. Parkes (£5,049) T. Robson, 6–7–0
    2. Cagirama,   **3.** Inyanga.   4, 1½.   16 ran
1966 Aegean Blue (6–4f) L. Piggott (£4,430) R. Houghton, 4–8–5
    2. Champ,   **3.** Royal Rubicon.   2½, Sht Hd.   16 ran
1967 Sweet Story (3–1) J. Etherington (£1,849) R. Peacock, 5–9–4
    2. Dromoland,   **3.** Farm Walk.   1, Hd.   9 ran
1968 First Phase (3–1) G. Oldroyd (£1,842) J. Mulhall, 5–8–4
    2. Lone Wolf,   **3.** Dodge City.   3, ½.   8 ran

Race 178: GREAT JUBILEE HANDICAP
1 mile 2 furlongs. Kempton. First run 1887

1900	Sirenia, 5–8–6	(20)		1927	Abbot's Speed, 4–7–8	(21)
1901	Santoi, 4–8–9	(22)		1928	Abbot's Speed, 5–8–6	(14)
1902	Royal George, 4–6–9	(17)		1929	Athford, 4–8–2	(17)
1903	Ypsilanti, 5–8–1	(19)		1930	Lucky Tor, 5–7–8	(14)
1904	Ypsilanti, 6–9–5	(16)		1931	Racedale, 5–8–3	(14)
1905	Ambition, 4–7–1	(14)		1932	Venturer, 4–7–9	(15)
1906	Donnetta, 6–8–11	(15)		1933	Colorado Kid, 4–7–12	(16)
1907	Polar Star, 3–7–12	(12)		1934	Cotoneaster, 4–7–11	(14)
1908	Hayden, 4–6–12	(12)		1935	Wychwood Abbot, 4–9–2 and	
1909	Ebor, 4–7–7	(14)			British Quota, 4–7–6	(11)
1910	No race			1936	Inflation, 4–8–0	(16)
1911	Bachelor's Double, 5–8–11	(11)		1937	Commander III, 7–8–9	(16)
1912	Bachelor's Hope, 4–7–2	(12)		1938	Monument, 5–8–13	(14)
1913	Absolute, 4–6–12	(16)		1939	Antonym, 4–9–2	(13)
1914	The Curragh, 4–6–12	(20)		1940–45	No race	
1915	Diadumenos, 5–7–12	(15)				
1916–18	No race				**[AT HURST]**	
				1946	Paper Weight, 4–8–9	(10)
	[AT HURST]					
1919	Arion, 4–6–3	(11)			**[AT KEMPTON]**	
				1947	Royal Tara, 4–7–12	(18)
	[AT KEMPTON]			1948	Royal Tara, 5–8–11	(12)
1920	Tangiers, 4–7–9	(18)		1949	Fil d'Or II, 5–8–3	(7)
1921	Paragon, 4–8–4	(19)		1950	Peter Flower, 4–8–4	(12)
1922	Silver Image, 4–7–6	(15)		1951	Roman Way, 6–8–1	(11)
1923	Simon Pure, 4–8–6 and			1952	Durante, 4–7–7	(12)
	Diligence, 4–8–2	(11)		1953	Durante, 5–7–11	(13)
1924	Parth, 4–9–0	(12)		1954	Chatsworth, 4–8–10	(11)
1925	Amethystine, 4–6–7	(13)		1955	Swept, 4–7–0	(12)
1926	No race (general strike)			1956	Tudor Jinks, 4–7–7	(15)

1957 Orinthia (4–1f) G. Starkey (£2,898) C. F. Elsey, 4–6–13
    2. Rowland Ward,   3. Andros.
    (Royal Chief second, disqualified.) Original distances, 1, Hd, ¾.   14 ran
1958 Alcimedes (100–8) J. Mercer (£2,822) R. J. Colling, 4–8–3
    2. Sun Charger,   3. Falls of Shin.   Nk, Hd.   15 ran
1959 Alcimedes (10–1) J. Mercer (£2,864) R. J. Colling, 5–8–3
    2. Royal Chief,   3. Sinbad the Sailor. ½, ½.   12 ran
1960 Rocky Royale (3–1) D. Smith (£2,703) D. Whelan, 4–7–9
    2. Firecracker,   3. Above Suspicion. 1½, ½.   13 ran
1961 Chalk Stream (8–1) B. Lee (£2,816) E. Cousins, 6–7–5
    2. Sallymount,   3. Thames Trader.   Hd, 4.   16 ran
1962 Water Skier (100–7) P. Robinson (£2,643) E. Cousins, 5–7–10
    2. Test Case,   3. Darling Boy.   2, ½.   14 ran

1963 Water Skier (8–1) D. Yates (£4,912) E. Cousins, 6–7–11
    2. I Claudius,   **3.** London Gazette. 1½, Hd.   22 ran
1964 Commander in Chief (100–7) F. Durr (£3,167) E. Cousins, 5–8–7
    2. Owl,   **3.** Raccolto.   1, 1½.   16 ran
1965 Antiquarian (10–1) J. Sharman (£2,955) H. G. Blagrave, 4–7–9
    2. Minor Portion,   **3.** Noorose.   ½, 1.   12 ran
1966 Antiquarian (6–1) P. Cook (£2,965) H. Blagrave, 5–7–11
    2. Hotroy,   **3.** Rehearsed.   1, 1½.   13 ran
1967 Red Bar (20–1) R. P. Elliott (£2,582) H. Price, 5–8–2
    2. Le Cordonnier,   **3.** Castle Yard.   Nk, Sht Hd.   17 ran
1968 Pally's Double (33–1) J. Lowe (£2,629) J. F. Watts, 4–6–11
    2. Castle Yard,   **3.** Ben Novus.   2½, Hd.   15 ran

Race 179: AIREY OF LEEDS SPRING CUP

7 furlongs. York. Called Spring Handicap 6 furlongs until 1968

1960 Rolled Gold (100–8) G. Lewis (£3,361) P. Hastings-Bass, 5–8–5
    2. Shamrock Star and
    2. Accompanist.   ¾, Dd Ht.   18 ran
1961 Bourbon (20–1) P. Robinson (£3,123) J. Jarvis, 4–7–7
    2. Eternal Goddess,   **3.** Whistler's   Nk, 1½.   12 ran
                            Daughter.
1962 Non Proven (100–9) S. Smith (£2,316) J. Jarvis, 4–8–4
    2. Whistling Victor,   **3.** Earl Marshal.   1, 5.   16 ran
1963 Windscale (100–7) J. Sime (£2,358) S. Hall, 4–8–11
    2. Star Princess,   **3.** Burning Thoughts 4, ½.   18 ran
1964 No Argument (10–1) J. Mercer (£2,273) W. Wharton, 4–8–3
    2. King's Leap,   **3.** Marcher.   ¾, ½.   13 ran
1965 Weeper's Boy (9–1) G. Bougoure (£7,605) D. Hanley, 4–9–4
    2. No Argument,   **3.** Marcus Superbus. Hd, Hd.   21 ran
1966 Lucasland (100–8) E. Eldin (£8,017) J. A. Waugh, 4–8–4
    2. Spark,   **3.** Kamundu.   Sht Hd, 3.   25 ran
1967 Norton Priory (6–1) G. Sexton (£1,241) A. Vasey, 4–7–11
    2. Fair Samela,   **3.** Sound Number. 6, 3.   8 ran
1968 Quy (5–2f) E. Eldin (£1,784) R. Jarvis, 4–9–9
    2. Follywise,   **3.** In Bond.   ¾, ½.   9 ran

Race 180: JOHN DAVIES HANDICAP

1 mile 4 furlongs. Haydock. Run over 1 mile for three-year-olds in 1957. *Called Haydock Diamond Jubilee Stakes

1957 Mark Antony (10–1) E. Mercer (£1,620) J. Jarvis, 8–11
    2. Repetition,   **3.** Kingston-by-Pass. Sht Hd, 3.   15 ran

1958 Clear Night (7–1) D. Johnstone (£1,713) W. R. Whiston, 5–6–9
    2. No Comment,   3. Pampered King.   4, 3.   10 ran
*1959 Trimmer (10–1) S. Clayton (£2,297) W. Hern, 4–8–5
    2. Amazons Choice,   3. Cannebiere.   Nk, 3.   15 ran
1960 Si Furieux (100–7) C. Parkes (£1,680) C. F. Elsey, 3–7–5
    2. Persian Road,   3. Polar Way.   1½, 1½.   9 ran
1961 Little Buskins (11–4) L. Piggott (£1,699) C. Boyd-Rochfort, 4–8–9
    2. Welsh Border,   3. No Saint.   4, 5.   8 ran
1962 Sword Hilt (9–2f) W. Carr (£1,715) C. Boyd-Rochfort, 4–8–6
    2. Royal Glen,   3. Cracksman.   5, 3.   11 ran
1963 Best Song (6–4f) S. Clayton (£1,707) J. Gosden, 4–8–1
    2. Drumbeg,   3. Raccolto.   ½, 2.   8 ran
1964 Roman Scandal (9–1) D. Smith (£1,731) J. F. Watts, 4–7–10
    2. Young Lochinvar,   3. Best Song.   Sht Hd, 5.   9 ran
1965 Current Speech (6–5f) J. Sime (£1,559) S. Hall, 4–8–12
    2. Champ,   3. Golden Gorden.   2½, ½.   5 ran
1966 Thundridge (5–2) S. Clayton (£1,593) C. Boyd-Rochfort, 4–7–12
    2. Sans Pareil,   3. L'Homme Arme.   2, Nk.   5 ran
1967 Bunker (13–2) R. Maddock (£1,260) B. van Cutsem, 4–8–12
    2. New Liskeard,   3. Barnie Beatle.   Sht Hd, 5.   11 ran
1968 Farm Walk (8–1) J. Seagrave (£1,289) P. Beasley, 6–8–11
    2. Philistine,   3. Bugle Boy.   3, 1.   10 ran

Race 181: CECIL FRAIL HANDICAP

1 mile. Haydock. Three-year-olds

1958 Royal Painter (7–1) M. Hayes (£1,280) S. Hall, 7–5
    2. Aalsund,   3. Glendawn.   ½, 3.   8 ran
1959 Muckle John (100–9) G. Littlewood (£1,201) H. Peacock, 8–9
    2. Sirri,   3. Moonsprite.   1½, Hd.   8 ran
1960 Quadruple (9–4f) D. Smith (£1,172) J. F. Watts, 8–7
    2. Right Guy,   3. Silent Waters.   Nk, ½.   9 ran
1961 Double Bee (8–1) R. Fawdon (£1,208) L. Elwell, 8–4
    2. Bluecourt,   3. Foxstar.   ½, Sht Hd.   10 ran
1962 Gay Casino (8–1) H. Greenaway (£1,129) P. Beasley, 9–1
    2. Old Tom,   3. Luminous Sun.   1½, 2.   10 ran
1963 High Flown (9–2) F. Durr (£2,067) S. James, 9–5
    2. Ros Rock,   3. Clydeann.   4, 3.   11 ran
1964 Current Speech (6–1) J. Sime (£1,646) S. Hall, 8–11
    2. Gallegos,   3. Lobitos.   1, 6.   12 ran
1965 Danella (4–1) E. Hide (£1,635) W. Hide, 8–3
    2. Sweet Gem,   3. Sunderton.   3, 4.   8 ran
1966 Tracker (10–1) H. Greenaway (£1,780) R. Peacock, 7–11
    2. Palmy,   3. On Probation.   3, 1½.   15 ran
1967 Frankincense (7–2) G. Starkey (£2,120) J. Oxley, 8–7
    2. Hang On,   3. Moon King.   1½, 3.   7 ran

1968 Charlie's Pal (9–2) G. Duffield (£2,169) R. Jarvis, 7–3
    2. Delayed Tip,   **3.** Guildhall.   2½, ½.   10 ran

Race 182: THIRSK HUNT CUP

1 mile handicap. Thirsk

1957 King's Coup (7–2) D. Greening (£1,073) M. Easterby, 4–7–9
    2. Dionisio,   **3.** Argol.   2, 1.   6 ran
1958 King's Coup (3–1) D. Greening (£845) M. Easterby, 5–7–11
    2. QUORUM,   **3.** Dutton.   Sht Hd, ½.   7 ran
1959 King's Coup (9–4f) A. Hide (£1,069) M. Easterby, 6–8–7
    2. Dauber,   **3.** Bishop's Move.   2, 1½.   7 ran
1960 Guitarist (2–1f) F. Durr (£1,143) H. Jelliss, 5–9–0
    2. Hard and Soft,   **3.** Shamrock Star.   ½, 3.   11 ran
1961 Monawin (5–1) J. Sime (£1,101) R. Mason, 6–7–13
    2. Honeycomb Rock,   **3.** Torullo.   1½, 2.   10 ran
1962 My Timps (10–1) P. Robinson (£1,269) E. Cousins, 6–7–11
    2. Honeycomb Rock,   **3.** Royal Jester.   2, Nk.   21 ran
1963 Gay Casino (13–2) J. Sime (£2,605) P. Beasley, 4–9–2
    2. Chestergate,   **3.** Guard of Honour.   ¾, ½.   23 ran
1964 High Flown (100–8) E. Hide (£2,211) W. Wharton, 4–9–9
    2. Zaleucus,   **3.** Chief Inspector and
                        3. Wrangle.   Nk, 2.   11 ran
1965 Mandamus (5–2f) J. Roe (£2,172) B. van Cutsem, 5–9–1
    2. Shotley Mill,   **3.** Burning Torch.   2½, Hd.   18 ran
1966 Kentra (11–2) A. Robson (£2,030) G. Fenningworth, 5–7–12
    2. Footpath,   **3.** Raybelle.   1½, Sht Hd.   9 ran
1967 Danella (11–4f) R. Maddock (£1,738) P. Makin, 5–8–4
    2. Prince of Orange,   **3.** Matsur.   ½, 1½.   10 ran
1968 Emerilo (10–1) M. Thomas (£1,815) P. Allden, 4–7–11
    2. High Table,   **3.** Sunny Tunes.   ¾, 1.   16 ran

Race 183: HAREWOOD HANDICAP

1 mile 4 furlongs. Doncaster. Run over 1 mile 6 furlongs 132 yards until 1963

1957 FRENCH BEIGE (4–1) G. Littlewood (£1,684) H. Peacock, 4–9–4
    2. Dalstar,   **3.** Morecambe.   Sht Hd, 3.   8 ran
1958 Alexis (5–1) S. Clayton (£1,659) W. Hern, 4–8–10
    2. Milan,   **3.** Dark Heron.   2, 2.   8 ran
1959 All Serene (3–1) E. Britt (£1,663) N. Bertie, 4–8–5
    2. Huguenot,   **3.** Snow Leopard.
        (Predominate first, disqualified.) Original distances, Nk, 2, 2.   6 ran

1960 Great Gonerby (8–1) D. Greening (£1,490) W. Lyde, 4–7–1
    2. Freelight,   **3.** Beau Normand.   1½, Sht Hd.   4 ran
1961 Little Buskins (10–11f) D. Smith (£1,552) C. Boyd-Rochfort, 4–9–1
    2. Utrillo,   **3.** Fulminate.   ¾, 5.   6 ran
1962 Sunny Way (7–2) D. Smith (£1,552) N. Murless, 5–10–0
    2. Poetic Licence,   **3.** Cracksman.   2, 4.   3 ran
1963 Porky (7–2) J. Sime (£1,513) J. Walsh, 6–7–9
    2. Port Corsair,   **3.** Rapanni.   ½, 4.   7 ran
1964 Aviator (100–8) R. Maddock (£1,310) H. Rohan, 4–8–0
    2. Rapanni,   **3.** Peter Piper.   Sht Hd, 1½.   9 ran
1965 Inyanga (10–1) K. Stott (£1,192) G. N. Robinson, 4–6–9
    2. Mintmaster,   **3.** Osier.   1, 1.   5 ran
1966 Sweet Story (5–1) J. Etherington (£1,139) R. Peacock, 4–8–13
    2. Mintmaster,   **3.** Set to Music.   3, ½.   4 ran
1967 Renardier (11–2) D. Greening (£1,174) H. Cottrill, 5–7–10
    2. High Table,   **3.** Lariak.   1½, 1½.   11 ran
1968 No race

Race 184: ZETLAND HANDICAP

1 mile. Doncaster. Run over 6 furlongs until 1962

1957 Cheviot Hills (4–1f) G. Starkey (£2,198) P. Beasley, 3–6–12
    2. Light Harvest,   **3.** Prairie Emblem.   2, 1½.   8 ran
1958 D.T.J. (11–2) W. Snaith (£2,151) W. Lyde, 4–7–12
    2. Abbey Oaks,   **3.** Idler.   ½, ½.   11 ran
1959 Ryecroft (20–1) J. Sime (£2,283) W. Binnie, 4–7–9
    2. Welsh Abbot,   **3.** Sufi.   2, 3.   13 ran
1960 Deer Leap (2–1jf) G. Starkey (£2,092) J. Oxley, 4–8–9
    2. Helen Rosa,   **3.** Golden Light.   2, 2.   5 ran
1961 Palatina (4–5f) J. Sime (£2,045) F. Armstrong, 3–8–2
    2. Light of the Road,   **3.** Charbon.   Hd, 1½.   4 ran
1962 Arion (4–1) J. Sime (£2,232) S. Hall, 5–9–0
    2. Biarritz,   **3.** Church Stretton.   ½, 3.   8 ran
1963 Old Tom (8–1) J. Etherington (£2,381) M. H. Easterby, 4–8–1
    2. King of Saba,   **3.** Fury Royal.   1, 1½.   12 ran
1964 Salammbo (8–1) R. P. Elliott (£2,139) H. Wragg, 4–7–9
    2. Bobsbest,   **3.** Soueida.   ½, Nk.   9 ran
1965 Sovereign Edition (4–1) R. Maddock (£1,970) R. Mason, 3–7–11
    2. Finish Fast,   **3.** Heartburn.   3, Sht Hd.   9 ran
1966 Bobsbest (20–1) L. Pinder (£2,071) A. Bacon, 7–7–9
    2. Candid Picture,   **3.** Welcomed.   Sht Hd, 1.   13 ran
1967 Ben Novus (4–1) E. Hide (£1,979) W. Hide, 5–8–5
    2. Vibrant,   **3.** Regal Light.   ½, 2½.   8 ran
1968 Petros (4–1jf) R. Maddock (£2,018) B. van Cutsem, 4–8–6
    2. Common Pond,   **3.** Bobsbest.   Sht Hd, Hd.   14 ran

Race 185: ZETLAND GOLD CUP

1 mile 2 furlongs handicap. Redcar

1950 Near Way, 4–8–4	(17)	**1954** Prince d'Or, 5–7–13	(16)
1951 Socrates, 4–7–13	(8)	**1955** Blue Prince II, 4–8–10	(12)
1952 Mid View, 5–7–10	(10)	**1956** Tale of Two Cities, 5–7–8	(11)
1953 H.V.C., 4–8–7	(12)		

1957 Sunrise (100–8) G. Starkey (£3,380) G. Boyd, 4–7–1
    2. Rabbi,   **3.** Arctic Flower.   5, 1.   20 ran
1958 Cash and Courage (7–1) M. Hayes (£4,230) S. Hall, 5–8–2
    2. No Comment,   **3.** No Complaint.   2, 1½.   14 ran
1959 Maddalo (33–1) B. Jago (£6,760) P. Thrale, 4–8–0
    2. Warrior,   **3.** Cash and Courage. 1, ¾.   16 ran
1960 Hard and Soft (10–1) A. Russell (£4,910) T. Dent, 5–8–4
    2. Chino,   **3.** Royal Chief.   1½, Hd.   13 ran
1961 Beau Rossa (9–2f) J. Sime (£4,910) S. Hall, 5–8–10
    2. Fulshaw Cross,   **3.** Pannier.   ½, Nk.   18 ran
1962 Henry the Seventh (100–8) E. Hide (£4,910) W. Elsey, 4–9–10
    2. Better Honey,   **3.** Espresso.   2, ½.   11 ran
1963 Principal (100–7) M. Hayes (£4,910) F. Armstrong, 4–9–4
    2. Mighty Gurkha,   **3.** Space King.   2, Hd.   14 ran

1964 Red Tears (7–1) J. Mercer (£4,910) W. Hern, 4–8–11
    2. Raccolto,   **3.** King of Babylon. Sht Hd, ¾.   14 ran
1965 Dark Court (6–4f) A. Breasley (£4,176) Sir G. Richards, 4–8–2
    2. Burning Torch,   **3.** Forthright.   ½, 2½.   13 ran
1966 Preclusion (4–1) J. Sime (£4,159) S. Hall, 4–7–13
    2. Royalgo,   **3.** Space King.   ¾, 1½.   9 ran
1967 Sportaville (100–6) P. Hetherington (£2,519) P. Beasley, 5–7–8
    2. Raw Silk,   **3.** Kentra.   1, 6.   11 ran
1968 Castle Yard (11–2) S. Smith (£2,549) Sir C. Boyd-Rochfort, 5–8–4
    2. Midnight Marauder,   **3.** High Table.   2, Nk.   11 ran

Race 186: SANDOWN PARK WHITSUN CUP

1 mile handicap. Sandown. Three-year-olds only in 1963

1963 Tiger (4–5f) A. Breasley (£1,726) Sir G. Richards, 9–6
    2. John Cameron,   **3.** Wheatsheaf.   2, ¾.   6 ran
1964 Red Slipper (8–1) W. Williamson (£2,670) Sir Hugh Nugent, 4–9–7
    2. Mandamus,   **3.** Shoulder Arms. 2, Sht Hd.   10 ran
1965 Christmas Review (100–9) D. Cullen (£2,505) K. Cundell, 4–7–11
    2. Aberdeen,   **3.** Hasty Cloud.   ¾, 3.   10 ran
1966 Aberdeen (5–1) B. Raymond (£2,092) H. Cottrill, 5–8–8
    2. Grey Lord,   **3.** Christmas Review. 3, 2.   10 ran

1967 Morris Dancer (5–1) G. Lewis (£1,924) I. Balding, 6–8–4
    2. Lucky Biscuit,   **3.** Christmas Review. 1, 2.   10 ran
1968 Cumshaw (7–1) W. Williamson (£1,612) C. Benstead, 7–8–3
    2. Blazing Scent,   **3.** Morris Dancer. Hd, 1.   9 ran

Race 187: PAVILION HANDICAP

1 mile 2 furlongs. Brighton. Run over 1 mile 4 furlongs until 1966

1957 Poaching (2–1jf) W. Rickaby (£692) V. Smyth, 5–8–5
    2. Two Royals,   **3.** Brunel II.   6, 4.   6 ran
1958 Tuscar (5–1) L. Piggott (£1,006) T. H. Carey, 5–8–7
    2. Scamperdale,   **3.** Same.   6, 2.   9 ran
1959 Huguenot (4–1) E. Mercer (£1,031) J. Oxley, 5–9–7
    2. Illinois,   **3.** Trimmer. $\frac{1}{2}$, l.   10 ran
1960 Illinois (11–4) L. Piggott (£963) P. Payne-Gallwey, 5–9–5
    2. Operatic Society,   **3.** Alcimedes.   4, 2.   5 ran
1961 Illinois (7–4f) L. Piggott (£979) P. Payne-Gallwey, 6–9–4
    2. Nerograph.   **3.** Tudor Period.   3, 5.   10 ran
1962 Dispute (8–1) D. Keith (£935) H. Smyth 4–7–13
    2. Zeus Boy,   **3.** Family Tree.   2, 4.   8 ran
1963 Royal Sanction (4–1) D. Smith (£1,815) F. Winter, 4–8–5
    2. Spartan General,   **3.** Persian Kim.   6, 3.   9 ran
1964 Operatic Society (5–2) L. Piggott (£1,374) C. Benstead, 8–9–7
    2. Touroy,   **3.** Anassa.   1, 3.   6 ran
1965 I Claudius (5–2jf) A. Breasley (£1,333) G. Todd, 6–9–11
    2. One and Only,   **3.** Picture Palace.   5, 12.   5 ran
1966 Happy Haven (7–1) A. Breasley (£1,358) T. Corbett, 4–8–4
    2. Ballyconneely,   **3.** Cabouchon.   Nk, $\frac{3}{4}$.   10 ran
1967 Happy Haven (7–1) A. Barclay (£1,137) T. Corbett, 5–7–8
    2. Le Garcon,   **3.** Apollo.   1, Hd.   11 ran
1968 Royal Falcon (4–1) A. Barclay (£791) N. Murless, 4–9–3
    2. Lexicon,   **3.** Happy Haven. $2\frac{1}{2}$, $1\frac{1}{2}$.   13 ran

Race 188: BRIGHTHELMSTONE HANDICAP

7 furlongs. Brighton. Three-year-olds. Run over 1 mile 2 furlongs until 1966

1957 Table Wine (8–11f) A. Breasley (£729) S. Ingham, 8–13
    2. Shearwater,   **3.** Middle Watch. $1\frac{1}{2}$, 2.   7 ran
1958 Illinois (100–6) L. Piggott (£1,052) P. M. Nelson, 8–6
    2. Roxburgh,   **3.** Dalrymple.   3, $1\frac{1}{2}$.   7 ran
1959 Free Air (5–1) J. Mercer (£1,040) J. Jarvis, 8–6
    2. Polar Way,   **3.** Belafonte. $1\frac{1}{2}$, 1.   7 ran

1960 Delta Brava (10–1) A. Cash (£959) D. Marks, 6–5
    2. Allez,   **3.** Canton.   2, ¾.   5 ran
1961 Miss Biffin (3–1) G. Lewis (£987) P. Hastings-Bass, 9–1
    2. Pinhurst,   **3.** Vinca.   1, 4.   9 ran
1962 Royal Sanction (7–1) A. Breasley (£959) F. Winter, 8–11
    2. Santaway,   **3.** Sudden Thought.   3, 2.   6 ran
1963 Executor (7–2f) G. Lewis (£1,840) P. Hastings-Bass, 9–7
    2. King's Cavalier,   **3.** Martinsell.   Hd, ½.   10 ran
1964 Cabouchon (11–4f) D. Smith (£1,369) F. Winter, 8–13
    2. Faultless Image,   **3.** Nymet Tracey.   Sht Hd, 4.   5 ran
1965 Royal St George (9–4) P. Cook (£1,360) K. Cundell, 7–10
    2. Alyba,   **3.** Shaykh   2½, ¾.   5 ran
        Sulieman.
1966 Last Case (9–4f) A. Breasley (£1,379) P. Nelson, 8–12
    2. Last Chip,   **3.** Giuro.   1, 2.   11 ran
1967 St Chad (5–6f) G. Moore (£1,167) N. Murless, 9–6
    2. Skegness Camp,   **3.** Treble J.   Nk, 2.   9 ran
1968 Reita (33–1) P. Reavey (£815) D. Hanley, 6–12
    2. Stop Thief,   **3.** High Time.   ½, 2.   10 ran

Race 189: ROSEBERY MEMORIAL HANDICAP

2 mile 2 furlongs. Epsom

1957 Hammal II (13–2) G. Starkey (£1,047) H. Thomson-Jones, 4–7–11
    2. Combatant,   **3.** Gay Ballad.   4, 8.   6 ran
1958 Lucky White Heather (9–4) E. Smith (£1,443) G. Todd, 4–8–5
    2. Eiger,   **3.** Birthday Present.   2, 1.   6 ran
1959 Birthday Present (11–2) E. Mercer (£1,043) E. Parker, 5–8–1
    2. Prefairy,   **3.** Time and Again.   Hd, ¾.   7 ran
1960 Domesday (4–1) E. Larkin (£1,069) J. Jarvis, 4–8–13
    2. Come to Daddy,   **3.** Kaffirboom.   ½, 5.   7 ran
1961 Avon's Pride (4–1) B. Lee (£1,077) W. Hern, 4–8–12
    2. Cold Comfort,   **3.** Starliner.   1, 5.   10 ran
1962 Avon's Pride (5–1) W. Carr (£1,002) W. Hern, 5–9–8
    2. Parnear,   **3.** Rainstorm.   4, 2.   9 ran
1963 Utrillo (11–2) A. Breasley (£1,028) H. Price, 6–8–10
    2. Domesday,   **3.** Ulster Ranger.   1½, 2.   7 ran
1964 Roxburgh (100–30) R. Hutchinson (£1,535) W. Wightman, 9–7–11
    2. Woodleighs,   **3.** Singer.   ¾, 2.   7 ran
1965 Tree Leopard (13–2) J. Mercer (£1,274) W. Hern, 5–9–3
    2. Harvest Gold,   **3.** Philemon.   5, 3.   14 ran
1966 Sir Giles (13–2) W. Carson (£1,291) F. Walwyn, 5–7–10
    2. Gold Aura,   **3.** Happy Nick.   2, 2½.   14 ran
1967 Gold Aura (100–9) R. Hutchinson (£1,225) C. Boyd-Rochfort, 7–8–10
    2. Drumlanrig,   **3.** Black Justice.   Nk, 1.   12 ran

1968 Great Pleasure (7–1) J. Wilson (£1,213) H. Wallington, 4–8–8
    2. La Foire II,   **3.** Jacthelot.   2, 2½.   10 ran

Race 190: NEWBURY SUMMER CUP
1 mile 4 furlongs handicap. Newbury

1957 Rue de Romance (4–1jf) L. Piggott (£1,026) G. Todd, 4–8–9
    2. Midwest,   **3.** Andros.   ¾, 2.   8 ran
1958 Rabbi (5–2) J. Mercer (£1,511) R. J Colling, 6–9–1
    2. Rose Argent,   **3.** Aorangi.   ½, ¾.   6 ran
1959 Red Dragon (4–1) W. Rickaby (£1,638) N. Bertie, 4–8–8
    2. Trimmer,   **3.** Milan.   1½, ½.   9 ran
1960 Rue de Romance (7–4f) A. Breasley (£1,481) G. Todd, 7–8–2
    2. Huguenot,   **3.** Alcimedes.   Hd, 3.   7 ran
1961 Nerograph (5–1) T. Carter (£1,570) G. Todd, 5–7–8
    2. His Story,   **3.** Dear Gazelle.   2, 3.   11 ran
1962 Espresso (100–30f) W. Williamson (£1,536) H. Wragg, 4–8–9
    2. Powder Rock,   **3.** Entanglement.   Nk, 1½.   10 ran
1963 St Gulliver (11–2) W. Snaith (£2,917) F. Armstrong, 4–7–10
    2. Sherry Netherland,   **3.** Anassa.   2, Sht Hd.   12 ran
1964 Crepes d'Enfer (7–2jf) L. Piggott (£1,591) N. Murless, 4–8–7
    2. Osier,   **3.** Porky.   1, Sht Hd.   8 ran
1965 Valoroso (11–2) G. Lewis (£1,479) S. Ingham, 3–8–1
    2. Antiquarian,   **3.** Champ.   6, Hd.   9 ran
1966 Polymint (6–1) D. Maitland (£1,438) J. Sutcliffe jun., 6–7–5
    2. Antiquarian,   **3.** Vitruvius.   5, 1.   5 ran
1967 Sun Rock (13–8f) A. Barclay (£1,197) N. Murless, 3–7–10
    2. Patron Saint,   **3.** Operatic Society. 4, 4.   8 ran
1968 Duperion (6–1) D. Keith (£1,213) H. Wallington, 4–8–9
    2. Polymint,   **3.** Spunyarn.   5, 1½.   6 ran

Race 191: ASCOT STAKES
2 mile 4 furlongs handicap. Royal Ascot. First run 1839

2 MILES			
1900 Baldur, 4–7–2	(11)	1909 Rushcutter, 4–8–5	(15)
1901 Sinopi, 5–8–2	(16)	1910 Declare, 4–8–3	(14)
1902 Scullion, 4–6–12	(16)	1911 Willonyx, 4–8–4	(14)
1903 Genius, 5–7–0	(18)	1912 The Policeman, 4–7–12	(11)
1904 Merry Andrew, 5–7–6	(22)	1913 Rivoli, 4–9–1	(22)
1905 Sandboy, 5–8–7	(19)	1914 Broadwood, 4–6–2	(24)
1906 Pradella, a–8–4	(22)	1915–18 No race	
1907 Torpoint, a–8–4	(11)	1919 Haki, a–8–6	(14)
1908 Turbine, 5–7–11	(12)	1920 Happy Man, 4–9–3	(16)
		1921 Spearwort, 4–8–3	(13)

1922 Double Hackle, 4–7–3	(10)	1937 Valerian, 4–8–13	(29)
1923 Juniso, 5–8–1	(16)	**2M 4F**	
1924 Scullion, 4–7–11	(14)	1938 Frawn, 4–7–12	(25)
1925 Mandelieu, 4–7–8	(10)	1939 Frawn, 5–8–10	(30)
1926 Miss Sport, 5–6–7	(16)	1940–45 No race	
1927 Duke of Buckingham 4–7–10	(18)	1946 Reynard Volant, 4–7–12	(16)
1928 Brown Jack, 4–7–13	(21)	1947 Reynard Volant, 5–9–4	(23)
1929 Old Orkney, 5–8–4	(24)	1948 No Orchids, 5–8–11	(27)
1930 Bonny Boy II, 6–8–5	(20)	1949 Hilali, 5–7–4	(34)
1931 Noble Star, 4–7–10	(21)	1950 Honorable II, 6–8–4	(25)
1932 Son of Mint, 5–8–2 and		1951 Guerrier, 6–6–12	(25)
Sandy Lashes, 4–6–9	(24)	1952 Flighty Frances, 4–7–9	(23)
1933 Roi de Paris, 5–7–9	(23)	1953 Pluchino, 4–7–12	(24)
1934 Hands Off, 4–7–1	(20)	1954 Corydalis, 5–7–2	(20)
1935 Doreen Jane, 5–6–11	(24)	1955 Wildnor, 4–7–0	(15)
1936 Bouldnor, 4–7–6	(34)	1956 Zarathustra, 5–9–0	(23)

1957 Bonhomie (25–1) M. Hayes (£2,878) E. Cousins, 8–6–8
   2. Closebeck,   **3.** Chaseaway.   4, ½.   16 ran

1958 Sandiacre (100–7) W. Carr (£2,797) W. Dutton, 6–8–13
   2. Seleucus,   **3.** Garibaldi.   1½, 1.   19 ran

1959 Rugosa (100–7) E. Smith (£2,941) T. Leader, 4–7–12
   2. York Fair,   **3.** Ocho Rios.   ½, ¾.   21 ran

1960 Shatter (100–8) R. P. Elliott (£2,788) T. Masson, 4–7–9
   2. Elysium,   **3.** Trelawny.   Nk, 10.   17 ran

1961 Angazi (6–1f) D. Keith (£2,920) W. Nightingall, 5–8–1
   2. Augustine,   **3.** Minute Gun.   Sht Hd, ¾.   23 ran

1962 Trelawny (11–2jf) A. Breasley (£2,737) G. Todd, 6–9–8
   2. Fortwyn,   **3.** Domesday.   4, 3.   15 ran

1963 Trelawny (9–1) A. Breasley (£2,788) G. Todd, 7–10–0
   2. Sea Leopard,   **3.** Lost Property.   ¾, 1½.   22 ran

1964 Delmere (8–1) D. Cullen (£2,776) W. Stephenson, 4–7–2
   2. Trelawny,   **3.** Calyphas.   2, ½.   19 ran

1965 Harvest Gold (9–1) F. Durr (£2,699) T. Robson, 6–8–12
   2. Philemon,   **3.** Tropical Song.   Hd, Hd.   17 ran

1966 Tubalcain (100–6) G. Lewis (£2,822) E. Goddard, 5–8–0
   2. Shira,   **3.** Square Deal.   Sht Hd, 2.   24 ran

1967 Shira (6–1) J. Hayward (£2,515) G. Todd, 7–7–9
   2. Pilino,   **3.** All Found.   ½, 3.   20 ran

1968 King of Peace (8–1) A. Murray (£2,505) J. Hardy, 5–7–12
   2. Debach Girl,   **3.** Jacthelot.   2, 3.   19 ran

HORSES IN CAPITAL LETTERS
WERE TO BE, OR HAD BEEN,
PLACED IN THE CLASSICS

Race 192: BRITANNIA STAKES

1 mile handicap. Royal Ascot. Three-year-olds

1957 Pundit (8–1) G. Lewis (£1,438) S. Ingham, 8–2
    2. Sun Flight,   **3.** Wheatley.   2, Nk.   11 ran
1958 Legal Tie (9–2) E. Britt (£1,506) P. Beasley, 8–0
    2. Supreme Joy,   **3.** Barley.   1, 4.   14 ran
1959 Macquario (100–9) E. Smith (£1,659) N. Murless, 8–1
    2. Stratus,   **3.** Rocky Royale.   ¾, 4.   15 ran
1960 Right of Way (9–2jf) E. Hide (£1,621) C. F. Elsey, 8–12
    2. Blublue,   **3.** Adorn.   3, 1.   13 ran
1961 Firewalker (25–1) R. Hutchinson (£1,715) W. G. O'Gorman, 7–9
    2. World Peace,   **3.** Betray.   4, 4.   21 ran
1962 Fiacre (5–1) J. Sime (£1,774) P. Beasley, 8–13
    2. Tamerlo,   **3.** Flag.   3, Hd.   19 ran
1963 Ros Rock (100–8) J. Lindley (£1,651) J. Tree, 9–7
    2. Fine Bid,   **3.** Vijay.   2, Sht Hd.   16 ran
1964 Double Fall (100–6) J. Mercer (£1,693) D. Candy, 8–5
    2. Bexar,   **3.** Roman   ½, Nk.   18 ran
        Wedding.
1965 Sheridan (15–2) B. Raymond (£1,579) J. Clayton, 8–11
    2. Tromba,   **3.** Alan Adare.   3, ¾.   17 ran
1966 Corinto (100–7) R. Hutchinson (£1,569) H. Wragg, 8–9
    2. By Rights,   **3.** Gallic.   ¾, Nk.   16 ran
1967 Waterloo Place (25–1) W. Williamson (£1,374) H. Thomson-Jones, 8–7
    2. Nicois,   **3.** St Padarn.   2, Sht Hd.   14 ran
1968 Delayed Tip (7–1) J. Mercer (£1,356) J. F. Watts, 9–1
    2. Zambomba,   **3.** Marmaduke.   Sht Hd, 2½.   12 ran

Race 193: ROYAL HUNT CUP

1 mile handicap. Royal Ascot. First run 1843

7F 166Y				
1900 Royal Flush, a–7–0	(20)	**1912** Eton Boy, 4–7–10	(28)
1901 Stealaway, 4–6–7	(22)	**1913** Long Set, 6–9–1	(29)
1902 Solicitor, 4–7–4	(23)	**1914** Lie-a-Bed, 3–6–0	(25)
1903 Kunstler, 5–7–5	(25)	**1915–18** No race	
1904 Csardas, 5–7–5	(28)	**1919** Irish Elegance, 4–9–11	(26)
1905 Andover, 4–8–0	(25)	**1920** Square Measure, 5–8–0	(22)
1906 Dinneford, 4–7–7	(22)	**1921** Illuminator, 4–7–6	(22)
1907 Lally, 4–8–0	(24)	**1922** Varzy, 4–7–0	(20)
1908 Billy the Verger, 4–6–13	(20)	**1923** Weathervane, 4–6–12	(25)
1909 Dark Ronald, 4–7–2	(23)	**1924** Dinkie, 4–6–10	(20)
1910 Bachelor's Double, 4–8–4	(20)	**1925** Cockpit, 4–7–6	(30)
1911 Moscato, 5–7–2	(18)	**1926** Cross Bow, 4–9–0	(31)
		1927 Asterus, 4–8–13	(29)

1928 Priory Park, 6–8–12	(52)	1945 Battle Hymn, 3–7–11	(14)
1929 Songe, 5–8–11	(29)	1946 Friars Fancy, 5–7–12	(16)
		1947 Master Vote, 4–7–6	(28)
7F 155Y		1948 Master Vote, 5–8–10	(27)
1930 The McNab, 4–7–8	(22)	1949 Sterope, 4–8–12	(29)
1931 Grand Salute, 4–7–5	(18)	1950 Hyperbole, 5–8–8	(20)
1932 Totaig, 3–7–3	(31)	1951 Val d'Assa, 4–8–8	(23)
1933 Colorado Kid, 4–8–5	(28)	1952 Queen of Sheba, 4–8–4	(29)
1934 Caymanas, 4–8–4	(29)	1953 Choir Boy, 4–7–8	(21)
1935 Priok, 4–7–6	(37)	1954 Chivalry, 5–8–3	(26)
1936 Guinea Gap, 5–8–5	(31)		
1937 Fairplay, 4–8–3	(33)		
1938 Couvert, 5–7–12	(29)	**1M**	
1939 Caerloptic, 4–8–12	(24)	1955 Nicholas Nickleby, 4–7–9	(22)
1940–44 No race		1956 Alexander, 4–8–11	(27)

1957 Retrial (100–7) P. Robinson (£3,174) C. Boyd-Rochfort, 5–8–2
    2. MIDGET II,   **3.** Loppylugs.   1, ½.   18 ran
1958 Amos (20–1) P. Boothman (£2,928) S. Mercer ,4–7–1
    2. Empire Way,   **3.** Falls of Shin.   ¾, 2.   17 ran
1959 Faultless Speech (8–1) G. Lewis (£3,591) H. Wallington, 4–8–1
    2. PALL MALL,   **3.** Small Slam.   1½, 1½.   23 ran
1960 Small Slam (28–1) R. P. Elliott (£3,591) G. Barling, 5–8–2
    2. Mustavon,   **3.** Pheidippides.   Nk, Nk.   26 ran
1961 King's Troop (100–7) G. Lewis (£4,050) P. Hastings-Bass, 4–8–4
    2. Robson's Choice.   **3.** Midsummer   1, 3.   39 ran
                                          Night II.
1962 Smartie (22–1) J. Sime (£3,863) R. Mason, 4–7–9
    2. China Clipper,   **3.** Water Skier.   Sht Hd, Sht Hd. 31 ran
1963 Spaniards Close (25–1) L. Piggott (£3,961) F. Winter, 6–8–6
    2. Mystery,   **3.** Nereus.   Hd, Nk.   38 ran
1964 Zaleucus (100–7) D. Smith (£3,731) G. Brooke, 4–8–2
    2. Gelert,   **3.** Emerald Cross.   Hd, 1.   30 ran
1965 Casabianca (100–9) L. Piggott (£5,332) N. Murless, 4–8–7
    2. Weeper's Boy,   **3.** Zaleucus.   Hd, ½.   26 ran
1966 Continuation (25–1) J. Roe (£5,111) S. McGrath, 4–7–9
    2. Steeple Aston,   **3.** Midnight   5, Nk.   30 ran
                                          Marauder.
1967 Regal Light (100–9) G. Sexton (£3,618) S. Hall, 4–7–6
    2. Kibenka,   **3.** Midnight   Sht Hd, Hd.   15 ran
                                          Marauder.
1968 Golden Mean (28–1) F. Durr (£3,980) Doug Smith, 5–8–4
    2. Owen Anthony,   **3.** Straight Master.   ½, 2.   26 ran

Race 194: BESSBOROUGH STAKES

1 mile 4 furlongs handicap. Royal Ascot

1957 Tuscar (13–2) A. Breasley (£1,438) Sir G. Richards, 4–8–4
    2. Casmiri,   **3.** Roman Sand.   Hd, 1½.   12 ran
1958 Huguenot (7–1) E. Mercer (£1,633) G. Colling, 4–8–4
    2. Agreement,   **3.** Rhythmic Light.   3, 3.   18 ran
1959 Hyphen (5–1) D. Smith (£1,655) J. F. Watts, 4–8–4
    2. Rhythmic Light.   **3.** Fulminate.   1½, ¾.   9 ran
1960 Persian Road (7–1) J. Lindley (£1,715) J. Tree, 5–8–5
    2. Jock's Lodge,   **3.** Mistlethrush.   Nk, 1.   15 ran
1961 Thames Trader (100–7) A. Breasley (£1,834) S. Ingham, 5–9–2
    2. Hatton Garden,   **3.** Redoubt.   2, 3.   25 ran
1962 Better Honey (10–1) G. Littlewood (£1,766) G. Fenningworth, 4–8–3
    2. My Steel,   **3.** Henry's Choice.   1, 6.   21 ran
1963 Raccolto (11–4) L. Piggott (£1,732) S. Hall, 6–8–10
    2. Voivode,   **3.** Dahabeah.   Hd, 2.   12 ran
1964 Linnet Lane (8–1) G. Lewis (£1,744) I. Balding, 4–8–9
    2. Arctic Kanda,   **3.** Hinton Blewett.   1½, 1½.   8 ran
1965 Prince Hansel (100–8) G. Bougoure (£1,655) D. Thom, 4–8–12
    2. Forthright,   **3.** Ulster Prince.   6, 2.   19 ran
1966 Twelfth Man (8–1) J. Mercer (£1,770) H. Wragg, 5–8–4
    2. Menaphon,   **3.** Barkhan.   2, Nk.   22 ran
1967 Polmak (9–2f) L. Piggott (£1,392) F. Armstrong, 4–8–5
    2. Nous Esperons,   **3.** Bunker.   1, 1½.   14 ran
1968 Q.C. (7–1) G. Lewis (£1,431) E. Goddard, 7–8–6
    2. Tiber,   **3.** Pally's Double.   ½, 6.   13 ran

Race 195: KING GEORGE V STAKES

1 mile 4 furlongs handicap. Royal Ascot. Three-year-olds

1957 Clouds (7–2f) E. Mercer (£1,586) G. Colling, 7–12
    2. Wigandia,   **3.** Northern   4, 1.   21 ran
                                    Highway.
1958 Quick Decision (20–1) F. Durr (£1,625) C. F. Elsey, 7–13
    2. Miss McTaffy,   **3.** Mr Snake.   4. 2.   23 ran
1959 Suki Desu (100–7) S. Clayton (£1,727) W. Nightingall, 8–5
    2. Admiral's Lark and   **2.** Solo Singer.   2, Dd Ht.   15 ran
1960 Sunny Way (7–1) L. Piggott (£1,770) N. Murless, 8–6
    2. Spartan Green,   **3.** Ruby's Boy.   2, 5.   22 ran
1961 Vinca (100–9) R. P. Elliott (£1,774) E. Parker, 7–13
    2. Flambeau,   **3.** Jaxartes.   3, 2.   21 ran
1962 Panjandrum (11–2) E. Eldin (£1,817) J. A. Waugh, 8–0
    2. Magnus,   **3.** Orchardist.   2, Sht Hd.   15 ran

1963 Master Cappelle (11–2jf) B. Taylor (£1,625) H. Leader, 9–0
    2. Prophetess,   **3.** Aim High.   Nk, 2.   13 ran
1964 Abandoned
1965 Brave Knight (6–1) L. Piggott (£1,558) W. Nightingall, 9–5
    2. Barkhan,   **3.** Nearside.   Hd, 3.   12 ran
1966 Marcus Brutus (11–2) L. Piggott (£1,597) S. Hall, 8–10
    2. Nous Esperons,   **3.** Snob.   2, 10.   15 ran
1967 Sharavogue (9–1) G. Lewis (£1,428) I. Balding, 8–0
    2. Dicker,   **3.** Epidendrum.   1, Sht Hd.   14 ran
1968 Tudor Abbe (3–1f) R. Hutchinson (£1,341) P. Nelson ,7–13
    2. Sheil,   **3.** Rhine Maiden.   3, $\frac{1}{2}$.   9 ran

Race 196: WOKINGHAM STAKES

6 furlongs handicap. Royal Ascot. First run 1874

1900 Bridge, 4–7–12	(17)	**1928** Hera, 4–7–8	(22)
1901 Rose Tree, 5–7–9	(20)	**1929** Six Wheeler, 4–7–5	(23)
1902 His Lordship, 3–6–6	(25)	**1930** Grandmaster, 5–7–5	(17)
1903 Glass Jug, 4–7–9	(24)	**1931** Heronslea, 4–8–7	(22)
1904 Out o'Sight, 5–8–5	(29)	**1932** Concerto, 4–8–6	(15)
1905 Queen's Holiday, 4–8–2	(14)	**1933** Concerto, 5–9–3	(24)
1906 Golden Gleam, 4–8–0	(13)	**1934** Coroado, 4–8–9	(18)
1907 Forerunner II, 3–6–11	(23)	**1935** Theio, 3–7–5	(23)
1908 Portland Bay, 4–8–2	(22)	**1936** Cora Deans, 4–7–11	(26)
1909 Portland Bay, 5–8–2	(21)	**1937** Kong, 4–6–12	(31)
1910 Galleot, 6–8–4	(19)	**1938** Bold Ben, 4–8–9	(26)
1911 Meleager, 3–7–6	(21)	**1939** America, 4–8–12	(28)
1912 Borrow, 4–8–2	(19)	**1940–44** No race	
1913 Braxted, 5–8–0	(22)	**1945** Portamara, 4–7–5	(10)
1914 Mount William, 3–6–10	(24)	**1946** The Bug, 3–8–7	(21)
1915–18 No race		**1947** Lucky Jordan, 4–7–6	(24)
1919 Scatwell, 4–7–11	(11)	**1948** White Cockade, 4–7–7	(32)
1920 Golden Oil, 4–7–13	(23)	**1949** The Cobbler, 4–9–4	(35)
1921 Santaquest, 4–7–4	(9)	**1950** Blue Book, 3–7–11	(24)
1922 Proconsul, 4–8–3	(20)	**1951** Donore, 4–8–5	(23)
1923 Crowdennis, 5–9–2	(16)	**1952** Malka's Boy, 4–8–10	(22)
1924 Pandarus, 5–7–3	(20)	**1953** Jupiter, 3–7–3	(22)
1925 Compiler, 5–8–1	(22)	**1954** March Past, 4–9–0	(16)
1926 Capture Him, 4–8–1	(29)	**1955** The Plumber's Mate, 4–6–9	(19)
1927 Nothing Venture, 4–8–10	(23)	**1956** Light Harvest, 4–7–12	(28)

1957 Dionisio (5–1) E. Britt (£1,501) C. F. Elsey, 4–8–10
    2. Bigibigi,   **3.** Light Harvest.   3, Nk.   8 ran
1958 Magic Boy (20–1) D. Greening (£1,510) M. Bolton, 5–7–5
    2. Autonomy,   **3.** Earl Marshal.   2, $\frac{1}{2}$.   22 ran
1959 Golden Leg (33–1) R. P. Elliott (£1,948) M. Pope, 4–7–1
    2. Anxious Lady,   **3.** Logarithm.   Nk, $\frac{3}{4}$.   29 ran

1960 Silver King (15–2f) J. Sime (£1,965) S. Hall, 4–7–11
    2. Sovereign Path,   **3.** Dawn Watch.   3, Hd.   29 ran
1961 Whistler's Daughter (10–1jf) J. Sime (£1,872) S. Hall, 4–8–6
    2. Little Redskin,   **3.** Winna.   Nk, ½.   28 ran
1962 Elco (20–1) W. Williamson (£2,093) D. Whelan, 4–8–13
    2. Demerara,   **3.** Rins of Clyde.   1, ½.   35 ran
1963 Marcher (100–8) R. Hutchinson (£1,880) D. Hanley, 3–7–12
    2. Spring Wheat,   **3.** Creole.   3, 1.   27 ran
1964 Abandoned
1965 Nunshoney (33–1) D. East (£1,737) G. Beeby, 3–7–2
    2. Silver Churn,   **3.** Audience.   Nk, Nk.   25 ran
1966 My Audrey (20–1) G. Cadwaladr (£1,954) E. Cousins, 5–8–2
    2. Air Patrol,   **3.** Barrymore.   ½, 1½.   33 ran
1967 Spaniards Mount (100–6) D. Smith (£1,701) J. Winter, 5–8–6
    2. Lunar Princess,   **3.** Vibrant.   1, 2½.   19 ran
1968 Charicles (100–7) D. East (£1,677) E. Lambton, 3–7–6
    2. Gemini Six,   **3.** Directory.   1½, Hd.   21 ran

Race 197: FERN HILL HANDICAP
1 mile. Ascot. Three-year-old fillies

1957 Instow (100–7) F. Barlow (£1,302) G. Barling, 8–9
    2. Swallow Swift,   **3.** Sylphide.   1, ¾.   16 ran
1958 Gillylees (11–4) J. Sime (£1,277) P. Beasley, 8–0
    2. Verve,   **3.** Cross Talk.   1½, 4.   12 ran
1959 Vouchsafe (3–1) E. Britt (£1,613) P. Beasley, 8–6
    2. Drake's Affair,   **3.** Grecian Urn II.   1, 2.   10 ran
1960 Jeanne Michelle (4–1) F. Barlow (£1,723) B. Foster, 8–5
    2. Zoom,   **3.** Gallant Deal.   Nk, 2.   14 ran
1961 Violetta III (8–1) W. Carr (£1,778) H. Wragg, 8–6
    2. Melpomene,   **3.** Rachel.   2, 1.   20 ran
1962 Peroxide (5–2f) D. Smith (£1,744) F. Armstrong, 9–2
    2. Elsa,   **3.** Hidden Meaning. and
                3. La Belle.   1½, Nk.   11 ran
1963 Lachine (11–8f) A. Breasley (£1,617) Sir G. Richards, 9–4
    2. Outcrop,   **3.** Nautch Dance.   1, 1½.   12 ran
1964 Abandoned
1965 Petty Cash (5–2f) M. Thomas (£1,589) G. Barling, 8–4
    2. Vital Issue,   **3.** Toffee Nose.   ¾, ½.   12 ran
1966 Greek Streak (100–8) A. Breasley (£1,655) P. Nelson, 8–3
    2. Petite Marmite,   **3.** Swiftest.   Sht Hd, 1.   16 ran
1967 Lady Magistrate (3–1f) R. Hutchinson (£1,332) G. Smyth, 8–1
    2. Freeholder,   **3.** Tickle My Palm.   2, 2.   9 ran
1968 Pardina (5–2f) J. Mercer (£1,338) H. Wragg, 8–4
    2. Sage Rose,   **3.** Matilda III.   3, 4.   12 ran

Race 198: ANDY CAPP HANDICAP

1 mile 2 furlongs. Redcar. Three-year-olds

1962 Initial (10–1) B. Connorton (£955) W. Hall, 8–11
    2. Golstar,   3. Codicil.   Sht Hd, 8.   8 ran
1963 Dion (10–1) Donald Morris (£4,225) W. Elsey, 8–9
    2. Chandra Cross,   3. Red Tears.   Hd, Sht Hd.   12 ran
1964 Philanderer (9–2) D. Ryan (£4,220) W. Wharton, 9–2
    2. Oy-Oy,   3. Twelfth Man.   Nk, Hd.   14 ran
1965 Shai (10–1) F. Durr (£4,220) H. Wragg, 8–10
    2. Take Heed,   3. Northern Deamon.
                                              Hd, 1.   13 ran
1966 Sword Dancer (33–1) E. Larkin (£4,220) S. Hall, 8–0
    2. Sotuta,   3. Bunker. $\frac{1}{2}$, 1.   16 ran
1967 Pennant (100–8) E. Larkin (£4,479) S. Hall, 9–5
    2. Bosworth Field,   3. Strident and
                           3. Tiber.   1, Hd.   13 ran
1968 Hamood (7–1) E. Johnson (£4,452) S. Hall, 7–7
    2. Darda,   3. Orchard Boy. $\frac{3}{4}$, 4.   16 ran

Race 199: NORTHUMBERLAND PLATE

2 miles handicap. Newcastle. First run 1833

1900 Joe Chamberlain, 3–8–2	(8)	
1901 Reminiscence, 5–6–1	(12)	
1902 Osbech, a–9–0	(10)	
1903 Cliftonhall, 4–7–7	(8)	
1904 Palmy Days, 4–7–11	(10)	
1905 Princess Florizel, 4–6–7	(9)	
1906 Outbreak, 4–8–0	(12)	
1907 Killigrew, 6–6–7	(11)	
1908 Old China, 4–8–2	(11)	
1909 Sir Harry, 4–8–7	(11)	
1910 Elizabetta, 4–7–11	(11)	
1911 Pillo, 6–8–7	(10)	
1912 Mynora, 6–6–6	(9)	
1913 The Tylt, 4–7–13	(13)	
1914 The Guller, 5–8–0	(9)	
1915–18 No race		
1919 Trestle, 4–6–13	(6)	
1920 Irish Lake, 4–7–7	(10)	
1921 Hunt Law, 4–8–4	(12)	
1922 Double Hackle, 4–8–4	(14)	
1923 Carpathus, 4–7–10	(11)	
1924 Jazz Band, 5–8–3	(9)	

1925 Obliterate, 4–8–12	(10)
1926 Foxlaw, 4–7–13	(6)
1927 Border Minstrel, 4–7–3	(7)
1928 Primrose League, 5–7–6	(14)
1929 Ballynahinch, 6–7–1	(13)
1930 Show Girl, 4–8–4	(12)
1931 Blue Vision, 4–7–4	(8)
1932 Pomarrel, 5–7–5	(10)
1933 Leonard, 7–7–9	(10)
1934 Whiteplains, 4–7–11	(15)
1935 Doreen Jane, 5–7–8	(8)
1936 Coup de Roi, 4–7–13	(7)
1937 Nectar II, 4–7–12	(11)
1938 Union Jack, 4–8–0	(12)
1939 Oracion, 4–8–0	(13)
1940–45 No race	

[AT LIVERPOOL]

1946 Gusty, 4–9–2   (5)

[AT NEWCASTLE]

1947 Culrain, 6–7–7   (9)

1948	Pappatea, 5–9–5	(15)	1953	Nick la Rocca, 4–8–11	(14)
1949	Fol Ami, 4–7–1	(13)	1954	Friseur, 4–8–2	(20)
1950	Light Cavalry, 4–7–6	(8)	1955	Little Cloud, 4–8–4	(16)
1951	Sycomore II, 4–8–3	(15)	1956	Jardiniere, 4–8–0	(12)
1952	Souepi, 4–7–6	(6)			

1957 Great Rock (10–1) E. Hide (£2,025) W. Dutton, 4–7–8
    2. Devon Brew,   **3.** Staghound.   1, ½.   17 ran

1958 Master of Arts (7–2f) J. Mercer (£3,945) R. J. Colling, 5–8–4
    2. Little Topper,   **3.** Chamafleur.   1½, 5.   21 ran

1959 Cannebiere (100–7) Donald Morris (£4,455) A. Barclay, 6–7–9
    2. Persian Road,   **3.** Final Test.   4, ½.   17 ran

1960 New Brig (10–1) N. Stirk (£4,455) G. Boyd, 4–8–8
    2. Mistlethrush,   **3.** Poetic Licence.   1½, ½.   13 ran

1961 Utrillo (100–7) D. Cullen (£4,455) W. G. O'Gorman, 4–7–1
    2. Brocade Slipper,   **3.** Avon's Pride.   Nk, Nk.   20 ran

1962 Bordone (100–7) G. Littlewood (£5,045) G. Fenningworth, 4–8–5
    2. Optimistic,   **3.** Sostenuto.   Sht Hd, 1.   13 ran

1963 Horse Radish (8–1) P. Robinson (£5,045) F. Maxwell, 4–7–8
    2. Golden Oriole,   **3.** Acrophel.   1, Hd.   14 ran

1964 Peter Piper (28–1) J. Wilson (£5,045) R. Mason, 4–7–9
    2. Lomond,   **3.** Senior Steward.   5, ½.   18 ran

1965 Cagirama (9–1) N. McIntosh (£4,935) G. Boyd, 6–7–5
    2. Grey of Falloden,   **3.** Ravel.   5, Nk.   16 ran

1966 Sweet Story (100–7) J. Etherington (£4,992) R. Peacock, 4–8–4
    2. Cagirama,   **3.** Valoroso.   1½, 2½.   15 ran

1967 Piaco (100–30f) M. Thomas (£3,926) G. Barling, 4–9–1
    2. Sweet Story,   **3.** Chestergate.   Hd, 1.   13 ran

1968 Amateur (100–9) W. Carson (£4,000) B. van Cutsem, 4–7–9
    2. Quartette,   **3.** Farm Walk.   Nk, 2.   14 ran

Race 200: BRIGHTON MILE

1 mile handicap. Brighton. Three-year-olds

1957 Red Letter (5–1) G. Lewis (£1,270) W. Smyth, 8–12
    2. Lower Boy,   **3.** Epsom Lady.   Nk, 3.   8 ran

1958 Master of Boyden (100–8) D. Cullen (£1,485) W. Stephenson, 6–12
    2. Stunning,   **3.** Laurino.   1½, 1.   6 ran

1959 Stratus (7–4f) D. Smith (£1,430) Sir G. Richards, 9–5
    2. Polar Way,   **3.** Sirri.   2, 3.   6 ran

1960 Grasp (10–1) L. Piggott (£1,416) P. Walwyn, 8–12
    2. King's Rock,   **3.** Midsummer   ¾, 1.   12 ran
                                     Night II.

1961 Biarritz (7–2) J. Uttley (£1,446) S. Ingham, 8–13
    2. Eagle,   **3.** Piero.   Sht Hd, 4.   7 ran

1962 Tamerlo (15–8f) A. Breasley (£1,422) Sir G. Richards, 9–1
    2. Owl,   **3.** Good Flight.   2, $\frac{3}{4}$.   9 ran
1963 Fine Bid (3–1f) R. Hutchinson (£2,727) G. Todd, 8–12
    2. Hercules Boy,   **3.** Lincolnwood.   2, 1$\frac{1}{2}$.   12 ran
1964 Bivouac (11–10f) P. Robinson (£2,325) J. Jarvis, 9–0
    2. Vilmorence,   **3.** Filey Camp.   Sht Hd, Nk.   9 ran
1965 L.J. (9–2) R. Hutchinson (£1,788) K. Gethin, 7–12
    2. Scriventon,   **3.** Sheriff. $\frac{1}{2}$, 4.   9 ran
1966 Last Case (3–1) A. Breasley (£1,772) P. Nelson, 9–1
    2. By Rights,   **3.** Crepango.   2, Nk.   7 ran
1967 Nicois (3–1) R. Hutchinson (£1,489) P. Nelson, 7–10
    2. Broadway Melody,   **3.** Frankincense.   Sht Hd, Hd.   5 ran
1968 Town Crier (9–2) D. Keith (£1,168) P. Walwyn, 9–1
    2. Marmaduke,   **3.** Night Lot.   Nk, 3.   11 ran

Race 201: GREENALL WHITLEY GOLD CHALLENGE TROPHY

2 miles 2 furlongs 77 yards handicap. Chester

1965 Philemon (3–1) G. Lewis (£2,941) W. Marshall, 5–8–4
    2. Nireus,   **3.** Harvest Gold.   1, 3.   11 ran
1966 Alcalde (7–2f) D. Smith (£3,986) B. van Cutsem, 4–9–1
    2. High Proof,   **3.** Persian Lancer.   5, 1.   11 ran
1967 Grey of Falloden (7–1) J. Mercer (£3,186) W. Hern, 8–8–7
    2. C.E.D.,   **3.** All Found.   1, $\frac{1}{2}$.   11 ran
1968 Tubalcain (13–8f) G. Lewis (£3,240) E. Goddard, 7–8–13
    2. Shira,   **3.** La Foire II.   3, 2.   9 ran

Race 202: OLD CHESTER HANDICAP

1 mile 2 furlongs 10 yards. Chester

1965 Tudor Summer (100–6) W. Carson (£1,497) W. O'Gorman, 4–7–8
    2. Chestergate,   **3.** Royalgo.   2, Sht Hd.   10 ran
1966 Desacre (7–4f) R. Maddock (£1,459) J. Tree, 4–8–5
    2. Chestergate,   **3.** Make Haste. $\frac{3}{4}$, 4.   7 ran
1967 Paddykin (5–4f) G. Lewis (£1,136) S. Ingham, 3–8–11
    2. Astral Green,   **3.** Red Swan.   1, $\frac{1}{2}$.   4 ran
1968 Colonel Blimp (11–4f) L. Brown (£805) R. Peacock, 6–9–7
    2. Lord Sing,   **3.** Limuru.   2$\frac{1}{2}$, 2$\frac{1}{2}$.   7 ran

Race 203: SANDOWN ANNIVERSARY HANDICAP

1 mile. Sandown. *Run over 1 mile 2 furlongs

1957 Cardington Court (100–6) E. Mercer (£1,035) R. Jarvis, 5–8–2
    2. Bright Silk,   **3.** Canardeau.   ½, Hd.   8 ran
*1958 Wonder Belle (evens f) A. Breasley (£1,044) S. Ingham, 3–8–0
    2. Fair Victor,   **3.** Sunstart.   3, 1½.   7 ran
1959 Kingroy (10–1) S. Clayton (£1,027) W. Nightingall, 4–8–13
    2. Chinese Sun,   **3.** William F.   Hd, 3.   8 ran
1960 Thames Trader (4–1) A. Breasley (£945) S. Ingham, 4–8–11
    2. Sunstart,   **3.** Golden Vision.   ¾, 1½.   6 ran
1961 Givenaway (9–4f) J. Mercer (£1,053) F. Winter, 4–8–5
    2. Spring Madness,   **3.** Good Light.   Sht Hd, ½.   9 ran
1962 Marchakin (5–1) R. Hutchinson (£1,028) K. Cundell, 6–7–10
    2. Lohengrin,   **3.** Givenaway.   Hd, 1½.   8 ran
1963 Good Flight (4–1) R. Hutchinson (£1,621) G. Todd, 4–7–12
    2. Shady Case,   **3.** Popular Prince.   2, 3.   7 ran
1964 Red Slipper (7–1) W. Williamson (£1,441) Sir Hugh Nugent, 4–10–0
    2. Rescind,   **3.** Fine Bid.   1, 3.   10 ran
1965 Candid Picture (100–9) W. Snaith (£1,250) L. Hall, 5–7–12
    2. Mandamus,   **3.** Excel.   ¾, Sht Hd.   7 ran
1966 Birdbrook (9–2) R. Hutchinson (£1,274) M. Pope, 5–8–3
    2. Aberdeen,   **3.** Lucky Biscuit.   ¾, 1.   7 ran
1967 Giddaby (3–1) A. Breasley (£1,169) L. Hall, 4–8–6
    2. Mugatpura,   **3.** Midnight   1, 3.   5 ran
                                     Marauder.
1968 Privy Seal (9–4f) L. Piggott (£1,276) T. Waugh, 4–8–8
    2. Benroy,   **3.** Giddaby.   Hd, ½.   7 ran

Race 204: BUNBURY CUP

7 furlongs handicap. Newmarket

1962 Blue Over (100–7) G. Lewis (£2,656) F. Armstrong, 5–8–0
    2. Burning Thoughts,   **3.** Welsh Rake.   ¾, ¾.   16 ran
1963 Nereus (15–8f) A. Breasley (£2,494) K. Cundell, 4–9–7
    2. Sang Froid,   **3.** Grand Applause.   ¾, Sht hd.   12 ran
1964 Passenger (100–7) M. Thomas (£2,152) P. Moore, 5–9–9
    2. Dunme,   **3.** Spaniards Close.   Sht Hd, 4.   16 ran
1965 Grey Lord (6–1) F. Durr (£2,156) Sir G. Richards, 3–7–11
    2. BALUSTRADE,   **3.** Showoff.   Sht Hd, Hd.   12 ran
1966 Showoff (9–1) L. Piggott (£2,108) J. Winter, 4–8–9
    2. Dunme,   **3.** Creole.   2½, 1.   14 ran
1967 Vibrant (3–1f) P. Robinson (£1,674) E. Lambton, 4–9–10
    2. Enrico,   **3.** Above Water.   1½, 3.   11 ran
1968 Swinging Minstrel (8–1) R. Still (£1,654) W. Payne, 4–7–7
    2. Hadrian,   **3.** Right-Winger.   ½, 4.   9 ran

Race 205: SEAVIEW HANDICAP

1 mile. Brighton

1957 No Worry (3–1) J. Forte (£582) H. Price, 6–8–4
    2. Aidos,   **3.** Midelfin.   1, 1½.   7 ran

1958 Master Nicky (11–2) J. Gifford (£558) M. Feakes, 4–8–3
    2. No Worry,   **3.** Diplomatic Bag.   Nk, 3.   6 ran

1959 Caught Out (10–1) J. Friar (£603) G. Todd, 7–8–1
    2. Aidos,   **3.** Flash Past.   3, 1½.   13 ran

1960 Master of Boyden (11–2) D. W. Morris (£999) W. Stephenson, 5–7–6
    2. Westmarsh,   **3.** Master Nicky.   2, 1.   8 ran

1961 Master of Boyden (11–2) R. P. Elliott (£1,002) A. Kerr, 6–7–6
    2. Release,   **3.** Midsummer   3, 3.   6 ran
                                Night II.

1962 Barbary Pirate (20–1) W. Williamson (£500) R. Sturdy, 6–8–1
    2. Marchakin,   **3.** Spaniards Close.   Nk, ¾.   6 ran

1963 Dunme (5–2f) G. Lewis (£985) R. Read, 4–8–1
    2. Passenger,   **3.** Becket.   Nk, 2.   10 ran

1964 Greenhills Lad (100–7) J. Tulloch (£792) L. Dale, 5–9–4
    2. Dunme,   **3.** Sparrow Pie.   3, 2.   10 ran

1965 Toosin Tack (10–1) R. Hutchinson (£937) P. Nelson, 5–8–1
    2. Cheveley Lad,   **3.** Floral Tribute.   1½, 1½.   10 ran

1966 Welcomed (8–1) D. W. Morris (£1,341) John Waugh, 4–7–7
    2. Langley Park,   **3.** Riot Act.   1½, 1½.   8 ran

1967 Herbaceous (3–1f) A. Barclay (£1,151) N. Murless, 4–9–0
    2. Harvest Flame,   **3.** Peruvian Silk.   1, 1½.   11 ran

1968 Birdbrook (9–1) R. Hutchinson (£819) M. Pope, 7–9–10
    2. Straight Master,   **3.** Come April.   1, 2½.   9 ran

Race 206: SOUTHERN HANDICAP

1 mile 2 furlongs. Brighton. Three-year-olds. Run over 1 mile 4 furlongs until 1968. All ages until 1966, but three-year-olds only in 1961

1957 Roman Sand (4–11f) E. Mercer (£579) G. Colling, 4–9–6
    2. Red Urchin,   **3.** Candelabra.   1½, 1½.   6 ran

1958 Roxburgh (11–2) M. Hayes (£1,103) W. Wightman, 3–7–9
    2. Marron,   **3.** Ulanova,   10, 1½.   11 ran

1959 Kalydon (5–4) E. Smith (£1,120) B. van Cutsem, 3–9–0
    2. Calceolaria,   **3.** Glenborne.   1½, 4.   5 ran

1960 Prime Mover (1–4f) J. Mercer (£545) A. Budgett, 4–9–2
    2. Owenor,   **3.** Nakalanta.   8, 1.   5 ran

1961 Dispute (15–8f) D. Keith (£530) H. Smyth, 7–10
    2. Parthenon,   **3.** Patrick's Choice.   5, Nk.   5 ran

1962 Zeus Boy (5–4f) W. Williamson (£997) P. Nelson, 4–8–1
    2. Dispute,   **3.** Springmount.   3, 5.   5 ran
1963 Persian Kim (6–1) G. Lewis (£438) H. Wallington, 4–8–1
    2. Vandyke,   **3.** Owen Davis.   ¾, ½.   9 ran
1964 Cabouchon (3–1) D. Smith (£788) F. Winter, 3–7–9
    2. Operatic Society,   **3.** Sugar Daddy.   4, ½.   10 ran
1965 Singer (11–8f) D. East (£764) W. Wightman, 5–7–8
    2. Paper Boy,   **3.** Mid Field.   2, 2.   5 ran
1966 Gold Shalimar II (11–4) W. Carson (£633) F. Armstrong, 8–7
    2. Betatron,   **3.** Borodino.   ¾, 4.   8 ran
1967 Bayarin (8–11f) A. Breasley (£1,134) K. Cundell, 8–1
    2. Starbrush,   **3.** Psidiana.   2½, 1.   6 ran
1968 Pallarco (4–1) W. Williamson (£1,140) P. Nelson, 8–7
    2. Eastwell,   **3.** Greenacre.   2, ¾.   6 ran

Race 207: OLD NEWTON CUP

1 mile 4 furlongs handicap. Haydock

1957 Rhythmic Light (4–6f) P. Robinson (£1,939) S. Ingham, 3–7–3
    2. Roll Away,   **3.** Penitent.   ½, 4.   5 ran
1958 Huguenot (7–4f) E. Mercer (£1,969) G. Colling, 4–9–0
    2. Pampered King,   **3.** Great Rock.   1½, 3.   6 ran
1959 Mongoose (15–2) E. Hide (£2,147) C. F. Elsey, 4–7–13
    2. Solo Singer,   **3.** Chino.   1, 2.   10 ran
1960 Apostle (evens f) E. Hide (£1,994) S. Ingham, 3–8–3
    2. Midlander,   **3.** Illinois.   2, 1½.   6 ran
1961 Menelek (8–1) A. Rawlinson (£2,033) G. Brooke, 4–8–4
    2. Porky,   **3.** Welsh Border.   3, Sht Hd.   8 ran
1962 Cloudy Wyn (100–7) L. G. Brown (£1,802) M. H. Easterby, 4–7–13
    2. Port Corsair,   **3.** Latin Lover.   2, 1.   10 ran
1963 Young Lochinvar (7–2jf) W. Williamson (£3,437) H. Wragg, 4–8–12
    2. Menelek,   **3.** Risky.   5, 2.   11 ran
1964 Rapanni (9–1) P. Hetherington (£3,379) G. Boyd, 5–7–3
    2. Philanderer,   **3.** Roman Scandal.   5, ¾.   11 ran
1965 Atilla (100–30) M. Thomas (£3,379) H. Wragg, 4–7–3
    2. Valoroso,   **3.** Signal Rocket.   6, ½.   9 ran
1966 Ballywit (20–1) D. W. Morris (£3,414) A. Budgett, 4–7–4
    2. Lariak,   **3.** Menaphon.   8, ¾.   7 ran
1967 French Vine (13–2) D. Cullen (£3,092) W. Elsey, 3–7–7
    2. Par Value,   **3.** Polmak.   2, 1.   8 ran
1968 Tiber (7–4f) J. Lindley (£3,214) J. Tree, 4–8–9
    2. Great Pleasure,   **3.** Inyanga.   1, ¾.   11 ran

Race 208: MAGNET CUP

1 mile 2½ furlongs handicap. York

1960 Fougalle (9–1) N. McIntosh (£4,125) P. Beasley, 3–7–0
    2. Billum,   **3.** Royal Painter.   Hd, 3.   14 ran
1961 Proud Chieftain (5–2f) W. Carr (£4,211) W. Hern, 4–8–10
    2. Keystone Cop,   **3.** Henry's Choice.   2, Hd.   17 ran
1962 Nortia (100–9) F. Durr (£4,155) W. Hern, 3–8–4
    2. Fury Royal,   **3.** Water Skier.   ½, 3.   16 ran
1963 Raccolto (6–1) J. Sime (£4,282) S. Hall, 6–8–3
    2. Fury Royal,   **3.** Royal Magician.   1½, 1½.   19 ran
1964 Space King (25–1) E. Hide (£4,266) W. Hide, 5–8–9
    2. Owl,   **3.** Fraxinus.   1½, 2.   15 ran
1965 Dark Court (5–2f) A. Breasley (£4,240) Sir G. Richards, 4–8–6
    2. Burning Torch,   **3.** Flying Curtis.   2½, 1.   12 ran
1966 DAVID JACK (4–1f) P. Robinson (£4,266) E. Lambton, 3–7–6
    2. Haymaking,   **3.** Master Barry.   3, 1.   14 ran
1967 Copsale (8–1) L. Brown (£3,742) R. Smyth, 4–7–13
    2. Polymint,   **3.** Castle Yard.   2, 4.   11 ran
1968 Farm Walk (8–1) J. Seagrave (£3,822) P. Beasley, 6–8–13
    2. Castle Yard,   **3.** Private Room.   2, ½.   10 ran

Race 209: TENNENT TROPHY

1 mile 7 furlongs handicap. Ayr. Called John Kennedy Cup in 1962 and 1963

1962 Scorton Gold (9–2) J. Sime (£1,515) S. Hall, 4–8–2
    2. Zuchet,   **3.** Sauce Diable.   1½, ¾.   10 ran
1963 Dalnamein (7–1) J. Sime (£1,579) S. Hall, 8–8–5
    2. Dahabeah,   **3.** Pluit.   ¾, 3.   13 ran
1964 Arctic Kanda (9–1) R. Maddock (£2,253) W. Nightingall, 5–9–2
    2. Osier,   **3.** Harvest Gold.   Sht Hd, 6.   15 ran
1965 Cagirama (4–1) N. Stirk (£2,118) G. Boyd, 6–8–10
    2. Borlent Boy,   **3.** Inyanga.   2, ½.   12 ran
1966 Cagirama (4–1) B. Connorton (£2,092) G. Boyd, 7–8–11
    2. Mintmaster,   **3.** Tampion.   Nk, 3.   14 ran
1967 Montecello (5–2f) D. Smith (£1,806) B. van Cutsem, 4–9–0
    2. Farm Walk,   **3.** Shy Boy.   Nk, 4.   14 ran
1968 Dodge City (9–1) P. Hetherington (£1,856) E. Weymes, 4–7–8
    2. Lampardal,   **3.** Kentra.   1, ¾.   15 ran

Race 210: CHESTERFIELD CUP

1 mile 2 furlongs handicap. Goodwood. First run 1840

1900	Spectrum, 4–6–11	(9)
1901	Glenapp, 3–6–1	(14)
1902	Ypsilanti, 4–7–12	(6)
1903	Lady Help, 3–6–5	(10)
1904	Union Jack, 4–8–13	(9)
1905	Song Thrush, 3–6–13	(9)
1906	Gold Riach, 3–7–12	(8)
1907	Velocity, 5–9–10	(11)
1908	King's Courtship, 4–6–13	(12)
1909	Succour, 6–8–8	(12)
1910	Land League, a–8–3	(12)
1911	Dean Swift, a–8–3	(8)
1912	Southannan, a–8–6	(10)
1913	Junior, 4–8–7	(9)
1914	Kiltoi, 4–7–11	(14)
1915–18	No race	
1919	Tangiers, 3–7–9	(7)
1920	Alasnam, 4–7–9	(4)
1921	Illuminator, 4–8–11	(10)
1922	Statuary, 5–8–1	(13)
1923	Evander, 5–8–11	(12)
1924	Frater, 3–8–0	(9)
1925	Warden of the Marches, 3–8–0	(14)
1926	Warden of the Marches, 4–9–8	(11)

1927	Volta's Pride, 4–8–4	(9)
1928	Silver Hussar, 3–7–10	(14)
1929	Double Life, 3–7–5	(13)
1930	The McNab, 4–8–11	(18)
1931	Lord Bill, 4–8–1	(10)
1932	Seraph Boy, 3–7–1	(14)
1933	Colorado Kid, 4–9–6	(15)
1934	Alcazar, 3–7–9	(12)
1935	Irongrey, 4–8–1	(10)
1936	William of Valence, 4–8–8	(20)
1937	Finalist, 5–9–7	(14)
1938	Pylon II, 5–8–1	(15)
1939	Bacardi, 5–7–12	(11)
1940–45	No race	
1946	Signalman, 3–8–4	(9)
1947	Avignon, 4–7–13	(6)
1948	Royal Tara, 5–8–13	(10)
1949	Impeccable, 5–9–12	(7)
1950	Krakatao, 4–9–7	(10)
1951	Grani, 5–7–11	(12)
1952	Sunny Brae, 4–8–5	(9)
1953	Hilltop, 4–8–12	(16)
1954	Prefect, 4–8–3	(15)
1955	Royal Maid, 4–7–3	(7)
1956	Athenien II, 3–8–5	(15)

1957 Rowland Ward (100–8) E. Mercer (£1,583) J. Jarvis, 5–9–0
2. Venus Slipper,   3. Athenien II. $\frac{3}{4}$, $1\frac{1}{2}$.   13 ran

1958 London Cry (5–1) A. Breasley (£1,485) Sir G. Richards, 4–8–12
2. Chief Barker,   3. Aorangi. $1\frac{1}{2}$, 2.   8 ran

1959 Aggressor (100–30) J. Lindley (£1,600) J. Gosden, 4–8–13
2. Pundit,   3. Royal Chief.   1, 2.   8 ran

1960 Rocky Royale (100–8) W. Carr (£1,574) D. Whelan, 4–9–1
2. Pandour,   3. Dairialatan.   2, 2.   15 ran

1961 Stupor Mundi (7–1) W. Carr (£1,566) C. Boyd-Rochfort, 4–8–9
2. Iron Blue,   3. Marshall Hall.   Nk, $\frac{3}{4}$.   13 ran

1962 Robson's Choice (8–1) A. Breasley (£2,016) E. Goddard, 6–8–4
2. Smuggler's Joy,   3. Don't Look.   Sht Hd, 2.   11 ran

1963 St Gulliver (4–1f) L. Piggott (£2,131) F. Armstrong, 4–9–2
2. Kingbenitch,   3. Smuggler's Joy.   3, $1\frac{1}{4}$.   15 ran

1964 Early to Rise (10–1) G. Lewis (£2,040) I. Balding, 4–8–7
2. St Gulliver,   3. Fine Bid. $1\frac{1}{2}$, $\frac{1}{2}$.   11 ran

1965 Tarqogan (8–1) W. Williamson (£2,051) S. McGrath, 5–9–1
2. Space King,   3. Concealdem.   3, Nk.   13 ran

1966 Polymint (20–1) R. Dicey (£1,979) J. Sutcliffe, 6–6–9
    2. Langley Park,   **3.** Pally.   2, Nk.   10 ran
1967 Midnight Marauder (8–1) J. Mercer (£1,860) J. Tree, 5–8–3
    2. Le Cordonnier,   **3.** Hotroy. $1\frac{1}{2}, \frac{3}{4}$.   11 ran
1968 Scottish Sinbad (100–6) R. Hutchinson (£1,820) J. Dunlop, 4–8–13
    2. Copsale,   **3.** Castle Yard.   Hd, Sht Hd.   11 ran

Race 211: STEWARDS' CUP
6 furlongs handicap. Goodwood. First run 1840

1900 Royal Flush, a–7–13	(19)	
1901 O'Donovan Rossa, 4–7–0	(28)	
1902 Mauvezin, 6–8–2	(23)	
1903 Dumbarton Castle, 3–7–4	(21)	
1904 Melayr, 3–6–9	(19)	
1905 Xeny, 4–7–9	(17)	
1906 Rocketter, 3–7–6	(13)	
1907 Romney, 3–6–3	(15)	
1908 Elmstead, 3–7–0	(18)	
1909 Mediant, 3–7–13	(21)	
1910 Golden Rod, 4–8–1	(21)	
1911 Braxted, 3–7–5	(19)	
1912 Golden Rod, 6–8–13	(21)	
1913 Lord Annandale, 3–6–10	(20)	
1914 Golden Sun, 4–8–12 and		
Lord Annandale, 4–7–9	(23)	

1915–18 No race

1919 King Sol, 5–7–0	(14)	
1920 Western Wave, 4–8–7	(21)	
1921 Service Kit, 4–6–12	(20)	
1922 Tetrameter, 5–7–7	(30)	
1923 Epinard, 3–8–6	(14)	
1924 Compiler, 4–7–9	(24)	
1925 Defiance, 4–7–8	(24)	
1926 Perhaps So, 5–8–1	(29)	
1927 Priory Park, 5–9–0	(24)	
1928 Navigator, 3–7–5	(16)	
1929 Fleeting Memory, 4–8–1	(19)	

1930 Le Phare, 4–8–1	(28)	
1931 Poor Lad, 4–7–11	(15)	
1932 Solenoid, 3–7–10	(21)	
1933 Pharacre, 4–7–5	(26)	
1934 Figaro, 4–8–5	(22)	
1935 Greenore, 6–8–8	(17)	
1936 Solerina, 4–8–11	(20)	
1937 Firozepore, 3–8–3	(30)	
1938 Harmachis, 5–7–6	(25)	
1939 Knight's Caprice, 4–8–6	(23)	
1940 No race		

[AT NEWMARKET]

1941 Valthema, 4–7–2	(15)

1942–45 No race

[AT GOODWOOD]

1946 Commissar, 6–7–12	(15)
1947 Closeburn, 3–8–10	(19)
1948 Dramatic, 3–7–7	(16)
1949 The Bite, 4–7–7	(21)
1950 First Consul, 4–8–13	(21)
1951 Sugar Bowl, 4–7–12	(21)
1952 Smokey Eyes, 5–8–10	(18)
1953 Palpitate, 4–7–13	(22)
1954 Ashurst Wonder, 4–6–11	(28)
1955 King Bruce, 4–8–11	(26)
1956 Matador, 3–9–2	(24)

1957 Arcandy (100–7) T. Gosling (£2,556) G. Beeby, 4–8–9
    2. Sargent,   **3.** Persuader.   2, $\frac{1}{2}$.   16 ran
1958 Epaulette (33–1) F. Durr (£2,569) W. O'Gorman, 7–9–0
    2. Logarithm,   **3.** Deauville.   1, $\frac{1}{2}$.   20 ran
1959 Tudor Monarch (25–1) G. Lewis (£2,744) W. Nightingall, 4–7–13
    2. Deer Leap,   **3.** St Elmo.   Nk, $1\frac{1}{2}$.   21 ran
1960 Monet (20–1) J. Lindley (£3,032) J. Tree, 3–8–5
    2. Deer Leap,   **3.** Hawa.   Sht Hd, $1\frac{1}{2}$.   18 ran

1961 Skymaster (100–7) A. Breasley (£3,032) G. Smyth, 3–8–12
    2. Deer Leap,   **3.** Klondyke Bill.   Sht Hd, 2.   22 ran
1962 Victorina (10–1f) W. Williamson (£3,164) P. Nelson, 3–8–9
    2. Bullrush,   **3.** Klondyke Bill.   Nk, ¾.   26 ran
1963 Creole (20–1) S. Smith (£3,147) J. Jarvis, 4–9–1
    2. Highroy,   **3.** Tumbrel.   Sht Hd, 1½.   25 ran
1964 Dunme (9–1jf) P. Cook (£3,708) R. Read, 5–7–12
    2. Weeper's Boy,   **3.** Prince of Orange. ½, 1½.   20 ran
1965 Potier (100–7) R. Hutchinson (£3,859) J. Jarvis, 3–8–5
    2. Ron,   **3.** Weeper's Boy.   ¾, Sht Hd.   20 ran
1966 Patient Constable (33–1) R. Reader (£3,932) R. Smyth, 3–7–7
    2. French Parade,   **3.** Top of the Pops. ½, 1.   25 ran
1967 Sky Diver (20–1) D. Cullen (£3,859) P. Payne-Gallwey, 4–7–5
    2. Welshman,   **3.** More Money. 1½, 1.   31 ran
1968 Sky Diver (100–6) T. Sturrock (£3,538) P. Payne-Gallwey, 5–7–6
    2. Spaniards Inn,   **3.** Gold Pollen.   Sht Hd, Nk.   18 ran

Race 212: GOODWOOD STAKES

2 miles 3 furlongs handicap. Goodwood. First run 1823

1900 Jiffy II, 5–7–9	(10)	1928 Arctic Star, 4–8–5	(19)
1901 Avidity, 5–7–6	(14)	1929 Clear Cash, 4–7–9	(14)
1902 Templemore, 4–7–8	(10)	1930 Joyous Greetings, 6–7–2	(18)
1903 Genius, 5–7–13	(10)	1931 Noble Star, 4–8–11	(14)
1904 Sandboy, 4–7–6	(9)	1932 Forum II, 5–6–8	(13)
1905 His Majesty, 4–8–3	(8)	1933 Prince Oxendon, 5–7–13	(19)
1906 Winwick, 4–6–13	(12)	1934 Claran, 5–7–13	(12)
1907 Royal Dream, 4–8–1	(11)	1935 Hoplite, 4–8–11	(14)
1908 Asticot, 5–6–12	(14)	1936 Avondale, 8–7–4	(16)
1909 Lagos, 4–8–6	(7)	1937 Epigram, 4–7–8	(19)
1910 Queen's Journal, 4–7–4	(11)	1938 Naval Display, 4–7–12 and
1911 Ignition, 3–6–4	(6)	Snake Lightning, 4–7–9	(11)
1912 Irish Marine, 4–8–1	(9)	1939 Valedictory, 4–7–13	(18)
1913 Washing Day, 4–7–5	(10)	1940–45 No race
1914 Collodion, 3–6–7	(14)	1946 Reynard Volant, 4–8–10	(6)
1915–18 No race		1947 Strathmore, 4–7–0	(11)
1919 Haki, a–9–0	(11)	1948 Auralia, 5–9–6	(15)
1920 Rowland, 4–6–13	(11)	1949 Harlech, 4–8–8	(10)
1921 Arravale, 6–6–13	(7)	1950 Strathspey, 5–9–0	(16)
1922 Flint Jack, 5–8–3	(6)	1951 Veuillin, 4–7–13	(11)
1923 Trossach Girl, 3–7–0	(9)	1952 French Design, 5–6–12	(8)
1924 London Cry, 5–8–8	(13)	1953 Papillio, 4–8–6	(12)
1925 Diapason, 4–8–10	(9)	1954 Osborne, 7–9–7	(13)
1926 Broken Faith, 9–7–2	(8)	1955 French Design, 8–8–7	(17)
1927 Try Try Again, 5–7–10	(13)	1956 Terrington, 5–6–10	(12)

1957 Persian Flag (13–2f) W. Carr (£1,761) W. Nightingall, 4–8–7
    2. Tickled Pink,   **3.** Combatant. $\frac{1}{2}$, 2.   15 ran
1958 Predominate (100–9) E. Smith (£1,718) T. Leader, 6–8–8
    2. Tuscar,   **3.** Festive.   6, $\frac{3}{4}$.   14 ran
1959 Predominate (3–1) E. Smith (£1,557) T. Leader, 7–9–5
    2. All Serene,   **3.** Papy.   1, Sht Hd.   7 ran
1960 Predominate (15–8f) E. Smith (£1,629) T. Leader, 8–9–5
    2. Freelight,   **3.** Grecian Granite. 4, 2.   10 ran
1961 Alcove (11–2) D. Smith (£1,620) J. F. Watts, 4–8–5
    2. Sunny Way,   **3.** Angazi.   8, 1$\frac{1}{2}$.   8 ran
1962 Golden Fire (13–2) D. Yates (£1,574) D. Marks, 4–7–10
    2. Avon's Pride,   **3.** Agreement. $\frac{3}{4}$, 1.   11 ran
1963 Golden Fire (10–1) D. Yates (£1,735) D. Marks, 5–8–6
    2. Acrophel,   **3.** Utrillo. $\frac{3}{4}$, 2.   18 ran
1964 Tree Leopard (100–8) J. Mercer (£1,574) W. Hern, 4–8–8
    2. Gold Aura,   **3.** Sea Leopard. $\frac{1}{2}$, 4.   11 ran
1965 Gold Aura (5–1) S. Clayton (£1,497) C. Boyd-Rochfort, 5–7–12
    2. Sea Leopard,   **3.** Tropical Sky.   1$\frac{1}{2}$, 2.   10 ran
1966 All Found (10–1) D. Maitland (£1,566) H. Blagrave, 4–7–6
    2. Persian Lancer,   **3.** Peter Piper.   Nk, 1$\frac{1}{2}$.   14 ran
1967 Tubalcain (8–1) G. Lewis (£1,380) E. Goddard, 6–8–13
    2. Drumlanrig,   **3.** Gaudy $\frac{3}{4}$, Nk.   12 ran
                                 Commodore.
1968 Acharacle (100–8) B. Taylor (£1,407) T. Leader, 4–8–7
    2. Ginger Boy,   **3.** Zaloba. $\frac{1}{2}$, 1$\frac{1}{2}$.   14 ran

Race 213: NEWS OF THE WORLD STAKES

1 mile 2 furlongs handicap. Goodwood. Three-year-olds

1962 Tamerlo (100–7) A. Breasley (£8,899) Sir G. Richards, 9–0
    2. Mystery,   **3.** Space King.   1$\frac{1}{2}$, 1$\frac{1}{2}$.   26 ran
1963 Fraxinus (25–1) D. Yates (£8,633) W. Wightman, 7–7
    2. Peter Piper,   **3.** Early to Rise.   Nk, $\frac{1}{2}$.   21 ran
1964 French Possession (20–1) D. Smith (£8,581) G. Brooke, 7–9
    2. Priddy Maid,   **3.** Cabouchon.   3, 2.   19 ran
1965 Super Sam (5–1) P. Robinson (£8,752) J. F. Watts, 7–9
    2. Royal Rubicon,   **3.** Convamore.   7, 3.   16 ran
1966 Le Cordonnier (100–7) G. Lewis (£8,567) S. Ingham, 9–2
    2. Swift Harmony,   **3.** Proconsul. $\frac{1}{2}$, 1$\frac{1}{2}$.   19 ran
1967 Sucaryl (5–6f) G. Moore (£7,993) N. Murless, 8–8
    2. Lexicon,   **3.** Tiber.   1$\frac{1}{2}$, 4.   12 ran
1968 Principal Boy (4–1f) E. Eldin (£7,662) J. M. Clayton, 8–1
    2. Cheval,   **3.** Delayed Tip.   Sht Hd, 1.   12 ran

Race 214: VAUX GOLD TANKARD

1 mile 6 furlongs 132 yards handicap. Redcar. Called Redcar Fifteen Hundred Handicap until 1959

1957 Staghound (13–2) N. McIntosh (£1,185) G. Boyd, 6–7–9
    2. Cannebiere,   **3.** Fifty-Fifty.   1, 1½.   11 ran
1958 Cannebiere (9–2jf) Donald Morris (£1,185) A. Barclay, 5–8–3
    2. Grand Stand,   **3.** Coxcomb.   3, 4.   9 ran
1959 Morecambe (7–2f) J. Sime (£8,460) S. Hall, 6–9–3
    2. Cannebiere,   **3.** Grand Stand.   ½, ¾.   18 ran
1960 Red Dragon (100–8) J. Sime (£10,460) N. Bertie, 5–8–13
    2. Eborneezer,   **3.** Light Horseman.   ½, 4.   15 ran
1961 Off Key (100–7) L. Piggott (£10,460) N. Murless, 4–8–5
    2. Avon's Pride,   **3.** Balaji.   Nk, Sht Hd.   16 ran
1962 MONTERRICO (5–1jf) R. P. Elliott (£10,460) H. Wragg, 3–7–9
    2. Sostenuto,   **3.** Panjandrum.   Sht Hd, 1½.   12 ran
1963 Espresso (7–1) W. Williamson (£10,460) H. Wragg, 5–9–9
    2. Tropical Sky,   **3.** Young Lochinvar.   Hd, Nk.   14 ran
1964 I Titan (3–1f) S. Clayton (£10,450) N. Murless, 3–8–3
    2. Espresso,   **3.** Cagirama.   Nk, 2½.   14 ran
1965 Atilla (3–1f) F. Durr (£10,764) H. Wragg, 4–7–13
    2. Twelfth Man,   **3.** Cagirama.   ¾, 6.   11 ran
1966 Salvo (15–1) E. Johnson (£8,470) H. Wragg, 3–6–9
    2. Allenheads,   **3.** Alcalde.   2, 2½.   19 ran
1967 Farm Walk (10–1) L. Brown (£5,199) P. Beasley, 5–7–11
    2. Chicago,   **3.** Red Rumour.   4, 1.   15 ran
1968 Quartette (6–1) R. Maddock (£5,675) T. Gosling, 4–7–10
    2. Frog,   **3.** Inyanga.   1, 6.   19 ran

Race 215: WILLIAM HILL GOLD CUP

1 mile handicap. Redcar

1959 Faultless Speech (11–8f) G. Lewis (£6,760) H. Wallington, 4–8–7
    2. King's Coup,   **3.** Babu.   1, 2.   14 ran
1960 Silver King (2–1f) J. Sime (£6,560) S. Hall, 4–8–8
    2. Bellisle,   **3.** Sanctum.   Sht Hd, ½.   17 ran
1961 Sanctum (8–1) F. Durr (£6,560) A. Smyth, 5–8–2
    2. King's Troop,   **3.** Smuggler's Joy.   Nk, ¾.   15 ran
1962 Songedor (100–8) T. Carter (£6,550) C. H. Pratt, 3–7–9
    2. Persian Wonder,   **3.** Fury Royal.   1½, Nk.   21 ran
1963 Campaign (10–1) P. Robinson (£6,550) J. Jarvis, 3–7–8
    2. Songedor,   **3.** Wrangle.   ¾, 2.   21 ran
1964 Passenger (8–1) L. Piggott (£6,540) P. Moore, 5–9–12
    2. Mandamus,   **3.** March Wonder.   ½, 2½.   13 ran

1965 Mandamus (8–1) J. Roe (£8,347) B. van Cutsem, 5–8–10
    2. Northern Deamon,   **3.** Hasty Cloud.   1½, Hd.   16 ran
1966 Corinto (7–1) R. Hutchinson (£8,025) H. Wragg, 3–7–11
    2. Mayville,   **3.** Double-U-Jay.   Sht Hd, Sht Hd. 14 ran
1967 Frankincense (6–1) G. Starkey (£6,586) J. Oxley, 3–8–5
    2. Supreme Sovereign,   **3.** Porcha.   ¾, 1½.   12 ran
1968 Straight Master (100–30f) W. Williamson (£5,789) G. Smyth, 4–8–6
    2. Petros,   **3.** Ashford Lea.   Hd, ¾.   11 ran

Race 216: NOTTINGHAM STEWARDS' HANDICAP
6 furlongs. Nottingham. Called Nottingham Stewards' Cup until 1966

1957 Camille (13–2) D. Smith (£1,846) J. Jarvis, 3–7–8
    2. Jackie's Kuda,   **3.** Anchovy.   ¾, 1.   4 ran
1958 Jacintha (5–2f) A. Russell (£1,927) W. Lyde, 7–8–0
    2. Anxious Lady,   **3.** Radiopye.   Hd, 1½.   10 ran
1959 Deer Leap (7–2f) E. Mercer (£1,906) J. Oxley, 3–8–2
    2. Accompanist,   **3.** Logarithm.   2, ¾.   11 ran
1960 Faint Hope (100–30) P. Povall (£2,049) E. Cousins, 8–7–4
    2. Tingle,   **3.** Charbon.   ¾, ¾.   7 ran
1961 Dawn Watch (9–1) H. Greenaway (£2,027) E. Cousins, 6–7–10
    2. Deer Leap,   **3.** Crisper.   Sht Hd, Sht Hd. 11 ran
1962 Creole (5–1) P. Robinson (£2,185) J. Jarvis, 3–8–1
    2. Julia's Hamlet,   **3.** Royal Jester.   1½, 2.   9 ran
1963 Bullrush (8–1) D. Smith (£2,749) G. Brooke, 4–7–10
    2. Miladdo,   **3.** Chalkey.   2, 1½.   18 ran
1964 Gallegos (13–2) S. Clayton (£2,529) W. Lyde, 3–8–2
    2. Irish Gambol,   **3.** No Argument.   3, Nk.   12 ran
1965 Dondeen (100–9) H. Greenaway (£2,433) J. Calvert, 4–9–5
    2. No Argument,   **3.** Gently.   3, Nk.   18 ran
1966 Creole (5–1jf) P. Cook (£886) J. Jarvis, 7–8–8
    2. Drakes Drum,   **3.** Arrest and Trial. 2½, ½.   11 ran
1967 Fleece (100–8) L. Brown (£2,764) M. W. Easterby, 4–8–8
    2. My Enigma,   **3.** Highland Melody. 2, 1.   16 ran
1968 Backgammon (8–1) L. Piggott (£2,522) K. Cundell, 5–9–9
    2. Fleece,   **3.** Cease Fire.   ¾, 2.   13 ran

Race 217: GREAT ST. WILFRED HANDICAP
6 furlongs. Ripon

1957 Roman Vale (11–8f) R. Armstrong (£1,185) J. Fawcus, 7–7–11
    2. Prairie Emblem,   **3.** Judicature.   2, 1½.   7 ran
1958 Kandy-Sugar (11–2) J. Etherington (£1,530) W. Bellerby, 3–8–13
    2. Magic Moment,   **3.** Blessing.   1, 1.   10 ran

1959 Golden Leg (8–1) G. Starkey (£1,880) M. Pope, 4–8–3
   2. Sufi,　　　　　　　　　　**3.** Mannion.　　　1½, 1.　　　13 ran
1960 Whistler's Daughter (9–2) N. McIntosh (£2,275) S. Hall, 3–7–8
   2. Faint Hope,　　　　　　　**3.** Helen Rosa.　　1, Hd.　　　12 ran
1961 Galivanter (4–5f) W. Carr (£2,275) W. Hern, 5–9–7
   2. Tudor Flash,　　　　　　　**3.** Brigg Fair.　　Hd, 5.　　　13 ran
1962 Whistling Sands (4–1f) P. Tulk (£2,275) E. Cousins, 4–8–8
   2. Satan,　　　　　　　　　　**3.** Janeat.　　　Nk, 1.　　　16 ran
1963 Matatina (5–6f) L. Piggott (£3,925) F. Armstrong, 3–8–9
   2. Printer,　　　　　　　　　**3.** Burning　　　1, 3.　　　10 ran
　　　　　　　　　　　　　　　　　　　Thoughts.
1964 Miladdo (9–2) P. Robinson (£3,894) E. Duffy, 5–7–11
   2. Creole,　　　　　　　　　　**3.** High Sun.　　3, Nk.　　　13 ran
1965 Monkey Palm (100–9) W. Carson (£3,885) F. Armstrong, 4–7–5
   2. High Sun,　　　　　　　　**3.** Dondeen.　　Hd, 3.　　　15 ran
1966 Royal Yacht (100–8) D. Cullen (£4,092) W. Holden, 5–7–3
   2. Comonisi,　　　　　　　　**3.** America.　　½, 3.　　　16 ran
1967 Gemini Six (9–4f) G. Sexton (£3,235) H. Wragg, 3–7–7
   2. Green Park,　　　　　　　**3.** Juries Act.　　½, 3.　　　14 ran
1968 Morgan's Pride (20–1) D. Coates (£3,224) S. Nesbitt, 4–7–1
   2. Florescence,　　　　　　　**3.** Petite Path.　　5, ½.　　　16 ran

Race 218: ROSE OF YORK HANDICAP

1 mile. York. *Weight-for-age race in 1966

1957 Counsel (100–8) J. Mercer (£2,700) R. J. Colling, 5–8–2
   2. River Line,　　　　　　　**3.** Fairy Stone.　　Sht Hd, 2.　　19 ran
1958 Legal Tie (10–1) A. Breasley (£3,540) P. Beasley, 3–8–3
   2. Pheidippides,　　　　　　**3.** Old King Cole.　　¾, 1.　　19 ran
1959 King's Coup (8–1) D. Greening (£2,523) M. H. Easterby, 6–8–4
   2. Stratus,　　　　　　　　　**3.** Kingroy.　　　½, 4.　　　16 ran
1960 Sanctum (10–1) A. Breasley (£2,675) A. Smyth, 4–8–12
   2. Nice Guy,　　　　　　　　**3.** Bellisle.　　　½, Sht Hd.　　21 ran
1961 Zanzibar (100–9) E. Smith (£2,690) J. Oxley, 6–9–7
   2. Arctic Express,　　　　　　**3.** Le Levanstell.　　Nk, Hd.　　19 ran
1962 Gay Casino (9–2f) A. Breasley (£2,680) P. Beasley, 3–8–1
   2. Smartie,　　　　　　　　　**3.** Adrasto.
　　(Honeymoor second, disqualified.) Original distances, Sht Hd, Nk, 1.　18 ran
1963 Solar Charge (11–2) G. Bougoure (£2,690) P. J. Prendergast, 5–8–4
   2. Songedor,　　　　　　　　**3.** Old Tom.　　　6, Hd.　　　18 ran
1964 Wrangle (100–6) J. Sime (£2,630) S. Hall, 7–8–6
   2. Bobsbest,　　　　　　　　**3.** Gay Casino.　　Nk, ½.　　　21 ran
1965 Le Garcon (5–1) A. Breasley (£2,492) J. Gosden, 4–8–2
   2. Mayville,　　　　　　　　　**3.** Wrangle.　　　Sht Hd, 1.　　13 ran

*1966 Tesco Boy (11–4) R. Hutchinson (£2,297) S. Ingham, 3 yrs
    2. Promontory,   **3.** Mayville.   1½, 2.   7 ran
1967 Giddaby (100–8) D. Maitland (£2,508) L. Hall, 4–8–0
    2. Danella,   **3.** Good Match.   1½, 1.   19 ran
1968 Petros (11–2) L. Piggott (£2,632) B. van Cutsem, 4–8–11
    2. Tomdoun,   **3.** Resolved.   4, 1½.   15 ran

Race 219: HAREWOOD HANDICAP
5 furlongs. York

1957 Appilow (25–1) J. Lynch (£1,295) W. Wharton, 5–6–3
    2. Clear River,   **3.** Beckfoot.   ½, ½.   11 ran
1958 Earnest Alice (4–1) P. Robinson (£1,325) S. Hall, 4–7–6
    2. Home Secretary,   **3.** Newton.   4, 1.   11 ran
1959 Thyra Lee (2–1f) D. Smith (£1,239) L. Hall, 3–7–8
    2. Abernicky,   **3.** Bleep-Bleep.   2, ½.   16 ran
1960 Sleepless Night (20–1) B. Lee (£1,200) G. Laurence, 6–6–11
    2. Bourbon,   **3.** Whistle Me.   1½, ½.   8 ran
1961 Granville Greta (100–30) B. Lee (£1,190) E. Davey, 4–8–3
    2. Easter Rock,   **3.** Barnie Seton.   Nk, Nk.   11 ran
1962 Dipper (5–1) P. Robinson (£1,254) J. Jarvis, 3–8–5
    2. Comet,   **3.** Minstrel King.   1½, Hd.   17 ran
1963 Silent Whistle (100–7) P. Robinson (£1,366) I. Walker, 5–7–10
    2. Comefast,   **3.** Master Mariner.   ½, 3.   17 ran
1964 High Flying (100–9) J. Lindley (£1,330) A. Budgett, 4–9–8
    2. Grey Panther,   **3.** Avro Jet.   1, ¾.   14 ran
1965 Roughlyn (11–2) E. Hide (£1,334) W. D. Francis, 4–9–5
    2. Soft Collar,   **3.** Wind Song.   Nk, Hd.   15 ran
1966 Celo (100–6) J. Mercer (£1,362) J. Calvert, 4–8–5
    2. Knobbled,   **3.** Spring Cabbage.   2½, 1½.   15 ran
1967 Quy (4–1f) J. Lindley (£1,005) R. Jarvis, 3–9–6
    2. Salan,   **3.** Spark.   Sht Hd, 2.   12 ran
1968 Fearless Lady (11–2) G. Duffield (£1,062) T. Waugh, 4–7–3
    2. Close Call,   **3.** Spring Cabbage.   1, 4.   10 ran

Race 220: EBOR HANDICAP
1 mile 6 furlongs. York. First run 1843

1900	Jiffy II, 5–8–4	(9)	**1906**	Golden Measure, 4–8–5	(12)
1901	Gyp, 6–8–5	(16)	**1907**	Wuffy, 4–7–12	(9)
1902	Wargrave, 4–8–2	(17)	**1908**	Rousay, 4–8–12	(4)
1903	McYardley, 5–7–9	(13)	**1909**	Dibs, 4–8–0	(12)
1904	War Wolf, 5–7–9	(10)	**1910**	Claretoi, 6–6–10	(14)
1905	The Page, 5–7–6	(12)	**1911**	Pillo, 6–8–9	(19)

1912 Election, 5–7–4 (10)
1913 Junior, 4–9–0 (12)
1914–18 No race
1919 Race Rock, a–7–7 (9)
1920 Iron Hand, 4–6–12 (11)
1921 March Along, 4–9–1 (20)
1922 Flint Jack, 5–8–9 (15)
1923 Flint Jack, 6–8–12 (8)
1924 Marvex, 4–8–5 (20)
1925 Chapeau, 5–7–6 (13)
1926 Pons Asinorum, 4–8–10 (15)
1927 Cap-a-Pie, 3–6–7 (16)
1928 Cinq-a-Sept, 4–8–4 (14)
1929 Bonny Boy II, 5–8–1 (13)
1930 Gentleman's Relish, 4–7–5
    and Coaster, 4–8–0 (13)
1931 Brown Jack, 7–9–5 (19)
1932 Cat o'Nine Tails, 5–7–8 (19)
1933 Dictum, 5–7–4 (11)
1934 Alcazar, 3–8–5 (14)
1935 Museum, 3–7–13 (12)
1936 Penny Royal, 3–7–9 (14)

1937 Weathervane, 4–7–10 (17)
1938 Foxglove II, 3–8–1 (12)
1939 Owenstown, 5–8–8 (12)
1940–42 No Race

[AT PONTEFRACT]
1943 Yorkshire Hussar, 4–8–8 (19)
1944 The Kernal, 4–7–8 (14)

[AT YORK]
1945 Wayside Inn, 3–8–6 (14)
1946 Foxtrot, 3–7–13 (13)
1947 Procne, 4–8–4 (11)
1948 Donino, 4–8–12 (20)
1949 Miraculous Atom, 5–8–11 (16)
1950 Cadzow Oak, 4–7–12 (21)
1951 Bob, 4–6–12 (25)
1952 Signification, 3–7–12 (15)
1953 Norooz, 4–8–4 (21)
1954 By Thunder!, 3–6–12 (22)
1955 Hyperion Kid, 3–7–2 (25)
1956 Donald, 3–7–10 (17)

1957 Morecambe (100–8) J. Sime (£10,215) S. Hall, 4–7–9
    2. HORNBEAM,   3. Star Prince.   ½, 2.   30 ran
1958 Gladness (5–1f) L. Piggott (£10,215) M. V.O'Brien, 5–9–7
    2. Woodside Terrace,   3. Owen Glendower. 6, 2.   25 ran
1959 Primera (6–1) L. Piggott (£10,093) N. Murless, 5–9–0
    2. Water Wings,   3. Eborneezer.   1½, 3.   21 ran
1960 Persian Road (18–1) G. Moore (£10,238) J. Tree, 5–8–4
    2. Water Wings,   3. New Brig.   ½, ¾.   21 ran
1961 DIE HARD (11–2f) L. Piggott (£10,040) M. V. O'Brien, 4–8–9
    2. Tudor Period,   3. Utrillo.   2, 1.   21 ran
1962 Sostenuto (9–1) Donald Morris (£10,089) W. Elsey, 4–8–10
    2. Cracksman,   3. Le Prince.   8, Nk.   18 ran
1963 Partholon (100–6) J. Sime (£10,337) T. Shaw, 3–7–8
    2. Arctic Vale,   3. Best Song.   Hd, 1½.   22 ran
1964 Proper Pride (28–1) D. Smith (£10,209) W. Wharton, 5–7–11
    2. Cassim,   3. Mahbub Aly.   ¾, 3.   20 ran
1965 Twelfth Man (6–1jf) P. Cook (£10,419) H. Wragg, 4–7–5
    2. Alcalde,   3. Valoroso.   1½, 3.   25 ran
1966 Lomond (100–8) E. Eldin (£10,258) R. Jarvis, 6–9–2
    2. Valoroso,   3. Mehari.   Sht Hd, 1½.   23 ran
1967 Ovaltine (100–8) E. Johnson (£8,027) J. F. Watts, 3–7–0
    2. Hermes,   3. Bunker.   1½, 2.   22 ran
1968 Alignment (9–1) E. Johnson (£8,526) W. Elsey, 3–7–8
    2. Tiber,   3. Quartette.   Nk, 2½.   20 ran

Race 221: MELROSE HANDICAP
1 mile 6 furlongs. York. Three-year-olds

1957 Hesiod (8–1) E. Mercer (£1,635) W. Smyth, 8–12
    2. Eiger,   **3.** Nectar.   Sht Hd, ½.   19 ran
1958 Persian Road (100–8) E. Mercer (£1,620) J. Tree, 8–2
    2. Petty France,   **3.** Arctic Gittell.   2, 3.   14 ran
1959 Domesday (10–1) E. Mercer (£1,271) J. Jarvis, 8–1
    2. Saphira,   **3.** Gaymoss.   2, 2.   15 ran
1960 Brocade Slipper (8–1) J. Mercer (£1,364) R. J. Colling, 8–4
    2. Menelek,   **3.** Avon's Pride.   5, 6.   20 ran
1961 Persian Lancer (5–1jf) A. Breasley (£1,298) Sir G. Richards, 8–3
    2. Dictionary,   **3.** Winning Bid.   ½, 4.   15 ran
1962 Lametta (100–7) F. Durr (£1,436) A. Cooper, 8–0
    2. Golden Oriole,   **3.** Phaethusa.   ½, 1.   17 ran
1963 Tree Leopard (100–8) J. Mercer (£1,482) W. Hern, 9–0
    2. Linnet Lane,   **3.** Marcourt.   ½, 5.   22 ran
1964 Nanda Devi (5–1) D. Cullen (£1,622) W. Elsey, 7–3
    2. Celtic King,   **3.** Romp Home.   ¾, Nk.   18 ran
1965 PROVOKE (9–4f) J. Mercer (£1,442) W. Hern, 8–11
    2. Santa Vimy,   **3.** Banyan.   Hd, 6.   19 ran
1966 Major Oak (100–9) B. Connorton (£1,530) R. Jarvis, 7–12
    2. Showman's Fair,   **3.** Pick Me Up.   2½, 5.   21 ran
1967 Hipster (100–30f) J. Lindley (£1,071) W. Hern, 8–10
    2. Right Wheel,   **3.** Monte Carlo.   2½, 1.   13 ran
1968 Twiberry (100–9) F. Durr (£1,210) R. Smyth, 8–0
    2. Mustwyn,   **3.** Mad Hatter.   Sht Hd, 1½.   18 ran

Race 222: NORTHERN GOLDSMITHS' HANDICAP
1 mile. Newcastle. Three-year-olds

1961 Dock Green (7–1) G. Littlewood (£1,743) G. Barling, 8–9
    2. Foxstar,   **3.** Alba Rock.   Sht Hd, ¾.   16 ran
1962 Sovereign Star (20–1) B. Connorton (£1,737) W. Gray, 8–5
    2. Tom Cat,   **3.** Heiress.   2, Sht Hd.   13 ran
1963 Jambo (10–1) H. Greenaway (£1,668) W. Elsey, 7–11
    2. Merry Quip,   **3.** Brothertoft.   ½, ¾.   12 ran
1964 Maria Gabriella (100–7) E. Hide (£1,633) W. Elsey, 8–0
    2. Gloomy Portal,   **3.** Irish Rhythm.   Sht Hd, 2.   14 ran
1965 Northern Deamon (7–1) B. Connorton (£1,639) W. Gray, 9–10
    2. Unity,   **3.** Take the Plunge.   1, 1.   16 ran
1966 Double-U-Jay (9–4f) J. Lindley (£3,056) J. Winter, 9–1
    2. Red Swan,   **3.** Corinto.   8, 1½.   13 ran
1967 Resilience II (7–4f) B. Taylor (£2,512) H. Leader, 8–8
    2. Pennant,   **3.** Common Pond.   1, 5.   13 ran

1968 Mycropolis (20–1) D. Coates (£2,585) D. Williams, 7–2
    2. Diddler,   **3.** Pettyless.   1½, 1.   9 ran

Race 223: STEVE DONOGHUE APPRENTICE HANDICAP

1 mile 4 furlongs. Epsom. Run over 1 mile 110 yards until 1958

1957 Heavens Bequest (5–1) B. Mayne (£299) C. Mitchell, 5–6–6
    2. No Worry,   **3.** Aidos.   ½, Nk.   7 ran
1958 Buffer (5–2f) T. Stringer (£846) P. Hastings-Bass, 4–8–1
    2. Caught Out,   **3.** Listoke Invader.   1½, Nk.   11 ran
1959 Sveltana (100–7) A. Klimscha (£992) F. Armstrong, 4–6–10
    2. Tarquinian,   **3.** Glenborne.   3, 1.   9 ran
1960 Scaphander (6–1) B. Jones (£1,490) J. Oxley, 6–7–0
    2. Roxburgh,   **3.** Sveltana.   ¾, 6.   14 ran
1961 Caught Out (9–1) G. Foster (£1,763) G. Todd, 9–8–8
    2. Top 'C',   **3.** Dante's Inferno.   1½, 1½.   19 ran
1962 Induna (100–8) A. Kimberley (£1,682) Sir G. Richards, 9–9–4
    2. Kings Secret,   **3.** Caught Out.   1½, ¾.   13 ran
1963 Sable Skinflint (7–1) R. Styles (£1,639) W. Nightingall, 5–6–13
    2. Caught Out,   **3.** Singer.   6, 6.   5 ran
1964 Caught Out (5–1) G. T. Foster (£1,448) G. Todd, 12–8–3
    2. Rascasse,   **3.** Nahum.   ½, ½.   14 ran
1965 Cuillins (100–8) D. Maitland (£1,359) G. Smyth, 4–6–11
    2. Damredub,   **3.** Take Heart.   ½, 2.   8 ran
1966 Leadendale Lady (5–1) D. Maitland (£1,368) G. Smyth, 5–7–3
    2. Noirmont Buoy,   **3.** Le Dauphin.   ½, 3.   13 ran
1967 Resistance (3–1f) M. Haines (£1,183) J. Sirett, 5–8–3
    2. Gold Aura,   **3.** Q.C.   2, 1½.   8 ran
1968 Ulster Prince (9–1) M. Day (£1,188) C. Mitchell, 10–6–13
    2. Royal Rubicon,   **3.** Colonel Imp.   1½, 2.   6 ran

Race 224: RIPON ROWELS HANDICAP

1 mile. Ripon. Three-year-olds

1958 Offspring (5–4f) S. Clayton (£785) W. Hern, 8–11
    2. Hard and Sharp, **3.** Glendawn.   1¼, ½.   10 ran
1959 Scylla (100–8) P. Boothman (£1,205) G. Armstrong, 7–11
    2. Gallant Scholar, **3.** Pedlar's Fair.   3, 1½.   8 ran
1960 Mountain King (5–1) G. Littlewood (£1,208) E. Carr, 8–4
    2. Sind,   **3.** Buchan   Sht Hd, Nk.   10 ran
                                 Hummlie.
1961 Deton (3–1f) J. Sime (£1,500) S. Hall, 8–11
    2. Calf Love,   **3.** Nimbroke.   Hd, 5.   12 ran

1962 Miss D (9–2) F. Durr (£1,930) H. Wragg, 7–13
    2. Bewildroom,   3. Brother.   1½, Nk.   20 ran
1963 Yellow Sovereign (13–8f) J. Mercer (£2,280) W. Hern, 8–11
    2. Uhuru,   3. Tierra del Fuego. Nk, Sht Hd.   11 ran
1964 Lobitos (5–1) J. Sime (£2,104) S. Hall, 7–13
    2. Kentra,   3. Toughest.   Nk, 1.   7 ran
1965 Raybelle (15–2) L. Pinder (£2,092) S. Hall, 6–12
    2. Baranof,   3. Mirella.   Sht Hd, ½.   12 ran
1966 Marandis (6–1) B. Raymond (£1,967) H. Cottrill, 8–10
    2. Dunmore Lass II,   3. Selvedge.   ¾, 3.   9 ran
1967 Sir Herbert (4–1) J. Etherington (£1,888) M. H. Easterby, 8–7
    2. Burning Bright,   3. Copper's   ½, Nk.   9 ran
                                      Evidence.
1968 Paddy Me (9–4f) F. Durr (£1,924) P. Davey, 9–7
    2. Orchard Boy,   3. Fragrant Rose.   ½, 4.   11 ran

Race 225: LANARK SILVER BELL

1 mile 4 furlongs handicap. Lanark

1957 Cannebiere (6–1) N. Pearson (£1,052) A. Barclay, 4–8–5
    2. Orinthia,   3. Obadan.   2, 4.   11 ran
1958 Cannebiere (100–30f) Donald Morris (£908) A. Barclay, 5–8–6
    2. Antagonist,   3. No Comment.   6, ¾.   11 ran
1959 No Comment (4–1jf) A. Russell (£1,774) G. Boyd, 6–8–11
    2. Paul Jones,   3. Cannebiere.   Hd, 2.   10 ran
1960 Welsh Border (10–1) C. Parkes (£2,030) C. F. Elsey, 3–7–3
    2. Dalnamein,   3. Bognie Brae.   2, 4.   11 ran
1961 Falls of Cruachan (4–1f) A. Russell (£1,850) G. Boyd, 5–9–0
    2. Porky,   3. Variety King.   ½, ½.   9 ran
1962 Lanesborough (2–1f) J. Sime (£1,922) S. Hall, 3–8–8
    2. Drumbeg,   3. Le Prince.   2, ¾.   11 ran
1963 Hejaz (7–2) R. Maddock (£2,059) F. Armstrong, 3–7–11
    2. Peter Piper,   3. Porky.   Sht Hd, 1.   15 ran
1964 Casting Vote (evens f) J. Sime (£2,602) S. Hall, 4–8–9
    2. Cool Breeze,   3. Stargate.   10, 1½.   7 ran
1965 Current Speech (evens f) E. Larkin (£1,632) S. Hall, 4–9–5
    2. Inyanga,   3. Wild Flame.   1, 8.   8 ran
1966 Parcel Post (11–4) A. Barclay (£1,663) A. Thomas, 4–7–7
    2. Desacre,   3. Garland Knight.   2½, 2½.   9 ran
1967 Voldemo (7–4f) E. Larkin (£1,383) R. Peacock, 3–8–1
    2. Kentra,   3. Inyanga.   3, ¾.   10 ran
1968 Al-'Alawi (100–9) G. Kyle (£1,327) T. Robson, 5–7–11
    2. Lady Anna,   3. Old Sugar.   ¾, ¾.   10 ran

Race 226: GREAT YORKSHIRE HANDICAP

1 mile 6 furlongs 132 yards. Doncaster

1957 Induna (13–2) J. Purtell (£1,162) N. Cannon, 4–8–12
    2. Staghound,   **3.** Magnetic North. 4, 3.   10 ran
1958 Snow Leopard (4–1) J. Mercer (£1,132) R. J. Colling, 4–8–6
    2. Cannebiere,   **3.** Woodside   3, 3.   5 ran
                                     Terrace.
1959 Persian Road (4–11f) J. Lindley (£1,145) J. Tree, 4–8–12
    2. Tudor Style,   **3.** Petticoat Pocket. 4, 4.   3 ran
1960 Poetic Licence (13–2) R. Hutchinson (£2,156) H. Cottrill, 4–7–11
    2. Sabot,   **3.** Induna.   5, 2.   9 ran
1961 Tudor Period (11–4f) A. Breasley (£2,118) G. Smyth, 4–8–11
    2. No Saint,   **3.** Utrillo.   Nk, 1.   15 ran
1962 Tudor Tale (8–1) L. Piggott (£2,198) H. Cottrill, 4–9–0
    2. Princely Portion,   **3.** Optimistic.   Sht Hd, 3.   11 ran
1963 Credo (13–2) J. Roe (£2,313) P. J. Prendergast, 3–7–9
    2. Voivode,   **3.** Lomond.   4, 2.   12 ran
1964 Philemon (100–8) E. Smith (£2,156) B. van Cutsem, 4–8–2
    2. Arrigle Valley,   **3.** Mahbub Aly.   1½, ¾.   12 ran
1965 New Liskeard (100–8) G. Cadwaladr (£2,091) E. Cousins, 4–7–12
    2. Gyroscope,   **3.** Mintmaster.   2, 1½.   12 ran
1966 Farm Walk (9–4f) J. Sime (£2,156) P. Beasley, 4–7–8
    2. Bunker,   **3.** Kathyanga.   1, 3.   8 ran
1967 Bunker (7–4f) G. Moore (£1,761) N. Murless, 4–9–8
    2. Wallaroo,   **3.** Bugle Boy.   4, 1½.   9 ran
1968 Inyanga (9–2) D. Coates (£1,660) G. N. Robinson, 7–7–9
    2. National Gallery,   **3.** Home Park.   4, 5.   4 ran

Race 227: DONCASTER HANDICAP

1 mile. Doncaster. Called Doncaster High-weight Handicap until 1959

1957 Tudor Jinks (11–2) A. Breasley (£598) M. Feakes, 5–9–2
    2. King's Coup,   **3.** River Line.   3, ¾.   7 ran
1958 Amos (10–1) P. Boothman (£1,073) S. Mercer, 4–8–1
    2. Sunstart,   **3.** King's Coup.   4, Hd.   9 ran
1959 Small Slam (7–2) R. Singer (£1,081) G. Barling, 4–7–6
    2. Master Nicky,   **3.** Sunstart.   ½, 1½.   7 ran
1960 Blast (9–2f) L. Piggott (£1,183) A. Budgett, 3–8–12
    2. Kilrane,   **3.** Pheidippides.   3, ¾.   16 ran
1961 Miss Caroline (3–1) D. Smith (£1,086) H. Wragg, 4–7–12
    2. Monawin,   **3.** Guitarist.   ¾, 3.   6 ran
1962 Marche d'Or (100–7) G. Lewis (£1,353) H. Nicholson, 4–8–13
    2. Honeymoor,   **3.** TIME GREINE. 1, Nk.   13 ran

1963 Breck Road (100–8) N. McIntosh (£1,092) E. Weymes, 4–7–0
 2. Bobsbest,   **3.** Copper Horse. 1, 1. 13 ran
1964 Heartburn (7–1) C. Parkes (£1,350) W. Gray, 4–7–9
 2. Breck Road,   **3.** Yellow Sovereign.
             Sht Hd, Sht Hd. 10 ran
1965 Foxford Boy (11–4f) P. Cook (£1,272) H. Blackshaw, 4–7–7
 2. Bobsbest,   **3.** Aberdeen. ½, 1½. 7 ran
1966 Crosby Don (33–1) G. Sexton (£1,346) J. Calvert, 6–7–4
 2. Vital Issue,   **3.** Traffic Leader. ¾, ½. 19 ran
1967 Common Pond (100–30f) D. Letherby (£1,300) M. W. Easterby, 3–7–8
 2. Golden Mean,   **3.** Queen's Lane. 1, Sht Hd. 12 ran
1968 Starboard Watch (4–1jf) P. Tulk (£1,291) G. Harwood, 4–7–11
 2. Kushi,   **3.** Tudor Bar. Nk, Hd. 9 ran

Race 228: PORTLAND HANDICAP
5 furlongs 152 yards. Doncaster. First run 1855

1900	Lucknow, 5–7–4	(15)	1930	Polar Bear, 3–7–2	(18)
1901	Dieudonne, 6–8–0	(18)	1931	Xandover, 4–9–7	(11)
1902	Gladwin, 3–6–3	(23)	1932	Polar Bear, 5–8–8	(22)
1903	Nabot, 4–7–13	(22)	1933	Valkyrie, 4–7–5	(20)
1904	Santry, 3–7–13	(17)	1934	Rosemary's Pet, 5–8–12	(16)
1905	Xeny, 4–8–12	(18)	1935	Shalfleet, 4–9–7	(23)
1906	Nero, 3–6–5	(16)	1936	Shalfleet, 5–9–2	(23)
1907	Woolley, 5–6–7	(20)	1937	Carissa, 3–8–3	(25)
1908	The Welkin, 4–7–9	(20)	1938	The Drummer, 6–7–3	(27)
1909	Americus Girl, 4–8–13	(17)	**1939–40**	No race	
1910	Ballaton, a–8–6	(21)			
1911	Stolen Kiss, 4–8–0	(21)		**[AT NEWMARKET]**	
1912	Wethers Well, 4–9–1	(16)	1941	Comatas, 4–8–11	(15)
1913	Hornet's Beauty, 5–9–9	(11)			
1914	Flying Orb, 3–7–11	(17)		**[AT DONCASTER]**	
1915–18	No race		**1942–45**	No race	
1919	Irish Elegance, 4–10–2	(13)	1946	The Shah, 4–7–5	(14)
1920	Pelops, 3–7–12	(17)	1947	Good View, 5–8–0	(17)
1921	Glanmerin, 5–9–5	(14)	1948	Gold Mist, 3–7–12	(18)
1922	Two Step, 3–8–10	(14)	1949	Le Lavandou, 5–7–7	(28)
1923	Polydipsia, 6–8–5	(8)	1950	Paramount, 4–8–9	(19)
1924	Heverswood, 3–8–12	(14)	1951	Reminiscence, 4–8–10	(25)
1925	Diomedes, 3–9–2	(22)	1952	Stephen Paul, 4–9–3	(20)
1926	Sunstone, 5–8–0	(19)	1953	Reminiscence, 6–8–8	(29)
1927	Mayrian, 4–6–7	(19)	1954	Vilmoray, 4–9–0	(25)
1928	Tag End, 4–9–0	(19)	1955	Princely Gift, 4–9–4	(12)
1929	Tag End, 5–9–5	(10)	1956	Epaulette, 5–8–2	(19)

1957 Refined (9–1) D. Smith (£2,541) P. J. Prendergast, 3–8–10
 2. Camille,   **3.** Bowerchalke, 1, Nk. 18 ran

1958 Welsh Abbot (100–9) S. Clayton (£3,276) W. Nightingall, 3–9–2
    2. Idler,   **3.** Clear River.   5, Sht Hd.   14 ran
1959 New World (25–1) D. Greening (£3,183) G. Balding, 6–7–3
    2. Right Boy,   **3.** March Alone.   ¾, 2.   11 ran
1960 Accompanist (7–1) D. W. Morris (£3,089) F. Maxwell, 5–7–6
    2. Bleep-Bleep,   **3.** Faint Hope.   ½, ¾.   12 ran
1961 Winna (100–8) C. Parkes (£3,183) H. Wragg, 4–7–2
    2. Deer Leap,   **3.** Daisy Belle.   ½, 1½.   16 ran
1962 Harmon (9–1) A. Breasley (£3,472) P. Beasley, 3–8–2
    2. Prince Tor,   **3.** Atishoo.   ¾, 3.   18 ran
1963 Marcher (100–6) R. Hutchinson (£3,497) D. Hanley, 3–8–9
    2. Comefast,   **3.** Janeat.   2, Nk.   20 ran
1964 Comefast (9–1) E. Hide (£3,353) J. Vickers, 5–7–13
    2. High Flying,   **3.** High Sun.   Sht Hd, ½.   17 ran
1965 Go Shell (100–7) D. Smith (£3,018) B. van Cutsem, 3–8–7
    2. Compensation,   **3.** High Sun.   Nk, ½.   14 ran
1966 Audrey Joan (20–1) A. Barclay (£3,243) E. Cousins, 3–7–3
    2. Close Call,   **3.** Forlorn River.   1½, Hd.   21 ran
1967 Florescence (100–9) W. Williamson (£2,593) F. Armstrong, 3–8–13
    2. Forlorn River,   **3.** Go Shell.   Hd, 1.   15 ran
1968 Gold Pollen (11–4f) E. Johnson (£2,477) R. Jarvis, 3–7–7
    2. Polistina,   **3.** Charicles.   ¾, ¾.   12 ran

Race 229: NEWBURY AUTUMN CUP

2 miles handicap. Newbury

ABT 2M 1F		
1906 The White Knight, 3–7–11	(7)	
1907 The Page, 8–7–13	(9)	
1908 Maya, 4–6–9	(11)	
1909 Bridge of Earn, 3–7–0	(9)	
1910 Admiral Toga III, 6–7–6	(9)	
1911 Royal Realm, 6–8–8	(12)	
1912 Balscadden, 5–8–2	(7)	
1913 Balscadden, 6–8–7	(12)	
1914 Abandoned		
1915 Abandoned		
1916 Aboukir, 5–7–11	(12)	
1917–18 No race		
1919 Silver Bridge, 4–7–4	(8)	
1920 Aris, 5–7–7	(6)	
1921 Yutoi, 4–8–2	(12)	
1922 Norseman, 3–7–5	(9)	
1923 Ceinturon, 5–8–7	(14)	
1924 Diapason, 3–6–12	(11)	
1925 Seradella, 3–6–9	(11)	
1926 Try Try Again, 4–6–12	(8)	
1927 Lightning Artist 4–7–8	(12)	
1928 Troubadour, 3–7–0	(8)	
1929 Old Orkney, 5–9–0 and		
Show Girl, 3–6–4	(9)	
1930 Brumeux, 5–7–13	(13)	
1931 Sandals, 4–7–3	(15)	
1932 Roi de Paris, 4–7–9	(13)	
1933 Loosestrife, 4–7–9	(13)	
1934 Enfield, 3–7–5	(16)	
1935 Cecil, 4–9–0	(20)	
1936 Coup de Roi, 4–7–10	(14)	
1937 Severino, 4–8–2 and		
Dytchley, 4–8–9	(19)	
1938 Pylon II, 5–8–3	(12)	
1939–40 No race		
1941 Germanicus, 5–8–5	(9)	
1942–51 No race		

2M

1952	Absolve, 4–8–8	(15)	1954 Lepidoptic, 4–9–7	(12)
1953	Flighty Frances, 5–8–10	(15)	1955 Dragon Fly, 4–7–0	(11)
			1956 Straight Lad, 6–8–2	(12)

1957 Maelsheachlainn (6–1) W. Carr (£1,557) C. Boyd-Rochfort, 4–9–0
    2. Gads Hill,   3. Lightkeeper. $\frac{3}{4}$, 2.   10 ran
1958 Abandoned
1959 Red Dragon (9–2) A. Breasley (£1,727) N. Bertie, 4–9–3
    2. Bali Ha'i III,   3. Lacydon. $\frac{1}{2}$, 3.   13 ran
1960 Tarquinian (100–30) T. Stringer (£1,557) G. Todd, 5–7–9
    2. Archie,   3. Polar Way.   3, 15.   6 ran
1961 Optimistic (100–30f) D. W. Morris (£1,617) C. Boyd-Rochfort, 4–7–6
    2. Farrney Fox,   3. Prolific and   3, $\frac{3}{4}$.   11 ran
                        3. Sunny Way.
1962 Rainstorm (100–6) B. Raymond (£1,630) W. Stephenson, 5–7–6
    2. Orchardist,   3. Sublime.   3, 2.   10 ran
1963 Acrophel (11–4f) G. Lewis (£3,058) P. Hastings-Bass, 4–8–9
    2. Sublime,   3. Iron Blue.   Sht Hd, 2.   11 ran
1964 Ruantallan (6–1) J. Mercer (£2,947) W. Hern, 3–8–5
    2. Turf,   3. Chinese Lacquer. 1$\frac{1}{2}$, 4.   14 ran
1965 Abletai (5–1) J. Murtagh (£2,859) W. Byrne, 7–8–4
    2. Gold Aura,   3. Armagnac   2, Nk.   13 ran
                        Monarch.
1966 Salvo (8–1) G. Sexton (£2,874) H. Wragg, 3–7–4
    2. Mehari,   3. Tatarin.   1$\frac{1}{2}$, 6.   14 ran
1967 Major Rose (100–8) W. Jesse (£2,366) H. Price, 5–7–6
    2. Landigou,   3. Bric-Brac.   Nk, 5.   12 ran
1968 Abandoned

Race 230: AYR GOLD CUP

6 furlongs handicap. Ayr

1935	Greenore, 6–9–3	(14)	1949 Irish Dance, 6–9–1	(16)
1936	Marmaduke Jinks, 4–6–13	(15)	1950 First Consul, 4–9–7	(17)
1937	Daytona, 4–9–0	(19)	1951 Fair Seller, 5–9–4	(15)
1938	Old Reliance, 3–9–2	(13)	1952 Vatellus, 4–8–7	(13)
1939–45	No race		1953 Blue Butterfly, 4–8–9	(16)
1946	Royal Charger, 4–9–7	(19)	1954 Orthopaedic, 3–8–1	(18)
1947	Kilbelin, 4–7–13	(12)	1955 Hook Money, 4–7–11	(10)
1948	Como, 6–8–9	(9)	1956 Precious Heather, 4–7–7	(16)

1957 Jacintha (100–7) E. Larkin (£2,109) W. E. Lyde, 6–7–7
    2. Petigold,   3. Libator. $\frac{3}{4}$, Sht Hd.   17 ran
1958 Rhythmic (20–1) F. Durr (£3,387) W. Dutton, 3–8–5
    2. Golden Gittell,   3. Earl Marshal. Sht Hd, Sht Hd.   22 ran
1959 Whistling Victor (7–1) J. Sime (£3,463) G. Laurence, 3–7–8
    2. Faint Hope,   3. Deer Leap.   Nk, 3.   16 ran

1960 Dawn Watch (100–9) C. Parkes (£3,468) E. Cousins, 5–7–2
    2. Faint Hope,   **3.** Whistling Victor. 2, Nk.   23 ran
1961 Klondyke Bill (100–8) E. Smith (£3,509) C. J. Benstead, 3–8–7
    2. Bourbon,   **3.** Deer Leap. $1\frac{1}{2}$, $1\frac{1}{2}$.   17 ran
1962 Janeat (25–1) B. Henry (£3,715) A. Vasey, 3–7–11
    2. La Belle,   **3.** Dolau.   2, 2.   25 ran
1963 Egualita (10–1jf) F. Durr (£5,027) S. Hall, 3–8–0
    2. Field Master,   **3.** Light of the Road, 4, Nk.   18 ran
1964 Compensation (10–1) P. Robinson (£5,479) E. Lambton, 5–8–10
    2. Wiljotur,   **3.** Mayville.   3, Sht Hd.   18 ran
1965 Kamundu (100–8) G. Cadwaladr (£5,529) E. Cousins, 3–8–1
    2. Printer,   **3.** Creole. $2\frac{1}{2}$, $1\frac{1}{2}$.   20 ran
1966 Milesius (25–1) N. McIntosh (£5,875) G. Boyd, 4–7–12
    2. Top of the Pops,   **3.** Dondeen.   Sht Hd, 1.   24 ran
1967 Be Friendly (100–8) G. Lewis (£4,791) C. Mitchell, 3–8–9
    2. Go Shell,   **3.** Relian.   2, 1.   33 ran
1968 Petite Path (100–7) J. Higgins (£4,429) R. Mason, 4–7–6
    2. Saratoga Skiddy,   **3.** Spaniards Inn.   2, $\frac{1}{2}$.   21 ran

Race 231: IRISH CAMBRIDGESHIRE

1 mile handicap. Curragh

1957 Courts Appeal (3–1f) John Power (£1,065) M. V. O'Brien, 3–8–2
    2. Darn,   **3.** No Complaint.   5, 3.   18 ran
1958 Lavella (100–7) W. Berg (£1,035) D. J. Hayes, 3–7–7
    2. Bright Talk,   **3.** Courts Appeal.   3, 5.   18 ran
1959 Appreciation (10–1) J. Roe (£1,065) S. McGrath, 3–7–2
    2. Ballyogan Queen,   **3.** Check Abbess.   Sht Hd, 4.   18 ran
1960 Lavella (9–2f) W. Berg (£1,017) D. J. Hayes, 5–8–8
    2. Sword,   **3.** Perhapsburg.   6, 2.   26 ran
1961 Travel Light (10–1) G. Bougoure (£1,026) M. V. O'Brien, 3–8–12
    2. Che Bella,   **3.** Reliant.   Sht Hd, 5.   22 ran
1962 Che Bella (4–1f) N. Brennan (£1,042) E. M. Quirke, 5–7–12
    2. Lully Boy,   **3.** Captain's Yarn.   3, Nk.   18 ran
1963 Red Slipper (100–7) M. Kennedy (£1,109) Sir Hugh Nugent, 3–8–13
    2. Miss Cossie,   **3.** Lully Boy.   Nk, 2.   19 ran
1964 Belle Rosheen (100–7) A. C. McGarrity (£1,132) D. Ruttle, 4–6–11
    2. Courtwell,   **3.** Talgo Abbess.   Sht Hd, $2\frac{1}{2}$.   21 ran
1965 Courtwell (100–8) P. Vaughan (£1,093) C. L. Weld, 4–8–9
    2. Solwezi,   **3.** Queen's   Nk, $2\frac{1}{4}$.   27 ran
                Messenger.
1966 Willya (40–1) C. Roche (£1,060) P. Kearns, 4–7–1
    2. Mabrouk,   **3.** Talgo Abbess.   Hd, 2.   20 ran
1967 Khemis (100–6) J. Hunter (£2,207) K. Bell, 4–7–2
    2. Slipper Supreme,   **3.** Sweet Jewel.   1, $\frac{3}{4}$.   19 ran

1968 Hibernian (8–1) L. Ward (£2,282) M. V. O'Brien, 3–9–0
    2. Ivalo,   3. Imperius.   ¾, Sht Hd.   25 ran

Race 232: CESAREWITCH STAKES
2 miles 2 furlongs handicap. Newmarket. First run 1839

1900	Clarehaven, 4–7–13	(21)	**1930**	Ut Majeur, 3–8–3	(28)
1901	Balsarroch, 3–6–5	(23)	**1931**	Noble Star, 4–8–12	(26)
1902	Black Sand, 5–8–2	(17)	**1932**	Nitsichin, 4–8–9	(26)
1903	Grey Tick, a–6–9	(26)	**1933**	Seminole, 4–8–0	(33)
1904	Wargrave, 6–7–4	(19)	**1934**	Enfield, 3–7–10	(27)
1905	Hammerkop, 5–8–9	(19)	**1935**	Near Relation, 3–7–9	(29)
1906	Mintagon, 5–7–0	(24)	**1936**	Fet, 5–6–12	(24)
1907	Demure, 4–6–9	(14)	**1937**	Punch, 4–7–11	(31)
1908	Yentoi, 4–7–1	(16)	**1938**	Contravent, 3–6–10	(28)
1909	Submit, 3–6–13	(17)			
1910	Verney, 4–7–11	(19)		**2M 24Y**	
1911	Willonyx, 4–9–5	(16)	**1939**	Cantatrice II, 4–7–5	(36)
1912	Warlingham, 3–6–12	(18)	**1940**	Hunters Moon IV, 4–9–5	(14)
1913	Fiz Yama, 4–7–7	(24)	**1941**	Filator, 3–7–12	(21)
1914	Troubadour, 3–6–9	(21)	**1942–44**	No race	
1915	Son-in-Law, 4–8–4	(31)			
1916	Sanctum, 4–7–4	(19)		**2M 2F**	
1917	Furore, 4–8–6	(17)	**1945**	Kerry Piper, 4–8–1	(26)
1918	Air Raid, 3–8–1	(24)	**1946**	Monsieur l'Amiral, 5–8–5	(27)
1919	Ivanhoe, 6–7–12	(19)	**1947**	Whiteway, 3–7–12	(22)
1920	Bracket, 3–7–7	(32)	**1948**	Woodburn, 3–7–13	(32)
1921	Yutoi, 4–8–5	(17)	**1949**	Strathspey, 4–7–11	(37)
1922	Light Dragoon, 4–7–3	(31)	**1950**	Above Board, 3–7–10	(38)
1923	Rose Prince, 4–8–3	(29)	**1951**	Three Cheers, 3–7–8	(30)
1924	Charley's Mount, 3–7–10	(34)	**1952**	Flush Royal, 7–8–13	(36)
1925	Forseti, 5–8–3	(33)	**1953**	Chantry, 4–8–4	(25)
1926	Myra Gray, 6–6–1	(24)	**1954**	French Design, 7–8–3	(31)
1927	Eagle's Pride, 4–7–0	(30)	**1955**	Curry, 4–7–6	(21)
1928	Arctic Star, 4–8–2	(15)	**1956**	Prelone, 3–7–3	(19)
1929	West Wicklow, 5–7–6	(35)			

1957 Sandiacre (100–8) D. Smith (£3,102) W. Dutton, 5–7–8
    2. Morecambe,   3. Predominate.   ½, 3.   24 ran
1958 Morecambe (15–2f) J. Sime (£2,813) S. Hall, 5–9–1
    2. Predominate,   3. Kubba.   10, 2.   30 ran
1959 Come to Daddy (6–1jf) D. Smith (£3,854) W. Lyde, 4–7–8
    2. Seascape,   3. Bali Ha'i III.   5, 1½.   17 ran
1960 Alcove (100–30f) D. Smith (£3,570) J. F. Watts, 3–7–8
    2. Sea Wolf,   3. Hoy.   Nk, 3.   20 ran
1961 Avon's Pride (100–8) E. Smith (£3,714) W. Hern, 4–7–11
    2. Alcoa,   3. Persian Lancer.   Sht Hd, ¾.   27 ran

1962 Golden Fire (25–1) D. Yates (£3,829) D. Marks, 4–7–11
    2. Orchardist,   **3.** Grey of Falloden.
    (Orchardist first, disqualified.) Original distances, Nk, 2.   25 ran
1963 Utrillo (100–8) J. Sime (£3,833) H. Price, 6–8–0
    2. Tropical Sky,   **3.** Sea Leopard. $\frac{1}{2}$, $1\frac{1}{2}$.   25 ran
1964 Grey of Falloden (20–1) J. Mercer (£5,030) W. Hern, 5–9–6
    2. Magic Court,   **3.** Straight Die. $\frac{3}{4}$, Hd.   26 ran
1965 Mintmaster (13–2) J. Sime (£4,907) A. Cooper, 4–7–9
    2. Aureate,   **3.** Sayfar.   Nk, Sht Hd.   18 ran
1966 Persian Lancer (100–7) D. Smith (£6,020) H. Price, 8–7–8
    2. C.E.D.,   **3.** Miss Dawn. $\frac{3}{4}$, 8.   24 ran
1967 Boismoss (13–1) E. Johnson (£4,948) M. W. Easterby, 3–7–1
    2. Major Rose,   **3.** Farur.   4, 1.   23 ran
1968 Major Rose (9–1f) L. Piggott (£5,447) H. Price, 6–9–4
    2. Promotion Year,   **3.** Lone Wolf. $1\frac{1}{2}$, 8.   33 ran

Race 233: CAMBRIDGESHIRE STAKES

1 mile 1 furlong handicap. Newmarket. First run 1839

1900	Berrill, 4–7–9	(24)	**1927**	Medal, 3–7–4 and	
1901	Watershed, 3–7–7	(23)		Niantic, 4–6–3	(21)
1902	Ballantrae, 3–6–8	(24)	**1928**	Palais Royal II, 3–7–13	(27)
1903	Hackler's Pride, 3–6–10	(27)	**1929**	Double Life, 3–7–12	(36)
1904	Hackler's Pride, 4–8–10	(17)	**1930**	The Pen, 3–7–4	(31)
1905	Velocity, 3–6–5	(18)	**1931**	Disarmament, 3–7–11	(24)
1906	Polymelus, 4–8–10	(20)	**1932**	Pullover, 3–6–11	(33)
1907	Land League, 4–7–13	(15)	**1933**	Raymond, 3–8–4	(26)
1908	Marcovil, 5–7–11	(23)	**1934**	Wychwood Abbot, 3–8–6	(33)
1909	Christmas Daisy, 4–7–2	(18)	**1935**	Commander III, 5–7–11	(40)
1910	Christmas Daisy, 5–8–2	(21)	**1936**	Dan Bulger, 3–7–13	(22)
1911	Long Set, 4–6–12	(16)	**1937**	Artist's Prince, 4–6–12	(26)
1912	Adam Bede, 4–7–12	(20)	**1938**	Helleniqua, 5–6–12	(29)
1913	Cantilever, 3–7–12	(18)	**1939**	Class I Gyroscope, 3–7–7	(27)
1914	Honeywood, 3–7–8	(17)		Class II Orichalque, 6–8–10	(27)
1915	Silver Tag, 3–8–3	(25)			
1916	Eos, 3–7–6	(17)		**[AT NOTTINGHAM]**	
1917	Brown Prince, 3–7–7	(14)	**1940**	Caxton, 4–7–9	(15)
1918	Zinovia, 3–8–1	(22)			
1919	Brigand, 5–6–10	(18)		**[AT NEWMARKET]**	
1920	No race		**1941**	Rue de la Paix, 5–8–13	(9)
1921	Milenko, 3–7–1	(24)	**1942–44**	No race	
1922	Re-echo, 3–7–9	(34)	**1945**	Esquire, 3–6–3	(28)
1923	Verdict, 3–7–12	(23)	**1946**	Sayani, 3–9–4	(34)
1924	Twelve Pointer, 4–8–12	(27)	**1947**	Fairy Fulmar, 4–8–12	(39)
1925	Masked Marvel, 3–7–9	(24)	**1948**	Sterope, 3–7–4	(32)
1926	Insight II, 5–7–13	(32)	**1949**	Sterope, 4–9–4	(39)
			1950	Kelling, 3–7–10	(31)

1951 Fleeting Moment, 5–7–13	(45)	1954 Minstrel, 3–7–0	(36)
1952 Richer, 3–8–0	(42)	1955 Retrial, 3–7–1	(40)
1953 Jupiter, 3–8–3	(29)	1956 Loppylugs, 4–7–8	(34)

1957 Stephanotis (100–6) W. Carr (£3,187) J. Rogers, 4–8–5
    2. Heritiere,   3. Fairy Stone. $\frac{3}{4}$, $\frac{3}{4}$.   38 ran
1958 London Cry (22–1) A. Breasley (£3,038) Sir G. Richards, 4–9–5
    2. Falls of Shin,   3. Aggressor. $\frac{1}{2}$, 2.   33 ran
1959 Rexequus (25–1) N. Stirk (£4,071) G. Boyd, 3–8–7
    2. Anthelion,   3. Thames Trader. $\frac{1}{2}$, Hd.   36 ran
1960 Midsummer Night II (40–1) D. Keith (£4,160) P. Hastings-Bass, 3–7–12
    2. Fougalle,   3. Ides of March.   Hd, 2.   40 ran
1961 Henry the Seventh (100–8) E. Hide (£2,212) W. Elsey, 3–8–4 and
Violetta III (33–1) C. Parkes (£2,212) H. Wragg, 3–7–8
    3. Miss Biffin.   Dd Ht, Nk.   27 ran
1962 Hidden Meaning (7–1f) A. Breasley (£4,636) H. Leader, 3–9–0
    2. Hasty Cloud,   3. Bewildroom.   2, Sht Hd.   46 ran
1963 Commander in Chief (100–7) F. Durr (£4,033) E. Cousins, 4–8–0
    2. Principal,   3. Hasty Cloud.   Nk, 1$\frac{1}{2}$.   23 ran
1964 Hasty Cloud (100–8jf) J. Wilson (£5,536) H. Wallington, 6–7–10
    2. Commander in Chief,   3. Barwin. $\frac{3}{4}$, 4.   43 ran
1965 Tarqogan (100–8) W. Williamson (£5,158) S. McGrath, 5–9–3
    2. Karelia,   3. Langley Park.   Nk, 4.   30 ran
1966 Dites (33–1) D. Maitland (£6,220) H. Leader, 4–7–4
    2. Isis,   3. Tarqogan.   Hd, 1$\frac{1}{2}$.   34 ran
1967 LACQUER (20–1) R. Hutchinson (£5,193) H. Wragg, 3–8–6
    2. Straight Master,   3. Wolver Hollow.   2, $\frac{1}{2}$.   34 ran
1968 Emerilo (20–1) M. Thomas (£5,116) P. Allden, 4–7–9
    2. Wolver Hollow,   3. Bluerullah.   Nk, Sht Hd.   35 ran

Race 234: IRISH CESAREWITCH STAKES

2 miles handicap. Curragh

1957 Sword Flash (5–1f) J. Wright (£1,154) P. Sleator, 4–7–7
    2. Celestial Sucker,   3. Owen's Image.   2, 7.   28 ran
1958 Havasnack (11–4) L. Ward (£1,021) P. Sleator, 6–9–1
    2. Sorrel,   3. Maid of   Sht Hd, 4.   17 ran
                                     Galloway.
1959 Another Flash (6–4f) L. Ward (£1,063) P. Sleator, 5–8–5
    2. Rouge Scot,   3. Maid of   3, 2.   17 ran
                                     Galloway.
1960 Knight of the Morn (8–1) G. McGrath (£1,041) A. D. Turner, 7–7–7
    2. Ballyrichard,   3. Full Flight.   2$\frac{1}{2}$, Hd.   12 ran
1961 Orofino (20–1) G. McGrath (£1,082) K. Kerr, 3–7–7
    2. Miss Patsy,   3. In Trust.   2, Sht Hd.   24 ran

1962 Height o'Fashion (7–1) J. Wright (£1,074) P. Mullins, 5–7–5
    2. De Reszki,   3. Solpetre.   2, 5.   21 ran
1963 Arctic Kanda (8–1) P. Vaughan (£1,148) C. L. Weld, 4–8–3
    2. Linan Belle,   3. Persian Signal.   ¾, Nk.   22 ran
1964 Abletai (10–1) J. Murtagh (£1,126) W. J. Byrne, 6–8–4
    2. West Iran,   3. Garland Knight. 6, 8.   26 ran
1965 Agrippina (11–2) A. C. McGarritty (£1,229) J. C. Tonson-Rye, 6–6–12
    2. Say the Word,   3. Fuengirola.   3, ½.   22 ran
1966 Say the Word (100–6) C. Roche (£1,128) C. L. Weld, 5–7–2
    2. Regret,   3. Sparrow Hawk. 4, ½.   17 ran
1967 Mr Smarty (100–8) J. Murtagh (£2,207) J. O'Connell, 5–7–11
    2. Murpep,   3. Cathy B.   1, 10.   22 ran
1968 Arctic Serenade (100–1) M. Teelin (£2,080) M. Kiely, 5–6–7
    2. Storyville,   3. Donicom.   3, 5.   31 ran

Race 235: MANCHESTER HANDICAP

1 mile 4 furlongs. Doncaster. Called November Handicap at Manchester until 1964. First run 1876

1900	Lexicon, 6–6–13	(18)
1901	Carabine, 3–6–9	(22)
1902	St Maclou, 4–9–4	(15)
1903	Switchcap, 3–6–6	(24)
1904	No race	
1905	Ferment, 3–6–2	(19)
1906	Spate, 3–7–5	(17)
1907	Baltinglass, 3–7–11	(10)
1908	Old China, 4–7–11	(20)
1909	Admiral Togo III, 5–8–2	(16)
1910	The Valet, 6–6–9	(18)
1911	Ultimus, 4–7–3	(17)
1912	Wagstaff, 3–8–1	(16)
1913	Dalmatian, 6–7–8	(16)
1914	Wardha, 3–6–5	(21)
1915–16	No race	
1917	Planet, 3–8–1	(17)
1918	No race	
1919	King John, 4–8–6	(17)
1920	Pomme de Terre, 4–9–4	(12)
1921	Blue Dun, 4–8–5	(24)
1922	Torelore, 5–9–0	(14)
1923	Abandoned	
1924	Cloudbank, 3–7–10	(17)
1925	Abandoned	
1926	Abandoned	

1927	Old Orkney, 3–7–7	(6)
1928	Saracen, 3–7–8	(20)
1929	Promptitude, 5–6–13	(19)
1930	Glorious Devon, 3–7–5	(28)
1931	North Drift, 4–7–6	(42)
1932	Hypostyle, 3–7–5	(18)
1933	Jean's Dream, 3–7–5	(28)
1934	Pip Emma, 3–7–9	(29)
1935	Free Fare, 7–8–4	(19)
1936	Newtown Ford, 4–8–4	(21)
1937	Solitaire, 6–8–1	(31)
1938	Pappageno II, 3–8–6	(26)
1939	Tutor, 3–8–3	(24)
1940	Beinn Dearg, 5–8–2	(20)
1941	Crown Colony, 5–7–9	(18)

[AT PONTEFRACT]

1942	Golden Boy, 4–8–11	(16)
1943	Mad Carew, 4–7–6	(21)
1944	Kerry Piper, 3–8–0	(19)
1945	Oatflake, 3–7–13	(23)

[AT MANCHESTER]

1946	Las Vegas, 4–8–8	(23)
1947	Regret, 4–6–3	(34)
1948	Sports Master, 3–6–13	(40)

281

1949	Fidonia, 5–9–2	(41)	1953	Torch Singer, 4–6–5	(25)
1950	Coltbridge, 4–7–6	(37)	1954	Abandoned	
1951	Good Taste, 7–7–13	(31)	1955	Tearaway, 5–6–11	(38)
1952	Summer Rain, 3–7–13	(24)	1956	Trentham Boy, 5–7–6	(26)

1957 Chief Barker (late Polar Lodge) (33–1) D. W. Walker (£6,352) H. Price, 4–6–5
    2. Spaceman,   **3.** Floor Show.   Sht Hd, 1½.   40 ran

1958 Paul Jones (100–7) J. Mercer (£6,131) A. Budgett, 3–8–2
    2. Donna Lollo,   **3.** Brancusi.   2, 3.   30 ran

1959 Operatic Society (18–1) K. Gethin (£7,108) J. Benstead, 3–8–9
    2. Ross Sea,   **3.** Sunrise.   1, 2.   49 ran

1960 Dalnamein (28–1) H. Greenaway (£6,241) S. Hall, 5–7–10
    2. Windyedge,   **3.** Pandofell.   Nk, 1.   30 ran

1961 Henry's Choice (100–8) E. Hide (£6,462) P. Beasley, 4–8–2
    2. Damredub,   **3.** Greyburn.   2, 1½.   29 ran

1962 Damredub (20–1) M. Germon (£6,547) J. Gosden, 5–8–1
    2. Dalnamein,   **3.** White Park Bay.   4, 2.   35 ran

1963 Best Song (100–7) J. Lindley (£3,464) J. Gosden, 4–9–6
    2. Damredub,   **3.** Pluit.   Nk, Nk.   31 ran

1964 Osier (20–1) D. Smith (£4,471) B. van Cutsem, 4–7–10
    2. Space King,   **3.** Rapanni.
        (By Jupiter third, disqualified.) Original distances, ½, ½, 4.   28 ran

1965 Concealdem (100–8) R. Hutchinson (£4,023) J. Gosden, 6–8–10
    2. High Proof,   **3.** Osier.   2½, 1.   18 ran

1966 Polish Warrior (100–6) A. Barclay (£4,156) A. Budgett, 3–7–3
    2. Valoroso,   **3.** Concealdem.   Hd, 1.   26 ran

1967 Bugle Boy (22–1) A. Barclay (£4,074) A. Budgett, 4–7–8
    2. Easter Island,   **3.** Promotion Year.   ¾, 1.   25 ran

1968 Zardia (25–1) R. Still (£4,168) A. Vasey, 4–7–8
    2. Spunyarn,   **3.** Duperion.   2, 1½.   29 ran

HORSES IN CAPITAL LETTERS
(EXCLUDING RACE 245)
WERE TO BE, OR HAD BEEN,
PLACED IN THE CLASSICS

Section Five: National Hunt Events

Race 245: GRAND NATIONAL
4 miles 856 yards Handicap Chase. Liverpool

1837 The Duke	(6)	**1869** The Colonel, 6–10–7	(22)
1838 Sir Henry	(10)	**1870** The Colonel, a–11–12	(23)
1839 Lottery, 12–0	(17)	**1871** The Lamb, a–11–5	(25)
1840 Jerry, 12–0	(13)	**1872** Casse Tete, a–10–0	(25)
1841 Charity, 12–0	(10)	**1873** Disturbance, 6–11–11	(28)
1842 Gaylad, 12–0	(15)	**1874** Reugny, 6–10–12	(22)
1843 Vanguard, a–11–10	(16)	**1875** Pathfinder, a–10–11	(19)
1844 Discount, 6–10–12	(16)	**1876** Regal, 5–11–3	(19)
1845 Cureall, a–11–5	(15)	**1877** Austerlitz, 5–10–8	(16)
1846 Pioneer, 6–11–12	(22)	**1878** Shifnal, a–10–12	(12)
1847 Matthew, a–10–6	(28)	**1879** Liberator, a–11–4	(18)
1848 Chandler, a–11–12	(29)	**1880** Empress, 5–10–7	(14)
1849 Peter Simple, a–11–0	(23)	**1881** Woodbrook, a–11–3	(13)
1850 Abd-el-Kader, a–9–12	(32)	**1882** Seaman, 6–11–6	(12)
1851 Abd-el-Kader, a–10–4	(21)	**1883** Zoedone, 6–11–0	(10)
1852 Miss Mowbray, a–10–4	(24)	**1884** Voluptuary, 6–10–5	(15)
1853 Peter Simple, a–10–10	(21)	**1885** Roquefort, 6–11–0	(19)
1854 Bourton, a–11–12	(20)	**1886** Old Joe, a–10–9	(23)
1855 Wanderer, a–9–8	(20)	**1887** Gamecock, a–11–0	(16)
1856 Freetrader, a–9–6	(21)	**1888** Playfair, a–10–7	(20)
1857 Emigrant, a–9–10	(28)	**1889** Frigate, a–11–5	(20)
1858 Little Charley, a–10–7	(16)	**1890** Ilex, 6–10–5	(16)
1859 Half-caste, 6–9–7	(16)	**1891** Come Away, a–11–12	(21)
1860 Anatis, a–9–10	(19)	**1892** Father O'Flynn, a–10–5	(25)
1861 Jealousy, a–9–12	(24)	**1893** Cloister, a–12–7	(15)
1862 Huntsman, a–11–0	(13)	**1894** Why Not, a–11–13	(14)
1863 Emblem, a–10–10	(16)	**1895** Wild Man from	
1864 Emblematic, 6–10–6	(25)	Borneo, a–10–11	(19)
1865 Alcibiade, 5–11–4	(23)	**1896** The Soarer, a–9–13	(28)
1866 Salamander, a–10–7	(30)	**1897** Manifesto, a–11–3	(28)
1867 Cortolvin, a–11–13	(23)	**1898** Drogheda, 6–10–12	(25)
1868 The Lamb, 6–10–7	(21)	**1899** Manifesto, a–12–7	(19)

1900 Ambush II (4–1) A. Anthony (H.R.H. Prince of Wales) A. Anthony, 6–11–3
      2. Barsac,   3. Manifesto.   4, Nk.   16 ran
1901 Grudon (9–1) A. Nightingall (Mr B. Bletsoe) J. Holland, 11–10–0
      2. Drumcree,   3. Buffalo Bill.   4, 6.   24 ran

1902 Shannon Lass (20–1) D. Read (Mr A. Gorham) Hackett, 7–10–1

    2. Matthew,   **3.** Manifesto.   3, 3.   21 ran

1903 Drumcree (13–2f) P. Woodland (Mr J. S. Morrison) Sir Charles Nugent, 9–11–3

    2. Detail,   **3.** Manifesto.   3, 20.   23 ran

1904 Moifaa (25–1) A. Birch (Mr Spencer Gollan) O. Hickey, 8–10–7

    2. Kirkland,   **3.** The Gunner.   8, Nk.   26 ran

1905 Kirkland (6–1) F. Mason (Mr F. Bibby) Thomas, 9–11–5

    2. Napper Tandy,   **3.** Buckaway II.   3, 4.   27 ran

1906 Ascetic's Silver (20–1) Hon. A. Hastings (Prince Hatyfeldt) Hon. A. Hastings, 9–10–9

    2. Red Lad,   **3.** Aunt May.   10, 2.   23 ran

1907 Eremon (8–1) A. Newey (Mr S. Howard) Coulthwaite, 7–10–1

    2. Tom West,   **3.** Patlander.   6, Bad.   23 ran

1908 Rubio (66–1) H. Bletsoe (Maj. F. Douglas-Pennant) Costello, 10–10–5

    2. Mattie Macgregor,   **3.** The Lawyer III.   10, 6.   24 ran

1909 Lutteur III (100–9) G. Parfrement (Mr J. Hennessy) H. Escott, 5–10–11

    2. Judas,   **3.** Caubeen.   2, Bad.   32 ran

1910 Jenkinstown (100–8) R. Chadwick (Mr S. Howard) T. Coulthwaite, 9–10–5

    2. Jerry M,   **3.** Odor.   3, 3.   25 ran

1911 Glenside (20–1) Mr J. R. Anthony (Mr F. Bibby) Capt. Collis, 9–10–3

    2. Rathnally   **3.** Shady Girl   20, 3.   26 ran
    (fell, remount),   (fell, remount).

1912 Jerry M (4–1) E. Piggott (Sir C. Assheton-Smith) R. Gore, 9–12–7

    2. Bloodstone,   **3.** Axle Pin.   6, 4.   24 ran

1913 Covertcoat (100–9) P. Woodland (Sir C. Assheton-Smith) R. Gore, 7-11-6

    2. Irish Mail,   **3.** Carsey   Dist, Dist.   22 ran
                                (fell, remount).

1914 Sunloch (100–6) W. J. Smith (Mr T. Tyler) T. Tyler, 8–9–7

    2. Trianon III,   **3.** Lutteur III.   8, 8.   20 ran

1915 Ally Sloper (100–8) Mr J. R. Anthony (Lady Nelson) Hon. A. Hastings, 6–10–5

    2. Jacobus,   **3.** Father Confessor. 2, 8.   20 ran

AT GATWICK

1916 Vermouth (100–8) J. Reardon (Mr P. F. Heybourn) J. Bell, 6–11–10

    2. Irish Mail,   **3.** Schoolmoney.   2, 6.   21 ran

1917 Ballymacad (100–9) E. Driscoll (Sir G. Bullough) Hon. A. Hastings, 10–9–12

    2. Chang,   **3.** Ally Sloper.   8, 4.   19 ran

1918 Poethlyn (5–1) E. Piggott (Mrs H. Peel) A. Escott, 8–11–6

    2. Captain Dreyfus,   **3.** Ballymacad.   4, Bad.   17 ran

AT LIVERPOOL

1919 Poethlyn (11–4) E. Piggott (Mrs H. Peel) A. Escott, 9–12–7

    2. Ballyboggan,   **3.** Pollen.   8, 6.   22 ran

1920 Troytown (6–1) Mr J. R. Anthony (Maj. T. G. C. Gerrard) A. Anthony, 7–11–9

    2. The Turk II,   **3.** The Bore.   12, 6.   24 ran

1921 Shaun Spadah (100–9) F. B. Rees (Mr T. M. McAlpine) G. C. Poole, 10–11–7

    2. The Bore,   **3.** All White.   Dist, Dist.   35 ran

1922 Music Hall (100–9) L. B. Rees (Mr H. Kershaw) Owen Anthony, 9–11–8

    2. Drifter,   **3.** Taffytus.   12, 6.   32 ran

1923 Sergeant Murphy (100–6) Capt. G. H. Bennet (Mr S. Sanford) G. Blackwell, 13–11–3

    2. Shaun Spadah,   **3.** Conjuror II.   3, 6.   28 ran

1924 Master Robert (25–1) R. Trudgill (Lord Airlie) Hon. A. Hastings, 11–10–5

    2. Fly Mask,   **3.** Silvo.   4, 6.   30 ran

1925 Double Chance (100–9) Maj. J. P. Wilson (Mr D. Goold) F. Archer, 9–10–9

    2. Old Tay Bridge.   **3.** Fly Mask.   4, 6.   33 ran

1926 Jack Horner (25–1) W. Watkinson (Mr A. C. Schwartz) H. Leader, 9–10–5

    2. Old Tay Bridge,   **3.** Bright's Boy.   3, 1.   30 ran

1927 Sprig (8–1) T. Leader (Mrs M. Partridge) T. Leader, 10–12–4

    2. Bovril III,   **3.** Bright's Boy.   1, 1.   37 ran

1928 Tipperary Tim (100–1) Mr W. P. Dutton (Mr H. S. Kenyon) J. Dodd, 10–10–0

    2. Billy Barton.   Only two finished.   Dist.   42 ran

1929 Gregalach (100–1) R. Everett (Mrs M. A. Gemmall) T. Leader, 7–11–4

    2. Easter Hero,   **3.** Richmond II.   6, Bad.   66 ran

1930 Shaun Goilin (100–8) T. Cullinan (Mr W. H. Midwood) F. Hartigan, 10–11–7

    2. Melleray's Belle,   **3.** Sir Lindsay.   Nk, 1½.   41 ran

1931 Grakle (100–6) R. Lyall (Mr C. R. Taylor) T. Coulthwaite, 9–11–7

    2. Gregalach,   **3.** Annandale.   1½, 10.   43 ran

1932 Forbra (50–1) J. Hamey (Mr W. Parsonage) T. R. Rimell, 7–10–7

    2. Egremont,   **3.** Shaun Goilin.   3, Bad.   36 ran

1933 Kellsboro' Jack (25–1) D. Williams (Mrs E. Ambrose Clark) I. Anthony, 7–11–9

    2. Really True,   **3.** Slater.   3, Nk.   34 ran

1934 Golden Miller (8–1) G. Wilson (Miss D. Paget) A. Briscoe, 7–12–2

    2. Delaneige,   **3.** Thomond II.   5, 5.   30 ran

1935 Reynoldstown (22–1) Mr F. Furlong (Maj. N. Furlong) F. Furlong, 8–11–4

    2. Blue Prince,   **3.** Thomond II.   3, 8.   27 ran

1936 Reynoldstown (10–1) Mr F. Walwyn (Maj. N. Furlong) Maj. N. Furlong, 9–12–2

    2. Ego,   **3.** Bachelor Prince.   12, 6.   35 ran

1937 Royal Mail (100–6) E. Williams (Mr H. Lloyd Thomas) I. Anthony, 8–11–13

    2. Cooleen,   **3.** Pucka Belle.   3, 10.   33 ran

1938 Battleship (40–1) B. Hobbs (Mrs Marion Scott) R. Hobbs, 11–11–6

    2. Royal Danieli,   **3.** Workman.   Hd, Bad.   36 ran

1939 Workman (100–8) T. Hyde (Sir A. Maguire) J. Ruttle, 9–10–6

    2. Mac Moffat,   **3.** Kilstar.   3, 15.   37 ran

1940 Bogskar (25–1) M. Jones (Lord Stalbridge) Lord Stalbridge, 7–10–4

    2. Mac Moffat,   **3.** Gold Arrow.   4, 6.   30 ran

1941–45 No race

1946 Lovely Cottage (25–1) Capt. R. Petre (Mr J. Morant) T. Rayson, 9–10–8
    2. Jack Finlay,   **3.** Prince Regent.   4, 3.   34 ran
1947 Caughoo (100–1) E. Dempsey (Mr J. J. McDowell) H. McDowell, 8–10–0
    2. Lough Conn,   **3.** Kami.   20, 4.   57 ran
1948 Sheila's Cottage (50–1) A. P. Thompson (Mr J. Procter) N. Crump, 9–10–7
    2. First of the Dandies,   **3.** Cromwell.   1, 6.   43 ran
1949 Russian Hero (66–1) L. McMorrow (Mr W. F. Williamson) G. Owen, 9–10–8
    2. Roimond,   **3.** Royal Mount.   8, 1.   43 ran
1950 Freebooter (10–1) J. Power (Mrs L. Brotherton) R. Renton, 9–11–11
    2. Wot No Sun,   **3.** Acthon Major.   15, 10.   49 ran
1951 Nickel Coin (40–1) J. A. Bullock (Mr J. Royle) J. O'Donoghue, 9–10–1
    2. Royal Tan,   **3.** Derrinstown   6, Bad.   36 ran
                                  (fell, remount).
1952 Teal (100–7) A. P. Thompson (Mr H. Lane) N. Crump, 10–10–12
    2. Legal Joy,   **3.** Wot No Sun.   5, Bad.   47 ran
1953 Early Mist (20–1) B. Marshall (Mr J. H. Griffin) M. V. O'Brien, 8–11–2
    2. Mont Tremblant,   **3.** Irish Lizard.   20, 4.   31 ran
1954 Royal Tan (8–1) B. Marshall (Mr J. H. Griffin) M. V. O'Brien, 10–11–7
    2. Tudor Line,   **3.** Irish Lizard.   Nk, 10.   29 ran
1955 Quare Times (100–9) P. Taaffe (Mrs W. H. E. Welman) M. V. O'Brien,
9–11–0
    2. Tudor Line,   **3.** Carey's Cottage.   12, 4.   30 ran
1956 E.S.B. (100–7) D. V. Dick (Mrs L. Carver) T. F. Rimell, 10–11–3
    2. Gentle Moya,   **3.** Royal Tan.   10, 10.   29 ran

1957 SUNDEW (20–1) F. T. Winter (£8,868) (Mrs G. Kohn) F. Hudson, 11–11–7
    2. Wyndburgh   **3.** Tiberetta
       (M. Batchelor),   (A. Oughton),
    4. Glorious Twelfth,   **5.** Crofter,
    6. Goosander (5–1f).   Extended distances, 8, 6, 8, 5, 5.   35 ran
1958 MR WHAT (18–1) A. Freeman (£13,719) (D. J. Coughlan) T. Taaffe,
8–10–6
    2. Tiberetta (G. Slack),   **3.** Green Drill (G. Milburn),
    4. Wyndburgh (6–1f),   **5.** Goosander,
    6. E.S.B.   Extended distances, 30, 15, 15, 20, 12.   31 ran
1959 OXO (8–1) M. Scudamore (£13,646) (J. E. Bigg) W. Stephenson, 8–10–13
    2. Wyndburgh   **3.** Mr What (T. Taaffe)
       (T. Brookshaw),   (6–1f),
    4. Tiberetta.   Only four finished.
                        Extended distances, 1½, 8, 20.   34 ran
1960 MERRYMAN II (13–2f) G. Scott (£13,134) (Miss W. H. S. Wallace)
N. Crump, 9–10–12
    2. Badanloch (S. Mellor),   **3.** Clear Profit (B. Wilkinson),
    4. Tea Fiend,   **5.** Sabaria,
    6. Green Drill.   Extended distances, 15, 12, 12, 5, 20.   26 ran
1961 NICOLAUS SILVER (28–1) H. Beasley (£20,020) (C. Vaughan) T. F.
Rimell, 9–10–1
    2. Merryman II (D. Ancil),   **3.** O'Malley Point (P. Farrell),

4. Scottish Flight II,   **5.** Kilmore,
6. Wyndburgh.
(Jonjo 7–1f—7th.)   Extended distances, 5, Nk, 6, 5, 4. 35 ran

1962 KILMORE (28–1) F. T. Winter (£20,239) (N. Cohen) H. Price, 12–10–4
    2. Wyndburgh (T. Barnes),   **3.** Mr What (J. Lehane),
    4. Gay Navarree,   **5.** Fredith's Son,
    6. Dark Venetian.
(Frenchman's Cove 7–1f—b.d.) Extended distances, 10, 10, 4, 12, 10. 32 ran

1963 AYALA (66–1) P. Buckley (£21,315) (P. B. Raymond) E. K. Piggott, 9–10–0
    2. Carrickbeg (J. Lawrence),   **3.** Hawa's Song (P. Broderick),
    4. Team Spirit,   **5.** Springbok (10–1f),
    6. Kilmore.   Extended distances, $\frac{3}{4}$, 5, 6, Hd, 10. 47 ran

1964 TEAM SPIRIT (18–1) G. W. Robinson (£20,280) (J. K. Goodman)
F. Walwyn, 12–10–3
    2. Purple Silk   **3.** Peacetown (R. Edwards),
    (J. Kenneally),
    4. Eternal,   **5.** Pontin-Go,
    6. Springbok.
(100–7) co-favourites; Pappageno's Cottage—10th. Flying Wild, Time and
Laffy—fell.)   Extended distances, $\frac{1}{2}$, 6, 3, 8, 4. 33 ran

1965 JAY TRUMP (100–6) C. Smith (£22,041) (Mrs M. Stephenson)
F. T. Winter, 8–11–5
    2. Freddie (P. McCarron)   **3.** Mr Jones
    (7–2f),   (C. Collins),
    4. Rainbow Battle,   **5.** Vultrix,
    6. L'Empereur.   Extended distances, $\frac{3}{4}$, 20, $1\frac{1}{2}$, 15, 15. 47 ran

1966 ANGLO (50–1) T. Norman (£22,334) (S. Levy) F. T. Winter, 8–10–0
    2. Freddie (P. McCarron)   **3.** Forest Prince
    (11–4f),   (G. Scott),
    4. Fossa,   **5.** Jim's Tavern,
    6. Quintin Bay.   Extended distances, 20, 5, 20, 4, 6. 47 ran

1967 FOINAVON (100–1) J. Buckingham (£17,631) (C. P. Watkins)
J. Kempton, 9–10–0
    2. Honey End (J. Gifford)   **3.** Red Alligator (B. Fletcher),
    (15–2f),
    4. Greek Scholar,   **5.** Packed Home,
    6. Solbina.
(Only winner escaped 23rd fence pile-up. Other finishers were remounted or put
to the fence a second time.)   Extended distances, 15, 3, 8, 4, 8. 44 ran

1968 RED ALLIGATOR (100–7) B. Fletcher (£17,848) (J. Manners)
D. Smith, 9–10–0
    2. Moidore's Token   **3.** Different Class
    (B. Brogan),   (D. Mould) (17–2f),
    4. Rutherfords,   **5.** Fossa.
    6. Valbus.   Extended distances, 20, Nk, 12, 6, 10. 45 ran

Race 246: MACKESON GOLD CUP

2 miles 4 furlongs Handicap Chase. Cheltenham. Run over 2 miles until 1967–68

1960–61 Fortria (8–1) P. Taaffe (£4,385) T. Dreaper, 8–12–0
    2. Icanopit,   **3.** King.   6, 2.   19 ran
1961–62 Scottish Memories (9–2) C. Finnegan (£4,385) A. Thomas, 7–10–12
    2. Fortria,   **3.** Thataway.   3, $\frac{1}{2}$.   17 ran
1962–63 Fortria (5–1f) P. Taaffe (£4,385) T. Dreaper, 10–12–0
    2. School for Gamble,   **3.** Owen's Sedge.   3, $\frac{1}{2}$.   25 ran
1963–64 Richard of Bordeaux (20–1) H. Beasley (£4,385) F. Walwyn, 8–10–5
    2. Blue Dolphin,   **3.** Too Slow.   4, 10.   20 ran
1964–65 Super Flash (8–1) S. Mellor (£4,380) F. Cundell, 9–10–5
    2. Jungle Beach,   **3.** Flash Bulb. $1\frac{1}{2}$, 1.   9 ran
1965–66 Dunkirk (11–10f) W. Rees (£4,350) P. Cazalet, 8–12–7
    2. Choreographer,   **3.** Irish Imp. $\frac{1}{2}$, 6.   8 ran
1966–67 Pawnbroker (7–2) P. Broderick (£3,933) W. A. Stephenson, 8–11–9
    2. Tibidabo,   **3.** Mr Puffington.   5, $\frac{1}{2}$.   5 ran
1967–68 Charlie Worcester (7–1) J. Gifford (£4,218) H. Price, 10–10–11
    2. Arctic Sunset,   **3.** Border Grace.   4, 4.   13 ran
1968–69 Jupiter Boy (9–1) E. P. Harty (£4,000) T. F. Rimell, 7–10–3
    2. Specify,   **3.** Moonduster.   Sht Hd, $2\frac{1}{2}$.   13 ran

Race 247: MACKESON HANDICAP HURDLE

2 miles 200 yards. Cheltenham

1962–63 Beaver II (100–8) F. T. Winter (£2,246) H. Price, 4–11–4
    2. Alioop,   **3.** Old Mull.   3, 2.   24 ran
1963–64 Cash (50–1) P. Kelleway (£2,193) L. Dale, 5–10–6
    2. Running Rock,   **3.** Antiar.   3, 2.   16 ran
1964–65 Sky Pink (13–2) J. King (£2,134) J. Sutcliffe jun., 7–10–5
    2. Chinese Lacquer,   **3.** Barolo. $\frac{1}{2}$, $\frac{1}{2}$.   13 ran
1965–66 Makaldar (11–2) D. Mould (£2,225) P. Cazalet, 5–11–11
    2. Kirriemuir,   **3.** First Audition.   4, $\frac{3}{4}$.   16 ran
1966–67 Rackham (33–1) D. Mould (£2,117) R. Hobson, 5–10–6
    2. Tamorn,   **3.** Albinella.   3, Sht Hd.   19 ran
1967–68 Bric-Brac (20–1) J. Guest (£2,133) H. Hannon, 8–10–4
    2. Stubbs II,   **3.** Oberon.   2, 6.   18 ran
1968–69 No Race

Race 248: KIRK AND KIRK HANDICAP CHASE

3 miles. Ascot

1965–66	Rupununi (5–1) H. Beasley (£1,716) A. Thomas, 10–11–5			
	2. John O'Groats,	3. Montevideo II.	10, 15.	7 ran
1966–67	Regal John (15–2) J. Gifford (£2,120) H. Price, 8–10–10			
	2. Thorn Gate,	3. Indian Spice.	3, 1½.	9 ran
1967–68	Sixty-nine (6–1) B. Fletcher (£2,113) D. Smith, 7–11–4			
	2. Larbawn,	3. Hunter's Quest.	10, 2.	8 ran
1968–69	Laird (10–1) J. Jing (£2,162) R. Turnell, 7–12–7			
	2. Stalbridge Colonist	3. Hove	1½, 4.	7 ran

Race 249: BLACK AND WHITE GOLD CUP CHASE

2 miles. Ascot

1965–66	Flyingbolt (8–15f) P. Taaffe (£4,115) T. Dreaper, 6 yrs			
	2. Interosian,	3. Salmon Spray.	15, 2.	7 ran
1966–67	Dicky May (6–4f) P. Taaffe (£3,694) T. Dreaper, 7 yrs			
	2. Drinny's Double,	3. Laird.	1½, 12.	8 ran
1967–68	Makaldar (9–1) D. Mould (£3,973) P. Cazalet, 7 yrs			
	2. Stonehaven,	3. Certainement.	2½, 4.	10 ran
1968–69	Spanish Steps (10–1) J. Cook (£3,928) E. Courage, 5 yrs			
	2. Molar,	3. Hal's Farewell	8, 15.	7 ran

Race 250: HENNESSY GOLD CUP

3 miles 2 furlongs 82 yards handicap chase. Newbury. Run at Cheltenham until 1960–61; over 3 miles 1 furlong in 1957–58: 3 miles 3 furlongs 100 yards in 1958–59, 1959–60

1957–58	Mandarin (8–1) P. Madden (£5,272) F. Walwyn, 6–11–0			
	2. Linwell,	3. Bremontier.	3, 6.	19 ran
1958–59	Taxidermist (10–1) J. Lawrence (£5,302) F. Walwyn, 6–11–1			
	2. Kerstin,	3. Caesar's Helm.	Sht Hd, 4.	13 ran
1959–60	Kerstin (4–1jf) S. Hayhurst (£5,322) C. Bewicke, 9–11–10			
	2. Brunel II,	3. Croizet.	5, Nk.	26 ran
1960–61	Knucklecracker (100–7) D. Ancil (£5,218) D. Ancil, 7–11–1			
	2. Zonda,	3. Fearless Cavalier.	15, 10.	20 ran
1961–62	Mandarin (7–1) G. W. Robinson (£5,231) F. Walwyn, 10–11–5			
	2. John o'Groats,	3. Taxidermist.	1½, Hd.	22 ran
1962–63	Springbok (15–2) G. Scott (£5,272) N. Crump, 8–10–8			
	2. Rough Tweed,	3. Knucklecracker.	Hd, 6.	27 ran
1963–64	Mill House (15–8f) G. W. Robinson (£5,020) F. Walwyn, 6–12–0			
	2. Happy Spring,	3. Arkle.	8, ¾.	10 ran

1964–65 Arkle (5–4f) P. Taaffe (£5,516) T. Dreaper, 7–12–7
2. Ferry Boat,   3. Rip.   10, 12.   9 ran
1965–66 Arkle (1–6f) P. Taaffe (£7,099) T. Dreaper, 8–12–7
2. Freddie,   3. Brasher.   15, 3.   8 ran
1966–67 Stalbridge Colonist (25–1) S. Mellor (£5,713) K. Cundell, 7–10–0
2. Arkle,   3. What a Myth.   ½, 1½.   6 ran
1967–68 Rondetto (100–8) J. King (£5,941) R. Turnell, 11–10–1
2. Stalbridge Colonist,   3. What a Myth.   Hd, ½.   13 ran

Race 251: RHYMNEY BREWERIES HANDICAP CHASE

3 miles. Chepstow

1959–60 Bell (9–2) M. Tory (£1,960) T. W. Yates, 8–11–11
2. Oscar Wilde,   3. Highland Dandy. 3, 8.   15 ran
1960–61 Reprieved (6–1) C. Chapman (£1,993) W. Brookes, 7–10–0
2. Dandy Scot,   3. Chavara.   1½, Nk.   13 ran
1961–62 Pas Seul (11–10f) D. V. Dick (£1,964) R. Turnell, 8–12–0
2. Frenchman's Cove,   3. Limonali.   6, 10.   12 ran
1962–63 Happy Spring (100–8) R. Vibert (£2,028) J. S. Wright, 6–10–9
2. Meon Valley,   3. Owen's Sedge.   ½, 15.   16 ran
1963–64 Caduval (5–1) I. Balding (£1,950) G. Balding, 8–11–11
2. Limonali,   3. Regal Splendour. 3, 3.   11 ran
1964–65 Rupununi (11–4f) H. Beasley (£2,124) A. Thomas, 9–11–0
2. Sword Flash,   3. Beau Normand. 8, 2.   22 ran
1965–66 What a Myth (3–1f) P. Kelleway (£2,129) H. Price, 8–12–3
2. Princeful,   3. Highland   Dist., Bad.   11 ran
       Wedding.
1966–67 Kilburn (7–1) H. Beasley (£1,708) C. Nesfield, 8–12–7
2. Highland Wedding,   3. Game Purston.   ¾, ½.   11 ran
1967–68 Abandoned

Race 252: MASSEY-FERGUSON GOLD CUP

2 miles 4 furlongs handicap chase. Cheltenham. Run over 2 miles 5 furlongs 197 yards in 1963–64

1963–64 Limeking (100–9) T. Taaffe (£2,517) D. J. Morgan, 6–10–12
2. Flying Wild,   3. Happy Spring.   2, 1½.   14 ran
1964–65 Flying Wild (100–8) T. Carberry (£3,989) D. L. Moore, 8–10–6
2. Buona notte,   3. Arkle.   Sht Hd, 1.   7 ran

1965–66 Flyingbolt (5–2f) P. Taaffe (£4,435) T. Dreaper, 6–12–6
    2. Solbina,   **3.** Scottish   15, 1½.   11 ran
                                    Memories.
1966–67 Laird (13–2) J. King (£3,983) R. Turnell, 5–10–9
    2. Charlie Worcester,   **3.** Stalbridge   10, 5.   8 ran
                                      Colonist.
1967–68 Abandoned

Race 253: HENRY VIII CHASE

2 miles 18 yards. Sandown. Run over 2 miles 275 yards at Hurst Park until 1962–63

1957–58 Le Palatin (5–1) F. T. Winter (£680) H. Price, 6 yrs
    2. Double Star,   **3.** Caesar's Helm.   1½, 3.   9 ran
1958–59 Staghound (4–1) F. T. Winter (£680) H. Price, 7 yrs
    2. Wayward Bird,   **3.** Flame Royal.   Dist., 3.   8 ran
1959–60 Mariner's Dance (13–2) V. Speck (£680) P. Cazalet, 6 yrs
    2. Prudent King,   **3.** Quick Approach. 10, 12.   6 ran
1960–61 King's Nephew (13–2) M. Scudamore (£684) F. Cundell, 6 yrs
    2. Blessington Esquire,   **3.** Friendly Boy.   1, 10.   10 ran
1961–62 Granville (13–8f) R. McCreery (£684) H. Price, 5 yrs
    2. Wilmington II,   **3.** Firecracker.   4, 12.   17 ran
1962–63 Blue Rondo (11–2) J. Gifford (£685) K. Bailey, 8 yrs
    2. Irish Imp,   **3.** Sky Pink.   ½, 15.   7 ran
1963–64 Buona Notte (13–8) J. Haine (£1,042) R. Turnell, 6 yrs
    2. Dunkirk,   **3.** Lackapin.   4, 3.   5 ran
1964–65 Man of the East (8–1) J. Morrissey (£1,042) A. W. Jones, 6 yrs
    2. Salmon Spray,   **3.** Antiar.   3, 8.   5 ran
1965–66 Arctic Sunset (7–1) G. Milburn (£1,030) J. Oliver, 5 yrs
    2. Dicky May,   **3.** Stalbridge   8, 10.   10 ran
                                      Colonist.
1966–67 Irish Rover (7–4f) D. Mould (£1,030) P. Cazalet, 6 yrs
    2. Merry Stranger,   **3.** Wedding Dance. 15, Bad.   5 ran
1967–68 Abandoned

HORSES IN CAPITAL LETTERS
(EXCLUDING RACE 245)
WERE TO BE, OR HAD BEEN,
PLACED IN THE CLASSICS

Race 254: KING GEORGE VI CHASE

3 miles. Kempton

1947 Rowland Roy, 8 (10)		**1952** Halloween, 7	(6)	
1948 Cottage Rake, 9 (9)		**1953** Galloway Braes, 8 (7)		
1949 Finnure, 8 (4)		**1954** Halloween, 9	(8)	
1950 Manicou, 5 (7)		**1955** Limber Hill, 8	(8)	
1951 Statecraft, 6 (6)		**1956** Rose Park, 9	(6)	

1957–58 Mandarin (7–1) P. Madden (£2,983) F. Walwyn, 6 yrs
    2. Lochroe,   **3.** Kerstin.   1, 1½.   9 ran
1958–59 Lochroe (7–2) A. Freeman (£2,885) P. Cazalet, 10 yrs
    2. Roddy Owen,   **3.** Mandarin.   Hd, 15.   7 ran
1959–60 Mandarin (5–2f) P. Madden (£2,919) F. Walwyn, 8 yrs
    2. Pointsman,   **3.** Pas Seul.   Hd, 15.   9 ran
1960–61 Saffron Tartan (5–2f) F. T. Winter (£2,862) D. Butchers, 9 yrs
    2. King,   **3.** Knucklecracker.   3, 8.   10 ran
1961–62 Abandoned
1962–63 Abandoned
1963–64 Mill House (2–7f) G. W. Robinson (£4,933) F. Walwyn, 6 yrs
    2. Blue Dolphin,   **3.** Coleen Star.   20, Bad.   3 ran
1964–65 Frenchman's Cove (4–11f) S. Mellor (£4,723) H. Thomson-Jones, 9 yrs
    2. Jay Trump.   10.   2 ran
1965–66 Arkle (1–7f) P. Taaffe (£4,634) T. Dreaper, 8 yrs
    2. Dormant,   **3.** Arctic Ocean.   Dist., Dist.   4 ran
1966–67 Dormant (10–1) J. King (£3,689) J. C. Wells-Kendrew, 9 yrs
    2. Arkle,   **3.** Maigret.   1, Bad.   7 ran
1967–68 Abandoned

Race 255: FRED WITHINGTON HANDICAP CHASE

4 miles. Cheltenham

1956–57 Henry Purcell (25–1) R. Richards (£870) E. C. Smith, 10–10–4
    2. Polonius,   **3.** Rondino.   2, 1½.   16 ran
1957–58 Polar Flight (7–1) G. Slack (£1,007) G. Spann, 7–11–4
    2. Tea Fiend,   **3.** Athenian.   3, ¾.   16 ran
1958–59 Bell (8–1) B. Lawrence (£1,014) T. H. Yates, 7–10–2
    2. Hart Royal,   **3.** Wyndburgh.   10, 5.   13 ran
1959–60 Clover Bud (100–7) S. Mellor (£937) G. Llewellin, 9–9–8
    2. Rose's Pact,   **3.** Oscar Wilde.   15, Hd.   10 ran
1960–61 Vivant (13–2) R. Hamey (£996) W. Stephenson, 7–10–1
    2. Cannobie Lee,   **3.** Merganser.   4, ¾.   14 ran
1961–62 Abandoned

1962–63 Abandoned
1963–64 Pappageno's Cottage (10–1) J. Haldane (£1,413) J. Oliver, 9–11–4
    2. Pheberion,   **3.** Caduval.   3, 2.   18 ran
1964–65 Pappageno's Cottage (9–1) T. Biddlecombe (£1,427) J. Oliver, 10–11–10
    2. What a Myth,   **3.** Happy Arthur.   4, 12.   19 ran
1965–66 Mr Wonderful (4–1f) R. Vibert (£1,434) T. Forster, 10–10–3
    2. Kilburn,   **3.** Vulcano.   2½, 25.   12 ran
1966–67 Abandoned
1967–68 Abandoned

Race 256: MILDMAY MEMORIAL CHASE

3 miles 5 furlongs handicap. Sandown

1952 Cromwell, 11–11–10	(12)	**1955** Abandoned	
1953 Whispering Steel, 8–11–3	(16)	**1956** Linwell, 8–9–9	(10)
1954 Domata, 8–10–12	(10)		

1956–57 Much Obliged (12½–1) H. East (£2,147) N. Crump, 9–10–12
    2. Glorious Twelfth,   **3.** Hart Royal.   Nk, 3.   20 ran
1957–58 Polar Flight (11–2) G. Slack (£2,102) G. Spann, 8–10–7
    2. Hall Weir,   **3.** Tiberetta,   2, Hd.   14 ran
1958–59 Abandoned
1959–60 Team Spirit (10–1) G. W. Robinson (£2,077) D. L. Moore, 8–9–10
    2. Marcilly,   **3.** Mac Joy.   1½, ½.   12 ran
1960–61 Mac Joy (25–1) M. Scudamore (£1,986) K. Bailey, 9–10–7
    2. Wily Oriental,   **3.** Springbok.   3, 1.   13 ran
1961–62 Duke of York (6–1jf) D. Scott (£2,159) J. Tilling, 7–10–12
    2. John o'Groats,   **3.** Springbok.   3, 2.   18 ran
1962–63 Abandoned
1963–64 Dormant (11–4jf) P. Buckley (£2,048) N. Crump, 7–10–12
    2. John o'Groats,   **3.** Time.   8, ¾.   9 ran
1964–65 Freddie (2–1f) P. McCarron (£2,564) R. Tweedie, 8–10–5
    2. Vultrix,   **3.** Rip.   Sht Hd, 1½.   12 ran
1965–66 What a Myth (4–1) P. Kelleway (£2,355) H. Price, 9–12–0
    2. Stirling,   **3.** Kapeno.   6, 3.   5 ran
1966–67 Abandoned
1967–68 Stalbridge Colonist (7–1) S. Mellor (£2,479) K. Cundell, 9–12–0
    2. Red Rondo,   **3.** What a Myth.   Hd, 1½.   18 ran

Race 257: MANDARIN HANDICAP CHASE

3 miles 2 furlongs 82 yards. Newbury

1962–63 Mill House (5–6f) G. W. Robinson (£2,489) F. Walwyn, 6–12–5
    2. Border Sparkle,   **3.** Meon Valley.   8, 12.   6 ran

1963–64 Out and About (7–1) B. Gregory (£2,794) K. Cundell, 9–10–5
    2. Beau Normand,   **3.** Crobeg.   6, 15.   6 ran
1964–65 Mill House (6–4) G. W. Robinson (£1,980) F. Walwyn, 8–12–7
    2. Dormant,   **3.** Happy Spring.   Hd, 12.   7 ran
1965–66 Abandoned
1966–67 What a Myth (5–2f) P. Kelleway (£2,232) H. Price, 10–11–9
    2. Woodlawn,   **3.** Different Class.   1, 2½.   11 ran
1967–68 Abandoned

Race 258: THYESTES HANDICAP CHASE

3 miles 170 yards. Gowran Park

1956–57 Sandy Jane II (10–1) F. Shortt (£444) P. Murphy, 10–9–13
    2. Solwink,   **3.** Roddy Owen.   8, 20.   11 ran
1957–58 Copp (3–1jf) H. Beasley (£504) P. Sleator, 14–10–5
    2. Sandy Jane II,   **3.** Sam Brownthorn. 4, 4.   13 ran
1958–59 Slippery Serpent (11–2) P. Taaffe (£663) T. Dreaper, 8–10–3
    2. Zonda,   **3.** Mr What.   6, 4.   13 ran
1959–60 Blue Moth (10–1) F. Carroll (£844) P. Sleator, 11–10–1
    2. Nic Atkins,   **3.** Zonda.   3, 2½.   8 ran
1960–61 Hunter's Breeze (4–1) F. Carroll (£799) A. C. Bryce-Smith, 10–10–10
    2. Owen's Sedge,   **3.** Mr What.   4, 4.   11 ran
1961–62 Kerforo (6–1) L. McLoughlin (£787) T. Dreaper, 8–9–8
    2. Brown Diamond,   **3.** Fortria.   Nk, 2.   10 ran
1962–63 My Baby (6–1) F. Shortt (£990) P. Murphy, 8–9–7
    2. Last Link,   **3.** Clementine.   Nk, 15.   10 ran
1963–64 Arkle (4–6f) P. Taaffe (£900) T. Dreaper, 7–12–0
    2. Loving Record,   **3.** Springtime Lad II.
          10, 1.   9 ran
1964–65 Fort Leney (5–4f) L. McLoughlin (£1,307) T. Dreaper, 7–12 -0
    2. Greek Vulgan,   **3.** Greatrakes.   2, 1.   10 ran
1965–66 Flyingbolt (2–5f) P. Taaffe (£1,325) T. Dreaper, 7–12–0
    2. Height o'Fashion,   **3.** Flying Wild.   Dist., 25.   4 ran
1966–67 Greek Vulgan (4–1) B. Hannon (£1,375) T. Taaffe, 10–10–12
    2. Corrie-Vacoul,   **3.** Talbot.   8, 3.   10 ran
1967–68 Great Lark (8–1) T. S. Murphy (£1,379) W. T. O'Grady, 9–11–11
    2. Alice Maythorn,   **3.** Tobraheela.   4, 5.   13 ran

HORSES IN CAPITAL LETTERS
(EXCLUDING RACE 245)
WERE TO BE, OR HAD BEEN,
PLACED IN THE CLASSICS

Race 259: GREAT YORKSHIRE HANDICAP CHASE

3 miles 2 furlongs. Doncaster. Run over 3 miles and a few yards until 1966-67

1951 Arctic Gold, 6–11–0 (10)   **1954** Abandoned
1952 Abandoned   **1955** Bramble Tudor, 7–11–3 (14)
1953 Knock Hard, 9–11–7 (9)   **1956** Abandoned

1956–57 E.S.B. (10–1) T. Molony (£2,118) T. F. Rimell, 11–11–10
     2. De Combat,   3. Sundew.   8, 3.   13 ran
1957–58 Hall Weir (11–4f) W. Rees (£2,173) F. Cundell, 8–10–10
     2. Caesar's Helm,   3. Mariner's Hand.   3, 1½.   17 ran
1958–59 Abandoned
1959–60 Knightsbrook (11–4f) G. Slack (£1,982) W. Hall, 8–11–1
     2. O'Malley Point,   3. Spring Flight.   8, 2.   10 ran
1960–61 Chavara (10–1) S. Mellor (£2,092) G. R. Owen, 8–10–7
     2. O'Malley Point,   3. Northern King.   5, ½.   13 ran
1961–62 Nicolaus Silver (100–8) H. Beasley (£2,130) T. F. Rimell, 10–11–9
     2. Cocky Consort,   3. Springbok.   3, Sht Hd.   15 ran
1962–63 Abandoned
1963–64 King's Nephew (7–4jf) S. Mellor (£2,870) F. Cundell, 10–11–10
     2. Kapeno,   3. Major Hitch.   5, 10.   9 ran
1964–65 King of Diamonds (20–1) J. Kenneally (£3,070) G. Vergette, 7–10–4
     2. Limetra,   3. Honey End.   1, 12.   12 ran
1965–66 Freddie (2–1f) P. McCarron (£3,040) R. Tweedie, 9–11–7
     2. Stirling,   3. Imperator.   2, 3.   12 ran
1966–67 Spear Fir (100–6) J. Leech (£2,924) R. Fairbairn, 8–10–6
     2. Dormant,   3. Mill House.   ½, 2.   12 ran
1967–68 Sixty-nine (7–1) B. Fletcher (£2,464) D. Smith, 8–12–0
     2. Regal Wine,   3. Rutherfords.   Sht Hd, 15.   16 ran

Race 260: HAYDOCK PARK NATIONAL TRIAL

3 miles 4 furlongs handicap chase. Haydock

1956–57 Goosander (8–11f) H. East (£1,055) N. Crump, 9–11–8
     2. Red Menace,   3. Felias.   2, 1.   7 ran
1957–58 Giles Farnaby (100–7) P. Madden (£1,655) T. Lord, 12–9–7
     2. Pippykin,   3. Filon d'Or.   10, 1.   12 ran
1958–59 Abandoned
1959–60 Highland Dandy (6–1) R. Langley (£1,953) G. R. Owen, 8–10–3
     2. Pippykin,   3. Giles Farnaby.   2, 8.   10 ran
1960–61 Uncle Isaac (6–1) C. Scott (£1,959) T. Scott, 8-10-5
     2. Badanloch,   3. Scotch Prince.   ¾, 1½.   9 ran
1961–62 Solfen (4–1f) T. Taaffe (£2,071) W. O'Grady, 10–12–0
     2. John o'Groats,   3. Sham Fight.   5, 12.   15 ran

1962–63 Abandoned
1963–64 Reproduction (9–4) S. Mellor (£1,998) G. R. Owen, 11–9–7
    2. Border Sparkle,   **3.** Count.   2, 2.   6 ran
1964–65 Abandoned
1965–66 Ringer (5–2f) P. Broderick (£1,688) W. A. Stephenson, 7–10–4
    2. Rough Tweed,   **3.** Fossa.   Nk, 3.   11 ran
1966–67 Bassnet (13–2) D. Nicholson (£1,722) A. Kilpatrick, 8–10–12
    2. Game Purston,   **3.** Woodland   4, 3.   8 ran
                           Venture.
1967–68 Abandoned

Race 261: EIDER HANDICAP CHASE

4 miles 350 yards. Newcastle. Called Tote Investors Cup in 1956–57

1956–57 Wyndburgh (12½–1) M. Batchelor (£920) P. Wilkinson, 7–10–4
    2. Green Drill,   **3.** Moston Lane.   Nk, 1.   15 ran
1957–58 Wyndburgh (9–4f) M. Batchelor (£1,060) P. Wilkinson, 8–11–1
    2. Game Field,   **3.** Kari Sou.   4, Hd.   10 ran
1958–59 Turmoil (7–1) J. Hudson (£830) T. Hudson, 9–9–11
    2. Mainstown,   **3.** Border Bandit.   8, Dist.   14 ran
1959–60 Abandoned
1960–61 Carmen IV (5–1) R. Brewis (£845) R. Brewis, 9–11–3
    2. Master Perie,   **3.** Kinmont Wullie.   5, 6.   13 ran
1961–62 Ballydar (13–2) P. Buckley (£831) N. Crump, 9–10–7
    2. Kinmont Wullie,   **3.** Angostura.   3, 5.   11 ran
1962–63 Abandoned
1963–64 Vice Regent (6–1) S. Hayhurst (£1,040) T. Scott, 7–9–12
    2. Pontin-Go,   **3.** Moyrath.   6, 30.   5 ran
1964–65 Pontin-Go (10–1) J. Lehane (£640) W. Marshall, 13–9–9
    2. Away for Slates,   **3.** Major Hitch.   1½, 8.   16 ran
1965–66 Highland Wedding (6–1) O. McNally (£1,320) G. Balding, 9–10–11
    2. Major Hitch,   **3.** Vice Regent.   20, ¾.   10 ran
1966–67 Highland Wedding (evens f) O. McNally (£1,320) G. Balding, 10–12–0
    2. Mr Wonderful,   **3.** Kirtle-Lad.   7, 10.   7 ran
1967–68 Abandoned

Race 262: STONE'S GINGER WINE HANDICAP CHASE

2 miles 4 furlongs 68 yards. Sandown

1960–61 Pouding (5–1) F. T. Winter (£1,967) F. Walwyn, 8–10–1
    2. Northern King,   **3.** O'Malley Point.   4, 1.   10 ran

1961–62 Rough Tweed (6–1) D. Nicholson (£2,079) N. Crump, 8–10–4
    2. Cocky Consort,   **3.** Strat Royal.   1½, 8.   16 ran
1962–63 Abandoned
1963–64 Flying Wild (10–1) T. Carberry (£3,049) D. L. Moore, 8–11–9
    2. Dormant,   **3.** Kapeno.   2, Sht Hd.   14 ran
1964–65 Rondetto (9–2jf) J. King (£2,666) R. Turnell, 9–11–5
    2. Wayward Queen,   **3.** Sandy Abbot.   5, ¾.   12 ran
1965–66 Abandoned
1966–67 Laird (6–1) J. King (£2,435) R. Turnell, 6–11–10
    2. Hello Dolly,   **3.** Moonduster.   1½, 2.   16 ran
1967–68 Bowgeeno (7–2jf) J. Haine (£2,453) R. Turnell, 8–10–13
    2. Charlie Worcester,   **3.** Hypur II.   ¾, 8.   10 ran

Race 263: SCHWEPPES GOLD TROPHY

2 miles handicap hurdle. Newbury. Run over 2 miles 1 furlong at Liverpool in 1962–63

1962–63 Rosyth (20–1) J. Gifford (£7,825) H. Price, 5–10–0
    2. Royal Jenny,   **3.** Iron Blue.   1, Sht Hd.   41 ran
1963–64 Rosyth (10–1) J. Gifford (£7,639) H. Price, 6–10–2
    2. Salmon Spray,   **3.** Sempervivum.   2, 2.   24 ran
1964–65 Elan (9–2f) D. Nicholson (£7,821) J. Sutcliffe jun., 6–10–7
    2. Rosyth,   **3.** Spartan General.   1½, 2.   21 ran
1965–66 Le Vermontois (15–2) J. Gifford (£6,472) H. Price, 5–11–3
    2. Sempervivum,   **3.** Risky.   6, 1.   28 ran
1966–67 Hill House (9–1) J. Gifford (£6,634) H. Price, 7–10–10
    2. Celtic Gold,   **3.** Beau Caprice.   12, Sht Hd.   28 ran
1967–68 Persian War (9–2f) J. Uttley (£6,751) C. Davies, 5–11–13
    2. Major Rose,   **3.** Sempervivum.   ½, 2.   33 ran

Race 264: MANIFESTO HANDICAP CHASE

3 miles. Lingfield

1959–60 Bell (11–8f) B. Lawrence (£688) T. H. Yates, 9–11–2
    2. Pas Seul,   **3.** Laramie.   6, 8.   4 ran
1960–61 Pas Seul (evens f) D. V. Dick (£688) R. Turnell, 8–12–7
    2. King's Nickel,   **3.** Solonace.   5, 8.   5 ran
1961–62 Pas Seul (11–8f) D. V. Dick (£788) R. Turnell, 9–12–7
    2. King's Nephew.   Only two finished. 2.   4 ran
1962–63 Abandoned
1963–64 Laffy (5–1) D. Mould (£1,390) P. Cazalet, 8–10–11
    2. Rupununi,   **3.** Knockaphrumpa. 1½, 1½.   10 ran

1964–65 Laffy (8–15f) D. V. Dick (£1,380) P. Cazalet, 9–11–9
    2. Double March,   **3.** L'Empereur.   6, 6.   3 ran
1965–66 Abandoned
1966–67 Vultrix (7–4) S. Mellor (£1,380) F. Cundell, 9–11–8
    2. Vulcano,   **3.** Rondetto.   2½, 30.   3 ran
1967–68 Bowgeeno (11–4) J. Haine (£1,040) R. Turnell, 8–11–12
    2. Vultrix,   **3.** Chu-teh.   5, 4.   8 ran

Race 265: LEOPARDSTOWN CHASE
3 miles handicap. Leopardstown

1956–57 Tutto (12½–1) J. Lehane (£927) M. Pollard, 10–10–7
    2. Sentina,   **3.** Longmead.   5, Hd.   14 ran
1957–58 Roddy Owen (100–8) H. Beasley (£927) D. J. Morgan, 9–12–0
    2. Mr What,   **3.** Richardstown.   8, 2½.   16 ran
1958–59 Zonda (10–1) G. W. Robinson (£897) M. Geraghty, 8–9–10
    2. Nic Atkins,   **3.** Top Twenty.   1¼, 5.   12 ran
1959–60 Fredith's Son (100–8) F. Shortt (£1,342) P. Murphy, 9–10–1
    2. Zonda,   **3.** Blue Moth.   2¼, 4.   12 ran
1960–61 Jonjo (100–6) G. W. Robinson (£1,346) J. W. Osborne, 11–9–8
    2. Zonda,   **3.** Roman Folly.   3, Hd.   11 ran
1961–62 Kerforo (7–2jf) L. McLoughlin (£1,320) T. Dreaper, 8–9–11
    2. Fredith's Son,   **3.** Mr What.   ¾, 12.   9 ran
1962–63 Owen's Sedge (15–2) P. Taaffe (£1,436) T. Dreaper, 10–10–10
    2. Four Aces,   **3.** Carrickbeg.   4, 4.   13 ran
1963–64 Arkle (4–7f) P. Taaffe (£1,671) T. Dreaper, 7–12–0
    2. Greatrakes,   **3.** Vulsea.   12, 20.   6 ran
1964–65 Arkle (8–11f) P. Taaffe (£2,584) T. Dreaper, 8–12–7
    2. Scottish Memories,   **3.** Persian Signal.   1, 10.   9 ran
1965–66 Arkle (1–5f) P. Taaffe (£2,475) T. Dreaper, 9–12–7
    2. Height o'Fashion,   **3.** Splash.   Nk, 15.   4 ran
1966–67 Fort Leney (7–1) P. McLoughlin (£2,591) T. Dreaper, 9–12–4
    2. Talbot,   **3.** Corrie-Vacoul.   15, 4.   10 ran
1967–68 Fort Leney (5–2jf) P. McLoughlin (£2,617) T. Dreaper, 10–12–7
    2. Greek Vulgan,   **3.** Cottagebrook.   6, 4.   7 ran

Race 266: VICTOR LUDORUM HURDLE
2 miles. Haydock. Four-year-olds

1961–62 Pillock's Green (5–1) H. Beasley (£1,089) T. F. Rimell
    2. Wild Fast,   **3.** Merlins Oak.   1½, 8.   9 ran
1962–63 Abandoned

1963–64 Makaldar (8–11f) D. Mould (£2,819) P. Cazalet
    2. Master Cappelle,   **3.** Ballet Painting.   5, 4.   11 ran
1964–65 Anselmo (13–8f) T. Carberry (£2,907) K. Piggott
    2. Gambling Debt,   **3.** Chorus.   Nk, 2½.   15 ran
1965–66 Harwell (4–9f) H. Beasley (£2,732) A. Thomas
    2. Fuengirola,   **3.** Expedier.   2, 1½.   9 ran
1966–67 Persian War (5–4f) J. Uttley (£2,440) B. Swift
    2. Spearhead,   **3.** Beau Chapeau.   7, 2.   9 ran
1967–68 Wing Master (8–1) R. Reid (£2,452) J. R. Bower
    2. Tanlic,   **3.** Young Ash Leaf. 3, 3.   6 ran

Race 267: TOM COULTHWAITE HANDICAP CHASE

3 miles. Haydock. Run over 3 miles 4 furlongs until 1964–65

1956–57 Goosander (11–4f) H. East (£691) N. Crump, 9–11–5
    2. Game Field,   **3.** E.S.B.   4, 5.   8 ran
1957–58 Tea Fiend (4–1f) S. Mellor (£991) G. R. Owen, 9–9–12
    2. Goosander,   **3.** Copper Cable.   Hd, 6.   12 ran
1958–59 Abandoned
1959–60 John Jacques (5–1) G. Scott (£991) N. Crump, 11–11–13
    2. Badanloch,   **3.** Pattino.   1, 2.   9 ran
1960–61 Rock's Cross (100–8) H. East (£991) N. Crump, 9–11–11
    2. Knight Errant,   **3.** Badanloch.   6, 2.   11 ran
1961–62 Reproduction (100–6) R. Langley (£991) G. R. Owen, 9–9–7
    2. Happy Kid,   **3.** Couligarten.   ½, 3.   16 ran
1962–63 Union Pacific (6–1) D. Campbell (£691) C. Bell, 9–9–2
    2. Master Perie,   **3.** Longtail.   5, 2.   14 ran
1963–64 Springbok (15–2) G. Scott (£1,898) N. Crump, 10–11–0
    2. Union Pacific,   **3.** Snifter.   Hd, 8.   10 ran
1964–65 Game Purston (100–6) K. B. White (£1,965) J. P. Yeomans, 7–10–2
    2. Big George,   **3.** Mac's Flare.   10, ½.   13 ran
1965–66 Forest Prince (7–2f) G. Scott (£2,041) N. Crump, 8–12–1
    2. Ringer,   **3.** Imperator.   6, 3.   13 ran
1966–67 Rutherfords (9–2) E. Harty (£1,990) T. Molony, 7–11–3
    2. Fossa,   **3.** Kellsboro' Wood. ½, 3.   10 ran
1967–68 Abandoned

Race 268: PRINCESS ROYAL HANDICAP HURDLE

2 miles 140 yards. Doncaster

1956–57 Merry Deal (10–1) G. Underwood (£1,116) A. Jones, 7–10–9
    2. Oakdale,   **3.** Borgia.   4, 1½.   12 ran

1957–58 Celtic Night (25–1) J. Birch (£1,082) T. Sanger, 5–9–13
    2. Tokoroa,   **3.** Fare Time.   Sht Hd, 3.   12 ran
1958–59 Abandoned
1959–60 Saucy Model (10–1) B. Carr (£1,099) R. Dick, 7–10–4
    2. Breathlessly Smart,   **3.** Laird o'Montrose. $\frac{3}{4}$, $\frac{1}{2}$.   13 ran
1960–61 Speedwell (10–1) H. McCalmont (£1,147) H. Thomson-Jones, 5–10–10
    2. Cheerer,   **3.** Merry Deal. $1\frac{1}{2}$, 1.   23 ran
1961–62 Abandoned
1962–63 Abandoned
1963–64 Magic Court (11–4f) P. McCarron (£1,238) T. Robson, 6–11–9
    2. Mustard,   **3.** Old Mull. $1\frac{1}{2}$, $\frac{1}{2}$.   16 ran
1964–65 Abandoned
1965–66 Welcome News (11–4f) J. Gifford (£890) H. Price, 7–11–1
    2. Holder,   **3.** Tilmoray. $1\frac{1}{2}$, 6.   16 ran
1966–67 Rackham (4–1jf) R. Edwards (£887) R. Hobson, 6–11–4
    2. Spartae,   **3.** Tudor Legend.   Hd, $2\frac{1}{2}$.   11 ran
1967–68 Inyanga (10–1) R. Reid (£953) G. N. Robinson, 7–10–0
    2. Valoroso,   **3.** Mowden Magic.   5, Hd.   14 ran

Race 269: K.P. HURDLE

2 miles hurdle. Kempton. Four-year-olds. Called Friary Meux Gold Cup until 1967–68

1964–65 Bronzino (11–2) R. Broadway (£3,039) G. Todd
    2. Robber Baron,   **3.** West Boy.   5, 2.   10 ran
1965–66 Harwell (11–10f) H. Beasley (£3,004) A. Thomas
    2. Fair Play II,   **3.** Colonel Imp.   1, 6.   12 ran
1966–67 Acrania (20–1) H. Beasley (£2,552) G. Harwood
    2. Te Fou,   **3.** Persian War.   3, 4.   16 ran
1967–68 St Cuthbert (9–4jf) T. Biddlecombe (£1,375) T. F. Rimell
    2· Privy Seal,   **3.** Hully Gully.   2, $\frac{1}{2}$.   12 ran

Race 270: GLOUCESTERSHIRE HURDLE

2 miles 200 yards. Cheltenham

1956–57 Div. I—Tokoroa (5–4f) D. V. Dick (£685) T. F. Rimell, 6 yrs
    2. Cortego,   **3.** Son and Heir II.   5, $\frac{3}{4}$.   10 ran
    Div. II—Saffron Tartan (10–11f) T. P. Burns (£685) M. V. O'Brien, 6 yrs
    2. Predominate,   **3.** Northern King.   3, 5.   12 ran
1957–58 Div. I—Admiral Stuart (6–5f) T. P. Burns (£685) M. V. O'Brien, 7 yrs
    2. Green Light,   **3.** Flaming Star.   3, Sht Hd.   19 ran
    Div. II—Prudent King (3–1f) T. P. Burns (£685) M. V. O'Brien, 6 yrs
    2. Magical Approach,   **3.** Staghound. $\frac{1}{2}$, 2.   19 ran

1958–59 Div. I—York Fair (4–5f) T. P. Burns (£685) M. V. O'Brien, 5 yrs
    2. No Comment,   **3.** Sire de l'Adour II. 8, 3.   16 ran
Div. II—Albergo (9–1) D. Page (£685) C. Magnier, 5 yrs
    2. Courts Appeal,   **3.** Vic Rose.   6, 4.   19 ran
1959–60 Div. I—Blue Mountain (5–1) R. Broadway (£685) G. Todd, 6 yrs
    2. Birinkiana,   **3.** Hal's Hope.   4, ½.   20 ran
Div. II—Bastille (33–1) W. Woods (£685) T. Masson, 5 yrs
    2. Mozie Law,   **3.** Sea Wife.   1½, 4.   18 ran
1960–61 Div. I—Beau Normand (5–1) W. Rees (£1,360) R. Turnell, 5 yrs
    2. Bridal Choice,   **3.** Brasher.   1½, 3.   18 ran
Div. II—Greektown (100–8) M. Scudamore (£1,360) W. Stephenson, 5 yrs
    2. Milo,   **3.** Four Acres.   3, 4.   15 ran
1961–62 Div. I—Tripacer (20–1) T. Carberry (£1,360) D. L. Moore, 4 yrs
    2. Trelawny,   **3.** Ross Sea.   Nk, ¾.   18 ran
Div. II—Clerical Grey (100–8) G. W. Robinson (£1,360) P. Murphy, 4 yrs
    2. Eastern Harvest,   **3.** Water Skier.   2, 3.   18 ran
1962–63 Div. I—Honour Bound (3–1f) T. Biddlecombe (£1,360) T. F. Rimell, 5 yrs
    2. Bahrain,   **3.** Super Fox.   1, 3.   18 ran
Div. II—Deetease (9–1) C. Chapman (£1,360) B. Foster, 5 yrs
    2. Oedipe,   **3.** Dionysus III.   ¾, 3.   18 ran
1963–64 Div. I—Flyingbolt (4–9f) P. Taaffe (£1,380) T. Dreaper, 5 yrs
    2. Extra Stout,   **3.** Dionysus III.   4, 2.   11 ran
Div. II—Elan (9–2) D. V. Dick (£1,380) J. Sutcliffe, 5 yrs
    2. Minute Gun,   **3.** Le Pirate.   Nk, Nk.   18 ran
1964–65 Div. I—Red Tears (7–1) S. Mellor (£1,365) H. Thomson Jones, 5 yrs
    2. Comet Star,   **3.** Cloucourt.   4, 3.   19 ran
Div. II—Havago (11–8f) H. Beasley (£1,365) P. Sleator, 6 yrs
    2. Tristram,   **3.** Palycidon.   2, 8.   15 ran
1965–66 Div. I—Beau Caprice (6–1) T. Jennings (£1,365) F. Walwyn, 12 yrs
    2. AURELIUS,   **3.** Woodbow.   12, 1½.   14 ran
Div. II—Fosco (7–2) D. Moore (£1,365) M. Goswell, 5 yrs
    2. Albinella,   **3.** Coventry Express. 2, ½.   19 ran
1966–67 Div. I—Chorus (15–2) J. Haine (£1,365) H. Thomson Jones, 6 yrs
    2. Black Justice,   **3.** Indamelia.   4, 1½.   20 ran
Div. II—Early to Rise (11–2) J. King (£1,365) R. Turnell, 7 yrs
    2. Dogged,   **3.** Drumikill.   6, Sht Hd.   14 ran
1967–68 Div. I—King Cutler (85–40) B. Fletcher (£1,365) D. Smith, 5 yrs
    2. My Swanee,   **3.** Irish Rain.   6, 2½.   12 ran
Div. II—L'Escargot (13–2) T. Carberry (£1,365) D. L. Moore, 5 yrs
    2. Pick Me Up,   **3.** King Penny.   6, 15.   11 ran

Race 271: TOTALISATOR CHAMPION NOVICES' CHASE

3 miles 2 furlongs 170 yards. Cheltenham. Run over 3 miles and called Broadway Novices' Chase until 1963–64

1956–57	Mandarin (8–1) M. Scudamore (£685) F. Walwyn, 6 yrs			
	2. Gentle Colein,	**3.** Comedian's Folly. 25, 10.		14 ran
1957–58	Just Awake (100–7) A. Freeman (£685) P. Cazalet, 6 yrs			
	2. Limonali,	**3.** Galloway Hills. Sht Hd, 4.		19 ran
1958–59	Mac Joy (4–1) A. Freeman (£685) K. Bailey, 7 yrs			
	2. Team Spirit,	**3.** Dicksboro. 1, 1.		11 ran
1959–60	Solfen (5–4f) P. Taaffe (£685) W. O'Grady, 8 yrs			
	2. Scotch Prince,	**3.** Coleen Star. 25, 1.		21 ran
1960–61	Grallagh Cnoc (8–13f) P. Taaffe (£1,360) J. W. Osborne, 7 yrs			
	2. Solfenora,	**3.** Cadmore. 6, 5.		17 ran
1961–62	Caduval (11–2) L. Morgan (£1,360) B. Lubecki, 7 yrs			
	2. Rye Light,	**3.** Brittas. 2, 15.		13 ran
1962–63	Arkle (4–9f) P. Taaffe (£1,360) T. Dreaper, 6 yrs			
	2. Jomsviking,	**3.** Brasher. 20, 4.		15 ran
1963–64	Buona notte (11–8f) J. Haine (£6,035) R. Turnell, 7 yrs			
	2. Fort Leney,	**3.** Lackapin. ½, 6.		16 ran
1964–65	Arkloin (100–7) L. McLoughlin (£5,792) T. Dreaper, 6 yrs			
	2. Doone Valley,	**3.** Brasher. 4, 4.		17 ran
1965–66	Different Class (10–1) D. Mould (£6,092) P. Cazalet, 6 yrs			
	2. Jomsviking,	**3.** Richard's Jubilee. Sht Hd, 4.		17 ran
1966–67	Border Jet (4–1f) J. Gifford (£6,269) H. Price, 7 yrs			
	2. Bowgeeno,	**3.** Busty Hill. 8, 2.		19 ran
1967–68	Herring Gull (9–1) J. Crowley (£6,318) P. Mullins, 6 yrs			
	2. Gay Trip,	**3.** Freddie Boy. 6, 2.		16 ran

Race 272: NATIONAL HUNT HANDICAP CHASE

3 miles 1 furlong. Cheltenham. Run over 3 miles and a few yards until 1964–65

1956–57	Sentina (3–1f) P. Taaffe (£1,025) T. Dreaper, 7–10–4			
	2. Scottish Sea,	**3.** Sydney Jones. 15, 1½.		12 ran
1957–58	Sentina (7–1) T. Taaffe (£1,370) T. Dreaper, 8–11–7			
	2. Valiant Spark,	**3.** Cannobie Lee. 6, 1½.		14 ran
1958–59	Winning Coin (100–9) D. V. Dick (£1,370) G. Beeby, 7–11–7			
	2. Bell,	**3.** Rathronan. 4, 5.		14 ran
1959–60	Isle of Skye (100–8) A. Keen (£1,370) A. S. Kilpatrick, 9–10–5			
	2. Bob Tailed 'Un,	**3.** Lansallos. 1, 2.		12 ran
1960–61	Ravencroft (9–2) F. T. Winter (£1,360) F. Walwyn, 8–10–3			
	2. Owen's Sedge,	**3.** Chavara. 4, Nk.		10 ran

1961–62 Longtail (100–7) S. Mellor (£1,360) R. Curran, 7–11–0
    2. Solray,   **3.** Brown Diamond. 5, 6.   18 ran
1962–63 Team Spirit (100–8) G. W. Robinson (£1,360) F. Walwyn, 11–11–4
    2. Brown Diamond,   **3.** Hal's Hope.   1, 4.   24 ran
1963–64 Prudent Barney (10–1) T. Biddlecombe (£2,070) R. Renton, 10–10–11
    2. Aussie,   **3.** Caduval.   5, 1½.   10 ran
1964–65 Rondetto (11–2) J. Haine (£2,055) R. Turnell, 9–11–10
    2. Fort Leney,   **3.** Duke of York. 3, 3.   20 ran
1965–66 Arkloin (5–2f) P. Taaffe (£2,050) T. Dreaper, 7–12–5
    2. Easter Prince,   **3.** Plea in Bar.   1, 1½.   12 ran
1966–67 Different Class (13–2) D. Mould (£2,050) P. Cazalet, 7–11–13
    2. Tobraheela,   **3.** Penvulgo.   4, 6.   16 ran
1967–68 Battledore (3–1f) C. Stobbs (£2,050) W. A. Stephenson, 7–10–10
    2. Red Rondo,   **3.** Larbawn.   Hd, Nk.   8 ran

Race 273: NATIONAL HUNT TWO MILE CHAMPION CHASE

2 miles. Cheltenham

1958–59 Quita Que (4–9f) J. Cox (£2,172) D. L. Moore, 10 yrs
    2. Top Twenty,   **3.** Double Star. 6, 15.   9 ran
1959–60 Fortria (15–8f) P. Taaffe (£1,977) T. Dreaper, 8 yrs
    2. Blue Dolphin,   **3.** Brown Owen. 3, 3.   7 ran
1960–61 Fortria (2–5f) P. Taaffe (£1,883) T. Dreaper, 9 yrs
    2. Sandy Abbot,   **3.** Quita Que.   2, 8.   5 ran
1961–62 Piperton (100–6) D. V. Dick (£1,926) A. Tomlinson, 8 yrs
    2. Scottish Memories,   **3.** Blue Dolphin. 1½, 6.   7 ran
1962–63 Sandy Abbot (5–1) S. Mellor (£1,934) G. R. Owen, 8 yrs
    2. Scottish Memories,   **3.** Blue Dolphin. Sht Hd, ¾.   5 ran
1963–64 Ben Stack (2–1) P. Taaffe (£2,936) T. Dreaper, 7 yrs
    2. Blue Dolphin,   **3.** Scottish   2, 4.   5 ran
                                       Memories.
1964–65 Dunkirk (8–1) D. V. Dick (£2,949) P. Cazalet, 8 yrs
    2. Greektown,   **3.** Flash Bulb. 20, 3.   6 ran
1965–66 Flyingbolt (1–5f) P. Taaffe (£2,888) T. Dreaper, 7 yrs
    2. Flash Bulb,   **3.** Flying Wild. 15, ¾.   6 ran
1966–67 Drinny's Double (7–2) F. Nash (£2,946) R. Turnell, 9 yrs
    2. Pawnbroker,   **3.** Arctic Sunset. Nk, 2½.   8 ran
1967–68 Drinny's Double (6–1) F. Nash (£2,927) R. Turnell, 10 yrs
    2. Border Grace,   **3.** Ronan.   1½, 6.   5 ran

Race 274: NATIONAL HUNT CHASE
4 miles. Cheltenham

1934 Crown Piper, 9 (26) **1946** Prattler, 11 (20) **1952** Frosty Knight, 6 (19)
1935 Rod and Gun, 8 (20) **1947** Maltese **1953** Pontage, 7 (22)
1936 Pucka Belle, 10 (22) Wanderer, 8 (20) **1954** Quare Times, 8 (26)
1937 Hopeful Hero, 9 (20) **1948** Bruno II, 8 (37) **1955** Reverend
1938 St George II, 9 (26) **1949** Castledermot, 7 (17) Prince, 9 (26)
1939 Litigant, 8 (21) **1950** Ellesmere, 7 (26) **1956** Rosana III, 7 (22)
1940–45 No race **1951** Cushendun, 6 (18)

1956–57 Kari Sou (100–6) A. Lillingston (£2,138) A. H. Thomlinson, 8 yrs
    2. Copper Cable,   **3.** Rose's Pact.   Hd, 2.   24 ran
1957–58 Spud Tamson (13–2) G. Dun (£2,216) T. Dun, 7 yrs
    2. Kolpham,   **3.** Landshire Lane.   10, 3.   28 ran
1958–59 Sabaria (5–2f) J. Lawrence (£2,021) R. Turnell, 8 yrs
    2. Bantry Bay,   **3.** Calor.   Dist., 15.   17 ran
1959–60 Proud Socks (100–6) H. Thompson (£2,186) V. Bishop, 8 yrs
    2. Meldola,   **3.** Not a Link.   30, 1½.   22 ran
1960–61 Superfine (10–1) Sir W. Pigott-Brown (£2,118) F. Cundell, 8 yrs
    2. King's Nickel,   **3.** Beotien.   10, Nk.   33 ran
1961–62 Go Slow (10–1) G. Small (£2,040) A. Piper, 7 yrs
    2. Golden Seabright,   **3.** Bijou.   15, 4.   26 ran
1962–63 Time (8–1) I. Balding (£2,235) W. Stephenson, 8 yrs
    2. Croizet,   **3.** Big George.   20, 5.   35 ran
1963–64 Dorimont (4–1) C. Vaughan (£2,138) T. Taaffe, 10 yrs
    2. Pontoeuvre,   **3.** Sunbridge.   3, 1½.   30 ran
1964–65 Red Vale (100–8) G. Small (£1,826) A. Piper, 11 yrs
    2. Fascinating Forties,   **3.** Saintworthy.   1½, 1½.   26 ran
1965–66 Polaris Missile (100–6) M. J. Thorne (£1,874) M. J. Thorne, 7 yrs
    2. Sally Brook,   **3.** Saintworthy.   6, ¾.   29 ran
1966–67 Master Tammy (100–7) B. Fanshawe (£1,757) G. Guilding, 9 yrs
    2. Lizzy the Lizard,   **3.** Pearlita.   Nk, 10.   24 ran
1967–68 Fascinating Forties (9–1) M. Dickinson (£1,923) G. R. Owen, 9 yrs
    2. Cured,   **3.** Moon River.   ½, 10.   22 ran

Race 275: COTSWOLD CHASE
2 miles. Cheltenham

1956–57 Ballyatom (8–1) R. McCreery (£685) G. Beeby, 5 yrs
    2. Boys Hurrah,   **3.** Oasis.   4, 6.   13 ran
1957–58 Fortria (7–2) T. Taaffe (£685) T. Dreaper, 6 yrs
    2. Irish Jurist,   **3.** Regal Token.   5, 4.   17 ran
1958–59 Flame Gun (7–2) F. T. Winter (£685) C. Mallon, 8 yrs
    2. Cashel View,   **3.** Fellhound.   2, 8.   14 ran

1959–60 Mazurka (10–1) R. R. Harrison (£685) R. Smyth, 6 yrs
    2. Daily Telegraph,   3. Rock House   Nk, 1.   25 ran
                                Bridge.
1960–61 Mountcashel King (2–5f) P. Taaffe (£1,360) T. Dreaper, 6 yrs
    2. Rough Tweed,   3. Silver Dome.   5, 3.   12 ran
1961–62 Prudent Barney (20–1) H. East (£1,360) R. Renton, 8 yrs
    2. Double March,   3. One Seven Seven. 25, Bad.   9 ran
1962–63 Ben Stack (13–8f) P. Taaffe (£1,360) T. Dreaper, 6 yrs
    2. Irish Imp,   3. Another Flash.   ½, 8.   17 ran
1963–64 Greektown (13–2) M. Scudamore (£1,380) W. Stephenson, 8 yrs
    2. Snaigow,   3. High Power.   15, 10.   16 ran
1964–65 Flyingbolt (4–9f) P. Taaffe (£1,365) T. Dreaper, 6 yrs
    2. Princeful,   3. Ballinaclasha.   5, 4.   13 ran
1965–66 Arctic Sunset (3–1) G. Milburn (£1,365) J. Oliver, 6 yrs
    2. Thorn Gate,   3. Havago.   3, 1½.   9 ran
1966–67 Arctic Stream (8–1) B. Hannon (£1,365) P. Rooney, 7 yrs
    2. First Audition,   3. Tilmoray.   ¾, 10.   9 ran
1967–68 Hustler (20–1) B. Brogan (£1,365) Earl Jones, 6 yrs
    2. Monks Mead,   3. Get Stepping.   5, 5.   11 ran

Race 276: GRAND ANNUAL CHASE

2 miles handicap. Cheltenham

1956–57 Sir Edmund (6–1) R. Morrow (£1,025) A. S. Kilpatrick, 7–10–12
    2. Rosenkavalier,   3. Lancelot.   2, 1½.   11 ran
1957–58 Top Twenty (10–1) F. Shortt (£1,370) C. Magnier, 9–10–7
    2. Dove Cote,   3. Prince Nearco.   5, 1½.   18 ran
1958–59 Top Twenty (9–2jf) F. T. Winter (£1,370) C. Magnier, 10–12–6
    2. Lancelot,   3. Limeville.   2, 1.   12 ran
1959–60 Monsieur Trois Etoiles (3–1f) F. Carroll (£1,370) J. Brogan, 8–11–6
    2. Moretons,   3. Icanopit.   ½, 6.   9 ran
1960–61 Barberyn (3–1) M. Scudamore (£1,360) W. Stephenson, 6–11–0
    2. Fortron,   3. Icanopit.   ½, 1½.   10 ran
1961–62 Moretons (100–8) W. Rees (£1,360) P. Cazalet, 9–10–12
    2. Croise,   3. Barberyn.   1, 2.   14 ran
1962–63 Anner Loch (7–1) D. Nicholson (£1,360) J. Hicks, 8–10–6
    2. Richard of Bordeaux,   3. Prudent Barney.   5, 1½.   13 ran
1963–64 Richard of Bordeaux (9–1) G. W. Robinson (£1,380) F. Walwyn, 9–11–3
    2. Flash Bulb,   3. Too Slow.   2, ½.   14 ran
1964–65 Fort Rouge (13–2) G. Milburn (£1,365) J. Oliver, 7–11–0
    2. Well Packed,   3. Corrigadillisk.   ¾, 6.   10 ran
1965–66 Well Packed (100–7) T. Stack (£1,365) R. Renton, 8–10–11
    2. Ted Broon,   3. Moonduster.   ½, ½.   12 ran
1966–67 San Angelo (10–1) J. Buckingham (£1,365) E. Courage, 7–11–1
    2. Riversdale,   3. Flash Bulb.   4, ¾.   13 ran

1967–68 Hal's Farewell (5–1) J. King (£1,365) P. Bailey, 7–10–10
    2. Flash Bulb,   **3.** Certainement.   12, 4.   10 ran

Race 277: CHAMPION HURDLE
2 miles 200 yards. Cheltenham

1927 Blaris, 6	(4)	**1939** African Sister, 7	(13)	**1949** Hatton's	
1928 Brown Jack, 4	(6)	**1940** Solford, 9	(8)	Grace, 9	(14)
1929 Royal Falcon, 6	(6)	**1941** Seneca, 4	(6)	**1950** Hatton's	
1930 Brown Tony, 4	(5)	**1942** Forestation, 4	(20)	Grace, 10	(12)
1931 No race		**1943–44** No race		**1951** Hatton's	
1932 Insurance, 5	(3)	**1945** Brains Trust, 5	(16)	Grace, 11	(8)
1933 Insurance, 6	(5)	**1946** Distel, 5	(8)	**1952** Sir Ken, 5	(16)
1934 Chenango, 7	(5)	**1947** National		**1953** Sir Ken, 6	(7)
1935 Lion Courage, 7	(11)	Spirit, 6	(14)	**1954** Sir Ken, 7	(13)
1936 Victor Norman, 5	(8)	**1948** National		**1955** Clair Soleil, 6	(21)
1937 Free Fare, 9	(7)	Spirit, 7	(12)	**1956** Doorknocker, 8	(14)
1938 Our Hope, 9	(5)				

1956–57 Merry Deal (28–1) G. Underwood (£3,729) A. Jones, 7 yrs
    2. Quita Que,   **3.** Tout ou Rien.   5, 5.   16 ran
1957–58 Bandalore (20–1) G. Slack (£4,813) J. S. Wright, 7 yrs
    2. Tokoroa,   **3.** Retour   2, 3.   18 ran
                      de Flamme.
1958–59 Fare Time (13–2) F. T. Winter (£4,587) H. Price, 6 yrs
    2. Ivy Green,   **3.** Prudent King.   4, 1.   14 ran
1959–60 Another Flash (11–4f) H. Beasley (£4,290) P. Sleator, 6 yrs
    2. Albergo,   **3.** Saffron Tartan.   2, 3.   12 ran
1960–61 Eborneezer (4–1) F. T. Winter (£5,211) H. Price, 6 yrs
    2. Moss Bank,   **3.** Farmer's Boy.   3, 1½.   17 ran
1961–62 Anzio (11–2) G. W. Robinson (£5,143) F. Walwyn, 5 yrs
    2. Quelle Chance,   **3.** Another Flash.   3, 1½.   14 ran
1962–63 Winning Fair (100–9) A. Lillingston (£5,585) G. Spencer, 8 yrs
    2. Farrney Fox,   **3.** Quelle Chance.   3, Nk.   21 ran
1963–64 Magic Court (100–6) P. McCarron (£8, 161) T. Robson, 6 yrs
    2. Another Flash,   **3.** Kirriemuir.   4, ¾.   24 ran
1964–65 Kirriemuir (50–1) G. W. Robinson (£8,042) F. Walwyn, 5 yrs
    2. Spartan General,   **3.** Worcran.   1, 1½.   19 ran
1965–66 Salmon Spray (4–1) J. Haine (£7,921) R. Turnell, 8 yrs
    2. Sempervivum,   **3.** Flyingbolt.   3, ¾.   17 ran
1966–67 Saucy Kit (100–6) R. Edwards (£8,857) M. H. Easterby, 6 yrs
    2. Makaldar,   **3.** Talgo Abbess.
        (AURELIUS second, disqualified.) Original distances, 4, 1, 1½. 23 ran
1967–68 Persian War (4–1) J. Uttley (£7,798) C. H. Davies, 5 yrs
    2. Chorus,   **3.** Black Justice.   4, 5.   16 ran

Race 278: UNITED HUNTS CHALLENGE CUP

3 miles 2 furlongs 170 yards chase. Cheltenham. Run over 3 miles 4 furlongs until 1960–61, then 3 miles 2 furlongs until 1964–65

1956–57 Gay Roger (6–1) J. Daniell (£342) Miss L. Jones, 10 yrs
    2. Chandie IV,   **3.** Solbay.   8, 1.   16 ran
1957–58 Dark Island (5–1) W. Jones (£685) Miss D. Williams, 9 yrs
    2. Felhampton,   **3.** Mighty's Niece.   4, 3.   22 ran
1958–59 Mr Teddy (7–1) D. Oseman (£685) H. Rushton, 8 yrs
    2. J'Arrive,   **3.** Felhampton.   6, 15.   15 ran
1959–60 Master Copper (11–4) C. H. Davies (£685) C. H. Davies, 9 yrs
    2. Bannut Beauty,   **3.** Gay Roger.   3, 3.   14 ran
1960–61 Chaos (4–1jf) A. Frank (£680) W. J. A. Shepherd, 7 yrs
    2. Culleenpark,   **3.** Mr Teddy.   1½, 2.   18 ran
1961–62 Mr Teddy (7–2) A. Biddlecombe (£680) H. Rushton, 11 yrs
    2. Corn Star,   **3.** Chaos.   ¾, Sht Hd.   11 ran
1962–63 Baulking Green (5–2) G. Small (£680) T. Forster, 10 yrs
    2. Andy II,   **3.** Fun.   8, Hd.   11 ran
1963–64 Baulking Green (11–8f) A. Frank (£680) T. Forster, 11 yrs
    2. Chaos,   **3.** Moeda d'Ouro.   Nk, 25.   11 ran
1964–65 Baulking Green (15–8f) G. Small (£680) T. Forster, 12 yrs
    2. Mr Worth,   **3.** Dumbo II.   5, 15.   11 ran
1965–66 Snowdra Queen (5–2) H. Oliver (£680) Mrs J. Brutton, 7 yrs
    2. Mr Worth,   **3.** Pay Out.   5, 1½.   9 ran
1966–67 Baulking Green (5–4f) G. Small (£680) T. Forster, 14 yrs
    2. Snowdra Queen,   **3.** Persian Barrier.   6, Nk.   9 ran
1967–68 Snowdra Queen (13–2) D. Edmunds (£680) Mrs J. Brutton, 10 yrs
    2. Baulking Green,   **3.** Bartlemy Boy.   Hd, ½.   14 ran

Race 279: GEORGE DULLER HANDICAP HURDLE

3 miles. Cheltenham. Called Birdlip Handicap Hurdle until 1962–63

1956–57 Buckingham (4–1f) H. Sprague (£685) H. Nicholson, 8–10–13
    2. Pentathlon,   **3.** Sedgebrook.   Nk, Hd.   19 ran
1957–58 Springsilver (5–2f) H. Beasley (£1,025) C. Magnier, 8–10–10
    2. P.X.,   **3.** Hurry Home.   1, 3.   22 ran
1958–59 Sword Flash (100–8) A. Freeman (£1,025) H. T. Smith, 6–10–13
    2. Profit,   **3.** Cool Reception.   Sht Hd, Hd.   24 ran
1959–60 Cool Reception (100–7) G. Milburn (£1,025) C. Bewicke, 9–11–4
    2. Union Pacific (first, disq.) **3.** Sword Flash
                      Original distances, 3, 2.   25 ran
1960–61 Couligarten (25–1) M. Batchelor (£1,020) J. Wight, 7–10–6
    2. Union Way,   **3.** Oakleigh Way.   1½, 3.   18 ran
1961–62 St Stephen (100–6) F. T. Winter (£1,020) H. Price, 9–10–7
    2. Devon Cawvoge,   **3.** Carrigeen Duff.   3, 2.   28 ran

1962–63 Happy Arthur (4–1f) T. Brookshaw (£1,360) J. Oliver, 6–10–8
    2. Gideon,   **3.** Black Caprice.   8, 8.   21 ran
1963–64 Do or Die (25–1) T. Norman (£1,380) A. S. Neaves, 7–10–7
    2. Coral Cluster,   **3.** Rainbeam.   1½, Sht Hd.   21 ran
1964–65 Coral Cluster (8–1) T. Biddlecombe (£1,365) D. Gandolfo, 8–10–13
    2. No Restrictions,   **3.** Ribobo.   Nk, 3.   32 ran
1965–66 Harvest Gold (5–1) J. Fitzgerald (£1,365) T. Robson, 7–11–2
    2. Roman Scandal,   **3.** Eloped.   Sht Hd, 5.   20 ran
1966–67 Stepherion (100–9) N. Bampton (£1,365) J. Holt, 6–9–8
    2. Chancer,   **3.** Clonroche.   4, Hd.   24 ran
1967–68 Spaniard (8–1) B. Brogan (£1,365) J. K. Oliver, 6–12–2
    2. Go Gailey,   **3.** Tipperty.   ½, 1.   28 ran

Race 280: KIM MUIR MEMORIAL CHALLENGE CUP

3 miles 1 furlong handicap chase. Cheltenham. Run over 3 miles and a few yards until 1964–65

1956–57 Mighty Apollo (25–1) R. Brewis (£685) D. Machin, 8–10–13
    2. Oscar Wilde,   **3.** Mr Chippendale. Nk, 5.   16 ran
1957–58 Lochroe (10–11f) E. Cazalet (£685) P. Cazalet, 10–12–2
    2. Taxidermist,   **3.** Eastern Chance. 20, 5.   11 ran
1958–59 Irish Coffee (100–30) G. Kindersley (£685) C. McCartan, 9–10–13
    2. E.S.B.,   **3.** Wartown.   2, 3.   12 ran
1959–60 Solray (7–1) N. Upton (£685) F. Cliffe, 6–11–3
    2. Joan's Rival,   **3.** E.S.B.   1, 3.   9 ran
1960–61 Nicolaus Silver (10–1) W. Tellwright (£680) T. F. Rimell, 9–10–5
    2. Carmen IV,   **3.** Not a Link.   6, ½.   11 ran
1961–62 Carrickbeg (7–1) G. Pitman (£680) D. Butchers, 6–9–12
    2. Lizawake,   **3.** Naval Law.   4, 2.   10 ran
1962–63 Centre Circle (6–1) B. Ancil (£680) D. Ancil, 8–10–12
    2. Claymore,   **3.** Malacca III.   4, 5.   18 ran
1963–64 Jim's Tavern (10–1) G. Pitman (£690) J. Hicks, 7–10–4
    2. Pheberion,   **3.** Centre Circle.   4, ¾.   11 ran
1964–65 Burton Tan (10–1) R. Collie (£680) R. Collie, 10–11–3
    2. Pioneer Spirit,   **3.** Son of Tam.   2½, 2.   15 ran
1965–66 Jimmy Scot (6–1) J. Lawrence (£680) F. Walwyn, 10–10–9
    2. Oedipe,   **3.** Leslie.   6, Bad.   14 ran
1966–67 Chu-Teh (9–2) N. Gaselee (£680) K. Cundell, 8–10–8
    2. Border Fury,   **3.** Green Parrot.
          (Devon View third, disqualified.) Original distances, 5. 6. ½.   11 ran
1967–68 Chu-Teh (3–1f) D. Crossley-Cooke (£680) K. Cundell, 9–10–6
    2. Fossa,   **3.** Border Fury.   2, 1½.   8 ran

Race 281: MILDMAY OF FLETE CHALLENGE CUP

2 miles 4 furlongs handicap chase. Cheltenham. Run over 2 miles 5 furlongs and a few yards in 1963–64 and 1964–65

1956–57 Madras (100–7) J. A. Bullock (£685) M. L. Marsh, 9–10–2
    2. Bollinger,   **3.** Solar City.   4, 1.   12 ran
1957–58 Caesar's Helm (9–2) F. T. Winter (£685) R. Renton, 7–11–6
    2. Irish Coffee,   **3.** Fine Point.   ½, 8.   14 ran
1958–59 Siracusa (9–4f) B. Wilkinson (£685) R. Renton, 6–10–12
    2. Clanyon,   **3.** Flowering Lime.   6, 4.   12 ran
1959–60 Devon Customer (100–7) J. Guest (£685) S. Bowler, 8–10–4
    2. Plummers Plain,   **3.** Bachelor King.   3, 4.   12 ran
1960–61 Malting Barley (5–1) O. McNally (£680) G. Balding, 6–10–4
    2. Monsieur Trois Etoiles,   **3.** Major.   3, 8.   8 ran
1961–62 Spring Greeting (100–8) J. Lehane (£680) C. Bewicke, 7–10–6
    2. Clanyon,   **3.** Ballyfinaghy.   1, ½.   19 ran
1962–63 Milo (11–2) J. Gifford (£1,020) H. Blagrave, 8–10–4
    2. Limeking,   **3.** Dandy Tim.   ¾, 15.   19 ran
1963–64 Take Plenty (100–9) R. Vibert (£1,035) T. Forster, 8–10–1
    2. Sir Percy,   **3.** Loving Record.   12, 2.   12 ran
1964–65 Snaigow (100–6) J. Lehane (£1,020) C. Bewicke, 6–10–3
    2. Ben Voy,   **3.** Trunk Call.   8, 2.   15 ran
1965–66 Tibidabo (7–1) J. King (£1,020) A. Freeman, 6–10–4
    2. San Jacinto,   **3.** Shanlis.   ¾, 12.   12 ran
1966–67 French March (25–1) B. Hanbury (£1,020) T. Hanbury, 7–9–9
    2. Border Grace,   **3.** Kapeno.   4, 6.   14 ran
1967–68 Merrycourt (20–1) J. Gifford (£1,020) R. Renton, 7–10–3
    2. Sir Giles,   **3.** First Audition.   8, 1½.   14 ran

Race 282: FOXHUNTERS CHALLENGE CUP

4 miles chase. Cheltenham. Run over 3 miles 6 furlongs 160 yards in 1957–58

1956–57 Callant (10–11f) J. Scott-Aiton (£685) J. S. Wight, 9 yrs
    2. Colledge Master,   **3.** Royal Lark.   3, 12.   9 ran
1957–58 Whinstone Hill (7–1) R. Brewis (£1,025) R. Brewis, 9 yrs
    2. Royal Lark,   **3.** Surprise Packet.   2, 4.   16 ran
1958–59 Some Baby (100–8) M. Thorne (£1,025) T. D. Rootes, 10 yrs
    2. R.U.C.D.,   **3.** Flick.   ½, Bad.   15 ran
1959–60 Whinstone Hill (11–8f) R. Brewis (£1,025) R. Brewis, 11 yrs
    2. Jolly Fiddler,   **3.** Liveryman.   30, 4.   15 ran
1960–61 Colledge Master (7–2) L. Morgan (£1,020) L. Morgan, 11 yrs
    2. Whinstone Hill,   **3.** Peter Rock.   8, Bad.   17 ran
1961–62 Colledge Master (9–2) L. Morgan (£1,020) L. Morgan, 12 yrs
    2. Donation,   **3.** Glen Weather.   1½, 4.   17 ran

1962–63 Grand Morn II (15–2) R. Bloomfield (£1,020) G. Shepheard, 9 yrs
    2. Sea Knight,   **3.** Chaos.   Nk, 5.   20 ran
1963–64 Freddie (1–3f) A. Mactaggart (£1,020) R. Tweedie, 7 yrs
    2. Pomme de Guerre,   **3.** Sea Knight.   6, 4.   10 ran
1964–65 Woodside Terrace (33–1) R. Woodhouse (£1,020) R. Woodhouse, 12 yrs
    2. Prilliard,   **3.** Deb's Delight. $\frac{1}{2}$, 1$\frac{1}{2}$.   19 ran
1965–66 Straight Lady (100–8) R. Shepherd (£1,020) W. Shepherd, 10 yrs
    2. Puddle Jumper,   **3.** Corrielaw   3, 8.   21 ran
                             Diamond.
1966–67 Mulbarton (evens f) N. Gaselee (£1,020) I. H. Pattullo, 11 yrs
    2. Minto Burn,   **3.** Bright Beach.   8, 1.   13 ran
1967–68 Bright Beach (5–1) C. Macmillan (£1,020) G. Dun, 8 yrs
    2. Regal Mist,   **3.** Minto Burn.   1, 4.   12 ran

Race 283: DAILY EXPRESS TRIUMPH HURDLE

2 miles 200 yards. Cheltenham. Four-year-olds. Run at Hurst Park until 1964–65

1950 Abrupto	(19)	**1953** Clair Soleil	(13)	**1955** Kwannin	(12)
1951 Blue Song II	(12)	**1954** Prince		**1956** Square Dance	(11)
1952 Hoggar	(15)	Charlemagne	(12)		

1956–57 Meritorious (20–1) D. Dillon (£2,545) P. Thrale
    2. Pierian Springs,   **3.** Doxford.   3, 1$\frac{1}{2}$.   14 ran
1957–58 Pundit (5–2f) H. Sprague (£2,477) S. Ingham
    2. Hindu Penny,   **3.** Nostalgia.   6, 1.   14 ran
1958–59 Amazon's Choice (7–1) J. Gilbert (£2,698) P. Thrale
    2. Maddalo,   **3.** Ferryman's   5, 3.   13 ran
                             Image.
1959–60 Turpial (7–1) A. Freeman (£2,639) P. Cazalet
    2. Scarron,   **3.** Gun Smoke.   3, 6.   13 ran
1960–61 Cantab (4–1) F. T. Winter (£2,724) H. Price
    2. Anzio,   **3.** Babel.   Hd, 6.   15 ran
1961–62 Beaver II (100–6) J. Gifford (£2,562) H. Price
    2. Catapult II,   **3.** Tudor Treasure.   6, 8.   11 ran
1962–63 No race
1963–64 No race
1964–65 Blarney Beacon (8–1) G. Ramshaw (£2,518) R. Smyth
    2. Toledan II,   **3.** Bronzino.   2, 2.   7 ran
1965–66 Black Ice (9–2) H. Beasley (£3,558) A. Thomas
    2. Chiron,   **3.** Colonel Imp.   1$\frac{1}{2}$, Sht Hd.   11 ran
1966–67 Persian War (4–1) J. Uttley (£3,457) B. Swift
    2. Te Fou,   **3.** Al-'Alawi. $\frac{3}{4}$, 8.   13 ran
1967–68 England's Glory (9–2) J. Uttley (£3,769) S. Ingham
    2. Privy Seal,   **3.** Nothing Higher.   10, 4.   16 ran

Race 284: CHELTENHAM GOLD CUP
3 miles 2 furlongs 76 yards. Cheltenham

1924	Red Splash, 5	(9)	1936	Golden Miller, 9	(6)	1948	Cottage Rake, 9 (12)
1925	Ballinode, 8	(4)	1937	No race		1949	Cottage Rake, 10 (6)
1926	Koko, 8	(8)	1938	Morse Code, 9	(6)	1950	Cottage Rake, 11 (6)
1927	Thrown In, 11	(8)	1939	Brendan's		1951	Silver Fame, 12 (6)
1928	Patron Saint, 5	(7)		Cottage, 9	(5)	1952	Mont
1929	Easter Hero, 9	(10)	1940	Roman Hackle, 7	(7)		Tremblant, 6 (13)
1930	Easter Hero, 10	(4)	1941	Poet Prince, 9	(10)	1953	Knock Hard, 9 (12)
1931	No race		1942	Medoc II, 8	(12)	1954	Four Ten, 8 (9)
1932	Golden Miller, 5	(6)	1943-44	No race		1955	Gay Donald, 9 (9)
1933	Golden Miller, 6	(7)	1945	Red Rower, 11	(16)	1956	Limber Hill, 9 (11)
1934	Golden Miller, 7	(7)	1946	Prince Regent, 11	(6)		
1935	Golden Miller, 8	(5)	1947	Fortina, 6	(12)		

1956–57 Linwell (100–9) M. Scudamore (£3,996) C. Mallon, 9 yrs
    2. Kerstin,   **3.** Rose Park.   1, 5.   13 ran

1957–58 Kerstin (7–1) S. Hayhurst (£5,788) C. Bewicke, 8 yrs
    2. Polar Flight,   **3.** Gay Donald. $\frac{1}{2}$, Bad.   9 ran

1958–59 Roddy Owen (5–1) H. Beasley (£5,363) D. Morgan, 10 yrs
    2. Linwell,   **3.** Lochroe.   3, 10.   11 ran

1959–60 Pas Seul (6–1) W. Rees (£5,414) R. Turnell, 7 yrs
    2. Lochroe,   **3.** Zonda.   1, 5.   12 ran

1960–61 Saffron Tartan (2–1f) F. T. Winter (£6,043) D. Butchers, 10 yrs
    2. Pas Seul,   **3.** Mandarin. $1\frac{1}{2}$, 3.   11 ran

1961–62 Mandarin (7–2) F. T. Winter (£5,720) F. Walwyn, 11 yrs
    2. Fortria,   **3.** Cocky Consort.   1, 10.   9 ran

1962–63 Mill House (7–2f) G. W. Robinson (£5,958) F. Walwyn, 6 yrs
    2. Fortria,   **3.** Duke of York.   12, 4.   12 ran

1963–64 Arkle (7–4) P. Taaffe (£8,004) T. Dreaper, 7 yrs
    2. Mill House,   **3.** Pas Seul.   5, 25.   4 ran

1964–65 Arkle (300–100f) P. Taaffe (£7,986) T. Dreaper, 8 yrs
    2. Mill House,   **3.** Stoney Crossing.   20, 30.   4 ran

1965–66 Arkle (1–10f) P. Taaffe (£7,674) T. Dreaper, 9 yrs
    2. Dormant,   **3.** Snaigow.   30, 10.   5 ran

1966–67 Woodland Venture (100–8) T. Biddlecombe (£7,999) T. F. Rimell, 7 yrs
    2. Stalbridge Colonist,   **3.** What a Myth. $\frac{3}{4}$, 2.   8 ran

1967–68 Fort Leney (11–2) P. Taaffe (£7,713) T. Dreaper, 10–12–0
    2. Laird,   **3.** Stalbridge   Nk, 1.   5 ran
     Colonist.

> *HORSES IN CAPITAL LETTERS*
> *(EXCLUDING RACE 245)*
> *WERE TO BE, OR HAD BEEN,*
> *PLACED IN THE CLASSICS*

Race 285: COUNTY HANDICAP HURDLE

2 miles 200 yards. Cheltenham

1956–57	Flaming East (100–6) P. Pickford (£1,025) G. R. Vallance, 8–10–5		
	2. Grand Morn,	3. Happy Prospect. 2, 1.	19 ran
1957–58	Friendly Boy (3–1f) W. Brennan (£1,370) J. W. Osborne, 6–10–5		
	2. Siamois,	3. Approval. 1½, 3.	18 ran
1958–59	Approval (10–1) D. Leslie (£1,370) S. Mercer, 13–11–2		
	2. Branca Doria,	3. Green Light. 2, ½.	20 ran
1959–60	Albergo (7–4f) D. Page (£1,370) C. Magnier, 6–12–5		
	2. Branca Doria,	3. Costa Brava. ½, 4.	26 ran
1960–61	Most Unusual (100–7) J. Gifford (£1,360) W. Ransom, 6–10–7		
	2. Sea Wife,	3. Chouchou II. 3, 2.	23 ran
1961–62	Sky Pink (100–8) F. T. Winter (£1,360) H. Price, 5–10–11		
	2. Irish Imp,	3. Red Hackle. 2, Nk.	20 ran
1962–63	Bahrain (11–2) T. Carberry (£1,360) D. L. Moore, 6–10–6		
	2. Antiar,	3. Kirtella. 3, 6.	19 ran
1963–64	Icy Wonder (11–2) J. King (£1,380) V. Cross, 5–10–2		
	2. Pillock's Green,	3. Anner Banks. 1½, Hd.	17 ran
1964–65	Mayfair Bill (100–7) A. Turnell (£1,365) R. Turnell, 6–10–4		
	2. Enlightenment,	3. Risky. Hd, Nk.	25 ran
1965–66	Roaring Twenties (10–1) G. Milburn (£1,365) J. Oliver, 6–11–2		
	2. Severn Bore,	3. Playlord, 1½, ¾.	16 ran
1966–67	Cool Alibi (20–1) R. Reid (£1,365) J. R. Bower, 5–10–9		
	2. Jolly Signal,	3. Pike's Fancy. 6, 2½.	28 ran
1967–68	Jolly Signal (6–1) J. Uttley (£1,365) Earl Jones, 6–10–11		
	2. Pony Express,	3. Even Keel. ¾, 5.	16 ran

Race 286: CATHCART CHALLENGE CUP

2 miles and a few yards chase. Cheltenham

1956–57	Rose's Quarter (3–1) D. V. Dick (£685) G. Beeby, 10 yrs		
	2. Limb of the Law,	3. Royal Approach. 2, 4.	7 ran
1957–58	Quita Que (10–11f) J. Cox (£685) D. L. Moore, 9 yrs		
	2. Lion Noir,	3. Gruline. Dist., ¾.	7 ran
1958–59	Gallery Goddess (11–2) F. T. Winter (£685) C. Mallon, 8 yrs		
	2. Silvogan's Hook,	3. Spring Flight. ½, Bad.	7 ran
1959–60	Dove Cote (2–1f) M. Batchelor (£685) J. S. Wight, 10 yrs		
	2. Icanopit,	3. Skate Up. 8, 4.	8 ran
1960–61	Quita Que (8–11f) G. W. Robinson (£680) D. L. Moore, 12 yrs		
	2. Up the Vale,	3. Lancelot. Nk, 8.	7 ran
1961–62	Hoodwinked (8–1) D. Nicholson (£680) N. Crump, 7 yrs		
	2. Mariner's Dance,	3. Rolling Rapture. 12, 6.	8 ran
1962–63	Some Alibi (9–4f) G. W. Robinson (£680) F. Walwyn, 8 yrs		
	2. Plummers Plain,	3. Ivy Green. 4, Sht Hd.	13 ran

312

1963–64 Panisse (7–2) M. Scudamore (£690) W. Stephenson, 9 yrs
    2. Wayward Muse (first,   **3.** Super Flash.
        disq.)   Original distances, Hd, 2.   10 ran
1964–65 Scottish Memories (4–9f) H. Beasley (£680) P. Sleator, 11 yrs
    2. Bonnie Mac,   **3.** Quick Approach. 5, 10.   5 ran
1965–66 Flying Wild (5–4jf) T. Carberry (£680) D. L. Moore, 10 yrs
    2. Skeedalagh,   **3.** Banzai.   20, 6.   6 ran
1966–67 Prince Blarney (100–8) R. Barry (£680) John Barclay, 7 yrs
    2. Jungle Beach,   **3.** Yellowhammer. 8, 6.   5 ran
1967–68 Muir (10–11f) P. Taaffe (£680) T. Dreaper, 9 yrs
    2. Sir Thopas,   **3.** Slave Driver.   6, 1½.   8 ran

Race 287: IMPERIAL CUP

2 miles handicap hurdle. Sandown

1956–57 Camugliano (20–1) R. Emery (£2,306) H. T. Smith, 7–10–10
    2. Limeville,   **3.** Hilarion.   4, 1½.   29 ran
1957–58 Flaming East (100–9) J. Lawrence (£2,276) G. Vallance, 9–10–5
    2. Approval,   **3.** Camugliano. 2, Hd.   23 ran
1958–59 Langton Heath (100–6) R. Martin (£2,204) T. Griffiths, 5–10–9
    2. Mariner's Dance,   **3.** Green Light.   1½, 3.   21 ran
1959–60 Farmer's Boy (25–1) D. Nicholson (£2,132) W. Stephenson, 7–11–7
    2. Albergo,   **3.** Branca Doria.   1½, ¾.   20 ran
1960–61 Fidus Achates (25–1) C. Chapman (£2,339) M. James, 6–10–4
    2. Granville,   **3.** Gay Tricks.   Nk, 3.   23 ran
1961–62 Irish Imp (10–1) G. Ramshaw (£2,424) R. Smyth, 5–10–12
    2. Anzio,   **3.** Scottish Final.   3, ½.   26 ran
1962–63 Antiar (7–1jf) D. Mould (£1,952) P. Cazalet, 5–11–2
    2. Roxburgh,   **3.** Smogland.   2, 1.   21 ran
1963–64 Invader (6–1) T. M. Jones (£2,235) L. Dale, 6–11–4
    2. Pediment,   **3.** Lars Porsena.   8, ½.   15 ran
1964–65 Kildavin (100–7) J. King (£2,742) J. Sutcliffe jun., 7–10–7
    2. Sempervivum,   **3.** Lars Porsena.   1½, Sht Hd.   19 ran
1965–66 Royal Sanction (10–1) R. Pitman (£2,634) F. T. Winter, 7–10–1
    2. First Audition,   **3.** Rosador.   4, 2.   18 ran
1966–67 Sir Thopas (100–9) J. Haine (£2,440) R. Turnell, 6–11–8
    2. Spartae,   **3.** Rosador.   1, ¾.   20 ran
1967–68 Persian Empire (4–1jf) B. Scott (£2,393) C. H. Davies, 5–11–4
    2. Bric-Brac,   **3.** Tamorn.   2, 2.   18 ran

Race 288: TOPHAM TROPHY HANDICAP CHASE
2 miles 6 furlongs. Liverpool

1956–57 Roughan (100–7) H. East (£1,793) N. Crump, 9–10–8
    2. Sentina,   **3.** Spate.   Dist., Bad.   14 ran
1957–58 Roughan (11–2jf) F. T. Winter (£1,763) N. Crump, 10–11–0
    2. Irish Coffee,   **3.** Turmoil.   2, 1.   16 ran
1958–59 Clanyon (6–1) G. Underwood (£1,814) W. Johns-Powell, 11–11–2
    2. E.S.B.,   **3.** Melted Ice.   8, 12.   19 ran
1959–60 Fresh Winds (100–7) S. Mellor (£1,772) W. Whiston, 9–11–1
    2. Scottish Flight II,   **3.** E.S.B.   20, 3.   21 ran
1960–61 Cupid's Charge (9–1) W. Rees (£1,687) P. Cazalet, 6–11–3
    2. Nobbutjust,   **3.** Clanyon.   4, 3.   13 ran
1961–62 Dagmar Gittell (100–8) J. Gifford (£1,805) R. Renton, 7–10–11
    2. College Don,   **3.** Peacetown.   1, 2.   22 ran
1962–63 Barberyn (7–1f) M. Scudamore (£1,845) W. Stephenson, 8–11–9
    2. Shavings,   **3.** Lizawake.   Nk, 1.   20 ran
1963–64 Red Tide (10–1) J. King (£2,130) R. Turnell, 7–10–6
    2. Siracusa,   **3.** Silver Dome.   2, 15.   14 ran
1964–65 Hopkiss (11–2f) E. Harty (£1,772) A. Kilpatrick, 7–10–12
    2. Spring Greeting,   **3.** Royal Ruse.   Nk, 12.   13 ran
1965–66 Walpole (10–1) J. Gifford (£1,800) H. Price, 10–11–5
    2. Bassnet,   **3.** Sandy Abbot.   2½, 1.   24 ran
1966–67 Georgetown (100–8) P. Mahoney (£1,770) N. Kusbish, 7–10–7
    2. Go-Pontinental,   **3.** Dear John.   ¾, 15.   23 ran
1967–68 Surcharge (100–8) S. Davenport (£1,757) John Barclay, 10–10–8
    2. Royal Ruse,   **3.** First Audition.   5, 30.   16 ran

Race 289: SPA HURDLE
3 miles. Cheltenham

1956–57 Bold Baby (13–8f) P. Powell jun. (£685) M. Dawson, 11 yrs
    2. Mac Joy,   **3.** Axim.   4, 6.   12 ran
1957–58 Mac Joy (4–1) A. Freeman (£685) K. Bailey, 6 yrs
    2. Baby Don,   **3.** Axim.   ¾, 4.   17 ran
1958–59 Clair Soleil (5–1) F. T. Winter (£685) H. Price, 10 yrs
    2. Fireglow,   **3.** Chantry.   2, 4.   10 ran
1959–60 Solfen (5–2f) H. Beasley (£685) W. O'Grady, 8 yrs
    2. Ferryman's Image,   **3.** Dunnock.   1, 6.   21 ran
1960–61 Sparkling Flame (9–4f) H. Beasley (£680) P. Sleator, 10 yrs
    2. Duke of York,   **3.** Bandalore.   Nk, 15.   15 ran
1961–62 Merry Deal (7–1) I. Markham (£680) A. W. Jones, 12 yrs
    2. Raes Gill,   **3.** Perfect Mate.   ½, 2.   14 ran
1962–63 Beau Normand (5–1f) W. Rees (£1,020) R. Turnell, 7 yrs
    2. Union Pacific,   **3.** Sartorius.   8, 4.   15 ran

1963-64 Nosey (100–30) H. Beasley (£1,035) G. Todd, 8 yrs
    2. Comandeer,   **3.** Ballinaclasha.   4, 8.   17 ran
1964-65 Antiar (6–1) D. V. Dick (£1,020) P. Cazalet, 7 yrs
    2. Tobago,   **3.** Imperator. $1\frac{1}{2}$, 6.   17 ran
1965-66 Trelawny (11–4f) T. Biddlecombe (£1,020) T. F. Rimell, 10 yrs
    2. Man of the East,   **3.** Caduval.   8, 4.   12 ran
1966-67 Beau Normand (6–1) J. King (£1,020) R. Turnell, 11 yrs
    2. King Vulgan,   **3.** Middleton Tower. $\frac{3}{4}$, 4.   14 ran
1967-68 Park Ranger (100–30) S. Mellor (£1,020) H. Thomson Jones, 5 yrs
    2. Whaddon Hero,   **3.** Tapina. $2\frac{1}{2}$, 2.   9 ran

Race 290: IRISH GRAND NATIONAL

3 miles 2 furlongs. Fairyhouse. Run over 3 miles until 1920, then 3 miles 4 furlongs until 1961–62. First run 1870

1900 Mavis of Meath, 6–12–12	(5)	
1901 Tipperary Boy, a–12–0	(9)	
1902 Patlander, 6–11–0	(7)	
1903 Kirko, 6–11–7	(9)	
1904 Ascetic's Silver, a–11–7	(12)	
1905 Red Lad, 5–10–7	(13)	
1906 Brown Bess, 5–10–11	(6)	
1907 Sweet Cecil, 6–11–4	(5)	
1908 Lord Rivers, 6–11–12	(6)	
1909 Little Hack II, a–10–0	(9)	
1910 Oniche, a–9–3	(8)	
1911 Repeater II, a–10–6	(13)	
1912 Small Polly, a–10–10	(17)	
1913 Little Hack II, a–10–10	(15)	
1914 Civil War, 5–10–7	(14)	
1915 Punch, a–11–8	(19)	
1916 All Sorts, 6–11–0	(11)	
1917 Pay Only, 7–12–0	(14)	
1918 Ballyboggan, 7–11–4	(14)	
1919 No race		
1920 Halston, 8–10–5	(11)	
1921 Bohernore, 8–10–7	(11)	
1922 Halston, 10–12–11	(16)	
1923 Be Careful, 14–10–2	(11)	
1924 Kilbarry, 9–10–1	(16)	
1925 Dog Fox, 11–10–2	(19)	
1926 Amberwave, 8–10–0	(15)	
1927 Jerpoint, 7–12–0	(15)	
1928 Don Sancho, 8–12–1	(19)	

1929 Alike, 6–10–5	(11)
1930 Fanmond, 7–9–8	(22)
1931 Impudent Barney, a–10–3	(11)
1932 Copper Court, a–10–9	(15)
1933 Red Park, 7–11–5	(16)
1934 Poolgowran, 5–9–11	(12)
1935 Rathfriland, a–9–10	(9)
1936 Alice Maythorn, 6–10–1	(19)
1937 Pontet, a–10–2	(14)
1938 Clare County, a–11–3	(9)
1939 Shaun Peel, a–9–7	(16)
1940 Jack Chaucer, 9–11–11	(14)
1941 No race	
1942 Prince Regent, 7–12–7	(10)
1943 Golden Jack, 8–10–3	(8)
1944 Knight's Crest, 7–9–7	(13)
1945 Heirdom, 13–9–7	(12)
1946 Golden View II, a–12–7	(11)
1947 Revelry, 7–11–5	(17)
1948 Hamstar, a–9–7	(17)
1949 Shagreen, 8–10–10	(20)
1950 Dominick's Bar, 6–10–6	(12)
1951 Icy Calm, 8–10–3	(19)
1952 Alberoni, 9–10–1	(11)
1953 Overshadow, 13–10–4	(15)
1954 Royal Approach, 6–12–0	(11)
1955 Umm, 8–10–5	(16)
1956 Air Prince, 12–10–0	(19)

1956–57 Kilballyown (10–1) G. W. Robinson (£2,044) P. Norris, 10–9–10
    2. Brookling,   **3.** Royal Assent.   7, 4.   26 ran
1957–58 Gold Legend (100–8) J. Lehane (£2,017) J. Brogan, 8–9–7
    2. Knight Errant,   **3.** Fair Gale.   Hd, 8.   21 ran
1958–59 Zonda (5–1) P. Taaffe (£1,879) M. Geraghty, 8–10–6
    2. Knightsbrook,   **3.** Mazzibell.   4, 6.   15 ran
1959–60 Olympia (6–1) T. Taaffe (£2,256) T. Dreaper, 6–9–11
    2. Take Time,   **3.** Zonda.   6, 2½.   16 ran
1960–61 Fortria (17–2) P. Taaffe (£2,301) T. Dreaper, 9–12–0
    2. Owen's Sedge,   **3.** Fredith's Son.   4, ½.   14 ran
1961–62 Kerforo (9–1) L. McLoughlin (£2,245) T. Dreaper, 8–10–3
    2. Team Spirit,   **3.** Brown Diamond. 1½, 4.   11 ran
1962–63 Last Link (7–1) P. Woods (£2,870) T. Dreaper, 7–9–7
    2. Willow King,   **3.** Brown Diamond. 6, 3.   10 ran
1963–64 Arkle (1–2f) P. Taaffe (£2,630) T. Dreaper, 7–12–0
    2. Height o'Fashion,   **3.** Ferry Boat.   1¼, 8.   7 ran
1964–65 Splash (6–4) P. Woods (£4,237) T. Dreaper, 7–10–13
    2. Devon Breeze,   **3.** Duke of York.   3, 10.   4 ran
1965–66 Flyingbolt (8–11f) P. Taaffe (£4,470) T. Dreaper, 7–12–7
    2. Height o'Fashion,   **3.** Splash.   2, 10.   6 ran
1966–67 Vulpine (7–1) M. Curran (£4,537) P. Mullins, 6–11–6
    2. Reynard's Heir,   **3.** Fort Ord.   3, ½.   12 ran
1967–68 Herring Gull (5–2f) J. Crowley (£4,759) P. Mullins, 6–11–13
    2. Knockaney,   **3.** Splash.   Sht Hd, 8.   12 ran

Race 291: SCOTTISH GRAND NATIONAL

4 miles 120 yards handicap chase. Ayr. Run over 3 miles 7 furlongs at Bogside until 1965–66

1956–57 Bremontier (10–1) A. Rossio (£1,030) P. Taylor, 10–10–12
    2. Merry Windsor,   **3.** Moston Lane.   6, 1.   13 ran
1957–58 Game Field (9–1) J. Boddy (£1,030) J. Fawcus, 8–11–10
    2. Tiger William,   **3.** Glorious Twelfth. 8, Nk.   14 ran
1958–59 Merryman II (100–8) G. Scott (£1,035) N. Crump, 8–10–12
    2. Stop List,   **3.** Punch Bowl   12, 4.   18 ran
                            Hotel.
1959–60 Fincham (9–4f) M. Batchelor (£1,035) J. S. Wight, 8–10–0
    2. Fair Gale,   **3.** French Window. 5, 20.   8 ran
1960–61 Kinmont Wullie (8–1) C. Stobbs (£1,380) W. A. Stephenson, 7–10–7
    2. Carmen IV,   **3.** Uncle Isaac.   ½, 10.   18 ran
1961–62 Sham Fight (100–6) T. Robson (£1,380) T. Robson, 10–10–10
    2. Threepwood,   **3.** Skish.   10, 4.   18 ran
1962–63 Pappageno's Cottage (100–8) T. Brookshaw (£5,436) J. Oliver, 8–10–9
    2. Master Perie,   **3.** Threepwood. 20, 15.   18 ran
1963–64 Popham Down (8–1) J. Haine (£4,935) F. Walwyn, 7–10–0
    2. Freddie,   **3.** Rainbow Battle. ½, 20.   14 ran

1964–65 Brasher (4–1) J. Fitzgerald (£3,444) T. Robson, 9–10–5
 2. Happy Arthur,   **3.** Union Pacific. 2, ½.   9 ran
1965–66 African Patrol (10–1) J. Leech (£4,350) R. Fairbairn, 7–10–7
 2. Norther,   **3.** Craigbrock. 2, 1½.   17 ran
1966–67 Fossa (8–1) A. Turnell (£4,552) T. F. Rimell, 10–9–12
 2. Reynard's Heir,   **3.** Pappageno's Nk, 1½.   18 ran
              Cottage.
1967–68 Arcturus (4–1) P. Buckley (£4,311) N. Crump, 7–10–4
 2. Roborough,   **3.** Rondetto. 8, 10.   10 ran

Race 292: WHITBREAD GOLD CUP

3 miles 5 furlongs 18 yards handicap chase. Sandown

1956–57 Much Obliged (10–1) H. East (£4,842) N. Crump, 9–10–12
 2. Mandarin,   **3.** Pointsman. Nk, 10.   24 ran
1957–58 Taxidermist (100–6) J. Lawrence (£5,790) F. Walwyn, 6–10–8
 2. Mandarin,   **3.** Kerstin. 4, 2.   31 ran
1958–59 Done Up (100–6) H. Sprague (£6,240) H. Price, 9–10–13
 2. Mandarin,   **3.** Brunel II. Sht Hd, 6.   23 ran
1959–60 Plummers Plain (20–1) R. R. Harrison (£8,240) L. Dale, 7–10–0
 2. Pas Seul,   **3.** Brunel II. 1½, 25.   21 ran
1960–61 Pas Seul (8–1) D. V. Dick (£8,235) R. Turnell, 8–12–0
 2. Nicolaus Silver,   **3.** Springbok. 4, 2.   23 ran
1961–62 Frenchman's Cove (7–2f) S. Mellor (£8,235) H. Thomson-Jones, 7–11–3
 2. Carrickbeg,   **3.** Springbok. 1, 8.   22 ran
1962–63 Hoodwinked (100–7) P. Buckley (£8,235) N. Crump, 8–10–9
 2. Purple Silk,   **3.** Master Perie. 5, 6.   32 ran
1963–64 Dormant (11–4) P. Buckley (£8,235) N. Crump, 7–9–7
 2. Mill House,   **3.** Laffy. 3, 3.   11 ran
1964–65 Arkle (4–9f) P. Taaffe (£8,230) T. Dreaper, 8–12–7
 2. Brasher,   **3.** Willow King. 5, 20.   7 ran
1965–66 What a Myth (5–4f) P. Kelleway (£7,380) H. Price, 9–9–8
 2. Dormant,   **3.** Kapeno. 1½, 6.   8 ran
1966–67 Mill House (9–2f) D. Nicholson (£7,350) F. Walwyn, 10–11–11
 2. Kapeno,   **3.** Kellsboro' Wood. 1½, 1½. 13 ran
1967–68 Larbawn (8–1) M. Gifford (£7,510) M. L. Marsh, 9–10–9
 2. Fort Leney,   **3.** Bowgeeno. Nk, 4.   16 ran

HORSES IN CAPITAL LETTERS
(EXCLUDING RACE 245)
WERE TO BE, OR HAD BEEN,
PLACED IN THE CLASSICS

Race 293: FINAL CHAMPION HUNTERS' CHASE

3 miles 2 furlongs. Stratford. Sponsored by Horse and Hound after 1960–61

1956–57 Jumna (2–1) R. Megginson (£406) J. Calvert, 7 yrs
  2. Happy Morn II,   **3.** Colonel Wynn. $\frac{3}{4}$, 15.   9 ran
1957–58 Dark Island (100–8) W. Jones (£431) Miss D. Williams, 9 yrs
  2. Happy Morn II,   **3.** Middlegate. $\frac{1}{2}$, 3.   13 ran
1958–59 Speylove (25–1) J. Jackson (£649) V. R. Bishop, 10 yrs
  2. J'Arrive,   **3.** Merryman II.   3, $\frac{1}{2}$.   15 ran
1959–60 Bantry Bay (6–1) M. Tory (£645) H. Dufosee, 9 yrs
  2. Sleigh Run,   **3.** Duplicator.   4, 5.   17 ran
1960–61 Bantry Bay (8–1) M. Tory (£685) H. Dufosee, 10 yrs
  2. Megsbridge,   **3.** Precious Gem.   3, Sht Hd.   8 ran
1961–62 Baulking Green (11–2) R. Willis (£916) J. Reade, 9 yrs
  2. False Bay,   **3.** Cauliflower.   5, 4.   16 ran
1962–63 Baulking Green (7–4f) A. Frank (£1,017) T. Forster, 10 yrs
  2. Rosie's Cousin,   **3.** Leyton Orient.   3, 2.   17 ran
1963–64 Royal Phoebe (100–7) M. Gifford (£906) W. Whiston, 8 yrs
  2. Rosie's Cousin,   **3.** Sizzle-On.   Nk, 6.   13 ran
1964–65 Baulking Green (4–7f) G. Small (£983) T. Forster, 12 yrs
  2. Pomme de Guerre,   **3.** Royal Phoebe.   4, 2.   8 ran
1965–66 Santa Grand (7–1) C. Collins (£1,071) W. A. Stephenson, 7 yrs
  2. Royal Phoebe,   **3.** Cauliflower. $2\frac{1}{2}$, 5.   10 ran
1966–67 Cham (3–1) J. Lawrence (£1,063) F. Cundell, 10 yrs
  2. Royal Phoebe,   **3.** Pomme de $1\frac{1}{2}$, 12.   16 ran
       Guerre.
1967–68 Green Plover (33–1) A. Maxwell (£1,003) J. Ford, 8 yrs
  2. Queen's Guide,   **3.** Veronica Bell.   Sht Hd, 4.   8 ran

Some Important Foreign Races

(Not included in index)

WASHINGTON INTERNATIONAL
1 mile 4 furlongs. Laurel Park

1952	Wilwyn (G.B.)	1960	Bald Eagle (U.S.A.)
1953	Worden II (Fr.)	1961	T.V. Lark (U.S.A.)
1954	Fisherman (U.S.A.)	1962	Match (Fr.)
1955	El Chama (Venezuela)	1963	Mongo (U.S.A.)
1956	Master Boing (Fr.)	1964	Kelso (U.S.A.)
1957	Mahan (U.S.A.)	1965	Diatome (Fr.)
1958	Sailor's Guide (Australia)	1966	Behistoun (Fr.)
	Tudor Era 1st, disqualified	1967	Fort Marcy (U.S.A.)
1959	Bald Eagle (U.S.A.)	1968	Sir Ivor (Ireland)

FRENCH OAKS

1 mile 2½ furlongs. Chantilly.
Prix de Diane

1950	Aglae Grace	(24)
1951	Stratonice	(23)
1952	Seria	(17)
1953	La Sorellina	(18)
1954	Tahiti	(14)
1955	Douve	(17)
1956	Apollonia	(14)
1957	Cerisoles	(19)
1958	Dushka	(19)
1959	Barquette	(25)
1960	Timandra	(19)
1961	Hermieres	(22)
1962	La Sega	(14)
1963	Belle Ferranniere	(13)
1964	Belle Sicambre	(6)
1965	Blabla	(16)
1966	Fine Pearl	(15)
1967	Gazala	(20)
1968	Roseliere	(22)

FRENCH DERBY

1 mile 4 furlongs. Chantilly.
Prix du Jockey Club

1950	Scratch II	(15)
1951	Sicambre	(14)
1952	Auriban	(13)
1953	Chamant	(20)
1954	Le Petit Prince	(19)
1955	Rapace	(15)
1956	Philius II	(16)
1957	Amber	(14)
1958	Tamanar	(17)
1959	Herbager	(16)
1960	Charlottesville	(16)
1961	Right Royal	(15)
1962	Val de Loir	(18)
1963	Sanctus	(13)
1964	Le Fabuleux	(7)
1965	Reliance	(9)
1966	Nelcius	(13)
1967	Astec	(13)
1968	Tapalque	(22)

319

GRAND PRIX DE PARIS

1 mile 7 furlongs. Longchamp

1950	Vieux Manoir	(18)
1951	Sicambre	(15)
1952	Orfeo	(16)
1953	Northern Light	(22)
1954	Popof	(17)
1955	Phil Drake	(20)
1956	Vattel	(19)
1957	Altipan	(13)
1958	San Roman	(15)
1959	Birum	(18)
1960	Charlottesville	(20)
1961	Balto	(18)
1962	Armistice	(13)
1963	Sanctus	(19)
1964	White Label	(14)
1965	Reliance	(10)
1966	Danseur	(20)
1967	Phaeton	(13)
1968	Dhaudevi	(15)

PRIX DE L'ARC DE TRIOMPHE

1 mile 4 furlongs. Longchamp

1950	Tantieme (3)	(12)
1951	Tantieme (4)	(19)
1952	Nuccio (4)	(18)
1953	La Sorellina (3)	(25)
1954	Sica Boy (3)	(21)
1955	Ribot (3)	(23)
1956	Ribot (4)	(20)
1957	Oroso (4)	(24)
1958	Ballymoss (4)	(17)
1959	Saint Crespin (3)	(25)
1960	Puissant Chef (3)	(17)
1961	Molvedo (3)	(19)
1962	Soltikoff (3)	(24)
1963	Exbury (4)	(15)
1964	Prince Royal II (3)	(22)
1965	Sea Bird II (3)	(20)
1966	Bon Mot (3)	(24)
1967	Topyo (3)	(30)
1968	Vaguely Noble (3)	(17)

Index to Horses

THIS INDEX is a complete list of all horses appearing in the FULL results. It comprises the name of the horse, the sex—for simplicity's sake described as either a colt (c) or filly (f)—followed by the sire and dam and then the reference numbers of the races in which it took part, brackets around the figure indicating a win.

It should be remembered that while this section will give a guide to the best performances of each horse, it is certainly not a complete record of that animal's career. Note too that each horse's 'race figures' follow in numerical, but not necessarily chronological, order.

A

A.20 f (Panorama—Loved One) (11).
Aalsund c (Palestine—Herringbone) 181.
Abadesa f (Panorama—St Bride) 136.
Abanilla f (Abernant—Nella) (20), 43.
Abat Jour c (Free Man—Abaka) 103.
Abbey Oaks c (Golden Cloud—Elstree) 184.
Abbie West f (Abernant— Key West) 29, (69), 109.
Abelia f (Abernant—Queen of Peru) (11), (16), (23), 29, 43, (44), 115.
Aberdeen c (Abernant—Golden Gulf) 162, 168, 171, 186, (186), 203, 227.
Aberdovey c (Abernant—Umidzaneh) 168, 174.
Aberflight f (Abernant—Queen's Flight) 166.
ABERMAID f (Abernant—Dairymaid) (2), (12), 86, 106, 121.
Abernicky c (Abernant—Pernickity) 219.
Abletai c (Impeccable—Taimone) (229), (234).
Above Suspicion c (Court Martial—Above Board) 3, 76, 100, (105), (128), 178.
Above Water c (Skymaster—Low Water) 1, 12, 59, 204.
Abscond c (Elopement—Trenoon) 1, 74, 85.
Accompanist f (Tudor Minstrel—Amaica) 179, 216, (228)
Accuser, The c (Javelot—Allegation) (104), 135, (140) 148.
Acer c (Abernant—Flighty) 1, 21, 105.
Acharacle c (Alycidon or Alcide—Golden Gulf) (212).
Acrania c (Acropolis—Azania) 63, (78), 81, (269).
Acrophel c (Acropolis—Helsinki II) 199, 212, (229).
Acros c (Acropolis—Briquette) 68.
Admiral's Lark c (Infatuation—Admiral's Frolic) (130), 195.
Admiral Stuart c (Sea Lover—Nee Stuart) (270).
Adorn c (Djebe—Hazy Moon) 192.
Adowa f (Auriban—Salamis) 40.
Adrasto c (Macherio—Lady Luck) 218.

Adriatic Star c (Milesian—Venarctic) (15), (25).
Adropejo c (Privy Councillor—Kitty Quick) 31, 39.
Aegean Blue c (Botticelli—Tenebel) (165), (175), (177).
Aerial Lady f (Alcide—Bride Elect) 20, 75, 93.
African Patrol c (Big Game—Castelloza) (291).
After the Show f (Phideas—Apres l'Ondee) (66), 86, (102), (118).
After Twelve c (Nearco—Rendezvous) 7.
Aggravate f (Aggressor—Raven Locks) 34
Aggressor c (Combat—Phaetonia) (31), 47, (59), (72), (77), 77, 113, (124), (143), (210), 233.
Agile f (Court Martial—Ballet) (132).
Agogo c (Never Say Die—Speed Bird) 135.
Agreement c (Persian Gulf—Northern Hope) (60), 91, 114, 114, 127, (140), (140), 165, 172, (175), (194), 212.
Agricola c (Precipitation—Aurora) 5, 72, 73, 135.
Agrippina f (Black Tarquin—Hot Point) (234).
Ahascragh c (Como—Queens Prize) 65.
Ahmose c (Rigolo—Ji Bar Ka) 116.
Aidos c (My Babu—Mystification) 205, 205, 223.
Aigle Gris c (Klairon—Aglae Grace) 1.
Aiguillette f (Epaulette—Fair One) 17.
Aim High c (Grey Sovereign—Steady Aim) 195.
Aiming High f (Djebe—Annie Oakley) (107).
Air Patrol c (King's Bench—Naval Patrol) 32, 196.
Al-'Alawi c (Aureole—Andromeda Nebula) 64, (163), (225), 283.
Alamo City f (Sovereign Lord—Apprehension) 8, 136.
Alan A'Dale c (Tudor Minstrel—Mystification) 67.
Alan Adare c (Alcide—Andante) (47), 99, 192.
Alaska Way f (Honeyway—Aleutian) (26), 43.
Alastair c (Preciptic—X-Ray) 109.
Alba Rock c (Rock Star—Chambiges) 24, 222.
Albatros c (Persian Gulf—Sea Parrot) 60.
Albergo c (Dante—Bill of Fare) 85, 128, (270), 277, (285), 287.
Alberta Blue c (Blue Peter—Rock Goddess) 3.
Albinella c (Alibi II—Serenella) 247, 270.
Alborada f (Fastnet Rock—Light of Day) (69), 90, (121).
ALCAEUS c (Alycidon—Marteline) 3, (84), (85), 117.
Alcalde c (Alcide—Sundry) (78), 92, 111, 142, 175, (201), 214, 220.
Alcan c (Princely Gift—Alcoa) (48).
Alcastus c (Alycidon—Anna Lucasta) 92, 169.
Alceste c (Alcide—Honeysuckle) 22.
ALCIDE c (Alycidon—Chenille) (5), (48), 76, (82), (92), 110, (124), (135), 148.
Alciglide c (Alcide—Silken Glider) (114).
Alcimedes c (Alycidon—Honey Hill) (178), (178), 187, 190.
Alcoa f (Alycidon—Phyllis Court) 138, 232.
Alcove f (Alycidon—Hortentia) (212), (232).
Aldium c (Psidium—Alcatraz) 34.
Alexis c (Alycidon—Participation) 78, 140, (183).

322

Alf's Caprice c (Mustang—Miss Caprice) 174, (174).
Alice Delysia f (Alycidon—Daring Miss) 71.
Alice Maythorn f (Bowsprit—Alice Greenthorn) 258.
Alignment c (Alcide—Blue Line) 5, 166, 176, (220).
Alioop c (Ali Pacha II—September Lady) 247.
Alizio c (Alizier—Lovely Princess) 81.
All-a-Gogg c (Tamerlane—Goggles) (34).
All A'Light c (Major Portion—Queen of Light) 106.
Allenheads c (Alcide—Blue Line) 82, 161, 175, 214.
Allez c (Alycidon—Fiction) 188.
All Found c (Alycidon—Lady Carina) 191, 201, (212).
All Hail f (Alcide—None Nicer) 40.
Alloway Lad c (Duel—Honey High) (166).
All Saved f (Never Say Die—Silken Glider) 4, 41, 49.
All Serene c (Alycidon—Serangela) (78), 111, 133, (183), 212.
Allurement f (Infatuation—Tarsia) 47.
Al Mabsoot c (Mat de Cocagne—Rose o'Lynn) 100, 124.
Almeria f (Alycidon—Avila) 93, (108), 124, (134), (139), 140.
Almiranta f (Alycidon—Rosario) (75), 134, (139).
ALPINE BLOOM f (Chamossaire—Fragrant View) 2, 17, 71, 121.
Alpine Scent f (Chamossaire—Fragrant View) (19), 23, 29.
Althrey Don c (Fighting Don—Slainte) (136).
Alyba f (Alycidon—Love Bird) 188.
Alzara f (Alycidon—Zabara) 40, 93, 139.
AMANTE f (Tehran—Pale Ale) 2, 108, (131).
Amateur c (Charlottesville—Dilettante) (199).
Amazon's Choice c (Bois Roussel—Fair Amazon) 165, 180, (283).
AMBERGRIS f (Sicambre—Quarterdeck) 2, 4, (32), (90), 107, (131).
Ambericos c (Darius—Ambergris) 1, 3, 62.
Amber Light c (Borealis—Killashee) 96, (103).
America f (Buisson Ardent—Lucky Verdict) (6), 9, 61, 217.
Amerigo c (Nearco—Sanlinea) (10), 18.
Amicable f (Doutelle—Amy Leigh) 4, (69), (93), 134.
Amorella f (Crepello—Amora) (75), 94.
Amos c (Mossborough—Candrena) (193), (227).
Amourrou c (Worden II—Army Flirt) (116).
Ampney Princess f (Wilwyn—Fama) 13, (146).
Amstel f (Denturius—Red Duchess) 6.
Analupus f (Hugh Lupus—Anaphalis) 71.
Anaphora c (Zarathustra—Anaphalis) 68, 80.
Anassa f (Pardal—Janie Mou) 2, (71), 187, 190.
Ancasta f (Ballymoss—Anyte II) (118), (131), 134, 139.
Anchovy c (Hard Sauce—Blue Style) 216.
Ancient Lights c (Supreme Court—Queen of Light) (46), 89.
Andromeda Nebula f (Arctic Star—Salvinia) 15.
Andros c (Borealis—Nassau) 170, 178, 190.
Andy II f (pedigree unknown) 278.
Angazi f (Anwar—Burdekin) (191), 212.

Angel Baby f (My Babu—Cutaway) 98.
ANGELET f (Nimbus—Toujours) 2, 86, 107.
Angers c (Worden II—Gwynedd) 3.
Anglo (late Flag of Convenience) c (Greek Star—Miss Alligator) (245).
Angostura c (Annatom—Icewater) 261.
Anguilla f (Primera—Fiji) 26.
Anippe f (Aggressor—River Clyde) 97.
Anitra f (Borealis—Faerie Lore) 131.
ANNE LA DOUCE f (Silnet—Sweet Anne) 4.
Anne of Hollins f (Tudor Minstrel—Anne of Essex) (21).
Anner Banks c (Black Tarquin—Mill Vine) 102, 285.
Anner Loch f (Flamenco—Loch Cash) (276).
Annotation f (Sayajirao—Light Comment) 139.
Another Flash c (Roi d'Egypte—Cissie Gay) 275, (277), 277, 277.
Anselmo c (Aureole—Aranda) 3, (81), (266).
Antagonist c (Amour Drake—Nearly) 225.
Antelami c (Botticelli—Allegra II) 5.
Anthelion f (Zucchero—Cumulus) 23, (26), 34, (47), 83, 121, 233.
Anthony c (Merry Boy—Grey Anna) (102), 117.
Antiar c (Antares—V Day II) 247, 253, 285, (287), (289).
Antiquarian c (Relic—Rosy Starling) 164, (178), (178), 190, 190.
Anxious Lady f (Golden Cloud—Solicitous) 146, 196, 216.
Anzio c (Vic Day—Lido Lady) (277), 283, 287.
Aorangi c (Bois Roussel—My Bonnie II) 190, 210.
Apache c (Vimy—Sophronia) 48.
Apex II c (Fine Top—Armande) (45).
Aphrodita f (Vandale II—Semoule d'Or) 83, (121).
Apollo c (Panaslipper—Saving Grace) 187.
Apostle c (Blue Peter—Bellani) 116, (120), 135, (148), 149, (207).
Appiani II c (Herbager—Angela Rucellai) 119.
Appilow f (Appian Bridge—Pappalow) (219).
Appoline f (Abernant—Temple Bar) 27, 75.
Appreciation f (Valerullah—Nameless) (231).
Apprentice c (Aureole—Young Entry) (91), 104, 114, 114, (127).
Approval c (Dubonnet—Applause) 285, (285), 287.
Arawak f (Seminole II—Ilonka II) 131, 134.
Arbitrate f (Arbar—Above Board) 93.
Arcandy c (Archive—Ann Denise) (146), (211).
Archangel Gabriel c (Above Suspicion—Angel III) (30).
Archie c (Pappageno II—Crested Gem) 229.
ARCOR c (Arbar—Corejada) 3.
Arcticeelagh c (Arctic Star—Inchigeelagh) (41), 102, 116, 135, 148.
Arctic Explorer c (Arctic Prince—Flirting) (77), (111), (119), 119.
Arctic Express c (Arctic Prince—The Brighton Belle) 218.
Arctic Flower c (Arctic Prince—Fuchsia) 84, 185.
Arctic Gittell c (Arctic Prince—Tiffin Bell) 221.
Arctic Hope c (Arctic Star—Star of Hope) 42.
Arctic Jelly c (Arctic Storm—Wintersweet) 7.

Arctic Kanda c (Arctic Star—Kandahar) 194, (209), (234).
Arctic Lace f (Arctic Chevalier—Alace) 41
Arctic Melody f (Arctic Slave—Bell Bird) (66), (90).
Arctic Ocean c (Pluchino—Light Arctic) 254.
Arctic Run c (Borealis—Run Honey) 60, 76.
Arctic Sea c (Arctic Star—Chloris II) (30), 48, 87, 116, 163.
Arctic Serenade f (Straight Deal—Arctic Blaze) (234)
Arctic Storm c (Arctic Star—Rabina) 25, 30, (87), 117, 124, (149).
Arctic Stream c (Vulgan—Arctic Lady) (275).
Arctic Sunset c (Arctic Slave—Golden Sunset) 246, (253), 273, (275).
Arctic Vale c (Arctic Time—Mill Baby) (84), 91, 140, (142), 175, 220.
Arcturus c (Arctic Slave—Snow Goose) (291).
Ardent Dancer f (Buisson Ardent—June Ball) (86).
Arenaria f (Aureole—Abanilla) 103.
Argol c (Pharis II—Argolide) 182.
Argosy Royal c (Golden Cloud—Scandinavia) 6.
Arion c (Sayajirao—Maneva's Daughter) (45), (184).
Arise c (Grey Sovereign—Rising Wings) 34.
Aristarchus c (Hill Gail—Black Chiffon) 175.
Ark, The c (Relic—Arctic Polly) 27.
Arkle c (Archive—Bright Cherry) 250, (250), (250), 250, 252, (254), 254, (258), (265), (265), (265), (271), (284), (284), (284), (290), (292).
Arkloin c (Archive—Knockiel) (271), (272).
Armagnac Monarch c (Court Harwell—Turkish Delight) 172, 229.
Armour Star c (Arctic Star—Shevaun) 67.
Arodstown Boy c (Fighting Don—Valerie Rose) 25.
Arrest and Trial c (High Treason—Preza) 216.
Arrigle Valley c (Aureole—Val d'Assa) 226.
Art Nouveau c (Gentle Art—My Charger) 8.
Arvak c (Supreme Court—Garden City) 74.
As Before c (Alcide—None Nicer) 5, 128.
Ashavan f (Persian Gulf—Ash Plant) 62, 118, 131, 142.
Ashford Lea c (Sound Track—Sheila's Cabin) 215.
Ash Lawn f (Charlottesville—Crystal Palace) 17, 138.
Ashling f (Nashua—No Strings) 66, 71.
Asiago c (Abernant—Val d'Assa) 37.
Assurance c (The Phoenix—Bernice) (65).
Astrador c (Court Martial—Pensacola) 48, 99.
Astral Green c (Aureole—Edie Kelly) 202.
At-a-Venture c (Alycidon—Caress) 10, 59.
Atbara c (Crepello—Kassala II) (48).
Athenian c (The Phoenix—Felorbia) 255.
Athenien II c (Chateauroux—Athena) 210.
Atherstone Wood c (Buisson Ardent—Reine des Bois) (87), (102), 137.
Atilla c (Alcide—Festoon) 100, (207), (214).
Atishoo f (Hyacinthus—Louby Lou) 228.
Atlantis c (Milesian—Atlantida) 128.
Atlas c (Djebel—Young Entry) 175.

Atonement f (Palestine—Malapert) 29.
Atopolis c (Acropolis—Tudor Top) 105.
Atrax c (Pharis II—Sembrana) (111).
Atrevida f (Sunny Boy III—Palariva) 75, 86.
Attacker c (Aggressor—Diction) 48, 92.
Attalus c (Shantung—Antalya) 39, 74, 85, 120, (143).
Attitude f (Gratitude—Troy-Weight) (20), 71.
Attractor c (Migoli—The Lady in Red) 130.
Aubusson c (Aureole—Terra-Cotta) (99).
Audience c (Requested—Serene Highness) (27), (34), 44, 196.
Audrey Joan f (Doutelle—Zoom) (35), (228).
Augustine c (Aureole—Young Entry) 191.
Aunt Audrey c (Aureole—Jojo) 71.
Aunt Edith f (Primera—Fair Edith) 90, (91), (124), (129).
Aura f (Aureole—Fougalle) 138.
Aura c (Aureole—Cedilla) 45.
Aurabella f (Aureole—Montebella) 86, (131).
Aureate c (Aureole—Fair Maiden) 169, 172, 175, 232.
AURELIUS c (Aureole—Niobe II) (5), 64, (67), 95, (111), (113), 124, 135, 270, 277.
Aurianda f (Aureole—Statuette) 45, 94, 101.
AUROY c (Aureole—Millet) 1, 3, 59, 92.
Auskerry c (Aureole—All Honesty) (19).
Aussie c (Ossian II—Happy Flower) 272.
Autonomy c (Orthodox—Avenue) 196.
Autre Prince c (Beau Prince—Argosy II) 78, 84, 110.
Autumn Melody f (Aureole—Melodious Charm) 129.
Aviator c (Airborne—Julia Caesar) (183).
Avon's Pride c (Arctic Prince—Verdura) 8, 169, 169, (189), (189), 199, 212, 214, 221, (232).
Avril Sprite f (Beau Sabreur—Sprite) 142.
Avro Jet f (Polly's Jet—Avra) 219.
Away for Slates c (Royal Challenger—Meadowbrook) 261.
Axe, The c (Mamoud—Blackball) (37).
Axim c (Marsyas II—Pretty Lady) 289, 289.
Ayala c (Supertello—Admiral's Bliss) (245).
Aznip c (Pinza—Persian Lilac) 39, 46, 73.
Azurine f (Chamossaire—Blue Dun) 84, 86, 118.

B

Babel c (Cagire II—Babylon) 283.
Babu c (My Babu—Nella) (36), 98, 215.
Babur c (My Babu—Reseda) 144, (162), (162).

Baby Don c (Donatello II—Baby Blue) 289.
Bacchanalia f (Nearco—Solar Rhythm) 71.
Bachelor King c (King Hal—Castlecomer Beauty) 281.
Backgammon c (Vilmorin—Meiriona) (216).
Badanloch c (Bakhtawar—Mischievous) 245, 260, 267, 267.
Bagoas c (Darius—Martica) 163.
Bahrain c (Tulyar—Brolly) 270, (285).
Baiser f (Brunel—Yorkshire Rose) 6.
Balaji c (Sayajirao—Ashoka Kumari) 89, 120, 128, 214.
Balbo c (Apple Pie—Blue Bottle) 124.
Bald Eagle c (Nasrullah—Siama) 1, (45), (67), (89), 105.
BALDRIC II c (Round Table—Two Cities) (1), 3, 119, (149).
Bali H'Ai III c (Marco Polo II—Honeywood) (114), 229, 232.
Baljour c (Ballymoss—Day Dreaming) (102).
Ballet Painting c (Valerullah—French Ballet) 266.
Ballette f (Ballymoss—Crotchet) (40).
Ballinaclasha c (Goldwell—Felotte) 275, 289.
Ballyatom c (Annatom—Ballytouchy) (275).
Ballyciptic c (Preciptic—Bally Tickle) 103, 119, 141, 144, 149.
Ballyconneely c (Stephanotis—Tena Mariata) 187.
Ballydar c (Bidar—Ballyfermott) (261).
Ballyfinaghy c (Pappageno II—Coeur Brise) 281.
Ballygoran c (Larkspur—Celia III) (38), 102.
Bally Joy c (Ballymoss—Gladness) 113.
Ballymacad c (Kelly—Ballycade) (12).
Ballymarais c (Ballymoss—Skylarking) 5, 77, (89), 128, 135, (176).
BALLYMOSS c (Mossborough—Indian Call) 3, (5), (84), (100), (117), (119), (124), 135.
Ballyogan Queen f (Ballyogan—Stone Crop) 231.
Bally Precious c (Ballyogan—Precious Rose) 65, 87.
Ballyrichard c (Whitehall—Corabelle) 234.
Ballyrullah c (Ballyogan—Starullah) 10, 30.
Bally Russe c (Ballymoss—Dame Melba) (104), 111, 127, 133.
Bally Vimy c (Vimy—Cambalee) 1, (63).
Ballywit c (Ballymoss—Witness) (207).
Bal Masque c (Nasrullah—Ballerina) (78).
Balto c (Wild Risk—Bouclette) (110), 127.
BALUSTRADE c (Ballymoss—Minstrel's Gallery) 1, 67, 123, 125, 204.
Bamboozle f (Alcide—Claudette) 100, (145).
Bandalore c (Tambourin—Smart Woman) (277), 289.
Bannut Beauty f (Fortina—Dandies Castle) 278.
Bantry Bay c (April the Fifth—Stalbridge Weston) 274, (293), (293).
Banyan c (Zarathustra—Aralia) 221.
Banzai c (Pheroc—Greyluc) 286.
Baranof c (Canadian Champ—La Vodka) 224.
Barbaresque f (Ocarina—Barbara) (107).
Barbary Pirate c (L'Amiral—Ghader) (205).
Barberyn c (Bewildered—Mary Stuart) (276), 276, (288).

Barclay c (Guersant—Tahiti) 77, 113, (142), 149.
Bargello c (Auriban—Isabelle Brand) 77, 81.
Barkhan c (French Beige—Distant Hills) 194, 195.
Barley c (Orthodox—White Label) 192.
Barleycroft c (Wilwyn—Lady Barle) 45, 74.
Barlow Fold f (Monet—Bright and Breezy) 29.
Barnegat f (Mossborough—Four o' Clock) (40).
Barney Fagan c (Fighting Don—Sueberius) (163).
Barnie Beatle c (Dumbarnie—Chanteuse) 180.
Barnie Seton c (Dumbarnie—Mary Seton) 219.
Baroco II c (Fontenay II—Bonne Princesse) 3.
Barolo c (Botticelli—Twilight Hour) 247.
Baron's Folly c (Blue Peter—Fairnington) 84, (103).
Barrymore c (Relic—Even Star) 10, 196.
Bartlemy Boy c (Archive—Beresina) 278.
Barton Street c (Watling Street—Scarborough Lily) 164.
Barwin f (Wilwyn—Barbie) (171), 233.
Bassnet c (Manet—Bassenden) (260), 288.
Bass Rock c (Fastnet Rock—Browband) (174).
Bastille c (Beau Sabreur—Cheveley Lass) (270).
Bastion c (Buisson Ardent—La Bastille) (60).
Battledore c (Combat—Samanda) (272).
Baulking Green c (Coup de Myth—Niccotine Nellie) (278), (278), (278), (278), 278, (293), (293), (293).
Bayarin c (Kythnos—Pin Tray) (206).
Beatle, The c (Pinza—Mount Rosa) 85, 164.
Beau Caprice c (Whim II—Fair Flint) 263, (270).
Beau Chapeau c (High Hat—Beau Co Co) 266.
Beau Court c (Alycidon—Forecourt) 13.
Beaufront f (Mossborough—Sylvan) 4, (80), (93), 134.
Beau Ideal f (Beau Sabreur—Cambalee) (26).
Beau Lavender c (Javelot—Downhill) (172).
Beau Normand c (Bouton Rose—Ma Normandie) 91, 183, 251, 257, (270), (289), (289).
Beau Rossa c (Beau Sabreur—Cara Rossa) (185).
Beau Tudor c (Beau Sabreur—Blue Sapphire) 92.
Beaver II c (Fast Fox—Anne III) (247), (283).
Bebop f (Prince Bio—Cappellina) 129.
Be Careful f (My Babu—Fair Freedom) (28), (32), 61.
Becket c (Eudaemon—Fanai Tire) 162, 205.
Beckfoot c (Court Martial—Choice Bloom) 219.
Beddard c (Quorum—Miss Pepita) (104).
Bedecked f (Rockefella—Easter Day) 86.
Be Friendly c (Skymaster—Lady Sliptic) (59), (115), 136, (151), (151), (230).
Beige Lee c (French Beige—Pat Lee) 88.
Belafonte c (Nearco—Solar Rhythm) 120, 188.
Bel Baraka II c (Worden II—Fleur des Neiges II) 127.
Bell, The c (Bellman—Lincoln's Inn) (251), (255), (264), 272.

BELLA PAOLA f (Ticino—Rhea II) (2), (4), (149).
Bella Voce f (Chanteur II—Monarchia) 68.
Bellborough c (Mossborough—Church Bell) 1, 144.
Belle Rosheen f (Beau Sabreur—Roseian) (231).
Bellisle f (King's Bench—Garrydoolis) 215, 218.
Bell Top f (Doutelle—Blue Jean) (83).
Belmura c (Mossborough—Chakita) 165, 175.
Beneficiary c (Rockefella—Grandpa's Will) 76, 96.
Bengal Lancer c (Nearco—Jungle Music) 48.
Ben Novus c (Ben Hawke—Novelty) (162), 178, (184).
Benroy c (Rockefella—Banka) 203.
Ben Stack c (Tangle—Sweet Vernal) (273), (275).
Ben Voy c (Fortina—Sweet Vernal) 281.
Beotien c (Pot o'Luck—Berylune) 274.
Berber c (Princely Gift—Desert Girl) (22), 42, (99), 105.
BERKELEY SPRINGS f (Hasty Road—Virginia Water) 2, 4, (43).
Bernie f (Beau Sabreur—Artetta) (83).
Best Song c (Chanteur II—Best Seller) 77, 113, (180), 180, 220, (235).
Beta f (Alycidon—Second Barrel) (39).
Betatron c (Pardal—Verve) 206.
Betray c (High Treason—Nicolarta) 192.
Better Honey c (Honey Way—Mieux Rouge) 185, (194).
Bewilder f (Crepello—Tantalizer) 97.
Bewildroom c (Bewildered—Whinbroom) 224, 233.
Bexar c (Princely Gift—Parnassia) 192.
Beyond the Moss c (Mossborough—Solitaire) 169.
Bianconi Lady f (Sovereign Lord—Clematis) 30.
Biarritz c (Buisson Ardent—Asti Spumanti) 184, (200).
Big Deal c (Pirate King—Riddlemeree) 37.
Big George c (Gay Presto—Miss Muffet V) 267, 274.
Big Hat c (High Hat—Gay Natasha) 176.
Bigibigi c (Hard Sauce—Spirille) 196.
Bijou c (Goldwell—Beresina) 274.
Billum c (Arctic Prince—Catchit) (46), 73, 208.
Biomydrin c (Ballymoss—Collyria) (84), 110.
Birdbrook c (Mossborough—Game Bird) 21, (123), (203), (205).
Birinkiana c (Birikan—Salmiana II) 270.
Birthday Present c (Precipitation—Persian Maid) 189, (189).
Biscayne c (Talgo—Marjorie Castle) (142).
Bishop's Move c (Langton Abbot—Marsh Marigold) 182.
Bivouac c (Darius—Camp Fire) 16, (200).
Black Caprice c (Black Tarquin—Quel Caprice) 279.
Black Gold f (Aureole—Brunetta) 4, 66, (118), 131.
Black Ice c (Arctic Chevalier—Indian Queen) (283).
Black Justice c (Jock Scot—Triangle) 189, 270, 277.
Black King c (Nimbus—Reel In) (104), 172.
Black Nanny f (Black Tarquin—Jenny Lind) 145.
Blackness c (Black Tarquin—Keystone) (60), 85.

BLACK PRINCE II c (Arctic Prince—Rose II) 3, 82, (92), 135, 148.
Blackwood c (Narrator—Faro) 130.
Blakeney c (Hethersett—Windmill Girl) (47).
Blarney Beacon c (Ballymoss—Fluorescent) (283).
Blast c (Djebe—Gale Warning) 10, 42, 60, (103), 119, 119, (227).
Blaze of Glory II c (Tyrone—Blazing) (19).
Blazing Scent c (Blason—Frigid Flower) (174), 186.
Bleep Bleep c (Hard Sauce—Curtsey) 22, (126), 126, (136), 219, 228.
Blessing, The c (Devonian—Circassia) 217.
Blessington Esquire c (Escamillo—Lady Blessington II) 253.
Bleu Azur f (Crepello—Blue Prelude) 90, 138.
Blizzard f (Borealis—No Appeal) 121.
Blockhaus c (Relic—Belle Princesse) 144.
Blublue c (The Phoenix—French Ballad) 192.
Bluecourt f (Court Martial—Alcyone) 138, 181.
Blue Dolphin c (Domaha—Rock Pigeon) 246, 254, 273, 273, 273, 273.
Blue Galleon f (Alycidon—Set Sail) 108, 129, 134.
Blue Marine c (Hook Money—Bedecked) 12, (15).
Blue Moth c (Blue Archer—Lady Pearl) 258, 265.
Blue Mountain c (Krakatao—Mont Bleu) (270).
Blue Net II c (Fastnet III—Blue Stone II) 116.
Blue Over f (Democratic—Skindles) (204).
Blue Riband f (Blue Peter—Stream of Light) 97.
Blue Rondo c (Blue Speck—Lady Rondo) (253).
Blueroy c (Persian Gulf—Blue Galleon) 5.
Bluerullah c (Valerullah—Windsor Blue) 77, (98), 125, 233.
Blue Sails c (Blue Peter—Miss Mabel) 10.
Bluest f (Infatuation—Two Blues) (166).
Blue Streak c (Firestreak—White Shoulders) 14.
Blue Wolf c (Romulus—Blue Mark) 30.
Blue Yonder c (Crepello—Soldier's Song) 49.
Bobar II c (Bozzetto—Balatame) (149).
Bob Barker c (Robert Barker—The Bog) 164.
Bobsbest c (Tamerlane—Coolmaine) 184, (184), 184, 218, 227, 227.
Bob Tailed 'Un c (Tambourin—Hunting Morn) 272.
Bognie Brae c (Pandemonium—Vainglory) 225.
Bois Belleau c (Bois Roussel—War Loot) 30, 36, 117.
Boismoss c (Mossborough—Branches Park) (232).
Bold Baby c (Bellacose—Baby Blue) (289).
Bold Lad c (Bold Ruler—Barn Pride) 1, (10), (32), (42), (65), 98, 105.
Bold Lover c (Never Say Die—Chaste and Fair) 10.
Boleslas c (Botticelli—Ascension II) (41).
Bollinger c (Reynard Volant—Wedding Day) 281.
Bombazine f (Shantung—Whimsical) 4.
Bonda c (Floribunda—B.B.Bognor) 15.
Bonhomie c (Dubonnet—Golden Grain) (161), (191).
Bonnard c (Tenerani—Buonamica) 140.
Bonnie Mac c (Falls of Clyde—Retort) 286.

Bonny Creeper c (Democratic—Ashley's Pride) 79.
Bookmarker c (Nearula—Booklet) (60).
Border Bandit c (Bakhtawar—Eva's Pet) 261.
Border Bounty f (Bounteous—B.Flat) 90, 134, 139.
Border Fury c (Border Chief—Pre Fleuri) 280, 280.
Border Grace c (Olein's Grace—Oola) 246, 273, 281.
Border Jet c (Zalophus—Border Girl) (271).
Border Sparkle c (Border Legend—Champagne Wyn) 257, 260.
Bordone c (Botticelli—Blue Ballad) 177, (199).
Borghetto c (Bozzetto—l'Alma) 114.
Borgia c (Niccolo Dell'arca—Fairly Hot) 268.
Borlent Boy c (Borealis—Lentolia) 209.
Born Free f (Alycidon—Queen of Sheba) 83, 97, 138.
Borodino c (Wild Risk—Tamora II) 206.
Bo'sun, The c (Crepello—All Aboard) (74), (170).
Bosworth Field c (Henry the Seventh—Lentolia) 10, 19, 27, 198.
Bothered c (Bewildered—Roseblush) (161).
BOUNTEOUS c (Rockefella—Marie Elizabeth) 5, (46), 82.
Bourbon c (Le Lavandou—Lady Victoria) (179), 219, 230.
Bowerchalke f (Robert Barker—Herstmonceux) 228.
Bowgeeno c (Bowsprit—Avageeno) (262), (264), 271, 292.
Bow Tie c (Golden Cloud—Scarf) 14.
Bowzen c (Bowsprit—Zendy) 116.
Boys Hurrah c (Baman—Ballypact) 275.
Bracey Bridge f (Chanteur II—Rutherford Bridge) (108), 131, 134, (139), (145).
Brackley c (Lucero—Chain Bridge) 163.
Branca Doria c (Dante—White Vision) 285, 285, 287.
Brancusi c (Donatello II—Buxted) 235.
Brand New c (Milesian—Early Call) 27.
Brasher c (Fortina—Broken Dawn) 250, 270, 271, 271, (291), 292.
Brassia f (Buisson Ardent—Discorea) (11), 66, 86.
Brave Buck c (Blue Peter—Fire Song) 5, 76.
Brave Knight c (Court Harwell—Lady Into Fox) 31, 49, 74, (195).
Bravery f (Hillsdale—Victoria Cross II) (30), 43, 107.
Bravi c (Wild Risk—Undecided) (172).
Breathlessly Smart c (Vic Day—Cadre) 268.
Breck Road c (Lord of Verona—Dararole) (227), 227.
Bremontier c (Labrador—Heve) 250, (291).
Brent c (Tyrone—Pink Foot) 35.
Bric-Brac f (Aureole—La Brigantine) 229, 247, 287.
Bridal Choice c (Black Tarquin—Bridal Bay) 270.
Brief Chorus f (Counsel—B. Flat) 27, 134.
Brief Flight f (Counsel—Par Avion) 106, (166).
Brigg Fair f (Como-Gorsetra) 217.
Bright Beach f (Little Cloud—Badger's Beech) 282, (282).
Bright Silk f (Bright News—Sylko) 203.
Bright Talk f (Bright News—Golden Shilling) (163), 231.
Bright Will c (Will Somers—Bright Set) 48.

Brilliant Stone f (Borealis—Cobble Stone) 26, (40).
Bringley f (Poaching—Gondolette II) 97, (139).
BRIOCHE c (Tantieme—Eudemis) 5, 73, 84, (91), 111, (113), (135), 140, 148.
British Empire c (Court Martial—Iroquoise II) 18, 22, 67.
Brittas c (Riding Mill—Mairin's Law) 271.
Brittle II f (Djebe—Emulsion) 121.
Broadway Melody f (Tudor Melody—Goldwyn Girl) 11, (61), 106, 200.
Brocade Slipper c (Solar Slipper—Brocade) (116), 199, (221).
Broken Doll f (Relic—China Maid) 101.
Bromelia f (Bois Roussel—Ocean Lore) 17.
Bronzino c (Botticelli—Herringbone) (269), 283.
Brookling c (Brooksby—Emily Square) 290.
Brooky c (Pinza—Bottalina) 6.
Brother c (Nearula—Aunt Agnes) 21, 32, 122, 224.
Brothertoft c (Epaulette—Herodiade) 222.
Brown Diamond c (Vulgan—Little Blue Star) 258, 272, 272, 290, 290.
Brown Owen (Late Onthejob) c (Owenstown—Red Lady) 273.
Brunel II c (Norseman—Irlande) 187, 250, 292, 292.
Brunton c (Solar Slipper—Fair Treat) (163).
Bryonia f (Honeyway—Belladonna) 61.
Buchan Hummlie c (Rocket—Caerlissa) 224.
Buckingham c (Bakhtawar—No Medals) (279).
Budge Blue c (Le Lavandou—Nova) 14.
Buffer c (Auralia—Coupling) (223).
Bugle Boy c (Tudor Melody—Moss Maiden) 31, 180, 226, (235).
Bull Dancer c (Matador—Good as Gold) 10.
Bullrush c (Matador—Meadowsweet) 211, (216).
Bunker c (Kalydon—Coal Board) (180), 194, 198, 220, 226, (226).
Bun Penny c (Hook Money—Lady Victoria) 65, (109).
Bunratty Castle c (Henry the Seventh—Winter Solstice) (7), 19.
Buona notte c (Lake Placid—Jenny Lind) 252, (253), (271).
Burglar c (Crocket—Agin the Law) 14, (16), 22, 42.
Burning Bright c (Buisson Ardent—Messua) 224.
Burning Thoughts c (Buisson Ardent—Parnassia) (16), 179, 204, 217.
Burning Torch c (Tropique—Miss Olympia) 99, 182, 185, 208.
Burn the Candle c (Midnight Sun—Wallis III) 104.
Burton Tan c (Foroughi—Brown Bess III) (280).
Bush Fire c (Buisson Ardent—Escasida) 45.
Busted c (Crepello—Sans le Sou) (77), (102), (119), (124).
Busty Hill c (Prince Richard—Fort Field) 271.
Butiaba f (Prince Chevalier—Bodala) (86).
But Why f (Pandemonium—Mulligatawny) 163.
By Jupiter! c (By Thunder!—Grande Corniche) (177), 235.
Byng c (Vimy—Riding Rays) (161), (169).
By Rights c (Right Boy—Chart Room) 192, 200.

C

Cabouchon c (Tamerlane—Sunol) 187, (188), (206), 213.
Cadenza f (Chanteur II—Delia) 129.
Cadmore c (Fortina—Inver Hope) 271.
Caduval c (Lacaduv—La Francaise) (251), 255, (271), 272, 289.
CAERGWRLE f (Crepello—Caerphilly) (2), (61), 101.
Caerphilly f (Abernant—Cheetah) 126.
Caesars Helm c (Arctic Star—Roman Galley) 250, 253, 259, (281).
Cagirama c (Cagire II—Pet Girl) 161, 172, (172), 177, 177, (199), 199, (209), (209), 214, 214.
Cagliari c (Cagire II—Alanna) 62.
Caistor Top f (Reverse Charge—Coriona) (143).
Calceolaria f (Aureole—Flying Slipper) 4, 206.
Calf Love c (Infatuation—Ibex) 224.
Caliph, The c (Persian Gulf—Joyce Grove) 7.
Callant, The c (St Michael—Windywalls) (282).
Call of the Wild c (High Treason—Wild Harvest) 7.
Calor c (Nack—Dream Again) 274.
Calyphas c (Tamerlane—Ovada) 191.
CAMBREMER c (Chamossaire—Tomorrow II) 110.
Cambridge c (Saint Crespin III—Cantelo) 3, (74).
Camille f (Abernant—Camp Fire) 167, (216), 228.
Camisado c (Chamier—Ballora) 37.
Campaign c (Aureole—Camp Fire) 7, 26, (60), 174, (215).
Camugliano c (Verso II—Camuccina) (287), 287.
Canardeau c (Admiral Drake—La Petite) 203.
Canarina f (Zarathustra—Campanette) 68.
Candelabra c (Niccolo Dell'Arca—Incandescent) 206.
Candid Picture c (Dionisio—Picture Gallery) 37, 184, (203).
Candy Cane c (Crepello—Candy Gift) 36, (64), 149.
Canisbay c (Doutelle—Stroma) (68), 88, 116, (119).
Cannebiere c (Alycidon—Apparition) 180, (199), 214, (214), 214, (225), (225), 225, 226.
Cannobie Lee c (Soldado—Droptown) 255, 272.
Cantab c (Cantaber—Balek) (283).
Cantadora f (Matador—Kantara) (9).
Canteen f (Kings Troop—Picnic Party) (9), 14, 23.
CANTELO f (Chanteur II—Rustic Bridge) 4, (5), (39), (83), (108), 139.
CANTERBURY c (Charlottesville—Cavatina) 5, 133.
Canton c (The Phoenix—Star Island) 188.
Caperer f (Persian Gulf—River Test) (101).
Capitaine c (Krakatao—La Capitane) 142.
Capitaine Corcoran c (Wild Risk—Partie Carree) 111.
Captain Kidd c (Nearula—All Aboard) 16, (18), 28.
Captain's Yarn c (Great Captain—Solar Serial) 231.
Capuchon c (Abernant—Sun Cap) 109.
Caramel f (Crepello—Maple Leaf) 94.

Carbon Copy c (Fair Copy—Clara Barton) 89.
Cardington Court c (Court Martial—Danse d'Espoir) (203).
Carlemont c (Charlottesville—Torbella III) (45), (125).
Carmen IV f (Bellman—Caramel II) (261), 280, 291.
CARNOUSTIE c (Dante—Winged Foot) 1, 3, (14), 32, (73), 105, 128.
Carrack c (Acropolis—Felucca) (120).
Carrickbeg c (Control—Florida) 245, 265, (280), 292.
Carrigeen Duff c (Hill Gail—Beauty Royal) 172, 279.
CARROZZA f (Dante—Calash) 2, (4), (75).
Carsina f (Hethersett—Whimsical) 11, 19.
Caruso c (Sing Sing—Donna) 8, 18.
Casabianca c (Never Say Die—Abelia) (39), (193).
Casey c (Black Tarquin—Ready) 92.
Cash c (Hook Money—Dinorama) (247).
Cash and Courage c (Rockefella—Daring Miss) (185), 185.
Cashel View c (The Phoenix—Bellevue III) 275.
Casmiri c (Bright News—Ranee) 194.
Casque c (Vatellor—Gay's the Word) (76), 92.
Cassarate f (Abernant—Cassydora) (115), 136.
Cassim c (Tamerlane—Prudent Polly) 64, 64, 72, 163, (163), 220.
Casting Vote c (Quorum—Lenaea) (225).
Castle Yard c (St Paddy—Spanish Court) 80, 128, 178, 178, (185), 208, 208, 210.
Castro c (Nearco—Chione) (130).
Catapult III c (Norseman—Eastern Stream) 283.
Catchpenny c (Grey Sovereign—Besides) 24, 173.
Catchpole c (King of the Tudors—Catchmay) 1, 46, 87, 99, (106).
Caterina f (Princely Gift—Radiopye) 126, 136, (136).
Catherine f (King of the Tudors—Danae) 9.
Cathy B f (Beau Sabreur—Vinaigrette) 234.
Catterline c (Premonition—Darrica) 13.
Caught Out c (Court Martial—Long Cast) (205), 223, (223), 223, 223, (223).
Cauliflower f (Colonist II—Dancing Flower) 293, 293.
Causerie f (Cagire II—Happy Thought) (26), 101, 138.
Cease Fire f (Martial—Blank Day) 11, (17), 216.
C.E.D. c (Fidalgo—Papoose) 201, 232.
Celestial Sucker c (Donatello II—Faith in China) 234.
Celina f (Crepello—Rose of Medina) 20, 71, (94), 108, (131).
Celo f (Live Spirit—Kingsway Lady) (219).
Celtic Gold c (Cash and Courage—Welsh Ballad) 263.
Celtic King c (Schapiro—Kildonan) 221.
Celtic Night c (Owen Tudor—Fairly Hot) (268).
CELTIC SONG c (Sing Sing—Caledonie II) 1, (32).
Centaurus c (Premonition—Kate's Way) 35.
Centra f (Tit for Tat II—Lavandou Mink) 25.
Centre Circle c (Hyacinthus—Royal Circle) (280), 280.
Ceremony f (Grandmaster—Glory Din) 161.
Certainement f (Doubtless II—French Colleen) 249, 276.
Chalkey c (Grit—Queencote) 216.

Chalk Stream c (Midas—Sabie River) 162, (178).
Cham c (Cagire II—Pharosia II) (293).
Chamafleur c (Chamossaire—Safe Conduct) 199.
Chamarre c (Chamier—Bemore) 30, 36.
Chambord f (Chamossaire—Life Hill) 134, 139.
Chamour c (Chamier—Cracknel) (102), (117).
Champ c (Chamossaire—Miss Deal) 177, 177, 180, 190.
Chancer f (Chamier—Romancer) 279.
Chandie IV c (Chinde—Sapphire VII) 278.
Chandra Cross c (Sayajirao—War Ribbon) 198.
Chandulal c (Narrator—In Doubt) 81.
Chanter f (Chanteur II—Marie Therese) 37.
Chantha f (Chanteur II—Naptha) 6.
Chantry c (Chanteur II—Tiffin Bell) 289.
Chaos c (Bewildered—Speedway) (278), 278, 278, 282.
Chapmans Peak c (Major Portion—Seascape) 47.
Chappaqua c (Big Game—Snow Shower) 167.
Charbon c (King's Bench—Golden Gay) 184, 216.
Charicles c (Bleep-Bleep—Candida) (196), 228.
Charlie's Pal c (Gratitude—Our Dark Lady) (181).
Charlie Worcester c (Mustang—Beylough) (246), 252, 262.
CHARLOTTOWN c (Charlottesville—Meld) (3), 5, (31), (48), (72), 92, (100), 117, (133).
Charmed Life f (Petition—Niobe) 167.
Chaseaway c (Chanteur II—Hailea) 191.
Chasmarella f (Rockefella—Chasse Maree) 138.
Chatellerault f (Abernant—Duke's Delight) 6.
Chatting f (Arctic Star—Murmuration) 131.
Chavara c (Royal Tara—Cherubim) 251, (259), 272.
Che Bella f (Beau Sabreur—Victory Bells) (231).
Chebs Lad c (Lucky Brief—Cheb) 1, (6), (19), 28, (32), (35), (73), 99.
Check Abbess f (Raincheck—Mount Abbess) 231.
Cheerer c (Naucide—Blank Day) 268.
Cherry f (Prince Bio—Baghichen) 131.
Chestergate c (Buisson Ardent—Abadek) 182, 199, 202, 202.
Cheval c (Javelot—Shevaun) 60, 213.
Chevalier c (Prince Chevalier—Lady Midge) 26, 37.
Chevastrid c (Prince Chevalier—Panastrid) (105).
Cheveley Lad c (Tamerlane—Special Request) 205.
Cheviot Hills c (Panorama—Northumbria) (184).
Chicago c (Fidalgo—Grischuna) (95), 214.
Chief Barker (late Polar Lodge) c (Arctic Star—Viceregal) 210, (235).
Chief Inspector c (Constable—Two Blues) 182.
China Clipper c (Migoli—Taipeh) (24), 42, 193.
China Rock c (Rockefella—May Wong) (72), 72, (81), 113, 148.
Chinese Lacquer c (Tenerani—Chinese Cracker) 177, 229, 247.
Chinese Sun c (Hyperion—Chinese Cracker) 128, 168, 203.
Chino c (Faubourg II—Golden Polly) 168, 185, 207.

Chinwag c (Pinza—Chinky Bu) (96), 105.
Chiron c (Saint Crespin III—Ballechin) 283.
Choir Practise f (Guersant—Agar's Plough) 131.
Choreographer c (Artist's Son—Eagle's Law) 246.
Chorus c (Beau Sabreur—May) 266, (270), 277.
Chota Hazri f (Sayajirao—Salmi) 83.
Chouchou II c (Lacaduv—Choupette II) 285.
Chris c (Vilmorin—Tie Silk) (115).
Christmas Island c (Court Harwell—Tahiti) (62), (82), 133, (142).
Christmas Night c (Maharaj Kumar—Hellebore) 47.
Christmas Review c (March Past—Hellebore) 162, (171), (186), 186, 186.
Chrona f (Princely Gift—Duckling) (17), (121).
Chrysler III c (Cranach—Hurrylor) 5.
Church Stretton c (Dumbarnie—Noble Belle) 184.
Chu-Teh c (Big Game—In Doubt) 264, (280), (280).
Cipriani c (Never Say Die—Carezza) 3, (77), 85, 125.
Clair Soleil c (Maravedis—La Divine) (289).
Clanyon c (Canyonero—Miss Clare) 281, 281, (288), 288.
Clara Bow f (Solar Slipper—Nero's Lady) 86.
Claymore c (Cameron—Clemency) 280.
Clean Verdict f (Whistler—Pip and Polish) 9.
Clear Night c (Alycidon—Request) 169, (180).
Clear Profit c (High Profit—Rent Free) 245.
Clear River c (Abernant—Fairbourne) 219, 228.
Clear Round c (Final Score—Noble Link) (163), 163.
Clear Sound c (Whistler—Fleeting Beauty) 1, (32).
Clementine f (Vulgan—Clemency) 258.
Clerical Grey c (Migoli—Ephese) (270).
Clever Dick c (Democratic—Sophronia) 27.
Clichy c (Clarion III—Carrere) 127.
Clonroche f (Arctic Slave—Mulberry Bay) 279.
Closebeck c (Closeburn—Arksey) 191.
Close Call c (Whistler—Newsy Nook) 219, 228.
Close Up f (Nearula—Horama) 9.
Cloth of Gold f (Tudor Minstrel—Sun Glory) 9.
Cloucourt c (Court Harwell—Clouette) 270.
Clouds c (Nimbus—Aurora) (195).
Cloudy Symbol f (Alcide—Veritas II) (97).
Cloudy Wyn f (Wilwyn—Cloudy Walk) (207).
Clover Bud f (Phebus—The Hayseed) (255).
Clydeann f (Anamnestes—Bridge of Clyde) 181.
Cocky Consort c (Happy Monarch—Sporty Ann) 259, 262, 284.
Codicil f (Prince Chevalier—Grandpa's Will) 198.
Colchicum c (Colonist II—Slovak) 114.
Cold Comfort c (Arctic Prince—Careless Coquette) 189.
Cold Slipper c (Arctic Time—Blaith na Greine) 65, 114.
COLD STORAGE f (Never Say Die—Snow Court) 5, 83.
Coleen Star c (Nearcolein—May Star) 254, 271.

Coliseum c (Umberto—Cornice) 39, 82.
Colledge Master c (Grandmaster—Collence) 282, (282), (282).
College Don c (Donatello II—School Days) 288.
Collyria f (Arctic Prince—Eyewash) 4, 37, (139).
Colonel Blimp c (Aggressor—Ratho) (202).
Colonel Imp c (Colonist II—Mushtara) 165, 165, 169, 169, 169, 223, 269, 283.
Colonel in Chief c (Princely Gift—Colonel's Lady) 173.
Colonel Wynn c (Cariff—Rose Sprite) 293.
Colony f (Constable—Rambling Way) (6).
Colour Blind c (Solonaway—Amberley) (34).
Colour Plate c (Whistler—Instant) 22.
Comandeer c (Combat—Eastags) 289.
Combatant c (Chanteur II—Mercy) 175, 189, 212.
Come April f (March Past—Meadow Grass) (173), 205.
Comedian's Folly c (Jubilee Day—Swift Eagle) 271.
Comefast c (Como—Waterspout) 219, 228, (228).
Comet c (Buisson Ardent—My Anne) 219.
Come to Daddy c (Niccolo Dell'Arca—Snow Bunting) 189, (232).
Comet Star c (Star Signal—Trigennie) 270.
Comma f (Chamossaire—Cedilla) 93.
Commander in Chief c (Court Martial—Seria) (178), (233), 233.
Common Pond c (Skymaster—Saucy Nell) 184, 222, (227).
Comonisi c (Como—Nisi) 44, 217.
Compensation c (Gratitude—Shillelagh) (37), (109), 146, 228, (230).
Compere c (Como—Star of France) 27, 126.
Compromise c (Nearco—Idealist) 81, 104, 175.
Compton Martin c (Guersant—Martinhoe) 161.
Con Brio c (Ribot—Petronella) (35), 82, (88).
Concealdem c (Damremont—The Bog) 210, (235), 235.
Coney Island c (Palestine—Iberia) 14.
Confidence f (Preciptic—Bernice) (26), 66.
Conjuror c (Crepello—No Saint) 32, (37).
Connaissance c (King's Bench—La Pilleuse) 13, (59), 98, 98, (143).
CONNAUGHT c (St Paddy—Nagaika) 3, 5, 27, 70, 82, (111), (135).
Connamara Kid c (Dumbarnie—Royal Ensign) 171.
Constans c (March Past—Constantia) 44, (59), 79.
Continuation c (Ballyogan—Damians) (193).
Convamore c (Court Harwell—Absolution) 3, (111), 117, 213.
Coogee f (Relic—Last Judgement) 8.
Cool Alibi c (Alibi II—Coolnakisk) (285).
Cool Breeze c (Anwar—Blue Breeze) 225.
Cool Debate c (Arctic Prince—Debate) (26).
Cool Reception c (Iceberg II—Miss Hopkins) 279, (279).
Copenhagen c (Royal Charger—All Aboard) 59, 99.
Copp c (Pinxit—Crested Plover) (258).
Copper Cable c (Penny Royal—Gold Airgraph) 267, 274.
Copper Horse, The c (Royal Charger—Windbourne) 227.
Coppers Evidence c (Hook Money—Fleeting Interest) 224.

Copsale c (King's Bench—Chrysoprase) (208), 210.
Coral Cluster c (Pink Flower—Filigrana) 279, (279).
Coralinda f (Palestine—Papido) 6.
Corbalton f (Milesian—Corbally Princess) 129.
Corifi c (Acropolis—Peterkin) (67).
Corinto c (Grey Sovereign—Mistress Gwynne) (192), (215), 222.
Corn Star c (Cacador—Dawn Star) 278.
Coronado c (Whistler—Vertige) 1, 45.
Coronation Year c (Petition—Trixie) (170).
CORPORA c (Ribot—Lady Lufton) 1, 3.
Corrielaw Diamond c (Exodus—Tipperary Flame) 282.
Corrie Vacoul c (Vulgan—Lady Mustang) 258, 265.
Corrigadillisk c (Vulgan—Dark Mist) 276.
Cortachy c (Court Martial—Briquette) (45), 123.
Cortego c (Coaraze—Pharelle) 270.
Costa Brava c (Greek Star—Solebay) 285.
Cottagebrook c (Nearcolein—Cottage Bride) 265.
Couligarten (late Hasty Hints) c (Flamenco—Hasty Chance) 267, (279).
Couloir f (Court Martial—Golden Gulf) 43.
Counsel c (Court Martial—Wheedler) (218).
Count, The c (Oxonian—Kilcranatan) 260.
Countermarch c (Hard Ridden—Ballyogan Queen) 26, 46.
Country Path f (Mossborough—Passerelle) 48, 90.
Coup f (Hook Money—Touch) 61.
Court Command c (Precipitation—Forecourt) 72, 140.
Courtesan f (Supreme Court—Anna Lucasta) (83).
Court Gift c (Tanerko—Courtesan) (133).
COURT HARWELL c (Prince Chevalier—Neutron) 5, 72, (78), 78, 80, (130), (133).
Court One f (Supreme Court—Moonstone) (121).
Court Prince c (Supreme Court—Capital Issue) (78), 148.
Courts Appeal c (Petition—Da Ve) 163, (231), 231, 270.
Court Sentence c (Court Martial—Nagaika) 10, (105).
Courtwell f (Court Harwell—Courtlier) 66, 231, (231).
Covent Garden c (Crepello—Lavender Girl) 80.
Coventry Express c (Cagire II—Devon Violet) 270.
Covert Side f (Abernant—Cub Hunt) 2.
Coxcomb c (Honeyway—Lady Grand) 214.
Cracker f (Court Harwell—Isetta) 94, (129).
Cracksman c (Chamossaire—Nearly) 82, 180, 183, 220.
Craigbrock c (Vulgan—Goldenstown) 291.
Craighouse c (Mossborough—Tarbert Bay) (68), 135, (142).
Crampon c (Arctic Prince—Canvas Shoe) 70.
Cranberry Sauce f (Crepello—Queensberry) (69), (94), 134, (147).
Crazy Paving c (Sovereign Path—Verbena) 27.
Creditor, The f (Crepello—The Accused) (98), (106), (144), 149.
Credo c (Crepello—Marsyaka) 104, 127, 133, (175), (226).
Crenelle f (Crepello—Mulberry Harbour) 90, 138.
Creole c (Tropique—Camille) 174, 196, 204, (211), (216), (216), 217, 230.

Crepango c (Crepello—Panga) 200.
Crepe Clover c (Crepello—Honey Flower) 62, 102.
Crepe de Chine f (Crepello—Carrozza) 83.
CREPELLO c (Donatello II—Crepuscule) (1), (3).
Crepello's Daughter f (Crepello—Sybil's Niece) (17).
Crepes d'Enfer c (Crepello—No Angel) 133, (190).
Crepone c (Crepello—Sweet One) 78, 103, 164.
Crest of the Wave c (Crepello—Mulberry Harbour) 80.
Crete c (Mossborough—Carezza) 3, 87, 128.
Cretencia f (Crepello—Vertencia) 108.
Crevette f (Crepello—Fair Amazon) 107, (121).
Crimea II f (Princequillo—Victoria Cross) 2, (23), (43), 126.
Crisp and Even c (Saint Crespin III—Polar Myth) 3, 5, 88, 111, (130).
Crisper f (Court Martial—Tripaway) 11, 18, (79), 216.
Crispian c (Saint Crespin III—Phoenissa) 32.
Crisp Piece f (Saint Crespin III—Peacemaker) 40, 69.
Crobeg c (Iceberg II—Astrography) 257.
Crocket c (King of the Tudors—Chandelier) 1, (10), (28), (42), (67), (105).
Crofter, The c (Tartan—Dawn Cottage) 245.
Croise c (Ksarinor—Prime Croisee) 276.
Croizet c (Hahnhof—Caro Mio II) 250, 274.
Crosby Don c (Counsel—Haycock) (227).
Cross Talk f (Pardal—Criss-Cross) 197.
Crotchet f (Chanteur II—Nelia) 4, 83, (93), 134, 139, 145.
Crowded Room c (Pinza—Amatali) 31.
Crozier c (Zarathustra—Vimere) (78), 111, 128, (140).
Crystal Bay c (Persian Gulf—Blue Sapphire) (80).
Crystal Clear f (Chamossaire—Six of Diamonds) 83, 145.
Crystal Palace f (Solar Slipper—Queen of Light) (121), (129), 144.
Cuaran Riona f (Panaslipper—Banri Calma) 41.
Cuillins c (Doutelle—Far Hills) (223).
Culleenpark c (Hyacinthus—Culleen's Coup) 278.
Cullen f (Quorum—Phrygia) (169).
Cumshaw c (Djebe—Remuneration) 168, (186).
Cupid's Charge c (Reverse Charge—Lace Bow) (288).
Cured c (No Worry—Nae Drappie) 274.
Current Coin c (Hook Money—Frances) (25), (38), (109), 146.
Current Speech c (Narrator—Tumbling Waters) (180), (181), (225).
Curry c (Sayajirao—Calorie) 169, (175).
Curry's Kin c (Wilwyn—Calorietrix) 161.
Cursorial f (Crepello—None Nicer) 93, 130, (139).
CUTTER f (Donatello II—Felucca) 4, (72), (91), (139).
Cynara f (Grey Sovereign—Ladycroft) (11), (23), 29, 126, 136.
Cyrus c (Darius—Good Line) 16, (26), (74), 98, 105, 144.
Czar Alexander e (Pampered King—War Ribbon) 13.

D

Daffodil f (Dante—Sweet Nan) (30), 66.
Dagmar Gittell c (His Slipper—Dagmar) (288).
Dahabeah c (Aureole—Felucca) 113, 194, 209.
Dahban c (Princely Gift—Dover Lassie) 79.
Daily Telegraph c (Hotspur—Sug Plant) 275.
Dairialatan c (Pardal—Kunj Lata) 210.
Daisy Belle f (Abraxas—Burnt Sienna) (27), 146, 228.
Daisy Chain f (Darius—Casual) (101).
Dalesa c (Pardal—Solesa) (99).
Dalnamein c (Rockefella—June Ball) (209), 225, (235), 235.
Dalry c (Hethersett—Lindylee) 1, (45), 48, 87.
Dalrymple c (Dante—Ringtime) 188.
Dalstar c (Pardal—Windfall) 183.
Dame Melba f (Chanteur II—Armada) 40, (97), 108, 145.
Damredub c (Damremont—Rub-a-Dub) (164), 223, 235, (235), 235.
Dancing Moss c (Ballymoss—Courbette) 111, 142, (148).
Dan Cupid c (Native Dancer—Vixenette) 1, 42.
Dandini c (Sovereign Path—Fleeting Beauty) 87.
Dandy Scot c (Pearl Orient—Heroic China) 251.
Dandy Tim c (Last of the Dandies—Carbery's Hall) 281.
Danella c (Rockefella—Daneway) 162, 168, 171, (181), (182), 218.
Dan Kano c (Dicta Drake—Gilly Lees) 81, 100, (142).
Danseur c (Tantieme—La Danse) 110.
Dan Somers c (Will Somers—Lady Dandy) (21).
Dante's Hill c (Hill Gail—Dainty Dancer) 63.
Dante's Inferno c (Dante—Big Romance) 223.
Daphne f (Acropolis—Donna) 83.
Darda c (Darius—Daisy) 198.
Dark Court c (Supreme Court—Darlene) (185), (208).
Dark Heron c (Heron Bridge—Dark Duet) 183.
Dark Island c (Chinde—dam said to be by Embargo) (278), (293).
Dark Sovereign c (Grey Sovereign—Black Rage) 12.
Dark Venetian f (Black Tarquin—Malcontenta) 245.
Darlene f (Dante—Admiral's Love) 2, (129), 134.
Darling Boy c (Darius—Sugar Bun) (78), (116), 170, 178.
Darn f (Devonian—Bermaline) 231.
DART BOARD c (Darius—Shrubswood) 3, 5, (46), (88), 117.
Dats One c (Ratification—Garnet) 168.
Dauber c (Daumier II—Danissa II) 182.
Davedasee f (My Babu—Little Honey) 66.
DAVID JACK c (Pampered King—Judy Owens) 5, 78, (84), (176), (208).
Davids Boy c (Queen's Hussar—Floss) 8.
Davy Crockett c (Donatello II—Starcross) 60.
Dawn Watch c (Tehran—Javotte) 196, (216), (230).
Daybreak c (Golden Cloud—Julie) (12), 22.
Daylight Robbery c (Hook Money—Luminant) (27), (122).

Dear Gazelle c (Petition—Giselda) 190.
Dear John c (Fil d'Or II—dam said to be Fir Park) 288.
Death Duties c (Rockefella—Grandpa's Will) 40.
Deauville c (Grey Sovereign—Andree) 211.
Deauville Dandy c (Alizier—Rushed) 31.
Debach Girl f (Fighting Don—Flowing Lava) 191.
Deb's Delight c (Idle Rich—Wild Almond) 282.
De Combat c (Speculation—Campaspe) 259.
Decree c (Rockefella—Authority) 47.
Deep Gulf c (Persian Gulf—Sweetcake) 63.
Deep Run c (Pampered King—Trial by Fire) (41), 46.
Deep Sapphire c (Red God—Blue Solitaire) 143.
Deer Leap c (Stephen Paul—Star Island) 146, (184), 211, 211, 211, (216), 216, 228, 230, 230.
Deetease c (Rabirio—Tudor Princess) (270).
Delayed Tip c (Gratitude—Wait Now) 173, 181, (192), 213.
Delmere c (Worden II—Avis) 161, 172, (191).
Delta Brava c (Fairey Fulmar—Prologue) (188).
Demagog c (Democratic—Charming) (47).
Demerara c (Persian Gulf—Cachou) 196.
Democrat c (Pinza—Fair Plea) 36.
Denim c (Denturius—Papita) 25.
Denosa f (Worden II—Rimosa) (40), 75.
Dentivate c (Denturius—Activate) 122.
De Reszki (see Middleton Tower).
Derring-Do c (Darius—Sipsey Bridge) 18, (37), (44), 125, (132), 144, (144).
Derry, The c (King's Bench—Ballisland) 24, 79.
Desacre c (Rustam—Scottish Lass) (202), 225.
Desaix c (Djebe—Cydonia) 27, 39.
Desert Beauty f (Dante—Desert Girl) 71, (129), 145.
Desert Call c (Palestine—Trace) 146, 150.
Desert Call II c (Klairon—Princess of Bagdad) 133, 140.
Desert Moss f (Mossborough—Desert Girl) 108.
Deton c (Elopement—Limereagh) 85, (224).
Devastation c (Tamerlane—Daughter of Sylvia) 85, (143).
Devon Breeze c (Devonian—Speedy Breeze) 290.
Devon Brew f (Whiteway—Entangle) 91, 199.
Devon Cawvoge f (Devonian—Kellsboro' Cottage) 279.
Devon Customer c (Tiverton—Another Customer) (281).
Devon View c (Devonian—Bath View) 280.
Diamonds Galore f (Luminary—Lady Dandy) 15.
Dickens c (Precipitation—Dickneos) (60), (89), (91), (127).
Dicker c (Swaps—Blue Star) 195.
Dicksboro' c (Prince Richard—Lady Kellsboro') 271.
Dicky May c (Migoli—Bay Polly) (249), 253.
DICTA DRAKE c (Phil Drake—Dictature) 3, 5, (100).
Dictionary c (We Don't Know—Setback) 221.
Diddler, The c (King's Bench—Criterion Maid) 222.

Didon f (Prince Bio—Djebellica) 43.
DIE HARD c (Never Say Die—Mixed Blessing) 3, 5, (63), 113, (220).
Dieudonne c (Hornbeam—Tarara) (26).
Different Class c (Beau Sabreur—Wiolette) 245, 257, (271), (272).
Diffidence f (Fastnet Rock—Bashful) 61.
DILETTANTE II c (Sicambre—Barizonette) 3, (130), 135.
Dinant f (Abernant—Dairymaid) 40, 69.
Dion c (Guersant—Anadem) (198).
Dionisio (c My Babu—Candida) (174), 182, (196).
Dionysus III c (Rapace—Bishop's Vine) 270, 270.
Diplomatic Bag f (Krakatao—Peace Terms) 205.
Dipper f (Donore—Lark) (6), (219).
Directory c (Kelly—Fine Fiction) 196.
Discorea f (Dante—Stella Polaris) 93, (131), 139.
DISPLAY f (Rustam—Review) 2, (18), (43), (107).
Dispute f (Narrator—Quoin) (187), (206), 206.
Dites c (Doutelle—Parlez-Vous) (233).
Diving Suit (see Kadir Cup).
Djebe Boy c (Djebe—Sea Princess) 102.
Djebel Traffic c (Coastal Traffic—Djebel Armour) 144.
Djehad c (Milesian—Zenobia) 112.
Dock Green c (Constable—Tosca) (222).
Doctor F c (Hindostan—Gillian Ann) 175.
Doctor Tadgh c (Orthodox—Blandford Alice) 168.
Dodge City c (Marshal Pil—Fair Clippie) 177, (209).
Dogged c (Never Say Die—Sonsa) 270.
Dolau f (King's Bench—Postlip) 230.
Dollar Piece c (Luminary—Wishy Washy) (22).
Domesday c (Supreme Court—Fair Edith) 169, (172), (189), 189, 191, (221).
Dominate c (Hyperion—Donatella III) (8), 32, 82.
Dominion Day c (Charlottesville—Running Blue) 5, 36.
Donald c (Honeyway—Donah) 82, 100, 127.
Donated c (Princely Gift—Meld) 10.
Donatellina II f (Nearula—Donatella III) 121.
Donation c (Domaha—Matchless Guide) 282.
Donato c (Alycidon—Mamounia) 5, 78.
Dondeen c (Donore—Blue Rosette) 122, 146, 146, 151, (216), 217, 230.
Done Up c (Donatello II—Fasten) (292).
Donicom c (Fighting Don—Icomkill) 234.
Donna f (Donore—Bashful) 61, 71.
Donna Lollo f (Donatello II—Camerita) 235.
Donna Lydia f (Hyperion—Donatella III) 108.
Don't Look c (March Past—King's Maid) 123, 210.
Doon c (Polly's Jet—Bright Idea) 49.
Doone Valley f (Devonian—Shady Customer) 271.
Do or Die c (Doubtless II—Duelette) (279).
Dorimont c (Domaha—Monacrasia) (274).
Dormant c (Domaha—Miss Victoria) 254, (254), (256), 257, 259, 262, 284, (292), 292.

Dorney Common c (Democratic—Pastures Green) (15), (63).
Double Bee f (Borealis—Barosa) (181).
Double Fall c (Falls of Clyde—Two-Timer) (192).
Double Handful f (Major Portion—Nubis) 8.
Double Jump c (Rustam—Fair Bid) (18), (28).
Double March c (March Past—Soft Rain) 264, 275.
Double Quick c (Dual—Magali) 148.
Double Red c (Signal Light—Lady Fell) 81, 116.
Double Star c (Arctic Star—Bright Star) 253, 273.
Double-u-Jay c (Major Portion—Renounce) 45, 99, 105, (141), 215, (222).
Doutelle c (Prince Chevalier—Above Board) (59), (72), (84), (92), 110, 124.
Dove Cote c (Wood Cot—Glory Din) 276, (286).
Doxford c (Krakatao—Lexia) 283.
Drake's Affair f (Armour Drake—Fair Jean) 197.
Drakes Drum c (Fighting Don—Harvest Maid) 216.
Drinny's Double c (John Constable—Donomore) 249, (273), (273).
Driven f (Hard Ridden—Send) 68.
Dromoland c (Umberto—Lily Ophelia) (30), 177.
Drum Beat c (Fair Trial—Respite) (115), 122, 146.
Drumbeg c (Dumbarnie—Empire Fairytale) 180, 225.
Drumikill c (Pampered King—Owenbeg) 270.
Drumlanrig c (Right Royal V—Eildon) 189, 212.
D.T.J. c (Nakamuro—Ortolan) (174), (184).
Dual c (Chanteur II—Duplicity) (31), 39, (59), 72, 77, 88, (143).
Duke of York c (Flush Royal—Queen of the Dandies) (256), 272, 284, 289, 290.
Dumbo II c (Domaha—Tondoneyo) 278.
Dumelle c (Supreme Court—Topaz) 47, 60.
Dunce Cap f (Tom Fool—Bright Coronet) 2, 18, (24), (29), 43, (132).
Dunkirk c (Domaha—Tolldown) (246), 253, (273).
Dunlin c (Donore—Lark) 16, 22.
Dunme c (Dumbarnie—Bonnie Flora) 168, 204, 204, (205), 205, (211).
Dunmore Lass II f (Nashua—La Sylphide II) 224.
Dunnock c (Pardal—Dora Zack) 289.
Duperion c (Dual—Beau Bijou) (190), 235.
Duplation c (Vimy—Duplicity) (92).
Duplex c (Aureole—Duplicity) 78, 120.
Duplicator c (Control—Copycat) 293.
D'Urberville c (Klairon—Courtessa) (14), (33), 46, (115).
Dusky Boy c (Sayajirao—Dusky Slipper) 41, 63.
Dusky Prince c (Zucchero—Blue Sallamah) 133.
Dutch Bells c (Poaching—Peal o'Bells) 7, (39).
Dutton c (Tudor Minstrel—Persian Maid) 182.

E

Eagle c (Court Martial—Ark Royal) 67, 98, 105, 123, 125, (132), 144, 144, 200.
Earldom c (Mossborough—Lady Carina) 72, 113.
Earl Marshal c (Court Martial—Ferry Pool) 73, 179, 196, 230.
Early to Rise c (Ribot—Night Sound) 85, (210), 213, (270).
Earnest Alice f (Grey Sovereign—Ardue) (219).
Easter Island c (Buisson Ardent—Tahiti) 235.
Eastern Chance c (Turkhan—Sanchance) 280.
Eastern Harvest c (Anwar—Ukraine) 270.
Eastern Nip c (Tamerlane—Libation) (170).
Easter Prince c (River Prince—Carilyn) 272.
Easter Rock f (Rockefella—Easter Bride) 219.
Eastwell c (Narrator—Lavender Girl) 206.
Eborneezer c (Ocean Swell—Priory Princess) (165), 214, 220, (277).
E.B.S. f (Infatuation—Final Sweep) 21.
Edmundo c (Owen Tudor—Weighbridge) 115.
Edwalton Boy c (Hard Sauce—L-S-D) 14.
Eglee f (Norseman—Emma) 66, 118.
Egualita f (Democratic—Ballymaginathy) (230).
Eiger c (Chamossaire—Lady Grand) (161), 189, 221.
Ela Marita f (Red God—Fantan II) (71), (90).
Elan c (Elopement—Annetta) (263), (270).
Elco c (King's Bench—Bellani) (196).
Elf Arrow c (Precipitation—Titania) 165.
El Gallo c (Matador—Discipliner) (109).
El Giza c (Gilles de Retz—Queen of Cairo) 74, 82.
Elite Royale f (Rockefella—Avocet) 4, (83), 145.
Elk, The c (Only For Life—Sambur) (49).
El Mighty c (Sheshoon—Delicious II) 49, 85.
Eloped c (Elopement—French Moss) 279.
El Relicario c (Relic—Saponite) 144.
Elsa f (Migoli—Fair and True) 197.
El Surpriso f (Beau Sabreur—Villa Medici), 175.
El Toro c (Cagire II—Early Milkmaid) (87), 175.
Elysium c (Hyperion—Elysian) 191.
Emerald Cross c (Borealis—Faro) 193.
Emerilo c (Emerson—Dorila) (182), (233).
Empire Way c (Honeyway—Brave Empress) 164, 193.
Empress Sissi f (Martial—Young Empress) 109, 136.
Enchanter c (Palestine—Starlighter) 38.
Endless Honey c (Never Say Die—Run Honey) (16).
End Money f (My Babu—Bold Maid) (163).
Englands Glory c (Match III—Snow Baby) (283).
English Slipper c (Greek Star or His Slipper—Coramere) 65.
Enlightenment c (Premonition—Lightning) 285.
Ennis c (Golden Cloud—First House) 126, 126.
Enrico c (Sica Boy—Zanzara) 1, (99), 132, (174), 204.

Entanglement c (King of the Tudors—Filigrana) 148, 190.
Epaulard c (Epaulette—Cockles and Mussels) 143.
Epaulette c (Court Martial—Golden Sari) (211).
Epidauros c (Relic—Fair Rosamond) 68.
Epidendrum c (Ribot—Parthenope) 195.
Epsom Lady f (Midas—Bridgette) 200.
Eratosthenes c (Guersant—Lady Electra) 26.
Ergina f (Fair Trial—Ballechin) 40, 45.
Ernest Henry c (Shackleton—Nameless) 25.
Erudite c (Donore—Thoughtful Light) (106), (167).
E.S.B. c (Bidar—English Summer) 245, (259), 267, 280, 280, 288, 288.
Escort c (Palestine—Warning) 1, 3, (39), 49, 73, 91, 95, 111.
Espresso c (Acropolis—Babylon) 84, 185, (190), (214), 214.
Essoldo (see Sereno).
Eternal c (The Phoenix—Constant Nymph) 245.
Eternal Goddess f (The Phoenix—Railing) 179.
Eucumbene f (Sica Boy—Hypericum) 93, 129, 134.
Europa f (Lucero—Vienna Coup) (21).
Eutrippa f (Eudaemon—Doll Dance) 94.
Evening Shoe f (Panaslipper—Evening Belle) (66), 86.
Even Keel c (Even Money—Officer's Pet) 285.
Even Money c (Krakatao—Vendome) (104).
Even Star f (Abernant—Safari Moon) (61), 71, (86).
Everanick c (The Phoenix—Little Mary) (68).
Every Blessing f (Parthia—Mixed Blessing) (75), 101.
Exar c (Arctic Prince—Excelsa) 78, 91, 110, (127), (140).
Exbury c (Le Haar—Greensward) (100).
Excel c (Saint Crespin III—Grey Rhythm) (70), 203.
Exchange f (Tudor Jinks—Nyke) 20, 34, (90), 108, (134).
Exchange Student c (Faubourg II—Loved One) 87.
Excuse (see Franciscan).
Executor c (Ratification—St Lucia) (188).
Exhorbitant c (Exploitation—Henalore) 161, 169.
Expedier c (Hard Ridden—Nile Bird) 266.
Explode c (Exbury—Mitraille) (27).
Extra Stout c (Blue Chariot—Irish Wine) 270.
Extra Time f (Never Say Die—Respite) 20, 37, 40, 121.
Eyrefield c (Palestine—Neemah) 123.
Eze c (Star Gazer—Derrycarne) 79.

F

Fab f (Acropolis—Riddlemeree) 37, (40), 121.
FABERGE II c (Princely Gift—Spring Offensive) 1, 32, 42, 96.
Fabius c (Babu's Pet—Folastra) 114.
Faerie Ring f (Royal Palm—Galloway Queene) 9.
Fagus c (Fair Trial—Tea Time) 103, (132).
Faint Hope c (Petition—Miss Skeggs) (216), 217, 228, 230, 230.
Fair Astronomer f (Star Gazer—Fair Temair) (44), 61, (94), 121, (123), 162.
Fair Future f (Denturius—Railing) 27.
Fair Gale c (Galingale—Fair Mildred) 290, 291.
Fair Journey c (Sayajirao—Danae) 36.
Fair Patricia f (Parthia—Auspicious) 93, 138.
Fair Play II c (Free Man—Lady Fair) 269.
Fair Samela f (Constable—Samaritaine) 179.
Fair Saying c (Never Say Die—Pamorpee) 73.
Fairullah c (Immortality—Clorinda) 32.
Fair Victor c (Vic Day—Fair Rosemary) 203.
Fair Winter f (Set Fair—Winter Gleam) 96, (129).
Fairy Path f (Sovereign Path—Fairy Whistle) 37, 43.
Fairy Stone (late Queen of Egypt) f (Court Martial—Stone of Fortune) 103, 218, 233.
Faith Healer c (Petition—Heala Ray) (106).
Falcon c (Milesian—Pretty Swift) (12), (18), 28.
Fall in Love II f (Swaps—Never Too Late II) 43.
Falls of Cruachan c (Mossborough—Hunter's Quay) (225).
Falls of Shin c (Falls of Clyde—Helsinki II) (164), 178, 193, 233.
False Bay c (False Colours—Salmon Gilt) 293.
Family Tree c (Owen Tudor—Faggot) 187.
Fan Light f (Wilwyn—Light of Day) (17), 29.
Farandole c (Floribunda—Lepanto) 30.
Fare Time c (Thoroughfare—Septime) 268, (277).
Farmer's Boy c (Hyperbole—Bashful) 277, (287).
Farm Walk c (Kribi—Monastery Garden) 177, (180), 199, (208), 209, (214), (226).
Farrney Fox c (Archive—Foxy Jane) 104, 114, (163), 163, 229, 277.
Farur c (Fidalgo—Persian Romance) 232.
Fascinating Forties c (Roaring Forties—Secret Pact) 274, (274).
Fatima's Gift f (Hook Money—Corrine) (25).
Fatralo c (Babu's Pet—Bella VI) 128.
Faultless Image c (Impeccable—King's Model) 188.
Faultless Speech c (Impeccable—Light Comment) (167), 173, (193), (215).
Faust c (Pinza—No Angel) 111.
Fauvallon c (Faubourg II—Hunting Vale) 79.
Favorita f (Abernant—La Montespan) (16), 29, (44), (106), 122.
Favour c (Darling Boy—Aylesford) 47.
Fearless Cavalier c (Cavalin—Fearless Queen) 250.
Fearless Lady f (Privy Councillor—Anxious Lady) (219).
Feather Bed f (Gratitude—Sweet Cygnet) 75, 86, 132, 144.
Featheredge f (Nashua—No Strings) 106, 146.

Feevagh Hill f (Hill Gail—Feevagh) 41.
Felhampton c (Sir Lancelot—Dainty VII) 278, 278.
Felias c (Phideas—Feluce) 260.
Felicio II c (Shantung—Fighting Edie) 124.
Feliptica f (Preciptic—Feline) 26.
Fellhound c (Rockefella—Queen of the Chase) 275.
Fern c (Free Man—La Petite Princesse) (80).
Ferncliffe c (My Babu—Bonnet o'Blue) (161).
Ferneley c (Aureole—Flirting) (76), 89, 119.
Ferry Boat c (Buckhound—Boat Race) 250, 290.
Ferrymans Image c (Charon—Sculptress) 283, 289.
Festive c (Alycidon—Sunny Morning) 212.
Fez c (Tehran—Gertimurfi) (161), 165.
Fiacre c (Faubourg II—Pumpkin) (192).
FIDALGO c (Arctic Star—Miss France) 3, 5, 47, (82), (117).
Fidelio c (Princely Gift—Second Fiddle) 1, 43.
Fidus Achates c (Le Lavandou—Collosol) (287).
Field Master c (Fair Trial—Huntress) 230.
Fifty Fifty f (Arco—Half a Chance) 214.
Fighting Charlie c (Tenerani—Flight of the Heron) 81, 91, 95, (95), (110), (110), 135.
FIGHTING SHIP c (Doutelle—Jane) 5, (70), (78), 82, (95), 111.
Fight On c (Fighting Don—Collogue) 30.
Fiji f (Acropolis—Rififi) (107).
Filey Camp c (Pall Mall—Baltic Exchange) (173), 200.
Filipepi c (Botticelli—Honey Hill) (70).
Filon d'Or c (Labrador—Alexandrovna) 260.
Final Move c (Botticelli—Checkmate) 63.
Final Test c (Petition—Sea Idol) 199.
Fincham c (Devonian—Rose of Stefan) (291).
Fine Bid c (Set Fair—High Calling) 60, 192, (200), 203, 210.
Fine Feathers f (Set Fair—Sun Finch) 17.
Fine Point c (Steel-Point—Stuart Plaid) 281.
Finish Fast c (Fidalgo—Javotte) 68, 184.
Fiorentina f (Tulyar—Leventina) 75, (86).
Firecracker c (Krakatao—Reseda) 89, 178, 253.
Fireglow f (Limekiln—Lat-Le-Poo) 289.
Firestreak c (Pardal—Hot Spell) (123), (170).
Firewalker c (Buisson Ardent—Bootless) (192).
First Audition c (Narrator—The Test) 247, 275, 281, 287, 288.
First Date f (Royal Palm—Golden Footprints) 9.
First Phase c (Nulli Secundus—Sonatina) (177).
First Pick c (Immortality—Fast Lady) 31.
First Sea Lord c (Supreme Court—Naval Patrol) 7.
Fix the Date f (Swaps—Never Too Late II) 2.
Flag c (Border Chief—Unfurl) 192.
Flag of Convenience (see Anglo).
Flambeau c (The Phoenix—Light Amber) 46, 76, 195.
Flame Gun c (Flamenco—Lady Mustang) (275).

Flame Royal c (Flamenco—Terba) 253.
Flaming East c (Taj Ud Din—Cinderwench) (285), (287).
Flaming Red c (Red God—Rosheen) 62.
Flaming Star c (Flamenco—Vestarsome) 270.
Flare f (Premonition—Maritime) 20.
Flash Bulb c (Hyacinthus—Cissie Gay) 246, 273, 273, 276, 276, 276.
Flash Past c (Petition—Marcelette) 173, 205.
Flattering f (Abernant—Flatter) (9), 23, 29, 43.
Fleece c (Palestine—Poplin) 35, (216), 216.
FLEET f (Immortality—Review) (2), 4, (20), (43), 107.
Fleur de Lys f (Palestine—Fine Flower) 118.
Flick c (Pylon II—American Lady) 282.
Flip-a-Disc c (Sound Track—Singing Lady) 176.
Floor Show c (Stardust—Rainbow Room) 235.
Floosie f (Fortino II—Hot Dish) 11, 18.
Floral Mile c (Royal Highway—Polycanthus) 38.
Floral Tribute c (Alibhai—Bayrose) 205.
Florescence c (Floribunda—Papido) 126, 150, 217, (228).
Floribunda c (Princely Gift—Astrentia) (12), 28, 115, (126), (136).
Flower Drum c (Honeyway—La Marseillaise) 143.
Flowering Lime f (Limekiln—Happy Flower) 281.
Flyingbolt c (Airborne—Eastlock) (249), (252), (258), (270), (273), (275), 277, (290).
Flying By f (Bleep Bleep—Japhette) (8), 126, 136.
Flying Curtis c (Colonist II—Joyful Christine) 208.
Flying Flag II c (Sunny Boy III—Finlandia) (114), (148).
Flying Fur f (Pinza—Wild Cat) 94.
Flying Legs f (Palestine—Alona) (23), (29).
Flying Wild f (Airborne—Wild Delight) 245, 252, (252), 258, (262), 273, (286).
Flyover c (Denturius—Bridle Way) (8).
Foinavon c (Vulgan—Ecilace) (245).
Folle Rousse f (Red God—Ballymiss) (9).
Follow Suit c (Ballymoss—Persian Lilac) 46, 105, 120, 128, 143.
Follywise c (Infatuation—Sibella) 179.
Fontex c (Exar—Fontana Angelica) (34).
Fool's Gold f (Tom Fool—Track Medal) 2, 69, (90).
Foothill c (Aggressor—Buckham Hill) 26, (48), 82, 92.
Footpath c (Sovereign Path—Dolcis) 182.
Forearmed c (Premonition—Armentieres) 46, 48.
Foreign Account f (Final Score—Credit Lyonnais) 15.
Forest Prince c (Devon Prince—Forest) 245, (267).
Forlorn River c (Fighting Don—Starflight) (122), (136), (150), 151, 228, 228.
Fortezza f (Botticelli—Title Deed) (106).
Forthright c (Quorum—Rustic Maid) 185, 194.
Fortissimo c (Fortino II—Choir Practice) (72), 91, 113, 140, 148.
Fort Knox II c (Mourne—Foretaste) 68, 89.
Fort Leney c (Fortina—Leney Princess) (258), (265), (265), 271, 272, (284), 292.
Fort Ord c (Fortina—Appropriate) 290.
Fortria c (Fortina—Senria) (246), 246, (246), 258, (273), (273), (275), 284, 284, (290).

Fortron c (Fortina—Castle Saffron) 276.

Fort Rouge c (Fortina—Golden Sunset) (276).

Fortune's Darling f (Fair Trial—Tinted Venus) (29).

Fortwyn f (Wilwyn—Fortunate Lass) 191.

Fosco c (Tosco—Fleche) (270).

Fossa, The c (Jena II—Fustian) 245, 245, 260, 267, 280, (291).

Fougalle f (Djefou—Galatina) (208), 233.

Four Aces f (Straight Deal—Little Trix) 265, 270.

Fourth of June f (King of the Tudors—Arquebuse) 165.

Foxford Boy c (Kelly—Lady Sliptic) (227).

Foxstar c (Infatuation—Paravane) 12, 166, 181, 222.

Fragrant Rose f (King's Bench—Rose Walk) 224.

Franciscan (late Excuse) c (Grey Sovereign—Ursuline) 59, 70.

Frangipan c (Fair Trial—Tea Time) 45.

Frankincense c (Princely Gift—Amethea) 103, 125, (162), (181), 200, (215).

Fraxinus c (Supreme Court—Ash Tray) 208, (213).

Fray Bentos c (Hard Tack—Dedica) 102.

Freddie c (Steel Chip—dam by Soldado) 245, 245, (250), (256), (259), (282), 291.

Freddie Boy c (High Endeavour—Another Hope) 271.

Frederique II f (Malka's Boy—Ginevra) 23.

Fredith's Son c (Jubilee Day—Tidal Wave) 245, (265), 265, 290.

Free Air c (Nimbus—Liberty) (188).

Freeholder f (Pinza—Title Deed) 197.

Freelight c (Borealis—Freedar) 183, 212.

FRENCH BEIGE c (Bois Roussel—Nivea) 91, 110, 127, (140), 140, 148, (148), (183).

French Cream f (Faubourg II—Nivea) (131).

French Fern f (Mossborough—Star of France) 97, (108), 139.

Frenchman's Cove c (Airborne—Frenchman's Creek) 245, 251, (254), (292).

French March c (March Past—Taza II) (281).

French Parade f (March Past—Bienfaisant) 211.

French Patrol c (French Beige—Dittany) 161.

French Plea c (Petition—Djelleba III) 44, 59, 136.

French Possession f (French Beige—Rose of Tudor) (145), (213).

French Tutor c (Tudor Melody—French Ballad) 19, 33.

French Vine c (French Beige—Princess Jasmine) 46, (85), 128, (207).

French Window c (Contrevent—French Lesson) 291.

Fresh Winds c (Roaring Forties—Lough Beg) (288).

Fric c (Vandale—Fripe) (100), 100, (113), 149.

Friendly Boy c (Flamenco—Mrs Josser) 253, (285).

Frigolet c (Pinza—Harfleur) 13, (60), 70.

Frimas (see Sinbad the Sailor).

Frog c (French Beige—Rock Snake) 175, 214.

Front Row f (Epaulette—Panaview) (86), 107.

Frozen Blonde f (Arctic Time—Northern Beauty) 145.

Fuchsia Cottage f (Ossian II—Topping News) 172.

Fuel c (The Cobbler or Abadan—Fylgia) 106, 168.

Fuengirola c (Prince Chevalier—Viviparus) 234, 266.

Full Dress II f (Shantung—Fusil) (34).

Full Flight f (Limekiln—Atlatouan) 234.
Fulminate c (Fairey Fulmar—La Rixe) 183, 194.
Fulshaw Cross f (Roc du Diable—Mary Clare) (173), 174, 185.
Fun c (Mustang—Little Episode) 278.
Fury Royal c (Flush Royal—Commotion) 89, 184, 208, 215.
Fusil f (Fidalgo—Mitraille) 108.
Fusion f (Preciptic—Off the Fash) 27.
Futurama f (Borealis—Midsummer Fair) 97, (108).

G

Gads Hill c (Nicolaus—Verity) (172), 229.
Gailowind c (Hill Gail—Mindy) 36, 111, 128.
Gail Prince c (Hill Gail—Certosa) 13.
Gail Royal f (Hill Gail—Arctic Royal) 40.
Gail Time f (Arctic Time—Certogail) 163.
Gainstrive c (Golden Cloud—Ballynulta) 14.
Galipar c (Galivanter—Pink Parrot) (24).
Galivanter c (Golden Cloud—Lycia) 12, 16, (79), (122), 136, 146, (217).
Gallant Deal f (Straight Deal—Galante) 197.
Gallant Knight c (Prince Chevalier—Hustle) (48), (89).
Gallant Scholar c (Vilmorin—Hunt the Slipper) 224.
Gallegos c (Vilmorin—Akimbo) 181, (216).
Gallery Goddess f (Limekiln—Ronnie D) (286).
Gallic c (Galivanter—La Marseillaise) 192.
Galloping Shoe f (Ferriol—Verona) 17.
Gallop On f (Grey Sovereign—Tinted Venus) (9), 17.
Galloway Hills c (St Clement—Little Jess) 271.
Gambling Debt c (Flush Royal—Brazen Polly) 266.
Game All f (Alcide—Game Bird) 123.
Game Ball c (Ballyogan—Tracked Down) 99, 106.
Game Field c (Camfield—Be Game) 261, 267, (291).
Game Hide f (Big Game—Spyado) 146.
Game Purston c (Prince's Game—Little Purston) 251, 260, (267).
Gang Warily c (Premonition—Lady Godiva) 106, 132.
Garibaldi c (Nearco—Mitrailleuse) 172, 191.
Garland Knight c (Sadani—Garland) 143, 225, 234.
Gaska f (Gilles de Retz—Sally Deans) 9.
Gaudy Commodore c (Worden II—Cloth of Gold) 212.
Gaul c (Alycidon—Bignonia) (78), 84, (95), 95, (111), 133, 133, (148).
Gaulois c (Auriban—Gallega) 76, 104, (127).
Gay Ballad c (Owen Tudor—Straight Tune) (169), 189.
Gay Casino c (Trouville—Gala Night) (181), (182), (218), 218.

350

Gay Challenger c (Royal Challenger—Thrilled) 102, 116, (128).
Gay Donald c (Gay Light—Pas de Quatre) 284.
Gay Garland c (Shantung—Festoon) 72, (89), 128.
Gay Glory c (Galivanter—Coral Wreath) 16.
Gay Henry c (Henry the Seventh—Button Boots) 63.
Gay Mairi f (Vilmorin—Hyacinthia Girl) 11, (21), (24), (136).
Gaymoss c (Mossborough—Golden Revelry) 221.
Gay Navarree c (Rio de Navarre II—Intuition) 245.
Gaynora f (Gratitude—Amnora) 21.
Gay Palm c (Royal Palm—Bottoms Up) (24).
Gay Roger c (Lobau—dam by Gough's Auction) (278), 278.
Gay Tricks f (Vulgan—Miss Gaiety) 287.
Gay Trip c (Vulgan—Turkish Tourist) 271.
Gazpacho f (Hard Sauce—Red Cloak) (71), (86).
Gelert c (Owen Tudor—Westerlands Rosebud) 193.
Gemini Six c (Princely Gift—Speed Bird) 196, (217).
Gem of Gems f (Grey Sovereign—Twice Blessed) 121.
General Gordon c (Never Say Die—Camp Fire) 68, (82).
Genius (late Vagilistria) f (Le Tyrol—Virofla) 81.
Gentle Art c (Whistler—Tessa Gillian) (7), 18, (22), 28, (99).
Gentle Colein f (Nearcolein—Fair Abbey) 271.
Gently f (Grey Sovereign—Be Careful) (69), 216.
Georges c (Ratification—Amoureuse) 30.
George's Girl f (Ossian II—Dawn Chorus) 66, 118, (138).
Georgetown c (Colonist II—Zapala) (288).
Geraldine Too f (Parthia—Nan) 129.
Gerome c (Tenerani—Doll Tearsheet) 80, 85.
Getaway c (Solonaway—Fragilite) (25).
Get Stepping c (Grey Sovereign—Tripaway) 275.
Get There f (Gratitude—Tinted Venus) 9.
Giddaby f (Constable—Ceremonial) (203), 203, (218).
Gideon c (Palestine—Mitrailleuse) 279.
Gift Token f (Firestreak—Gracious Gift) 20.
Gigi f (Infatuation—Enagh) (25).
Gilboa f (Palestine—Giselda) (66), 106, 132.
Giles Farnaby c (Dastur—Spinet) (260), 260.
GILLES DE RETZ c (Royal Charger—Ma Soeur Anne) (77).
Gillylees f (The Bug—Chanting Hill) (197).
Gilroy c (Delirium—Thrifty Princess) 163.
Ginetta f (Tulyar—Diabletta) 107.
Ginger Boy c (Colonist II—Sea Princess) 169, 212.
Giolla Mear c (Hard Ridden—Jacobella) (63), (102), (142).
Giuro c (Gilles de Retz—Sweet Ursula) 188.
Givenaway c (Solonaway—For Nothing) 103, (203), 203.
Glad Hand c (Proud Chieftain—Palm Court) 38.
Gladness f (Sayajirao—Bright Lady) (110), 124, (127), 163, (220).
GLAD ONE f (Milesian—Gladness) 4, 86, 131, 143.
GLAD RAGS f (High Hat—Dryad) (2), 39, 107.

Gladys f (Borealis—Grolldochnicht) 41, 102.
Glenborne c (Airborne—Royal Patent) 206, 223.
Glendawn c (Preciptic—Solomon's Choice) 47, 181, 224.
Gleniry c (Hindostan—Polperro) 163.
Glenrowan c (Kelly—Rosheen) 63, (64).
Glen Weather c (Grand Weather—Naya) 282.
Gloomy Portal f (Mossborough—Brillante II) 90, 143, 222.
Glorious Twelfth c (Cadenazzo—Fading Glory) 245, 256, 291.
Glyndebourne c (Pinza—Beausite) 77, 103.
Godiva's Pink Flower c (Pink Flower—Lady Godiva) 12.
Go Gailey c (Worden II—Parakeet) 279.
Gol Brig c (Golestan—Empress Catharine) 24.
Gold Aura c (Aureole—In Need) (169), 189, (189), 212, (212), 223, 229.
Golden Apollo f (Princely Gift—Gold Fury) 44, 115, 126.
Golden Bolt c (Parthia—Star of Gold) 34.
Golden Dipper c (Gratitude—Huntress) 42.
Golden Fire c (Worden II—Golden Cascade) 172, (175), (212), (212), (232).
Golden Game c (Golden Cloud—Queen's Gambit) (15).
Golden Gittell c (Golden Cloud—Tutelina) 230.
Golden Gloves c (Fighting Don—Final Decision) 173.
Golden Gorden c (Golden Cloud—Lycia) 180.
Golden Harmony f (Aureole—Duckling) 20.
Golden Hind f (Aureole—All Aboard) 8.
Golden Horus c (Tudor Melody—Persian Union) 1, (16), 22, (28), 42, 99, 123, 167.
Golden Inca c (Nearula—Maltreated) 16.
Golden Leg f (Golden Cloud—Kings Well) (196), (217).
Golden Light c (Luminary—Fainne Oir) 184.
Golden Mean c (Taboun or Hill Gail—Oweninny) (171), (193), 227.
Golden Merle c (Golden Cloud—Merlette) 12.
Golden Oriole c (Aureole—In Need) 199, 221.
Golden Pal c (Palestine—Gilded Spirit) 79.
Golden Plume c (Golden Cloud—Perennial) (8).
Golden Rain f (Precipitation—Palmy Days) 20.
Golden Reward f (Major Portion—West Side Story) 75.
Golden Sands f (Persian Gulf—Magnificent) 47.
Golden Scene c (Golden Vision—Anneen) 63, 65.
Golden Seabright c (Seasick—Main Rock) 274.
Golden Sicamore c (Sica Boy—Parhelia) 70.
Golden Sovereign c (Whistler—Bridge of Stars) 12, (15).
Golden Vision c (Golden Cloud—Merryland) 170, 203.
Golden Voice c (Pinza—Treasure Trove) 70.
Goldhill c (Le Dieu d'Or—Gilded Rose) (14), (115), 122.
Gold Legend c (Legend of France—French Gold) (290).
Gold Pollen f (Klondyke Bill—Black Pollen) 211, (228).
Gold Shalimar II c (Royal Note—Shalimar) (206).
Golstar c (Vimy—Green Tipperary) 198.
Gondolier c (Crepello—Titian Hair) 130.
Good Flight c (Gratitude—Rocket Flight) 200, (203).

Good Light c (Beau Sabreur—Lustrous) 203.
Good Match c (Match III—Dolphinet) 48, 76, (103), 141, 218.
Good Old Days c (Tudor Minstrel—Better Days) 59, 99.
Goody Two Shoes f (Solar Slipper—Pantomime Queen) 36.
Goosander c (Sandyman—Josie Blink) 245, 245, (260), (267), 267.
Goose Creek c (Requested—Virginia Water) 31, 39.
Go Pontinental c (Eble—Volige) 288.
Gorm Abu f (My Babu—Cnoc Gorm) 66.
Go Shell c (Ennis—Summerlands) 47, 106, (228), 228, 230.
Go Slow c (Linoral—Misdeed) (274).
Goupi c (Premonition—Marie de Medeci) 95, (96), (116), 120, (148), 176.
Grallagh Cnoc c (Fortina—Fairy Hill) (271).
Grand Applause c (Gratitude—Queen of Song) 204.
Grand Morn c (Grandmaster—Easter Morn) 285.
Grand Morn II c (Spiritus—Grand Mare) (282).
Grandpa's Legacy f (Zeus Boy—Codicil) 61, 97, 129.
Grand Stand c (Jock Scot—Stadium) 214, 214.
Granville c (Neron—Sylmar) (253), 287.
Granville Greta f (Grandmaster—Mickrita) 136, (219).
Grasp f (Torbido—Clasp) (200).
Gratin c (Hard Sauce—Gentilezza) 173.
Gratitude c (Golden Cloud—Verdura) 126, (136).
Graunuaile f (Proud Chieftain—Western Sun) 25.
Great Bear c (Star Gazer—Blue Polly) (146), 146, 150, 150.
Great Faith c (Nearula—Avocet) 73.
Great Gonerby c (Souverain—Snow Bunting) (183).
Great Host c (Sicambre—Abermaid) 5, (82), (135).
Great Lark f (Great Captain—Flarke) (258).
GREAT NEPHEW c (Honeyway—Sybil's Niece) 1, 98, 99, 103, 119.
Great Occasion f (Hornbeam—Golden Wedding) 68.
Great Pleasure c (Hugh Lupus—Pleasure Cruise) 74, 92, (189), 207.
Greatrakes c (Cacador—First Quarter) 258, 265.
Great Rock c (Black Rock—M.E.F.) (199), 207.
Great Society c (Buisson Ardent—Visor) (80).
Grecian Bridge f (Acropolis—San Luis Rey) 40.
Grecian Granite c (Greek Star—Rockface) 212.
Grecian Urn II f (Heliopolis—War Tide) 17, 197.
Greek Honey c (Honeyway—Ariadne) 47.
Greek Scholar c (Dionisio—Highbrow) 245.
Greek Sovereign c (Grey Sovereign—Bridge of Hellas) 14, (16), 44.
Greek Streak f (Firestreak—Pygmalion) (197).
Greektown c (Midas—Flying Exit) (270), 273, (275).
Greek Vulgan c (Vulgan—Wendy) 258, (258), 265.
Greenacre c (Ballymoss—Title Deed) 206.
Green Banner c (Palestine—Fainne Oir) (30), 65, (87).
Green Drill c (Gold Drill—Verdant) 245, 245, 261.
Greengage f (Primera—Sugar Plum) (17), 43, (101), (107).
Green Halo f (Aureole—Green Opal) (138).

Greenhills Lad c (Colonist II—So Alone) (205).
Green Light c (Signal Light—Fair Appeal) 270, 285, 287.
Green Opal f (Persian Gulf—Sea Parrot) 93, (97), 108, (121), 129, 134, (145).
Green Park c (Pall Mall—Ballerina) (44), 151, 217.
Green Parrot f (Jock Scot—Lundy Parrot) 280.
Green Plover c (Democratic—Lapwing) (293).
Greyburn c (Battle Burn—Grey Sun) 235.
Grey Fashion f (Grey Sovereign—La Mode) 23.
Grey Goose f (Grey Sovereign—Jojo) 43.
Grey Hawk c (Rise 'n Shine II—Ballora) 41.
Grey Imp c (Red God—Magic Lass) 173.
Grey Lord c (Quorum—Romosa) 186, (204).
Grey Marsh c (Grey Sovereign—Ardue) 6.
Grey Moss c (Ballymoss—My Poppet) 38, (85).
Grey of Falloden c (Alycidon—Sister Grey) 91, 95, (95), 114, (114), 114, (140), 140,
    148, (165), 165, 165, 175, 199, (201), 232, (232).
Grey Panther f (Right Boy—Scargill) 219.
Grey Portal c (Grey Sovereign—Gloomy Portal) 16.
Grey Streak f (Palestine—La Cascade) 21.
Grey Wave f (Grey Sovereign—Heatwave) (6).
Grischuna f (Ratification—Mountain Path) 75.
Grizel f (Grey Sovereign—Polly Gilles) (11), 23, 29.
Gruline c (Fairwell—Flaunted) 286.
Guano c (Sica Boy—Mouette) 13.
Guarani c (The Phoenix—Gloriana) 74.
Guard of Honour c (Court Martial—Most Beautiful) 168, 182.
Gudmenarmist c (Legend of France—Wahine) 165.
Guersillus c (Guersant—Cantarilla) 3, 105, 113, (128), 135, (170).
Guildhall c (Le Dieu d'Or—Rossenhall) 181.
Guinea Sparrow f (Grey Sovereign—Parakeet) 11, 17, 29, 71.
Guitarist c (Tudor Minstrel—Salvadora) (182), 227.
Gulf Pearl c (Persian Gulf—Nan) (37), 82, 96.
Gun Smoke c (Tenerani—Chantry's Daughter) 283.
Gustav c (Grey Sovereign—Gamesmistress) 34, (42).
GWEN f (Abernant—Donna) 2, 29, (61).
Gypsy Refrain f (Romany Air—Halidom) 169, 175.
Gyropolis f (Acropolis—Whirlibird) 97, 108.
Gyroscope c (Golden Cloud—Transplendent) 21, 59, 226.

H

Hadji Mourad c (Petition—Capital Issue) 68.
Hadrian c (Saint Crespin III—Rosebag) (173), (174), 204.
Hall Weir c (Fairy Prince—Lady Craigie) 256, (259).
Hal's Farewell f (King Hal—Lady Tartwell) 249, (276).
Hal's Hope c (King Hal—Inver Hope) 270, 272.
Hambleden c (Elopement—Game Maria) (13), (22), 32, 88.
Hametus c (High Hat—Villa Medici) (37), (46), 59.
Hammal II c (Kerlor—Hama) 161, (189).
Hamood c (Chamier—Ishkoodah) (198).
Hanassi c (Nearula—Soldanel) 130.
Hand in Hand f (High Hat—Pleasure) 7, 13.
Hang On c (Hornbeam—Lucky Verdict) 176, 181.
Hannah Darling f (Match III—Sweetcake) 4, 86.
Hans Andersen c (Borealis—Faerie Lore) 41.
Happy Arthur c (Artist's Son—Hopeful Lady) 255, (279), 291.
Happy Haven c (Eudaemon—Fair Sylvia) (187), (187), 187.
Happy Kid f (Happy Landing—Colorado Canyon) 267.
Happy Morn II f (Hurrican—Marchella) 293, 293.
Happy Nick c (Lucero—Nick of Time) 189.
Happy Omen c (Hugh Lupus—Royal Applause) 10, (31), 42, 88, 171.
Happy Prospect c (Happy Landing—Latin Quarter) 285.
Happy Spring c (Tambourin—Smart Woman) 250, (251), 252, 257.
Hard and Sharp f (Hard Sauce—Karina II) 224.
Hard and Soft c (Hard Sauce—Sophia) 182, (185).
Hard as Nails c (Chanteur II—Sugar Bun) 170.
Hardicanute c (Hard Ridden—Harvest Maid) (32), (49), (64).
Hardiesse f (Hornbeam—Stage Fright) 4, 83, 134.
Hard Master c (Hard Sauce—Old Mistress) (161), 177.
Hard Match c (Hard Tack—Wedding Morn) (173).
HARD RIDDEN c (Hard Sauce—Toute Belle II) (3), 65, (87).
Hard Tack c (Hard Sauce—Cowes) 126.
Hard Water c (Hard Tack—Winmarine) 122.
Hardy Annual c (Hard Sauce—Astrentia) 15.
Harley Street c (Count Fleet—Gallant Nurse) 48.
Harmon c (Whistler—Ballymaginathy) (228).
Harolds Cross f (Tudor Jinks—Tory Victory) 29.
Harry c (Hill Gail—War Loot) (65).
Harry Lauder c (Pinza—Bonnie Flora) 80.
Hart Royal c (Atout Royal—Roe Deer) 255, 256.
Harvest Flame c (Buisson Ardent—Yga) 205.
Harvest Gold c (Aureole—Harvest Festival) 68, (175), 189, (191), 201, 209, (279).
Harwell c (Court Harwell—East Africa) (266), (269).
Hassan c (Rustam—Muscat) 106.
Hasty Cast f (Preciptic—Greenheart) 9.
Hasty Cloud c (Preciptic—Clouette) 186, 215, 233, 233, (233).
Hasty Hints (see Couligarten).

Hatton Garden c (Palestine—Precious Stone) 194.
Havago c (Richard Louis—What a Daisy) (270), 275.
Havasnack c (Tenerani—Ad Hoc) 114, (234).
Haven c (Borealis—Quick Arrow) 117.
Hawa c (Golden Cloud—Eastern Fairy) 211.
Hawa's Song c (El Hawa—Serenading) 245.
Haymaking f (Galivanter—Haytime) 77, 96, (107), 123, (129), 208.
Hazy f (My Smokey—Well Whistled) 6.
Hazy Sky f (Sica Boy—Moonmist) 23.
Heartburn c (Abernant—Greenheart) 184, (227).
Heathen c (Hethersett—Verdura) 24, 26, 46, (70).
Heath Rose f (Hugh Lupus—Cherished) (37).
Heathtolt c (Kelly—Abaddon) 6.
Heave Ho c (Le Levanstell—Vallombrosa) (92).
Heavenly Boss c (Skymaster—Star Gail) 21.
Heavenly Sound f (Sound Track—Clorinda) (79), 115.
Heavens Bequest c (Golden Cloud—Donation) (223).
Hedge Rose f (Hugh Lupus—Noretta) 85, 138.
Height o'Fashion f (Artist's Son—Dress Parade) (234), 258, 265, 290, 290.
Heiress f (Rockefella—Martial Air) 222.
Hejaz c (Hafiz II—Plume II) (225).
Helen Rosa f (Nearula—Aunt Agnes) 184, 217.
Hello Dolly f (Nuage Dore—The Igloo) 262.
Hell's Angels f (Hook Money—Luminant) (40).
Helluvafella c (Little Buskins—Manetta) 3.
Henry Purcell c (Sol Oriens—Spinet) (255).
Henry's Choice c (King of the Tudors—Vestal Girl) 194, 208, (235).
Henry the Seventh c (King of the Tudors—Vestal Girl) 32, 73, (119), (123), (185), (233).
Hera f (Grey Sovereign—Cumulus) 2, 11, (21), 37, 44, (61).
Herbaceous c (Crepello—Persian Lilac) (205).
Hercules Boy c (Buisson Ardent—Home Game) 200.
Hereford c (Royal Challenger—Flyola) (104).
Heritiere f (Rockefella—Star of France) 145, 233.
Hermes c (Aureole—Ark Royal) 5, (47), 72, 72, (73), 78, (89), (135), 140, (148), 220.
Heron c (Pardal—Show a Leg) 39, 48, 76, 88.
Heron's Plume c (High Hat—Heron Bay) 76, 130.
Hero's Mead c (Honeyway—Brave Empress) 82.
Herring Gull c (Devonian—Lonely Wings) (271), (290).
Hesiod c (Hyperion—Serocco) (221).
Hespero c (Chamier—Weaving Spider) (38).
Heswall Honey c (Honeyway—Kess) (80), 133.
HETHERSETT c (Hugh Lupus—Bride Elect) 3, (5), (45), 78, (88), 100, (135), 149.
Hibernia III f (Masetto—Horatia) 66, 86, (118), (131).
Hibernian c (Hethersett—Hibernia III) (41), 62, (231).
Hidden Meaning f (Woodcut—Conceal) (31), (61), 197, (233).
Hiding Place f (Doutelle—Jojo) 2, 4, (69).
Hieroglyph c (Heliopolis—Pocket Edition) (10), (22), 42, 111.

High Camber f (His Highness—Cambalee) 29.
High Finance c (Como—Berylfelic) 136.
High Flown c (Hill Gail—Cherished) 123, 181, (182).
High Flying c (High Treason—Sophronia) (219), 228.
High Hat c (Hyperion—Madonna) 1, 78, (81), (133), 133.
Highland Dandy c (Last of the Dandies—Highland Witch) 251, (260).
Highland Melody c (Tudor Melody—Follow Elizabeth) 216.
Highland Wedding c (Question—Carrick Princess) 251, 251, (261), (261).
High Noon c (Sayajirao—Shining Hour) 1, (67).
High Order f (Hugh Lupus—Bride Elect) 45.
High Perch c (Alycidon—Phaetonia) (72), 133, 143.
High Pitch f (Big Game—Sea Symphony) (40).
High Power c (Vulgan—April the Second) 275.
High Powered f (Hugh Lupus—Pharsalia) 11, (20), (101).
High Proof c (Above Suspicion—Gaskella) 130, 201, 235.
Highroy c (High Treason—Rise and Fall) 211.
High Sun c (High Treason—Solar Telegram) 217, 217, 228, 228.
High Table c (Dignitary—Trimontium) 143, 182, 183, 185.
High Time c (Bleep Bleep—Daylight Saving) 188.
High Veldt c (Hyperion—Open Country) 100, 113.
Hilarion c (Hyperion—Laitron) 287.
Hilary Term f (Supreme Court—Spring Running) 4.
Hillgrove c (Sheshoon—Donna Lollo) 104.
Hill House c (By Thunder! or Indian Blue—Pretty Baby) (263).
Hill Rise c (Hillary—Red Curtain) (123), (144).
Hill Royal c (Democratic—Fair Alycia) (162).
Hill Run c (Hillary—Red Curtain) (19).
Hill Shade f (Hillary—Penumbria) 2, 4, 40, 45, 75, (129), (147).
Hill Town c (Acropolis—Sweet Caroline) 48.
Hindu Festival c (Hindostan—Nasturtium) (84), 87, 117.
Hindu Penny c (Hindostan—Penny on the Jack) 283.
Hinton Blewett c (Princely Gift—Pearl Fishing) 194.
Hipster c (Alcide—Blue Jean) 60, 165, (221).
His Legend c (His Slipper—Pretty Legend) (15), 30.
His Story c (His Slipper—Pretty Legend) (36), 63, 72, 102, 116, 123, 190.
Hobson c (His Slipper—Better Choice) (15).
Holborn c (Pall Mall—Hattons Last) 59, 79, 109.
Holder c (Hook Money—Lady Barle) 268.
Hollyhock c (His Eminence II—Auricula) (165), (169).
Home Park c (Pardal—Alesia) 226.
Home Secretary c (Petition—Haste) 219.
HOMEWARD BOUND f (Alycidon—Sabia River) (4), (75), 100, (134), 140.
Honest Boy c (Straight Deal—Olan) 84, 133.
Honey Bear c (Aureole—Honey Bun) 22, 26, 85.
Honeycomb Rock c (Honeyway—Wildwood) 162, 182, 182.
Honey End c (Honeyway—Fair Donation) 245, 259.
Honey Lake f (Spy Song—Miss Grillo) 66.
Honey Line c (Pardal—Honey Ration) 22.

Honeymoor c (Honeyway—Lorelei) 162, 162, 218, 227.
Honey Portion f (Major Portion—Run Honey) 75, 107, 167.
Honeysucker f (Doutelle—Oh My Honey) 121.
Honeysuckle f (Darius—Honey Bun) 69.
Honour Bound c (Straight Deal—Fancy Ribbons) (91), (270).
Hoodwinked c (Monsieur l'Amiral—Josie Blink) (286), (292).
HOPEFUL VENTURE c (Aureole—White House) 5, (68), (84), 111, (113), (120),
  (133).
Hopiana f (Hook Money—Present Hope) (14).
Hopkiss c (Fortina—Miss Hopkins) (288).
Hopsack f (Abernant—Fleeting Storm) 24.
HORNBEAM c (Hyperion—Thicket) 91, 91, 110, 140, 220.
Hornblower c (Hornbeam—Blue Line) (73).
Horned Moon c (Hornbeam—Even Star) (35).
Horse Radish c (Hard Sauce—Spring Offensive) (199).
Hot Brandy c (Panaslipper—Angelicus) (72), 72, 78, 113, 116, (130), 148.
Hotfoot c (Firestreak—Pitter Patter) 32.
Hot Penny f (Red God—Harmonius) 17, 20
Hotroy c (Aureole—Jungle Jewel) 47, 164, (164), (170), 178, 210.
House Proud c (Proud Chieftain—Glasshouse) (36), 41, 102.
Hove c (Coxcomb—All Square) 248.
Hovercraft c (Pardal—Wave Crest III) 102.
How Far f (Hethersett—Pharsalia) 18.
Hoy c (Orthodox—Secret Code) (175), 232.
Huguenot c (Hyperion—Martinhoe) 183, (187), 190, (194), (207).
HULA DANCER f (Native Dancer—Flash On) (2), (149).
Hullabaloo c (Aureole—Babua) 80.
Hully Gully c (Emerson—Third Slip) 170, 269.
Hunter's Breeze c (Cacador—Mountain Breeze) (258).
Hunter's Quest c (Cacador—Ton Rettour) 248.
Hurada c (Precipitation—Pharada) 161.
Hurry Home c (Shahpoor—Sudden Dawn) 279.
Hurry Hurry c (Hornbeam—Hustle) (34), 92, 104.
Hustler, The c (Welsh Abbot—Anezzula) (275).
Hyphen c (Nearco—Hortentia) 120, 130, (194).
Hypur II c (Copernicus—Pampas Girl) 262.

I

Icanopit c (Domaha—Easter Parade) 246, 276, 276, 286.
Icarian c (Precipitation—Sun Lane) 165.
Icarus c (Tenerani—Sun Chariot) 133.
Ice Ballet f (Ballymoss—Snow Shower) 94.
I Claudius c (Tantieme—Armada) 178, (187).
Icy Look f (Arctic Time—Eila) (118), 139.
Icy Wonder c (Distinctive—Old Icy) (285).
Ides of March c (Premonition—Roman Spice) 233.
Idle Dreams f (High Treason—My Dream) 9.
Idle Hour c (Persian Gulf—Dilettante) (130).
Idler c (The Cobbler—Sarala) 184, 228.
Idomeneo c (Alycidon—Arietta) 31.
Ileana f (Abernant—Romantica) 2, (101), (121).
Ilium c (Acropolis—Sarcelle) (47).
Illinois c (Tenerani—Lady Amy) 5, 148, 187, (187), (187), (188), 207.
Illuminous f (Rockefella—Picture Light) 90, (97).
Imagination c (Alcide—Limitless) 26.
IMBERLINE f (Ocarina—Barley Corn) 4.
Impatient c (Precipitation—Pharada) (113).
Impeached f (High Treason—Almond) 9, 14, 17.
Imperator c (Final Score—The Sweetest) 259, 267, 289.
Imperius c (Hugh Lupus—Impudent) 231.
Impudent f (Owen Tudor—Saucy Lass) (93).
In Bond c (Dionisio—Disdainful) 179.
In Command f (March Past—Boudicca) (130).
Indamelia f (Indian Ruler—Barton's Sister) 270.
INDIANA c (Sayajirao—Willow Ann) 3, (5), 76, (82), (84), 91, (135).
Indian Conquest c (Tamerlane—Nokomis) (30), 106, 173.
Indian Lad c (Hard Sauce—Papoose) (6).
INDIAN MELODY f (Sayajirao—Turkish Melody) 2, 4, 131.
Indian Order c (Crepello—Star of India) 143.
Indian Scene c (Sayajirao—Niccolo Scene) 65.
Indian Spice c (County Delight—Spice Wind) 248.
Induna c (Migoli—Solar Princess) 72, 77, 114, 172, 175, (223), (226), 226.
Initial c (Relic—Hazy Moon) (198).
Ink Spot f (My Babu—Blue Stain) 8, 18, 28.
Inquisitor c (Firestreak—Madrilene) 47.
Instow f (Big Game—Appledore) 121, (197).
Intermezzo c (Hornbeam—Plaza) 49.
Interosian c (Ossian II—Interrogated) 249.
Intervener c (Supreme Court—My Poppet) (31), 46.
In the Gloaming c (Crepello—Sun Cap) 76, 92, (130).
Intrepid c (Sheshoon—Maria Robusti) 163.
In Trust c (Arctic Prince—Honey Pound) 234.
Invader c (Norman—Bali Ha'I) (287).

Inyanga f (Lord of Verona—Di Vernon II) 161, 177, (183), 207, 209, 214, 225, 225, (226), (268).
Io f (Tenerani—Fatimite) 4.
IONIAN c (Milesian—Persian View) 1, (45), 105.
Irish Chorus f (Ossian II—Dawn Chorus) (25).
Irish Coffee c (Reynard Volant—Lady Walewska) (280), 281, 288.
Irish Gambol c (Stephen Paul—Watalic) 109, 216.
Irish Guard c (Martial—Shagreen) 15, 25.
Irish Imp c (Tangle—Gay Lydia) 246, 253, 275, 285, (287).
Irish Jurist c (Midas—Pomme de Reinette) 275.
Irish Penny c (Hindostan—Penny on the Jack) 142.
Irish Rain c (Raincheck—Split the Wind) 270.
Irish Rhythm f (Ennis—Tosca) 222.
Irish Rover c (Star Signal or Vulgan—Random Inn) (253).
Irma la Douce f (Nimbus—Primbush) (21).
Iron Blue c (Rockefella—Lady Barle) 85, 92, 120, 130, 165, 210, 229, 263.
Ironic c (Petition—Metallic) (48).
Iron Peg c (Dark Star—Hostage) 74.
Irristable f (Darius—Lady Blane) 101, 134, 139.
I SAY c (Sayajirao—Isetta) 3, (80), (100), 113.
Isis c (Ennis—Ice Carnival) 233.
Iskereen f (Hornbeam—Mor'a Bai) (118), 131, 147.
Islam c (Sayajirao—Istar) 41.
Island Lore f (Court Martial—Aleutian) 8.
Isle of Skye c (Cameron—Brotanault's Pride) (272).
Isola d'Asti f (Court Harwell—Asti Spumante) 35.
Italiano c (Molvedo—Zanzara) 60, 96.
I Titan c (Ballymoss—La Montespan) 5, (104), (214).
Ivalo c (Philius II—Agamma) 231.
Ivy Green f (Flyon—Hedge Law) 277, 286.

J

Jabula f (Sheshoon—White River) 61.
Jacintha f (Hyacinthus—Twin) (216), (230).
Jack & Jill c (Delirium—Astafa) (146), (146).
Jackies Kuda c (Coup de Lyon—Ailis) 216.
Jack Ketch c (Abadan—Law) (65), (87).
Jacobus c (Relic—Miss Klaire II) 70.
Jacthelot c (Javelot—Turkish Pearl) 161, 189, 191.
Jadeite f (Princely Gift—Alare) 2, (15), (25), (66).
Jalan-Besar c (Chamossaire—Cache) 72.
Jambo f (Babur—Kikuyu) (222).

Jamipego c (Luminary—Nix) 30.
Janeat f (Grey Sovereign—Shirley Pat) 217, 228, (230).
J'Arrive c (J'Accours—Ennis Girl) 278, 293.
Javata f (Javelot—Tena Mariata) (93).
Javelot c (Fast Fox—Djaina) 119, (119), 149.
Jaxartes c (Tamerlane—Heaven's Gate) 195.
Jay Trump c (Tonga Prince—Be Trump) (245), 254.
Jealous c (Above Suspicion—Leidenschaft) (41).
Jeanne Michelle f (Chamier—Umbria) (197).
Jebanette c (Djebe—Campanette) (47).
Jet Age c (Polly's Jet—Pastures Green) 15.
Jet Stream c (Alizier—Streamlace) 39, 81, 85, (92), 110, 111.
Jibuti f (Djebe—Queen of Sheba) 71, (101).
JIMMY REPPIN c (Midsummer Night II—Sweet Molly) 1, 99, (132), (137).
Jimmy Scot c (Jock Scot—Kandahar) (280).
Jim's Tavern c (Playhouse—Jim's Love) 245, (280).
Joan's Rival c (Vulgan—Black Arch) 280.
Jock's Lodge c (Jock Scot—Persian Ivy) 194.
John Cameron c (Colonist II—Dirrie-More) 186.
John Jacques c (Bellman—Tiber Whin) (267).
John o'Groats c (Jock Scot—Tonsure) 248, 250, 256, 256, 260.
John's Court c (Court Martial—Snow Shower) (162).
John's Key c (Off Key—Gold Tie) 166.
Joker, The c (Court Harwell—Sijui) 163.
Jolly Fiddler, The f (Shahpoor—Fiddling) 282.
Jolly Signal c (Reverse Charge—Ninotchka) 285, (285).
Jomsviking c (King Legend—Traveller's Pride) 271, 271.
Jongleur c (Sayajirao—Turkish Tune) 140, 148.
Jonjo c (Tartan—Clarion March) (265).
Joyful Scene f (Vilmorin—Bright Disguise) 17.
Judicature c (Supreme Court—Hyphenate) 217.
Julia's Hamlet c (Royal Hamlet—Julia) 216.
Jumna c (Dilawarji—Fairy Fleet) (293).
Jungle Beach c (King of the Jungle—Wild Beach) 246, 286.
Jupiter Boy c (Sayajirao—Ashoka Kumari) (246).
Juries Act f (Marsolve—Susie's Image) 217.
Just Awake c (Vulgan—Awakening) (271).
Just Great c (Worden II—Just Wyn) (76), (88), (135).
Just Verdict c (Fair Trial—Cats Corrie) 67.

K

Kadir Cup (late Diving Suit) c (Pearl Diver—Porters Choice) 169.
Kaffirboom c (Alycidon—Quickwood) (169), 189.
Kalimnos c (Dionisio—Wild Girl) 162, 170.
Kalydon c (Alycidon—Lackaday) (133), (206).
Kamasu c (Beau Sabreur—Shushoe) 166.
Kamundu c (Will Somers—Belle of Victor) 179, (230).
Kandy-Sugar c (Stardust—Bonbon) 24, (217).
Kanthral c (Chanteur II—Cold Response) 161.
Kapeno c (No Orchids—Kanjana) 256, 259, 262, 281, 292, 292.
Karabas c (Worden II—Fair Share) 111, (130).
Karelia f (Kelly—Larryta) 233.
Kari Sou c (Souverain—Karina II) 261, (274).
Karpathos c (Kythnos—Hymette) (34).
KASHMIR II c (Tudor Melody—Queen of Speed) (1).
Kathyanga c (Great Captain—Celestial Gold) (13), 22, 226.
Kathy Too f (Beau Sabreur—Celestial Gold) 16, (25), (29).
Kazanlik f (Ommeyad—Rose Supreme) 131, 134.
Kedge c (Petition—Ripeck) 99.
Keld f (Owen Tudor—Congo) 40.
Kellsboro Wood c (Woodcut—Kellsboro' Jane) 267, 292.
Kelly c (Panorama—Cottesmore) 22, (32), 42.
Kentra c (Set Fair—Pirate's Daughter) (182), 185, 209, 224, 225.
Kerforo f (Foroughi—Kerlogue Steel) (258), (265), (290).
Kerrabee f (Whistler—Sea Chorus) (9), (18), 23, 43, 136.
Kerstin f (Honor's Choice—Miss Kilcash) 250, (250), 254, 284, (284), 292.
Kew f (Princely Gift—Astrentia) 9.
Keystone Cop (late Normand II) c (Alizier—Clorinthe) 208.
Khalekan c (Alycidon—Tenebel) 46, 49, (128), 142.
Khalife c (Montaval—Jill Scott) 102, 142.
Khalkis c (Vimy—Merry Xmas) (62), 77, 100, (119).
Khemis c (Babur—Ma Davies) (231).
Kibenka c (King's Bench—Kathie) (8), 16, 19, 98, (99), 106, 132, (167), (171), 193.
Kilballyown c (Last of the Dandies—Cringer) (290).
Kilburn c (Battle Burn—dam by Steel-Point) (251), 255.
Kilcoran c (Gilles de Retz—Chislet) 102.
Kildavin c (Preciptic—Akkaraje) (287).
Kilmore c (Zalophus—Brown Image) 245, (245), 245.
Kilrane c (Le Sage—Kilashee) 227.
Kimono f (Court Martial—Almond Eyes) 24.
Kindling Chips c (Bois Roussel—Kindy) 132.
King c (Caldarium—Marquise) 246, 254.
King Aziru c (Sovereign Path—Davedasee) 21.
King Babar c (My Babu—Merayah) (82).
Kingbenitch c (King's Bench—Mainswitch) 210.
King Chesnut c (Alycidon—Equiria) 120.
King Cutler c (Black Tarquin—Shuleen) (270).

Kingfisher c (Alcide—Warspite) 87.
King Frank (late Praise) c (Stephen Paul—Rightful) 12, 16.
Kinglike c (King's Bench—Santamarina) 8.
King Log c (Relic—Queen's Beast) 46, (128).
King of Babylon c (King of the Tudors—Babylon) 1, 28, (32), (73), 185.
King of Diamonds c (Kingstone—Puretta) (259).
King of Peace c (Sovereign Path—Lucia di Lammermoor) (161), (191).
King of Saba c (Relic—Balkis III) (173), 174, 184.
King Penny c (Eudaemon—Penny on the Jack) 270.
Kingroy c (King's Bench—Bishopscourt) 1, 74, (173), (203), 218.
King's Barn c (Persian Gulf—Wiston) 106, 132.
King's Case c (King's Bench—Mareeba) 10.
King's Cavalier c (Coronation Year—Sister Sally) 188.
King's Coup c (Kingsway—Fair Coup) (182), (182), (182), 215, (218), 227, 227.
Kings Decision c (Pardal—Solomon's Choice) 26.
King's Favourite c (King of the Tudors—None Nicer) 19, 46.
King's Lane c (Tamerlane—Two Blues) (46).
King's Leap c (Princely Gift—Impala) 174, 179.
King's Mistress f (Rockefella—Equiria) 2, (40).
King's Nephew c (Cacador—Hal's Maiden) (253), (259), 264.
King's Nickel c (Kingsmead—Nickel Coin) 264, 274.
King's Petition c (Petition—Mistress Gwynne) 7.
King's Regulations c (Court Martial—Tante Rose) (47), 89.
King's Rock c (King's Bench—Rocketta) 200.
King's Secret c (Darius—Soft Whisper) 223.
Kingston-By-Pass c (Kingstone—Honours Degree) 180.
Kings Troop c (Princely Gift—Equiria) (193), 215.
King Vulgan c (Vulgan—Bright Princess) 289.
Kinmont Wullie c (El Hawa—Devonshire Cream) 261, 261, (291).
Kipling c (Narrator—Fair Ranger) (128).
Kirriemuir c (Tangle—Jonquille II) 247, 277, (277).
Kirsch Flambee c (Crepello—Kandy Sauce) 48, 105.
Kirtella f (King's Bench—La Goulue) 285.
Kirtle-Lad c (Exodus—Montlace) 261.
Kiss of Life c (Never Say Die—Poste Restante) 89.
Kitimat f (Preciptic—Maple Leaf) 138.
Klondyke Bill c (Golden Cloud—Reckless Lady) 122, 211, 211, (230).
Knight Errant c (Steel-Point—Amber Castle) 267, 290.
Knight of the Morn c (Sadani—Garland) (234).
Knightsbrook c (Orbit—Halo) (259), 290.
Knobbled c (Hook Money—Copper Knob) 219.
Knockaney c (Fortina—Bank Roll) 290.
Knockaphrumpa c (Foroughi—Wool Ball) 264.
Knotty Pine c (Tambourine II—Our Girl) 7.
Knucklecracker c (Caudillo—Allegorie II) (250), 250, 254.
K.O. c (Fighting Don—Final Decision) (163), 163, 163.
Kolpham c (Kolper—Ightham) 274.
Koolabah c (Eastern Lyric—Angelist) 172.

Koppernik c (Hyperion—Frying Pan) 7.
Krakenwake f (Krakatao—Dented Bell) (23), 115.
Kubba c (Persian Gulf—Periculum) 232.
Kulak c (Fast Fox—Katika) 80.
Kushi f (Paridel—Turkish Delight) 227.
Kylin f (Kythnos—Fortwyn) 4, 41, 86, 118, 131.
KYTHNOS c (Nearula—Capital Issue) 3, (65), (87), 124.

L

LA BAMBA f (Shantung—Frontier Song) 4.
La Belle f (Vilmorin—Kentucky Belle) (146), 197, 230.
La Bergerette f (Tornado—La Perie) 4.
Lachine f (Grey Sovereign—Loved One) (101), (138), (197).
Lackapin c (Pinza—Lackaday) 253, 271.
La Coquenne f (Migoli—La Li) 108, 131.
LACQUER f (Shantung—Urshalim) 2, (86), (233).
Lacydon c (Alycidon—Lackaday) 39, 229.
Lad's Love c (Tudor Melody—Goldwyn Girl) 18.
Lady Advocate f (Kings Bench—Villa Medici) (20), 23.
Lady Anna f (Panaslipper—Cherie Marie) 225.
Lady Arctic f (Arctic Prince—Lady Rosemary) 15.
Lady Clodagh f (Tyrone—Chloris II) 86.
LADY IN TROUBLE f (High Treason—Reseda) 2, 71, 101, 107, 121.
Lady Kyth f (Kythnos—Lady Preciptic) 93.
Lady Magistrate f (Privy Councillor—Magicoal) (197).
Lady Matador f (Matador—Utteradevi) (15).
Lady Pilot f (Blue Peter—Ferry Pool) 75.
Lady Salisbury f (Precipitation—Diamond Garter) 4.
Lady Senator f (The Phoenix—Peace Terms) 69, (86), 125.
Lady's View f (Tin Whistle—Crownless) (8), (24).
Laffy c (Rigolo—Vatelinde) 245, (264), (264), 292.
La Foire II f (Arabian—Forolla) 189, 201.
La Gamberge f (Vieux Manoir—Sun Beauty) 61.
Laird, The c (Border Chief—Pre Fleuri) (248), 249, (252), (262), 284.
Laird o'Montrose c (Nicolaus—Rays of Montrose) 161, 268.
LA LAGUNE f (Val de Loir—Landerinette) (4).
Lalibela f (Honeyway—Blue Mark) (43).
Lama f (Arctic Storm—Goggles) 30.
Lametta f (Alycidon—Golden Cascade) (221).
La Mome f (Princely Gift—La Parisienne) (75).
Lampardal c (Pardal—Lametta) 209.
Lanark c (Grey Sovereign—Vermillion o'Toole) 28.

Lanarkshire f (Grey Sovereign—Vermillion o'Toole) 166.
Lancelot c (Lancewood—Honey Sweet) 276, 276, 286.
Landigou c (Mourne—Lady Djebel) 3, 88, 114, 229.
Landshire Lane f (Thoroughfare—Stalbridge Common) 274.
Lanesborough c (Tamerlane—Fylgia) (225).
Langley Park c (Chamier—Country House) 205, 210, 233.
Langton Heath c (Langton Abbot—Roseneath) (287).
Lansallos c (King Hal—Miss Loobagh) 272.
Laramie c (Rococo—Pylilian) 264.
Larbawn c (Vulgan—Fly Book) 248, 272, (292).
Lariak c (Buisson Ardent—Traviata) 183, 207.
LARKSPUR c (Never Say Die—Skylarking) (3), 5, 36.
Larkspur Bloom c (Some Bloom—Rose Larkspur) 65.
Lars Porsena c (Black Tarquin—Lycia) 287, 287.
Last Case f (Firestreak—Court Case) 129, (168), (188), (200).
Last Chip c (King's Troop—Last Flutter) 188.
Lastime c (Fairey Fulmar—Colorado Girl) 173.
Last Line c (Cagire II—Tackler) 39.
Last Link f (Fortina—Senria) 258, (290).
Last Shoe c (El Gallo—Tireless) (7), 16.
La Tendresse f (Grey Sovereign—Isetta) (23), (24), (29), 115, (126).
Latin Lover c (Ribot—Hortentia) 3, 207.
Latour c (Lavandin—Chiffonier) 176.
Laudamus c (Lauso—Damarctic) 13, 102.
Lauravella f (Aureole—Lavella) 86.
Laureate c (Aureole—Sundry) 73, (85), (92).
Laurence O c (Saint Crespin III—Feevagh) 38, 135, 142.
Laurino c (Nearco—Lady Grand) 200.
Lavandier c (Le Lavandou—Double Dutch) 16, 162, 170.
Lavella f (Le Lavandou—Lilting Lullaby) 163, (231), (231).
Lawful c (King's Bench—Tiger Flower) 85.
Lawrence c (Abernant—Gregos) 15.
Lay About c (Aggressor—Free for All) (60).
Leadendale Lady f (Damremont—The Bog) (223).
Lead the Way c (Never Say Die—Flicka de Saint Cyr) 104.
Lebon M.L. c (Cote d'Or II—Leaupartie) 149.
LE CANTILIEN c (Norseman—La Perie) 3.
Le Cordonnier c (Saint Crespin III—Selindra) (26), 46, 49, 74, 164, 178, 210, (213).
Le Dauphin c (Tamerlane—Schonbrunn) 223.
Legal Measure c (Watch Your Step—Case Dismissed) 42.
Legal Tie c (Dogat—Aster Link) 143, (192), (218).
Le Garcon c (Damremont—Village Maid) 162, 170, 171, 187, (218).
Le Levanstell c (Le Lavandou—Stella's Sister) 36, 59, 106, (125), (144), 218.
Le Loup Garou c (Prince Bio—Roselane) 110.
Lemnos c (Alycidon—Hot Water) 104, 130.
L' Empereur c (Foxlight—Nosika) 245, 264.
Leonardo c (Doutelle—Seven Knots) 49.
Le Palatin c (Laurentis—My Lady) (253).

L'Epinay c (Buisson Ardent—Pantona) 1.
Le Pirate c (Zarathustra—Marsh Mallow) 78, 102, 161, (172), 270.
Le Pretendant c (Ocean Swell—Cy Bele II) 77, 116.
Le Prince c (Prince Bio—Atlantida) 103, 220, 225.
Lerida f (Matador—Zepherin) (11), 23.
L' Escargot c (Escart III—What a Daisy) (270).
Leslie c (Vulgan—Miss Gaiety) 280.
Le Vermontois c (Acropolis—Bethora) (263).
Levmoss c (Le Levanstell—Feemoss) (133).
Lexicon c (Hornbeam—Alexi) 164, 187, 213.
Leyton Orient c (Tiverton or Nearcolein—Beresina) 293.
L'Homme Arme c (Milesian—Palestrina) 87, 180.
Libator f (Gustator—June Jinks) 230.
Liberal Lady f (Abernant—Fair Freedom) 11, (29).
Liberty Truck c (Rapace—Armoured Train) 114.
Light Fantastic f (Denturius—Light Fantasy) 9.
Light Harvest c (Signal Light—Wild Harvest) 184, 196.
Light Horseman c (Guersant—Lumine) 72, (84), 130, 142, 214.
Lightkeeper c (Lighthouse II—Grape Fruit) 229.
Light of the Road c (Pink Flower—Akela) 184, 230.
Light Year c (Chamier—Spring Light) 36, 65, (87).
Lillet f (Anwar—Flash of Wit) 25, 86.
Lima f (Abernant—Queen of Peru) 18.
Limb of the Law c (Within-the-Law—Boltown) 286.
Limeking c (Limekiln—Scottish Princess) (252), 281.
Limetra c (Soletra—Limberette) 259.
Limeville c (Limekiln—Roseville) 276, 287.
Limonali c (Hyder Ali—Limonetta) 251, 251, 271.
Limuru f (Alcide—Princess Cecilia) 202.
Linacre c (Rockefella—True Picture) (87), 125, (144), 149, 149.
Linan Belle f (Ballylinan—Baby Bella) 234.
Lincoln c (Abernant—Never Give In) 167.
Lincolnwood c (Vilmoray—Lilliesleaf) 200.
Lindosa f (Aureole—Short Sentence) 121, 138.
Lindrick c (Nearula—Raven Locks) 1.
Lindsay f (Dante—Colombelle) 2, (24), (43).
Line Shooter c (Mossborough—Northern Line) (168).
Linnet Lane f (Chanteur II—Dale Street) (194), 221.
Linwell c (Rosewell—Rubia Linda) 250, (284), 284.
Lionhearted c (Never Say Die—Thunder) 67, 92, 117, 128.
Lion Noir c (Paul Beg—Virginian Cottage) 286.
Listoke Invader c (Mustang—Wiesbaden) 223.
Little Buskins c (Solar Slipper—Overboard) (169), (180), (183).
Little Hawk c (Aureole—Northern Circuit II) (163).
Little Miss Muffet f (Tourment—My Mascot) 93.
Little Mo f (Sayajirao—Little Mop) (118).
Little Redskin c (Luminary—Papoose) 196.
Little Sandy c (Migoli—Sandona) 102.

Little Topper, The c (Stardust—Cent Sous) 199.
Liveryman c (Le Pacha—Aromatic II) 282.
Livia f (Tyrone—La Diva II) 118, 145.
Lizawake c (Long Stop—Liza) 280, 288.
Lizzie the Lizard f (Romany Air—Sea Wedding) 274.
L.J. c (Zimone—Androyna) (200).
Lobelia f (Niccolo Dell'Arca—Alrabia) 93.
Lobitos c (Vilmorin—Home Game) 181, (224).
Lochailort f (Doutelle—Solar Path) 108, 129, 145.
Lochroe c (King Hal—Loch Cash) 254, (254), (280), 284, 284.
Lock Hard c (Hard Tack—Dunlavin Star) (63), 144.
Locris c (Venture VII—Ormara II) 149.
Logarithm f (Rock Star—Cabin) 196, 211, 216.
Lohengrin c (Tamerlane—Cygnet) 203.
Lombard c (High Treason—Panacea) 18.
Lomond c (Preciptic—Miss Prince) (116), (120), (120), 148, 199, (220), 226.
London Cry c (Pardal—Lavender) (68), 77, 100, (210), (233).
London Gazette c (Panaslipper—Court Circular) 92, (116), 120, 164, 178.
London Melody c (Pall Mall—French Ballad) 16, 46, 48.
Lone Wolf c (Hugh Lupus—Melusine) 177, 232.
Long John Silver c (Colonist II—Eastern Sunset) 46, 60.
LONG LOOK f (Ribot—Santorin) 2, (4), 131.
Longmead c (Pactolus—First Seller) 265.
Longtail c (Domaha—Device) 267, (272).
Look Sharp c (Crepello—Wake Up!) 34, (85).
Loppylugs c (Royal Tara—Lady Jitters) 193.
Loquacious f (Reverse Charge—Vivacious) 15, 109.
Lord John c (Sovereign Lord—Janita) 12, (25).
Lord Provost c (Borealis—Habeas Corpus) 161.
Lord Sing c (Sing Sing—Lady Chatter) 202.
Lorenzaccio c (Klairon—Phoenissa) (16), 32, 144, 167.
Lost Property (late Papy) c (Orcada—Piccadilly) 81, 175, 191, 212.
Love and Marriage c (Pinza—Amora) 68.
Love for Sale f (Crepello—Tudor Love) (47).
Lovely Gale f (Windy City—Mlle Lorette) (66), 86, 107.
Lovely Light f (Henry the Seventh—Queen of Light) 17.
Lovestone f (Amour Drake—Safari Moon) (132).
Loving Record c (Archive—Admiring) 258, 281.
Lower Boy c (Sayajirao—Duke's Delight) 200.
Lowna f (Princely Gift—Gillamoor) (23).
Loyal Lady f (Preciptic—British Colombia) (7).
Loyal Monarch c (Darius—Constantia) 27, 173.
Loyalty f (Above Suspicion—Bordeaux) 11, (66), 86, 131.
Lucasland f (Lucero—Lavant) (122), 136, (146), (179).
Lucaya f (Ossian II—Blue Solitaire) (83), 90, (147).
Lucem f (Guersant—Luminant) 34.
Luciennes f (Grey Sovereign—Courtship) 23.
Lucky Biscuit c (Hard Tack—Fortunata) (59), 141, 186, 203.

Lucky Brief c (Counsel—Welsh Rose) (35), (89).
Lucky Coin c (Tudor Melody—Lucky Cruzeiro) (27), 32.
Lucky Finish c (Milesian—Campanette) 42, (89).
Lucky Guy c (Pink Flower—Donna Anniversaire) (77), (103), 103.
Lucky Gwen f (Princely Gift—Ogwen) 23.
Lucky Match c (Match III—Dianella) 116.
Lucky Pigeon f (The Mongoose—Coronation Route) 118.
Lucky White Heather (late Romany Fair) c (Fairwell—Romanesque) 165, (189).
Lucyrowe f (Crepello—Esquire Girl) 43.
LUDHAM f (Pampered King—Sunward) 4, 83, (143).
Lullaby f (Relko—Siren) 40.
Lully Boy c (Beau Sabreur—Shushoe) 163, 231, 231.
Luminous Sun c (Luminary—Sunyasee) 166, 181.
Lunar Princess f (King's Bench—Lunar Way) 17, 122, 196.
Lupina f (Hugh Lupus—Salka) 40.
Luran f (Tehran—Lugano) 163.
Lutine f (Alcide—Mona) 45.
Lynch Law c (Court Martial—Camp Fire) 13.
Lynchris f (Sayajirao—Scollata) (41), (131), (134), (142).
Lysander c (Nearco—Meld) 130, 172.

M

MABEL f (French Beige—Aunt May) 2, 4, (134), 139.
Mabrouk c (Babur—Ma Davies) 231.
Machella f (Crepello—Vague Mary) 94.
Macip c (Marsyas II—Corejada) 127.
Mac Joy c (Canot—Pladda) 256, (256), (271), 289, (289).
Macmartin c (Falls of Clyde—Marietta) 24.
Macquario c (Precipitation—White River) (192).
Mac's Flare c (Fun Fair—dam said to be Border Girl) 267.
Mlle Barker f (Mossborough—Mlle Lorette) (138).
Maddalo c (The Phoenix—Cracknel) (185), 283.
Mad Hatter c (High Hat—Persian Queen) 221.
Madras c (Epaulette—Hot Curry) 6.
Madras c (Victrix—Brinda) (281).
Maeander f (Milesian—Open Court) 29, 43, 101.
Maelsheachlainn c (Erno—Maighdean Mara) 91, (229).
Magga Dan c (Krakatao—Monkeyshines) 84.
Magical Approach c (King's Approach—Magic Bright) 270.
Magic Boy c (Magic Red—Best of Luck) (196).
Magic Court c (Supreme Court—Blue Prelude) (161), 177, 232, (268), (277).
Magic Moment c (Magic Red—Quincey) 174, 217.

Magic North c (Norseman—Magic Noire) 114.
Magic Thrust f (Zarathustra—Pappagena) 121.
Magnetic North c (Borealis—Melitensis) 226.
Magnificat c (Pinza—Libera Nos) 76.
Magnifitant f (Preciptic—Lady Hunter) 161.
Magnus c (The Phoenix—Larryta) 195.
Mahal f (Tutankhamen—Suncourt) (138), 147.
Mahbub Aly c (Worden II—Mabiba) 104, 116, (175), 220, 226.
Maid of Galloway f (Scottish Union—Miss Valence) 234.
Maigret c (Snow King—Metra) 254.
Mainstown c (Owenstown—Ravine) 261.
Majetta c (King's Troop—Etta) 18, 122, 137.
Major, The c (Foroughi—Zazzaway) 281.
Major General c (Court Martial—Red Shoes) 162, 168.
Major Hitch c (Aeolian—Mantilla Vulgan) 259, 261, 261.
Majority Blue c (Major Portion—Gorm Abu) (65), (109), (146).
Majority Rule c (Democratic—Feline) (15), 25, (115).
Major Oak c (King's Bench—Miski) (221).
MAJOR PORTION c (Court Martial—Better Half) 1, (8), (13), (42), (105), (125), (144), 149.
Major Rose c (March Past—Rosefield) (175), (229), 232, (232,) 263.
Makaldar c (Makalu—La Madouna) (247), (249), (266), 277.
Make Haste c (Major Portion—Thunderstone) 59, 85, 202.
Malacca III c (Le Tyrol—Mehalla) 280.
Maldavan c (Pindari—Petigold) 13, 60.
Malting Barley f (Doubtless II—Barley Sugar) (281).
Manacle c (Sing Sing—Hard and Fast) 16, 136.
Mandamus c (Petition—Great Fun) (182), 186, 203, 215, (215).
Mandarin c (Deux Pour Cent—Manada) (250), (250), (254), 254, (254), (271), 284, (284), 292, 292, 292.
Mannion c (Erno—Resistance) 217.
Man of the East c (Manicou—Eastern Signal) (253), 289.
Man the Rail c (Turn-to—Dark Rose) 77.
Marandis c (Pinza—Martica) 22, (224).
Mara River f (Gratitude—Buckham Hill) 121.
Maratea c (Persian Gulf—Beausite) 26.
Marble Step f (Sovereign Path—Biotte) 163.
Marchakin c (March Past—Kintail) (203), 205.
March Alone f (March Past—Lone Beech) 228.
Marche d'Or c (Mieuxce—Guinea) 13, (227).
Marcher c (March Past—Wayside Singer) 122, 179, (196), (228).
March Wind c (Hill Gail—War Loot) 5.
March Wonder f (March Past—Worthy Wonder) (168), 215.
Marcia Royal f (Le Levanstell—Illuminate) 15, 25, (30).
Marcia's Mark c (Counsel—Impala) 163.
Marcilly c (Panipat—Marinella) 256.
Marco Polo c (Milesian—Taipeh) (45), (63).
Marcourt f (Court Harwell—Ma Michou) 221.

Marcus Brutus c (Preciptic—Poste Restante) 26, 73, 143, (195).
Marcus Superbus c (Lucero—Khosro Star) 179.
Marengo c (Premonition—Marietta) (76).
Margaret Ann f (Persian Gulf—Alassio) 17.
Margera f (Martial—Segera) 9.
Marguerite Vernaut f (Toulouse Lautrec—Marie Belle) (149).
Maria Gabriella f (Umberto—Viabella) (222).
Marians f (Macherio—Damians) 118.
Marie's Daughter f (Rockefella—Marie Therese) 118.
Marieson c (Tehran—Eiram) 166.
Mariner c (Acropolis—Kyak) 76, (111), 135, 148.
Mariners Dance c (Vulgan—Mariner's Match) (253), 286, 287.
Mariners Hand c (Lighthouse II—Winning Hand) 259.
Mark Antony c (Honeyway—Blue Mark) (180).
Mark Royal c (Monet—Royal Straight) (10), 22.
Mark Scott c (Milesian—Tonakhan) 65, 106.
Marmaduke c (Galivanter—Gaiety Girl) (173), 192, 200.
Marron c (Arciere—Chestnut Pole) 206.
Marshal Grey c (Grey Sovereign—Balkis III) 25.
Marshall Hall c (Supreme Court—Saving Grace) 76, 210.
Marshal Pil c (Rockefalla—Grandpa's Will) (162), 164.
Marsh King c (Grey Sovereign—May Meadow) 74, (177).
Marsh Meadow f (Grey Sovereign—May Meadow) 29.
Marsolve c (Court Martial—Absolve) 74, (122).
MARTIAL c (Hill Gail—Discipliner) (1), (10), 73, 125.
Martial Air f (Court Martial—Solar Myth) 121, 173.
Martian Lady f (Martial—Yga) 30.
Martinsell c (Guersant—High Rocks) 188.
Marton Lady f (March Past—Maid of Kintail) 35.
Mary Mine f (Infatuation—Ma Marie) 40.
MASHAM c (King of the Tudors—Mashaq) 1, (12), (42), (70).
Masquerade c (Cagire II—Garden City) 167, 173.
Massasoit c (Milesian—Syracuse) 22.
Master Barry c (Court Harwell—Slippery Fox) 208.
Master Buck c (Buckhound—Bezique) 62, (102).
Master Cappelle c (Quorum—Ephese) (195), 266.
Master Copper c (Copernicus—Tully Maid) (278).
Master Mariner c (Como—Carradora) 219.
Master Nicky c (Magic Red—Elegant Miss) (205), 205, 227.
Master of Arts c (Nearco—Amber Flash) 165, (199).
Master of Boyden c (Grandmaster—Reset) (200), (205), (205).
Master Perie c (Perion—Bargany Star) 261, 267, 291, 292.
Master Tammy c (Tambourin—Sarafand) (274).
Matador c (Golden Cloud—Spanish Gallantry) (109).
Matatina f (Grey Sovereign—Zanzara) 6, 23, 44, 79, 115, 122, 122, (126), (136), 136, (217).
Match III c (Tantieme—Relance III) (124).
Matchim c (Match III—Anticham) 133.

Matilda III f (Matador—Jane) 197.
Matsur c (Rustam—Preza) 182.
Mayfair Bill c (King's Bench—Love Parade) (285).
Mayhaw f (Parthia—Pal an Oir) 40.
Maystreak c (Firestreak—Mayflower) 6.
Mayville c (Trouville—Maggie Dungarvan) 215, 218, 218, 230.
Mazurka c (Menetrier—Farandole II) (275).
Mazzibell c (Mazarin—Miss Sibell) 290.
MEADOW COURT c (Court Harwell—Meadow Music) 3, 5, 62, 89, (117), (124).
Meadsville c (Charlottesville—Honey Flower) 63.
Medina f (Magic Red—Elegant Miss) (20).
Megsbridge f (Raid—dam's pedigree unknown) 293.
Mehari c (Lavandin—Eos) (76), (81), 89, 95, 110, 220, 229.
Meldola c (Donatello II—Trumps Queen) 274.
Meldon c (Neron—Alcantara) (123).
Meldrum c (Hard Sauce—Ruffino) (35).
Melodic Air c (Tudor Melody—Par Avion) 24, 73.
Melpomene f (Pardal—Melba) 197.
Melted Ice c (Iceberg II—Miss Yen) 288.
Menaphon c (Tamerlane—Whinchat) 194, 207.
Menelek c (Tulyar—Queen of Sheba) (130), (207), 207, 221.
Mentone c (Pink Flower—Favilla) 21.
Meon Valley c (Neron—Myrina) 251, 257.
MERCHANT VENTURER c (Hornbeam—Martinhoe) 3, 5, 39, 67, (89), 128, 135.
Merganser c (Vulgan—She Gone) 255.
Meriana f (Bois Roussel—Samaritaine) 118.
Meridian c (Nimbus—Brilliant Green) 45.
Meritorious c (Migoli—Laurelle II) (283).
Merlins Oak c (Relic—Eiluned) 266.
Merrycourt c (Buckhound—Clear Bay) (281).
Merry Deal c (Straight Deal—Merryland) (268), 268, (277), (289).
Merry Hell f (El Gallo—Mary Kelly) (6).
Merry Madcap f (Grey Sovereign—Croft Lady) (122), 146.
Merryman II c (Carnival Boy—Maid Marion) (245), 245, (291), 293.
Merry Mate f (Ballymoss—Gladness) (131).
Merry Quip f (Petition—Gold Mirth) 222.
Merry Stranger c (Sea Lover—Garryroe Lass) 253.
Merry Windsor c (Foxlight—Courcelle) 291.
Mesembryanthemum c (Migoli—Anaphalis) 65.
Mesopotamia f (Zarathustra—Agar's Plough) (13), 19, 36, 86.
Messene f (Ballyogan—Currarevagh) 30, (118).
Messmate c (Blue Peter—Run Honey) 3, 85, 111, 120.
Metellus c (Kelly—Stem Princess) 28.
Metropolita f (Palestine—Vendeuse) 6.
Meyerling f (Vienna—Dilemma) 47.
Miba f (Ballymoss—Stop Your Tickling) 2, 4, (75), (94), 108, 139, 145.
Michaelis c (Our Babu—Champac) 30.
Middlegate c (Nicolaus—Rissington) 293.

Middleham Matt c (Fidalgo—Maid of Middleham) 82.
Middleton Tower (late De Reszki) c (Chanteur II—Eastern Fairy) 234, 289.
Middle Watch c (Blue Peter—Sundial) 188.
Midelfin c (Midas—Fairyairy) 205.
Mid Field c (Final Score—Scented Night) 206.
MIDGET II f (Djebe—Mimi) (144), 193.
Midlander c (Nimbus—Claudette) 207.
Midnight Marauder c (Milesian—Eila) 123, (164), 185, 193, 193, 203, (210).
Midnight Press f (Borealis—Publication) 83.
Midsummer Dream c (Mark Ye Well—Orange Flash) (21).
Midsummer Night II c (Djeddah—Night Sound) 46, 123, 173, 193, 200, 205, (233).
Midwest c (Midas—Star Spangled) 190.
Mige f (Saint Crespin III—Midget II) (43).
Mighty Apollo c (Hyacinthus—Mighty Prudent) (280).
Mighty Gurkha c (Gratitude—Fatimite) (162), 185.
Mighty's Niece f (Azra—Miss Coleen) 278.
Migologan f (Ballyogan—Visite Migol) 15.
Miladdo c (Whistler—Phoenice) 216, (217).
Milan c (Migoli—La Bormida) 183, 190.
Milesius c (Milesian—Luz) 18, (230).
Miletus c (Milesian—Open Court) (59), 123, 167, 174.
Milistrina f (Milesian—Zanzara) 61.
Military c (Milesian—Burp) 37.
Military Pickle f (Pinza—Colonel's Lady) (94).
MILIZA II f (Mossborough—Polaire II) 2.
Mill House c (King Hal—Nas Na Riogh) (250), (254), (257), (257), 259, (284), 284, 284, 292, (292).
Millibar f (Nimbus—Marie de Medeci) 6.
Milltown c (Milesian—Moss Pink) 31, 67.
Milo c (Foroughi—Hal's Maiden) 270, (281).
Minehead Camp c (Panaslipper—Chaffer) 169.
Minera c (Crepello—Esquire Girl) 174.
Miner's Lamp c (Signal Light—Young Entry) 3, 39, (74), (120).
Minho c (Vigo—Mother Shipton) (166).
Minnehaha f (Mossborough—Indian Call) 131.
Minnie f (Migoli—Lady Wyn) 75, 101.
Minor Portion c (Major Portion—Light Comment) 1, (74), 144, (170), 178.
Minotaur c (Acropolis—Red Cloak) 104.
Minou f (Court Martial—Tiva) (66).
Minstrel King c (Tudor Minstrel—Shrimp Sauce) 219.
Mintmaster c (Colonist II—Joyful Christine) 91, 91, 110, 183, 183, 209, 226, (232).
Minto Burn c (Telegram II—Cousin Kate) 282, 282.
Minute Gun c (Mossborough—Turakina) 91, (165), 191, 270.
MIRALGO c (Aureole—Nella) 5, 28, (49), 82, 92, (96), (113), 119, 124, 128, 135.
Mirella f (Petition—English Miss) 69, 224.
Mirnaya f (Nearco—Solar System) 2, 4, (93), 107, 134, 145.
Miss Biffin f (Bewildered—Landlubber) (138), (188), 233.
Miss Butterfly f (Whistler—Turkish Pearl) 27.

Miss Caroline f (Mustang—Trubley) 47, (227).
Miss Cossie f (Le Lavandou—Monkey Puzzler) 231.
Miss D f (Darius—Ballisland) (224).
Miss Dawn f (Chanteur II—Heat Haze) 232.
MISSILE c (Milesian—Cyphia) 1.
Miss McTaffy f (Jock Scot—Pontypridd) 91, 145, (169), 195.
Miss Patsy f (Olein's Grace—Desla's Own) 234.
Miss Pixie f (Le Lavandou—Palmist) 20.
Miss Success f (Mister Gus—Succeed) 118.
Miss Tarara f (Hard Tack—Tarara) (27).
Miss Togs f (Royal Palm—Reign-Swept) 18.
Miss Wong f (Democratic—Fractious) 20.
Miss Worthington f (Crepello—Gaiety Girl) 97.
Mr Chippendale c (Domaha—Winsome Lady) 280.
Mr Dolittle c (Ossian II—Ardelle) 28.
Mr Higgins c (Nearula—Little Mary) (82).
Mr Jones c (Control—Copycat) 245.
Mr Puffington c (Falls of Clyde—Golden Milleress) 246.
Mr Smarty c (Rabirio—Golden Renny) (234).
Mr Snake c (Borealis—Rattlesnake) (7), 59, 85, 195.
Mr Teddy c (Epigram—Taurida) (278), 278, (278).
Mr What c (Grand Inquisitor—Duchess of Pedulas) (245), 245, 245, 258, 258, 265, 265.
Mr Wonderful c (Black Tarquin—Pale Ale) (255), 261.
Mr Worth c (Brightworthy—Mountain Mist) 278, 278.
Misti IV c (Medium—Mist) 110.
Mistigo c (Miralgo—Flowing Lava) 38, 63, (87).
Mistlethrush f (Tudor Minstrel—Mitrailleuse) 129, 175, 194, 199.
Mistral f (Whistling Wind—Miss Maverick) 14.
Mistress Gwynne f (Chanteur II—Daring Miss) 75.
Mistress Sophie f (Ridan—Sophistry) 9.
Mitsouko c (Ionian—Exultation) 31.
Moeda d'Ouro f (Moidore—Aprolon Light) 278.
Moidore's Token c (Moidore—Steel Token) 245.
Moira II f (Sicambre—Madrilene) 4.
Molar The, c (Paniko—Merry Mist) 249.
Molino c (Darius—Angelicus) (27), 36.
MONADE f (Klairon—Mormyre) (4).
Mona Louise f (Chamier—Black Books) 71, 107, 168.
Monamolin f (Golestan—Diana D) (14).
Monawin f (Hyperbole—Whinmoor) (162), (182), 227.
Monet c (Whistler—Gold Proof) 16, (27), 115, (211).
Mongolia II c (Mongo—Egyptian) 41.
Mongoose, The c (Supreme Court—Rikki Tikki) 89, (207).
Monkey Palm f (Royal Palm—Right Monkey) (217).
Monks Mead c (Welsh Abbot—Miss Honey) 275.
Monsieur Roc c (Roc du Diable—Bagdette) (99).
Monsieur Trois Etoiles c (Greek Star—Miss Maria) (276), 281.

Montana Girl f (Ballymoss—Lima) 121.
MONTAVAL c (Norseman—Ballynash) 119, (124).
Mont Blanc II c (Murghab—Tharsine) 88.
Monte Carlo f (Pandofell—Casino Lady) 221.
Montecello c (Charlottesville—Yola) 172, (209).
Montella f (Montaval—Fair Ranger) 83.
MONTERRICO c (Alycidon—Timid Tilly) 5, 81, 135, 148, (214).
Montesano c (Vilmorin—Hard and Sharp) 27.
Montevideo II c (Medium—Malonne) 248.
Moon Dancer f (Never Give In—Mamounia) 20.
Moonduster c (Pearl Orient—Flying Gem) 246, 262, 276.
Moon King c (King's Bench—Gulli Gulli) 181.
Moon River c (River Prince—Buried City) 274.
Moon Shot c (Gun Shot—Mamounia) 89.
Moonsprite f (Hard Sauce—Spellbound II) 181.
Moon Storm c (Preciptic—Sauroma) (169).
Moorings, The c (Parthia—Amorella) (60).
Morecambe c (Mossborough—Clara Barton) 183, (214), (220), 232, (232).
More Money f (Ennis—Paper Money) 211.
Moretons c (Harroway—Princess of Iran) 276, (276).
Morgan c (Blue Peter—Agin the Law) (60).
Morgan's Pride c (Marsolve—Torella) (217).
Morgat f (Vilmorin—Harfleur) (9), 167.
Moriarty c (Pardal—Loneliness) 5.
Morin f (Vilmorin—Irish Candy) 9.
Morning Star c (Arctic Star—Young Bebe) (7).
Morris Dancer c (County Delight—Polyanthus) 98, (123), 168, (186), 186.
Mossarco c (Mossborough—White Lodge) 60.
Moss Bank c (Mossborough—Gamesmistress) (114), 114, 277.
Mossy Bank c (Mossy Face—Virginia Waters) 91.
Moston Lane c (Gold Drill—Verdant) 261, 291.
Most Unusual c (Straight Deal—Smuggler's Cove) (285).
MOTHER GOOSE f (Escamillo—Folie Douce) 2, 4, (61), 93, 129, 139, (145).
Mountain Call c (Whistler—Cloudy Walk) 33, (79), (109), 122, 146, (150), 151.
Mountain King c (Grey Sovereign—Mountain Path) (224).
MOUNT ATHOS c (Sunny Way—Rosie Wings) 3, (120), (128), (176).
Mountcashel King c (King Hal—Alice Bithorn) (275).
Mount Melody c (Tudor Melody—Mountain Daisy) 37.
Moutiers c (Sicambre—Ballynash) 3.
Mowden Magic c (Guersant—Magic Lass) 143, 268.
Moyrath c (Fortina—Peg's Cottage) 261.
Mozart c (Alycidon—Candida) (8), 99.
Mozie Law c (Mossborough—Rosa Mundi) 270.
Much Obliged c (Cameron—May Sen) (256), (292).
Muckle John c (Supreme Court—Gay Florentine) (181).
Mugatpura c (Floribunda—Eglee) 203.
Muir c (Snow King—Metra) (286).
Mulbarton c (Domaha—Teazel II) (282).

Mulberry Harbour f (Sicambre—Open Warfare) (83).
Munch f (Mustang—Ate) (17), 31.
Murpep c (High Perch—Parknasilla) 234.
Murrayfield c (Match III—Erisca) (10), (31), 39, 46.
Musical Hall c (Manet—Soloneire) 35.
Mustard c (Mustang—School Days) 268.
Mustavon c (Mustang—Sunny Stream) (162), 193.
Must Fly c (Mustang—Lady Florrie) 84.
Mustwyn c (Off Key—Flying Past) 221.
My Aladdin c (Tourment—My Mascot) 1, 60, (74), 80.
My Audrey f (Pall Mall—Morsgail) (196).
My Baby c (Foroughi—Pucka-mem-Sahib) (258).
Mycropolis c (Acropolis—My Share) (222).
My Dream f (King of the Tudors—Summerlands) (11), 18.
My Enigma f (Klairon—Land of Hope) 14, 23, 61, 216.
My Goodness Me f (Abernant—Persian Dish) (43), 61, 115.
My Horace c (Never Say Die—My Goodness Me) 7.
My Kuda c (Chamier—Listowel) 64, 113, 127.
My Mary f (French Beige—Ma Marie) 93.
My Myosotis c (Infatuation—Scilla) (34), (85), 92, 103.
My Sett c (Hethersett—Lindylee) (21).
My Steel c (Persian Gulf—Fair Linda) 194.
Mystery c (Milesian—Paleo II) (36), 63, 193, 213.
Mystify f (Hyperion—Mystification) 2, 37, (75).
My Swanee c (Petition—Grey Rhythm) 96, (170), 270.
Mythic f (Pardal—Polar Myth) 75.
Mythical Return f (The Phoenix—Outspan) 20, 44.
My Timps c (Dante—Persian Mite) (182).

N

Nadir Shah c (Persian Gulf—Martial Air) 45, 111.
Nagaika f (Goyama—Naim) 2, (145).
NAGAMI c (Nimbus—Jennifer) 1, 3, 5, 46, 67, 84, (100).
Nahum c (Nahar—Jolie Jada) 170, 171, 223.
Nakalanta f (Nakamuro—Atalanta III) 206.
Nanavati f (Nearco—Dodoma) 115.
Nanda Devi f (Zarathustra—Nautch) (221).
Nanette f (Worden II—Claudette) 94.
Nardus c (Nimbus—Veronica Franchi) 45.
Narratus f (Narrator—Umid Ranee) (169), 169, (175).
Narrow Escape f (Narrator—Press Forward) (13), 35.
Nasram II c (Nasrullah—La Mirambule) (124).
National Gallery c (Immortality—Waterscape) 226.

Natterer f (Narrator—Simonia) 20.
Nautch Dance f (Nearula—Foxtrot) 197.
Naval Law c (The Solicitor—Sea Mist) 280.
Neanderthal c (Nearula—Marteline) 130.
Near Naples f (Nearula—Lady of Naples) (6).
Nearside c (Alcide—Neaera) (76), 195.
Nectar c (Honeyway—Necelia) 221.
Negotiator f (Narrator—Persuader) 20.
Negresco II c (Sica Boy—Folle Nuit) 140.
Nelcius c (Tenareze—Namagua) 100.
Nentego c (Never Say Die—Tideless) 46.
Neptune II c (Crafty Admiral—Timely Tune) 42.
Nereus c (Neron—Peaceful Match) (103), 125, 132, 193, (204).
Nerissa f (Court Martial—Mazarinade) (8), 23.
Nerium c (Pink Flower—Donna Lucia) 126.
Nerograph c (Neron—Heliographic) 164, (170), 187, (190).
Net c (Clarion III—Sans Tares) (68).
Never a Fear f (Never Say Die—Cherished) 4, (35), 39, 93.
Never Beat c (Never Say Die—Bride Elect) 76.
Never Red f (Romulus—Repartee) 118.
Never Say f (Never Say Die—Aliscia) (139).
Never Say No f (Never Say Die—Adolescence) 8.
NEVER TOO LATE II f (Never Say Die—Gloria Nicky) (2), (4), 149.
New Blood c (Narrator—Fragilite) 7, 99.
New Brig c (Solar Slipper—Foxella) 91, (199), 220.
Newbus c (Nimbus—Gameness) (13), 22, 28, 32, (73).
New Liskeard c (Cambremer—La Paix) (172), 180, (226).
New Move f (Umberto—New Moon) (13).
News Item c (Narrator—Patroness) 32.
New South Wales c (Abernant—Alor Star) 89, 105.
Newton c (Appian Bridge—View) 219.
New Warrior c (Nearula—Fire Song) 10.
New World c (The Cobbler—Enagh) (228).
Nicaria f (Nearco—Huntress) (71).
Nic Atkins c (Nicolaus—Bunty Atkins) 258, 265.
Nice Guy c (Democratic—Prudent Polly) 14, 25, (59), 218.
Nicholas Nickleby c (Niccolo Dell'Arca—Grande Corniche) 162, 168, (168), 174.
Nicky's Double c (Niccolo Dell'Arca—Daily Double) 68.
Nicois c (Nice Guy—Rosie V) 192, (200).
Nicolaus Silver c (Nicolaus—Rays of Montrose) (245), (259), (280), 292.
Nicomedus c (Nimbus—Angelus) 68, 92.
Night Appeal f (Petition—Luz Mala) (71).
Night Court f (Court Martial—Crepuscule) (101).
Night Lot c (Midsummer Night II—Ocelot) 200.
NIGHT OFF f (Narrator—Persuader) (2), (43), 107.
Night Patrol c (Welsh Abbot—Naval Patrol) 14.
Night Porter c (Alycidon—Pass Key) 130.
Night Signal f (Ennis—Battle Flare) 8.

Night Star c (Greek Star—Oliverie) (163).
Nikimas c (Ossian II—Honey Pie) 8.
NIKSAR c (Le Haar—Niskampe) (1), 3, 34, (59), 149.
Nimble Runner f (Narrator—Pharsalia) 21.
Nimbroke c (Nimbus—Expensive Hobby) 224.
Nimgem f (Nimbus—Geifang Gem) 21.
Nip Away c (Narrator—Wistful) 133.
Nireus c (Borealis—Chenille) 201.
No Argument c (Narrator—Persuader) 99, (179), 179, 216, 216.
Nobbutjust c (Happy Knight—Gold Chain) 288.
No Bidders c (Infatuation—Pambidian) 143.
Noble Record c (Chanteur II—Filco) 103.
NOBLESSE f (Mossborough—Duke's Delight) (4), (40), (49), (90).
Noblesse Oblige c (Gallant Man—Noblesse) 65.
No Comment c (Greek Star—dam said to be Tiger's Bay) 180, 185, 225, (225), 270.
No Complaint c (Greek Star—dam said to be Tiger's Bay) 149, 185, 231.
No Fiddling c (Guersant—Lady Godiva) (74), 174.
Noirmont Buoy c (Hornbeam—Brave Huntress) 223.
Nonchalance c (Le Lavandou—Careless Kate) 174.
NONE NICER f (Nearco—Phase) 4, 5, (27), 43, (93), 108, 128, (134).
Non Proven c (Court Martial—Adolescence) (179).
Noorose f (Court Harwell—Metition) (164), 170, 178.
No Restrictions c (Combat—Penelope Ann) 279.
Normand II (see Keystone Cop).
North Copse c (Taboun—Pamorpee) 73.
Norther c (Precipitation—Serenoa) 291.
Northern Deamon c (Eudaemon—Northern Beauty) 198, 215, (222).
Northern Highway c (Borealis—Celestial Way) 195.
Northern King c (King Hal—Castlecomer Beauty) 259, 262, 270.
Northmayne c (Borealis—Mistress Fair) 143.
Nortia f (Narrator—Maitrise) 4, (93), (129), 134, (208).
Norton Priory c (Quorum—Nixula) 162, (166), (179).
No Saint f (Narrator—Vellada) 4, 13, 31, (34), 108, 134, 145, 180, 226.
Nosey c (Big Game—Roman Justice) (289).
Nos Royalistes c (Nosca—Queen Vashti) 142.
Nostalgia c (Nosca—Tai-Koo) 283.
Not a Link c (Charles's Wain—Rough Crossing) 274, 280.
Nothing Higher c (Narrator—Verdura) 283.
Not So Cold c (Arctic Time—Rose Vale) (62), 87, 102.
Nougat f (Nimbus—Noisette) 101.
Nous Esperons c (Molvedo—Miss McTaffy) 194, 195.
Nova Gail f (Hill Gail—Nova Puppis) 9.
No Worry c (Royal Charger—Maid of Sind) (205), 205, 223.
Nubena f (Nuccio—Benane) 131.
Number One f (Never Say Die—Gambol) (40), 93.
Nun Neater f (Narrator—Pharsalia) 18.
Nunshoney f (Welsh Abbot—Miss Honey) (196).
Nymet Tracey c (Combat—Regal Ruby) 188.

O

Oakdale c (Limekiln—Vandra) 268.
Oakleigh Way c (Whiteway—Almholme) 279.
Oak Ridge c (Blue Peter—Rustic Bridge) 5, 28, 135.
Oakville c (Tantieme—Snow Shower) 73, 78, 81, (81), (85), 140, 140, 140, 148.
Oasis c (Seven Seas—Desert Sarah) 275.
Obadan c (Ridge Wood—June Ball) 225.
Oberon c (Fairey Fulmar—Nirvana) 247.
Ocean f (Petition—Ark Royal) (107).
Ocean Diamond c (Epaulette—Bluefin) 171.
Ocho Rios c (Niccolo Dell'Arca—Akimbo) 172, 191.
Oedipe c (Foxlight—Ondee de Fleurs) 270, 280.
Off Key c (Nearco—Key) 5, 172, (214).
Offspring c (Orthodox—Springwell) (6), (224).
Okaye c (Luminary—Fancy Inn) 167.
Old King Cole c (Arctic Prince—Briquette) 218.
Old Mull c (Tartan—Nodella) 247, 268.
Old Sugar c (Major Portion—Sweet Lola) 225.
Old Tom c (Relic—Sweetcake) (162), 166, 174, 181, (184), 218.
Olgiata f (Acropolis—Tesaura) (68), 90, 139, 145.
Oliver Hardy c (Hard Sauce—Gold Mirth) 27.
Olympia f (Fortina—Lady Lucinda) (290).
Olympius c (Polly's Jet—Greek Train) 30.
O'Malley Point c (Sea Lover—Ross' Pride) 245, 259, 259, 262.
Ombrello c (Botticelli—Brolly) 19.
Ominous c (Ommeyad—Peribanoo) 26.
Ommeyad c (Hyperion—Minaret) 78, 78, 100, (142).
Oncidium c (Alcide—Malcolmia) 5, 39, 60, (76), (92), (100), 124, 133, (148).
One and Only c (Infatuation—Particular) 187.
One Seven Seven c (Sadler's Wells—Biddy Early) 275.
Ongar c (Bois Roussel—Queen of Simla) (99).
ONLY FOR LIFE c (Chanteur II—Life Sentence) (1), 70, 72, 81, (111), 135.
On Probation f (King's Bench—Kantara) 181.
Onthejob (see Brown Owen).
On Your Mark c (Restless Wind—Superscope) (14).
Opaline II f (Hyperion—Martine) (43), 107.
Open Sky c (Court Martial—Per Ardua) 48.
Operatic Society c (Bewildered—Belle Bailey) 187, (187), 190, 206, (235).
Ophite c (French Beige—Rock Snake) 104.
Optimist c (Set Fair—Vivacious) 34, 132, 167.
Optimistic f (Never Say Die—Northern Hope) 199, 226, (229).
Orabella II f (Set Fair—Quest III) (61), 90, (94), 103, 121.
Orbit c (Ribot—Eyewash) 39.
Orchard Boy c (High Hat—Courtani) 198, 224.
Orchardist c (No Orchids—Partiality) (81), 91, (165), 169, 195, 229, 232.
Ordonez c (Matador—Starry Belle) 65.
Orinthia f (Ocarina—Orienne) 164, (178), 225.

Orleans f (Gilles de Retz—Beani) 97.
Ormolu II f (Tudor Jinks—Orsetta) 6.
Orofino f (Autumn Gold—Veille Fine) 118, (234).
Oroondates c (Botticelli—Orienne) 31, 35.
Orthology c (Orthodox—Historic's Field) 168.
Orthopaedic c (Orthodox—Rosa Walk) (168).
Orycida f (Alycidon—Orienne) (73).
Oscar Wilde c (Epigram—Quenington) 251, 255, 280.
Osier c (Mossborough—Willow Ann) 183, 190, 209, (235), 235.
Ostrya f (Hornbeam—Malcolmia) (108), 139.
Our Charger c (Royal Challenger—Ouranna) 65, 142.
Our Girl f (Supreme Court—Monarchia) 68.
Our Ruby f (Pardao—Pinchbeck) (93).
Out and About c (Cabrach—Lovely Out) (257).
Outcrop f (Rockefella—Chambiges) (134), (139), 197.
Out of Orbit c (Star Gazer—Last) 67.
Ovaltine c (Match III—Tina II) (127), 140, (220).
Owen Anthony c (Proud Chieftain—Oweninny) (168), 171, 193.
Owen Davis c (Owen Tudor—Septime) 206.
Owenello f (Owen Tudor—Uccello) 86, (118).
Owen Glendower c (Owen Tudor—Fair Ranger) 104, (133), 220.
Owenor c (Owen Tudor—Orseniga II) 206.
Owen's Image c (Owenstown—Brown Image) 234.
Owen's Sedge c (Owenstown—Lady Sedge) 246, 251, 258, (265), 272, 290.
Owl c (Our Babu—Night Sound) (168), 178, 200, 208.
Owlet f (Owen Tudor—Limicola) 75.
Oxo c (Bobsleigh—Patum) (245).
Oy-Oy c (Dignitary—Woofa) 198.

P

Pablo c (Court Martial—Snow Princess) (60).
Packed Home c (Cisco Kid—Ballinveney II) 245.
Padante f (St Paddy—Andante) 69.
Paddy Boy c (St Paddy—Nearaglia) 7.
Paddykin c (St Paddy—Kilifi) (202).
Paddy Me c (St Paddy—A.20) 106, (224).
PADDY'S POINT c (Mieuxce—Birthday Wood) 3, 41, 87, 117.
Paddy's Sister f (Ballyogan—Birthday Wood) (11), (28), (32).
Paddy's Song f (Chanteur II—Birthday Wood) 47, (83).
Padus f (Anwar—Cherry Way) 118.
PAIMPONT f (Chamossaire—Ballynash) 4.
Palatch f (Match III—Palazzoli) 2, 4, 67, 78, (90), 91, (134).

Palatina f (Palestine—Gainsborough Lady) 14, 17, (184).
Pale Sapphire f (Palestine—Kashmire Sapphire) 11.
Palesrullah f (Palestine—Chesa Veglia) (6).
Pal Fast c (Palestine—Flatter) 99.
Palinda f (Palestine—Clarinda) 43.
Palisander c (Palestine—Forest Law) 67.
Pallarco c (Pall Mall—Asti Spumante) (206).
PALL MALL c (Palestine—Malapert) (1), (12), 16, 28, 32, (73), (98), (98), 125, 193.
Pally c (Pall Mall—Mutual Consent) 98, 103, 171, 210.
Pally's Double c (Pall Mall—Mutual Consent) (178), 194.
Palmistry c (Premonition—Gipsy Girl) 45, 48.
Palm Springs f (Royal Palm—Bluefin) (20).
Palmural f (Palestine—Fresco) 29, 37.
Palm Way c (Royal Palm—Coupling) 16.
Palmy c (Pardal—Pampered) 181.
Palor c (Vatellor—Plaisante Amie) (85), 104.
Pals Passage c (Palestine—Judys Passage) 73, 166.
Palycidon c (Alycidon—Pyronia) 270.
Pamaloo (late Panella) f (Pall Mall—The Old Look) 166.
Pampalina f (Bairam II—Padus) 118, (131).
Pampered King c (Prince Chevalier—Netherton Maid) 180, 207.
Panastar c (Arctic Star—Panastrot) 18.
Pandofell c (Solar Slipper—Nadika) 72, 81, (91), (110), (140), (165), 235.
PANDORA BAY f (Pandofell—French Moss) 4, 83, (108).
Pandour c (Petition—Belle Sauvage) 31, (85), 210.
Panella (see Pamaloo).
Panga f (My Babu—Pyrethrum) 2, (17).
Panic c (Panaslipper—Rash Promise) 114.
Panisse c (Final Score—Koufre II) (286).
Panjandrum c (King of the Tudors—Memsahib) (195), 214.
Pannier c (Abernant—Creel) 80, 185.
Panpiper c (Whistler—La Melba) 87, (167).
Pan's Surprise c (Panaslipper—Goggles) 70, 89.
Panthera f (Supreme Court—La Montespan) 132.
Papaya II f (Tropique—Greensward) 149.
Papayer c (Persian Gulf—Seaway) 82, 99.
Paper Boy c (Persian Gulf—San Paulo) 206.
Pappageno's Cottage c (Pappageno II—Dawn Cottage) 245, (255), (255), (291), 291.
Papy (see Lost Property).
PARAGUANA f (Prince Chevalier—Tayeh) 2, 43.
Paramour c (Pardal—White Sapphire II) 170.
Parbury c (Pardal—Alconbury) 67, 81, (81), 95, (95), (110), 127, 127, 148.
Parcel Post c (Pardal—Solera) (225).
Pardallo II c (Pardal—Great Success) (110).
PARDAO c (Pardal—Three Weeks) 3, 5, 22, 31, 84, (92), (128), 135, (148).
Pardina f (Pardao—Winna) (197).
Pardon c (High Treason—Timely) 47.
Pardoner c (Pardal—Crayke) (168).

Pardonez-Moi f (Pollards—Mons Meg) 164, 170.
Paresa c (Pardal—Solesa) 1, 8, (70), 92.
Paridel c (Pardal—Tourinta) 143, (172).
Pari-Passu c (Pall Mall—Parthaon) 19.
Paris Princess f (Prince Chevalier—Viviparus) (36), (41), 108, 145.
Park Ranger c (Worden II—Royal Diana) (289).
Park Top f (Kalydon—Nellie Park) 84, (108), 133.
Parma c (Pardal—Marietta) 70.
Parnear c (Pardal—Nearosa) 169, 189.
Parquetta f (Pardal—Mighty Mo) (20).
Parrotia f (Krakatao—Precious Polly) (20).
Parthaon f (Acropolis—Chart Room) 104.
Parthenia f (Never Say Die—Fair Virgin) 45.
Parthenon c (Acropolis—Orangette) 206.
PARTHIA c (Persian Gulf—Lightning) (3), 5, 46, (80), (81), (85), (92), 100, 113, 148.
Parthian Glance f (Parthia—Tenacity) 93, (108), (134), (139).
Parthian Shot c (Parthia—Marteline) 80.
Parthica f (Parthia—Violetta III) 147.
Partholon c (Milesian—Paleo II) 30, (36), 49, (220).
Partner c (Nearco—Participation) 165.
Par Value c (Parthia—Parakeet) 207.
Passenger c (Star Signal—Preceptory) 98, (204), 205, (215).
Pas Seul c (Erin's Pride—Pas de Quatre) (251), 254, 264, (264), (264), (284), 284, 284, 292, (292).
Pastime Penny f (Fun Fair—Penny of the Jack) (66).
Path f (Pardal—Touch) 45.
Path of Glory c (Golden Cloud—Bishopscourt) 45.
Patient Constable f (Constable—Patience III) (211).
Patrick's Choice c (Tenerani—Pretty Girl II) 206.
Patroness f (Prince Chevalier—Verdura) 11.
Patron Saint c (Saint Crespin III—Lovely Lady II) 190.
PATTI f (Chanteur II—Eastern Fairy) 4, 5, 131.
Pattino c (Patton—Columstyria) 267.
Paul Jones c (Mossborough—Palais Glide) 116, 225, (235).
Paveh c (Tropique—Persian Shoe) 41, (63), (87), 117, (125).
Pavot c (Vimy—Nasturtium) (104).
Pawnbroker c (Straight Deal—Sparkling Gold) (246), 273.
Pay Out c (Krakatao—Fast Luck) 278.
Paysan c (Pardal—Good Humour) 161.
Peace f (Klairon—Sun Rose) (40).
Peacetown c (Phalorain—Maytown) 245, 288.
Pearlita f (Pearl Orient—Granterre) 274.
Pebble Ridge f (Big Game—Rose of Torridge) 20.
Pediment c (Acropolis—Pointe a Pitre) 287.
Pedlar's Fair c (Fun Fair—Highlea) 224.
Peeress f (Never Say Die—Bonneville) 66, 83.
Pellegrino f (Crepello—Greenbridge) 121, 129.
Pendlehill f (The Phoenix—Snowdonia) 122.

Pen-Emma f (Pindari—Cordelia Brown) 69.
Penhill c (Pinza—Phase) 60.
Penitent c (Persian Gulf—Nelia) 207.
Pennant c (Pampered King—Fainne Oir) 28, (73), (198), 222.
Penny Stall c (Ommeyad—Rockface) (31), 48, (59).
Pentathlon c (Nepenthe—Celanese) 279.
Penvulgo c (Vulgan—Pengo) 272.
Pepperpot c (Petition—Poetry) 67.
Perfect Friday f (Romulus—Sublime) 37.
Perfect Knight c (Narrator—Postscript) 130.
Perfect Mate c (Sunny Boy III—My Endeavour) 289.
Performance c (Petition—Palma Rose) 47.
Perhapsburg c (His Highness—Shady Reply) 231.
Peroxide f (Never Say Die—Feather Ball) (197).
Persian Barrier c (Persian Gulf—Coral Reef) 278.
Persian Empire c (Tamerlane—Persian Beauty) (45), 167, (287).
Persian Flag c (Tehran—High Beacon) (165), (212).
Persian Genius c (Persian Gulf—Caucasia) 80.
Persian Kim c (Persian Gulf—Little Honey) 187, (206).
Persian Lamb f (Rustam—Yalda) 8.
Persian Lancer c (Persian Gulf—Bay Lancer) 201, 212, (221), 232, (232).
Persian Road c (Persian Gulf—One for the Road) 180, (194), 199, (220), (221), (226).
Persian Signal c (Persian Gulf—Wood Alarm) 234, 265.
Persian Spark c (Darius—Scintillating) 63.
Persian War c (Persian Gulf—Warning) (263), (266), 269, (277), (283).
Persian Wheel f (Tulyar—Sun Chariot) 2, 75, 93, 107, 129.
Persian Wonder c (Persian Gulf—Lilac Belle) (85), 98, 103, 215.
Persister c (Proud Chieftain—Crisper) 35, 67.
Persuader f (Petition—Palma Rosa) 211.
Persuasive f (Tehran—Wheedler) 27.
Pertinacity f (Aggressor—Petty France) 75, 145.
Pertino c (Fortino II—Perfick) 24.
Peruvian Silk c (Counsel—Lima) 205.
Pervinca f (Relic—Woodflower) 2, 29, (166).
Peter Jones c (Mossborough—Palais Glide) (72).
Peterman c (Blue Peter—Marie Elizabeth) 111.
Peter Piper c (Faubourg II—Bacchanalia) 175, 183, (199), 212, 213, 225.
Peter Rock c (Blue Peter—Moon Rocket) 282.
Petersfield c (Preciptic—Anita II) 167.
Petigold f (Petition—Footbridge) 230.
PETINGO c (Petition—Alcazar) 1, (28), (42), (67), (105), (125), 137.
PETITE ETOILE f (Petition—Star of Iran) (2), (4), 23, (77), (100), (100), (123), 124, (125), (134), 144, (149), (167).
PETITE GINA f (Petition—Anxious Lady) 2, 101.
Petite Marmite f (Babur—Madrilene) 147, 197.
Petite Path f (Sovereign Path—Petite Lass) (11), 217, (230).
Petrone c (Prince Taj—Wild Miss) 110.
Petronella f (Petition—Danse d'Espoir) 40.

Petros c (Petition—Queen's Rhapsody) (184), 215, (218).
Petticoat Pocket f (Devancer—Rubber Neck) 226.
Petty Cash f (Pindari—Petigold) 174, (197).
Petty France f (Alycidon—Petticoat Lane) 221.
Pettyless c (Petition—Tideless) 222.
Phaethusa f (Chanteur II—Phaetusa) 221.
Phantom Star f (Persian Gulf—Neberna) 134.
Pheberion c (Phebus—Colleen's Tote) 255, 280.
Pheidippides c (Court Martial—Queen Eleanor) (28), 73, 99, 193, 218, 227.
Philanderer c (Pampered King—Awfully Jolly) (77), 84, (198), 207.
Philemon c (Never Say Die—Winged Foot) (30), 91, 127, 142, 189, 191, (201), (226).
Philistine c (Palestine—Gay Polly) 180.
Phoenix Star c (The Phoenix—Villette) 60.
PHOTO FLASH f (Match III—Picture Light) 2, (20), 33, 167.
PIA f (Darius—Peseta II) 2, (4), (17), (29), 43, 90, (139).
Piaco c (Pandofell—Pink Parrot) 95, 127, (140), (199).
Piccadilly c (Pall Mall—Catchmenot) 10, 103, 132, 167.
Picfort c (Fort de France—Piccadilly) 100.
Pick Me Up c (Pindari—Desirous) (169), 221, 270.
Picture Light f (Court Martial—Queen of Light) 61, 101, (132).
Picture Palace f (Princely Gift—Palais Glide) 170, 187.
Pieces of Eight c (Relic—Baby Doll) 64, 102, (119), 141, (149).
Pierian Springs c (Dante—Shining Hour) 283.
Piero f (Hard Sauce—Bagatelle) 138, 200.
Pike's Fancy c (The Admiral—Dawn Fancy) 285.
Pilgrims Journey c (High Treason—A.20) 79.
Pilino c (Pinza—Libera Nos) 191.
Pillar of Fire f (Luminary—Bridle Way) 9.
Pillock's Green c (Prince Chevalier—Princess Beautiful) (266), 285.
Pinched c (Pinza—The Accused) 22, (24), 28, (39), 67, (99).
PINDARI c (Pinza—Sun Chariot) 5, (31), 39, (67), (111), (135).
Pindaric c (Pinza—Festoon) 78, 80, (92).
Pindarique c (Pindari—La Valteline) 13.
Pinerolo c (Pinza—Setello) 82.
Pinhurst c (Pinza—Little Danehurst) 188.
Pinicola c (Pinza—Golden Pheasant) (123), 133.
Pink Gem f (Crepello—Topaz) (83), 90, 139.
Pinturischio c (Pinza—Natalina da Murano) 1, (68).
Pin Wheel f (Pinza—Cyclorama) (37).
Pinzon c (Pinza—Sweet One) 67, 78, (81), 91, 111, 120.
Piona f (Precipitation—Kings Well) 31.
Pioneer Spirit c (Colonist II—Elfin Princess) 280.
Pipaway c (Solonaway—Orange Pippin) 37.
PIPE OF PEACE c (Supreme Court—Red Briar) 1, 3, (70), 98, 105, (128).
Piperton c (Border Legend—Killibeg) (273).
Piping Rock c (Aureole—Sundry) 89, 105, 125.
Pippykin c (Escamillo—Relizane) 260, 260.
Pirate King c (Prince Chevalier—Netherton Maid) 113, 119.

Plaudit c (Petition—Concubine) (6).
Play High c (Tudor Melody—Double Cloud) (70).
Playlord c (Lord of Verona—Playwell) 285.
Plea in Bar c (Foroughi—Bartilast) 272.
Pleasure Cruise f (Blue Peter—Chaste and Fair) 83.
Pleiades c (Nearco—Solar System) 73.
Plotina f (Hugh Lupus—Sibell) 97, 108.
Pluit c (Preciptic—Doll Dance) (177), 209, 235.
Plummers Plain c (Jim Newcombe—Air Cover) 281, 286, (292).
Plump f (Pinza—Fatima) (75).
Plymouth Sound f (Rockefella—Witness) 26, 101.
Poaching c (Owen Tudor—Game Book) (187).
Poet and Peasant c (Pinza—Sylphide) 19.
Poetic Licence c (Dante—Pretexte) 91, 104, 169, 183, 199, (226).
Pointsman c (Control—Lady Fleche) 254, 292.
Polar Flight c (Iceberg II—More Pure) (255), (256), 284.
Polar Gold c (Arctic Storm—Pal an Oir) 15, 25, 30, 65.
Polaris Missile f (Woodcut—Air Wedding) (274).
Polar Legend c (Hard Sauce—Polar Myth) 99.
Polar Lodge (see Chief Barker).
Polar Venture c (Venture VII—Polar Way) 48.
Polar Way f (Borealis—Petticoat Lane) 180, 188, 200, 229.
Polish Warrior c (Aggressor—Polar Way) (235).
Polistina f (Acropolis—Altina) 173, 228.
Polly Toogood f (Darius—Barchester) 14.
Polmak c (Mossborough—Agamma) (194), 207.
Polo c (Ambiorix II—Old Game) (99).
Polonius c (Epigram—Charmain) 255.
Polybius f (Mr Busher—Arctic Weather) 79.
Polyfoto c (Polic—Brabantia) 79, (126), (136).
Polyktor c (Panaslipper—Lady into Fox) 88, 104.
Polymint c (Ossian II—Lilis) (190), 190, 208, (210).
Pomme de Guerre c (War Lord—French Fruit) 282, 293, 293.
Pontifex c (Darius—Cheville) (41).
Pontin-Go c (Roi de Navarre II—Intuition) 245, 261, (261).
Pontoeuvre c (Sunny Boy III—Jnana) 274.
Pony Express c (Mustang—Welsh Bay) 285.
Popham Down c (Combat—Penelope Ann) (291).
Poplin f (Vilmorin—Copper Knob) 24.
Popular Prince c (Prince Chevalier—Verdura) 203.
Porcha c (Royal Palm—Golden Pacha) 215.
Porky c (Infatuation—Dollar Crisis) (183), 190, 207, 225, 225.
Port Corsair c (Chamossaire—Aleria) 183, 207.
Port Merion c (Abernant—Fresco) 109, 122, (167).
Porto Bello c (Floribunda—Street Song) (8), (12), 18, 115.
Portofino c (Premonition—Lusignan) 3, (88).
Port Soderick f (King's Bench—Spit of Alys) 6.
Potier c (Major Portion—Morgat) 19, 31, 67, (211).

Pouding c (Nosca—La Pougue) (262).
Pouncer, The c (Luminary—Pounce) (166).
POUPONNE f (Owen Tudor or Prince Chevalier—Ela Tengam) 4, 129.
POURPARLER f (Hugh Lupus—Review) (2), (18), (29), 61, 107.
Powder Rock c (Rockefella—Cosmetic) 164, 190.
Prado c (Sicambre—Princess Charming) 80.
Praetorian c (Precipitation—Tesoro) 130.
Prairie Emblem c (Mustang—Coolshamrock) 184, 217.
Praise (see King Frank).
Precious Gem c (Pearl Orient—Paradise) 293.
Precious Heather c (Golden Cloud—Heather Thatcher) 162, (168).
Precious Hoard c (Midas—Precious Rose) 25, 30, 41.
Preclusion c (Preciptic—Leonina) (185).
Predicament f (Alcide—Dilemma) 134, 139, (145), 147.
Predominate c (Preciptic—Garryhinch) (114), 127, (127), 183, (212), (212), (212), 232, 232, 270.
Prefairy c (Precipitation—Fairyairy) 165, 169, 189.
Prescience c (Le Sage—Preza) 41.
PRESENT II c (Princely Gift—Djebe) 1.
Presentiment c (Persian Gulf—Trial Ground) (68).
Presto c (Primate—Cresting) (7).
PRETENDRE c (Doutelle—Limicola) 1, 3, 5, (46), 49, (74), (111), 119.
Pretentious c (Pinza—Verdura) 60, 73.
Pretty Asset f (Galivanter—Barathea) 101.
Pretty Cage f (Cagire II—Tudor Fair) 29.
Pretty Swift f (Petition—Fragilite) 20.
Pretty Wit f (King's Bench—Arquebuse) 97.
Prevale c (Tenerani—Meadow Grass) 26.
Priddy Fair f (Preciptic—Campanette) 97.
Priddy Maid f (Acropolis—Priddy Fair) 213.
Prilliard c (Preciptic—Bright Set) 282.
Primary f (Petition—Hymette) 7.
Prime Boy c (Denturius—Romosa) 44.
Prime Mover c (Prince Chevalier—Palais Glide) (206).
Primera c (My Babu—Pirette) (84), 84, (116), 116, 120, (120), (120), 132, 142, (220).
Primus c (Nimbus—Priceless) (70).
Prince Barle c (Kingsway—Lady Barle) 81.
Prince Blarney c (Nearula—Eyewash) (286).
Prince Chamier c (Chamier—Princess Janique) 117.
Prince d'Amour c (Tantieme—Princess d'Amour) 3.
Prince de Galles c (Welsh Abbot—Vauchellor) 47.
Princeful c (Devon Prince—Verite) 251, 275.
Prince Hansel c (The Phoenix—Saucy Wilhelmina) 106, (140), 148, (194).
Princelone c (Princely Gift—Prelone) (103), (174).
Princely Portion c (Prince Bio—Participation) 226.
Princely Strath c (Princely Gift—Royal Strath) 12.
Prince Midge c (Prince Chevalier—Lady Midge) (98).
Prince Moon c (Prince Bio—Port Luna) 170, 170.

Puddle Jumper c (Iceberg II—That's It) 282.
Pugnacity f (Pampered King—Ballynulta) 6, (19), (29), 77, (121), (126).
Punch Bowl Hotel c (Jock Scot—Mysticus) 291.
Pundit c (Hindostan—Senatrix) (192), 210, (283).
Pure Folly f (Pandofell—Fair Folly) 75.
Purple Silk c (Flush Royal—Pure Silk) 245, 292.
Pushful c (Petition—Press Forward) (21), (49), 76, 92.
P.X. c (Annatom—Katsu) 279.
Pytchley Princess f (Privy Councillor—Fairy Princess) (75).

Q

Q.C. c (Petition—Ma Marie) (194), 223.
Quadruple c (Palestine—Algebra) (181).
Quarterings f (Princely Gift—Fouri) 145.
Quartette c (Quorum—Touraileen) (172), 199, (214), 220.
Quaver f (Tudor Minstrel—Queen of Hearts) 20.
Queen Anne's Lace f (Mossborough—Marie Therese) 4.
Queen of Helena f (Saint Crespin III—Helen Rosa) 24, 35.
Queen of the Roses f (King of the Tudors—Warfare) 11.
Queensberry f (Grey Sovereign—Blackberry) 2, 11, (23), (29), (43), 44, (61).
Queen's Guide f (Guide—Regal Coin) 293.
Queens Hussar c (March Past—Jojo) 14, 79, (98), 106, (125), 132.
Queens Lane f (Tamerlane—Two Blues) 227.
Queens Messenger c (Babur—Ballyogan Queen) 231.
Queen's Tankard c (Tantieme—Queenpot) 70.
Que Guapo c (Quorum—Miss Pepita) (165), 172.
Quelle Chance c (Flush Royal—Quellenize) 277, 277.
Quentin c (Quorum—Romosa) 14, 22.
Quick Approach c (King's Approach—Flotation) 253, 286.
Quick Decision c (Precipitation—Last Judgement) (195).
Quick Thought c (Quorum—Pleasure) 60.
Quince c (Polly's Jet—Quincey) 6.
Quinita f (Quorum—Minita) 17.
Quintillian c (Sicambre—Quarterdeck) (65), 82.
Quintin Bay c (Copernicus—dam by Oojah) 245.
Quisling c (High Treason—Lake Lavandou) 25, 109, 132.
Quita II f (Lavandin—Eos) (93), 107.
Quita Que c (Mustang—Selection) (273), 273, 277, (286), (286).
QUORUM c (Vilmorin—Akimbo) 1, 103, (106), 123, (125), (167), 182.
Quy c (Midsummer Night II—Quenilda) 59, 79, 146, 174, (179), (219).

R

Rabbi, The c (Palestine—Miss Minx) 77, 185, (190).
Raccolto c (Como—Harvest Festival) 45, 178, 180, 185, (194).
Rachel f (Tudor Minstrel—Par Avion) (129), 197.
Racing Demon c (Sound Track—Creepy Crawley) 21.
Rackham c (Ratification—Amberley) (247), (268).
Radbrook c (Ballymoss—Alare) 36, (64).
Radiation c (Aureole—Hot Water) 76.
Radiopye f (Bright News—Silversol) 216.
Raes Gill c (Preciptic—Green Tipperary) 289.
Ragazzo c (Macherio—Mill Baby) 41, (135).
Raggoty Ann f (Bright News—Costume) 172.
Ragtime c (Tudor Melody—Pillowfight) (16), (22), 28, 42, 132.
RAGUSA c (Ribot—Fantan II) 3, (5), 85, (117), (119), (124), (135).
Rainbeam c (Raincheck—Beaming) 279.
Rainbow Battle f (Raincheck—Duel in the Sun) 245, 291.
Rain Coat c (Nimbus—Prudence III) 13.
Rainstorm c (Premonition—Lightning) 189, (229).
Raise You Ten c (Tehran—Visor) (76), 89, (91), 127, (127), (140), 140.
Rally c (Big Game—Mitrailleuse) (114).
Ram Lamb c (Niccolo Dell'Arca—Gentilezza) 99.
Rampant c (Petition—Doreuse) 109, 122.
Ranchiquito c (Foxlight—Rancune) 127.
Rangong c (Right Royal V—Crepina) 89.
Ranunculus f (Grey Sovereign—Astrentia) 15.
Rapanni c (Rapace—Miana) 183, 183, (207), 235.
Rapin c (Cobalt II—Bali) 48.
Rare Jewel c (Princely Gift—Royal Pageant) 87.
Rascasse c (Sicambre—Golden Sprat) 223.
Rathronan c (War Lord—Keep Smiling) 272.
Rave f (Court Martial—Raven Locks) 17.
Ravel c (Relic—Reel In) 80, 199.
Ravencroft c (Kolper—Holne Pippin) (272).
Raw Silk c (Shantung—Stop Your Tickling) 185.
Raybelle f (Ossian II—Twentyfive Percent) 182, (224).
Raymonda f (Primera—Pirouette) (71).
Reactor c (Blue Peter—Dornoch) 26, 82.
Rebel Prince c (Aggressor—Bonnie Flora) 26, 35.
Rebirth c (Never Say Die—Papoose) 130.
Reckless f (Prince Chevalier—Dasher) 101, (138).
Red Alligator c (Magic Red—Miss Alligator) 245, (245).
Red Bar c (King's Bench—Red Linnet) (178).
Red Dragon c (Owen Tudor—Limicola) 104, (190), (214), (229).
Red Gauntlet c (Nearula—Red Shoes) 18, 70, (106).
Red Hackle c (Jock Scot—Cerise) 285.
Red Letter c (Fair Copy—Exaltation) (164), 164, (173), (174), (200).
Red Menace f (Flamenco—Pucka Falloch) 260.

Redoubt c (Court Martial—Ambiguity) 116, 164, 194.
Red Quill f (Doutelle—Caperer) 101.
Red Rondo c (Rondo II—Another Beauty) 256, 272.
Red Rose Prince c (Henry the Seventh—Nerissa) 18.
Red Ross c (Preciptic—Chance's School) 87.
Red Rumour c (Hail to Reason—Red Sea) 48, 214.
Red Slipper c (Trouville—Ruby Slipper) 132, (163), (186), (203), (231).
Red Sovereign c (Grey Sovereign—Southwater Red) 109.
Red Spice c (Red God—Turkish Spice) 15.
Red Swan c (Red God—Cygnet) 202, 222.
Red Taffy c (Red God—Welsh Crest) 25.
Red Tears c (Palestine—Huntress) (164), (185), 198, (270).
Red Tide c (County Delight—Red Sea) (288).
Red Urchin c (Porphyros—Sea Flame) 206.
Red Vagabonde c (Red God—La Vagabonde) 119.
Red Vale c (Court Nez—Red Spring) (274).
Reet Lass f (Right Boy—Cheb) (23), (29).
Refined f (Abadan—Dolly's Brae) 61, 66, (126), (228).
Reform c (Pall Mall—Country House) 70, (99), (105), (125), 137, (144), (149).
Regal Cloud f (Golden Cloud—Regal Carriage) 66.
Regality f (Right Royal V—Be Careful) 66.
Regal John c (John Moore—Regal Chain) (248).
Regal Light c (Sovereign Path—Tudor Gleam) 184, (193).
Regal Mist c (Flush Royal—Sywell Haze) 282.
Regal Pink f (Red God—Welsh Crest) (23).
Regal Rock c (Rock Star—Royal Pact) 143.
Regal Splendour c (Dante—Bessbrook) 251.
Regal Token c (Prince Richard—Gift Token) 275.
Regal Wine c (Roi d'Egypte—Honey Wine) 259.
Regiment, The c (Tamerlane—Babushka) 34.
Regret c (Milesian—Answer Me) 234.
Rehearsed c (Aggressor—Diction) (31), 39, 113, (143), (164), 178.
Reita f (Gilles de Retz—Hindu Express) (188).
Release f (Court Martial—Salka) 2, 43, 75, (101), 144, 205.
Relentless c (Ratification—Boudicca) 67.
Relian c (Relic—My Jean) 230.
RELKO c (Tanerko—Relance III) (3), (100), 117.
Remainder c (Relic—Vermeil) (173).
Remand c (Alcide—Admonish) 3, (31), (39), (82).
Renardier c (Chamossaire—Better) (183).
Repetition f (Petition—Full Speed) 180.
Reprieved c (pedigree unknown) (251).
Reproduction c (Last of the Dandies—Bulgaden Ivy) (260), (267).
Rescind c (Darius—Scintillating) 70, 203.
Resilience II f (Parthia—Eternal Spring) 83, 94, (97), (121), (222).
Resistance c (Pardal—Odette) (223).
Resolved c (Ratification—Disdainful) 218.
Restaurant c (Guersant—Dark Caprice) 132.

Restoration c (Persian Gulf—Hypericum) 5, 78, (111), 113, 119.
Resurge f (Blue Peter—Resurgam) 71.
Retour de Flamme c (Samaritain—Reine du Bearn) 277.
Retrial c (Court Martial—Princesse Rose II) (193).
Reubens c (Panaslipper—Peribanoo) (36), 62, (143).
Rexequus c (King of the Tudors—Under Canvas) 98, 103, (233).
Reynard's Heir c (Reynard Volant—Pride of Skilligalee) 290, 291.
Rhinelander c (Tamerlane—Blaue Nelke) 36.
Rhine Maiden f (Crepello—Lorelei) 195.
Rhythmic c (Maharaj Kumar—Metric) (230).
Rhythmic Light c (Persian Gulf—Golden Twilight) 98, 194, 194, (207).
RIBERO c (Ribot—Libra) (5), 89, 111, (117).
Ribes f (Ribot—Big Berry) 101.
Ribobo c (Ribot—Naseema) 279.
Riboccare c (Ribot—Easy Eight) 5, (13), 39, 49, 135, (148), 148.
RIBOCCO c (Ribot—Libra) 3, (5), 32, (49), 85, (117), 124.
Ribofilio c (Ribot—Island Creek) (13), (32), (46).
Rich and Rare f (Rockefella—Palmy Days) (14), (43), (47).
Richard of Bordeaux c (Royal Hamlet—Diana D) (246), 276, (276).
Richard's Jubilee c (Richard Louis—Hot Day) 271.
Richardstown c (Starmond—Magic Bright) 265.
Richmond c (Royal Palm—Tekka) (30), 36, (41), 63.
Richmond Fair c (Psidium—Martha) (116).
Ricky Joe c (Chanteur II—Tenebel) 34.
Rift, The c (Major Portion—Ol Arabel) 8, 21.
Right Boy c (Impeccable—Happy Ogan) (109), (109), (115), (122), (122), (126), (126),
    136, (136), (136), 228.
Right Guy c (Guersant—Rightful) 181.
Right Honourable Gentleman c (Silnet—Old England) 74.
Right Noble c (Right Royal V—Princess Marie) 3, 41, (80).
Right of the Line f (King's Troop—Good Line) 43.
Right of Way c (Honeyway—Magnificent) 123, (192).
Right Royal V c (Owen Tudor—Bastia) (124).
Right Strath c (Right Boy—Royal Strath) (25), (126).
Right Tack c (Hard Tack—Polly Macaw) (37), (42).
Right Wheel c (Right Royal V—Persian Wheel) 221.
Right Winger c (Right Boy—Dittany) 204.
Rigvada c (My Babu—Nile Bird) 170.
Rimark f (Ribot—Marker) (66), (118).
Ringer, The c (Water Serpent—Mantilla Vulgan) (260), 267.
Rins of Clyde c (Grey Sovereign—River Clyde) 167, 196.
Rio Santo c (Guersant—Ria Geno) 70.
Riot Act c (Ribot—Rave Notice) (162), 205.
Rip, The c (Manicou—Easy Virtue) 250, 256.
Rising Wings f (The Phoenix—Skylarking) 66.
Risky c (Elopement—Gold Sandal) 207, 263, 285.
Ritudyr c (King of the Tudors—Scamal Fanach) 25, 87, 146.
Ritz, The c (Gilles de Retz—Portray) 42.

River Chanter c (Chanteur II—River Test) 7, (46), 88.
Riverdare c (Nearula—Showbird) 105.
River Line c (Court Martial—Tributary) 218, 227.
Riversdale c (Eastern Venture—Turnberry) 276.
River Whistle c (Whistler—Boat Race) (143).
Roaming Star c (Star Gazer—Romaway) 173.
Roan Rocket c (Buisson Ardent—Farandole II) 98, (105), 119, (125), 125, (132).
Roaring Twenties c (Roaring Forties—Secret Pact) (285).
Robber Baron c (Rockefella—Ksarina) 269.
Roborough c (Devonian—Boro's Pet) 291.
Robson's Choice c (Set Fair—Arab Lady) 162, 174, 193, (210).
Rockamour c (Amour Drake—Rocket Flight) 164.
ROCKAVON c (Rockefella—Cosmetic) (1), 124.
Rock House Bridge c (Goldwell—Kraytion) 275.
Rock's Cross c (Foroughi—Pucka-mem-Sahib) (267).
Rock Tan c (Rockefella—Tanya) 68.
Rocky Royale (late Joe Winders) c (Rockefella—Narcisse) 170, (178), 192, (210).
Roddy Owen c (Owenstown—Desla's Star) 254, 258, (265), (284).
Roll Away c (Merry Boy—Snow Cloud) 207.
Rolled Gold c (Fair Copy—Gold Lily) (179).
Rolling Rapture c (Rolling On—Divinity) 286.
Roman Empire c (Nearco—Solanum) 81.
Roman Folly c (Papist—Foliday) 265.
Roman Sand c (Sandjar—Roman Fleet) 194, (206).
Roman Scandal c (Tenerani—Alimony) (180), 207, 279.
Romantic c (Princely Gift—Big Romance) 12, (16), (22), 32, 42.
Romantica f (Never Say Die—Vertige) 4, 129, 139, (145).
Roman Vale c (Watling Street—Vale of Stenigot) (217).
Roman Wedding c (Orsini—Marriage Day) 192.
Romany Fair (see Lucky White Heather).
Rome c (Red God—Fylgia) 63, 98, (174).
Romp Home f (Chanteur II—Rutherford Bridge) (169), 221.
Romsey f (Precipitation—River Test) 31.
ROMULUS c (Ribot—Arietta) 1, 32, (70), 98, (125), (132), (144).
Ron c (Vilmoray—Vigorous Eva) 211.
Ronan c (Bowsprit—Nas na Riogh) 273.
Rondetto c (Caporetto—Roundandround) (250), (262), 264, (272), 291.
Rondino c (Rondo—Louise of Rheims) 255.
Rosador c (Chanteur II—Rose Bay Willow) 287, 287.
ROSALBA f (Court Martial—Rose Coral) 2, (27), 43, (44), (71), (107), 122, (144).
Rosaura f (Court Martial—Belle of All) (9).
Rose Argent c (Owen Tudor—Zepherin) 76, 168, 190.
Rose d'Or f (Court Harwell—Phoney Gold) 30, 36.
Rose Knight c (Anwar—Young Rose) 168.
Rosenkavalier c (Prince Chevalier—Nizou) 276.
ROSE OF MEDINA f (Never Say Die—Minaret) 2, 4, 11, (75), 129, (145).
Rose of Mooncoin f (Ratification—Ablaze) 2.
Rose Park c (Pactolus—Primulas) 284.

Rose Rock f (Court Harwell—Rockabye Baby) 75.
ROSE ROYALE II f (Prince Bio—Rose of Yeroda) (2), 4, 75, (149).
Rose's Pact f (Pactolus—Rose of Rosetown) 255, 274.
Rose's Quarter c (Quarteroon—Princess Rose) (286).
Rosie's Cousin c (Moidore—Light Princess) 293, 293.
Rosie Wings f (Telegram II—Wynway) (177).
Ros Rock c (Rockefella—Fair Rosamond) (167), 181, (192).
Ross Sea c (Arctic Star—Chloris II) 65, 235, 270.
Rosyth c (Admiral's Walk—Rossenhall) (263), (263), 263.
Rothesay c (Falls of Clyde—Kiss Me Kate) 6.
Roughan c (Snow King—Flaming Bird) (288), (288).
Roughlyn c (Ballylinan—Sun Garden) (115), (219).
Rough Tweed c (Tartan—Rippling Wave) 250, 260, (262), 275.
Round Trip f (Grey Sovereign—Spinetta) (17).
Rover c (Signal Box—Nubis) 6.
Rowland Ward c (Big Game—Model) 178, (210).
Roxburgh c (Mossborough—Brighton Rock) 188, (189), (206), 223, 287.
Royal Agreement f (Ratification—Princesse Plucky) 103.
Royal Approach c (King's Approach—Flotation) 286.
Royal Assent c (King's Approach—Lady Allow) 290.
Royal Avenue c (Royal Palm—Wayfarer) (72), 77, 87, 100, (102), 120, 123, 124.
Royal Cavalier c (Prince Chevalier—Rose of Tudor) (161).
Royal Chant c (Fury Royal—Chanlana) 27.
Royal Chief c (Prince Chevalier—Chinese Cracker) (164), 178, 178, 185, 210.
ROYAL CYPHER f (Royal Palm—Star Telegrams) 2.
ROYAL DANSEUSE f (Prince Chevalier—Star Dancer) 2, (66), (86), 118.
Royal Desire c (Royal Living—Faint Hope) (47).
Royal Display f (Right Royal V—Short Sentence) 118.
Royal Falcon c (St Paddy—Indian Game) 77, (187).
Royal Flirt f (Above Suspicion—Saucy Nell) 34, (97).
Royal Garden c (Princely Gift—Radiant Rose II) 15, 25.
Royal Glen c (Nimbus—Glen Tromie) 180.
Royalgo c (Aureole—Laura) (26), 73, 185, 202.
Royal Heiress f (Royal Palm—Hiera II) 8.
Royal Highway c (Straight Deal—Queens Highway) 117, 133, (142), 148.
Royal Indiscretion f (Princely Gift—Affair) (23).
Royal Jenny f (Flush Royal—Dens Jenny) 263.
Royal Jester c (King's Bench—Mingled Mirth) 182, 216.
Royal Justice f (Supreme Court—Sun Princess) 17.
Royal Lark c (King's Caprice—dam by Constant Sol) 282, 282.
Royal Magician c (Royal Hamlet—Magic Harp) 208.
Royal Painter c (Faubourg II—Royal Palette) (181), 208.
ROYAL PALACE c (Ballymoss—Crystal Palace) (1), (3), (26), (39), (77), (100), (112), (119), (124), 149.
Royal Phoebe f (Phebus—Royal Croft) (293), 293, 293, 293.
Royal Ridge c (Vimy—Queenpot) 161, (165).
Royal Rocket c (Sovereign Path—Farandole II) 128.
Royal Rubicon c (Royal Palm—Demarcation) 116, 120, 177, 213, 223.

Royal Ruse c (Prince Chevalier—Pretexte) 288, 288.
Royal Saint f (Saint Crespin III—Bleu Azur) (71), 93, 107.
Royal St George c (Sica Boy—Snow Shower) (188).
Royal Sanction c (Ratification—Fairy Princess) (187), (188), (287).
Royal Scot c (Palestine—Turkish Castle) 15.
Royal Showband (late Senior Steward) c (Mossborough—Madame Pompadour) 199.
Royal Smoke c (Royal Serenade—Hickery Smoke) 10.
Royal Sword c (Right Royal V—The Blonde) 3, 64.
Royalties f (Dickens—Enticement) 97.
Royalty Cash f (Rustam—Purple Queen) 6.
Royal Whistler f (Whistler—Royal Strath) 27.
Royal Yacht c (Grey Sovereign—Rolling Barge) (217).
Royaumont c (Prince Bio—Montenica) 3.
Ruantallan c (Ribot—Tarbert Bay) 130, 148, (229).
Ruby Laser f (Red God—Dilly Dilly) (79).
Ruby's Boy c (Nomellini—Persian Ruby) 195.
RUBY'S PRINCESS f (Fidalgo—Persian Ruby) 4, 17, 19.
R.U.C.D. f (Clever Lad—Southernmore) 282.
Rue de Romance c (Watling Street—Chaste and Fair) (190), (190).
Ruffian c (High Treason—Fair Ranger) 132.
Rugosa c (Nearco—Tante Rose) (191).
RUNNING BLUE f (Blue Peter—Run Honey) 2, 10, (93), 107, (167).
Running Rock c (Royal Challenger—Ouranna) 247.
Running Words c (Worden II—Run Honey) 7.
Runnymede c (Petition—Dutch Clover) (79), 136.
Rupununi c (Grand Inquisitor—Lisnisky Tigress) (248), (251), 264.
Rusheen f (The Solicitor—Luggeen) 15.
Rustana f (Rustam—Brunetta) 17.
Rutherfords c (Doubtless II—Soldado Maid) 245, 259, (267).
Ruthin f (Abernant—Liberty) (9), 23.
RUYSDAEL II c (Right Royal V—Rossellina) 5.
Ryecroft c (Golden Cloud—Rigolade) (184).
Rye Light c (Lighthouse II—Ryecrop) 271.

S

Sabaria c (Lighthouse II—Pannonia) 245, (274).
Sable Skinflint c (Arctic Star—Junita) (223).
Sabot c (Stardust—Lower Abbey) 226.
Sabot d'Or f (Princely Gift—Amber Slipper) 30.
Sacarole c (Preciptic—Melitensis) (165), 169.
Safety Match c (Match III—Fiji) (76).
Saffron Tartan c (Tartan—Kellsboro' Witch) (254), (270), 277, (284).

Sagacity c (Le Sage—Double Charm) 68, 81, (91), 104, 110, 120, (127), (133), 140, 140.
Sage Rose f (Fortina II—Sageway) 197.
Sahib c (Sir Gaylord—Hideout) 36.
Sail Aniar f (Nearco—Staffa) 118, 131.
St Alphage c (Red God—Sally Dean) 126.
Saint Anne f (Aureole—Ma Soeur Anne) 4, 93.
St Antonius c (Aureole—Biotte) 68.
St Cecilia f (Milesian—Palestrina) 11.
St Chad c (St Paddy—Caerphilly) 44, (106), (132), (137), 144, 167, (188).
Saint Christopher c (Aureole—Aunt Clara) 38.
Saint Crespin III c (Aureole—Neocracy) 3, (37), (119).
St Cuthbert c (Herbager—The Veil) (269).
Saint Denys c (Dionisio—Fand) 87, (102).
St Elmo c (Signal Light—Little Witch) 211.
St Gulliver c (Nimbus—Gulabi) (190), (210), 210.
St Lucia f (Alycidon—Nassau) 40, 83, (107), 145.
St Padarn c (St Paddy—Abella) 34, 192.
ST PADDY c (Aureole—Edie Kelly) 1, (3), (5), (39), (78), (89), (113), (119), 124,
    128, (135), 149.
ST PAULI GIRL f (St Paddy—Martica) 2, 4, 17, 108, (138), 139, 147.
St Puckle c (St Paddy—Browband) 78, 84, 92, 116, 143, 164, 170.
Saints and Sinners c (Saint Crespin III—On Holiday) 130.
St Stephen c (Solferino—Stamina) (279).
Saintworthy c (Brightworthy—Saint Bridget) 274, 274.
Salammbo c (Lucero—Tropicana) (184).
Salan c (Ballylinan—Anne Scarlett) 219.
Sally Brook f (Iceberg II—Steel Latch) 274.
Sallymount c (Tudor Minstrel—Queen of Shiraz) 106, 144, 178.
Sally Stream f (Royal Challenger—Cheveley Lass) 118.
Salmon King c (Final Score—Irish Rose) 35.
Salmon Spray c (Vulgan—Fly Book) 249, 253, 263, (277).
Salvo c (Right Royal V—Manera) 47, (67), 72, 89, (91), (113), 124, (214), (229).
Sam Brownthorn c (Samarkand—Alice Brownthorn) 258.
Same, The c (Auralia—Sesame) 187.
Sammy Davis c (Whistler—Samaria) 27, (79), (146).
Samos c (Sheshoon—Solotanzerin) 110.
Samothraki c (Beau Sabreur—La Pucelle) (80).
San Angelo c (Fortina—Tiberina) (276).
Sanctum c (Solonaway—Angelus) 173, (174), 215, (215), (218).
Sandiacre c (Torbido—Snow Bunting) 127, (175), 175, (191), (232).
Sandiment c (Experiment—Sandra) 63.
Sandro c (Botticelli—Seria) 10, 120, (161), 169, (172).
Sandy Abbot c (Langton Abbot—Sylmar) 262, 273, (273), 288.
Sandy Jane II f (Sandyman—Mamma II) (258), 258.
Sang Froid c (Sailing Light—Royal Route) 204.
San Jacinto c (Bowsprit—Help Yourself) 281.
Sannazaro c (Zucchero—Reel In) 114, 127.
Sans Pareil c (Damremont—Sailing Eve) 165, 180.

Sans Souci f (His Highness—Cambalee) (9).
SANTA CLAUS c (Chamossaire—Aunt Clara) (3), (36), (87), (117), 124.
Santa Grand c (Dumbarnie—Grande Vedette) (293).
Santa Vimy f (Vimy—Merry Xmas) 221.
Santaway c (Solonaway—Santa Baby) 188.
Saphira f (Sunny Boy III—Sarny) 221.
Saragan c (Sicambre—Ash Plant) 142.
Saratoga Skiddy c (King of the Tudors—Nambiorix 230.
Sarcelle f (Amour Drake—Sarie) 107.
Sargent c (Panorama—Croquette) 211.
Sartorius c (Prince Chevalier—Warning) 289.
Satan c (Buisson Ardent—Persian View) (146), 217.
Sauce Diable c (Hard Sauce—Helsinki II) 209.
Saucepan f (Panaslipper—More Sauce) (37).
Sauchrie f (Le Lavandou—Dunure) (30).
Saucy Kit c (Hard Sauce—Reckitts) (277).
Saucy Model f (Hard Sauce—Summer Model) (268).
Saulisa f (Hard Sauce—L.S.D.) 23, 44.
Sayfar c (Sayajirao—Farandole II) 232.
Sayitagain c (Sayajirao—Beyond Belief) 15.
Say No More f (Sayajirao—Turkish Tune) 36.
Say the Word f (Sayajirao—Firm Offer) 234, (234).
Scabbard c (King's Bench—Scammell) 109.
Scala f (Chanteur II—Palazzo) 34.
Scamperdale c (The Phoenix—Cosmetic) 187.
Scaphander c (Pearl Diver—Ice) (223).
Scarron c (Lacaduv—Saucy II) 283.
Scatter c (Sicambre—Dasher) (80), 92.
Scholar Gypsy c (Honeyway—School for Scandal) (48).
School for Gamble c (School for Botany—All the Time) 246.
Scipio c (Twilight Alley—Mistress Ann) 19, 28, 76, 130.
Scissors c (Milesian—Dalila) (41), 49.
Scorton Gold f (Reverse Charge—In Love) (209).
Scotch Prince c (Prince Richard—Tartanvilla) 260, 271.
Scotch Woodcock c (Hard Sauce—Limicola) 98.
Scots Fusilier c (March Past—Jojo) (168).
Scottish Court f (Midas—Glenythan) 143.
Scottish Final c (Jock Scot—Final Line) 287.
Scottish Flight II c (Jai Hind or Scottish Rambler—Gemma) 245, 288.
Scottish Mary f (High Treason—Solar Telegram) 9.
Scottish Memories c (Scottish Union—Souvenir d'Un Ami) (246), 252, 265, 273,
    273, 273, (286).
Scottish Sea c (Scottish Union—Tide Time) 272.
Scottish Sinbad c (Tamerlane—Rosie Wings) (210).
Scriventon c (Milesian—My Valley) 200.
Scryer f (Precipitation—Mysticus) (83).
Scylla f (Cagire II—Ice Run) (224).
SEA BIRD II c (Dan Cupid—Sicalade) (3).

Seacroft c (Vigo—Helen Rosa) (21), 24.
Sea Knight c (Sea Lover—Knight's Kwan) 282, 282.
Sea Lavender f (Never Say Die—Abelia) 29.
Sea Leopard c (Persian Gulf—Wood Leopard) 191, 212, 212, 232.
Sea Lichen f (Ballymoss—Golden Sands) 2, (21), 24, 61.
Seascape f (Naucide—La Joliette) (34), (48), 83, 232.
Sea Wife f (Archive—She Gone) 270, 285.
Sea Wolf c (Arctic Prince—Flatter) 232.
Sebring c (Aureole—Queen of Speed) 3, 5, (63), 117.
Secret Ray f (Privy Councillor—Highland Beam) 71, (146).
Secret Session f (Court Martial—Code Militaire) 17, 101, 129.
Secret Step f (Native Dancer—Tap Day) 40, (122), (126), 136, 146.
Sedgebrook c (Airborne—Watercress) 279.
Sejamus c (Psidium—Sijui) 85.
Seleucus c (Alycidon—Emotion) 191.
Selvedge c (Sallymount—Sarah) 224.
Sempervivum c (Sayajirao—Veronica Franchi) 5, 263, 263, 263, 277, 287.
Senior Steward (see Royal Showband).
SENSUALITA f (Polynesian—Peace of Mind) 2, 123.
Sentier f (Parthia—Persian Shoe) (48).
Sentina c (Fortina—Senria) 265, (272), (272), 288.
Sereno (late Essoldo) c (Relic—Diamantine) 176.
Set Going c (Set Fair—Sayonara) 34.
Setting Star c (Signal Light—Phase) 162, (170).
Set to Music c (Chanteur II—Setback) 183.
Severn Bore c (Borealis—Sabie River) 285.
Shadow f (Alycidon—Sunshade) 93, 108.
Shady Case c (Court Martial—Shady Lane) 203.
Shady Knight c (Petition—Luz Mala) 164, 168.
Shahlala f (Tehran—Melody Inn) 83.
Shai c (Shantung—Io) 48, (198).
Sham Fight c (Carnival Boy—Strife) 260, (291).
Shamrock Cross f (Sheshoon—Alcora) 83.
Shamrock Queen f (Primera—Rockabye Baby) 145.
Shamrock Star c (Rock Star—Chambiges) 146, 179, 182.
Shandon Belle f (Hook Money—Merlette) 25, (86).
Shanlis c (Control—Skedog) 281.
SHANTUNG c (Sicambre—Barley Corn) 3.
Sharavogue c (Sallymount—Helsinki II) (195).
Shatter c (Arctic Prince—Dasher) 127, (191).
Shavings c (Vulgan—Headcap) 288.
Shaykh Sulieman c (Jock Scot—Marion) 188.
Shearwater c (My Babu—Sea Parrot) (67), 188.
Sheil c (Sheshoon—Past Experience) 195.
Sheridan c (Kelly—Floral Park) (192).
Sheriff, The c (Hill Gail—Discipliner) 200.
Sherry Netherland c (Montaval—Ithaca) 26, 190.
Sheshoon c (Precipitation—Noorani) 5, (110), 135.

She Wolf f (Hugh Lupus—Dilettante) 69.
Shikar II c (Souverain—Mehmany) 72.
Shining Orb c (Hyperion—Niccolite) 85.
Shira c (Coronation Year—Campion) 175, 191, (191), 201.
Shoemaker c (Saint Crespin III— Whipcord) 34.
Shortcastle c (Galivanter—Velma) 15.
Short Commons f (Hard Tack—Padus) 121, (167).
Short Sentence f (Court Martial—Three Weeks) 173.
Shotley Mill c (Babur—Turkish Castle) 35, (166), 182.
Shot Silk f (High Treason—Vahred) (11).
Shoubad f (Vimy—After the Show) 66.
Shoulder Arms c (Epaulette—Gay Princess) 186.
Showdown c (Infatuation—Zanzara) 1, (10), (42), 59, 98, (103), 125.
Showman's Fair c (Fidalgo—Reef Knot) 143, 221.
Showoff c (Whistler—Fair Amazon) 204, (204).
Shut Up II f (Shut Out—Tien Lan) 123.
Shy Boy c (Alycidon—Timid Tilly) 209.
Shy Girl f (Supreme Court—Palma Rosa) (21), 61.
Shylock c (Hook Money—Seguidilla) 6.
Siamois c (Sir Fellah—La Tramoise) 285.
Sica Dan c (Sica Boy—Scarlet Plume) 21, 24, 33.
Sicilia f (Die Hard—Syracuse) 94.
Sidon c (Milesian—Mrs Siddons) 77, (96), 132.
Siesta Time f (Ommeyad—Time Call) 35, 61.
Si Furieux c (Sicambre—Hell's Fury) (180).
Signa Infesta c (Saint Crespin III—Certosa) (62), (63), 64.
Signal Rocket c (Hugh Lupus—Like a Flash II) (73), 207.
Sijui f (Sayajirao—Eyewash) (71).
Silent Waters f (My Babu—Reel In) 181.
Silent Whistle c (Whistler—Shining Pearl) (219).
Siliconn c (Princely Gift—Fair Share) 99, 109, 132, 136.
Silken Glade f (Buisson Ardent—Brocade) 11.
SILKEN GLIDER f (Airborne—Silken Slipper) 2, 4, (131), 139.
Silken Yogan f (Ballyogan—Silken Star) 25.
SILLY SEASON c (Tom Fool—Double Deal) 1, (10), (46), (70), (98), (105), 123,
    125, (132), 144, (149).
Silver Churn c (Princely Gift—Sayula) 196.
Silver Cloud c (Aureole—Brolly) 74, (82), 96, 111, (120), 120.
Silver Dome c (Domaha—Silverina) 275, 288.
Silver King c (Grey Sovereign—Carol's Lady) (196), (215).
Silver Moon c (Pardal—Moonstone) 142.
Silver Tor c (Grey Sovereign—Theadora) 44, (115), 115, 136.
Silverware c (Red God—Silver Frame) (7), 12, 18.
Silvia f (Romulus—Monrovia) 9.
Silvogan's Hook f (Bakhtawar—Silvogan) 286.
Sinbad the Sailor (late Frimas) c (Lacaduv—Neige) 178.
Sind f (Darius—Scintillating) 224.
Sindon c (Hyperbole—Cotton Wool) 87, 102, (117), 142, 149.

Snow Cat c (Arctic Prince—Calash) (76), (123), 132.
Snow Court f (King's Bench—Snow Cloud) 116.
Snowdra Queen f (Brightworthy—Irish Jig II) (278), 278, (278).
Snow Leopard c (Prince Chevalier—Wood Leopard) 183, (226).
Snow White f (Narrator—Snow Princess) 20.
So Blessed c (Princely Gift—Lavant) 1, (44), 70, 115, (122), (126), (136).
Society c (Sheshoon—Blue Society) 3, (30), 36, (74).
So Cozy c (Sicambre—Seraglio) 74, 80.
SODERINI c (Crepello—Matuta) 5, (34), 46, (72), 100, (113), 124, 127.
SODIUM c (Psidium—Gambade) 3, (5), 39, 80, (88), 113, (117), 124, 133.
Sofico c (Hill Gail—Fair Alycia) 62.
Soft Angels f (Crepello—Sweet Angel) 2, (20), (39), 90.
Soft Collar c (Quorum—Scarf) 219.
Soho Lad c (El Gallo—Grand Day) (15).
Solar Beam c (Skymaster—Lil) 27.
Solar Charge c (Solar Slipper—Liam) (218).
Solar City c (Solar Prince—Okehampton) 281.
Solartickle c (Solar Slipper—Ballytickle) 142.
Solbay f (Baman—Soldeneeze) 278.
Solbina c (Soldado—Baygina) 245, 252.
Soldier c (Milesian—Kilcarn Victory) 41.
Soldiers Song f (Court Martial—Verse) (71).
Solfen c (Soldado—Fenora) (260), (271), (289).
Solfenora c (Soldado—Fenora) 271.
Solonace c (Trimbush—Bright Virginia) 264.
Solo Singer c (Chanteur II—Solisequious) 143, 195, 207.
Solpetre c (Sunny Boy III—Blue Pet) 234.
Solray c (Soletra—Rayvic) 272, (280).
SOLSTICE c (Solar Slipper—Thirty Cents) 5, 84, (92).
Solwezi c (Zimone—Solfarana) 231.
Solwink c (Soldado—Drop a Wink) 258.
Some Alibi c (Starmond—Another Alibi) (286).
Some Baby c (Holywell—Sweet Caprice) (282).
Somerville c (Chamier—Miss Fairville) 31.
Son and Heir II c (Menow—Piquet) 270.
Song c (Sing Sing—Intent) (12), 28.
Songedor c (Matador—Fazeley) 125, (215), 215, 218.
Sonnet II c (Sayajirao—Easter Bonnet II) 169.
Son of Tam c (Tambourin—Polly) 280.
Sorrel f (Distingue—Golden Call) 234.
Sorrentina f (Will Somers—Etta) (15), 66.
Soslaio c (Djebe—Clara Barton) 89.
Sostenuto c (Never Say Die—Arietta) 199, 214, (220).
Sotuta f (Amber X—Solarienne) 198.
Soueida c (Dumbarnie—Two-Timer) 184.
Sound Number f (Sound Track—Three Fours) 179.
Sound of Music f (Chanteur II—Bebe Grande) 129, 138, 145.
Sound Track c (Whistler—Bridle Way) (12), (16), 44, (115).

Sous Etoile f (Stardust—Susa) 36.
Southern Belle f (Charlottesville—Ribelle) 26.
Southern Cross f (Hornbeam—Stella Polaris) 118.
Souverlone c (Souverain—Lonely Maid) (91).
Souvrillus c (Souverain—Cantarilla) 161.
SOVEREIGN f (Pardao—Urshalim) 2, (11), (18), (29), (107).
Sovereign Crest c (Grey Sovereign—Oserian) 22.
Sovereign Edition c (Sovereign Path—Latest Edition) 42, 87, 105, (184).
Sovereign Flame c (Grey Sovereign—Vestal Girl) 60.
Sovereign Lord c (Grey Sovereign—Ardue) (22), (28), 42, 105.
Sovereign Path c (Grey Sovereign—Mountain Path) 25, 59, (65), (98), 109, 125, (144), 174, 196.
Sovereign Ruler c (Crepello—Empress Rina) 74.
Sovereign Service c (Sovereign Lord—Musardise) 12.
Sovereign Slipper c (Fortino II—Solar Echo) (41), 65.
Sovereign Star f (Joan's Star—Platinum Grey) (222).
Sovrango c (Krakatao—Painted Vale) 3, 5, 72, (82), (84), (84), 84, (133), (133).
Soysambu c (Sicambre—Safari Moon) 102, 117.
Space King c (King's Bench—Lunar Way) 185, 185, (208), 210, 213, 235.
Spaceman c (Cagire II—Talitha) 235.
Spaniard, The c (Sayajirao—Perle o'Espagne) (279).
Spaniards Close c (Solonaway—Under Canvas) (174), (193), 204, 205.
Spaniards Inn c (Matador—Blue Sash) 211, 230.
Spaniards Mount c (Monet—Old Flo) (44), 115, 126, 167, (196).
Spanish Express c (Sovereign Path—Sage Femme) 37, (42), 70.
Spanish Steps c (Flush Royal—Tiberetta) (249).
Spare Filly f (Beau Sabreur—La Pucelle) 172.
Spark c (Quorum—Beau Co Co) 122, 179, 219.
Sparkling Flame c (Flamenco—Jazzaway) (289).
Sparrow Hawk c (Honeyway—Antonia) (62), 234.
Sparrow Pie c (Pardal—Daphne's Delight) 205.
Spartae c (Eudaemon—China Sarah) 268, 287.
Spartan General c (Mossborough—Grecian Garden) 165, 187, 263, 277.
Spartan Green c (Mossborough—Grecian Garden) 195.
Spate c (Vigorous—Vltava) 288.
Spear Fir f (Straight Deal—Miss Rigton) (259).
Spearhead c (Javelot—Sunny Morning) 266.
Specify c (Specific—Ora Lamae) 246.
Speed of Sound c (Buisson Ardent—Dame Melba) (31).
Speedwell c (Big Game—Le Rossignol) (268).
Speylove c (Spey Royal—Cri de Coeur) (293).
Spice f (Arctic Prince—Turkish Delight) (61).
Spin Out f (Pall Mall—Outspan) 8.
Spithead c (Guersant—Review) 12.
Splash c (Fortina—Tackler) 265, (290), 290, 290.
Sportaville c (Trouville—Gala Night) (185).
SPREE f (Rockefella—Emancipation) 2, 4, 71, (129), 144.

Straight Arrow c (Nashua—Noblesse) 45.
Straight Die c (Never Say Die—Straight Offer) 232.
Straight Lad c (Straight Deal—Olan) (161).
Straight Lady f (Straight Deal—Griosach) (282).
Straight Master c (Skymaster—Royal Straight) 60, 193, 205, (215), 233.
Strait-Jacket c (Straight Deal—Cutaway) 114.
Strand Station c (Nashua—Ament) 28.
Strathallander c (Henry the Seventh—Arca) 73.
Strat Royal c (Spey Royal—Strategy) 262.
Stratus c (Nimbus—Straight Offer) 192, (200), 218.
Streetfighter c (Aggressor—Cloche Merle) 59.
Street Singer f (Kingsway—Record Serenade) 75.
Strident c (Javelot—Syringe) 198.
Stubbs II c (Acropolis—Suzanne Valadon) 247.
Stung f (Galivanter—Bee Hive) 11.
Stunning c (Stardust—Running Wild) 200.
Stupor Mundi c (Tulyar—Engulfed) 77, (210).
Sturdy Man c (Polynesian—Sly Vixen) 42.
Stype f (Arctic Star—Boreal) (40).
Sublime f (Neckar—Sylvia) 229, 229.
Sucaryl c (St Paddy—Sweet Angel) 117, (213).
Sudden Thought f (Pardal—Sudden Light) 13, 188.
Sufi c (Persian Gulf—Farman Hill) 184, 217.
Sugar Apple c (Crepello—Sweet Angel) (68).
Sugar Daddy c (Zucchero—Yorkshire Rose) 206.
Suki Desu c (Malka's Boy—Doublure II) (195).
Sultry Day c (Tornado—Kypris) (172).
Summer Day f (Golden Cloud—Sweet Resolve) (14).
Sunbridge c (Foroughi—Archstar) 274.
Sunburnt Country f (Hyperion—Open Country) 101.
Sun Charger c (Royal Charger—Sungown) (76), 92, 120, 128, 178.
Sunderton c (Polic—Sundorne Alice) 181.
Sundew c (Sun King—Parsonstown Gem) (245), 259.
Sundown c (Hyperion—Open Country) 44.
Sun Flight c (Fairey Fulmar—Golden Sunlight) 192.
Sunland f (Charlottesville—Sunny Gulf) 139.
Sunny Court c (Supreme Court—Sunny Eve) (41), 63, 102, (116), 163.
Sunny Cove f (Nearco—Sunny Gulf) 97, 131, (139).
Sunny Tunes c (Epaulette—Aroon) 182.
Sunny Way c (Honeyway—Red Sunset) (183), (195), 212, 229.
Sunrise c (Grand Weather—Heroic China) (185), 235.
Sun Rock c (Ballymoss—Blue Prelude) (76), 78, 82, (128), (141), (190).
Sun Rose f (Mossborough—Suntime) 101.
Sunseeker c (Aureole—Sun Deck) 117, (133), 142.
Sunspeck f (Nearula—Sonsa) 9, (101).
Sunstart c (Hyperion—Aralia) 203, 203, 227, 227.
Sunsuit f (Alycidon—Herringbone) 4.
Superfine c (Supertello—Cocotte) (274).

Super Flash c (Hyacinthus—Cissie Gay) (246), 286.
Superfluous c (Supertello—Superlative) 133.
Super Fox c (Supertello—Foxy Jane) 270.
Super Gay c (Supreme Court—Gay Florentine) 26.
Super Sam c (Above Suspicion—Samaria) (77), (96), (213).
Super Snipe c (Supreme Court—Avocet) 59, 130.
Superstition c (Golden Cloud—Best of Luck) 21, 60, (98).
Supreme Courage c (Supreme Court—Hymette) 5, 74, 84, 104.
Supreme Joy c (Supreme Court—Gold Mirth) 192.
Supreme Sovereign c (Sovereign Path—Valtellina) (98), 125, (167), 174, 215.
Surcharge c (Reverse Charge—Very Fishy) (288).
Sure Shot f (Court Martial—Steady Aim) 80, 93.
Surprise Packet f (Jim Newcombe—Faerie Queene) 282.
Sutherland c (Vilmorin—Dornoch) 166.
Suvretta c (Never Say Die—Iberia) 84, 120, (130), 140.
Sveltana f (Grey Sovereign—Patum) (223), 223.
Swallowswift f (Nimbus—Skitop) (129), 197.
Swallow Tail II c (Alcide—Oh My Honey) 48.
Sway c (Preciptic—Lady Osway) 80, (81), (116).
Sweet Gem f (Hard Sauce—Pandora's Box) 181.
Sweet Jewel f (Will Somers—Diamond Deuce) 231.
Sweet Lola f (Zucchero—Armada) 97.
Sweet Moss c (Ballymoss—Sweet Angel) 73, (85), (89), (123), 123, 128.
SWEET SOLERA f (Solonaway—Miss Gammon) (2), (4), 11, (17), (61), (73).
Sweet Sovereign c (Grey Sovereign—Sweet One) (8), 29.
Sweet Story c (Zucchero—Queen's Fable) 80, 81, (91), (177), (183), (199), 199.
Swiftest f (Tamerlane—Like a Flash II) 197.
Swift Harmony f (Elopement—Syncopation) (13), 170, 213.
Swinging Bird c (Democratic—Bell Bird) 166.
Swinging Minstrel c (Tudor Minstrel—Rose Cloud) (204).
Sword c (Luminary—Answer Me) 231.
Sword Dancer c (Eudaemon—Doll Dance) (198).
Sword Flash c (Fair Copy—Sword Knot) (234), 251, (279), 279.
Sword Hilt c (Court Martial—Monrovia) (180).
Sybils Comb f (Honeyway—Sybil's Niece) 23.
Sydney Jones c (Davy Jones—Prudence II) 272.
Sylphide f (Supreme Court—Amidwar) (121), 125, 197.
Symona f (Sayajirao—Lendal) (17).

T

Table Wine c (Le Lavandou—Moll Flagon) (188).
TABOUN c (Tabriz—Queen of Basrah) (1), 10.
Tacitus c (Talgo—Activate) 13, 70, (77), (77), (96), 164.
Tadolina f (Neckar—Trevisana) 149.
Tahiri f (Persian Gulf—Dickneos) 75, 101, (170).

Taine c (Vandale II—Tanchere) 110.
Taittinger f (Tehran—Asti Spumante) 4, (143).
TAJ DEWAN c (Prince Taj—Devinette) 1, 119, 149.
Take Heart c (Tamerlane—Desirous) 223.
Take Heed c (Prince Chevalier or Mark-Ye-Well—Miss Advertencia) 198.
Take Plenty c (Gypse—McKeogh's Girl) (281).
Take the Plunge c (Cash and Courage—Chorus Girl) 222.
Take Time c (Grand Inquisitor—McKeogh's Girl) 290.
Talahasse c (Rustam—Mary Ellard) (19), (28), (32).
Talbot c (Maelsheachlainn—Hillman Minx) 258, 265.
Talgo c (Krakatao—Miss France) 77.
Talgo Abbess c (Talgo—Mount Abbess) 231, 231, 277.
Talisman c (Supreme Court—Samovar) 70.
Talmud c (Tulyar—Respite) (36).
Tamasha f (Tamerlane—Oh My Honey) 97.
Tambourine II c (Princequillo—La Mirambule) (117).
Tamerella f (Tamerlane—Ella Retford) 45, 71.
Tamerlo c (Tamerlane—Admiral's Love) 192, (200), (213).
Tamerslip c (Tamerlane—Amber Slipper) 31.
Tamino c (Sing Sing—Fair and True) 44, (79).
Tamorn c (Tambourin—Preciptic Morning) 247, 287.
Tamper f (Tantieme—Mitrailleuse) 104.
Tampion c (Tamerlane—Ovada) 209.
Tana Dante f (Dante—Chart Room) 20, 27.
Tang c (Vieux Manoir—Tanina) 119.
Tanlic c (Relic—Tanya III) 266.
Tanned f (Sunny Boy III—Neaera) (97).
Tantalizer f (Tantieme—Indian Night) 26, 80, 108, 131.
Tapina c (Tapioca II—La Tafna) 289.
Tapis Rose c (Tissot—Rosacre) 82, 113.
Tarqogan c (Black Tarquin—Rosyogan) 3, 15, 96, 119, 123, 124, 162, (210), (233), 233.
Tarquinian c (Dogat—Tarsia) 223, (229).
Tatarin c (Aureole—La Montespan) 130, 229.
Taurus c (Narrator—Moonstone) 70.
Taxidermist c (Ujiji—Rage Bleue) (250), 250, 280, (292).
Tea Fiend c (Colombo—Maureen's Lass) 245, 255, (267).
Team Spirit c (Vulgan—Lady Walewska) 245, (245), (256), 271, (272), 290.
Ted Broon c (Reynard Volant—Prestlass) 276.
Te Fou c (Djefou—Tawhida) 269, 283.
Tempest c (Court Martial—Squall) 3, 5, (74), 105, 125, 135.
Tenacity f (Wilwyn—Ella Tengam) 71, (134), (145).
Tendentious f (Tenerani—Ambiguity) 108.
TENDER ANNIE f (Tenerani—Annie Oakley) 4, (108), 113.
Tender Word f (Tenerani—Wheedler) (26), 61, 90, (97), 145.
Tenet c (Tenerani—Top Table) 168.
Tenterhooks c (Tenerani—Sweet and Rough) (104), (127).
Tesco Boy c (Princely Gift—Suncourt) (68), 96, (103), 125, 144, 149, (218).
Test Ban c (Court Harwell—Arctic Peace) 64.

Test Case c (Supreme Court—Tessa Gillian) (28), 105, 178.
Texana f (Relic—Tosca III) 115.
Texanita f (Relic—Tosca III) 2.
Teynham c (Wilwyn—Devon Vintage) 45, (103).
Thames Trader c (Honeyway—Ballochbuie) 178, (194), (203), 233.
Tharp c (Limekiln—Mother Rectress) (65), (102), 103.
Thataboy c (Mourne—Gilboa) (36).
Thataway f (Ujiji—Submission) 246.
There She Goes f (Tamerlane—Cheveley Beauty) 40, (47).
Thik Hai c (Anamnestes—Lusie Boudour) (143).
Thoralgo c (Fidalgo—Author) 176.
Thorn Gate c (Vulgan—Culleen's Coup) 248, 275.
Threepwood c (Melody Maker—Milady Jill) 291, 291.
Thundridge c (Ballymoss—Thunder) (180).
Thyra Lee f (Grey Sovereign—Romany Belle) (219).
Ti Amo c (Nearula—Hyphenate) 65.
Tiber c (Hugh Lupus—River Run) (176), 194, 198, (207), 213, 220.
Tiberetta f (Tiberius—Drumrora) 245, 245, 245, 256.
Tibidabo c (Vimy—Tawhida) 246, (281).
Tickled Pink c (Honeyway or Pink Flower—Idle Jest) 212.
Tickle My Palm f (Royal Palm—Ink Spot) 197.
Ticklish f (Greek Star—Stop Your Tickling) 81, 118.
Tierra Del Fuego c (Buisson Ardent—Patagonia) (7), 12, 224.
Tiger c (Tamerlane—Desert Girl) 117, (128), (186).
Tiger William c (King of the Jungle—Ellen O'Hara) 291.
Tilmoray c (Vilmoray—Tilton Rose) 268, 275.
Timarum c (Rustam—Lebanon) 8.
Timber King c (Tenerani—Personality) 127.
Time c (Colonist II—Cash Column) 245, 256, (274).
Time and Again c (The Phoenix—Ria Geno) 189.
TIME GREINE c (Arctic Time—Blaith na Greine) 1, (65), 227.
Timon c (Acropolis—Gwen) 13.
Tingle f (Tangle—Genesis) 216.
Tin King c (Tin Whistle—Shandrim Queen) (12), 16, (44).
Tin Whistle c (Whistler—Sister Miles) 21, (24), (109), 115, (122), 122, 126, 136.
Tipperty c (Sheshoon—Three Feathers) 279.
Tirconail c (Proud Chieftain—Sea Gipsy) 30.
Tired Monarch c (Hard Ridden—Queen Vashti) 142.
Tissot c (Tenerani—Tiepoletta II) 110.
Title Deed f (Supreme Court—Urshalim) 109.
Tobago c (Borealis—Nassau) 80, 133, 289.
Tobraheela c (Hyacinthus—Cullyvore) 258, 272.
Toffee Nose f (Alegrador—Astelie) 9, 11, 129, 197.
Tok c (Hill Gail—Eastern Fairy) 45.
Tokoroa c (Flamenco—Habiba) 268, (270), 277.
Toledan II c (Prince Taj—La Vanda) 283.
Tomahawk IV c (War Relic—Therapia) 65.
Tom Cat c (Luminary—Feline) 222.

405

Tomdoun c (Rockefella—Straight Off) 218.
Tom Pom c (Tudor Minstrel—Papido) 14.
Toosin Tack c (Hard Tack—Dagmar) (205).
Too Slow c (El Hawa—Ambassadress) 246, 276.
Top 'C' c (Chanteur II—Ortlinde) 223.
Top of the Milk f (King of the Tudors—Creme Maurice) 2, (19), 29, 93.
Top of the Pops f (Tudor Melody—Fairey Logic) 211, 230.
Top Song f (Greek Song—I Tops) 66, 109.
Top Twenty c (Tambourin—Sister Miles) 265, 273, (276), (276).
Topyo c (Fine Top—Deliriosa) 124.
Torano c (Tenerani—Street Singer) 142.
Torbella III f (Tornado—Djebellica) 4, (46), 131.
Tordo c (Tudor Minstrel—Beau Jet) (19).
Torero c (Matador—Nautch) 10, 16, 132.
Toro f (Tudor Minstrel—L'Horizon) (107).
Torpid c (Match III—Cutter) 3, 47, (80), 92, 128.
Torullo c (Nearula—Tourinta) 74, 182.
Toughest c (French Beige—Polly Doodle) 224.
Tournella f (King of the Tudors—Myrrha II) (121), 167.
Touroy c (Tourment—La Castigata) 170, 187.
Tout ou Rien c (Anemos—Triple Couronne) 277.
Tower Walk c (High Treason—Lorrikeet) (18), (33), 42.
Town Crier c (Sovereign Path—Corsley Bell) 106, 132, 173, (200).
Town Life c (Mossborough—Charmed Life) 68, 103
Tracker c (Sound Track—Bullen) 166, (181).
Track Spare c (Sound Track—Rosy Myth) 12, (42), (105), 144.
Trade Wind c (Never Say Die—Following Breeze) (143).
Trafalgar c (Pardal—Nelson Touch) (120).
Traffic Leader c (Traffic Judge—Party Leader) 227.
Traitress f (Court Martial—Nadika) 123.
Travel Light c (Royal Palm—Croix de Lorraine) 87, (231).
Travelling Fair f (Vienna—Harlotta) 2, 101.
Travel Man c (Buisson Ardent—Asti Spumante) 10, 22.
Traviata f (Pinza—Kennie II) 46.
Treble J c (Quorum—Santa Babu) 188.
Tree Leopard c (Hornbeam—Wood Leopard) (189), (212), (221).
Trelawny c (Black Tarquin—Indian Night) (114), (114), 127, (127), (175), 175, 175,
    191, (191), (191), 191, 270, (289).
Trial Note f (Pinza—Test Match) 101.
Tribord c (Bozzetto—Troie) 124.
Triborough c (Mossborough—Oracabessa) 76.
Trident Jet c (Polly's Jet—Bright Scene) 44.
Trimmer c (Tenerani—Nelia) 5, 10, 18, 37, (180), 187, 190.
Triona f (Never Say Die—Donna Lydia) 69, 83.
Tripacer c (Owen Tudor—Bishop's Vine) (270).
Tristram c (Tornado—Chloris II) 62, 270.
Tromba c (Whistler—Deuteron) 192.
Tropical Breeze f (Migoli—Squall) 61.

Tropical Sky c (Nimbus—Coral Reef) 212, 214, 232.
Tropical Song c (Ocarina—Coral Reef) 191.
Tropic Star f (Tropique—Patricia's Star) (83), 97, (118), 138.
Troubadour c (Guersant—Fair and True) 12, 132.
True Code c (Petition—Verity) 113.
True Course f (Hill Gail—Arctic Rullah) (27).
Truly f (Tulyar—Star Telegrams) 66.
Trumpet Major c (Klairon—Big Berry) 34.
Trunk Call c (Reverse Charge—Queen's Parade) 281.
Tuba f (Hornbeam—Grand Sing) 27.
Tubalcain c (Tantieme—Orycida) 95, (114), (191), (201), (212).
Tudor Abbe c (Will Somers—Lower Abbey) (195).
Tudor Bar c (King of the Tudors—Barbie) 227.
Tudor Black c (Sovereign Path—Artist's Licence) 44.
Tudor Court c (King of the Tudors—Fountain Court) 32.
Tudor Flash c (Signal Box—Rose of Tudor) 217.
Tudor Gal f (Henry the Seventh—La Brigantine) (97).
Tudor Grand c (Tudor Minstrel—Grand Sing) 109.
Tudor Grey c (Tudor Minstrel—Earnest Alice) 16, 24, 126.
Tudorich c (Tudor Minstrel—Ropencha) (67).
Tudor Jinks c (Owen Tudor—The Poult) (227).
Tudor Legend c (Tudor Jinks—La Doutelle) 268.
Tudor Love f (Owen Tudor—Amora) 138.
Tudor Melody c (Tudor Jinks—Matelda) (13).
Tudor Monarch c (Abernant—Madonna) (211).
Tudor Music c (Tudor Melody—Fran) (22), (28), 32.
Tudor Period c (Owen Tudor—Cornice) 60, (80), 187, 220, (226).
Tudor Style f (Owen Tudor—Cornice) 226.
Tudor Summer c (Will Somers—Snowdonia) (202).
Tudor Tale c (King of the Tudors—Royal Myth) 22, 128, (226).
Tudor Top f (Tudor Minstrel—Kirby Top) 69.
Tudor Treasure c (King of the Tudors—Turkish Treasure) 70, (105), (174), 283.
Tudor Warning c (King of the Tudors—Warning Light) 79.
Tuesday Eve f (Silnet—Catch) 94.
Tulyartos c (Tulyar—Certosa) 1, (7), 41, 119.
Tumbled c (Pandofell—Fair Folly) 120.
Tumbrel f (Djebe—La Marseillaise) 211.
Tuna Gail f (Hill Gail—Ituna) 4, 15, (66), 86.
Turbo Jet c (Polly's Jet—Spring Offensive) 36, (59), 87, 109.
Turf f (Ballymoss—Woodfire) 229.
Turmoil c (Lighthouse II—Capitation) (261), 288.
Turn Coat c (High Treason—Red Cloak) 44.
Turn Right c (Pall Mall—Rightful) 74, 99.
Turpial c (Babu's Pet—Evangelique) (283).
Turret c (Donore—Chilcombe Belle) (173).
Tuscar, The c (Tenerani—Falmouth Bay) (187), (194), 212.
Tutto c (Totaig—Tut Tartan) (265).
Twelfth Man c (Fidalgo—Test Match) (194), 198, 214, (220).

Twelve Oaks c (Polly's Jet—In Orbit) 15.
Twiberry c (Twilight Alley—Whinberry) (221).
Twilight Alley c (Alycidon—Crepuscule) 95, (110).
Twister c (Soleil Levant—Spleen) 76.
Two Francs c (Reverse Charge—Flying Pearl) 106, 125.
Two Royals c (Royal Tara—Royal View) 187.
Twosome f (Sicambre—Twofold) 20.
Tyler's Hill c (Solonaway—Fair Comet) 7.
Typhoon c (Honeyway—Kingsworthy) (10), (22).
Tyrone c (Tornado—Statira) 1.
Tywydd Teg c (Set Fair—Pontyfair) 14.
Tzigane f (Tudor Minstrel—Big Berry) (17).

U

Uhuru f (Petition—Postscript) 224.
Ulanova f (Torbido—Ebb & Flow) 206.
Ulpion c (Petition—Ulipi's Sister) 31, 37.
Ulster Prince c (Exploitation—Orient Princess) 95, (165), 194, (223).
Ulster Ranger c (Exploitation—Orient Princess) 165, 169, 189.
Ultima c (Umberto—Nearly) (172).
Ultimate II c (Endeavour II—Italian Mist) (65), 87.
Uncle Isaac c (Prickly—dam by Lighthouse) (260), 291.
Uncle Percy c (Djeddah—Tap Day) 42.
Union Pacific c (Union Jack—Paul's Daughter) (267), 267, 279, 289, 291.
Union Way c (Union Jack—Steel Owl) 279.
Unity f (Tudor Melody—Real Tesoro) 20, (24), 167, 222.
Up the Vale c (Pay Up—Cool Vale) 286.
Usurper c (Niccolo Dell'Arca—Snow Bunting) 161.
Utrillo c (Zucchero—Mont Bleu) 175, 183, (189), (199), 212, 220, 226, (232).

V

Vacarme c (Vandale II—Hajibibi) (81), (148).
Vagilistria (see Genius).
Vaguely Noble c (Vienna—Noble Lassie) (49).
Valbus c (Phebus—Valerita) 245.
Val d'Aoste c (Val de Loir—Nounouche) 117.

Valdesta f (Persian Gulf—Circassia) 17, (61).
Val d'Oisans c (My Babu—Valcamonica) 1.
Valentine c (Alycidon—Val d'Assa) (48), 67, 119.
Valentine's Day c (Acropolis—Pin Tray) 114.
Valentine Slipper c (His Slipper—Sandra) 102, 117.
Valiant Spark c (Pylon II—Valiant Nymph) 272.
Vallauris c (Nearco—L'Horizon) 74, 87.
VALORIS f (Tiziano—Vali) (4), 40, (86).
Valoroso c (Vimy—Bellaggio) 114, (161), (190), 199, 207, 220, 220, 235, 268.
Vandyke c Vandale II—Gritli) 206.
Vanita f (Cagire II—Bright Circlet) 8.
Variety King c (Tudor Minstrel—La Brigantine) 225.
VARINIA f (Charlottesville—Eyewash) 4, 47, 83, (93), 108, 139.
Veejlee f (Vilmorin—Dittany) 9.
Veneer c (Tenerani—Social Gulf) 76.
Vent Neurf f (Matador—Minstrel's Pride) 126.
VENTURE VII c (Relic—Rose o'Lynn) 1, (37), (42), (105), (125).
Venus Slipper c (Windsor Slipper—Bright Venus) 210.
Verbena f (Vimy—Val d'Assa) 2, (69), 90, 108.
Veronese c (Dante—Donatella III) 82.
Veronica Bell f (Lord of Verona—Viper Bell) 293.
Vertigo c (Acropolis—Venezia) 19, 30, (65).
Verve f (Nearco—Straight Verse) 197.
Vestogan f (Ballyogan—Star of Hope) (25).
Vhairi f (Narrator—Marie Therese) (145).
Vi f (Vilmorin—Dotterel) 20, 24.
Via Tenerana c (Tenerani—Via Devana) 99.
Vibrant c (Vilmorin—Heliographic) (106), 184, 196, (204).
Viburnum f (Guersant—Aralia) 26.
Vice Regent c (Border Legend—Kylescarlet) (261), 261.
Vic Mo Chroi c (Chamier—Vic Girl) 65, (102), 117.
Vic Rose c (Vic Day—Rose's Lime) 270.
Victoria Quay f (King's Bench—Hunters Quay) 25.
Victorina f (The Phoenix—Dryad) 61, 122, (211).
Victory Way c (Never Say Die—Winning Ways) 67.
VIENNA c (Aureole—Turkish Blood) 5, (74), 77, 100, 113, 149, 170.
Vif Argent c (Fast Fox—Djaina) 119.
Vigo c (Vilmorin—Thomasina) (122), 136.
Vijay c (Vigo—Chanterie) 14, 162, 192.
Village Cross c (Vilmorin—Grand Cross) 12.
Village Square c (Sir Gaylord—Two Cities) 1.
Vilmorence c (Vilmorin—Experience II) 200.
Vimadee c (Vimy—Upadee) (142).
Vinca c (Pink Flower—Velia) 188, (195).
Vinnie f (Vimy—Signeala) (35).
Violetta III f (Pinza—Urshalim) (197), 233.
Virginia Gentleman c (Crocket—Vivien) (103).
Viscount, The c (Whistling Wind—First Sail) 25, 59.

Visp f (Nantallah—Vestment) (7), (11).
Visualise f (Premonition—Miss Olympia) 13.
Vital Error f (Javelot—Aunt Florrie) 69, 79.
Vital Issue f (Immortality—Violtis) 197, 227.
Vitality Plus f (Nearco or Never Say Die—Gays the Word) 129.
Vital Link c (Panaslipper—Vacillate) 161.
Vitruvius c (Never Say Die—Venezia) 190.
Vivant c (Trois Moulins—La Rosay) (255).
Vivara f (Mossborough—Caronia) 94.
Vivat Rex c (Vimy—Kings Well) (81), 127.
Vivi Tarquin c (Black Tarquin—Viviparus) (104).
Voivode c (Worden II—Grandezza) 194, 226.
Voldemo c (Molvedo—St Citrus) (225).
Vouchsafe f (Petition—Full Speed) (197).
Vrai c (Die Hard—Verity) 104.
Vulcano c (Vulgan—Sanolien) 255, 264.
Vulpine c (Vulgan—Queen Astrid) (290).
Vulsea c (Vulgan—Sea Mera) 265.
Vultrix c (Vulgan—Little Trix) 245, 256, (264), 264.

W

Wage War c (Aggressor—Monrovia) (116), 116.
Wake Up! f (Persian Gulf—Arousal) (120).
Waldmeister c (Wild Risk—Santa Isabel) 110.
Wallaby II c (Fast Fox—Wagging Tail) 3, (110).
Wallaroo f (Wallaby II—Ripcord) 226.
Walpole c (My Babu—Warning) (288).
Wanjohe f (My Babu—Pyrethrum) 40.
War Dancer c (Zucchero—Kennie II) 32.
Warrior c (Le Sage—War Angel) 185.
Warrior Prince c (Tamerlane—Maralinni) 7.
Warsite f (Relic—Alhambra) 7.
Wartown c (Bakhtawar—Maytown) 280.
Warwick c (Abernant—Bali Ha'i) 15.
Washington c (Golden Cloud—Scarf) 115.
Wasps Fifteen f (The Phoenix—Oola Hills) 109.
Water Diviner c (Premonition—Seph) 19, 37.
Watergate c (Sovereign Path—Free and Easy) 105.
Waterloo Place c (Pall Mall—Bonne Bouche) 162, 171, (192).
Water Skier c (Rockefella—Free Dip) (178), (178), 193, 270.
Water Wings f (Nearco—Swallow Falls) 220, 220.
Wayne II c (Petition—Aurelie II) 1.

Wayward Bird c (The Pelican—Wayward Lass) 253.
Wayward Muse f (Phebus—Lady Mustang) 286.
Wayward Queen f (Pay Up—Wayward Lass) 262.
Weaver Bird c (Royal Palm—Weaving Spider) 37.
Wedding Dance c (Rondo II—Landlady) 253.
Wedding Present c (Macherio—Muscosa) 36, 117.
Weeper's Boy c (Whistler—Firesong) 146, (179), 193, 211, 211.
Welcomed c (Worden II—Pampered) 184, (205).
Welcome News c (Three Cheers—Last Port) (268).
Welford Lad c (Abernant—Baby Flinders) (8).
Well Packed c (Devonian—Pactona) 276, (276).
Welsh Abbot c (Abernant—Sister Sarah) 59, 115, 122, 126, 136, 146, 184, (228).
Welsh Border c (Abernant—Frieze) 68, 180, 207, (225).
Welsh Guard c (Royal Charger—Pelisse) 106, 125.
Welshman c (Welsh Abbot—Cyclamen) 109, 211.
Welsh Mistress f (Abernant—Ulupi's Sister) (9), 23.
Welsh Pageant c (Tudor Melody—Picture Light) 16.
Welsh Rake c (Abernant—Wayward Belle) 7, (103), 174, 174, 174, 204.
Welsh Reine f (Welsh Abbot—Soft Rain) 9.
Welsh Violet f (Welsh Abbot—April Violet) 173.
Welsh Warrior c (Abernant—Career Girl) 21, 24.
Wenona f (Larkspur—Pocahontas II) 147.
West Boy c (Rigolo—Mouxina) 269.
Western Wind c (Milesian—Palestrina) (62).
West Iran f (Zarathustra—Catchit) 234.
Westmarsh c (Fairwell—Westrol) 103, 205.
West Shaw f (Grey Sovereign—Irish Candy) 21.
WEST SIDE STORY f (Rockefella—Red Shoes) 2, 4, 43, (69), (134), 139.
Whaddon Hero c (Gilles de Retz—Nix) 289.
What a Myth c (Coup de Myth—What a Din) 250, 250, (251), 255, (256), 256, (257), 284, (292).
Wheatley c (Happy Knight—Quick Stitch) 170, 192.
Wheatsheaf c (Dumbarnie—Vilmorina) 186.
Whinstone Hill c (War Lord—Carrigeen Lady) (282), (282), 282.
Whipsnade f (Big Game—Felonia) (101).
Whirled f (Globemaster—Petara) 71, 107, 121.
Whiskey a Go Go c (Panaslipper—Goggles) 68, 74, 88, 99.
Whistle Me f (Whistler—Star of Knowledge) 219.
Whistler's Daughter f (Whistler—Signeala) 43, 179, (196), (217).
Whistle Stop f (Whistler—Signeala) 21.
Whistling Buoy c (Chanteur II—Dented Bell) 37, 106.
Whistling Fool c (Whistler—Meadow Music) 167, 173.
Whistling Sands f (Whistler—Dante's Dream) (217).
Whistling Top c (High Hat—Whistling Star) 10.
Whistling Victor c (Whistler—Port Victoria) 179, (230), 230.
Whistling Willie c (Whistler—Orum Star) 79.
Whistling Wind c (Whistler—Good as Gold) (18).
White Gloves c (High Hat—Gallamoud) (64), 100, (142).

White Label II c (Tanerko—Alba Nox) 5.
White Park Bay c (Straight Deal—Scarlet Myth) 235.
White Rajah c (Grey Sovereign—Widow's Peak) 8.
Whiz c (Whistler—Dream Girl) 12, 16.
Who Can Tell f (Worden II—Javotte) 61, 71.
Who's Caprice c (Tamerlane—Queens Caprice) 8.
Who You c (Stardust—Caerlissa) 162.
Widden f (Nimbus—Tenebel) 69.
Wide Awake f (Major Portion—Wake Island) 69, (101).
Wigandia f (Windsor Slipper—Lafayette) 195.
Wild Fast c (Wild Risk—Fastnella) 41, 266.
Wild Flame c (Infatuation—Fireproof) 225.
Wild Root c (Tudor Melody—Charity Concert) 166.
Wilhelmina Henrietta f (Chamier—Thebaine) (164).
Wiljotur c (Nearula—Shirley Pat) 73, 230.
William F c (Pink Flower—Persian Ivy) 203.
Willies, The c (King of the Tudors—Timid Tilly) 70.
Willies Kuda c (Polly's Jet—Listowel) 126.
Willipeg c (Will Somers—Eye Tooth) 126.
Willow King c (Snow King—Glenwillow) 290, 292.
Willowtale f (Olein's Grace—Mariana) 118.
Will Reward c (Wilwyn—See Red) 85.
Will Somers c (Tudor Minstrel—Queen's Jest) 12, 27.
Willya f (Trouville—Maggie Dungarvan) (231).
Wilmington II c (Babu's Pet—Tivoli) 253.
Wily Oriental c (Bidar—Twist) 256.
Wily Trout c (Le Sage—Luggeen) 84, 163.
Wimpole Street f (Reverse Charge—Inquisitive Rose) 75, 90, 108.
Windbag f (Borealis—Miss Know All) 83.
Winden c (Mossborough—Sylvan) 36.
WINDMILL GIRL f (Hornbeam—Chorus Beauty) 4, (108), 131.
Windscale c (Whistler—Signeala) 47, (73), 146, (179).
Wind Song f (Tudor Melody—Blizzard) 11, 23, 219.
Windyedge c (Rocket—Antipathy) 235.
Windy Gay f (Whistling Wind—Mrs Topham) 66.
Wing Master c (Master Owen—Phantom Wings) (266).
Winkie f (Bleep-Bleep—Luminant) 29.
Winna f (Wilwyn—Hot Rally) 196, (228).
Winning Bid f (Great Captain—Straight Bid) 221.
Winning Coin c (Vic Day—Florin Link) (272).
Winning Fair c (Fun Fair—Winning Hazard) (277).
Winning Move c (Pardal—Checkmate) 67.
Wishful Thinking f (Petition—Musidora) 129.
Wiskhert c (Alycidon—Salka) 76.
Wistful f (Worden II—Odilla) 134.
Wolver Hollow c (Sovereign Path—Cygnet) 12, 70, 144, 233, 233.
Wonder Belle f (Faubourg II—Battle View) (203).
Woodbow c (Bowsprit—Littlewoods) 270.

X

Y

Young Man's Fancy f (Alycidon—Spring Beauty II) (94), (138).
Your Highness c (Chamossaire—Lady Grand) 100, (117), 120, 142.
Yours c (Noor—Yutta) 115.
Ysolda f (Elopement—You'll Be Lucky) 40.

Z

Statistics (Flat)

JOCKEYS
APPRENTICES
TRAINERS
OWNERS
SIRES
TOP MONEY WINNERS (HORSES)
BREEDERS

Riding Records (Flat)

PAST CHAMPIONS

Year	Champion	Wins	Year	Champion	Wins
1846	E. Flatman	81	1881	F. Archer	220
1847	E. Flatman	89	1882	F. Archer	210
1848	E. Flatman	104	1883	F. Archer	232
1849	E. Flatman	94	1884	F. Archer	241
1850	E. Flatman	88	1885	F. Archer	246
1851	E. Flatman	78	1886	F. Archer	170
1852	E. Flatman	92	1887	C. Wood	151
1853	J. Wells	86	1888	F. Barrett	108
1854	J. Wells	82	1889	T. Loates	167
1855	G. Fordham	70	1890	T. Loates	147
1856	G. Fordham	108	1891	M. Cannon	137
1857	G. Fordham	84	1892	M. Cannon	182
1858	G. Fordham	91	1893	T. Loates	222
1859	G. Fordham	118	1894	M. Cannon	167
1860	G. Fordham	146	1895	M. Cannon	184
1861	G. Fordham	106	1896	M. Cannon	164
1862	G. Fordham	166	1897	M. Cannon	145
1863	G. Fordham	103	1898	O. Madden	161
1864	J. Grimshaw	164	1899	S. Loates	160
1865	G. Fordham	142	1900	L. Reiff	143
1866	S. Kenyon	123	1901	O. Madden	130
1867	G. Fordham	143	1902	W. Lane	170
1868	G. Fordham	110	1903	O. Madden	154
1869	G. Fordham	95	1904	O. Madden	161
1870	W. Gray and		1905	E. Wheatley	124
	C. Maidment	76	1906	W. Higgs	149
1871	G. Fordham and		1907	W. Higgs	146
	C. Maidment	86	1908	D. Maher	139
1872	T. Cannon	87	1909	F. Wootton	165
1873	H. Constable	110	1910	F. Wootton	137
1874	F. Archer	147	1911	F. Wootton	187
1875	F. Archer	172	1912	F. Wootton	118
1876	F. Archer	207	1913	D. Maher	115
1877	F. Archer	218	1914	S. Donoghue	129
1878	F. Archer	229	1915	S. Donoghue	62
1879	F. Archer	197	1916	S. Donoghue	45
1880	F. Archer	120	1917	S. Donoghue	42

	1918 S. Donoghue	66		1930 F. Fox	129
	1919 S. Donoghue	129		1931 G. Richards	145
	1920 S. Donoghue	143		1932 G. Richards	190
	1921 S. Donoghue	141		1933 G. Richards	259
	1922 S. Donoghue	102		1934 G. Richards	212
	1923 S. Donoghue and			1935 G. Richards	210
	C. Elliott	89		1936 G. Richards	177
	1924 C. Elliott	106		1937 G. Richards	214
	1925 G. Richards	118		1938 G. Richards	206
	1926 T. Weston	95		1939 G. Richards	155
	1927 G. Richards	164		1940 G. Richards	68
	1928 G. Richards	148		1941 H. Wragg	71
	1929 G. Richards	135		1942 G. Richards	67

**Only the top forty riders in each of the last twelve seasons are included in the following table. Figure in brackets is number of mounts.
† indicates the Champion and * a rider in top ten.**

	1957	1958	1959	1960	1961
Barclay, A.	—	—	—	—	—
Barlow, F.	22(160)	15(158)	—	—	—
Boothman, P.	—	37(217)	17(155)	—	—
Bougoure, G.	—	—	—	—	—
Breasley, A.	173(659)†	148(638)*	150(538)*	153(657)*	171(635)†
Britt, E.	62(375)*	52(339)	31(227)	—	22(272)
Brown, L. G.	—	—	—	—	—
Buckle, D.	23(94)	—	—	—	—
Cadwaladr, G.	—	—	—	—	—
Carr, W. H.	102(504)*	77(518)*	55(375)	84(483)*	64(426)*
Carson, W.	—	—	—	—	—
Clayton, S.	39(375)	60(520)*	48(480)	45(456)	35(336)
Coates, D.	—	—	—	—	—
Connorton, B.	22(191)	—	—	—	27(154)
Cook, P.	—	—	—	—	—
Cracknell, E. J.	21(240)	35(290)	34(379)	39(341)	23(196)
Cullen, D.	—	—	—	17(203)	26(289)
Dicey, R.	—	—	—	—	—
Duffield, G.	—	—	—	—	—
Durr, F.	46(341)	34(276)	26(345)	32(318)	66(427)*
Eldin, E.	—	—	—	25(323)	27(263)
Elliott, R. P.	—	—	26(310)	39(405)	35(437)
Elliott, W.	21(112)	18(245)	17(202)	36(288)	22(284)
Etherington, J.	33(231)	22(284)	33(279)	36(316)	39(319)
Faggotter, V.	—	—	—	—	—
Fawdon, R.	—	19(172)	34(221)	19(191)	—
Gethin, K.	43(226)	15(159)	18(119)	—	—
Gifford, J.	28(315)	—	—	—	—
Gosling, T.	33(210)	—	—	—	—
Greenaway, H. J.	—	27(301)	26(302)	36(322)	28(308)
Greening, D.	—	15(279)	—	—	—
Hayes, M.	—	23(229)	—	—	—
Henry, B.	—	25(162)	26(180)	43(298)	62(366)*
Hetherington, P.	—	—	—	—	—
Hide, E.	131(716)*	116(646)*	118(608)*	90(592)*	92(529)*
Hutchinson, R.	—	—	—	—	29(142)
Jago, B.	—	32(283)	17(201)	—	—
Johnson, E.	—	—	—	—	—

1943	G. Richards	65	1956	D. Smith	155
1944	G. Richards	88	1957	A. Breasley	173
1945	G. Richards	104	1958	D. Smith	165
1946	G. Richards	212	1959	D. Smith	157
1947	G. Richards	269	1960	L. Piggott	170
1948	G. Richards	224	1961	A. Breasley	171
1949	G. Richards	261	1962	A. Breasley	179
1950	G. Richards	201	1963	A. Breasley	176
1951	G. Richards	227	1964	L. Piggott	140
1952	G. Richards	231	1965	L. Piggott	160
1953	G. Richards	191	1966	L. Piggott	191
1954	D. Smith	129	1967	L. Piggott	117
1955	D. Smith	168	1968	L. Piggott	139

962	1963	1964	1965	1966	1967	1968
—	—	—	—	71(473)*	55(474)	116(528)*
—	—	—	—	—	—	—
—	—	—	—	22(301)	—	—
79(715)†	176(746)†	123(622)*	103(560)*	97(405)*	109(536)*	47(365)
41(324)	29(336)	42(349)	58(362)	38(391)	43(415)	34(346)
—	—	27(217)	—	—	—	—
—	—	—	—	31(275)	23(272)	—
47(336)	43(364)	—	—	—	—	—
—	—	—	37(313)	35(336)	35(358)	61(424)*
43(403)	28(374)	30(332)	33(416)	23(380)	34(346)	29(287)
—	—	—	—	—	—	40(356)
42(308)	23(316)	23(208)	29(139)	30(337)	30(315)	36(268)
—	—	46(344)	62(572)*	83(613)*	47(439)	26(322)
47(301)	—	—	—	—	—	—
—	21(318)	32(317)	—	—	25(289)	22(253)
—	—	—	—	—	32(306)	40(418)
—	—	—	—	—	—	39(275)
39(397)	28(396)	45(267)	48(397)	37(327)	—	78(492)*
44(318)	25(302)	34(298)	41(300)	60(435)*	37(389)	41(362)
46(383)	23(364)	24(363)	27(386)	—	—	—
39(325)	29(279)	—	—	—	—	—
43(260)	28(295)	—	50(307)	37(348)	42(356)	26(183)
—	38(256)	20(139)	—	—	26(242)	—
—	—	—	—	—	—	—
—	—	—	—	—	—	—
40(284)	36(321)	24(256)	23(315)	27(291)	—	—
43(125)	—	—	—	—	—	—
43(242)	25(313)	—	—	—	26(215)	—
—	—	—	—	—	25(229)	34(288)
43(545)*	68(508)*	72(483)*	78(517)*	59(495)*	56(480)	52(400)
47(649)*	109(675)*	136(678)*	113(654)*	95(638)*	111(575)*	111(527)*
—	—	—	—	22(365)	24(374)	—
—	—	—	—	30(261)	39(231)	62(423)*

	1957	1958	1959	1960	1961
Keith, D.	23(224)	30(281)	21(335)	38(396)	62(581)*
Klimscha, A.	—	—	—	17(261)	—
Lappin, T.	—	21(159)	16(149)	—	—
Larkin, E.	73(382)*	71(417)*	66(337)*	68(426)*	35(296)
Lee, B.	—	—	—	27(254)	54(428)
Letherby, D.	—	—	—	—	—
Lewis, G.	23(269)	32(292)	86(466)*	62(470)*	76(509)*
Lindley, J.	—	51(328)	47(333)	41(415)	58(338)
Littlewood, G.	33(313)	46(293)	32(328)	52(361)	42(359)
Lynch, J.	21(322)	30(329)	—	—	—
MacCaskill, W.	—	—	—	—	—
McIntosh, N.	26(200)	20(211)	—	37(281)	27(333)
McKeown, J.	—	—	—	—	—
Maddock, R.	—	—	—	—	40(317)
Maitland, D.	—	—	—	—	—
Masters, T.	—	—	—	—	—
Mercer, E.	105(511)*	125(624)*	100(510)*	—	—
Mercer, J.	75(389)*	84(470)*	87(495)*	95(519)*	87(446)*
Millbanks, S.	19(281)	15(225)	—	—	—
Mooney, B.	—	22(117)	—	—	—
Moore, G.	—	—	—	—	21(107)
Morris, Donald	—	—	24(257)	36(394)	32(378)
Morris, D. W.	—	—	—	25(233)	—
Moss, C.	—	—	—	—	—
Murray, A.	—	—	—	—	—
Oldroyd, G.	—	—	—	—	—
Parkes, L. C.	—	—	—	41(322)	—
Piggott, L.	122(557)*	83(536)*	142(558)*	170(634)†	164(701)*
Povall, P.	—	15(214)	24(180)	—	—
Purtell, K.	33(312)	23(206)	—	—	—
Rawlinson, A. C.	28(192)	—	—	34(215)	24(278)
Raymond, B.	—	—	—	—	—
Reader, R.	20(277)	—	—	—	—
Rickaby, W.	34(354)	45(381)	62(368)	35(294)	32(320)
Robinson, P.	51(387)	45(331)	43(277)	22(207)	33(339)
Robson, A.	—	—	—	—	—
Roe, M. J.	—	—	—	—	—
Russell, A. J.	60(328)	54(304)	34(202)	33(255)	21(237)
Ryan, D.	21(199)	—	—	17(227)	23(225)
Seagrave, J.	—	—	—	—	—
Sexton, G.	—	—	—	—	—
Sharman, J.	—	—	—	—	—
Sime, J.	58(424)	56(379)	84(415)*	108(536)*	77(470)*
Singer, R.	—	—	24(248)	—	—
Smith, D.	119(777)*	165(823)†	157(811)†	144(829)*	144(845)*
Smith, E.	70(475)*	71(488)*	79(539)*	62(491)*	50(411)
Smith, S.	—	—	—	20(233)	35(298)
Snaith, W.	62(514)*	53(433)	57(504)	42(500)	—
Starkey, G.	45(258)	22(164)	23(203)	26(230)	60(411)
Still, R.	—	—	—	—	—
Stirk, N.	—	18(133)	29(141)	28(168)	26(227)
Stringer, T.	—	—	15(102)	—	—
Swift, B.	34(136)	—	16(156)	—	—
Swinburn, W.	—	—	—	—	39(280)
Taylor, B.	—	—	—	—	—
Temple-Nidd, K.	—	—	—	18(214)	—
Thomas, M. L.	—	—	—	—	—
Tulk, P.	21(283)	—	25(231)	25(245)	—
Turner, G.	—	—	—	—	—
Ward, D.	—	—	—	17(241)	—
Willett, P. J.	18(174)	—	—	—	—
Williams, C.	—	—	—	—	—
Williamson, W.	—	—	—	—	—
Wilson, J.	—	—	—	—	—
Yates, D.	—	—	—	—	—

420

1962	1963	1964	1965	1966	1967	1968
58(512)	54(510)	27(278)	24(137)	42(430)	44(322)	54(306)
—	—	—	—	—	—	—
27(245)	21(213)	—	27(203)	—	25(181)	27(209)
20(271)			25(270)		—	—
			24(284)	47(430)	35(378)	
71(500)*	73(505)*	51(506)*	97(591)*	77(563)*	90(554)*	73(501)*
51(421)	71(376)*	55(403)*	62(391)*	51(385)	42(316)	26(168)
45(339)	—				—	
—	—	—	—	—	—	25(185)
—	—	—	—	—	—	—
—	—	24(207)	—	—		
51(363)	75(468)*	75(443)*	60(500)	51(471)	48(359)	36(337)
				30(303)		
25(224)	19(221)	—	—	—	—	—
85(485)*	88(471)*	106(507)*	106(587)*	89(541)*	78(340)*	68(435)*
—	—	—	—	—	—	—
—	—	—	—	—	72(233)*	—
26(150)	26(139)	33(207)	26(234)	—	—	—
—	—	—	—	—	—	—
—	—	—	—	—	37(434)	31(306)
—	—	—	—	—		39(240)
—	—	—	—	20(253)	—	—
96(456)*	175(652)*	140(625)†	160(650)†	191(672)†	117(552)†	139(580)†
—	—	—	—	—	—	—
—	—	—	—	—	—	—
—	—	—	25(244)	25(271)	22(212)	21(259)
38(367)	—	21(259)	—	—	—	—
60(386)*	35(324)	40(362)	37(281)	42(271)	58(270)*	25(210)
—	21(138)	45(345)	40(373)	42(313)	—	—
			44(400)			
25(260)	22(203)	27(242)	—	27(258)	—	36(276)
25(263)	22(271)	24(261)	—			
		18(134)	36(248)	43(362)	65(376)*	55(349)*
—	—	—		21(159)	29(217)	22(166)
—	—	18(118)	22(231)			
72(347)*	86(439)*	67(400)*	78(392)*	56(345)	37(285)	—
27(683)*	121(696)*	86(635)*	69(439)*	44(445)	67(484)*	—
51(453)*	44(368)	27(300)	25(220)	—	—	—
—	41(305)	19(194)	21(177)	—	—	—
26(349)	21(267)	31(379)	—	—	—	—
44(358)	44(417)	49(406)	25(327)	38(302)	51(305)	47(325)
—	—	—	—	—	—	38(280)
—	—	—	—	—	—	—
—	—	—	—	—	—	—
21(266)	23(338)	20(260)	—	—	—	—
35(207)	—	32(246)	49(300)	66(401)*	63(335)*	63(420)*
25(244)	—	—	23(220)	—	—	—
		43(322)	33(347)	40(402)	41(322)	33(242)
21(260)	26(301)	—			30(306)	24(312)
—	—	—	32(219)	24(177)	—	—
—	—	—	—	—	—	—
—	—	—	—	24(233)	—	—
1(327)	36(317)	42(315)	42(308)	28(360)	32(291)	29(265)
—	24(323)	22(335)	28(346)	—	—	28(227)
—	23(251)	26(344)	—	—	—	

421

TOP APPRENTICES (FLAT)

Year	Name		Year	Name		Year	Name	
1922	R. A. Jones	58	**1938**	G. Wells	27	**1954**	E. Hide	53
1923	E. C. Elliott	89	**1939**	K. Mullins	29	**1955**	P. Robinson	46
1924	E. C. Elliott	106	**1940**	G. Littlewood	13	**1956**	E. Hide	75
1925	C. Smirke	70	**1941**	K. Mullins	9	**1957**	G. Starkey	45
1926	C. Smirke	71	**1942**	K. Mullins	7	**1958**	P. Boothman	37
1927	S. Wragg	38	**1943**	J. Sime	5	**1959**	R. P. Elliott	27
1928	G. Baines and		**1944**	J. Sime	9	**1960**	R. P. Elliott	39
	L. Cordell	33	**1945**	F. Durr and		**1961**	B. Lee	52
1929	C. Adley	35		T. Gosling	10	**1962**	B. Raymond	13
1930	J. Simpson	28	**1946**	J. Sime	40	**1963**	D. Yates	24
1931	F. Rickaby	44	**1947**	D. Buckle	20	**1964**	P. Cook	46
1932	F. Rickaby	37	**1948**	D. Buckle	25	**1965**	P. Cook	62
1933	E. Smith	52	**1949**	W. Snaith	31	**1966**	A. Barclay	71
1934	E. Smith	36	**1950**	L. Piggott	52	**1967**	E. Johnson	39
1935	E. Smith	76	**1951**	L. Piggott	51	**1968**	D. Coates and	
1936	W. Wing	37	**1952**	J. Mercer	26		R. Dicey	40
1937	D. Smith	45	**1953**	J. Mercer	61			

LEADING TRAINERS (FLAT)

Amount of prize money followed by number of races won.

1900	R. Marsh	£43,321(31)		1935	Frank Butters	£59,688(48)
1901	J. Huggins	£29,142(42)		1936	J. Lawson	£61,773(49)
1902	R. S. Siever	£23,686(10)		1937	C. Boyd-Rochfort	£61,213(43)
1903	G. Blackwell	£34,135(24)		1938	C. Boyd-Rochfort	£51,350(44)
1904	P. P. Gilpin	£35,694(44)		1939	J. L. Jarvis	£56,219(34)
1905	W. T. Robinson	£34,466(52)		1940	F. Darling	£16,166(25)
1906	Hon. G. Lambton	£34,069(46)		1941	F. Darling	£19,026(37)
1907	A. Taylor	£24,708(31)		1942	F. Darling	£12,843(20)
1908	C. Morton	£26,431(20)		1943	W. Nightingall	£13,834(29)
1909	A. Taylor	£47,825(49)		1944	Frank Butters	£17,585(34)
1910	A. Taylor	£52,364(47)		1945	W. Earl	£29,557(41)
1911	Hon. G. Lambton	£49,769(48)		1946	Frank Butters	£56,140(60)
1912	Hon. G. Lambton	£22,884(55)		1947	F. Darling	£65,313(56)
1913	R. Wootton	£28,284(66)		1948	N. Murless	£66,542(63)
1914	A. Taylor	£52,052(39)		1949	Frank Butters	£71,721(42)
1915	P. Gilpin	£15,324(12)		1950	C. H. Semblat	£57,044(11)
1916	R. Dawson	£16,386(32)		1951	J. L. Jarvis	£56,397(62)
1917	A. Taylor	£17,924(25)		1952	M. Marsh	£92,093(30)
1918	A. Taylor	£36,629(33)		1953	J. L. Jarvis	£71,547(60)
1919	A. Taylor	£33,208(41)		1954	C. Boyd-Rochfort	£65,326(39)
1920	A. Taylor	£35,907(47)		1955	C. Boyd-Rochfort	£74,424(38)
1921	A. Taylor	£48,280(51)		1956	C. F. Elsey	£61,621(83)
1922	A. Taylor	£52,059(55)		1957	N. Murless	£116,898(48)
1923	A. Taylor	£49,190(46)		1958	C. Boyd-Rochfort	£84,186(37)
1924	R. C. Dawson	£48,857(26)		1959	N. Murless	£145,730(63)
1925	A. Taylor	£56,570(51)		1960	N. Murless	£118,298(42)
1926	F. Darling	£63,408(48)		1961	N. Murless	£95,972(36)
1927	Frank Butters	£57,468(54)		1962	W. Hern	£70,206(39)
1928	Frank Butters	£67,539(50)		1963	P. Prendergast	£125,294(19)
1929	R. C. Dawson	£74,754(58)		1964	P. Prendergast	£128,103(17)
1930	H. .S Persse	£49,487(46)		1965	P. Prendergast	£75,324(11)
1931	J. Lawson	£93,899(69)		1966	M. V. O'Brien	£123,849 (8)
1932	Frank Butters	£72,436(62)		1967	N. Murless	£256,699(60)
1933	F. Darling	£44,277(64)		1968	N. Murless	£141,509(47)
1934	Frank Butters	£88,844(79)				

The top forty trainers in each of the last twelve years are included in the following table with the amount of prize money collected and number of races won.

† indicates the champion trainer. * trainers in the top ten.

	1957	1958	1959	1960	1961
Armstrong, F.	£10,614(20)	£11,493(33)	—	£20,790(42)	£12,075(32)
Balding, I.	—	—	—	—	—
Balding, J.	—	—	—	—	—
Barling, G.	£9,679(29)	£12,343(27)	—	—	—
Bartholomew, C. (Fr.)	—	—	—	—	—
Beasley, P.	£13,854(24)	£22,480(30)	£11,895(28)	£16,662(30)	£12,204(19)
Bellerby, W.	£10,768(25)	—	—	—	—
Benstead, C.	—	—	—	—	£15,315(17)
Bertie, N.	£13,743(29)	£22,854(29)	£22,059(33)	£17,108(16)	£12,193(24)
Blackshaw, H.	£9,690(34)	£12,988(43)	£14,983(43)	—	—
Boutin, F. (Fr.)	—	—	—	—	—
Boyd, G.	£24,820(59)*	£15,867(43)	£23,463(54)	£19,724(51)	£38,528(38)*
Boyd-Rochfort, C.	£75,227(47)*	£84,186(37)†	£109,389(34)*	£18,852(13)	£34,739(24)
Bridgland, G. (Fr.)	£23,090(1)	—	—	—	—
Brooke, G.	£14,051(39)	£24,769(46)	£18,336(36)	£27,347(57)	£54,845(61)*
Budgett, A. M.	£13,784(32)	£23,265(39)	£14,989(48)	£19,520(37)	£12,897(35)
Calvert, J.	—	—	—	—	—
Candy, D.	—	£11,121(23)	£11,805(22)	£12,044(28)	—
Cannon, N.	£18,452(29)	—	—	—	—
Carter, P. (Fr.)	—	—	—	£16,186(1)	—
Clayton, J.	—	—	—	—	—
Colling, G.	£17,469(33)	£27,572(41)*	—	—	—
Colling, R. J.	£24,043(52)*	£36,538(54)*	£25,889(37)	£24,774(59)	£35,816(56)
Corbett, T.	—	—	—	—	—
Cottrill, H.	£29,187(46)*	—	£13,389(13)	£12,828(15)	£11,678(16)
Cousins, E.	—	—	—	£15,155(22)	£16,148(22)
Cundell, K.	—	—	—	—	—
Davey, E.	—	—	—	£12,603(41)	—
Davey, P.	—	—	—	—	—
Day, R.	—	£13,549(19)	£13,599(26)	—	£48,400(19)*
Dent, T.	—	—	—	£13,518(23)	—
Dunlop, J.	—	—	—	—	—
Dutton, W.	£21,353(43)	£28,486(47)*	—	—	—
Easterby, M. H.	—	—	—	£15,796(24)	£10,906(28)
Easterby, M. W.	—	—	—	—	—
Elsey, C. F.	£65,482(73)*	£72,119(72)*	£67,827(60)*	£40,428(70)*	—
Elsey, W.	—	—	—	—	£39,570(75)*
Fellows, E. (Fr.)	—	—	—	—	—
Fenningworth, G. O.	—	—	—	—	—
Gosden, J.	£12,134(25)	£15,351(22)	£18,824(27)	£46,271(30)*	£17,059(31)
Gray, W.	—	—	—	—	—
Hall, L.	—	—	£11,617(15)	—	—
Hall, S.	£20,086(29)	£26,425(45)	£24,458(36)	£55,383(64)*	£23,283(37)
Hastings-Bass, P. R. H.	£12,776(34)	£15,874(26)	£15,824(40)	£30,055(26)*	£29,604(45)
Head, A. (Fr.)	£29,711(4)*	£13,828(2)	£44,583(6)*	£20,861(4)	—
Hern, W. R.	—	£41,266(40)*	£28,435(41)*	£14,778(27)	£39,227(37)*
Hobbs, B.	—	—	—	—	—
Houghton, R. F. Johnson	—	—	—	—	—
Ingham, S.	£29,118(51)*	£12,321(26)	£16,589(27)	£25,181(25)	£41,809(51)*
Jarvis, J.	£32,529(39)*	£48,108(69)*	£27,532(42)*	£37,865(43)*	£29,988(36)
Jarvis, M.	—	—	—	—	—
Jarvis, R.	£11,131(22)	—	£14,863(43)	£16,708(35)	£11,365(33)
Lambton, E.	—	—	—	—	—
Laurence, G.	—	—	£11,748(28)	—	£10,922(22)
Leader, H.	£10,068(25)	—	—	—	—
Leader, T.	£25,779(16)*	£26,925(20)*	£18,277(15)	£17,676(23)	—
Lieux, J. (Fr.)	—	—	—	—	—

1962	1963	1964	1965	1966	1967	1968
29,642(65)	£49,473(59)*	£24,786(47)	£39,646(76)	£50,634(70)*	£53,946(68)*	£39,940(47)*
—	—	£17,841(19)	£70,216(43)*	—	—	£13,874(17)
—	—	—	—	£23,523(29)	—	—
—	£21,507(18)	£14,000(22)	—	£18,206(19)	—	£24,408(22)
—	—	—	—	£30,596(1)	—	—
14,975(18)	—	—	—	—	£14,993(16)	—
—	—	—	—	—	£19,402(28)	£14,748(24)
13,591(28)	—	—	—	—	—	—
—	—	—	—	—	—	£28,774(1)
—	—	£13,462(24)	—	—	—	—
27,719(22)	£30,664(20)	£23,393(22)	£40,509(11)	—	—	—
62,234(49)*	£36,428(50)	£39,041(37)	£16,757(31)	—	£14,763(26)	—
14,724(34)	£34,817(50)	£33,615(35)	£19,690(20)	£21,293(28)	£17,548(23)	—
—	£16,963(26)	—	—	—	—	—
—	—	—	—	£18,450(32)	£24,861(27)	£14,172(20)
15,817(22)	—	—	—	—	—	—
32,332(56)	—	—	—	—	—	—
19,800(34)	£52,828(42)*	—	—	£26,158(38)	£23.644(34)	—
14,764(18)	—	—	£21,911(25)	£18,148(17)	£15,699(23)	—
18,050(21)	£20,514(17)	£17,177(18)	£17,714(17)	£17,588(28)	—	—
—	£15,975(21)	—	£16,743(31)	£16,516(35)	£16,218(28)	£24,095(27)
—	—	—	—	—	—	£17,551(29)
—	—	—	—	£18,930(33)	£22,117(43)	£33,978(44)*
—	£14,957(26)	—	£37,560(55)	£17,163(36)	£18,867(41)	£21,992(35)
—	—	—	—	—	£21,282(31)	—
55,399(74)*	£45,332(73)*	£52,639(82)*	£26,120(48)	£28,687(39)	£42,875(16)*	£31,455(32)
—	—	£98,270(3)*	—	—	—	—
25,354(52)	£13,623(30)	£20,229(47)	£16,528(38)	£20,557(40)	—	—
20,830(27)	£21,806(18)	£14,105(18)	£31,577(26)	—	£16,449(21)	—
—	—	—	£25,980(29)	—	—	—
—	—	£28,802(13)	—	—	—	—
33,023(59)	£41,291(48)	£45,272(60)	£33,959(63)	£29,758(40)	£38,768(56)*	£20,669(37)
28,057(32)	£38,004(38)	—	—	—	—	—
70,206(39)†	£39,719(62)	£49,121(43)*	£68,198(39)*	—	£47,164(60)*	£22,192(21)
—	—	—	£20,910(23)	—	—	£17,495(33)
20,111(25)	—	—	£23,255(29)	£66,969(35)*	£58,150(29)*	£70,079(25)*
—	£19,151(28)	£17,667(25)	£43,633(34)	£32,965(35)	£19,427(25)	£15,217(21)
—	—	—	—	—	—	£18,457(27)
46,078(58)*	£55,437(52)*	£48,396(54)*	£48,466(34)*	£40,456(43)*	—	£29,500(23)
3,126(33)	£15,849(33)	£15,314(31)	£23,153(46)	£35,381(42)	—	£28,002(51)
—	—	£16,212(16)	—	£30,734(38)	£21,641(43)	£17,802(22)
5,857(43)	£15,263(19)	—	£20,842(34)	£30,685(33)	£26,166(34)	£33,557(38)*
4,104(10)	—	—	—	—	—	—
8,435(1)	—	—	—	—	—	—

o*

	1957	1958	1959	1960	1961
Lyde, W.	£15,178(27)	£13,648(30)	—	—	—
McGrath, S.	—	—	—	—	—
Mason, R.	—	—	—	—	—
Mathet, F. (Fr.)	—	£35,004(3)*	—	—	—
Maxwell, F.	—	—	—	—	£25,528(28)
Meaney, S.	—	—	—	—	—
Mercer, S.	—	£14,841(26)	—	—	—
Mitchell, C.	—	—	—	—	—
Moore, P.	—	—	—	—	—
Murless, N.	£116,898(48)†	£24,332(25)	£145,730(63)†	£118,298(42)†	£95,972(36)†
Nelson, P.	—	£14,727(29)	£18,320(42)	£25,519(31)	£30,904(47)
Nightingall, W.	£19,430(37)	£16,836(20)	£26,388(25)*	£27,898(25)	£39,247(39)*
O'Brien, M. V.	£15,755(2)	£67,543(9)*	—	—	£11,516(2)
Oxley, J.	—	—	£17,292(28)	£14,525(24)	£15,806(31)
Oxx, J.	—	—	—	—	—
Peacock, H.	£12,641(24)	£15,900(44)	—	—	—
Peacock, R. D.	—	£17,358(23)	—	—	—
Perryman, R.	£9,825(42)	—	—	—	—
Pollet, E. (Fr.)	—	—	—	£31,859(2)*	£24,884(2)
Prendergast, P. J.	—	—	£18,468(8)	£33,619(9)*	£39,301(17)*
Price, H. R.	£12,452(23)	—	—	—	—
Richards, Sir G.	£23,859(40)	£22,984(43)	£26,173(45)*	£28,834(52)*	£27,668(53)
Robson, T.	—	—	—	—	—
Rogers, J.	—	£21,033(2)	—	—	—
Rohan, H.	—	—	£20,786(40)	£14,091(30)	£11,391(37)
Shaw, T.	—	—	—	—	—
Sheddon, L.	—	—	—	—	—
Smith, Doug.	—	—	—	—	—
Smyth, A.	—	—	—	£13,001(18)	£14,273(16)
Smyth, G.	—	—	—	—	£30,171(37)
Smyth, R.	—	—	—	£13,916(24)	—
Smyth, W.	£22,697(40)	£12,590(18)	£18,897(26)	£19,147(26)	—
Stephenson, W.	—	£14,955(28)	—	—	—
Stephenson, W. A.	—	—	—	—	—
Sutcliffe, J. jnr	—	—	—	—	—
Taylor, P.	£10,689(33)	—	—	—	—
Thompson, J.	—	—	—	—	—
Thrale, P.	—	—	£14,293(19)	—	—
Thrale, R.	£9,933(25)	—	—	—	—
Todd, G.	£13,824(26)	£12,024(26)	£13,715(25)	—	£25,802(28)
Tree, J.	—	£11,080(17)	£11,884(16)	£20,336(13)	—
van Cutsem, B.	—	—	£11,835(18)	—	—
Vasey, A.	—	—	—	—	—
Wallington, H.	—	—	£15,032(9)	—	—
Walwyn, F.	—	—	—	—	—
Walwyn, P.	—	—	£18,855(44)	£15,589(28)	—
Ward, R.	—	—	—	—	£12,378(33)
Watson, G.	—	—	—	—	—
Watts, J. F.	—	£10,944(17)	£29,935(42)*	—	£16,569(21)
Waugh, J. A.	£12,931(26)	—	£15,474(18)	£12,272(25)	£12,647(22)
Waugh, T.	—	—	—	—	—
Wharton, W.	—	—	—	—	—
Whelan, D.	—	—	—	—	—
Wightman, W.	—	—	—	—	—
Winter, F., snr	—	—	—	—	£19,645(30)
Wragg, H.	£11,688(29)	£15,255(34)	£35,221(42)*	£30,227(28)*	£91,645(38)*

1962	1963	1964	1965	1966	1967	1968
—	—	—	—	—	£18,193(3)	—
—	—	£15,263(10)	£25,884(14)	—	—	—
27,485(2)	—	£14,222(1)	—	—	—	—
—	£15,300(23)	£13,453(23)	£29,325(29)	£23,618(29)	—	—
—	£33,098(15)	—	—	—	—	—
—	—	—	—	—	—	—
—	—	—	—	—	£16,831(13)	—
—	—	£13,415(9)	—	—	—	—
35,063(35)*	£55,468(42)*	£66,024(50)*	£54,977(35)*	£92,485(49)*	£256,699(60)†	£141,509(47)†
22,642(29)	£14,592(31)	£16,607(34)	£16,710(35)	£24,596(36)	£19,615(35)	—
20,100(27)	£26,592(35)	£25,483(36)	£57,431(34)*	£28,301(21)	£30,937(18)*	—
36,891(2)*	—	—	£32,168(2)	£123,849(8)†	—	£99,632(5)*
14,191(33)	£29,833(37)	£66,703(28)*	—	£19,776(16)	£29,685(28)	£19,804(23)
15,438(2)	—	—	—	—	—	—
—	—	—	—	£20,761(27)	£20,947(24)	£13,806(23)
—	£50,848(2)*	—	£65,301(1)*	—	—	—
53,060(13)*	£125,294(19)†	£128,103(17)†	£75,324(11)†	£41,587(10)*	£17,931(10)	£19,101(8)
—	£15,587(27)	—	—	—	—	£22,333(21)
40,066(64)*	£52,235(54)*	£20,532(37)	£42,094(33)	£38,171(47)*	£62,238(30)*	£18,698(32)
—	—	—	£18,301(8)	—	—	—
—	—	£72,067(1)*	—	—	—	—
—	£25,368(43)	£25,306(41)	£19,543(31)	£22,171(45)	£19,438(49)	£18,386(52)
—	£20,121(5)	—	—	—	—	—
—	—	—	—	—	—	£15,433(33)
—	—	—	—	—	—	£28,949(36)
17,227(29)	£20,205(28)	£21,420(38)	£29,985(40)	£101,867(32)*	£27,201(21)	£15,365(17)
—	—	—	£18,833(22)	—	—	£14,862(26)
—	—	£15,202(33)	—	—	—	—
—	—	—	—	—	£17,465(28)	—
—	—	—	—	—	—	£42,335(31)*
—	—	—	—	—	£20,810(30)	—
—	—	—	—	—	—	—
3,458(18)	£29,373(30)	£42,102(17)	£36,389(24)	£69,870(26)*	—	£17,213(21)
—	£50,496(19)*	£30,832(16)	—	£21,520(22)	£30,064(30)*	£48,073(32)*
—	—	£22,138(37)	£33,398(28)	£29,875(43)	£28,272(36)	£32,593(35)*
3,801(27)	—	—	—	—	£16,497(31)	—
—	—	—	—	£19,023(37)	—	—
—	—	—	—	—	£18,959(41)	£27,840(47)
—	£13,457(1)	—	—	—	—	—
6,181(27)	—	£67,236(19)*	£49,060(32)*	£25,272(30)	£21,218(26)	£16,771(19)
3,166(43)	£23,429(33)	£13,925(17)	£16,919(29)	£28,539(38)	—	—
0,156(22)*	—	—	—	—	—	—
—	—	£54,863(37)*	£52,523(27)*	£24,458(27)	£28,392(18)	—
2,274(20)	—	—	—	—	—	—
—	£18,929(21)	—	—	—	—	—
—	£43,104(36)	—	—	—	—	—
9,284(38)*	£44,077(29)*	£21,452(25)	£50,284(28)*	£44,871(37)*	£47,300(34)*	£37,870(33)*

LEADING OWNERS (FLAT)

The amount of prize money collected is followed by number of races won.

1900	H.R.H. Prince of Wales	£29,585 (9)	1934	H.H. Aga Khan	£64,898(45)
1901	Sir G. Blundell Maple	£21,370(58)	1935	H.H. Aga Khan	£49,201(23)
1902	Mr R. S. Sievier	£23,686(10)	1936	Lord Astor	£38,131(19)
1903	Sir James Miller	£24,768(15)	1937	H.H. Aga Khan	£30,655(30)
1904	Sir James Miller	£28,923(25)	1938	Lord Derby	£34,434(50)
1905	Col. W. Hall Walker	£23,687(18)	1939	Lord Rosebery	£38,465(14)
1906	Lord Derby (late)	£32,926(44)	1940	Lord Rothermere	£6,869 (5)
1907	Col. W. Hall Walker	£17,910(13)	1941	Lord Glanely	£8,762(21)
1908	Mr J. B. Joel	£26,246(19)	1942	His Majesty	£10,536(10)
1909	Mr 'Fairie'	£37,719(23)	1943	Miss D. Paget	£13,146(26)
1910	Mr 'Fairie'	£35,352(17)	1944	H.H. Aga Khan	£13,985(23)
1911	Lord Derby	£42,781(30)	1945	Lord Derby	£25,067(26)
1912	Mr T. Pilkington	£20,822 (5)	1946	H.H. Aga Khan	£24,118(33)
1913	Mr J. B. Joel	£25,430(31)	1947	H.H. Aga Khan	£44,020(28)
1914	Mr J. B. Joel	£30,724(22)	1948	H.H. Aga Khan	£46,393(28)
1915	Mr L. Neumann	£13,546 (7)	1949	H.H. Aga Khan	£68,916(39)
1916	Mr E. Hulton	£13,764(22)	1950	M. M. Boussac	£57,044(11)
1917	Mr 'Fairie'	£11,751(10)	1951	M. M. Boussac	£39,340(17)
1918	Lady James Douglas	£14,735 (5)	1952	H.H. Aga Khan	£92,519(29)
1919	Lord Glanely	£30,514(45)	1953	Sir Victor Sassoon	£58,579(39)
1920	Sir Robert Jardine	£19,385(29)	1954	Her Majesty	£40,994(19)
1921	Mr S. B. Joel	£33,048(37)	1955	Lady Zia Wernher	£46,345 (6)
1922	Lord Woolavington	£32,090(21)	1956	Maj. L. B. Holliday	£39,327(43)
1923	Lord Derby	£40,388(29)	1957	Her Majesty	£62,211(30)
1924	H.H. Aga Khan	£44,367(19)	1958	Mr J. McShain	£63,264 (6)
1925	Lord Astor	£35,723(20)	1959	Prince Aly Khan	£100,668(13)
1926	Lord Woolavington	£47,256(15)	1960	Sir Victor Sassoon	£90,069(29)
1927	Lord Derby	£40,355(37)	1961	Maj. L. B. Holliday	£39,227(37)
1928	Lord Derby	£65,603(45)	1962	Maj. L. B. Holliday	£70,206(39)
1929	H.H. Aga Khan	£39,886(35)	1963	Mr J. R. Mullion	£68,882 (9)
1930	H.H. Aga Khan	£46,259(23)	1964	Mrs H. E. Jackson	£98,270 (3)
1931	Mr J. A. Dewar	£39,034(15)	1965	Mr J. Ternynck	£65,301 (1)
1932	H.H. Aga Khan	£57,778(28)	1966	Lady Zia Wernher	£78,075 (2)
1933	Lord Derby	£27,559(16)	1967	Mr H. J. Joel	£120,923(34)
			1968	Mr R. R. Guest	£97,076(4)

1957

1. Her Majesty £62,211(30)
2. Sir Victor Sassoon £58,522(26)
3. Maj. L. B. Holliday £30,015(47)
4. Mr H. J. Joel £28,884(20)

1958

1. Mr J. McShain £63,264 (6)
2. Her Majesty £47,417(21)
3. Maj. L. B. Holliday £41,266(40)
4. M. F. Dupre £35,004 (3)

1959

1. Prince Aly Khan £100,668(13)
2. Sir H. de Trafford £68,682 (8)
3. Her Majesty £38,137(16)
4. Mr W. Hill £36,187(10)

1960

1. Sir Victor Sassoon £90,069(29)
2. Mrs H. E. Jackson £31,859 (2)
3. Sir H. Wernher £31,836 (9)
4. Mr H. J. Joel £24,411(31)

1961

1. Maj. L. B. Holliday £39,227(37)
2. Mrs V. Lilley £38,749 (9)
3. Mrs S. M. Castello £36,989 (4)
4. Mrs Arpad Plesch £36,806 (8)

1962

1. Maj. L. B. Holliday £70,206(39)
2. Mr H. J. Joel £38,588(17)
3. Mr R. R. Guest £34,786 (1)
4. Maj. G. Glover £34,400 (3)

1963

1. Mr J. R. Mullion £68,882 (9)
2. Mrs P. A. B. Widener £50,848 (2)
3. Maj. L. B. Holliday £42,513(27)
4. Lady Sassoon £36,411(19)

1964

1. Mrs H. E. Jackson £98,270 (3)
2. Mr J. R. Mullion £75,328 (6)
3. Mr C. W. Engelhard £72,461(19)
4. Mr J. Ismay £72,067 (1)

1965

1. Mr J. Ternynck £65,301 (1)
2. Mr Paul Mellon £59,453(18)
3. Mr J. J. Astor £53,484(18)
4. Maj. L. B. Holliday £52,521(27)

1966

1. Lady Zia Wernher £78,075 (2)
2. Mr C. W. Engelhard £58,460(26)
3. Countess de la Valdene £54,298 (2)
4. Mr R. J. Sigtia £45,196 (5)

1967

1. Mr H. J. Joel £120,923(34)
2. Mr Stanhope Joel £64,120(26)
3. Mr C. W. Engelhard £56,747(23)
4. Mr M. Sobell £52,112(19)

1968

1. Mr R. R. Guest £97,076(4)
2. Mr H. J. Joel £87,182(30)
3. Mr C. W. Engelhard £63,841(27)
4. Mr David Robinson £44,140(47)

LEADING SIRES (FLAT)

1901 St Simon	£28,672
1902 Persimmon	£36,810
1903 St Frusquin	£26,526
1904 Gallinule	£30,105
1905 Isinglass	£24,642
1906 Persimmon	£21,737
1907 Gallinule	£23,383
1908 Persimmon	£24,485
1909 Cyllene	£35,550
1910 Cyllene	£38,001
1911 Sundridge	£33,284
1912 Persimmon	£21,993
1913 Desmond	£30,973
1914 Polymelus	£29,607
1915 Polymelus	£17,738
1916 Polymelus	£16,081
1917 Bayardo	£12,337
1918 Bayardo	£15,650
1919 The Tetrarch	£27,976
1920 Polymelus	£39,704
1921 Polymelus	£34,307
1922 Lemberg	£32,988
1923 Swynford	£37,897
1924 Son-in-Law	£32,476
1925 Phalaris	£41,475
1926 Hurry On	£59,109
1927 Buchan	£45,918
1928 Phalaris	£46,393
1929 Tetratema	£53,026
1930 Son-in-Law	£44,755
1931 Pharos	£43,922
1932 Gainsborough	£34,790
1933 Gainsborough	£38,139
1934 Blandford	£75,706

1935 Blandford	£57,538
1936 Fairway	£57,931
1937 Solario	£52,889
1938 Blandford	£31,840
1939 Fairway	£53,441
1940 Hyperion	£13,407
1941 Hyperion	£22,700
1942 Hyperion	£13,801
1943 Fairway	£12,134
1944 Fairway	£15,704
1945 Hyperion	£39,727
1946 Hyperion	£52,961
1947 Nearco	£42,554
1948 Big Game	£40,690
1949 Nearco	£52,546
1950 Fair Trial	£37,887
1951 Nasrullah	£44,664
1952 Tehran	£83,177
1953 Chanteur II	£57,164
1954 Hyperion	£46,895
1955 Alycidon	£54,954
1956 Court Martial	£49,238
1957 Court Martial	£58,174
1958 Mossborough	£65,966
1959 Petition	£75,444
1960 Aureole	£89,076
1961 Aureole	£90,532
1962 King of the Tudors	£61,480
1963 Ribot	£121,288
1964 Chamossaire	£136,507
1965 Court Harwell	£112,708
1966 Psidium	£101,376
1967 Ballymoss	£113,601
1968 Ribot	£112,736

The top thirty sires in each of the last dozen seasons are in the following list. Prize money won is followed by number of offspring who collected it.

1963 includes stakes won in Ireland.

1964 includes stakes won in Ireland from November 14, 1963, to October 31, 1964.

1965 includes stakes won in Ireland with exception of period from June 21, 1965, to October 22, 1965.

1966 includes stakes won in Ireland from November 27, 1965, to November 5, 1966.

1967 includes stakes won in Ireland from November 10, 1966, to November 1, 1967.

1968 includes stakes won in Ireland from November 4, 1967 to October 26, 1968.

	1957	1958	1959	1960	1961
Abernant ('46)					
by Owen Tudor	£33,300(23)*	£13,016(18)	£15,499(19)	£20,994(19)	£20,251(24)
Above Suspicion ('56)					
by Court Martial	—	—	—	—	—
Acropolis ('52)					
by Donatello II	—	—	—	—	—
Alcide ('55)					
by Alycidon	—	—	—	—	—
Alycidon ('45)					
by Donatello II	£37,558(24)*	£59,246(19)*	£60,209(21)*	£27,018(17)*	£14,416(15)
Arctic Prince ('48)					
by Prince Chevalier	£19,585(15)	£19,707(16)	—	£19,358(12)	—
Aureole ('50)					
by Hyperion	—	—	£25,020(14)	£89,076(13)†	£90,532(13)†
Bairam II ('55)					
by Nearco	—	—	—	—	—
Ballymoss ('54)					
by Mossborough	—	—	—	—	—
Ballyogan ('39)					
by Fair Trial	—	—	£14,669(3)	—	—
Beau Sabreur ('45)					
by His Highness	—	—	—	—	—
Bewildered ('47)					
by Dante	—	—	£15,747(12)	—	—
Big Game ('39)					
by Bahram	£13,928(20)	—	—	—	—
Blue Peter ('36)					
by Fairway	—	—	£15,883(17)	£17,897(13)	—
Bois Roussel ('35)					
by Vatout	£12,330(12)	—	—	—	—
Bold Ruler ('54)					
by Nasrullah	—	—	—	—	—
Borealis ('41)					
by Brumeux	£14,242(20)	—	—	—	£16,237(18)
Buisson Ardent ('53)					
by Relic	—	—	—	—	—
Chamossaire ('42)					
by Precipitation	£18,343(18)	£16,820(14)	—	—	—
Chanteur II ('42)					
by Chateau Bouscaut	—	£18,597(21)	£42,585(17)*	—	£15,976(11)
Charlottesville ('57)					
by Prince Chevalier	—	—	—	—	—
Combat ('44)					
by Big Game	£12,733(18)	—	£16,154(17)	£36,322(19)*	—

432

1962	1963	1964	1965	1966	1967	1968
7,820(26)*	£25,983(28)	£22,225(21)	£22,280(20)	—	—	£19,983(15)
—	—	—	£22,244(9)	—	—	—
—	£30,138(14)	—	—	—	—	—
—	—	£23,606(13)	£40,442(12)*	£25,458(21)	£29,169(16)	£31,734(18)*
9,445(17)*	£26,022(15)	£62,637(13)*	—	—	—	—
—	—	—	—	—	—	—
3,558(19)	£32,864(22)	£23,852(22)	£85,519(22)*	£28,309(20)	£30,655(22)*	£27,961(17)
—	—	—	—	—	£22,689(5)	—
—	—	£49,718(16)*	£25,417(15)	£47,742(19)*	£113,601(13)†	£73,041(9)*
—	—	—	—	—	—	—
—	—	£19,814(11)	—	—	—	—
—	—	—	—	—	—	—
—	—	—	—	—	—	—
—	—	—	—	—	—	—
—	—	—	—	—	—	—
—	—	—	—	£21,106(1)	—	—
—	—	—	—	—	—	—
—	—	£39,277(17)*	—	—	£24,123(12)	—
—	—	£136,507(9)†	—	—	—	—
—	£57,052(21)*	—	£25,161(14)	—	—	—
—	—	—	£27,592(6)	£88,566(8)*	£23,610(12)	—
—	—	—	—	—	—	—

	1957	1958	1959	1960	1961
Constable ('52)					
by Panorama	—	—	—	—	—
Counsel ('52)					
by Court Martial	—	—	—	—	—
Court Harwell ('54)					
by Prince Chevalier	—	—	—	—	—
Court Martial ('42)					
by Fair Trial	£58,174(27)†	£42,832(26)*	£37,494(22)*	£18,429(17)	£37,907(32)*
Crepello ('54)					
by Donatello II	—	—	—	—	—
Dan Cupid ('56)					
by Native Dancer	—	—	—	—	—
Dante ('42)					
by Nearco	£33,850(20)*	£18,458(11)	—	—	—
Darius ('51)					
by Dante	—	—	—	—	£18,119(15)
Democratic ('52)					
by Denturius	—	—	—	—	—
Donatello II ('34)					
by Blenheim	£34,297(6)*	—	—	—	—
Doutelle ('54)					
by Prince Chevalier	—	—	—	—	—
Fast Fox ('47)					
by Fastnet	—	—	—	£16,186(1)	—
Faubourg II ('49)					
by Vatellor	—	—	—	—	—
Fidalgo ('56)					
by Arctic Star	—	—	—	—	—
Floribunda ('58)					
by Princely Gift	—	—	—	—	—
French Beige ('53)					
by Bois Roussel	—	—	—	—	—
Golden Cloud ('41)					
by Gold Bridge	£17,209(23)	£18,123(24)	£28,097(21)*	£20,031(21)	£28,803(18)*
Gratitude ('53)					
by Golden Cloud	—	—	—	—	—
Grey Sovereign ('48)					
by Nasrullah	—	£29,957(27)*	£21,550(20)	£39,780(20)*	£33,257(19)*
Hard Ridden ('55)					
by Hard Sauce	—	—	—	—	—
Hard Sauce ('48)					
by Ardan	—	£33,436(23)*	—	£17,220(17)	—
Hard Tack ('55)					
by Hard Sauce	—	—	—	—	—
Hethersett ('59)					
by Hugh Lupus	—	—	—	—	—
High Hat ('57)					
by Hyperion	—	—	—	—	—
High Treason ('51)					
by Court Martial	—	—	—	—	—
Hill Gail ('49)					
by Bull Lea	—	—	—	£19,843(7)	—
Honeyway ('41)					
by Fairway	£20,274(26)	£14,502(21)	—	£24,665(17)*	—
Hook Money ('51)					
by Bernborough	—	—	—	—	—
Hornbeam ('53)					
by Hyperion	—	—	—	—	—
Hugh Lupus ('52)					
by Djebel	—	—	—	—	—
Hyperion ('30)					
by Gainsborough	£14,543(10)	£18,787(16)	—	—	£23,931(8)
Immortality ('56)					
by Never Say Die	—	—	—	—	—

1962	1963	1964	1965	1966	1967	1968
—	—	—	—	£19,165(15)	—	—
43,579(14)*	—	—	—	—	—	—
—	£18,638(14)	—	£112,708(14)†	—	—	—
18,889(14)	—	—	—	—	—	—
—	£42,567(27)*	£35,903(21)*	£40,867(18)*	—	£68,945(21)*	£53,609(15)*
—	—	—	£65,301(1)*	—	—	—
—	—	—	—	—	—	—
17,821(16)	£23,399(16)	—	—	£22,127(12)	£41,868(11)*	—
—	£18,497(22)	—	—	—	—	—
—	—	—	—	—	—	—
—	—	—	£70,244(16)*	£28,854(18)	—	—
—	—	—	—	—	—	—
20,737(23)	—	—	—	—	—	—
—	—	—	£18,679(11)	—	—	—
—	—	—	—	—	£25,568(24)	—
—	—	—	—	—	£25,775(13)	—
25,649(20)	—	—	—	—	—	—
—	—	£24,073(19)	—	—	—	—
27,274(27)	£38,798(31)*	£21,698(22)	£36,995(23)*	£28,564(17)	—	—
—	—	£34,879(8)*	—	—	—	£25,281(14)
—	£17,965(9)	—	—	—	—	—
—	—	—	—	—	—	£26,248(14)
—	—	—	—	—	—	£18,040(15)
—	—	—	—	£44,035(7)*	£19,975(15)	—
—	—	—	—	—	—	£22,518(19)
—	—	—	—	—	—	—
20,502(20)	—	—	—	—	—	—
—	£18,048(20)	£18,542(23)	—	—	£24,241(18)	—
—	—	£18,258(15)	—	—	—	—
41,757(3)*	—	£38,431(11)*	—	—	—	—
—	—	—	—	—	—	—
—	—	—	—	—	£35,291(5)*	—

	1957	1958	1959	1960	1961
Impeccable ('44)					
by His Highness	—	—	£18,226(4)	—	—
Infatuation ('51)					
by Nearco	—	—	—	—	—
King of the Tudors ('50)					
by Tudor Minstrel	—	—	£13,272(9)	—	£41,025(22)*
King's Bench ('49)					
by Court Martial	—	£16,461(23)	£16,092(17)	£24,068(21)	£22,812(23)
Klarion ('52)					
by Clarion III	—	—	—	—	—
Karakatao ('46)					
by Nearco	—	£13,958(12)	—	—	—
Le Haar ('54)					
by Vieux Manoir	—	—	—	—	—
Le Lavandou ('44)					
by Djebel	—	—	—	—	£16,306(6)
Le Levanstell ('53)					
by Le Lavandou	—	—	—	—	—
Lucero ('53)					
by Solonaway	—	—	—	—	—
Major Portion ('55)					
by Court Martial	—	—	—	—	—
March Past ('50)					
by Petition	—	—	—	—	—
Matador ('53)					
by Golden Cloud	—	—	—	—	—
Match III ('58)					
by Tantieme	—	—	—	—	—
Midsummer Night ('57)					
by Djeddah	—	—	—	—	—
Milesian ('53)					
by My Babu	—	—	—	—	—
Mossborough ('47)					
by Nearco	£33,517(16)*	£65,966(20)†	£16,941(17)	£18,531(18)	£16,499(13)
My Babu ('45)					
by Djebel	£26,196(27)*	£29,457(18)*	£28,488(21)*	—	—
Narrator ('51)					
by Nearco	—	—	—	—	—
Nasrullah ('40)					
by Nearco	—	—	—	—	—
Native Dancer ('50)					
by Polynesian	—	—	—	—	—
Nearco ('35)					
by Pharos	£12,377(16)	£27,483(18)*	£16,339(10)	£15,235(11)	—
Never Say Die ('51)					
by Nasrullah	—	—	—	£37,285(9)*	£23,533(10)
Nimbus ('46)					
by Nearco	—	—	£21,931(20)	£14,480(19)	—
Norseman ('40)					
by Umidwar	£23,366(2)	—	—	—	—
Only for Life ('60)					
by Chanteur II	—	—	—	—	—
Owen Tudor ('38)					
by Hyperion	—	—	—	£18,924(15)	£32,904(10)*
Palestine ('47)					
by Fair Trial	£12,743(11)	£26,467(14)*	—	—	£17,144(11)
Pall Mall ('55)					
by Palestine	—	—	—	—	—
Pampered King ('54)					
by Prince Chevalier	—	—	—	—	—
Panaslipper ('52)					
by Solar Slipper	—	—	—	—	—
Panorama ('36)					
by Sir Cosmo	£17,735(16)	—	—	—	—

1962	1963	1964	1965	1966	1967	1968
9,626(22)	—	—	—	£24,238(29)	£19,473(16)	—
0,688(4)	—	—	—	—	—	—
—	—	—	—	—	—	—
—	—	—	£31,648(1)*	—	—	—
—	—	—	—	—	—	—
—	—	—	—	—	—	£18,492(14)
—	—	—	—	£18,350(5)	—	—
—	—	—	£21,699(14)	—	—	—
0,549(17)	£41,172(24)*	£19,914(19)	£17,704(25)	£22,077(17)	£21,052(20)	£20,838(19)
—	—	—	—	—	—	—
—	£33,573(17)	—	—	—	—	—
1,480(18)†	£19,291(16)	—	—	—	—	—
1,001(21)	£25,203(28)	—	—	—	—	—
—	—	—	—	—	£25,086(13)	£24,844(12)
—	—	—	—	—	—	£20,442(8)
—	£31,069(23)	—	—	£38,339(24)*	—	£21,148(26)
1,923(15)*	£37,507(16)*	£19,829(16)	£18,175(12)	—	£19,181(13)	—
—	—	—	—	—	—	—
3,416(16)	—	—	£29,440(5)	—	—	—
—	—	£30,740(1)	—	—	—	—
—	£57,492(3)*	—	—	—	—	—
—	—	—	—	—	—	—
0,348(16)*	£20,118(23)	—	—	—	—	—
—	—	—	—	—	—	—
—	—	—	—	—	—	—
—	—	—	—	—	—	£21,127(1)
—	—	—	—	—	—	—
—	—	—	—	—	—	—
—	—	—	£17,281(20)	£24,474(22)	£53,542(21)*	£21,260(20)
—	—	—	—	£22,305(16)	£25,865(22)	—
5,889(12)	—	—	—	—	—	—
—	—	—	—	—	—	—

	1957	1958	1959	1960	1961
Pardal ('47)					
by Pharis II	—	£23,366(25)	£16,432(21)	£24,651(17)	£60,288(26)*
Parthia ('56)					
by Persian Gulf	—	—	—	—	—
Persian Gulf ('40)					
by Bahram	£30,115(14)*	£24,530(17)	£60,107(15)*	£26,706(15)*	£19,188(14)
Petition ('44)					
by Fair Trial	—	£25,800(26)	£75,444(21)†	—	£20,851(19)
Phoenix, The ('40)					
by Chateau Bouscaut	—	—	£13,515(13)	—	—
Pinza ('50)					
by Chanteur II	£13,938(3)	—	£24,258(9)	£14,390(13)	£16,472(18)
Poaching ('52)					
by Owen Tudor	—	—	—	—	—
Precipation ('33)					
by Hurry On	—	£13,002(14)	£27,470(19)*	£18,351(12)	—
Preciptic ('42)					
by Precipitation	£12,800(17)	£13,809(19)	—	£21,515(18)	£18,815(18)
Primera ('54)					
by My Babu	—	—	—	—	—
Prince Bio ('41)					
by Prince Rose	£19,955(3)	—	—	—	—
Prince Chevalier ('43)					
by Prince Rose	£30,657(17)*	£18,539(17)	—	£14,897(16)	—
Princely Gift ('51)					
by Nasrullah	—	—	—	—	£15,782(15)
Psidium ('58)					
by Pardal	—	—	—	—	—
Quorum ('54)					
by Vilmorin	—	—	—	—	—
Red God ('54)					
by Nasrullah	—	—	—	—	—
Relic ('45)					
by War Relic	—	—	—	—	£15,133(16)
Ribot ('52)					
by Tenerani	—	—	—	—	—
Rockefella ('41)					
by Hyperion	£24,819(20)*	£13,396(12)	£13,186(12)	£25,977(15)*	£33,749(*14)
Round Table ('54)					
by Princequillo	—	—	—	—	—
Royal Palm ('52)					
by Royal Charger	—	—	—	—	—
Rustam ('53)					
by Persian Gulf	—	—	—	—	—
Saint Crespin III ('56)					
by Aureole	—	—	—	—	—
St Paddy ('57)					
by Aureole	—	—	—	—	—
Sayajirao ('44)					
by Nearco	£12,513(19)	£30,437(10)*	—	—	—
Shantung ('56)					
by Sicambre	—	—	—	—	—
Signal Light ('36)					
by Pharos	—	£14,508(9)	—	—	—
Sing Sing ('57)					
by Tudor Minstrel	—	—	—	—	—
Sir Gaylord ('59)					
by Tantieme	—	—	—	—	—
Skymaster ('58)					
by Golden Cloud	—	—	—	—	—
Solar Slipper ('45)					
by Windsor Slipper	—	—	—	—	£27,164(4)*
Solonaway ('46)					
by Solferino	—	—	—	£26,779(19)*	£54,505(19)*

1962	1963	1964	1965	1966	1967	1968
—	£17,707(18)	—	—	—	—	—
—	—	—	—	£24,980(14)	—	—
—	—	—	—	—	—	—
—	£35,005(16)*	£22,877(22)	£30,551(20)*	—	£27,199(16)	£30,708(11)*
5,479(12)	—	—	—	—	—	—
—	—	—	—	—	—	—
—	—	—	—	—	—	£18,060(7)
—	—	—	—	—	—	—
—	—	£18,733(10)	—	£25,463(11)	—	—
—	—	—	£21,472(7)	£38,524(12)*	—	—
—	—	—	—	—	—	—
—	—	£27,960(17)	—	—	—	—
8,080(24)*	—	£27,356(24)	£23,244(21)	£36,822(19)*	£49,588(24)*	£30,235(20)*
—	—	—	—	£101,376(10)†	—	—
—	—	—	£23,726(26)	—	—	—
—	—	£20,193(13)	—	—	£17,983(21)	£29,595(21)*
—	—	—	£23,506(11)	£72,271(17)*	—	—
2,021(11)	£121,288(7)†	£44,860(8)*	£39,752(3)*	£31,715(4)	£105,769(5)*	£112,736(6)†
1,028(5)	£43,372(15)*	—	—	—	—	—
—	—	£67,530(1)*	—	—	—	—
5,484(13)	—	—	£20,695(14)	—	—	—
—	£23,821(8)	£25,015(19)	—	—	—	—
—	—	—	—	£23,401(15)	£25,745(11)	£21,452(13)
—	—	—	—	—	£38,445(14)*	£24,470(14)
—	—	£60,255(18)*	—	£24,181(17)	—	—
—	—	—	—	—	£19,056(9)	—
—	—	—	—	—	—	—
—	—	—	—	—	—	£19,171(19)
—	—	—	—	—	—	£101,471(2)*
—	—	—	—	£18,920(15)	£33,251(19)*	£19,517(18)
—	—	—	—	—	—	—
—	—	—	—	—	—	—

	1957	1958	1959	1960	1961
Sound Track ('57)					
by Whistler	—	—	—	—	—
Sovereign Path ('56)					
by Grey Sovereign	—	—	—	—	—
Supreme Court ('48)					
by Persian Gulf or					
Precipitation	£13,208(17)	—	£34,362(23)*	£19,978(16)	—
Tabriz ('47)					
by Tehran	—	—	£15,341(1)	—	—
Tamerlane ('52)					
by Persian Gulf	—	—	—	—	—
Tanerko ('53)					
by Tantieme	—	—	—	—	—
Tantieme ('47)					
by Deux Pour Cent	—	—	—	—	—
Tenerani ('44)					
by Bellini	£13,823(11)	—	—	—	—
Ticini ('39)					
by Athanasius	—	£35,004(1)*	—	—	—
Tiziano ('57)					
by Sicambre	—	—	—	—	—
Tropique ('52)					
by Fontenay	—	—	—	—	—
Tudor Melody ('56)					
by Tudor Minstrel	—	—	—	—	—
Tudor Minstrel ('44)					
by Owen Tudor	—	£19,261(21)	£30,276(20)*	£14,605(17)	—
Val de Loir ('59)					
by Vieux Manoir	—	—	—	—	—
Vienna ('57)					
by Aureole	—	—	—	—	—
Vilmorin ('43)					
by Gold Bridge	£18,383(17)	£12,843(19)	£16,759(18)	—	—
Vimy ('52)					
by Wild Risk	—	—	—	—	—
Whistler ('50)					
by Panorama	—	—	£24,956(21)	£29,863(22)*	£19,190(23)
Will Somers ('55)					
by Tudor Minstrel	—	—	—	—	—
Wilwyn ('48)					
by Pink Flower	—	—	—	—	£20,800(17)
Worden II ('49)					
by Wild Duck	—	—	—	—	£14,438(5)

1962	1963	1964	1965	1966	1967	1968
—	—	—	£26,054(10)	—	—	—
—	—	£24,663(9)	—	£19,244(19)	£26,587(30)	£29,548(23)*
—	£22,020(12)	—	—	—	—	—
—	—	—	—	—	—	—
30,253(22)*	£31,604(25)	£22,696(20)	£23,648(27)	—	£19,185(23)	—
—	£35,339(1)*	—	—	—	—	—
27,987(6)*	—	—	—	—	—	—
15,759(13)	—	—	—	—	—	—
—	—	—	—	—	—	—
—	—	—	—	£41,732(1)*	—	—
—	—	—	—	£29,708(6)	—	—
—	—	—	—	£56,095(22)*	—	£35,565(22)*
—	—	—	—	—	—	—
—	—	—	—	—	—	£28,774(1)
—	—	—	—	—	£25,228(7)	—
16,611(19)	—	—	—	—	—	—
—	£30,132(20)	—	—	—	—	—
25,608(20)	£31,475(24)	£23,755(25)	£19,961(18)	—	—	£19,161(13)
—	—	—	£16,848(15)	—	—	—
—	—	—	—	—	—	—
—	—	—	—	—	—	—

CHAMPION RACEHORSES (FLAT)

Prize money is followed by number of wins. From 1963 Irish winnings are included.

1900	Diamond Jubilee (3y)	£27,985(5)	1934	Windsor Lad (3y)	£24,903(5)
			1935	Bahram (3y)	£31,328(4)
1901	Epsom Lad (4y)	£18,242(3)	1936	Rhodes Scholar (3y)	£12,466(2)
1902	Spectre (3y)	£23,195(6)	1937	Mid-day Sun (3y)	£15,273(5)
1903	Rock Sand (3y)	£18,425(5)	1938	Rockfel (3y)	£22,094(6)
1904	Rock Sand (4y)	£19,719(5)	1939	Blue Peter (3y)	£31,964(4)
1905	Cherry Lass (3y)	£13,119(6)	1940	Pont l'Eveque (3y)	£6,390(3)
1906	Keystone II (3y)	£12,837(5)	1941	Owen Tudor (3y)	£5,622(3)
1907	Lally (4y)	£11,555(3)	1942	Sun Chariot (3y)	£6,470(4)
1908	Your Majesty (3y)	£19,286(4)	1943	Straight Deal (3y)	£5,358(3)
1909	Bayardo (3y)	£24,797(11)	1944	Ocean Swell (3y)	£6,980(3)
1910	Lemberg (3y)	£28,224(7)	1945	Sun Stream (3y)	£13,865(2)
1911	Stedfast (3y)	£16,079(8)	1946	Airborne (3y)	£20,345(5)
1912	Prince Palatine (4y)	£20,730(4)	1947	Migoli (3y)	£17,215(6)
1913	Jest (3y)	£11,350(2)	1948	Black Tarquin (3y)	£21,423(3)
1914	Black Jester (3y)	£11,008(5)	1949	Nimbus (3y)	£30,236(4)
1915	Pommern (3y)	£11,200(4)	1950	Palestine (3y)	£21,583(5)
1916	Cannobie (3y)	£7,829(3)	1951	Supreme Court (3y)	£36,016(4)
1917	Gay Crusader (3y)	£10,180(7)	1952	Tulyar (3y)	£75,174(7)
1918	Gainsborough (3y)	£13,410(4)	1953	Pinza (3y)	£44,101(3)
1919	Tetratema (2y)	£11,494(5)	1954	Never Say Die (3y)	£30,332(2)
1920	Cinna (3y)	£8,529(2)	1955	Meld (3y)	£42,562(4)
1921	Craig an Eran (3y)	£15,345(3)	1956	Ribot (4y)	£23,728(1)
1922	Royal Lancer (3y)	£14,522(5)	1957	Crepello (3y)	£32,258(2)
1923	Tranquil (3y)	£20,707(6)	1958	Ballymoss (4y)	£38,686(3)
1924	Straitlace (3y)	£17,958(6)	1959	Petite Etoile (3y)	£55,487(6)
1925	Saucy Sue (3y)	£22,155(5)	1960	St Paddy (3y)	£71,256(4)
1926	Coronach (3y)	£39,624(5)	1961	Sweet Solera (3y)	£36,989(4)
1927	Booklaw (3y)	£27,745(6)	1962	Hethersett (3y)	£38,498(3)
1928	Fairway (3y)	£29,707(4)	1963	Ragusa (3y)	£114,744(4)
1929	Trigo (3y)	£23,690(3)	1964	Santa Claus (3y)	£132,103(3)
1930	Rustom Pasha (3y)	£13,933(3)	1965	Meadow Court (3y)	£87,158(2)
1931	Cameronian (3y)	£29,484(3)	1966	Sodium (3y)	£95,232(3)
1932	Firdaussi (3y)	£17,441(4)	1967	Ribocco (3y)	£100,286(2)
1933	Hyperion (3y)	£23,179(1)	1968	Sir Ivor (3y)	£97,076(4)

TOP BREEDERS (FLAT)

1909 Mr 'Fairie'	£37,719	**1924** Lady Sykes	£36,409
1910 Mr 'Fairie'	£35,311	**1925** Lord Astor	£36,323
1911 Lord Derby (late)	£42,999	**1926** Lord Woolavington	£39,869
1912 Col. W. Hall Walker	£26,141	**1927** Lord Derby	£41,039
1913 Mr J. B. Joel	£25,391	**1928** Lord Derby	£64,944
1914 Mr J. B. Joel	£33,092	**1929** Lord Derby	£30,644
1915 Mr L. Neuman	£14,482	**1930** Lord Derby	£35,681
1916 Mr E. Hulton	£13,379	**1931** Lord Dewar (late)	£40,837
1917 Mr 'Fairie'	£11,751	**1932** H.H. Aga Khan	£59,087
1918 Lady James Douglas	£15,980	**1933** Sir Alec Black	£35,229
1919 Lord Derby	£22,419	**1934** H.H. Aga Khan	£57,733
1920 Lord Derby	£17,048	**1935** H.H. Aga Khan	£49,285
1921 Mr S. B. Joel	£32,004	**1936** Lord Astor	£38,290
1922 Lord Derby	£32,277	**1937** H.H. Aga Khan	£46,252
1923 Lord Derby	£39,275	**1938** Lord Derby	£31,847

The top thirty breeders for each of the last dozen seasons are included in the following tables with the amount of prize money collected and the number of winning horses.

† indicates the champion. * in the top ten.

	1957	1958	1959	1960	1961
H.M. The Queen	£36,685(10)*	£39,626(13)*	£20,517(6)*	—	—
H.R.H. Princess Royal	—	£8,383(5)	£9,153(4)	£11,318(3)	—
Aga Khan, H.H., and Prince Aly	£26,914(5)*	£15,357(4)	£100,668(7)†	£24,608(5)*	—
Ainsworth, Lady	—	—	—	—	—
Airlie Stud	—	—	£15,314(3)	—	—
Allendale, Lord	—	—	—	—	—
Askew, A. B.	—	—	—	—	—
Astor Studs	£19,769(22)*	£20,615(14)*	—	£25,070(25)*	£27,859(22)*
Baillie, J. U.	—	—	—	—	—
Ball, R.	£21,442(4)*	£46,653(3)†	—	—	—
Ballykisteen Stud	—	£14,509(17)	£22,145(10)*	£18,183(18)*	£10,704(13)
Ballymacoll Stud Farm	—	—	—	—	—
Banstead Manor Stud Ltd	—	—	£8,696(8)	—	—
Barnett, A.	—	—	—	£9,693(4)	—
Baroda, Maharaja of	—	—	£16,131(1)	—	—
Basset, Lady Elizabeth	—	—	£12,777(1)	—	—
Bates, S.	—	—	—	—	—
Batthyany, Countess Margit	—	—	—	—	—
Beatty, Mrs S.	—	—	—	—	—
Bell, Mrs Reynolds W.	—	—	—	—	—
Benson, M. H.	—	—	—	—	£8,906(4)
Biddle, Mrs A.	—	—	—	—	—

9 Lord Rosebery	£37,377	**1954** Maj. L. B. Holliday	£45,651
0 Mr H. E. Morris	£7,647	**1955** Someries Stud	£50,125
1 Lord Glanely	£8,288	**1956** Maj. L. B. Holliday	£37,333
2 National Stud	£11,990	**1957** Eve Stud	£53,823
3 Miss D. Paget	£20,001	**1958** Mr R. Ball	£46,653
4 Lord Rosebery	£9,549	**1959** Prince Aly Khan and the late	
5 Lord Derby	£27,763	H.H. Aga Khan	£100,668
6 Lt.-Col. H. Boyd-Rochfort		**1960** Eve Stud Ltd	£90,124
	£23,059	**1961** Eve Stud Ltd	£41,354
7 H.H. Aga Khan	£41,165	**1962** Maj. L. B. Holliday	£72,629
8 H.H. Aga Khan	£38,509	**1963** Mr H. F. Guggenheim	£66,012
9 H.H. Aga Khan	£69,976	**1964** Mrs H. E. Jackson	£98,270
0 M. M. Boussac	£59,859	**1965** Mr J. Ternynck	£65,301
1 M. M. Boussac	£44,444	**1966** Someries Stud	£80,154
2 H.H. Aga Khan	£93,058	**1967** Mr H. J. Joel	£109,882
3 Mr F. Darling (late)	£48,099	**1968** Mrs R. W. Bell	£97,076

1962	1963	1964	1965	1966	1967	1968
—	—	£10,807(9)	£44,076(14)*	—	—	—
—	—	—	£25,122(2)*	—	—	—
—	—	—	—	—	—	—
—	—	£26,378(5)	—	—	—	—
—	—	—	—	—	—	£13,375(2)
—	—	—	£16,520(3)	—	—	—
2,759(20)*	£31,100(24)*	£33,600(16)*	£62,745(18)*	—	£39,122(23)*	£18,002(13)*
—	—	—	—	£15,712(2)	—	—
6,822(9)	£18,373(17)	£12,648(13)	£20,287(16)	£25,075(16)	£11,750(14)	£9,847(15)
				£29,378(13)*	£39,268(9)*	
—	—	—	—	—	—	—
—	—	—	—	—	—	—
—	—	—	—	—	—	£11,770(1)
—	—	—	—	—	—	—
—	—	—	—	—	£32,284(2)*	—
—	—	£11,652(1)	—	—	—	—
—	—	—	—	—	—	£97,076(1)†
—	£20,121(5)	—	—	—	—	—

	1957	1958	1959	1960	1961
Biddlesden Park Stud	—	—	—	—	£24,094(3)
Blackwell, T. F.	—	—	—	—	—
Brady, J. Cox	—	—	—	—	—
Brennan, D. B.	—	—	—	—	—
Brooke Stud	—	—	—	—	—
Broughton, Maj. H. R.	—	—	—	—	—
Bull, P.	£27,340(12)*	£12,657(7)	£11,052(8)	—	—
Burton Agnes Stud Co.	—	£8,985(8)	£10,286(7)	—	£28,541(9)*
Bury, Lady Mairi	—	—	—	—	—
Carroll, Miss E. M.	—	—	—	—	—
Celbridge Estate Ltd	—	—	—	—	—
Chambure, Comtesse de	—	—	—	—	—
Churchill, Sir Winston	—	—	—	£12,933(4)	£20,270(6)
Citadel Stud Establishment	—	—	—	—	—
Courtois, Mme G.	—	—	—	—	£10,342(2)
De Burgh, Maj. J. H.	—	—	—	—	—
Dennis, Maj. P.	—	—	—	—	—
Dormello-Olggiata, Razza	—	—	—	£10,223(1)	—
Dunne, Capt. P. R.	—	£8,994(4)	—	—	—
Dunraven, Lord	£10,016(8)	—	—	—	—
Dupre, M. F.	—	£35,004(1)*	—	—	—
Egan, M.	—	—	—	£13,401(6)	—
Eve Stud	£53,823(17)†	£17,004(21)	£18,545(21)*	£90,124(17)†	£41,354(10)†
Fagan, B. J.	—	—	—	—	—
Farr, T. H.	£14,540(5)	—	—	—	—
Fitzgerald, Commander P. J.	—	—	—	—	£11,072(4)
Floors Stud Co.	—	—	—	—	—
Fonthill Stud	—	—	—	—	—
Forget, M. R.	—	—	—	—	—
Fould, M. A.	—	—	—	—	—
Fremont Tousch, Mlle	—	—	—	—	—
Glover, Maj. G.	—	—	—	—	—
Granard Beatrice, Lady	—	—	—	—	—
Gray, Sir Harold	£11,588(1)	—	—	—	—
Greene, R.	—	—	—	—	—
Green Meadows Stud	£7,778(2)	—	—	—	—
Guggenheim, H. F.	—	—	—	—	—
Halifax, Lady	—	—	—	—	—
Halifax, Lord	—	—	—	—	—
Hall, E. N.	—	—	—	—	—
Hanstead Studs	—	—	—	—	—
Harrington, Lord	—	—	—	—	—
Harris, A. P.	—	—	—	—	—
Harris, G. A.	—	—	—	—	—
Harwood Stud Ltd	£8,797(12)	—	—	—	—
Hawkins, A. L.	—	—	£10,627(2)	—	—
Hely-Hutchinson, D. E.	£7,876(7)	—	—	—	—
Hill, W.	—	—	£35,054(2)*	—	—
Hindley, J. R.	—	—	£12,676(9)	—	—
Holliday, Maj. L. B.	£30,769(31)*	£40,113(26)*	£29,128(24)*	£18,181(24)*	£38,207(28)*
Hollingsworth, R. D.	—	—	—	—	—
Holt, Maj. H. P.	—	—	—	—	—
Hoole, Miss O. E.	—	—	—	—	£13,105(4)
Hue-Williams, Mrs V.	—	—	—	—	—
Hyde, S.	—	—	—	—	—
Hylton, J.	—	—	—	—	—
Jackson, Mrs H. E.	—	—	—	£31,859(1)*	—
Jarvis, Sir Adrian	—	—	—	£10,136(3)	—
Joel, H. J.	£29,256(16)*	£19,973(11)*	£16,209(8)*	£13,284(13)	£24,839(12)
Johnson, Maj. and Mrs S. C.	—	—	—	—	—
Kilcarn Stud Ltd	—	—	—	—	—
King, Mrs Audrey	—	—	—	—	—

1962	1963	1964	1965	1966	1967	1968
—	—	—	—	—	—	£9,840(6)
—	—	—	£31,093(2)*	—	—	—
—	—	—	—	£15,764(1)	—	—
2,680(8)	—	£9,779(8)	—	£14,085(5)	£17,723(7)	£9,613(7)
3,564(6)*	—	£12,377(9)	—	—	—	£16,249(6)
—	£15,212(11)	—	£15,645(9)	—	—	—
—	—	—	£13,599(1)	—	—	—
0,083(1)	—	—	—	—	£11,042(3)	—
—	—	—	£15,636(1)	—	—	—
—	—	—	—	—	—	£18,593(5)*
—	—	—	—	—	—	—
—	—	£21,780(2)	—	—	—	—
—	£16,328(3)	—	—	—	—	—
—	—	—	—	—	—	—
3,515(1)*	£35,339(1)*	£14,222(1)	—	—	—	—
—	—	—	—	—	£11,605(4)	—
—	—	£30,195(3)*	—	£15,550(6)	£37,719(5)*	—
—	—	—	—	—	£11,016(3)	—
—	—	—	—	—	£12,160(6)	—
—	—	—	—	£35,712(1)*	—	—
8,435(1)	—	—	—	—	—	—
1,481(2)	—	—	—	—	—	—
4,400(2)*	—	—	—	£21,848(3)	—	—
—	—	£30,259(2)*	—	—	—	—
—	£66,012(1)†	£35,691(2)*	—	—	—	—
—	£12,033(7)	—	—	—	£13,024(4)	£10,062(3)
—	—	—	—	£55,908(5)*	£18,056(8)	£19,858(4)*
—	£35,831(3)*	—	—	—	—	—
0,327(3)	—	£20,820(7)	—	—	—	—
—	—	—	£17,320(12)	—	—	—
—	£13,816(17)	£23,508(19)	£52,811(12)*	£22,808(10)	£11,507(15)	—
2,629(28)†	£43,395(22)*	£64,850(30)*	£64,084(29)*	£28,481(25)*	£34,295(16)*	—
—	—	£13,002(5)	—	£13,152(5)	—	—
—	—	—	—	—	£10,326(2)	—
1,771(2)	—	£21,111(8)	—	£13,652(9)	£23,167(9)	—
—	—	—	£10,220(1)	—	—	—
—	£28,523(5)*	£98,270(2)†	—	—	—	—
6,855(13)*	—	—	—	£15,184(11)	£109,882(14)†	£80,280(13)*
—	—	—	£21,484(3)	—	—	—
—	—	—	—	£49,492(9)*	—	—
—	—	—	—	—	—	£12,597(2)

	1957	1958	1959	1960	1961
Larkin, P.	—	—	—	—	—
Lambart, Sir Oliver	—	£20,727(3)*	—	—	—
Lawrence, L. L.	—	—	—	—	—
Lilley, J. A. C.	—	—	—	—	£11,332(6)
Lilley, T.	—	—	£15,710(1)	£10,620(6)	—
Limestone Stud	£9,186(13)	—	—	£11,137(15)	—
Loder, Lt.-Col. Giles	£15,720(6)	—	—	—	—
Loraine, Sir Percy, and O'Ferrall, R. More	—	—	—	£10,233(5)	£30,860(5)*
Love Ltd, Messrs Philip A.	—	—	—	—	—
McAlpine, Miss M. E. H.	—	—	£9,981(1)	—	—
McAlpine Farms	—	—	—	£12,479(1)	—
McCalmont, Maj. D.	—	£8,331(8)	—	—	£12,258(10)
Macey, S.	—	—	—	—	—
Macdonald-Buchanan, Mrs R.	£8,944(11)	£8,455(12)	£12,892(9)	—	—
McGrath Trust Co.	—	—	—	—	£10,984(5)
McGregor, S., and Venn, T.	—	£24,786(2)*	—	—	—
McIntyre, A. W.	—	—	—	£10,617(6)	—
Madden, W. J.	—	—	—	—	—
Margetts, Mrs P. C.	—	—	—	—	—
Measures Farms Ltd	—	—	—	—	£9,517(3)
Mellon, Paul	—	—	—	—	—
Milford, Lord	—	£12,289(10)	—	—	—
Mitchell, late W. J. and Exors	—	—	—	—	—
Moore, Mrs A. Levins	—	—	—	—	—
Moyns Park Stud	—	—	—	—	—
Murless, Mrs Noel	—	—	—	—	—
National Stud	£26,386(8)*	£9,365(7)	£20,010(9)*	—	—
Nicolay, Marquise de	—	—	—	—	—
Northmore Stud Farms Ltd	—	—	£8,897(5)	—	—
O'Brien, Messrs M & D.	—	—	—	—	—
O'Kelly, Maj. E.	£10,350(7)	—	—	—	—
Orbell, J. W.	—	—	—	—	—
O'Toole, F. B.	—	—	—	—	£9,200(13)
Overbury Stud	—	—	—	—	—
Paget, Miss D.	£13,137(20)	£11,640(18)	£15,086(19)	£24,580(16)*	£27,733(21)*
Phillips, J. P.	—	—	—	—	£9,165(9)
Plesch, Mrs Arpad	—	—	—	—	£36,220(3)*
Plummer, F. L. C.	£10,595(1)	—	£8,847(2)	—	—
Poe, Mrs Parker	—	—	—	—	—
Prendergast, J.	—	—	—	—	—
Prendergast, P. J.	—	—	—	—	—
Rathcannon Stud	—	—	—	—	—
Riley-Smith, W. H. D.	—	—	—	—	—
Robinson, Sir Foster	—	—	—	—	—
Rogers, Capt. A. A. D.	—	—	—	£25,082(5)*	—
Rogers, Mrs Julian G.	—	—	—	—	—
Rosebery, Lord	£18,153(15)	£22,875(17)*	£12,265(14)	£19,126(14)*	£13,260(18)
Rothschild, Baron Guy de	—	—	—	—	—
Sassoon Studs	—	—	—	—	—
Sefton, Lord	—	£10,103(5)	—	£16,008(8)	—
Sezincote Stud Ltd	—	—	—	—	£9,783(14)
Sledmere Stud	£16,174(13)	£12,163(11)	—	—	£15,298(8)
Smorfitt, Dr F. A.	—	—	—	—	—
Snailwell Stud Co. Ltd	—	—	—	—	£9,486(10)
Someries Stud	£12,845(7)	£10,478(7)	£23,045(10)*	£42,444(10)*	£8,762(6)
Southdown Stud	—	—	—	£11,125(6)	£10,664(7)
Stafford Smith, A.	—	—	—	£14,188(2)	—
Stanley Estate and Stud Co.	£8,883(9)	£11,093(12)	£14,564(10)	£9,984(7)	—
Stenigot Ltd	£9,275(9)	—	—	—	—
Stephens, G. S.	—	—	—	—	—

1962	1963	1964	1965	1966	1967	1968
—	—	—	—	—	—	£18,322(2)*
—	—	—	—	—	—	—
—	—	—	£14,830(2)	—	—	—
—	—	—	—	—	—	—
—	£18,016(7)	—	—	—	—	—
—	£14,435(15)	—	—	£17,767(14)	—	£15,573(13)
25,719(12)*	—	£9,064(4)	—	—	—	—
23,810(4)*	—	—	—	—	—	—
35,200(2)*	—	—	—	—	—	—
—	—	—	—	—	—	—
3,040(10)	—	—	—	—	—	—
—	£15,247(1)	—	—	—	—	—
—	£14,008(12)	—	—	—	—	—
—	—	—	—	—	—	—
25,801(1)*	£20,643(1)	—	—	—	£13,291(2)	—
4,526(5)	—	—	—	—	—	—
—	£16,313(8)	£11,064(5)	£51,428(5)*	£17,266(5)	—	—
—	—	—	£18,796(5)	£42,714(4)*	—	£9,913(7)
—	—	—	—	£16,169(9)	£12,820(7)	—
—	—	—	—	—	£11,864(2)	£21,319(2)*
—	—	—	£31,691(1)*	—	£10,017(6)	£10,452(3)
—	—	—	—	—	—	£22,776(4)*
9,636(10)	—	—	—	—	—	£9,708(1)
3,056(16)	£22,193(14)*	—	£10,229(10)	—	—	£14,715(10)
0,776(12)	—	—	—	—	—	—
—	—	—	£43,987(2)*	—	—	—
—	—	£9,793(1)	—	—	—	£13,760(4)
—	£18,262(2)	—	—	—	—	—
—	—	£42,783(3)*	—	£17,684(3)	—	—
—	—	—	—	£39,833(4)*	£43,083(2)*	—
1,862(20)	£34,212(16)*	£23,026(15)	£12,145(15)	£19,525(15)	£10,089(14)	£11,098(13)
—	£14,206(2)	—	—	—	—	—
8,842(23)	£49,522(25)*	£26,601(19)*	£15,205(14)	£14,659(19)	£23,773(12)*	—
—	£11,440(9)	—	—	—	—	—
—	—	£72,067(1)*	—	—	£10,537(4)	—
—	—	—	—	£14,767(9)	£60,353(11)*	—
—	£14,170(12)	—	£11,480(2)	£80,154(2)†	£14,439(3)	—
9,596(8)	—	£9,893(8)	£10,290(10)	£16,304(8)	—	£12,591(6)
6,097(12)	—	£23,082(10)	—	—	—	—
—	£19,765(3)	—	—	—	—	—

P

	1957	1958	1959	1960	1961
Stirling, W.	—	—	£14,597(2)	—	—
Strassburger, R. B.	£23,366(2)*	—	—	—	—
Tally Ho Stud	—	—	—	£17,602(10)	£39,457(4)*
Ternynck, M. J.	—	—	—	—	—
Torr, Brig. W., and Lambourn Stud	—	—	—	—	—
Trafford, Sir Humphrey de	—	£30,249(4)*	£70,750(6)*	—	—
Tuthill, F, F.	—	£11,181(9)	—	£12,195(8)	£25,878(10)*
Tweedie, Mrs R. R.	—	—	—	—	—
Vivier, Marquis du and Vivier, B du	—	—	—	—	—
Walden, Lord Howard de	—	—	—	—	—
Waldner, Baron G. de	—	—	£10,950(1)	£16,185(1)	—
Walker, Mrs D. M.	—	—	—	—	£37,436(2)*
Watson, R. F.	—	—	—	—	—
West Grinstead Stud Ltd	£11,521(2)	—	—	—	—
Westminster, Anne Duchess of	£14,872(10)	£8,134(8)	—	—	—
White Lodge Stud	—	—	—	—	—
Whitsbury Farm and Stud Ltd	£7,928(9)	£13,425(5)	—	—	—
Widener, P. A. B.	—	—	—	—	—
Woodpark Ltd	—	—	—	£11,010(6)	—
Wright, Col. P. L.	—	£10,022(5)	—	—	—
Wright, R. C.	—	—	—	—	—
Wyfold, Lady	—	—	£12,081(7)	—	—
Yeomans, I. M.	—	—	—	—	—
U.S.A.	—	—	—	—	—

1962	1963	1964	1965	1966	1967	1968
—	—	—	—	—	—	—
—	—	—	—	—	—	—
£2,696(4)	—	—	—	—	—	—
—	—	—	£65,301(1)†	—	—	—
—	£12,798(2)	—	—	—	—	—
£10,202(12)	£21,204(15)	£68,553(13)*	£11,846(11)	£19,253(5)	—	—
—	—	—	—	—	—	£15,113(2)
—	—	—	—	—	—	£28,774(1)*
£16,580(5)	—	£10,828(3)	£18,369(5)	—	—	£9,440(7)
—	—	—	—	—	—	—
—	—	—	£16,305(2)	—	—	—
—	—	—	—	£34,770(3)*	—	—
—	—	—	—	—	—	—
—	—	—	£13,487(4)	—	£22,174(8)	£10,198(7)
—	—	—	—	—	—	—
—	£50,848(1)*	—	—	£15,351(1)	—	—
£9,662(11)	£12,671(13)	£17,842(19)	£10,291(9)	—	—	—
—	—	—	—	—	£10,453(1)	—
—	—	—	—	—	—	—
—	—	—	—	—	—	£10,343(1)
—	—	—	—	£49,748(12)*	£26,531(19)*	£71,582(15)*

Statistics (National Hunt)

JOCKEYS
AMATEUR RIDERS
TRAINERS
SIRES

National Hunt Riding Records

PAST CHAMPIONS

Until 1925–26 statistics are for period January to December.

1900	Mr H. S. Sidney	53	1934–35	G. Wilson	73
1901	F. Mason	58	1935–36	G. Wilson	57
1902	F. Mason	67	1936–37	G. Wilson	45
1903	P. Woodland	54	1937–38	G. Wilson	59
1904	F. Mason	59	1938–39	T. Rimell	61
1905	F. Mason	73	1939–40	T. Rimell	24
1906	F. Mason	58	1940–41	G. Wilson	22
1907	F. Mason	59	1941–42	R. Smyth	12
1908	P. Cowley	65	1942–43	No Racing	
1909	R. Gordon	45	1943–44	No Racing	
1910	E. Piggott	67	1944–45	H. Nicholson and	
1911	W. Payne	76		T. Rimell	15
1912	I. Anthony	78	1945–46	T. Rimell	54
1913	E. Piggott	60	1946–47	J. Dowdeswell	58
1914	Mr J. R. Anthony	60	1947–48	B. Marshall	66
1915	E. Piggott	44	1948–49	T. Molony	60
1916	C. Hawkins	17	1949–50	T. Molony	95
1917	W. Smith	15	1950–51	T. Molony	83
1918	G. Duller	17	1951–52	T. Molony	99
1919	Mr H. Brown	48	1952–53	F. Winter	121
1920	F. Rees	64	1953–54	R. Francis	76
1921	F. Rees	65	1954–55	T. Molony	67
1922	J. Anthony	78	1955–56	F. Winter	74
1923	F. Rees	64	1956–57	F. Winter	80
1924	F. Rees	108	1957–58	F. Winter	82
1925	E. Foster	76	1958–59	T. Brookshaw	83
1925–26	T. Leader	61	1959–60	S. Mellor	68
1926–27	F. Rees	59	1960–61	S. Mellor	117
1927–28	W. Stott	88	1961–62	S. Mellor	80
1928–29	W. Stott	76	1962–63	J. Gifford	70
1929–30	W. Stott	77	1963–64	J. Gifford	94
1930–31	W. Stott	81	1964–65	T. Biddlecombe	114
1931–32	W. Stott	77	1965–66	T. Biddlecombe	102
1932–33	G. Wilson	61	1966–67	J. Gifford	122
1933–34	G. Wilson	56	1967–68	J. Gifford	82

Only the top dozen riders in each of the last twelve seasons are included in the following table. Figure in brackets is number of mounts. Star indicates Champion.

	1956–57	1957–58	1958–59	1959–60	1960–61
Ancil, D.	25(200)	35(256)	26(193)	—	—
Atkins, R.	—	—	—	—	—
Barnes, T.	—	—	—	—	31(174)
Batchelor, M.	—	39(197)	25(180)	29(176)	—
Beasley, H.	—	—	—	—	—
Biddlecombe, T.	—	—	—	—	—
Broderick, P.	—	—	—	—	—
Brogan, J. B.	—	—	—	—	—
Brookshaw, T.	—	60(309)	83(419)*	30(173)	90(490)
Chapman, C.	—	—	—	—	—
Cook, J.	—	—	—	—	—
Davenport, S.	—	—	—	—	—
Davies, B. R.	—	—	—	—	—
Dillon, D.	25(155)	—	—	—	—
East, H. J.	29(159)	—	—	—	—
Edwards, R.	—	—	—	—	—
Farrell, P. A.	—	—	—	39(205)	39(252)
Fletcher, B.	—	—	—	—	—
Freeman, A.	35(261)	53(282)	50(247)	37(171)	—
Gifford, J.	—	—	—	—	31(221)
Gilbert, J.	26(138)	—	—	38(163)	—
Haine, J.	—	—	—	—	—
Harty, E. P.	—	—	—	—	—
Hayhurst, S.	—	—	—	33(167)	—
King, J.	—	—	—	—	—
Leech, J.	—	—	—	—	—
Lehane, J.	—	—	47(311)	41(385)	29(328)
Leslie, D.	—	29(224)	—	—	—
Madden, P. J.	—	—	26(171)	—	—
Major, P.	27(213)	—	—	—	—
Mellor, S.	—	26(193)	32(277)	68(437)*	117(602)*
Milburn, G.	35(174)	—	33(164)	—	—
Molony, T.	48(309)	35(283)	—	—	—
Mould, D.	—	—	—	—	32(249)
Nicholson, D.	—	—	25(158)	36(287)	57(395)
Power, J.	27(226)	—	—	—	—
Rees, W.	48(247)	51(326)	30(232)	44(317)	52(306)
Robinson, W.	—	—	—	—	—
Scudamore, M.	58(366)	23(306)	45(348)	35(327)	33(344)
Shone, T.	—	25(238)	—	—	—
Speck, V.	—	30(210)	—	—	—
Sprague, H.	32(184)	—	—	—	—
White, K. B.	—	—	—	—	—
Wilkinson, B.	—	—	—	—	32(234)
Winter, F.	80(323)*	82(362)*	74(306)	67(346)	82(388)

1961–62	1962–63	1963–64	1964–65	1965–66	1966–67	1967–68
—	—	—	—	—	—	39(336)
33(180)	—	—	—	—	—	—
65(338)	35(220)	36(285)	46(219)	58(240)	34(235)	—
39(339)	41(288)	56(368)	114(532)*	102(467)*	83(363)	68(286)
—	24(143)	35(184)	48(201)	34(215)	50(260)	—
—	—	—	—	—	—	57(283)
38(365)	36(317)	—	—	—	—	—
30(220)	—	—	—	36(270)	47(212)	32(206)
—	—	—	35(234)	—	—	40(244)
—	—	—	—	—	—	—
—	—	—	—	—	—	—
—	50(298)	55(466)	46(310)	36(304)	64(280)	60(330)
45(261)	32(165)	—	—	—	—	—
—	—	—	—	—	—	77(268)
61(415)	70(371)*	94(415)*	—	49(155)	122(545)*	82(440)*
—	—	45(254)	52(278)	34(250)	34(255)	—
—	—	—	—	—	48(272)	—
—	—	38(241)	40(249)	41(333)	—	33(272)
—	—	—	—	39(177)	—	—
29(364)	—	—	—	—	—	—
—	—	—	—	—	—	—
80(481)*	64(306)	46(433)	71(407)	75(487)	63(481)	59(315)
—	—	—	—	34(152)	—	—
—	—	64(378)	—	62(369)	73(399)	55(319)
35(391)	37(355)	—	58(401)	53(390)	63(424)	36(347)
59(311)	33(186)	38(254)	53(225)	—	—	—
—	30(165)	46(220)	40(204)	—	—	—
—	—	—	43(338)	43(363)	—	—
—	—	—	—	—	—	—
—	—	—	—	—	—	—
—	—	—	—	—	34(259)	—
—	—	—	—	—	—	—
62(306)	29(171)	43(173)	—	—	—	—

P*

LEADING NATIONAL HUNT AMATEUR RIDERS

1956–57
McCreery, R.	24(142)
Moralee, A. H.	16(111)
Small, G.	9(42)

1957–58
Lawrence, J.	18(95)
Tory, M.	11(58)
McCreery, R.	10(68)

1958–59
Sutcliffe, J.	18(74)
Lawrence, J.	14(97)
Renfree, J.	13(73)
McCreery, R.	13(61)

1959–60
Kindersley, G.	22(102)
McCreery, R.	20 (72)
Renfree, J.	18 (85)

1960–61
Pigott-Brown, Sir W.	28(118)
Kindersley, G.	16 (87)
Shanks, W.	13 (53)

1961–62
Biddlecombe, A.	30(199)
Scott, D.	16(115)
McCreery, R.	14 (56)

1962–63
Pigott-Brown, Sir W.	20(82)
Balding, I.	15(83)
Lawrence, J.	10(61)

1963–64
Davenport, S.	32(160)
Renfree, J. A.	29(132)
Moore, D.	14 (81)
Sheddon, D.	14 (66)

1964–65
Gifford, M.	15(151)
Gorman, C.	9 (63)
Brewis, R.	8 (21)
Cann, J.	8 (35)
Macmillan, G.	8 (56)

1965–66
Collins, C.	24(138)
Macmillan, G.	13 (65)
Cann, J.	12 (49)
Gaselee, N.	12 (82)

1966–67
Collins, C.	33(124)
Gaselee, N.	24(197)
Scott, B.	23(183)

1967–68
Tate, R.	30(155)
Collins, C.	18 (67)
Gaselee, N.	13(104)

NATIONAL HUNT TRAINING RECORDS

In the following table only the top dozen trainers in each of the last twelve seasons are listed.
* indicates Champion. Prize money is followed by number of wins in brackets.

	1956–57	1957–58	1958–59	1959–60	1960–61
Ancil, D.	—	—	—	—	£9,183(19)
Balding, G.	—	—	—	—	£9,291(45)
Bell, C. H.	—	—	—	—	—
Bewicke, C.	£9,685(44)	£14,975(42)	£9,196(46)	£20,797(50)	—
Butchers, D.	—	—	—	£8,428(32)	£16,668(36)
Cazalet, P.	£15,083(39)	£17,446(51)	£16,635(48)	£22,220(58)*	£14,132(42)
Crump, N.	£18,495(39)*	£9,546(23)	£8,982(24)	£21,196(29)	—
Cundell, F.	£5,762(24)	£7,664(19)	—	—	£10,471(29)
Cundell, K.	—	—	—	—	—
Dale, L.	—	—	—	£10,143(8)	—
Davies, C. H.	—	—	—	—	—
Dreaper, T.	—	—	—	—	—
Easterby, M. H.	—	—	—	—	—
Fairbairn, R.	—	—	—	—	—
Hall, W.	—	—	£8,291(24)	£11,502(29)	—
Hudson, F.	£10,060(4)	—	—	—	—
Jones, A. W.	£6,509(6)	—	—	—	—
Kempton, J. H.	—	—	—	—	—
Mallon, C.	£6,402(10)	—	£5,829(15)	—	—
Marshall, W.	—	—	£9,629(42)	—	—
Oliver, J.	—	—	—	—	—
Owen, G. R.	—	£7,135(30)	—	£6,827(20)	£10,468(33)
Piggott, K.	—	—	—	—	—
Price, H. R.	£17,315(79)	£13,940(57)	£26,545(52)*	£11,487(37)	£16,379(33)
Renton, R.	—	—	—	—	—
Rimell, T. F.	£10,752(41)	£7,012(33)	£12,336(44)	£7,919(32)	£34,820(58)*
Robson, T.	—	—	—	—	—
Smith, Denys	—	—	—	—	—
Stephenson, W.	£10,756(37)	£7,497(29)	£17,488(17)	—	—
Stephenson, W. A.	—	—	—	—	£13,065(53)
Sutcliffe, J.	—	—	—	—	—
Taaffe, T.	—	£13,720(1)	—	—	—
Thomas, A.	—	—	—	—	—
Thomson-Jones, H.	—	—	—	—	—
Turnell, R.	£6,235(28)	—	£8,232(20)	£12,815(23)	£18,697(31)
Walwyn, F.	—	£23,013(35)*	£10,615(26)	£9,658(27)	£12,410(35)
Warren, S.	—	—	£6,159(33)	—	—
Whiston, W. R.	—	—	—	£10,528(47)	£9,340(49)
Wight, J. S.	£6,916(43)	£7,436(40)	—	—	—
Winter, F.	—	—	—	—	—
Wright, J. S.	—	£7,070(8)	—	—	—

1961–62	1962–63	1963–64	1964–65	1965–66	1966–67	1967–68
—	—	£11,865(34)	—	£13,459(35)	—	—
—	£11,363(44)	—	—	—	—	—
£7,211(25)	—	—	—	—	—	—
£18,412(55)	£20,499(49)	£27,791(62)	£36,157(82)*	£32,086(47)	£27,570(49)	£23,196(56)
£11,222(27)	£22,251(24)	£16,900(21)	£11,350(34)	£17,757(44)	£16,168(48)	—
—	£8,645(34)	£13,494(31)	£12,738(27)	—	£11,868(31)	£14,469(41)
—	—	—	—	—	—	£14,038(22)
—	—	—	—	—	—	£20,823(17)
—	£8,425(5)	£13,010(4)	£28,895(5)	£38,861(9)	—	—
—	—	—	—	—	£11,872(5)	—
—	—	—	—	£14,315(37)	—	—
—	—	—	—	—	—	—
—	—	—	—	—	£18,107(4)	—
—	—	—	—	—	—	—
—	£9,891(17)	—	—	—	—	£18,154(56)
—	—	£13,486(40)	—	—	—	—
—	£23,091(6)*	—	—	—	—	—
£40,950(64)*	£18,830(36)	£24,080(59)	—	£42,276(65)*	£41,232(73)*	£21,380(43)
£7,188(17)	—	—	—	—	—	—
£13,141(35)	—	£12,736(40)	£25,951(66)	£20,351(55)	£34,173(71)	£25,772(69)
—	—	£13,182(20)	£14,393(24)	—	£12,098(37)	£37,945(55)*
—	£7,294(9)	—	—	—	—	—
£12,246(50)	£11,507(46)	£17,786(59)	£22,160(68)	£19,504(65)	£26,942(85)	£23,100(72)
—	—	—	£17,579(18)	—	—	—
£13,581(27)	—	—	—	£23,783(43)	—	—
£14,530(24)	—	—	£13,931(20)	—	—	—
£11,826(33)	£11,913(35)	£33,049(59)	£27,325(52)	£28,954(46)	£27,988(42)	£22,921(30)
£26,252(40)	£19,540(32)	£67,229(59)*	£22,991(39)	£18,631(46)	£24,606(55)	£14,828(44)
£8,386(43)	—	—	—	—	—	—
—	—	—	—	—	—	—
—	—	—	£32,191(25)	£34,189(30)	£13,719(39)	£14,344(36)
—	—	—	—	—	—	—

LEADING NATIONAL HUNT SIRES

In the following table only the top dozen sires over the past twelve years are listed. The amount of prize money is followed by the number of offspring who collected it. * indicates champion.

1963–64 includes Irish sires from June 20, 1963 to June 13, 1964.
1964–65 includes Irish sires from June 11, 1964 to June 12, 1965.
1965–66 includes Irish sires from June 14, 1965 to June 8, 1966.
1966–67 includes Irish sires from June 9, 1966 to June 20, 1967.
1967–68 includes Irish sires from June 22, 1967 to June 17, 1968.

	1956–57	1957–58	1958–59	1959–60	1960–61
Admiral's Walk ('36) by Hyperion	—	—	—	—	—
Airborne ('43) by Precipitation	—	—	—	—	—
Archive ('41) by Nearco	—	—	—	—	—
Arctic Slave ('50) by Arctic Star	—	—	—	—	—
Arctic Star ('42) by Nearco	—	£4,996(6)	—	—	—
Artist's Son ('36) by Gainsborough	—	—	—	—	—
Aureole ('50) by Hyperion	—	—	—	—	—
Bakhtawar ('38) by Windsor Lad	£3,860(11)	—	—	—	—
Beau Sabreur ('45) by His Highness	—	—	—	—	—
Bellman ('36) by Achtoi	—	—	—	£6,812(7)	—
Bewildered ('47) by Dante	—	—	—	—	£6,294(13)
Black Tarquin ('45) by Rhodes Scholar	—	—	—	—	—
Bobsleigh ('32) by Gainsborough	—	—	£16,040(5)*	—	—
Bois Roussel ('35) by Vatout	—	—	£5,244(5)	—	—
Border Chief ('51) by Big Game	—	—	—	—	—
Border Legend ('48) by King Legend	—	—	—	—	—
Bowsprit ('52) by Blue Peter	—	—	—	—	—
Cacador ('35) by Foxhunter	—	—	£6,427(7)	—	—
Cameron ('37) by Cameronian	£8,948(8)	—	—	—	—
Caporetto ('47) by Dante	—	—	—	—	—

462

1961–62	1962–63	1963–64	1964–65	1965–66	1966–67	1967–68
—	£8,403(3)	—	—	—	—	—
£10,575(4)	—	£9,185(5)	£15,720(7)	£19,062(4)	—	—
—	—	£17,271(9)	£38,380(14)*	£35,260(14)	—	—
—	—	—	—	—	£10,947(22)	£12,433(17)
—	—	—	—	—	—	—
—	—	—	£9,647(16)	—	—	—
—	—	—	£9,976(9)	—	—	—
—	—	—	—	—	—	—
—	—	—	—	—	—	£9,917(9)
—	—	—	—	—	—	—
£5,497(16)	—	—	—	—	—	—
—	—	£8,936(15)	—	—	—	£12,786(24)
—	—	—	—	—	—	—
—	—	—	—	—	—	—
—	—	—	—	—	£11,174(6)	—
£6,403(11)	—	—	—	—	—	—
—	—	—	—	—	£11,510(12)	—
—	—	£8,314(10)	—	—	—	—
—	—	—	—	—	—	—
—	—	—	—	—	—	£10,876(7)

	1956–57	1957–58	1958–59	1959–60	1960–61
Carnival Boy ('41)					
by Colombo	—	—	—	£13,948(2)*	—
Caudillo ('39)					
by Solario	—	—	—	—	£5,835(1)
Colonist II ('46)					
by Rienzo	—	—	—	—	—
Combat ('44)					
by Big Game	—	—	—	—	—
Coup de Myth ('42)					
by Coup de Lyon	—	—	—	—	—
Court Harwell ('54)					
by Prince Chevalier	—	—	—	—	—
Dante ('42)					
by Nearco	—	—	—	£4,412(6)	—
Deux Pour Cent ('41)					
by Deiri	—	£9,663(2)	—	—	—
Devonian ('38)					
by Hyperion	—	—	—	£4,485(6)	—
Domaha ('34)					
by Vatout	—	—	—	£8,355(12)	£6,181(15)
Donatello II ('34)					
by Blenheim	—	—	£8,289(6)	—	—
Doubtless II ('44)					
by Cute Eyes	—	—	—	—	—
Eastern Venture ('50)					
by Marsyas II	—	—	—	—	—
Erin's Pride ('45)					
by Fairfax	—	—	—	£5,600(2)	£9,881(1)
Flamenco ('31)					
by Flamingo	£4,465(13)	£5,227(10)	£6,607(9)	—	£8,793(18)
Flush Royal ('45)					
by Majano	—	—	—	—	—
Fortina ('41)					
by Formor	—	£6,113(10)	—	£5,767(11)	£17,181(20)
Fun Fare ('40)					
by Fair Trial	—	—	—	—	—
Grand Inquisitor ('39)					
by His Reverence	—	£14,060(3)*	—	—	—
Greek Star ('41)					
by Hyperion	—	—	—	—	—
Hard Sauce ('48)					
by Ardan	—	—	—	—	—
Honor's Choice ('35)					
by Embargo	—	£6,945(5)	—	£9,633(4)	—
Hyacinthus (38)					
by Hyperion	—	—	—	—	—
Iceberg II ('35)					
by Van	—	£4,794(4)	—	—	—
Jim Newcombe ('34)					
by Embargo	—	—	—	£10,173(2)	—
Jock Scot ('45)					
by Scottish Union	—	—	—	—	—
King Hal ('37)					
by Windsor Lad	£5,061(4)	£5,046(8)	£7,098(7)	—	—
Lake Placid ('45)					
by Bobsleigh	—	—	—	—	—
Lighthouse II ('37)					
by Pharos	£5,458(15)	—	£8,124(14)	—	—
Magic Red ('41)					
by Link Boy	—	—	—	—	—
Maquis ('42)					
by Bois Roussel	—	£6,582(3)	—	—	—
Migoli ('44)					
by Bois Roussel	£4,421(6)	—	—	—	—

1961–62	1962–63	1963–64	1964–65	1965–66	1966–67	1967–68
—	—	—	—	—	—	—
—	—	—	—	—	—	—
—	—	—	—	£10,872(10)	£9,870(4)	—
—	—	£12,686(10)	—	—	—	—
—	—	—	—	£17,499(4)	—	—
—	—	—	—	£10,177(5)	—	—
—	—	—	—	—	—	—
£11,649(1)	—	—	—	—	—	—
—	—	—	—	—	—	£16,827(5)
£10,997(16)	£7,470(13)	£21,227(12)	£9,538(7)	£11,169(11)	—	—
—	—	—	—	—	—	—
—	£6,712(12)	—	—	£8,778(11)	£10,381(14)	£11,057(16)
—	—	—	—	—	£13,206(6)	—
—	—	—	—	—	—	—
—	—	—	—	—	—	—
£8,111(8)	—	—	£10,973(11)	—	—	£9,339(13)
£8,760(14)	£9,522(12)	£12,532(23)	£25,989(23)	£15,585(21)	£21,827(23)	£22,796(28)
—	£6,233(3)	—	—	—	—	—
—	—	—	—	—	—	—
—	—	—	—	£24,415(5)	—	—
—	—	—	—	—	£12,670(5)	—
—	—	—	—	—	—	—
—	—	—	£14,043(12)	—	—	—
—	—	—	—	—	—	—
—	—	—	—	—	—	—
£6,126(13)	£9,036(8)	—	£10,340(13)	£10,422(11)	£10,867(12)	—
—	£10,396(5)	£14,173(12)	—	—	—	—
—	—	£11,136(1)	—	—	—	—
—	—	—	—	—	—	—
—	—	—	—	—	—	£19,712(2)
—	—	—	—	—	—	—
—	—	—	—	—	—	—

	1956–57	1957–58	1958–59	1959–60	1960–61
Monsieur L'Amiral ('41)					
by Admiral Drake	—	—	—	—	—
Mustang ('41)					
by Mieuxce	—	£5,693(15)	£4,824(12)	—	—
Nicolaus ('39)					
by Solario	—	—	—	—	£23,182(6)*
Nosca ('39)					
by Abjer	—	—	—	—	£5,593(4)
Ocean Swell ('41)					
by Blue Peter	—	—	—	—	£6,324(3)
Owenstown ('34)					
by Apron	—	—	£7,865(8)	—	—
Pactolus ('35)					
by Pharos	£5,245(3)	—	—	—	—
Pappageno II ('35)					
by Prince Rose	—	—	—	—	—
Persian Gulf ('40)					
by Bahram	—	—	—	—	—
Rio d'Egypte ('35)					
by Van	—	—	—	£5,115(3)	—
Rosewell ('35)					
by Orwell	£9,540(7)	—	—	—	—
Scottish Union ('35)					
by Cameronian	£3,756(7)	—	—	—	—
Straight Deal ('40					
by Solario	£10,097(11)*	—	—	£4,573(10)	£5,841(9)
Sun King ('39)					
by Hyperion	£9,930(2)	—	—	—	—
Supertello ('46)					
by Donatello II	—	—	—	—	—
Supreme Court ('48)					
by Persian Gulf					
or Precipitation	—	—	—	—	—
Tambourin ('39)					
by Biribi	—	£8,491(5)	—	—	—
Tangle ('47)					
by Mustang	—	—	—	—	—
Tartan ('30)					
by Ellangowan	—	—	—	—	£13,551(8)
Thoroughfare ('38)					
by Fairway	—	—	£6,022(5)	—	—
Tonga Prince ('52)					
by Polynesian	—	—	—	—	—
Ujiji ('39)					
by Umidwar	—	£8,552(9)	£6,449(5)	—	—
Vic Day ('45)					
by Prince Rose	—	—	£5,014(5)	—	—
Vulgan ('43)					
by Sirlan	—	—	—	£12,061(15)	£5,825(18)
Wood Cot ('41)					
by Bois Roussel	£3,775(6)	—	—	—	—
Zalophus ('39)					
by Tetratema	—	—	—	—	—

1961–62	1962–63	1963–64	1964–65	1965–66	1966–67	1967–68
—	£9,354(3)	—	—	—	—	—
—	—	—	—	—	£11,131(12)	£11,380(10)
£6,002(5)	—	—	—	—	—	—
—	—	—	—	—	—	—
—	—	—	—	—	—	—
—	—	—	—	—	—	—
—	£6,386(5)	—	—	—	—	—
—	—	—	—	—	—	£15,710(3)
—	—	—	—	—	—	—
—	—	—	—	—	—	—
£6,499(3)	—	—	—	—	—	—
—	£8,444(7)	—	—	£10,028(13)	£18,164(20)	—
—	—	—	—	—	—	—
—	£23,500(5)*	—	—	—	—	—
—	—	£13,342(7)	—	—	—	—
—	—	—	—	—	—	—
—	—	£13,485(5)	£10,677(6)	—	—	—
—	—	—	—	—	—	—
—	—	—	—	—	—	—
—	—	—	£23,237(1)	—	—	—
—	—	—	—	—	—	—
£7,469(4)	—	—	—	—	—	—
—	£7,581(16)	£42,751(31)*	£23,392(34)	£45,482(48)*	£62,109(53)*	£38,662(47)*
—	—	—	—	—	—	—
£20,239(1)*	—	—	—	—	—	—

Racing Fixtures for 1969

Racing Fixtures for 1969

Subject to alterations. National Hunt fixtures in italics

Figure in brackets is number of days. † **Evening Racing.** ‡ **Evening Racing first day only.** § **Evening Racing second day only.**

Jan.	1	(Wednesday)	*Catterick Bridge* (1)
„	1	(Wednesday)	*Plumpton* (1)
„	1	(Wednesday)	*Cheltenham* (2)
„	2	(Thursday)	*Ayr* (2)
„	3	(Friday)	*Haydock Park* (2)
„	3	(Friday)	*Sandown Park* (2)
„	4	(Saturday)	*Teesside Park (Stockton)* (1)
„	6	(Monday)	*Leicester* (1)
„	7	(Tuesday)	*Sedgefield* (1)
„	8	(Wednesday)	*Windsor* (1)
„	9	(Thursday)	*Warwick* (1)
„	10	(Friday)	*Newbury* (2)
„	11	(Saturday)	*Catterick Bridge* (1)
„	13	(Monday)	*Wolverhampton* (2)
„	15	(Wednesday)	*Plumpton* (1)
„	16	(Thursday)	*Wincanton* (1)
„	17	(Friday)	*Lingfield Park* (2)
„	18	(Saturday)	*Catterick Bridge* (1)
„	18	(Saturday)	*Haydock Park* (1)
„	18	(Saturday)	*Warwick* (1)
„	20	(Monday)	*Leicester* (1)
„	21	(Tuesday)	*Wetherby* (1)
„	22	(Wednesday)	*Windsor* (1)
„	23	(Thursday)	*Taunton* (1)
„	23	(Thursday)	*Towcester* (1)
Jan.	24	(Friday)	*Fontwell Park* (1)
„	25	(Saturday)	*Doncaster* (1)
„	25	(Saturday)	*Sedgefield* (1)
„	25	(Saturday)	*Windsor* (1)
„	27	(Monday)	*Worcester* (1)
„	28	(Tuesday)	*Market Rasen* (1)
„	29	(Wednesday)	*Plumpton* (1)
„	30	(Thursday)	*Warwick* (1)
„	31	(Friday)	*Kempton Park* (2)
Feb.	1	(Saturday)	*Newcastle* (1)
„	1	(Saturday)	*Stratford-on-Avon* (1)
„	3	(Monday)	*Nottingham* (2)
„	5	(Wednesday)	*Haydock Park* (2)
„	7	(Friday)	*Sandown Park* (2)
„	8	(Saturday)	*Ayr* (1)
„	8	(Saturday)	*Wetherby* (1)
„	10	(Monday)	*Plumpton* (1)
„	10	(Monday)	*Leicester* (2)
„	12	(Wednesday)	*Fontwell Park* (1)
„	13	(Thursday)	*Wincanton* (1)
„	14	(Friday)	*Newbury* (2)
„	15	(Saturday)	*Catterick Bridge* (1)
„	17	(Monday)	*Wolverhampton* (2)
„	19	(Wednesday)	*Ascot Heath* (2)
„	21	(Friday)	*Lingfield Park* (2)

Feb.	22	(Saturday)	Chepstow (1)
"	22	(Saturday)	Newcastle (1)
"	22	(Saturday)	Stratford-on-Avon (1)
"	24	(Monday)	Nottingham (1)
"	24	(Monday)	Plumpton (1)
"	25	(Tuesday)	Sedgefield (1)
"	26	(Wednesday)	Windsor (1)
"	27	(Thursday)	Wincanton (1)
"	28	(Friday)	Kempton Park (2)
Mar.	1	(Saturday)	Kelso (1)
"	1	(Saturday)	Market Rasen (1)
"	1	(Saturday)	Warwick (1)
"	3	(Monday)	Warwick (1)
"	3	(Monday)	Wye (1)
"	3	(Monday)	Doncaster (2)
"	5	(Wednesday)	Ludlow (2)
"	7	(Friday)	Haydock Park (2)
"	7	(Friday)	Newbury (2)
"	8	(Saturday)	Hereford (1)
"	8	(Saturday)	Wetherby (1)
"	8	(Saturday)	Ayr (1)
"	10	(Monday)	Ayr (1)
"	10	(Monday)	Wolverhampton (1)
"	11	(Tuesday)	Worcester (1)
"	12	(Wednesday)	Plumpton (1)
"	13	(Thursday)	Stratford-on-Avon (1)
"	14	(Friday)	Grand Military M. (Sandown Park) (2)
"	15	(Saturday)	Bangor-on-Dee (1)
"	15	(Saturday)	Sedgefield (1)
"	15	(Saturday)	Taunton (1)
"	17	(Monday)	Southwell (1)
"	17	(Monday)	Worcester (1)
"	17	(Monday)	Wye (1)
"	18	(Tuesday)	National Hunt M. (Cheltenham) (3)
"	21	(Friday)	Lingfield Park (2)
"	22	(Saturday)	Market Rasen (1)
"	22	(Saturday)	Newcastle (1)
"	22	(Saturday)	Uttoxeter (1)

Mar.	24	(Monday)	*Folkestone* (1)
"	24	(Monday)	**Doncaster** (3)
"	24	(Monday)	**Doncaster** (3)
"	26	(Wednesday)	Plumpton (1)
"	27	(Thursday)	Wincanton (1)
"	27	(Thursday)	**Liverpool** (3)
"	27	(Thursday)	**Liverpool** (3)
"	29	(Saturday)	**Catterick Bridge** (1)
"	31	(Monday)	Fontwell Park (1)
"	31	(Monday)	*Nottingham* (1)
Apr.	1	(Tuesday)	*Folkestone* (1)
"	2	(Wednesday)	Worcester (2)
"	3	(Thursday)	Southwell (1)
"	5	(Saturday)	**Doncaster** (1)
"	5	(Saturday)	Southwell (1)
"	5	(Saturday)	**Teesside Park (Stockton)** (1)
"	5	(Saturday)	*Carlisle* (1)
"	5	(Saturday)	**Kempton Park** (1)
"	5	(Saturday)	*Newton Abbot* (1)
"	5	(Saturday)	Plumpton (1)
"	5	(Saturday)	Towcester (1)
"	5	(Saturday)	**Warwick** (1)
"	7	(Easter Monday)	*Carlisle* (1)
"	7	(Easter Monday)	**Kempton Park** (1)
"	7	(Easter Monday)	*Newton Abbot* (1)
"	7	(Easter Monday)	Plumpton (1)
"	7	(Easter Monday)	Towcester (1)
"	7	(Easter Monday)	**Warwick** (1)
"	7	(Easter Monday)	Fakenham (1)
"	7	(Easter Monday)	Hereford (1)
"	7	(Easter Monday)	Huntingdon (1)
"	7	(Easter Monday)	Market Rasen (1)
"	7	(Easter Monday)	**Nottingham** (1)
"	7	(Easter Monday)	Wincanton (1)
"	7	(Easter Monday)	Chepstow (2)
"	7	(Easter Monday)	**Newcastle** (2)
"	7	(Easter Monday)	*Uttoxeter* (2)
"	7	(Easter Monday)	*Wetherby* (2)
"	9	(Wednesday)	Royal Artillery M. (Sandown Park) (1)

(continued overleaf

Apr. 10	(Thursday)	Cheltenham (3)
,, 10	(Thursday)	**Ascot Heath (2)**
,, 11	(Friday)	Ascot Heath (1)
,, 11	(Friday)	Bangor-on-Dee (1)
,, 12	(Saturday)	**Catterick Bridge (1)**
,, 12	(Saturday)	Kelso (1)
,, 12	(Saturday)	Leicester (1)
,, 14	(Monday)	Leicester (1)
,, 14	(Monday)	Wye (1)
,, 15	(Tuesday)	**Newmarket Craven (3)**
,, 16	(Wednesday)	Fontwell Park (1)
,, 16	(Wednesday)	Newcastle (1)
,, 16	(Wednesday)	**Pontefract (1)**
,, 17	(Thursday)	Plumpton (1)
,, 17	(Thursday)	Stratford-on-Avon (1)
,, 18	(Friday)	**Newbury (2)**
,, 18	(Friday)	**Thirsk (2)**
,, 19	(Saturday)	**Ayr (1)**
,, 19	(Saturday)	Ayr (1)
,, 19	(Saturday)	Uttoxeter (1)
,, 19	(Saturday)	Hexham (1)
,, 21	(Monday)	Hexham (1)
,, 21	(Monday)	**Alexandra Park (1)**
,, 21	(Monday)	Edinburgh (1)
,, 22	(Tuesday)	**Epsom (3)**
,, 23	(Wednesday)	Devon & Exeter (1)
,, 23	(Wednesday)	**Ripon (1)**
,, 23	(Wednesday)	Ludlow (2)
,, 23	(Wednesday)	Perth (2)
,, 24	(Thursday)	Wincanton (1)
,, 25	(Friday)	†Teesside Park (Stockton) (1)
,, 25	(Friday)	**Sandown Park (2)**
,, 26	(Saturday)	Sandown Park (1)
,, 26	(Saturday)	Bangor-on-Dee (1)
,, 26	(Saturday)	**Hamilton Park (1)**
,, 26	(Saturday)	Redcar (1)
,, 26	(Saturday)	Towcester (1)
,, 28	(Monday)	Southwell (1)
,, 28	(Monday)	United Hunts M. (Folkestone) (1)
Apr. 28	(Monday)	Warwick (1)
,, 29	(Tuesday)	‡Kelso (2)
,, 29	(Tuesday)	**Newmarket Spring (3)**
,, 30	(Wednesday)	**Catterick Bridge (1)**
,, 30	(Wednesday)	‡Worcester (2)
May 1	(Thursday)	Taunton (2)
,, 2	(Friday)	†Chepstow (1)
,, 2	(Friday)	**Ascot Heath (2)**
,, 2	(Friday)	‡Beverley (2)
,, 3	(Saturday)	Huntingdon (1)
,, 3	(Saturday)	†Newcastle (1)
,, 3	(Saturday)	Uttoxeter (1)
,, 3	(Saturday)	**Lanark (1)**
,, 5	(Monday)	**Lanark (1)**
,, 5	(Monday)	†Nottingham (1)
,, 5	(Monday)	Plumpton (1)
,, 6	(Tuesday)	‡Alexandra Park (1)
,, 6	(Tuesday)	**Chester (3)**
,, 7	(Wednesday)	†Wetherby (1)
,, 7	(Wednesday)	Newton Abbot (2)
,, 8	(Thursday)	‡Carlisle (1)
,, 8	(Thursday)	†Hereford (1)
,, 9	(Friday)	Perth Hunt (1)
,, 9	(Friday)	‡Teesside Park (Stockton) (1)
,, 9	(Friday)	**Kempton Park (2)**
,, 9	(Friday)	**Leicester (2)**
,, 10	(Saturday)	Market Rasen (1)
,, 10	(Saturday)	**Newcastle (1)**
,, 10	(Saturday)	**Pontefract (1)**
,, 10	(Saturday)	**Hamilton Park (1)**
,, 12	(Monday)	**Hamilton Park (1)**
,, 12	(Monday)	†Southwell (1)
,, 12	(Monday)	**Windsor (1)**
,, 12	(Monday)	†Wolverhampton (1)
,, 12	(Monday)	Wye (1)
,, 13	(Tuesday)	**York (3)**
,, 14	(Wednesday)	Devon & Exeter (1)
,, 14	(Wednesday)	†Hexham (1)
,, 14	(Wednesday)	**Salisbury (2)**

May 15	(Thursday)	†Plumpton (1)
,, 15	(Thursday)	†Uttoxeter (1)
,, 16	(Friday)	†Sedgefield (1)
,, 16	(Friday)	†Stratford-on-Avon (1)
,, 16	(Friday)	Lingfield Park (2)
,, 16	(Friday)	‡Ayr (2)
,, 17	(Saturday)	Ayr (1)
,, 17	(Saturday)	Bath (1)
,, 17	(Saturday)	Newmarket (1)
,, 17	(Saturday)	Ripon (1)
,, 17	(Saturday)	Worcester (1)
,, 19	(Monday)	Ayr (1)
,, 19	(Monday)	Nottingham (1)
,, 19	(Monday)	†Windsor (1)
,, 20	(Tuesday)	†Alexandra Park (1)
,, 20	(Tuesday)	Market Rasen (1)
,, 21	(Wednesday)	Catterick Bridge (1)
,, 21	(Wednesday)	Perth Hunt (1)
,, 21	(Wednesday)	Goodwood (2)
,, 22	(Thursday)	Carlisle (1)
,, 23	(Friday)	†Taunton (1)
,, 23	(Friday)	†Windsor (1)
,, 23	(Friday)	†Teesside Park (Stockton) (2)
,, 23	(Friday)	Haydock Park (2)
,, 24	(Saturday)	Haydock Park (1)
,, 24	(Saturday)	Kempton Park (1)
,, 24	(Saturday)	†Southwell (1)
,, 24	(Saturday)	Warwick (1)
,, 24	(Saturday)	Cartmel (1)
,, 24	(Saturday)	Devon & Exeter (1)
,, 24	(Saturday)	Doncaster (1)
,, 24	(Saturday)	Hexham (1)
,, 24	(Saturday)	Towcester (1)
,, 26	(Bank Holiday)	Cartmel (1)
,, 26	(Bank Holiday)	Devon & Exeter (1)
,, 26	(Bank Holiday)	Doncaster (1)
,, 26	(Bank Holiday)	Hexham (1)
,, 26	(Bank Holiday)	Towcester (1)
,, 26	(Bank Holiday)	Fakenham (1)
May 26	(Bank Holiday)	Fontwell Park (1)
,, 26	(Bank Holiday)	Hereford (1)
,, 26	(Bank Holiday)	Huntingdon (1)
,, 26	(Bank Holiday)	Wetherby (1)
,, 26	(Bank Holiday)	Chepstow (2)
,, 26	(Bank Holiday)	Leicester (2)
,, 26	(Bank Holiday)	Redcar (2)
,, 26	(Bank Holiday)	Sandown Park (2)
,, 26	(Bank Holiday)	Uttoxeter (2)
,, 28	(Wednesday)	Ripon (1)
,, 28	(Wednesday)	Brighton (2)
,, 28	(Wednesday)	Newton Abbot (2)
,, 30	(Friday)	†Taunton (1)
,, 30	(Friday)	‡Ayr (2)
,, 30	(Friday)	Newbury (2)
,, 30	(Friday)	‡Stratford-on-Avon (2)
,, 30	(Friday)	†Thirsk (2)
,, 31	(Saturday)	†Market Rasen (1)
,, 31	(Saturday)	†Newcastle (1)
,, 31	(Saturday)	Newmarket (1)
June 2	(Monday)	†Edinburgh (1)
,, 2	(Monday)	†Nottingham (1)
,, 2	(Monday)	Windsor (1)
,, 3	(Tuesday)	Salisbury (1)
,, 4	(Wednesday)	†Ripon (1)
,, 4	(Wednesday)	Epsom (4)
,, 6	(Friday)	‡Haydock Park (2)
,, 6	(Friday)	Lanark (2)
,, 6	(Friday)	†Thirsk (2)
,, 7	(Saturday)	†Warwick (1)
,, 9	(Monday)	Folkestone (1)
,, 9	(Monday)	†Newcastle (1)
,, 9	(Monday)	‡Wolverhampton (2)
,, 10	(Tuesday)	‡Alexandra Park (1)
,, 10	(Tuesday)	Hamilton Park (1)
,, 11	(Wednesday)	‡Kempton Park (1)
,, 11	(Wednesday)	‡Beverley (1)
,, 11	(Wednesday)	Yarmouth (2)
,, 12	(Thursday)	Carlisle (1)

(continued overleaf)

June 13 (Friday) ‡Bath (2)
,, 13 (Friday) ‡Hamilton Park (2)
,, 13 (Friday) Sandown Park (2)
,, 13 (Friday) York (2)
,, 14 (Saturday) Newmarket (1)

,, 16 (Monday) Brighton (1)
,, 16 (Monday) †Edinburgh (1)
,, 16 (Monday) ‡Leicester (1)
,, 16 (Monday) †Teesside Park (Stockton) (1)
,, 17 (Tuesday) Royal Ascot (4)
,, 18 (Wednesday) †Catterick Bridge (1)
,, 20 (Friday) ‡Ayr (2)
,, 20 (Friday) ‡Pontefract (2)
,, 20 (Friday) Redcar (2)
,, 21 (Saturday) Ascot Heath (1)
,, 21 (Saturday) Brighton (1)

,, 23 (Monday) †Edinburgh (1)
,, 23 (Monday) Nottingham (1)
,, 23 (Monday) †Ripon (1)
,, 23 (Monday) †Windsor (1)
,, 24 (Tuesday) †Alexandra Park (1)
,, 24 (Tuesday) Catterick Bridge (2)
,, 25 (Wednesday) Newbury (2)
,, 26 (Thursday) Newcastle (3)
,, 27 (Friday) ‡Chepstow (2)
,, 27 (Friday) ‡Doncaster (2)
,, 27 (Friday) ‡Kempton Park (2)
,, 28 (Saturday) Newmarket (1)

,, 30 (Monday) †Wolverhampton (1)
,, 30 (Monday) Brighton (1)
July 2 (Wednesday) ‡Pontefract (2)
,, 2 (Wednesday) Salisbury (2)
,, 2 (Wednesday) Yarmouth (2)
,, 2 (Wednesday) ¶Carlisle (3)
,, 3 (Thursday) †Warwick (1)
,, 4 (Friday) ‡Bath (2)
,, 4 (Friday) ‡Beverley (2)
,, 4 (Friday) ‡Haydock Park (2)

July 4 (Friday) Sandown Park (2)
¶ Evening Racing on Wednesday and Friday.

,, 7 (Monday) Nottingham (1)
,, 7 (Monday) †Edinburgh (1)
,, 7 (Monday) †Teesside Park (Stockton) (1)
,, 7 (Monday) †Windsor (1)
,, 8 (Tuesday) Folkestone (1)
,, 8 (Tuesday) †Thirsk (1)
,, 8 (Tuesday) Newmarket July (3)
,, 9 (Wednesday) †Brighton (1)
,, 9 (Wednesday) †Doncaster (2)
,, 11 (Friday) Newbury (2)
,, 11 (Friday) York (2)
,, 12 (Saturday) Brighton (1)
,, 12 (Saturday) †Newcastle (1)
,, 12 (Saturday) †Wolverhampton (1)

,, 14 (Monday) Wolverhampton (1)
,, 14 (Monday) †Edinburgh (1)
,, 14 (Monday) †Windsor (1)
,, 15 (Tuesday) §Kempton Park (2)
,, 16 (Wednesday) Warwick (1)
,, 16 (Wednesday) Redcar (2)
,, 17 (Thursday) †Carlisle (1)
,, 17 (Thursday) Folkestone (1)
,, 18 (Friday) ‡Chester (2)
,, 18 (Friday) ‡Hamilton Park (2)
,, 18 (Friday) Lingfield Park (2)
,, 18 (Friday) ‡Pontefract (2)
,, 19 (Saturday) Salisbury (1)

,, 21 (Monday) Folkestone (1)
,, 21 (Monday) †Windsor (1)
,, 21 (Monday) Ayr (2)
,, 21 (Monday) §Leicester (2)
,, 22 (Tuesday) †Alexandra Park (1)
,, 23 (Wednesday) Bath (1)
,, 23 (Wednesday) Catterick Bridge (2)
,, 23 (Wednesday) Lanark (2)
,, 23 (Wednesday) Sandown Park (2)
,, 25 (Friday) †Teesside Park (Stockton) (1)

July	25	(Friday)	Ascot Heath (2)
„	25	(Friday)	Ayr (2)
„	26	(Saturday)	Ripon (1)
„	26	(Saturday)	Sworol Warwick (1)
„	28	(Monday)	†Alexandra Park (1)
„	28	(Monday)	Newcastle (1)
„	28	(Monday)	†Nottingham (1)
„	29	(Tuesday)	Redcar (3)
„	29	(Tuesday)	Goodwood (4)
Aug.	1	(Friday)	Thirsk (2)
„	2	(Saturday)	Lanark (1)
„	2	(Saturday)	Newmarket (1)
„	2	(Saturday)	*Market Rasen* (1)
„	2	(Saturday)	*Newton Abbot* (1)
„	2	(Saturday)	Windsor (1)
„	4	(Monday)	*Market Rasen* (1)
„	4	(Monday)	*Newton Abbot* (1)
„	4	(Monday)	†Windsor (1)
„	4	(Monday)	Folkestone (1)
„	4	(Monday)	Ripon (1)
„	4	(Monday)	Wolverhampton (2)
„	5	(Tuesday)	Redcar (1)
„	5	(Tuesday)	Brighton (3)
„	6	(Wednesday)	Ayr (1)
„	6	(Wednesday)	Bath (2)
„	6	(Wednesday)	*Devon & Exeter* (2)
„	6	(Wednesday)	Pontefract (2)
„	6	(Wednesday)	Yarmouth (2)
„	8	(Friday)	Lingfield Park (2)
„	8	(Friday)	Newmarket (2)
„	8	(Friday)	Redcar (2)
„	9	(Saturday)	Southwell (1)
„	9	(Saturday)	Warwick (1)
„	11	(Monday)	Newcastle (1)
„	11	(Monday)	Nottingham (2)
„	11	(Monday)	†Windsor (2)
„	13	(Wednesday)	†*Fontwell Park* (1)
„	13	(Wednesday)	Catterick Bridge (2)
„	13	(Wednesday)	Haydock Park (2)
Aug.	13	(Wednesday)	*Newton Abbot* (2)
„	13	(Wednesday)	Salisbury (2)
„	14	(Thursday)	†Alexandra Park (1)
„	15	(Friday)	Newbury (1)
„	16	(Saturday)	Folkestone (1)
„	16	(Saturday)	*Market Rasen* (1)
„	16	(Saturday)	Ripon (1)
„	16	(Saturday)	†Wolverhampton (1)
„	18	(Monday)	Warwick (1)
„	18	(Monday)	Windsor (1)
„	19	(Tuesday)	Folkestone (1)
„	19	(Tuesday)	York (3)
„	20	(Wednesday)	*Devon & Exeter* (2)
„	20	(Wednesday)	Goodwood (2)
„	22	(Friday)	Haydock Park (2)
„	22	(Friday)	Lingfield Park (2)
„	22	(Friday)	Teeside Park (Stockton) (2)
„	23	(Saturday)	Newmarket (1)
„	23	(Saturday)	Worcester (1)
„	25	(Monday)	Worcester (1)
„	25	(Monday)	†Alexandra Park (1)
„	25	(Monday)	Pontefract (1)
„	26	(Tuesday)	Folkestone (1)
„	27	(Wednesday)	*Newton Abbot* (1)
„	27	(Wednesday)	Beverley (1)
„	27	(Wednesday)	Brighton (2)
„	27	(Wednesday)	Yarmouth (2)
„	28	(Thursday)	Carlisle (1)
„	29	(Friday)	Goodwood (2)
„	29	(Friday)	†Windsor (2)
„	30	(Saturday)	Bath (1)
„	30	(Saturday)	*Hereford* (1)
„	30	(Saturday)	Leicester (1)
„	30	(Saturday)	*Market Rasen* (1)
„	30	(Saturday)	Pontefract (1)
„	30	(Saturday)	Newcastle (1)
Sept.	1	(Bank Holiday)	Newcastle (1)
„	1	(Bank Holiday)	*Cartmel* (1)
„	1	(Bank Holiday)	Folkestone (1)

(continued overleaf)

475

Sept.	1	(Bank Holiday)	Huntingdon (1)
,,	1	(Bank Holiday)	Wolverhampton (1)
,,	1	(Bank Holiday)	Newton Abbot (1)
,,	1	(Bank Holiday)	Chepstow (2)
,,	1	(Bank Holiday)	Epsom (2)
,,	1	(Bank Holiday)	Ripon (2)
,,	3	(Wednesday)	Southwell (2)
,,	3	(Wednesday)	Fontwell Park (1)
,,	3	(Wednesday)	Devon & Exeter (2)
,,	4	(Thursday)	York (2)
,,	5	(Friday)	Brighton (1)
,,	5	(Friday)	Chester (2)
,,	6	(Saturday)	Sandown Park (2)
,,	6	(Saturday)	Bath (1)
,,	6	(Saturday)	Lanark (1)
,,	6	(Saturday)	Stratford-on-Avon (1)
,,	6	(Saturday)	Thirsk (1)
,,	8	(Monday)	Warwick (1)
,,	8	(Monday)	Windsor (1)
,,	9	(Tuesday)	Alexandra Park (1)
,,	9	(Tuesday)	Doncaster (4)
,,	10	(Wednesday)	Ludlow (2)
,,	10	(Wednesday)	Salisbury (2)
,,	11	(Thursday)	Folkestone (1)
,,	12	(Friday)	Newbury (2)
,,	12	(Friday)	Newton Abbot (2)
,,	13	(Saturday)	Fakenham (1)
,,	13	(Saturday)	Ripon (1)
,,	13	(Saturday)	†Sedgefield (1)
,,	13	(Saturday)	Wolverhampton (1)
,,	15	(Monday)	Edinburgh (1)
,,	15	(Monday)	Worcester (1)
,,	15	(Monday)	Goodwood (2)
,,	16	(Tuesday)	Wincanton (1)
,,	16	(Tuesday)	Yarmouth (3)
,,	17	(Wednesday)	Fontwell Park (1)
,,	17	(Wednesday)	Cheltenham (2)
,,	17	(Wednesday)	Pontefract (2)
,,	17	(Wednesday)	Western M. (Ayr) (4)
Sept.	19	(Friday)	Kempton Park (2)
,,	20	(Saturday)	Bangor-on-Dee (1)
,,	20	(Saturday)	Newmarket (1)
,,	20	(Saturday)	Redcar (1)
,,	20	(Saturday)	Taunton (1)
,,	22	(Monday)	Folkestone (1)
,,	22	(Monday)	Leicester (2)
,,	23	(Tuesday)	Plumpton (1)
,,	24	(Wednesday)	Lingfield Park (1)
,,	24	(Wednesday)	Beverley (1)
,,	24	(Wednesday)	Devon & Exeter (2)
,,	24	(Wednesday)	Haydock Park (2)
,,	24	(Wednesday)	Perth Hunt (2)
,,	25	(Thursday)	Hereford (1)
,,	25	(Thursday)	Ascot Heath (3)
,,	27	(Saturday)	Catterick Bridge (1)
,,	27	(Saturday)	Market Rasen (1)
,,	27	(Saturday)	Stratford-on-Avon (1)
,,	27	(Saturday)	Hamilton Park (1)
,,	27	(Saturday)	Hexham (1)
,,	29	(Monday)	Hamilton Park (1)
,,	29	(Monday)	Hexham (1)
,,	29	(Monday)	Nottingham (2)
,,	30	(Tuesday)	Fontwell Park (1)
Oct.	1	(Wednesday)	Teeside Park (Stockton) (1)
,,	1	(Wednesday)	Worcester (2)
,,	1, 2, and 4	(Wednesday, Thursday and Saturday)	Newmarket October (3)
,,	2	(Thursday)	Folkestone (1)
,,	3	(Friday)	Wincanton (1)
,,	4	(Saturday)	Devon & Exeter (1)
,,	4	(Saturday)	Redcar (1)
,,	4	(Saturday)	Uttoxeter (1)
,,	4	(Saturday)	Windsor (1)
,,	4	(Saturday)	Carlisle (1)
,,	6	(Monday)	Carlisle (1)
,,	6	(Monday)	Wolverhampton (1)
,,	6	(Monday)	Wye (1)
,,	7	(Tuesday)	Lingfield Park (2)

Oct. 8	(Wednesday)	Ludlow (2)
,, 8	(Wednesday)	York (2)
,, 9	(Thursday)	Ascot Heath (1)
,, 10	(Friday)	Ascot Heath (2)
,, 11	(Saturday)	Chepstow (1)
,, 11	(Saturday)	Fakenham (1)
,, 11	(Saturday)	Teesside Park (Stockton) (1)
,, 11	(Saturday)	York (1)
,, 11	(Saturday)	Ayr (1)
,, 13	(Monday)	Ayr (1)
,, 13	(Monday)	Plumpton (1)
,, 13	(Monday)	Southwell (1)
,, 13	(Monday)	Warwick (1)
,, 14	(Tuesday)	Warwick (1)
,, 15	(Wednesday)	Wetherby (1)
,, 15	(Wednesday)	Cheltenham (2)
,, 16	(Thursday)	Newmarket Houghton (3)
,, 17	(Friday)	Kempton Park (2)
,, 18	(Saturday)	Bangor-on-Dee (1)
,, 18	(Saturday)	Beverley (1)
,, 18	(Saturday)	Kelso (1)
,, 18	(Saturday)	Taunton (1)
,, 20	(Monday)	Leicester (1)
,, 20	(Monday)	Fontwell Park (1)
,, 21	(Tuesday)	Plumpton (1)
,, 22	(Wednesday)	Newcastle (1)
,, 22	(Wednesday)	Sandown Park (1)
,, 22	(Wednesday)	Sandown Park (1)
,, 22	(Wednesday)	Worcester (1)
,, 23	(Thursday)	Newbury (3)
,, 23	(Thursday)	Newbury (3)
,, 24	(Friday)	Doncaster (2)
,, 24	(Friday)	Doncaster (2)
,, 25	(Saturday)	Huntingdon (1)
,, 25	(Saturday)	Kelso (1)
,, 25	(Saturday)	Stratford-on-Avon (1)
,, 27	(Monday)	Wye (1)
,, 27	(Monday)	Nottingham (2)
,, 29	(Wednesday)	Ayr (1)
Oct. 29	(Wednesday)	Hereford (1)
,, 30	(Thursday)	Uttoxeter (1)
,, 30	(Thursday)	Wincanton (1)
,, 31	(Friday)	Haydock Park (2)
,, 31	(Friday)	Haydock Park (2)
,, 31	(Friday)	Newmarket (2)
Nov. 1	(Saturday)	Cheltenham (1)
,, 1	(Saturday)	Market Rasen (1)
,, 1	(Saturday)	Teesside Park (Stockton) (1)
,, 1	(Saturday)	Towcester (1)
,, 3	(Monday)	Doncaster (1)
,, 3	(Monday)	Leicester (2)
,, 4	(Tuesday)	Hexham (1)
,, 5	(Wednesday)	Warwick (1)
,, 5	(Wednesday)	Newbury (2)
,, 6	(Thursday)	Sedgefield (1)
,, 7	(Friday)	Sandown Park (2)
,, 8	(Saturday)	Newcastle (1)
,, 8	(Saturday)	Taunton (1)
,, 8	(Saturday)	Wetherby (1)
,, 8	(Saturday)	Worcester (1)
,, 10	(Monday)	Fontwell Park (1)
,, 10	(Monday)	Wolverhampton (1)
,, 11	(Tuesday)	Plumpton (1)
,, 11	(Tuesday)	Kelso (1)
,, 12	(Wednesday)	Chepstow (1)
,, 12	(Wednesday)	Windsor (1)
,, 13	(Thursday)	Carlisle (1)
,, 13	(Thursday)	Stratford-on-Avon (1)
,, 14	(Friday)	Cheltenham (2)
,, 15	(Saturday)	Catterick Bridge (1)
,, 15	(Saturday)	Windsor (1)
,, 17	(Monday)	Ayr (1)
,, 17	(Monday)	Nottingham (2)
,, 18	(Tuesday)	Devon & Exeter (1)
,, 19	(Wednesday)	Wetherby (1)
,, 19	(Wednesday)	Kempton Park (2)
,, 20	(Thursday)	Wincanton (1)
,, 21	(Friday)	Ascot Heath (2)

(continued overleaf)

Nov. 21 (Friday) ...... Doncaster (2)
" 22 (Saturday) ...... Warwick (1)
" 24 (Monday) ...... Folkestone (1)
" 24 (Monday) ...... Leicester (2)
" 25 (Tuesday) ...... Lingfield Park (1)
" 26 (Wednesday) ...... Fontwell Park (1)
" 26 (Wednesday) ...... Teesside Park (Stockton) (1)
" 27 (Thursday) ...... Taunton (1)
" 27 (Thursday) ...... Wolverhampton (1)
" 28 (Friday) ...... Liverpool (2)
" 28 (Friday) ...... Newbury (2)
" 29 (Saturday) ...... Newcastle (1)
Dec. 1 (Monday) ...... Windsor (1)
" 1 (Monday) ...... Wolverhampton (1)
" 2 (Tuesday) ...... Huntingdon (1)
" 2 (Tuesday) ...... Wetherby (1)
" 3 (Wednesday) ...... Worcester (1)
" 3 (Wednesday) ...... Haydock Park (2)
" 4 (Thursday) ...... Towcester (1)
" 5 (Friday) ...... Lingfield Park (2)
" 6 (Saturday) ...... Catterick Bridge (1)
" 6 (Saturday) ...... Cheltenham (1)
" 6 (Saturday) ...... Southwell (1)
" 8 (Monday) ...... Southwell (1)
" 9 (Tuesday) ...... Warwick (1)
" 10 (Wednesday) ...... Ayr (1)
" 10 (Wednesday) ...... Newton Abbot (1)

Dec. 11 (Thursday) ...... Uttoxeter (1)
" 11 (Thursday) ...... Wincanton (1)
" 12 (Friday) ...... Sandown Park (2)
" 13 (Saturday) ...... Chepstow (1)
" 13 (Saturday) ...... Sedgefield (1)
" 15 (Monday) ...... Teesside Park (Stockton) (1)
" 16 (Tuesday) ...... Kelso (1)
" 17 (Wednesday) ...... Plumpton (1)
" 18 (Thursday) ...... Uttoxeter (1)
" 19 (Friday) ...... Ascot Heath (2)
" 20 (Saturday) ...... Catterick Bridge (1)
" 22 (Monday) ...... Catterick Bridge (1)
" 26 (Boxing Day) ...... Huntingdon (1)
" 26 (Boxing Day) ...... Newton Abbot (1)
" 26 (Boxing Day) ...... Sedgefield (1)
" 26 (Boxing Day) ...... Wincanton (1)
" 26 (Boxing Day) ...... Kempton Park (2)
" 26 (Boxing Day) ...... Market Rasen (2)
" 26 (Boxing Day) ...... Wetherby (2)
" 26 (Boxing Day) ...... Wolverhampton (2)
" 27 (Saturday) ...... Newcastle (1)
" 27 (Saturday) ...... Taunton (1)
" 29 (Monday) ...... Fontwell Park (1)
" 29 (Monday) ...... Warwick (1)
" 30 (Tuesday) ...... Taunton (1)
" 31 (Wednesday) ...... Catterick Bridge (1)
" 31 (Wednesday) ...... Fakenham (1)

Notes

Notes